ديوان المتنبي

The Diwan of Abu Tayyib Ahmad ibn al-Husayn al-Mutanabbi

Translated from the Text of
Abu al-Hasan Ali ibn Ahmad
al-Wahidi al-Naishaburi (d 468/1075)

Arthur Wormhoudt

ABC International Group, Inc.

© 2002 ABC International Group, Inc.

All rights reserved. No part of this book may be reproduced, stored in a retrieval system, or transmitted, in any form or by any means, electronic, mechanical, photocopying, recording or otherwise, without the written permission of the publishers.

Library of Congress Cataloging-in-Publication Data

Abu Tayyib Ahmad ibn al-Husayn al-Mutanabbi, *Diwan*
 1. Arabic Poetry. I. Title.

ISBN: 1-930637-38-1

Published by
ABC International Group, Inc.

Distributed by
**KAZI Publications, Inc.
3023 W. Belmont Avenue
Chicago IL 60618
Tel: 773-267-7001; FAX: 773-267-7002
email: info@kazi.org /www.kazi.org**

For Sarah and Pearl
and Jody and Michael

Contents

Translator's Introduction . . . 7
I. *Al-Shawmiyat*: Syrian Poems . . . 15
   The Prison: Poems 1-48
   Lament for Jesus—Ibn Ishaq: Poems 49-68
   The Full Moon—Badr ibn Ismail: Poems 69-112
   The Horse Tail Banner—Ibn Tugj: Poems 113-145
   Father of the Family—Abu Ashair: Poems 146-160

II. *Al-Saifyat*: Poems for Saif al-Daula
   Elegy for the Mother: Poems 161-167
   For the Son: Poems 168-174
   For Solomon—Ibn Dawud: Poems 175-190
   For General Patch—Yamak: Poems 191-230
   For the Sisters: Poems 231-240

III. *Al-Misriyat*: Egyptian Poems
   Black Camphor—Kafur: Poems 241-261
   Red Journey—Wardan: Poems 262-268
   Mad Fatik—Majnun: Poems 269-272
   The Lock—Dabba: Poem 273
   Spoken Honors—Dallar: Poem 274

IV. *Al-Amidiyat*: Poems for Ibn Amid
   The Swaggering Pen: Poem 275
   Incense: Poem 276
   New Year's Sword: Poem 277
   The Letter: Poem 278

THE UNBROKEN BOND: POEM 279

V. *AL-ADUDIYAT*: POEMS FOR ADUD AL-DAULA
EDEN'S GARDEN—SHIB BAWWAN: POEMS 280-281
SCATTERED ROSES: POEM 282
LAMENT FOR AN AUNT: POEMS 283-284
FORGIVENESS—WAHSUDHAN: POEM 285
THE HUNT AND THE WAY: POEMS 286-287

REFERENCES   535

Translator's Introduction

Abu Tayyib al-Mutanabbi was born in Kufa in southern Iraq in 915. He was raised by his grandmother and his father who fostered his poetic abilities from an early age. He spent some of his boyhood with the bedouin in the desert who were thought to speak a purer form of Arabic than the people of the cities whose language was corrupted by non-Arabs. The bedouin also cultivated the verse forms which had been developed in the centuries during which Islam spread beyond the confines of Arabia.

These forms included the meters and rhythms of the couplet in which the last word of the second half of the couplet was a word whose rhyming sound was maintained throughout the poem which could consist of forty or more couplets. The two halves of the couplet, when seen in written form, appeared as two columns parallel to each other and suggested the duality of reader and writer, listener and speaker or other forms of dialogue. This parallel was enhanced by the fact that Arabic words are formed on triliteral consonantal roots which form patterns that can be repeated in the two halves of the couplet in various ways.

In addition to the couplet form which tended to make each couplet independent of each other there were larger patterns that encompassed the entire poem. The most important of these was the *qasida*, or poem of search, which had a basically three part form. In the first part a lover stood at the deserted campsite of his beloved and lamented her loss. He was like the infant who is temporarily left alone by its nurse. In the middle part of the poem the lover mounted his horse or camel and made a journey through the wasteland. In this part he suggested the child who is learning to crawl as it develops the ability to speak. Finally the lover arrived at a patron whose praises he would celebrate.

The praise of the patron thus develops out of the erotic prelude, called the *nasi*b or genealogy, by way of the desert journey, called the *rahla*, to conclude in praise, called the *madih*. For al-Mutanabbi and for other poets who used the *qasida* form the praise tends to be exaggerated as does the gratitude expressed by the poet in return for the favors granted by the patron. This exaggeration can be traced to the fact that the infant in its earliest relation to the nurse has little knowledge of the external world which might temper its description of the nurse and patron. Since it is an erotic relationship which has its origin in the infant's need for food that the nurse alone can provide there is an additional motivation to exaggerate the virtues of the patron The use of the four legs of the child in search of the patron provides a further impetus to the activity of the lover.

The *qasida* in one form or another has a long history in the traditions of Middle Eastern literature. The fragmentary poem of the Gilgamesh story was written on twelver tablets which can be reduced to a three part grouping of episodes. The Gilgamesh was written twenty centuries before Christ in a syllabic script. The Babylonian Creation Epic, too, was written fifteen centuries before the Christian era and has a seven part pattern which reappears in the book of Genesis. The second, fourth and sixth parts of this same pattern form a three part series. In Genesis itself the creation story is repeated and a five part pattern is apparent in the Torah or Pentateuch. The Hebrew scriptures in their entirety consist of Torah, Former Prophets, Latter Prophets, Twelve Minor Prophets and Writings such as Psalms, etc

It was assumed in Mutanabbi's day that by far the largest group of readers were the Christians whose New Testament consists of the five Gospels plus the Letters that begin with Acts and end with the Apocalypse. The New Testament has some of its roots in the Homeric poems which have three part patterns into which their twenty-four books can be divided. But they are also amenable to a five part division of 4/6/4/6/4. A similar division is possible for the Quran which comes closest to the New Testament in the number of its readers. The Quran has 114 Surahs which divide into three groups of thirty-eight Surahs or five groups of 20/27/20/27/20.

The Greek philosopher Aristotle generalized these patterns in his book on poetry by saying that a poem has a beginning, a middle and an end which distinguishes it from a history which has neither beginning nor end. In his book on psychology Aristotle also mentioned five powers of the soul in terms of a nutritive or *threptikos* power, an *esthetikos* or aesthetic power, an *orektikos* or appetitive power, a *kinetikos kata topon* or movement as to place power, and a *dianetikos* or intellectual power. These powers may be related to five muscular positions which the child occupies in a developmental sequence. They are horizontal, seated, crawling, standing and walking. Each of these has a characteristic means of communication which are: cooing, crying, babble in terms of vowel and consonant syllables, speaking and listening, lettering, and finally written language

The purpose of these patterns is to give readers access to their own communication habits as developed in childhood and by means of this kind of stimulus to allow them to become productive writers, or builders, painters or musicians. In so doing they become stimuli to another kind of writer, the scientific writer, whose interest lies in the description of the external world as distinct from the inner world of the communication habits. The world of science that is thus produced may be either good or bad in its effects but part of its roots lie in the inner world revealed by literary writers

After the New Testament and Quran the chief literary works that make up the literary tradition include Mutanabbi's *Diwan*, Dante's *Comedy*, and possibly Jalal al Din's *Mathnavi*, Shakespeare's Plays, Cervantes' *Don Quixote*, and the writings of Goethe and Victor Hugo, all of whom have been compared to al-Mutanabbi.

In the three centuries that elapsed between the revelation of the Quran and the *Diwan* of al-Mutanabbi there were many poets writing in Arabic and most of their collected poems were arranged in alphabetical order according to rhyme. This arrangement drew attention to the importance of the new Quranic script but paid little attention to the biography of the poet. A few collections were arranged according to subject matter such as wine poems, love poems, praise poems, etc. But here again the poet's biography as it developed through time was neglected. Mutanabbi's poems do exist in early editions which are arranged alphabetically but the edition of Wahidi, used in this translation, has the form of a kind of autobiography and was approved by the poet himself. It is therefore a map of the communication habits.

The *Diwan* has five main parts which consist of poems written in Syria, called the *Shawmiyat* or left hand work. Poems written for Saif al-Daula, called the *Saifiyat*, to the ruler of Aleppo to whom the caliph gave the title of the Sword of State. Poems written in Egypt called the *Misriyat* for the densely populated land of the Nile. Poems written for ibn al-Amid called *Amidiyat* for the Persian minister whose name means "the son of the column." And finally poems for Adud al-Daula, the Adudiyat, for the ruler of south Persia whose name means the Forearm of State. Each of these five parts can be further divided into five sub-parts.

I. The *Shawmiyat*: In the part one of the *Shawmiyat* the poet alludes to his imprisonment as a way of suggesting that the infant in the horizontal position—due to its inability to move—lives in an inner world with limited knowledge of the external world. In poem 29 he compares himself to a pearl in an oyster shell. In Poem 30 he calls his prison mates monkeys and says that his crime was committed before it was his duty to kneel in prayer and between his birth and his learning to sit. He urges his patron not to listen to disputes of the Jews who condemned Jesus and compares them to the Thamud, a people who rejected the Quranic prophet Salih by hamstringing his camel. In Poems 33-39 he speaks of his unwillingness to drink wine except under protest. This suggests the infant's substitution of its own excretion, brought on by wine drinking, for the nourishment the nurse does not give. In place of that the poet becomes a fluent producer of sounds:

cooing and crying. He is Abu Tayyib, Father of Goodness who in modesty claims to be a prophet, al-Mutanabbi, worthy of praise, Ahmad son of the little beauty, Husayn.

In part two of the *Shawmiyat* the poet is commissioned to compose a series of elegies on the death of Ibn Ishaq al-Tanukhi, the son of Isaac, that is, Jesus who kneels, root *nukh*. Poem 58 in this series praises Ali ibn Ibrahim al-Tanukhi and concludes with a passage describing the lake of Galilee whose depths suggest the underworld of the seated infant. It is here that the pull of gravity forces a new kind of breathing which produces the babbling sounds of consonant and vowel as preliminary to speech. But the folk of Galilee are hateful to the poet.

In part three of the *Shawmiyat* a series of poems are dedicated to Badr al-Tabaristani. His name means the Full Moon and so represents the reflected light of the sun. This light is felt in the spoken word. It has a fluency represented by the flow of blood noted in Poem 70 where Badr is bled for an illness. In Poem 73 Badr goes on a lion hunt to suggest the child's use of the four feet in the crawling phase as well as a certain self-centeredness implied in speech as contrasted with writing.

In part four, a group of poems dedicated to the Turk Abu Muhammad ibn Tugj turns attention to the child's standing position. The word *tugj* means a horse's tail which is used as a banner in a military troop. It thus alludes to some of the problems that the child confronts in the seated and crawling positions but elevates them so as to free the hands which the child can now use to write letters. In the poems for Badr some of these problems were hinted at in the fall of the dancing girl in Poem 93 and the death of the grandmother in Poem 101 and the colt in 139.

In part five of the *Shawmiyat* there are poems dedicated to Abu Ashatir ibn Hamdan whose name means Father of the Ten (fingers) of the writer's hand. Poems 146-8 describe a fantastic melon which is a feast for the reader's eyes. There is also a satire on Ibn Kaigalag in poems 140-2 who tried to control the poet's inspiration by forcing him to write for him but it is only inner motivations that can do this.

II. The second fifth of the *Diwan, al-Saifyat,* is taken up with poems dedicated to Saif al-Daula, the ruler of Aleppo, the milky city, whose raids against the Byzantines and bedouin tribes suggest that he is the sword that cuts up the cooing crying sounds into the syllables represented in the Quranic script which differs from the Greco-Roman script and that used by the bedouin which lacks vowels signs. These poems are divided into seven sections separated by six elegies which suggest the destruction of the sounds produced in the horizontal position. The first elegy is for Saif's mother and so the infant's nurse. Poem 164 tells of a raid against Kharijites, extremists. in the Kalb (dog) tribe who do not make use of syllables.

The second elegy is for Saif's son who represents the offspring resulting from the pull of gravity on the seated infant's production of sounds. Following this elegy the poet's rewarded with the gift of a horse and a girl for whom he promises a dowry in poem 173. She may become the mother of his son.

The third elegy is for Saif's kinsman Abu Wail ibn Dawud. Poem 185 tells of a tent which Saif set up but was blown down by the kind of winds that motivate the articulate syllables formed in this fifth. These articulate sounds are alone useful for the spoken word in the middle fifth of the pattern. They form a tent that is more durable than tents made of cloth.

The fourth elegy is for Yamak, a Turkish commander of Saif's forces. His name means "patch" and thus the way in which the letters formed in the standing position cover and patch up the sounds of speech produced in the middle fifth. Poem 191 tells of the building of Martash, root *rsh* meaning to shiver. Poem 197 describes the conflict felt in the poet as he realizes that the activity of Saif's sword produces a coldness between them. It deprives him of the emotional depth and warmth of the cooing crying sounds while burdening him with the intellectual ability implied in the use of vowel consonant syllables. Poems 212, 225 and 228 tell of raids against Arab rebels and Saif's illness from an abscess and flooding of the Quwaiq river near Aleppo. The building of the fort Hadath, root *hdth* meaning excrement, shows the power of the Quranic vowel script on the vertical axis as compared to the Greco-Roman vowel script on the horizontal axis. Consonant signs are formed by gripping the pen and when vowel signs are made in the same way their inner reference is lost. This is due to the fact that spoken vowels are free of tactile experience. The Hebrew and Arabic vowels in ordinary writing are not written. But in classical texts the vowels are placed on a vertical axis to represent the seated and standing positions as contrasted with the horizontal and crawling positions. Poem 236 tells of a broken oath of the Byzantine commander to suggest the weakness of his script

The fifth elegy is for the younger sister of Saif who along with the elder sister presides over the poet's ability to write. Poem 232 personifies the fort of Hadath as a coquette who merits Saif's defense. But 235 shows Saif withdrawing from the lands of the Byzantines. It is left for others to further the cause of Islam.

III. The middle fifth of the *Diwan, al-Misriyat,* contains the poems written in Egypt the land of the Nile as representing the fluency of the spoken word. It is ruled by the black Kafur, white camphor, who like the front feet of the crawling child which have been in the filth of the underworld in the seated position but now looks forward to the role of the writer's hand, is thus both praised and mocked. Poem 243 shows his constructive side in building a palace which becomes a source of plague. In Poem 252 the poet is rumored to be dead by Saif's courtiers in Aleppo but like the child who is resurrected in the crawling position revives in Egypt. In poem 254 Shabib, lover, is a rebel beaten by Kafur but in Poem 255 the poet suffers from a fever.

In the part two of the *Misriyat* the poet makes his escape from Kafur to suggest the crawling phase as related to the production of syllables. He encounters Wardan who drives Majnun insane by forbidding his love for Laila, the night. His name means red and he makes his wife prostitute herself to the poet's slaves in poems 263-5. Poem 267 details the trip from Egypt to Iraq.

Part three of the *Misriyat* has Majnun reappear in poems 270-2 as the Greek born Fatik, the bold one, whom the poet praises and then laments when he dies. Like Wardan he represents the strange madness of the spoken word though his rebellion has a nobility which Wardan and Shabib lack. He is also associated with the apple that seduces Eve.

Part four of the Misriyat has a single poem in 273 that mocks Dabba, the lizard or lock, in filthy language to suggest the union of the letters with the spoken word in the standing position. The pull of gravity again draws waste products from the upright body as the vertical vowel script reveals some of the contents of the underworld before the written word appears.

In part five, another single poem, 274, praises the caliph's lieutenant who comes to rescue Kufa from the Kharijite attack. He arrives too late since the extremists have already left but he suggests that speech plays a role in the future script.

IV. In this part of the *Diwan, al-Amidiyat*, the poet travels to north Persia to praise the Wazir of Rukn al-Daula, the support of the state, Ibn Amid, the pillar of the state. In this standing position the letters of the script are produced by the hands freed of their role as front feet. Ibn Amid was himself a writer and in poem 275 he is compared to Aristotle, Alexander and Ptolemy, Greeks from up north, to suggest that the Arabic vowel script is superior to the Greco-Roman externalization of the vowel signs.

In part two of this part, poem 276 describes an incense burner producing the perfumes derived from the seated position where the syllables of speech are formed. These fumes rise from the feet to the head.

Part three is dedicated to the Persian New Year which is determined by the course of the sun at the spring equinox as the light rises to suggest the resurrection of the child in the crawling phase. Ibn Amid receives his due share of praise.

Part four is expressed in poem 278 which is a response to Ibn Amid's letter criticizing the poet's earlier comparison of Ibn Amid to the Greeks. The Quranic script remains superior to the Greco-Roman

Part five bids farewell to Ibn Amid and grants the truth of the patron's criticism as the ultimate flattery from one poet to another.

V. The fifth last part of the *Diwan, al-Aduiyat,* has poems. for Adud al-Daula, the Forearm of State and of the the writer and reader. In poem 280 he recalls his youth in Syria and Samawa, the heavenly, *ouranios*, desert where he was taken prisoner. In poem 281 he describes his approach to the court of Adud al-Daula as he travels through the Shib Bawwan, a kind of earthly paradise, from which Adam and Eve have not been driven.

In part two, poem 282 tells of the scattering of the roses to suggest the breakup of the cooing-crying sounds in the syllables of the consonant babble of the rose leaves. A new form of the red Wardan.

In part three, poem 283 tells of Adud al-Daula's conquest of the Kurdish rebel Wahsudhan to suggest the way the four feet of the crawling child mobilize the first two-fifths of the pattern. Poem 284 is an elegy for Adud al-Daula's aunt, a final farewell to the nurse all of whose representatives in the *Diwan* were eulogized in laments or *nasib* for the absent beloved.

In part four the rout of Wahsudhan is again detailed to demonstrate the superiority of the forearm which was once a front foot

In the last part poem 286 describes a hunting scene which echoes the Apocalypse at the end of the New Testament. And poem 287 is a farewell poem that seems to suggest the death of the poet on his return from southern Fars to his home in Kufa. This was in the year 965. The sun's eye is now his shoe.

(١)

«من البسيط»

قال أيضًا في صباه:

أَبْلى الهوى أَسَفًا يومَ النَّوى بَدَني   وَفَرَّق الهجرُ بينَ الجَفْنِ والوَسَنِ
رُوحٌ تَرَدَّدَ في مثلِ الخِلالِ إذا   أطارَتِ الرِّيحُ عنه الثوابَ لم يَبِنِ
كَفى بجِسمي نُحولاً أنَّنى رجُلٌ   لو لا مُخاطَبَتي إيّاكَ لم تَرَني

(٢)

«من الخفيف»

او شعر نظمه ارتجالا قوله وهو صبى:

بأبي مَن وَدِدْتُهُ فافترَقْنا   فافترَقْنا حَوْلاً فلمَّا التقَيْنا
وقَضى اللهُ بعدَ ذاكَ اجتماعًا   كان تَسليمُهُ عليَّ وَداعا

(٣)

«من المنسرح»

قال أيضًا فى صباه يمدح محمد بن عبيد الله العلوي المشطب:

أهلاً بدارٍ سَباكَ أغْيَدُها   أبْعَدُ ما بانَ عنكَ خُرَّدُها
ظِلْتَ بها تنطوي على كبدٍ   نضيجةٍ فوقَ خِلْبِها يَدُها
يا حادِيَيْ عيرِها وأحْسَبُني   أوحَدُ مَيْتًا قُبَيْلَ أفْقِدُها
قِفا قليلاً بها عليَّ فلا   أقَلِّ مِن نظْرَةٍ أُزَوَّدُها
ففي فؤادِ المحِبِّ نارُ جَوًى   أحَرُّ نارِ الجحيمِ أبْرَدُها
شابَ مِن الهجرِ فَرْقُ لِمَّتِهِ   فصارَ مِثلَ الدَّمَقْسِ أسْوَدُها
بانو بخُرْعُوبةٍ لها كَفَلٌ   يَكادُ عندَ القِيامِ يُقعِدُها
رَبْحَلةٍ أسْمَرَ مُقَبَّلُها   سَبَحْلَةٍ أبيضَ مُجَرَّدُها
يا عاذِلَ العاشِقينَ دَعْ فِئَةً   أضلَّها اللهُ كيفَ تُرشِدُها
ليسَ يُحيكُ الملامُ في هِمَمٍ   أقرَبُها منكَ عنكَ أبعَدُها
بئسَ الليالي سَهِدْتُ من طَرَبٍ   شَوْقًا إلى مَن يبيتُ يَرقُدُها

I. *al-Shawmiyat*: Syrian Poems
1
Abu Tayyib ibn al Husayn al Mutanabbi was born in Kufa in Kinda in the year 303 and grew up in Syria and the desert. He spoke poetry as a boy and these are among his first words in his youth.
(Outspread ni)

Love wastes my body sadly on parting day;
    Abandonment frightens sleep from my eyelids
The wind comes and goes on this toothpick;
    As breezes blow cloth from it and yet not seen
Enough emaciation in my body, I am a man:
    But for my speech with you, you would not see

2
And he spoke also in his youth impromptu.
(Perfect a)

My father was one we loved and we parted
    But God decided after that for this reunification
Thus we parted a year and when we met
    His salutation to me was like to a valediction

3
He spoke also in his youth praising Muhammad ibn Ubaidallah the 'Alawi.
(Flowing ha)

Hail to a camp whose virgin held you
    Its girls the farthest of those who departed
You remained writhing over the liver
    Roasted, her hand set upon its membrane
O both drivers of her camel I feel
    I'll be found dead just before I lost her
Stop a little with her even if I am
    Not nourished by the last bit of a look
In a lover's heart is a fire of love
    Hell's hottest fire is cooler than this
His locks' parting grays with flight
    Their black becomes like raw white silk
They took a fine woman whose flanks
    Almost if she rose seemed to make her sit
A tall woman whose lips were dark red
    A soft woman who is whitest when disrobed
O you who blame lovers, let them be
    God lured them, how can you guide them?
Reproof has no effect on the passions
    The closer you are to them the farther you
Evil nights when I waked with grief
    Longing to be him who spent them asleep

أحْيَيتُها والدُّمـــوعُ تُنجِدُنــي	شُؤونُها والظَّلامُ يُنجِدُهـــا
لا نــاقَتي تَقبَـــلُ الرَّديفَ ولا	بالسَّوطِ يَومَ الرِّهـانِ أُجهِدُهـا
شِراكُها كُورُهــا ومِشفَرُهــا	زِمامُها والشُّمــوعُ مِقوَدُهــا
أشَدُّ عَصفِ الرِّياحِ يَسبِقُهُ	تَحتي مِــن خَطوِهــا تَأَوُّدُهــا
في مِثلِ ظَهرِ المِجَنِّ مُتَّصِلٍ	مِثلَ بَطنِ المِجَــنِّ قَردَدُهـا
مُرتَمِيــاتٍ بنــا إلى ابنِ عُبَيـ	ـدِ اللهِ غِيطانُهـــا وَفَدفَدُهـا
إلى فتًى يُصدِرُ الرِّمـاحَ وقَد	أنهَلَها في القُلــوبِ مُورِدُهـا
لَــه أيــادٍ إلَيَّ ســابِقَةٌ	أعُـدُّ مِنهـا ولا أعَدُّدُهـــا
يُعطي فَــلا مَطلَـةٌ يُكَدِّرُهـا	بهـا ولا مَنَّــةٌ يُنَكِّدُهــا
خَيـرُ قُرَيـشٍ أبـاً وَجَدُّهـا	أكثَرُهــا نــائِلاً وأجوَدُهــا
أطعَنُهــا بالقَنــاةِ أضرِبُهــا	بالسَّيفِ جَحجاحُهــا مُسَــوَّدُها
أفرَسُــها فارِســاً وأطوَلُهـا	باعـــاً ومِغوارُهــا وسَــيِّدُها
تــاجُ لُـؤَيّ بـنِ غــالِبٍ وبِــهِ	سَما لهــا فَرعُهــا ومَحتِدُهــا
شَمسُ ضُحاها هِلالُ لَيلَتِها	دُرُّ تَقاصيرِهــا زَبَــرجَدُهـا
يا لَيـتَ بي ضربـةً أتيــحَ لهـا	كما أتِيحَـت لــهُ مُحَمَّدُهــا
أثَــرَ فيهــا وفي الحَديــدِ ومـا	أثَــرَ في وجهِــهِ مُهَنَّدُهـا
فاغتَبَطَت إذ رأت تَزَيُّنَهـا	بِمِثلِــهِ والجِــراحُ تَحسُـدُها
وأيقَـنَ النــاسُ أنّ زارِعَهــا	بالمَكرِ في قَلبِــهِ سَيَحصِدُها
أصبَــحَ حُسّــادُهُ وأنفُسُــهُم	يُحدِرُهــا خَوفُــهُ ويُصعِدُها
تَبكـي علـى الأنصُـلِ العُمُــودِ إذا	أنذَرَهــا أنَّــهُ يُجَرِّدُهــا
لِعِلمِهــا أنّهــا تَصيــرُ دَمــاً	وأنَّـهُ في الرِّقـابِ يُغمِدُها
أطلَقَهــا فــالعَدُوُّ مِــن جَـزَعٍ	يَذُمُّهــا والصَّديــقُّ يَحمَدُها
تَنقَــدِحُ النَّــارُ مِــن مَضارِبِها	وصَبُّ مــاءِ الرِّقـابِ يُخمِدُها
إذا أضَـلَّ الهُمــامُ مُهجَتَــهُ	يَومــاً فأطرافُهُــنَّ تُنشِــدُها
قد أجمَعَــت هذِهِ الخَليقَــةُ لي	أنَّــكَ يــا ابــنَ النبـيِّ أوحَدُها
وأنـكَ بالأمسِ كُنـتَ مُحتَلِمــاً	شَيــخَ مَعَــدٍّ وأنــتَ أمرَدُها
وكَم وكَــم نِعمَــةٍ مُجَلَّلــةٍ	رَبَّيتَهــا كــانَ مِنــكَ مَولِدُها

I lived through them, tears helped me
    Their channels and darkness aided them
My camel takes on no extra rider nor
    Do I urge her by the whip on racing days
A shoe strap her saddle, sandal tongue
    Her bridle the shoestring her leading rope
The winds' hardest blow is outdistanced
    Beneath me, in her step she sways slowly
Over seeming shield fronts as if joined
    To the insides of shields in the rocky hills
Tossing us toward Ubaidallah
    With their valleys and rough high peaks
To a young man who brings back lances
    After he gives them their drink in the hearts
He has gifts for me making a precedent
    I count some but I cannot make full census
He gives and his delay makes no muddle
    In them, nor is his favor wasted by the gifts
Best of Quraysh as to father, most famed
    Greatest of them in giving, most generous
Most piercing by spear, best slasher
    With the sword, their chief who leads them
Most chivalrous riding, longest armed
    If he shakes hands, their raider and lord
The crown of Luayy ibn Galib
    The branches spread for them and the root
Their morning sun and night's new moon
    Pearl of their necklace, and their ring's topaz
O would I had suffered such a scar for them
    As was given to him who is their Muhammad
He left a trace on it and on iron but
    The Indian steel impressed not his face
It was happy when it saw it adorned it
    On such as him and some wounds envied
Men were sure that he who planted this
    By craft, in his heart would reap from that
The jealous appear and their souls
    His fear ruins them as it aroused them
The sheaths weep over sword blades
    As he warns them he is unsheathing them
They know that the swords are bloody
    And that he will sheathed them in necks
He sets them free, and the foe in fear
    Blames them but the faithful praise them
A fire is flashed from the concussion
    Gushing blood from necks extinguishes it
If a warrior must lose heart's blood
    One day their edges will seek it out
These folk have agreed with me that you
    O son of the prophet are unique for them
You when you were just coming of age
    Were a shaikh of Ma'add yet of their youth
How many, how many splendid graces
    You nurtured after they were born in you

18   Diwan al-Mutanabbi

أقرَبُ مِنّي إلَيَّ مَوعِدُها	وكَمْ وكَمْ حاجَةٍ سَمَحْتَ بها
سَبِّرٍ إلى مَنزِلي تَرَدُّدُها	ومَكرُماتٍ مَشَتْ على قَدَمِ الـ
أقدِرُ حتى المَماتِ أجحَدُها	أقَرَّ جِلدي بها عَلَيَّ فلا
خَيرُ صِلاتِ الكريمِ أعوَدُها	فَعُدْ بها لا عَدِمْتُها أبَدًا

(٤)

«من السريع»

قيل له وهو في المكتب: ما أحسن هذه الوفرة! فقال:

| مَنشورَةَ الضَّفْرَينِ يَومَ القِتالْ | لا تَحسُنُ الوَفرَةُ حتى تَرى |
| يَعُلُّها مِنْ كُلِّ وافي السِّبالْ | على فَتًى مُعْتَقِلٍ صَعْدَةً |

(٥)

«من المتقارب»

مر برجلين قد قتلا جردا وأبرزاه يعجبان الناس من كبره، فقال:

أسيرَ المَنايا صَريعَ العَطَبْ	لقد أصبَحَ الجُرَذُ المُستَغيرْ
وتَلاهُ للوَجهِ فِعلَ العَرَبْ	رماهُ الكِنانيُّ والعامِريُّ
فأيُّكُما غَلَّ حُرَّ السَّلَبْ	كِلا الرَّجُلَينِ أتَلَّى قَتلَهُ
فإنّ به عَضَّةً في الذنَبْ	وأيُّكُما كانَ مِنْ خَلْفِهِ

(٦)

«من البسيط»

قال في صباه يهجو القاضي الذهبي:

ثمَّ اختُبِرتَ فلَمْ تَرجِعْ إلى أدَبِ	لمّا نُسِبْتَ فكُنتَ ابنًا لغيرِ أبِ
مُشتَقَّةً مِنْ ذَهابِ العَقلِ لا الذَّهَبِ	سُمِّيتَ بالذَّهَبيِّ اليَومَ تَسميَةً
يا أيُّها اللَّقَبُ المُلقى على اللَّقَبِ	مُلَقَّبٌ بِكَ ما لُقِّبتَ وَيكَ بِهِ

How many, how many needs satisfied
    Their vows were nearer to me than myself
Fine robes appear on virtue's feet
    Making their coming and going in my home
He delights my skin by them for my sake
    I'll not be able to disown them until death
Come back with them so I never lack
    The best of gifts is their reappearance

4
One said to him
when he was in a bookshop:
How fine these locks are!
So he spoke:
(Swift 1)

Locks are not fine until seen with
    Both braids undone on a day of battles
On a youth grasping a lance and giving
    It double drinks from all the bearded ones

5
He spoke in his youth
when he was passing by
two men who
had killed a rat
and were showing it.
(Tripping b)

The raiding rat has come to light
    Death has plunged him down to ruin
Kinany and 'Amr aimed at him
    Pursued him in a way that Arabs know
Both men were near to the kill
    Which of you looted the good spoil?
Which of you was closest behind
    He has the tooth marks on his tail!

6
He spoke in his youth
mocking the
Qadi al Dhahabi.
(Outspread bi)

When you were named you had no father
    You inquired about it but you had no breeding
You were al Dhahabi on the naming day
    Got from Lost Wits, not from the Golden One
Named by you O you not named by it
    O nickname dumped upon such a surname!

(٧)

«من الكامل»

قال وهو في المكتب يمدح رجلاً، وأراد أن تستكشفه عن مذهبه:

هَمٌّ أقامَ عَلى فُؤادٍ أنْجَمـا	كُفِّي! أراني،وَيْـلِكِ، لَوْمَـكِ ألوَمـا،
لَحْمـاً فَيُنْجِلَـهُ السَّقـامُ ولا دَمـا	وَخَيـالُ جِسْـمٍ لَـمْ يُخَـلِّ لـهُ الهَـوى
يـا جَنَّتـي لَظَنَنْـتِ فيـهِ جَهَنَّمـا	وخَفْـوْقُ قَلْـبٍ لَـوْ رأيْـتِ لَهيبَـهُ
تَرَكَـتْ حَـلاوَةَ كُـلِّ حُـبٍّ عَلْقَمـا	وَإذا سَحابَـةَ صَـدِّ حِـبٍّ أبْرَقَـتْ
أكَلَ الضّنى جسدي وَرَضَّ الأعظُما	يـا وَجْـهَ داهِيَـةِ الَّـذي لَـوْلاكَ مـا
أمْسَيْـتُ مِـن كَبِـدي ومنهـا مُعْدِمـا	إنْ كـانَ أغْنـاهـا السُّلُـوُّ فـإنّـي
شمسُ النَّهارِ تِقِـلُّ لَيـلاً مُظْلِمـا	عُصْـنٌ عَلـى نَقْـوَيْ فَـلاةٍ نابِـتٌ
إلّا لِتَجْعَلَنـي لِغُرْمـي مَغْنَمـا	لَمْ تُجْمَـعِ الأضـدادُ في مُتَشابِـهِ
بَهَـرَتْ فَأنْطَـقَ واصِفيـهِ وأفْحَمـا	كَصِفـاتِ أوْحَدِنـا أبي الفَضْلِ الّتي
أعطاكَ مُعْتَذِراً كَمَـنْ قَـدْ أجْرَمـا	يُعْطِيـكَ مُبْتَـدِراً فـإنْ أعْجَلْتَـهُ
وَيَـرى التَّواضُـعَ أنْ يُـرَى مُتَعَظِّمـا	وَيَـرى التَّعَظُّـمَ أن يُـرَى مُتَواضِعـاً
خـالَ السّـؤالَ عَلـى النَّـوالِ مُحَرَّمـا	نَصَـرَ الفِعـالَ علـى المِطـالِ كَأنَّمـا
من ذاتِ ذي المَلكوتِ أسمى مِن سَما	يـا أيُّهـا المَلَـكُ المُصَفَّـى جَوْهَـراً
فتَكـادُ تَعْلَـمُ عِلْـمَ مـا لَـنْ يُعْلَمـا	نُـورٌ تَظاهَـرَ فيـكَ لاهُوتِيُّـهُ
مِن كُـلِّ عُضْـوٍ مِنـكَ أنْ يَتَكَلَّمـا	وَيَهِـمُّ فيـكَ إذا نَطَقْـتَ فَصاحَـةً
مَـنْ كـانَ يَحْلُـمُ بالإلَـهِ فَأحْلُمـا	أنـا مُبْصِـرٌ وَأظُـنُّ أنّـي نـائِـمٌ
صـارَ اليَقيـنُ مِـنَ العِيـانِ تَوَهُّمـا	كَبُـرَ العِيـانُ عَلـيَّ حتـى إنَّـهُ
نِقَـمٌ تَعُـودُ علـى اليَتامـى أنْعُمـا	يـا مَـنْ لجُـودِ يَدَيْـهِ في أمْوالِـهِ
وَيَقُـولُ بَيْـتُ المالِ ما ذا مُسْلِمـا	حتـى يَقُـولُ النـاسُ مـا ذا عـاقِـلاً
إذْ لا تُريـدُ لِمـا أُريـدُ مُتَرْجِمـا	إذ كـارُ مِثْلِـكَ تَـرْكُ أذ كـارِي لَـهُ

7
He spoke also in his youth and he wanted to reveal his points of view.
(Perfect ma)

O cease, anxiety shows me your reproach
    Painfully arising in this breast without stars
A ghost of a body, love has not left
    It flesh or blood since an illness wastes it
A throbbing heart, if you saw its flame
    You'd suspect it, O my heaven, to be hell
So clouds on love's mountainside flash
    Leaving the sweetness of each love bitter
O trickster face, but for you languor
    Would not gnaw my body or crush my bone
If consolation enriches her then indeed
    I am impoverished due to my liver and her
Sapling growing on a double sand hill
    A sun of day that bears the darkest night
Contrasts unite in seeming likeness
    Only to make me the plunder of affliction
Like traits of our unique Abu Fadl that
    Win as he inspires and quiets his poets
He gives to you first, if you press him
    He gives with excuses like one who sins
He looks at pride so it seems to be low
    He sees humility as if it were a greatness
He keeps a good deed from delay as if
    He thought a request for a gift forbidden
O king made as pure as a jewel by one
    Who has the kingdom, highest of the high
A divine light shines out from you
    You almost know a wisdom not to be known
It desires as you speak eloquently to
    Make an utterance by each of your limbs
I have vision yet I feel I am asleep
    But who dreams of God as I am dreaming?
The eyes enlarge in me till it's clear
    To these eyes that they are led by fancy
O he, by gifts given from his wealth,
    Is revenge that returns as mercy to orphans
Until mankind says: This is not wise
    And the treasury says: This is not Muslim
Memory of such as you is my neglect
    For you need no reminder of what I want

(٨)

«من الطويل»

قال في صباه:

بَريئًا مِنَ الجَرْحى سَليمًا مِن القَتلِ	مُحبّي قيامي ما لِذلِكُمُ النَّصلِ
وَجُودةُ ضَربِ الهامِ في جُودةِ الصَّقلِ	أرى مِن فِرِنْدي قِطعَةً في فِرِنْدِهِ
أرَتكَ احمِرارَ المَوتِ في مَدرَجِ النَملِ	وَخُضرةُ ثَوبِ العَيشِ في الخُضرةِ التي
فَما أحدٌ فَوقي وَلا أحدٌ مِثلي	أمِطْ عَنكَ تَشبيهي بِما وَكأنَّهُ
نَكُنْ واحِدًا يَلقى الوَرى وانظُرَنْ فِعلي	وَدَعني وَإيّاهُ وَطَرفي وَذابِلي

(٩)

«من الطويل»

قال في صباه:

وَحَتّى مَتى في شِقْوةٍ وَإلى كَم	إلى أيِّ حينٍ أنتَ في زيِّ مُحرِمِ
تَمُتْ وَتُقاسِ الذُّلَّ غَيرَ مُكَرَّمِ	وَإلّا تَمُتْ تَحتَ السُّيوفِ مُكرَّمًا
يَرى المَوتَ في الهيجا جَنى النَحلِ في الفَمِ	فَثِبْ واثِقًا باللهِ وِثْبَةَ ماجِدٍ

(١٠)

«من البسيط»

يمدح سعيد بن عبد الله بن الحسين الكلابي المنبجي:

وَالبَينُ جارَ على ضُعفي وَما عَدَلا	أحْيا وَأيْسَرُ ما قاسَيْتُ ما قَتَلا
وَالصَّبرُ يَنحَلُ في جِسمي كَما نَحَلا	وَالوَجدُ يَقوى كَما تَقوى النَّوى أبدًا
لَها المَنايا إلى أرواحِنا سُبُلا	لَوْ لا مُفارَقةُ الأحبابِ ما وَجَدَت
يَهوى الحَياةَ وَأمّا إنْ صَدَدتِ فَلا	بِما بِجَفنَيكِ مِن سِحرٍ صَلي دَنِفًا
شَيبًا إذا خَضَبَتهُ سَلوةٌ نَصَلا	إلّا يَشِبْ فَلَقد شابَت لَهُ كَبِدٌ
تَزورُهُ مِن رياحِ الشَرقِ ما عَقَلا	يَحِنُّ شَوقًا فَلَولا أنْ رائِحَةً
مَن لَم يَذُقْ طَرَفًا مِنها فَقد وَأَلا	ها فانظُري أو فَظُنّي بي تَرَيْ حُرَقًا
إلى الّتي تَرَكَتني في الهَوى مَثَلا	عَلَ الأميرَ يَرى ذُلّي فَيَشفَعَ لي
لَمّا بَصُرتُ بِهِ بالرُمحِ مُعتَقِلا	أيقَنتُ أنّ سَعيدًا طالِبٌ بِدَمي

8
He spoke in his youth also.
(Long li)

O friend of my stance, is that blade
    Free of wounds and innocent of death?
I see in my temper a bit of the cut
    Good to strike skulls if it is finely honed
Life's green garment on a branch to
    Show you red death in the ant's tracks
Cease comparing me with like and as
    For none is above me and none like me
Leave it to me with horse and spear
    We are one to hit men, so watch my work

9
He spoke in his youth also.
(Long mi)

How long will you go in pilgrim dress
    Until when in misery and how many years?
If you die not under swords generously
    Die and suffer basely without the nobility
Jump, trusting in God, in glory's leap
    See death in war as honeycomb in mouth

10
He spoke in his youth
in Syria
praising Said ibn
Abdallah ibn al-Husayn al-Kilabi
(Outspread la)

I live, the easiest I suffer is deadly
    But parting oppresses my weakness unjustly
Love increases as distance grows greater
    Patience wears thin in my body as it wastes
But for the beloved's departure the fates
    Would not find in her the way to our souls
By your eyes' magic, give me mortal ills
    That love life but if you thwart it, then not
If he has not aged yet his liver is gray
    With age, and if solace lent color it faded
He sighs in love, if it weren't that odors
    Visited him on an east wind he'd not be sane
See or think of me whom you know aflame
    As one not tasting a glimpse of her as fleeing
Maybe the Amir sees my shame and pleads
    With her who left love and made me a proverb
I am sure Said will seek revenge for me
    When I see him with his lance held at ready

24 Diwan al-Mutanabbi

ونـائِـلٌ دونَ نَيْلي وَصْفَـهُ زُحَـلا	وأنّي غَيْرُ مُحْصٍ فَضْلَ والِـدِهِ
في الأفْقِ يَسْألُ عَمّنْ غَيْرهُ سَألا	فَيْـلٌ بَمَنْبِـجَ مَثْـواهُ ونـائِـلُـهُ
ويَحْمِلُ المَوْتُ في الهيجاءِ إنْ حَمَلا	يَلـوحُ بَـدْرُ الدُّجَى في صَحْنِ غُرَّتِـهِ
وسَيْفُهُ في جَنابٍ يَسْبُـقُ العَـذَلا	تُرابُـهُ في كِـلابٍ كُحْـلُ أعْيُنِـها
حُلْوٌ كَـأَنَّ عَلـى أخْلاقِـهِ عَسَـلا	مُهَـذَّبِ الجَدِّ يُسْتَسْقَى الغَمامُ بِـهِ
لَوْ صاعَدَ الفكرَ فيهِ الدَّهرَ ما نَـزَلا	لِنـورِهِ في سَماءِ الفخرِ مُخْـتَـرقٌ
قِدْماً وسـاقَ إلَيْهـا حَيْنُهـا الأجَـلا	هـوَ الأميـرُ الذي بـادَتْ تَميـمٌ بـهِ
والحربُ غَيْرُ عَوانٍ أسلمـوا الحِلَـلا	لَمّا رَأَوْهُ وخَيْـلُ النَّصْـرِ مُقْبِـلَـةٌ
إذا رَأى غَيْـرَ شَـيْءٍ ظَنّـهُ رَجُـلا	وضاقَتِ الأرْضُ حتى كـانَ هارِبُـهُمْ
بالخَيْلِ في لَهَواتِ الطِّفْلِ ما سَعَـلا	فَبُعْدَهُ وإلى اليَـوْمِ لَـوْ رَكَضَتْ
وقد قَتَلْتَ الأُلى لَـمْ تَلْقَهُـمْ وَجَـلا	فَقَـدْ تَرَكْـتَ الأُلى لاقَيْتَهُـمْ جَـزَرا
قلْـبَ المُحِبِّ قضانـي بعدمـا مَطَـلا	كَمْ مَهْمَـهٍ قَـذَفٍ قلْبُ الدّليـلِ بـهِ
وحُـرَّ وَجْهـي بَحَـرَّ الشّمْسِ إذْ أفَـلا	عَقَـدْتُ بـالنَّجْمِ طَـرْفي في مَفـاوِزِهِ
تَعَشْمَـرَتْ بـي إلَيْكَ السهْـلَ والجَبَـلا	أوْطَـأْتُ صُـمَّ حَصاهـا خُـفَّ يَعْمَلَـةٍ
سَمِعْتَ للجِنِّ في غيطانِهـا زَجَـلا	لَـوْ كُنتَ حشْـوَ قَميصي فَـوْقَ نُمرُقَهـا
ولَيْتَنـي عِشْـتُ منهـا بالـذي فَضَـلا	حتى وَصَلْتُ بنفْسٍ مـاتَ أكثرُهـا
يا مَنْ إذا وَهَـبَ الدّنيا فقـد بَخِـلا	أرْجـو نَداكَ ولا أخشَى المِطـالَ بـهِ

(١١)

«من الخفيف»

قال في صِباه:

لِبيـاضِ الطُّلَى وَوَرْدِ الخُـدودِ	كَـمْ قَتيـلٍ كمـا قُتِلْـتُ شَهيـدٍ
فَتَكَـتْ بالمُتَيَّـمِ المَعْمُـودِ	وعُيـونُ المَهـا ولا كَعُيـونٍ
رَ ذيولي بدارِ أثْلَـةَ عُـودي	دَرَّ دَرُّ الصِّبـا أيّـامَ تَجـريـ
طَلَعَـتْ في بَراقِـعَ وعُقُـودِ	عَمْـرَكَ الله! هَـلْ رأيْـتَ بُـدوراً
بَ تشُـقُّ القُلـوبَ قبـلَ الجُلودِ	راميـاتٍ بأسْهُـمٍ ريشُها الهُـدْ
هُـنَّ فيـهِ حَـلاوةُ التّوحيـدِ	يَترَشَّفْـنَ مِـنْ فَمـي رَشَفـاتٍ

I surely cannot count his father's favors
    Gifts like Zuhal beside my gift of limping
A lord whose seat is Manbij whose gifts
    Afar seek those who do not plead for them
A moon at dusk shines on his forehead
    Death attacks in the battle if he sallies forth
His dust on Kilab was collyrium to their eyes
    His sword against Janab outstripped blame
Ancestral honesty a rain cloud in him
    Sweetness as if his character were honey
A way for his star is in honor's heaven
    If the idea rose it would never set there
He is the Amir by whom the Tamim lost
    And their defeat led them to their destruction
When they saw him and winning horses
    And continuous war they yielded their camp
Earth was too narrow until their fugitive
    Thought he saw nothing yet thought it a man
After him to this day if they were to run
    Horses in a babe's throat it wouldn't cough!
You left those you met meat for beasts
    Killed with terror those you did not meet
Many a far desert where a guide's heart
    Is a lover's heart rewards me after the delay
I fixed my eyes on a star in the wasteland
    My face was free to the hot sun when it set
I trod its hot stones with camel's hoofs
    Taking me by force on plain and peak to you
If you were in my clothes on that saddle
    You would hear jinn howling in the hollows
I come with soul most of which is dead
    Would I could live on that which remains
I hope for your bounty, I fear no delay
    O if he gave the world he would be miserly

11
He spoke in his youth also
(Nimble di)

How many slain, as I was, are martyrs
    To the white throat and those rosy cheeks!
To eyes of a wild fawn, not like eyes
    That overcome some passionately enslaved
May youth's stream flow as if my skirt
    Was dragged in Dar Athla—O return to me!
Your life in God! have you seen such
    Moons rising among veils and necklaces?
Shooting arrows feathered by eyelashes
    To penetrate the hearts and before the skin
They suck from my mouth some drops
    Which there are sweeter than that of Unity

بِقَلْبٍ أَقْسى مِنَ الجُلْمودِ	كُلُّ خُمْصانَةٍ أَرَقُّ مِنَ الخَمْــ
بَرُّ فيهِ ماءُ وَرْدٍ وَعودِ	ذاتِ فَرْعٍ كَأَنَّما ضُرِبَ العَنْــ
جِيُّ أَثيثٍ جَعْدٍ بِلا تَجْعيدِ	حالِكٍ كَالغُدافِ حَثْلٍ دَجودِ
ـحِ وَتَفْتَرُّ عَنْ شَنيبٍ بَرودِ	تَحْمِلُ المِسْكَ عَن غَدائِرِها الرّيـ
ـمِ وَبَيْنَ الجُفونِ وَالتَسْهيدِ	جَمَعَتْ بَيْنَ جِسْمِ أَحْمَدَ وَالسُقْـ
فَانْقُصي مِنْ عَذابِها أَوْ فَزيدي	هَذِهِ مُهْجَتي لَدَيْكِ لَحَيْني
ـدَ بِتَصْفيفِ طُرَّةٍ وَجِيدِ	أَهْلُ ما بي مِنَ الضَنى بَطَلٌ صِيـ
شُرْبُهُ ما خَلا ابْنَةَ العُنْقودِ	كُلُّ شَيْءٍ مِنَ الدِماءِ حَرامٌ
مِنْ غَزالٍ وَطارَ في وَتَليدي	فَاسْقِنيها فِدًى لِعَيْنَيْكَ نَفْسي
وَدُموعي عَلى هَواكَ شُهودي	شَيْبُ رَأْسي وَذُلِّي وَنُحولي
لَمْ تَرُعْني ثَلاثَةٌ بِصُدودِ	أَيَّ يَوْمٍ سَرَرْتَني بِوِصالِ
كَمُقامِ المَسيحِ بَيْنَ اليَهودِ	ما مُقامي بِأَرْضِ نَخْلَةَ إِلّا
ـنَّ قَميصي مَسْرودَةٌ مِنْ حَديدِ	مَفْرِشي صَهْوَةُ الحِصانِ وَلَكِـ
أَحْكَمَتْ نَسْجَها يَدا داوُدِ	لِأَمَةٍ فاضَةٍ أَضاةَ دِلاصٍ
ـرَ بَعِيشٍ مُعَجَّلِ التَنكيدِ	أَيْنَ فَضْلي إِذا قَنِعْتُ مِنَ الدَهْـ
قَ قِيامي وَقَلَّ عَنهُ قُعودي	ضاقَ صَدْري وَطالَ في طَلَبِ الرِزْ
في نُحوسٍ وَهِمَّتي في سُعودِ	أَبَداً أَقْطَعُ البِلادَ وَنَجْمي
ـلُغُ بِاللَطْفِ مِنْ عَزيزٍ حَميدِ	وَلَعَلَّ مُؤَمَّلٍ بَعْضَ ما أَبْـ
نِ وَمَرْوِيَّ مَرْوَ لِبْسَ القُرودِ	لِسَرِيٍّ لِباسُهُ خَشِنَ القُطْـ
بَيْنَ طَعْنِ القَنا وَخَفْقِ البُنودِ	عِشْ عَزيزاً أَوْ مُتْ وَأَنتَ كَريمٌ
ـظِ وَأَشْفى لِغُلِّ صَدْرِ الحَقودِ	فَرُؤوسُ الرِماحِ أَذْهَبُ لِلغَيْـ
وَإِذا مُتَّ مُتَّ غَيْرَ فَقيدِ	لا كَما قَد حَييتَ غَيْرَ حَميدٍ
ـلِّ وَلَوْ كانَ في جِنانِ الخُلودِ	فَاطْلُبِ العِزَّ في لَظًى وَدَعِ الذُّ
جِزُ عَنْ قَطْعِ بَخْنَقِ المَولودِ	يُقْتَلُ العاجِزُ الجَبانُ وَقَدْ يَعْـ
ضَ في ماءِ لَبَّةِ الصِنديدِ	وَيُوَقّى الفَتى المِخَشُّ وَقَدْ خَوْ
وَبِنَفْسي فَخَرْتُ لا بِجُدودي	لا بِقَوْمي شَرُفْتُ بَل شَرُفوا بي
دَ وَعَوذُ الجاني وَغَوْثُ الطَريدِ	وَبِهِم فَخْرُ كُلِّ مَنْ نَطَقَ الضا

Each slim waisted one softer than wine
    Has a heart that is harder than one of stone
Possessed of locks amber drenched
    Mingled with rose water and with aloes
Black as a raven, full of darkness
    Very thick in waves but not frizzled
The wind carries musk from the braids
    She smiles with cool even spaced teeth
She unites Ahmad's body with sickness
    And then his eyelids with his sleeplessness
Here is my heart for you at my death
    Diminish its pain in me or increase it
I welcome emaciation I suffer as hero
    Hunted by ringlets on a brow and a neck
Ail that pertains to gore is forbidden
    For drinking except the blood of the grape
So pour since I am ransom for your eyes
    Among gazelles in my goods and heritage
My head's gray hair, shame, emaciation
    And tears are my witnesses to your passion
Which day do you delight me by embrace
    And don't scare me three days with denial?
My stay in Dar Nakhia is nothing but
    The stay of the Messiah among the Jews
My bed is the back of my stallion
    But yet my shirt is of the woven iron
Close knit, supple as a bright pool
    With David's hand they worked its weave
Where is my profit if I accept fate
    As life rushes onward in its harshness?
My breast anxious, my stay in search
    Of food is long with little respite for me
Ever I traverse lands and my stars
    Are in decline, but my purpose aspires
Perhaps I can somehow fulfill hopes
    By kindness of the power most praised
By a prince dressed in coarse cotton
    For Mervian silk is a dress for the apes
Live strong or die if you are noble
    Amid thrusting lances as flags flutter
Spearheads are best to melt wrath
    Best cure for boiling rage in a breast
Not as you live without any praise
    And you die, die without being missed!
Seek glory in fire, leave humiliation
    Even though it be in immortal paradise
A coward weakling is done to death
    He faints at a bit of a child's head cloth
But the bold youth is guarded and has
    Penetrated the liquor of the brave breast
I glory not in my folk, they do so in
    Me, I boast of myself not of my ancestors
They were the pride of all who used dad
    Asylum for culprits and an aid to refugees

28   Diwan al-Mutanabbi

إنْ أكنْ مُعجَباً فَعُجْبٌ عَجيبٌ	لَمْ يَجِدْ فَوقَ نَفْسِهِ مِن مَزيدِ
أنا تِرْبُ النَّدَى وَرَبُّ القَوافي	وَسِمامُ العِدَى وغَيظُ الحَسودِ
أنا في أُمَّةٍ تَدارَكَها اللّـهُ غَريبٌ كصالِحٍ في ثَمودِ	

(١٢)

«من المنسرح»

قال في صباه ارتجالاً وقد أهدى إليه عبيد الله بن خلكان هدية فيها سمك من سكر ولوز في عسل:

قَدْ شَغَلَ النّاسَ كَثرَةُ الأمَلِ	وأنتَ بالمَكرُماتِ في شُغُلِ
تَمَثَّلوا حاتِماً وَلَوْ عَقَلوا	لَكُنْتَ في الجُودِ غايَةَ المَثَلِ
أهلاً وَسَهْلاً بِما بَعَثْتَ بِهِ	إيهاً أبا قاسِمٍ وبالرَّسُلِ
هَدِيَّةً ما رَأيتُ مُهديها	إلّا رَأيتُ العِبادَ في رَجُلِ
أقَلُّ ما في اقَلِّها سَمَكٌ	يَسْبَحُ في بِركَةٍ مِنَ العَسَلِ
كَيفَ أكافي على أجَلِّ يَدٍ	مَنْ لا يَرَى أنَّها يَدُّ قَبْلي

(١٣)

«من الكامل»

وأرسل إليه جامة فيها حلوى فردها وكتب فيها بالزعفران:

أقصِرْ فَلَسْتَ بزائِدي وُدّا	بَلَغَ المَدَى وتَجاوَزَ الحَدّا
أرسَلْتَها مَملوءَةً كَرَماً	فَرَدَدْتُها مَملوءَةً حَمْدا
جاءَتْكَ تَطفَحُ وَهيَ فارِغَةٌ	مَثْنىً بِهِ وَتَظُنُّها فَرْدا
تَأبَى خَلائِقُكَ التي شَرُفَتْ	ألّا تَحِنَّ وَتَذْكُرَ العَهْدا
لَوْ كُنتَ عَصراً مُنبِتاً زَهَراً	كُنتَ الرَّبيعَ وكانَتِ الوَرْدا

If I am amazing yet a wonder of wonders
    Is that one finds none higher than this one
I am twin of reward, master of rhyme
    Poison to the foe and the rage of envy
I am among these folk, God pity them
    A stranger like Salih among the Thamud

12
He spoke impromptu in his youth when Ubaidallah ibn Khurasan had just given him a gift of a candy fish with almonds and honey.
(Flowing li)

Many expectations have kept men busy
    While you were busy with noble activities
They idealized Hatim but if they knew
    You would be the point of bounty's proverb
Welcome, greetings to what you sent
    Enough for Abu Qasim and the messengers
A gift whose giver I did not know
    Unless I knew mankind as a single man
The least of the platter is the fish
    That is swimming in the pool of honey
How do I repay the best of presents
    To one who sees it as no reward for me?

13
He wrote to him also on the sides of the platter in saffron.
(Perfect da)

Stop, you cannot increase love for me
    That attains the goal and exceeds the limit
You sent it overflowing with bounty
    And I returned it filled with gratitude
It comes to you brimful though empty
    Double praise but you thought it single
Your character denied what it ennobled
    Does it not yearn for and recall the bond?
If you were a season to bring flowers
    You would be spring and that the roses

(١٤)

«من الطويل»

يهجو سواراً الديلمي:

وَأَنْضاءُ أَسْفارٍ كَشَرْبِ عُقارِ	بَقِيَّةُ قَوْمٍ آذَنوا بِبَوارِ
عَلَيْنا لَها ثَوْباً حَصىً وَغُبارِ	نَزَلْنا عَلى حُكْمِ الرِياحِ بِمَسْجِدٍ
فَشُدّا عَلَيْها وَارْحَلا بِنَهارِ	خَليلَيَّ ما هذا مُناخاً لِمِثْلِنا
قِرى كُلِّ ضَيْفٍ باتَ عِنْدَ سِوارِ	وَلا تُنكِرا عَصْفَ الرِياحِ فَإِنَّها

(١٥)

«من الكامل»

قال في صباه يمدح أبا المنتصر شجاع بن محمد بن أوس بن معن بن الرضى سالازدي:

وَحَوى يَزيدُ وَعَبْرَةٌ تَتَرَقْرَقُ	أَرَقٌ عَلى أَرَقٍ وَمِثْلي يَأْرَقُ
عَيْنٌ مُسَهَّدَةٌ وَقَلْبٌ يَخْفِقُ	جُهْدُ الصَبابَةِ أَنْ تَكونَ كَما أَرى
إِلّا اِنْثَنَيْتُ وَلي فُؤادٌ شَيِّقُ	ما لاحَ بَرْقٌ أَوْ تَرَنَّمَ طائِرٌ
نارُ الغَضا وَتَكِلُّ عَمّا يُحْرِقُ	جَرَّبْتُ مِنْ نارِ الهَوى ما تَنْطَفي
فَعَجِبْتُ كَيْفَ يَموتُ مَنْ لا يَعْشَقُ	وَعَذَلْتُ أَهْلَ العِشْقِ حَتّى ذُقْتُهُ
عَيَّرْتُهُمْ فَلَقيتُ مِنْهُ ما لَقوا	وَعَذَرْتُهُمْ وَعَرَفْتُ ذَنْبي أَنَّني
أَبَداً غُرابُ البَيْنِ فيها يَنْعَقُ	أَبَني أَبينا نَحْنُ أَهْلُ مَنازِلٍ
جَمَعَتْهُمُ الدُنْيا فَلَمْ يَتَفَرَّقوا	نَبْكي عَلى الدُنْيا وَما مِنْ مَعْشَرٍ
كَنَزوا الكُنوزَ فَما بَقينَ وَلا بَقوا	أَيْنَ الأَكاسِرَةُ الجَبابِرَةُ الأُلى
حَتّى ثَوى فَحَواهُ لَحْدٌ ضَيِّقُ	مِنْ كُلِّ مَنْ ضاقَ الفَضاءُ بِجَيْشِهِ
أَنَّ الكَلامَ لَهُمْ حَلالٌ مُطْلَقُ	خُرْسٌ إِذا نودوا كَأَنْ لَمْ يَعْلَموا
وَالمُسْتَعِزُّ بِما لَدَيْهِ الأَحْمَقُ	فَالمَوْتُ آتٍ وَالنُفوسُ نَفائِسٌ
وَالشَيْبُ أَوْقَرُ وَالشَبيبَةُ أَنْزَقُ	وَالمَرْءُ يَأْمُلُ وَالحَياةُ شَهِيَّةٌ
مُسْوَدَّةً وَلَماءُ وَجْهي رَوْنَقُ	وَلَقَدْ بَكَيْتُ عَلى الشَبابِ وَلِمَّتي
حَتّى لَكِدَّتْ بِماءِ جَفْني أَشْرَقُ	حَذَراً عَلَيْهِ قَبْلَ يَوْمِ فِراقِهِ

14
He spoke impromptu about pilgrims and the rain and wind were attacking them.
(Long ri)

A remnant of folk called to perdition
    Exhausted by travel like the wine drinkers
We pause in a mosque by winds' decree
    Upon us, with it a cloak of the sand and dust
My two friends, this place is not for us
    So saddle up and be off while it is light
Do not dread blowing winds for they
    Are rest to guests staying a night with Siwar

15
He spoke also in his youth praising Abu Muntasir Shuja ibn Muhammad ibn Aws ibn Maan ibn Rida al-Azdi.
(Perfect qu)

Waking on waking and such as I wakeful
    Grief increases and tears beginning to flow
Passion's hardship is to be as I seem
    A sleepless eye and a palpitating heart
Lightning does not flash or bird sing
    Without my turning away with torn heart
I feel a fire of love inextinguishable
    A hard wood fire is weak in its burning
I blamed folk of love until I tasted it
    Then wondered how one died who loved not
I excused them and knew my sin when
    I reproached them, for I met what they met
O sons of our father, we are camp folk
    Always the raven of parting croaks for us
We weep for a world but none go that
    The world collects and does not scatter
Where are the bold Kisras who stored
    The treasure that did not stay, nor they
To each plains too small for armies
    Until he died and a narrow tomb held him
Silent when called as if they knew not
    The words were permitted and free to them
Death comes even to most precious souls
    One beguiled by his wealth is most absurd
A man hopes, and living is longing
    And age is burdened and youth headlong
I wept for youth when locks over my ear
    Were black and sweat on my face colored
Worrying about it before its parting day
    Till I almost choked with my eyelid's tears

فَأَعَزُّ مَنْ تُحْدَى إِلَيْهِ الأَيْنُقُ	أَمَّا بَنُو أَوْسِ بْنِ مَعْنِ بْنِ الرِّضَى
مِنْها الشُّمُوسُ وَلَيْسَ فِيها المَشْرِقُ	كَبَّرْتُ حَوْلَ دِيارِهِمْ لَمَّا بَدَتْ
مِنْ فَوْقِها وَصُخُورُها لا تُورِقُ	وَعَجِبْتُ مِنْ أَرْضٍ سَحابُ أَكُفِّهِمْ
لَهُمُ بِكُلِّ مَكانَةٍ تَسْتَنْشَقُ	وَتَفُوحُ مِنْ طِيبِ الثَّناءِ رَوائِحٌ
وَحْشِيَّةٌ بِسِواهُمُ لا تَعْبَقُ	مِسْكِيَّةُ النَّفَحاتِ إِلَّا أَنَّها
لا تَبْلُنا بِطِلابِ ما لا يُلْحَقُ	أَمُرِيدَ مِثْلِ مُحَمَّدٍ فِي عَصْرِنا
أَحَداً وَظَنِّي أَنَّهُ لا يَخْلُقُ	لَمْ يَخْلُقِ الرَّحْمَنُ مِثْلَ مُحَمَّدٍ
أَنَّى عَلَيْهِ بِأَخْذِهِ أَتَصَدَّقُ	يا ذا الَّذِي يَهَبُ الكَثِيرَ وَعِنْدَهُ
وَانْظُرْ إِلَيَّ بِرَحْمَةٍ لا أَغْرَقُ	أَمْطِرْ عَلَيَّ سَحابَ جُودِكَ ثَرَّةً
ماتَ الكِرامُ وَأَنْتَ حَيٌّ يُرْزَقُ	كَذَبَ ابْنُ فاعِلَةٍ يَقُولُ بِجَهْلِهِ

(١٦)

«الطويل»

قال في صباه يمدح علي بن أحمد الطائي:

فَلَمْ أَدْرِ أَيَّ الظَّاعِنَيْنِ أُشَيِّعُ	حُشاشَةُ نَفْسٍ وَدَّعَتْ يَوْمَ وَدَّعُوا
تَسِيلُ مِنَ الآماقِ وَالسَّمُّ أَدْمُعُ	أَشاوِرُ بِتَسْلِيمٍ فَجُدْنا بِأَنْفُسٍ
وَعَيْناي فِي رَوْضٍ مِنَ الحُسْنِ تَرْتَعُ	حَشايَ عَلى جَمْرٍ ذَكِيٍّ مِنَ الهَوى
غَداةَ افْتَرَقْنا أَوْشَكَتْ تَتَصَدَّعُ	وَلَوْ حُمِّلَتْ صُمُّ الجِبالِ الَّذِي بِنا
إِلَيَّ الدَّياجِي وَالخَلِيُّونَ هُجَّعُ	بِما بَيْنَ جَنْبَيَّ الَّتِي خاضَ طَيْفُها
وَكَالمِسْكِ مِنْ أَرْدانِها يَتَضَوَّعُ	أَتَتْ زائِراً ما خامَرَ الطِّيبُ ثَوْبَها
كَفاطِمَةٍ عَنْ دِرِّها قَبْلَ تُرْضِعُ	فَما جَلَسَتْ حَتَّى انْثَنَتْ تُوسِعُ الخُطى
مِنَ النَّوْمِ وَالتاعَ الفُؤادُ المُفَجَّعُ	فَشَرَّدَ إِعْظامِي لَها ما أَتى بِها
وَسُمُّ الأَفاعِي عَذْبُ ما أَتَجَرَّعُ	فَيا لَيْلَةً ما كانَ أَطْوَلَ بِتُّها
فَما عاشِقٌ مَنْ لا يَذِلُّ وَيَخْضَعُ	تَذَلَّلْ لَها وَاخْضَعْ عَلى القُرْبِ وَالنَّوى
عَلى أَحَدٍ إِلَّا بِلُؤْمٍ مُرَقَّعُ	وَلا ثَوْبُ مَجْدٍ غَيْرَ ثَوْبِ ابْنِ أَحْمَدٍ
بِهِ اللهُ يُعْطِي مَنْ يَشاءُ وَيَمْنَعُ	وَإِنَّ الَّذِي حابى جَدِيلَةَ طَيِّءٍ
عَلى رَأْسِ أَوْفى ذِمَّةً مِنْهُ تَطْلُعُ	بِذِي كَرَمٍ ما مَرَّ يَوْمٌ وَشَمْسُهُ

As For Banu Aws ibn Maan ibn Rida
    They are the best the camels are led to
I extol their house's power when suns
    Come out of it yet there is no dawn there
I wonder at earth as their cloud hands
    Move above and its rocks grow no leaves
Their winds of praise spread as incense
    In all of the places where odor is breathed
Musky in exhalation except that it is
    Foreign to others and clings not to them
O you seeking Muhammad's like now
    Trouble us not with unattainable search
The Merciful created none like Muhammad
    And it is my suspicion that he will never do so
O you who give so much and through whom
    I by taking it am able to give it others as alms
Rain down on me your rich bounty cloud
    Glance at me in mercy so I will not drown
A meddler's son lies saying ignorantly
    Bounty is dead when you live to provide it

16
He spoke also in his youth praising Ali ibn Ahmad al Khurasani. (Long u)

A bit of soul departed the day they went
    I know not which voyager's pall I escorted
They wave goodbye, we lavish with sighs
    Pouring from eyes but they are called tears
My guts are on coals ablaze with passion
    But my eyes are grazing meadows of beauty
If mountain tops were loaded as we were
    The morning we parted they'd quickly split
By my heart, it was she whose spirit came
    To me in darkness while the carefree slept
She visited, as scent warming her dress
    And like musk on her sleeve it spread afar
She hardly sat, then turned taking steps
    Like the weaning nurse before the suckling
My wonder at her scared what she had
    Of sleep and the distressed heart burned
O that night, how long it was I took it
    Poison of the snake was sweet as I drank
Submit to her, be meek if near or far
    He is no lover who is not not abased lowly
Nor glory garment but Ibn Ahmad's robe
    On anyone unless it is patched by meanness
He is one who gave richly to Tai's Jadila
    By him God gives as he wishes and refuses
This is nobility, no day passes that a sun
    Rises on a head richer in honesty than his

وَأَرْحَامُ مَالٍ مَا تَنِي تَتَقَطَّعُ	فَأَرْحَامُ شِعْرٍ يَتَّصِلْنَ لَدُنَّهُ
أَقَلُّ جُزَيْءٍ بَعْضُهُ الرَّأْيَ أَجْمَعُ	فَتَى أَلْفُ جُزْءٍ رَأْيُهُ فِي زَمَانِهِ
وَلَا البَرْقُ فِيهِ خُلَّباً حِينَ يَلْمَعُ	غَمَامٌ عَلَيْنَا مُمْطِرٌ لَيْسَ يُقْشِعُ
إِلَى نَفْسِهِ فِيهَا شَفِيعٌ مُشَفَّعُ	إِذَا عُرِضَتْ حَاجٌ إِلَيْهِ فَنَفْسُهُ
وَأَسْمَرُ عُرْيَانٌ مِنَ القِشْرِ أَصْلَعُ	خَبَتْ نَارُ حَرْبٍ لَمْ تَهِجْهَا بَنَانُهُ
وَيَحْفَى فَيَقْوَى عَدُوُّهُ حِينَ يُقْطَعُ	نَحِيفُ الشَّوَى يَعْدُو عَلَى أُمِّ رَأْسِهِ
وَيُفْهِمُ عَمَّنْ قَالَ مَا لَيْسَ يُسْمَعُ	يَمُجُّ ظَلَاماً فِي نَهَارٍ لِسَانُهُ
وَأَعْصَى لِمَوْلَاهُ وَذَا مِنْهُ أَطْوَعُ	ذُبَابُ حُسَامٍ مِنْهُ أَنْحَى ضَرِيبَةً
أُصُولَ البَرَاعَاتِ التِي تَتَفَرَّعُ	فَصِيحٌ مَتَى يَنْطِقْ تَجِدْ كُلَّ لَفْظَةٍ
لَمَا فَاتَهَا فِي الشَّرْقِ وَالغَرْبِ مَوْضِعُ	بِكَفِّ جَوَادٍ لَوْ حَكَتْهَا سَحَابَةٌ
إِلَى حَيْثُ يَفْنَى المَاءُ حُوتٌ وَضِفْدَعُ	وَلَيْسَ كَبَحْرِ المَاءِ يُشْتَقُّ قَعْرُهُ
زُعَاقٌ كَبَحْرٍ لَا يَضُرُّ وَيَنْفَعُ	أَبَحْرٌ يَضُرُّ المُعْتَفِينَ وَطَعْمُهُ
وَيَغْرَقُ فِي تَيَّارِهِ وَهْوَ مِصْقَعُ	يَتِيهُ الدَّقِيقُ الفِكْرِ فِي بُعْدِ غَوْرِهِ
وَهِمَّتُهُ فَوْقَ السِّمَاكَيْنِ تُوضَعُ	أَلَا أَيُّهَا القَيْلُ المُقِيمُ بِمَنْبِجٍ
وَأَنَّ ظُنُونِي فِي مَعَالِيكَ تَظْلَعُ	أَلَيْسَ عَجِيباً أَنَّ وَصْفَكَ مُعْجِزٌ
عَلَى أَنَّهُ مِنْ سَاحَةِ الأَرْضِ أَوْسَعُ	وَأَنَّكَ فِي ثَوْبٍ وَصَدْرُكَ فِيكُمَا
وَبِالجِنِّ فِيهِ مَادَرَتْ كَيْفَ تَرْجِعُ	وَقَلْبُكَ فِي الدُّنْيَا وَلَوْ دَخَلَتْ بِنَا
وَكُلُّ مَدِيحٍ فِي سِوَاكَ مُضَيَّعُ	أَلَا كُلُّ سَمْحٍ غَيْرَكَ اليَوْمَ بَاطِلٌ

(١٧)

«من المتقارب»

قال في صباه على لسان بعض التنوخيين وقد ساله ذلك:

ـذِي ادَّخَرَتْ لِصُرُوفِ الزَّمَانْ	قُضَاعَةُ تَعْلَمُ أَنِّي الفَتَى الَـ
عَلَى أَنَّ كُلَّ كَرِيمٍ يَمَانْ	وَمَجْدِي يَدُلُّ بَنِي خِنْدِفٍ
أَنَا ابْنُ الضِّرَابِ أَنَا ابْنُ الطِّعَانْ	أَنَا ابْنُ اللِّقَاءِ أَنَا ابْنُ السَّخَاءِ
أَنَا ابْنُ السُّرُوجِ أَنَا ابْنُ الرِّعَانْ	أَنَا ابْنُ الفَيَافِي أَنَا ابْنُ القَوَافِي

The wombs of poetry are attached to him
    And the wombs of wealth continue to divide
A man with a thousand ideas for his age
    The least bit of any is mind for all the others
Our cloud and rain that does not run off
    Nor is false lightning in him as it flashes
If needy ones turn to him then he himself
    Intercedes as mediator with himself for them
War flames die out if his fingers stir not
    A brown reed bare of bark is all too smooth
Slender ends in its head middle walk
    Barefoot and its run is fortified when cut
Its tongue pours darkness on the light
    What is unheard is grasped by all who speak
Sword's edge is more hasty in a stroke
    More rebel to its lord, this is the more loyal
If a cloud touches it in a generous hand
    The place won't be lacking in east or west
So eloquent if it talks it has each word
    As the root of beauty that ramifies itself
Not like sea water where whales or frogs
    Can plumb the depths to where water ends
Is a sea to deny the needy, have bitter
    Taste, like a sea that bars none but gives?
Finest thought strays in his far deeps
    And drowns in waves of his eloquent wit
Hail to you O chief who stays in Manbij
    Whose aspiration is set about the Simakain
No wonder your description is a miracle
    And that my thought limps to your heights
You are in robes and your heart in both
    And yet it is wider than the courts of earth
Your heart in a world if that entered it
    With us and jinn they would find no return
Is not all generosity but yours no now vain
    Is not every praise except yours misplace?

17
He spoke in his youth in the person of one of the Tanukhi who asked for it.
(Tripping ni)

Qudaa knows I am the young man
    Whom they saved for time's calamities
My renown points to Khindif
    Since everything noble is from Yaman
I'm son of a clash, son of giving
    Son of the blow and son of a thrust
I'm desert's son and caravan's son
    Son of saddle and son of mountain peak

طَويلُ القَناةِ طَويلُ السِّنانِ	طَويلُ النِّجادِ طَويلُ العِمادِ
حَديدُ الحُسامِ حَديدُ الجَنانِ	حَديدُ اللِّحاظِ حَديدُ الحِفاظِ
إليْهِمْ كَأنَّهُما في رِهانِ	يُسابِقُ سَيْفي مَنايا العِبادِ
إذا كُنْتُ في هَبْوَةٍ لا أَراني	يَرى حَدُّهُ غامِضاتِ القُلوبِ
وَلَوْ نابَ عَنْهُ لِساني كَفاني	سَأجْعَلُهُ حَكَماً في النفوسِ

(١٨)

«من الطويل»

قال في صِباه:

ولا تَخْشَيا خُلْفاً لِما أنا قائِلُ	قِفا تَرَيا وَدْقي فَهاتا المَخايِلُ
وآخِرُ قُطْنٌ مِنْ يَدَيْهِ الخَنادِلُ	رَماني خِساسُ النّاسِ مِن صائِبِ اسْتِهِ
وَيَجْهَلُ عِلْمي أنَّهُ بيَّ جاهِلُ	ومَنْ جاهِلٍ بي وهْوَ يَجْهَلُ جَهْلَهُ
وأنّي على ظَهْرِ السِّماكَيْنِ راجِلُ	وَيَجْهَلُ أنّي مالِكُ الأرْضِ مُعْسِرٌ
ويَقْصُرُ في عَيْني المَدى المُتَطاوِلُ	تُحَقَّرُ عِنْدي هِمَّتي كُلَّ مَطْلَبٍ
إلى أنْ بَدَتْ لِلضَّيْمِ في زَلازِلُ	وما زِلْتُ طَوْداً لا تَزُولُ مَناكِبي
قَلاقِلَ عيسٍ كُلُّهُنَّ قَلاقِلُ	فقَلْقَلْتُ بالهَمِّ الذي قَلْقَلَ الحَشا
بِقَدْحِ الحَصى ما لا تُريِنا المَشاعِلُ	إذا اللَّيْلُ وَارانا أَرَتْنا خِفافُها
رَمَتْ بي بِحاراً ما لَهُنَّ سَواحِلُ	كأنّي مِنَ الوَجْناءِ في ظَهْرِ مَوْجَةٍ
وأنِّيَ فيها ما تَقولُ العَواذِلُ	يُخَيَّلُ لي أنَّ البِلادَ مَسامِعي
تَساوَ المُحامي عِنْدَهُ والمُقاتِلُ	ومَنْ يَبْغِ ما أبْغي مِنَ المَجْدِ والعُلى
وَلَيْسَ لنا إلّا السّيوفَ وَسائِلُ	ألا لَيْسَتِ الحاجاتُ إلّا نُفوسَكُمْ
ولا صَدَرَتْ عَن باخِلٍ وهْوَ باخِلُ	فَما وَرَدَتْ رُوحَ امْرِىءٍ رُوحُهُ لَهُ
وَلَيْسَ بِغَثٍّ أنْ تَغَثَّ المَآكِلُ	غَثاثَةُ عَيْشي أن تَغَثَّ كَرامَتي

A long sword hanger, a high tent pole
    Long the lance shaft, high the point of it
Iron the grips and the iron glance
    Iron this saber and iron this buckler
My sword precedes mankind's deaths
    Moving towards them as if in the wager
Its blade sees into heart's darkness
    When I'm in a dust cloud I am not seen
I'll fix it as judgment on souls
    Tongue is agent for it and it will win

18
He spoke also in his youth.
(Long la)

Stay you two, see my rain as clouds rise
    And do not fear a broken vow when I speak
A vile man hit me with shit from his ass
    Another had cotton as stones in his hands
ignorant of me he was blind to ignorance
    A witness of my knowing that he was foolish
He knew not that as earth's king I'm poor
    Or if on the Simakain's back I'll still stride on
My desire makes contemptible every object
    And the distant goal is a limitation in my eyes
I'm a mountain whose height is unshaken
    Until an earthquake shows me to an injustice
I'm shaken by need that stirs my breast
    Disquiet of camels all of which are brisk
When night veils us their hoofs show us
    In sparks from stone s what flame never has
On a strong camel's back I am on a wave
    Driving me on the seas that have no shores
It seems to me wastelands are in my ears
    And I am for them what the gossips will whisper
He who wants what I want of glory or rank
    Finds life and death of equal value to himself
O there's no goal except it be your lives
    And no means between us except the swords
What they drink of man's soul is spirit
    They don't turn from a miser if he denies
Loss in my life is thinness in my honor
    And not the emaciation that no food makes

(١٩)

«من البسيط»

قال في صباه:

ألسَّيفُ أحسَنُ فِعلاً منهُ باللَّمَمِ	ضَيفٌ ألَمَّ برَأسي غَيرَ مُحتَشِمِ
لأنتَ أسوَدُ في عَيني مِنَ الظُّلَمِ	إبعَدْ بَعِدْتَ بَياضاً لا بَياضَ لَهُ
هَوايَ طِفلاً وشَيبي بالِغَ الحُلُمِ	بحُبِّ قاتِلَتي والشَّيبِ تَغذيتي
ولا بذاتِ خِمارٍ تَريقُ دَمي	فَما أُمَرُّ برَسمٍ لا أُسائِلُهُ
يَومَ الرَّحيلِ وشَعبٌ غَيرُ مُلتَئِمِ	تَنفَّسَتْ عن وَفاءٍ غَيرِ مُنصَدِعِ
وقَبَّلَتني على خَوفٍ فَما لَفَمٍ	قَبَّلتُها ودُموعي مَزجُ أدمُعِها
لَو صابَ تُرباً لأحيا سالِفَ الأُمَمِ	قد ذُقتُ ماءَ حَياةٍ مِن مُقَبِّلِها
وتَمسَحُ الطَّلَّ فَوقَ الوَردِ بالعَنَمِ	تَرنو إلَيَّ بعَينِ الظَّبي مُجهِشَةً
بالنّاسِ كُلِّهِمِ أفديكِ من حَكَمٍ	رُوَيدَ حُكمِكِ فينا غَيرَ مُنصِفَةٍ
ولم تَجَنِّي الذي أجنَيتُ من ألَمٍ	أبدَيتِ مِثلَ الذي أبدَيتُ من جَزَعٍ
وصِرتِ مِثلي في ثَوبَينِ مِن سَقَمِ	إذا لَبِزَّكِ ثَوبَ الحُسنِ أصغَرُهُ
ولا القَناعَةُ بالإقلالِ من شِيَمي	ليسَ التَّعلُّلُ بالآمالِ مِن أرَبي
حتّى تَسُدَّ عليها طُرقَها هِمَمي	ولا أظُنُّ بَناتِ الدَّهرِ تَترُكُني
برِقَّةِ الحالِ واعذِرْني ولا تَلُمِ	لُمِ اللّيالي التي أخنَتْ على جِدَتي
وَذِكرَ جُودٍ ومَحصولي على الكَلِمِ	أسرى أُناساً ومَحصولي على غَنَمٍ
لم يُثرِ منها كما أثرى مِنَ العَدَمِ	ورُبَّ مالٍ فَقيراً مِن مُروءَتِهِ
ويَنجَلي خَبَري عن صِمَّةِ الصَّمَمِ	سَيَصحَبُ النَّصلَ مِنّي مِثلَ مَضرِبهِ
فالآنَ أقحَمُ حتّى لاتَ مُقتَحَمِ	لقد تَصَبَّرتُ حتّى لاتَ مُصطَبَرِ
والحَربُ أقومُ مِن ساقٍ على قَدَمِ	لأترُكَنَّ وُجوهَ الخَيلِ ساهِمَةً
حتّى كانَ بها ضَرباً مِنَ اللَّمَمِ	والطَّعنُ يُحرِقُها والزَّجرُ يُقلِقُها
كَأنّما الصّابُ مَذرورٌ على اللُّجُمِ	قد كَلَّمتُها العَوالي فَهيَ كالِحَةٌ
حتّى أدَلْتُ لَهُ مِن دَولَةِ الخَدَمِ	بكُلِّ مُنصَلِتٍ ما زالَ مُنتَظِري
ويَستَحِلُّ دَمَ الحُجّاجِ في الحَرَمِ	شَيخٌ يَرى الصَّلواتِ الخَمسَ نافِلَةً

19
He spoke in his youth.
(Outspread mi)

A guest without shame lights on my head
    The sword would do this better for my braids
Be off! remove whiteness without splendor
    You are more black in my eye than the dark
My foe fed me with love and white hair
    My love was childish, my gray was puberty
I pass no camp traces without inquiring
    Nor a veiled one without shedding my blood
She sighed for a loyalty not divided
    On the parting day, and a flock not united
I kissed her so my tears mixed with hers
    And she kissed me in fear, mouth to mouth
I tasted the water of life from her lips
    If it fell on dust it would revive past mankind
She stared at me with tearful fawn eyes
    Touching the dew on roses with red fingers
Go slow with your unfair judgment on me.
    For I am the ransom with all men as judges
You discovered what I found of misfortune
    But you did not hide what I hid in my anguish
Then a bit of it stole your fine garment
    And you went as I in illness' double dress
There is no pretext for hope in my goal
    Nor any content with poverty in my nature
I know time's daughter's can't leave me
    Until my aspirations bar the way for them
Blame the nights who betray my good luck
    With poor estate; pardon but don't blame me
I see men, but my result is only sheep
    And memory of bounty but my pay is words
Some lord of wealth poor in manliness
    Not rich by it as he is rich in his nonentity
A blade has a friend in me like its edge
    My history as bravest of the brave is shining
I was patient till patience was no more
    Now I rush ahead until rushing is no more
I'll leave the face of horses mutilated
    While war is more fixed than a leg on foot
Thrusting burns as clamor shakes them
    Until it's as if they had a kind of madness
Long spears wound them, they are stern
    As if their bits were tinged by the colocynth
With each fighting man always expecting
    That I lead him to the kingdom of the slaves
A shaykh who sees five prayers as loot
    And justifies pilgrims' blood in sanctuary

أسَدُ الكَتائِبِ رامَتْهُ ولم يَرِمِ	وكُلَّما نُطِحَتْ تَحْتَ العَجاجِ بهِ
وتَكتفي بالدَّمِ الجاري عَنِ الدِّيَمِ	تُنسي البِلادَ بُروقَ الجَوِّ بارِقَتي
حِياضَ خَوْفِ الرَّدى للشّاءِ والنَّعَمِ	رِدي حِياضَ الرَّدى يا نَفسُ واترُكي
فلا دُعِيتُ ابنَ أُمِّ المَجدِ والكَرَمِ	إنْ لم اذَرْكِ على الارماحِ سائِلَةً
والطَّيرُ جائِعَةٌ لَحْمٌ على وَضَمِ	أَيَمْلِكُ المُلْكَ والأَسيافُ ظامِئَةٌ
ولَوْ عَرَضتُ لَهُ في النَّوْمِ لم يَنَمِ	مَن لَوْرَآني ماءً ماتَ مِن ظَمَإِ
ومَن عَصى مِن مُلوكِ العُرْبِ والعجمِ	مِيعادُ كلِّ رقيقِ الشَّفرَتَينِ غدا
وإنْ تَوَلَّوْا فَما أَرْضى لَها بِهِمِ	فإنْ أجابوا فَما قَصدي بها لَهُمْ

(٢٠)

«من الرجز»

وعذله أبو سعيد المجيمري على تركه لقاء الملوك فقال ارتجالا:

فَرُبَّ رَأيٍ أخطَأ الصَّوابا	أبا سَعيدٍ جَنِّبِ العِتابا
واستَوْقَفوا لِرَدَنا البَوّابا	فإنَّهُم قد أكْثَروا الحِجابا
والذَّابِلاتِ السُّمَرَ والعِرابا	وإنْ حَدَّ الصَّارِمَ القِرْضابا
	تَرْفَعُ فيما بَيْنَنا الحِجابا

(٢١)

«من الكامل»

قال في صباه ارتجالا على لسان رجل سأله ذلك:

فَارَقْتَني وأقامَ بَينَ ضُلوعي	شَوْقي إليكَ نَفى لَذيذَ هُجوعي
مِمّا أُرَقرِقُ في الفُراتِ دُموعي	أوَما وَجَدتُمْ في الصُّراةِ مُلوحَةً
حتى اغتَدى أسَفي على التَّوديعِ	ما زِلْتُ أحذَرُ مِن وَداعِكَ جاهِداً
أتْبَعْتُهُ الأنفاسَ للتَّشييعِ	رَحَلَ العَزاءُ برِحْلَتي فكأنَّما

Each time they are gored by him in dust
  A lion regiment flees him but he flees not
My fire makes towns forget sky lightning
  And suffices with flowing blood for showers
Drink from a pool of death my soul, leave
  Death's trough of fear to sheep and cattle
If I do not let you flow over spearpoints
  I'm not named son of mother glory or bounty
Shall one rule states with swords athirst
  Birds hungry that flesh on a butcher table?
Who if he saw me as water will die thirsty
  Or if I appeared to him in sleep he'd waken?
A rendezvous of all thin blades is soon
  With the Arab and foreign kings who disobey
If they reply my goal in this is not them
  If they turn I'll not feed these with them

20
He spoke also in his youth and Abu Said al Mukhaimari had just blamed him for his avoiding a meeting with kings.
(Trembling ba)

Abu Said put aside complaint
  Many an opinion misses the mark
For they multiply guardians and
  Set up doorkeepers to exclude us
But the sword's cutting edge
  And the brown lance and the horse
  Will raise those curtains between us

21
He spoke impromptu in his youth in the person of a man who asked him for it.
(Perfect i)

My love for you denies my sleep's joy
  You parted but it remained in my breast
O did you not find in Sara the salt
  That I poured into Furat with my tears?
I was wary of turmoil at your parting
  ˙ Until the pain overcame me at farewell
Patience was in my saddle as it seems
  I followed it with sighs as the pallbearers

(٢٢)

«من مجزوء الرجز»

أيَّ عَظيمٍ أتَّقي	أيَّ مَحَلٍّ أرْتَقي
سِهُ وما لَـمْ يَخْلُـقِ	وَكُلُّ ما قَدْ خَلَـقَ اللّـ
كَشَعْرَةٍ في مَفْرِقي	مُحْتَقَرٌ في هِمَّتي

(٢٣)

| فَقُمْ وَأطْلُبِ الشَّيْءَ الَّذي يَبْتُرُ العُمْرا | إذا لَمْ تَجِدْ ما يَبْتُرُ الفَقْرَ قاعِداً |
| لَعَلَّكَ أنْ تُبْقي بِواحِدَةٍ ذِكْــرا | هُمـا خَلَّتـانِ ثَـرْوَةٌ أوْ مَنِيَّـةٌ |

(٢٤)

«من الكامل»

قال له بعض إخوانه: سلمت عليك فلم ترد السلام، فقال معذرا:

مُتَعَجِّبٌ لِتَعَجُّبِكْ	أنـا عـاتِبٌ لِتَعَتُّبِكْ
مُتَوَجِّعـاً لِتَغَيُّبِكْ	إذ كُنْتُ حينَ لَقيتَني
مِ وكـانَ شُغْلي عنكَ بِكْ	فَشُغِلْتُ عَنْ رَدِّ السَّـلا

(٢٥)

«من البسيط»

قال عند وداعه بعض الأمرا:

| في الشَّرْقِ والغَرْبِ مِنْ عاداكَ مكبوتا | أنْصُـرْ بِجُـودِكَ ألفاظـاً تَرَكْـتُ بهـا |
| وذا وِداعٌ فَكُنْ أهلاً لِما شِيتا | فقد نَظَرْتُكَ حتى حانَ مُرْتَحَلي |

(٢٦)

«من البسيط»

قال في جعفر بن كيغلغ و لم ينشده إياها:

وَغَيَّضَ الدَّمْـعَ فـانْهَلَّتْ بَـوادِرُهُ	حاشَى الرَّقيبَ فَخانَتْـهُ ضَمـائِرُهُ
وصاحِبُ الدَّمعِ لا تَخفى سَرائِرُهُ	وكاتِمُ الحُبِّ يَـوْمَ البَيـنِ مُنهتِكٌ
وَلا بِرَبْرَبِهِـمْ لَـوْلا جَـآذِرُهُ	لَـوْلا ظِبـاءُ عَدِيٍّ مـا شُغِفْتُ بِهِمْ
خَمْـرٌ يُخامِرُهـا مِسْكٌ تُخامِـرُهُ	مِنْ كُلِّ أحْوَرَ في أنيابِـهِ شَنَـبٌ
حُمْـرٌ غَفائِرُهُ سُـودٌ غَدائِـرُهُ	نُعْـجٌ مَحاجِرُهُ دُعْـجٌ نَواظِـرُهُ

22
He spoke also in his youth impromptu.
(Trembling qi)

What place can I advance to
    What great thing can I be afraid of?
All that God has created
    And all that he has not created
Is despised by my ambition
    Like a white hair in my hair part

23
He spoke also in his youth.
(Long ra)

If you don't know how to kill poverty sitting
    Then rise, seek something to cut off the living
They are rich friends or deadly
    May if you survive one brings fame

24
He spoke answering a man who said:
I greeted you and you made no response.
(... k-)

I wonder at your criticism
    Am amazed at your amazement
Since I, When you met me
    Was complaining at your absence
I wanted to return your *salaam*
    And my neglect of you for your sake

25
He spoke also in his youth.
(Outspread fa)

Aid by your bounty words by which I make
    In east and west those who hate you abased
I waited for you till saddling time came
    And this farewell, so accept it as you will

26
He spoke also in his youth
and did not recite it to anyone.
(Outspread hu)

Wary of a guard as his thought gulls him
    He curbs tears but their streams fall heavy
Hidden love is revealed on parting day
    Tears' friend has secrets not to be hidden
But for Ady fawns I'd not feel for them
    Nor for their herd but for their young ones
For each black eye with white teeth
    Wine mingled with musk intoxicates them
Too bright his brow, dark his eyebrows
    Red his veils, black his braided hair plaits

مِنَ الهَوى ثِقلَ ما تَحوي مَآزِرُهُ	أَعارَني سُقمَ عَينَيهِ وَحَمَّلَني
وَمَن فُؤادي عَلى قَتلي يُضافِرُهُ	يا مَن تَحَكَّمَ في نَفسي فَعَذَّبَني
سَلَوتُ عَنكِ وَنامَ اللَيلَ ساهِرُهُ	بِعَودَةِ الدَولَةِ الغَرّاءِ ثانِيَةً
كَأَنَّ أَوَّلَ يَومِ الحَشرِ آخِرُهُ	مِن بَعدِ ما كانَ لَيلي لا صَباحَ لَهُ
كادَت لِفَقدِ اِسمِهِ تَبكي مَنابِرُهُ	غابَ الأَميرُ فَغابَ الخَيرُ عَن بَلَدٍ
وَخَبَّرَت عَن أَسى المَوتى مَقابِرُهُ	قَدِ اِشتَكَت وَحشَةَ الأَحياءِ أَربَعَةٌ
أَهَلَّ لِلَّهِ بادِيهِ وَحاضِرُهُ	حَتّى إِذا عُقِدَت فيهِ القِبابُ لَهُ
وَلا الصَبابَةُ في قَلبٍ تُجاوِرُهُ	وَجَدَّدَت فَرَحاً لا الغَمُّ يَطرُدُهُ
فَلا سَقاها مِنَ الوَسمِيِّ باكِرُهُ	إِذا خَلَت مِنكَ حِمصٌ لا خَلَت أَبَداً
وَنورُ وَجهِكَ بَينَ الخَلقِ باهِرُهُ	دَخَلَتها وَشُعاعُ الشَمسِ مُتَّقِدٌ
صَرفُ الزَمانِ لَمّا دارَت دَوائِرُهُ	في فَيلَقٍ مِن حَديدٍ لَو قَذَفتَ بِهِ
مِنها إِلى المَلِكِ المَيمونِ طائِرُهُ	تَمضي المَواكِبُ وَالأَبصارُ شاخِصَةٌ
في دِرعِهِ أَسَدٌ تَدمى أَظافِرُهُ	قَد حِرنَ في بَشَرٍ في تاجِهِ قَمَرٌ
تُحصى الحَصى قَبلَ أَن تُحصى مَآثِرُهُ	حُلوُ خَلائِقِهِ شُوسٌ حَقائِقُهُ
كَصَدرِهِ لَم تَبِن فيها عَساكِرُهُ	تَضيقُ عَن جَيشِهِ الدُنيا وَلَو رَحُبَت
مِن مَجدِهِ غَرِقَت فيهِ خَواطِرُهُ	إِذا تَغَلغَلَ فِكرُ المَرءِ في طَرَفٍ
كَأَنَّهُنَّ بَنوهُ أَو عَشائِرُهُ	تَحمي السُيوفُ عَلى أَعدائِهِ مَعَهُ
إِلّا وَباطِنُهُ لِلعَينِ ظاهِرُهُ	إِذا اِنتَضاها لِحَربٍ لَم تَدَع جَسَداً
وَقَد وَثِقنَ بِأَنَّ اللَهَ ناصِرُهُ	فَقَد تَيَقَّنَ أَنَّ الحَقَّ في يَدِهِ
عَلى رُؤوسِ فَلا ناسٍ مَغافِرُهُ	تَرَكنَ هامَ بَني عَوفٍ وَثَعلَبَةٍ
وَكانَ مِنهُ إِلى الكَعبَينِ زاخِرُهُ	فَخاضَ بِالسَيفِ بَحرَ المَوتِ خَلفَهُم
في الأَرضِ مِن جِيَفِ القَتلى حَوافِرُهُ	حَتّى اِنتَهى الفَرَسُ الجاري وَما وَقَعَت
وَمُهجَةٍ وَلَغَت فيها بَواتِرُهُ	كَم مِن دَمٍ رَوِيَت مِنهُ أَسِنَّتُهُ
فَالعَيشُ هاجِرُهُ وَالتَسَرُّ زائِرُهُ	وَحائِنٍ لَعِبَت شُمُّ الرِماحِ بِهِ
فَجَهلُهُ بِكَ عِندَ الناسِ عاذِرُهُ	مَن قالَ لَستَ بِخَيرِ الناسِ كُلِّهِمِ
بِلا نَظيرٍ فَفي روحي أَخاطِرُهُ	أَو شَكَّ أَنَّكَ فَردٌ في زَمانِهِمِ

He lends me his eye's languor, loads me
    With desire's weight like what his belt holds
O you who judge my soul and punish me
    Who assist my heart in this my destruction
In the lost state's second return I am
    Solaced for you and his night watch sleeps
After my night without any dawn it is
    As if the first of the last day was its end
The Amir went, good vanished from a town
    Its pulpits almost wept at his name's silence
Its quarters lamented life's desolation
    And its tombs told of the grief of the dead
Till the time when his tent was set here
    His town folk and the bedouin cried, God!
It renewed joy, grief did not pursue him
    Nor did affection in a heart stray from him
When Hims was empty of you no more
    Its dawn did not water it with first showers
You entered as sun's rays were kindled
    Light of your face among horsemen dazzled
If you attacked with iron cavalry like
    Changes of fate its reverses wouldn't occur
If a man's ideas look far to
    Glory his mind will drown in it
If swords rage against foes
    They seem his kin of neighbors
The procession moves on as eyes arise
    From it to a king whose augury is fortunate
They dazzle at a face in his crown, a moon
    In his armor, the lion whose claws are bloody
His tempers sweet, his values proud
    Pebbles counted where benefits are counted
A world too small for his army, if as wide
    As his bosom his troops wouldn't camp there
When he unsheathes in war there's nobody
    Unless the inside becomes outside to an eye
They make sure truth is in his hand
    And they ensure that God is his helper
Leaving skulls of Banu Auf and Thalab
    With helmets on heads without the bodies
With a sword he wades death's sea
    Behind them when its tide is up to ankles
Until a horse goes his gait and hoofs
    Do not touch earth due to the stinking dead
How much blood his points pour for him
    And how much gore his cutters lap up there
Many a death a brown lance jousts for him
    When life flees from and eagles approach him
One said you were not best of all men
    His ignorance was his excuse with mankind
Or doubted you were unique in their time
    Without a peer, but with my soul I pledge it

46 Diwan al-Mutanabbi

وَمَنْ أعُوذُ بِهِ مِمَّا أحاذِرُهُ	يا مَنْ ألُوذُ بِهِ فيما أؤمّلُهُ
جُوداً وأنّ عَطاياها جَواهِرُهُ	ومَنْ تَوَهّمَتْ أنَّ البَحرَ راحَتُهُ
ولا يَهيضُونَ عَظماً أنتَ جابِرُهُ	لا يَجْبُرُ النّاسَ عَظماً أنتَ كاسِرُهُ
يَدُ البِلَى وذَوَى فى السِجْنِ ناضِرُهُ	ارْحَمْ شَباب فتىً أوْدَتْ بجِدّتِهِ

(٢٧)

«من الطويل»

يمدح شجاع بن محمد الطائي المنبجي:

عَياءٌ بِهِ ماتَ المُحِبّونَ مِن قَبلُ	عَزيزٌ أساً مَن داؤهُ الحَدَقُ النُجْلُ
نَذيرٌ إلى مَن ظنّ أنّ الهَوَى سَهلُ	فَمَنْ شاءَ فَلْيَنْظُرْ إليّ فمنظَري
إذا نَزَلَتْ في قلبِهِ رَحَلَ العَقلُ	وما هيَ إلّا لَحظةٌ بَعْدَ لَحظةٍ
فأصبَحَ لي عَن كُلّ شُغلٍ بها شُغلُ	جرى حُبّها بمَجرى دَمي في مَفاصلي
تَكحُلُ عَينَيها وليسَ لها كُحلُ	سَبَتْني بِدَلّ ذاتِ حُسْنٍ يَزينُها
رَقيبٌ تَعَدّى أو عَدُوٌّ لهُ دَخلُ	كانَ لِحاظَ العَينِ في فَتْكِهِ بنا
فما فَوقَها إلّا وفيها لَهُ فِعلُ	ومِن جَسَدي لم يَترُكِ السُقمُ شَعرَةً
حُبَيبَتي قلبي فُؤادي هيا جُمَلُ	إذا عَذلُوا فيها أجَبتُ بأنّةٍ:
عَنِ العَذلِ حتى ليسَ يَدخلُها العَذلُ	كأنّ رَقيباً مِنكِ سَدّ مَسامِعي
فَبَينَهُما في كُلّ هَجرٍ لنا وَصلُ	كأنّ سُهادَ اللّيلِ يَعشَقُ مُقلَتي
وأشكُو إلى مَن لا يُصابُ لَهُ شِكلُ	أُحِبّ التي في البَدرِ مِنها مَشابَهٌ
شُجاعَ الذي للهِ ثَمّ لَهُ الفَضلُ	إلى واحِدِ الدّنيا إلى ابنِ مُحَمّدِ
فُرُوعٌ وقَحطانُ بنُ هُودٍ لها أصلُ	إلى الثّمَرِ الحُلوِ الذي طَيّءٌ لَهُ
بغَيرِ نَضيٍّ بَشّرَتنا بِهِ الرُّسلُ	إلى سَيّدٍ لَوْ بَشّرَ اللهُ أُمّةً
تُحَدّثُ عَن وَقفاتِهِ الخَيلُ والرّجلُ	إلى القابِضِ الأرواحِ والضَّيغَمِ الذي
تَجَمّعَ في تَشتيتِهِ للعُلَى شَملُ	إلى رَبّ مالٍ كُلّما شَتّتَ شَملَهُ
وعايَنتهُ لم تَدرِ أيّهُما النّصلُ	هُمامٌ إذا ما فارَقَ الغِمدَ سَيفُهُ
فشايينِ أهلِ الأرضِ لا نَقطَعُ النّسلُ	رأيتُ ابنَ أمّ المَوتِ لَوْ أنّ بأسَهُ
غَداةَ كأنّ النّبلَ في صَدرِهِ وَبلُ	على سابحٍ مَوجُ المَنايا بنَحرِهِ
فلم تُغضِ إلّا والسّنانُ لها كُحلُ	وكَمْ عَينِ قِرنٍ حَدَقَتْ لِنِزالِهِ

O one in whom I take refuge for my hope
    As one in whom I seek safety from all I fear
And one in whose hand I imagine a sea
    Of generosity with its gifts that are its pearls
Men do not mend a bone if you break it
    Nor break again the bone you have healed
Pity a young man for whom sorrow's hand
    Ruins his luck as his bloom fades in a prison

27
He spoke praising Shuja ibn Muhammad ibn Abd al-Aziz al-Manbiji. (Long lu)

Rare is a cure for one with wide eyed ill
    A disease from which lovers before this died
Let him who will look at me for view of me
    Is a warning to one who thinks love is easy
It is nothing but glimpse after glimpse
    If it settles in his heart reason saddles up
Her love runs my blood's course in limbs
    In that is labor in me apart from all my labor
She captured me decked with gay coquetry
    She put collyrium on her eyes but it was no remedy
As if eye's glance in its violence to us
    Were a hostile guard or the foe breaking in
Illness has preserved no hair of my body
    Nothing more, though it acts by means of that
If they blame me for her, I reply sighing
    My little darling heart, my soul, O my beauty!
As if your guard had prevented my hearing
    Blame, so complaint could not penetrate there
As if waking at night loved my eyeballs
    Our bond between them was in every parting
I love her whose comparison is a full moon
    And I appeal to one whom no shape surpasses
To the only one in the world Ibn Muhammad
    Shuja for whom virtue is with God then in him
For that sweet fruit of Tai's branches
    When Qahtan ibn Hud is the root of them
To a chief if God spoke to folk without
    The Prophet, the message would speak in him
To a grasper of souls and of lion heroes
    Whose wars the horsemen and soldiers tell
To a wealthy lord, if his ideas scatter
    A union gathers in dispersion to grandeur
A hero who when his sword leaves sheathe
    And you see him you know not which is blade
I saw mother death's son, if his courage
    Spread to men of earth the breed must cease
On a swimmer, death's wave at his throat
    Early as if arrows on his breast were the rain
How many heroes' eyes stare at his attack
    Unblinking, if spears are not as collyrium for them

وَحِلْمٌ في غَيرِ مَوْضِعِهِ جَهْلُ	إذا قيلَ رِفقاً قالَ للحِلمِ موْضِعٌ
عَنِ الأرضِ لانهدَّتْ وناءَ بها الجَملُ	ولَوْلا تَوَلَّي نَفسِهِ حَمْلَ حِلْمِهِ
وضاقَتْ بها إلاّ إلى بابِهِ السُّبْلُ	تَباعَدَتِ الآمالُ عن كلِّ مَقصِدٍ
فأسمَعهُمْ هُبّوا فقدْ هلكَ البُخْلُ	ونادى النَّدى بالنَّائمينَ عن السُّرى
فلَيسَ لَهُ إنجازُ وَعْدٍ ولاَ مَطْلُ	وَحالَتْ عَطايا كَفِّهِ دونَ وَعْدِهِ
وأيسَرُ مِن إحصائِها القَطرُ والرَّملُ	فأقْرَبُ مِن تَحديدِها رُدُّ فائِتٍ
لأخمَصِهِ في كلِّ نائبَةٍ نَعْلُ	وَما تَنْقِمُ الأيّامُ ممَّنْ وُجُوهُها
وإنْ عَزَّ إلاّ أن يكونَ لَـهُ مِثلُ	وَما عِزَّةٌ فيها مُرادٌ أرادَهُ
وَدَهرٌ لأنْ أمْسَيتَ مِن أهلِهِ أهلُ	كضفى تُعَلّاً فخراً بأنَّكَ منهُمْ
وَطُوبَى لعَينٍ ساعَةً منكَ لا تَخلو	رُوَيدَ لنَفسٍ حاوَلَتْ منكَ غِرَّةً
ولا في بِلادٍ أنتَ صَيِّبُها مَحْلُ	فَما بفَقيرٍ شامَ بَرقَكَ فاقةٌ

(٢٨)

«من الكامل»

يمدحه أيضًا:

هَيهاتِ ليسَ لِيَومِ عَهدِكُم غَدُ	اليَوْمَ عَهدُكمُ فأينَ المَوْعِدُ؟
والعَيشُ أبعَدُ منكُمُ لا تَبْعُدوا	المَـوتُ أقربُ مِخْلَباً مِـن بَينكُمْ
لمْ تَـدْرِ أنَّ دَمي الـذي تَتَقَلَّدُ	إنَّ التي سَفكَتْ دَمي بجُفُونِها
وتَنهَّدَتْ فأجَبْتُها المُتَنَهِّدُ	قالَتْ وقدْ رأتِ اصفِراري مِن بهِ
لَوني كَما صَبغَ اللُّجَينَ العَسجَدُ	فَمَضَتْ وقدْ صَبَغَ الحَياءُ بَياضَها
مُتَأوِّداً عُصنٌ بهِ يَتَأوَّدُ	فَرَأيتُ قَرْنَ الشَّمسِ في قَمَرِ الدُّجى
سَلبُ النُّفوسِ ونارُ حَربٍ توقدُ	غَدَويَّةٌ بَدَويَّةٌ مِـنْ دُونِها
وذَوابلٌ وتَوَعُّدٌ وتَهَـدُّدُ	وهَواجِـلٌ وصَواهِـلٌ ومَناصِـلُ
ومَشَى عَليها الدَّهرُ وهوَ مُقَيَّدُ	أبَلَـتْ مَوَدَّتهـا اللَّيالي بَعْدَنـا
مَرِضَ الطَّبيبُ لَـهُ وَعِيـدَ العُـوَّدُ	بَرَحْتَ يا مَـرَضَ الجُفون بمُمَـرِّضٍ
ولكُلِّ رَكبٍ شَأمَ عيسِـهُمْ ولفَقْـدُ	فَلَهُ بَنُـو عَبْـدِ العَزيزِ بنِ الرَّضَى
مَن فيكَ شأمُ سِوى شجاعٍ مَقصِدُ	مَن في الأنامِ مِنَ الكِرامِ ولا تَقُـلَّ
وَسْطا فقلتُ: لِسَيفِهِ ما يُولَـدُ	أعطى فقلتُ: لجودهِ ما يُقْتَنى،

If one calls: Friend! he says: Mercy!
    But man's pity out of place is a stupidity
But for trusting himself with pity's burden
    To earth the load would fall with its weight
The hopeful have been wide of every goal
    Roads are rough for them except to your door
Bounty calls sleepers to a night journey
    Tells them: Arise! stinginess is destroyed
Gifts of his hand come before his vows
    Nor does he break promises or make delays
Nearer than their limit the past's return
    Less than their number raindrops and sands
Days cannot punish one for whom ways
    Are the shoe on his foot in the rough places
Intentions he aims at do not conquer him
    If he weakened it would only be to his like
Enough praise for Thual you are of them
    For an age, that its people are your family
Grief to a soul who tries to forget you
    Blessed the eyes not free of you an hour
No need for the poor to sniff your flash
    No dearth in lands if you are their shower

28
He spoke also praising Shuja ibn Muhammad al-Tai al-Manbiji. (Perfect du)

Today your vow but when the rendezvous?
    O no tomorrow for the day of your departure
Death has easier claws than your going
    Life is more distant than you are, do not go!
She sheds my blood with her eyelashes
    But does not know my blood will be on her
She saw my pallor and said: What's wrong?
    She sighed and I said: The sighing sickness!
She went away and shame made her pale
    My color was as gilding that colors the silver
I saw the sun's horn on the dark moon
    Declining, a branch was bending near it
She is of the Ady bedouin, before her
    Booty of souls and a fire of war is flaring
Wayless deserts and horses and swords
    The spears and the menaces and the threats
She tests her love in nights after we go
    As fate trod against her and it was hobbled
You go too far, O eyelid ills in the sick
    His doctor is ill and the nurse is visited!
Yet his the folk of Abd al Aziz ibn Rida
    For other riders the deserts and their camels
Who among men of noble rank doesn't say
    Who among you, Syria, but Shuja is sought?

وتَحَيَّرَتْ فيهِ الصِّفاتُ لأنّها   ألْفَتْ طَرائِقَهُ عَلَيها تَبْعُدُ
في كلِّ مُعْتَرَكٍ كُلىً مَفْرِيّةٌ   يَذمُمْنَ مِنهُ ما الأسِنّةُ تَحْمَدُ
نِقَمٌ على نِقَمِ الزَّمانِ يَصُبُّها   نِعَمٌ على النِّعَمِ التي لا تُجْحَدُ
في شانِهِ ولِسانِهِ وبَنانِهِ   وَجَنانِهِ عَجَبٌ لِمَنْ يَتَفَقَّدُ
أسَدٌ دَمُ الأسَدِ الهِزَبْرِ خِضابُهُ   مَوْتٌ فَريصُ المَوْتِ مِنهُ يُرْعَدُ
ما مَنْبِجٌ مُذْ غِبْتَ إلّا مُقْلَةٌ   سَهِدَتْ وَوَجْهُكَ نَوْمُها والإثْمِدُ
فاللَّيلُ حينَ قَدِمْتَ فيها أبْيَضٌ   والصُّبْحُ مُنْذُ رَحَلْتَ عَنها أسْوَدُ
ما زِلْتَ تَدنو وهيَ تَعْلو عِزّةً   حتّى تَوارَى في ثَراها الفَرْقَدُ
أرضٌ لها شَرَفٌ سِواها مِثْلُها   لوْ كانَ مِثْلُكَ في سِواها يوجَدُ
أبْدَى العُداةُ بِكَ السُّرورَ كأنَّهُمْ   فَرِحوا وعِندَهُمُ المُقيمُ المُقْعَدُ
قَطَعْتَهُمْ حَسَداً أراهُمْ ما بِهِمْ   فَتَقَطَّعوا حَسَداً لِمَنْ لا يَحْسُدُ
حتّى انْثَنَوْا ولَوَ انَّ حَرَّ قُلوبِهِمْ   في قَلْبِ هاجِرَةٍ لَذابَ الجَلْمَدُ
نَظَرَ العُلوجُ فَلَمْ يَرَوْا مِن حَوْلِهِمْ   لَمّا رَأوْكَ وقيلَ هذا السَّيِّدُ
بَقِيَتْ جُموعُهُمْ كأنّكَ كُلَّها   وبَقِيتَ بَينَهُمْ كأنّكَ مُفْرَدُ
لَهْفانَ يَسْتوبي بِكَ الغَضَبُ الوَرَى   لوْ لم يُنَهْنِهْكَ الحِجى والسُّؤدُدُ
كن حَيثُ شِئتَ تَسِرْ إليكَ رِكابُنا   فالأرضُ واحِدَةٌ وأنتَ الأوْحَدُ
وصُنِ الحُسامَ ولا تُذِلْهُ فإنّهُ   يَشكو يَمينَكَ والجَماجِمُ تَشْهَدُ
يَيسَ النَّجيعُ عَلَيهِ وهوَ مُجَرَّدٌ   مِن غِمْدِهِ وكأنّما هوَ مُغْمَدُ
رَيّانُ لَوْ قَذَفَ الذي اسْتَقَيْتَهُ   لَجَرَى مِنَ المُهجاتِ بَحرٌ مُزْبِدُ
ما شارَكَتْهُ مَنِيّةٌ في مُهجَةٍ   إلّا وشَفْرَتُهُ على يَدِها يَدُ
إنَّ العَطايا والرَّزايا والقَنا   حُلَفاءُ طَيٍّ غَوَّروا أوِ انْجَدوا
صِحْ يا لَجُلْهُمَةٍ تُجِبْكَ وإنّما   أشْفارُ عَينِكَ ذابِلٌ ومُهَنَّدُ
مِن كلِّ أكبَرَ مِنْ جِبالِ تِهامَةٍ   قَلْباً ومِنْ جَوْدِ الغَوادي أجْوَدُ
يَلقاكَ مُرْتَدِياً بأحْمَرَ مِنْ دَمٍ   ذَهَبَتْ بِخُضْرَتِهِ الطُّلى والأكْبُدُ
حتّى يُشارَ إليكَ: ذا مَوْلاهُمُ   وهُمُ المَوالي الخَليقَةُ أعْبُدُ
أنّى يَكونُ أبا البَرِيّةِ آدَمُ   وأبوكَ والثَّقَلانِ أنتَ مُحَمَّدُ
يَفنى الكَلامُ ولا يُحيطُ بفَضْلِكُمْ   أيُحيطُ ما يَفنى بِما لا يَنْفَدُ

He gives so I said: What he owns is bounty
    He attacks, I said: All born are for his sword
Descriptions lose their way with him for
    They follow his paths on which they go far
In every battle the kidneys must suffer
    They blame in him what spearheads praise
Vengeance on vengeance of fate he sets
    As grace upon grace that can't be disowned
In his affairs his tongue, fingers, and
    His heart are wonderful to those who search
Courageous, fierce lion blood his dye
    Terrible, death's hackles tremble at him
Manbij if you are absent is only an eye
    Watching, your face its repose and eye shade
A night when you approach in it is bright
    And a dawn when you depart from it is dark
As you come slowly near it rises in pride
    Until the double pole star recedes in dust
Another city would have eminence like it
    If such as you were found in such another
Foes display joy for you as if they
    Rejoiced though they have lasting anxiety
You ruin them by envy to show them so
    They are ruined by envy of one without envy
If they make retreat their heart's heat
    In the heart of noon would melt the rocks
Foreign chiefs watch, see none of theirs
    When they see you so they say: The leader!
They remain as if you were all of them
    You stay among them as if you were alone
Disquieted, by your fury men are plagued
    Unless reason and leadership can deter you
Be where you like our camels reach you
    For earth is one and you are unique within it
Preserve the sword, degrade it not for it
    Pleads by your right hand as skulls witness
Blood dries on it, and though it is free
    From a scabbard it seems to be in a sheath
Copious, if it vomited what you give it
    As drink, a foaming sea of blood would flow
Death shares not in blood from the heart
    Unless his blade in her hand lends a hand
Truly the raids, bounty and spears are
    Allied to Tai whether defeating or rescuing
Cry, O Julhama, they rush to you so
    Fringes of your eye are spears and swords
Greater than all the mountains of Tihama
    In heart, more generous than morning shower
It meets you as if girded red with blood
    The liver and neck make its gems disappear
Until one explains: This is their lord!
    And they are helpers and people most loyal
How can Adam be father of mankind if
    Your father is Muhammad, you men and jinn?

(٢٩)

«من المنسرح»

أهدى أليه رجل يعرف بـأبي دلـف بـن كنـداج هدية وهـو معتقل بحمص، وكان قد بلغه أنه ثلبه عند الوالي الذي اعتقله فكتب إليه من السجن:

والسِّجنِ والقَيدِ يا أبا دُلَفِ	أهونُ بطولِ الثَّواءِ والتَّلَفِ
والجُوعُ يُرضي الأسودَ بالجِيَفِ	غيرَ اختيارٍ قبلْتُ بِرَّكَ لي
وَطَّنْتَ للمَوتِ نَفسَ مُعترِفِ	كُنْ أيُّها السِّجنُ كيفَ شئتَ فقد
لم يَكُنِ الدُّرُّ ساكِنَ الصَّدَفِ	لو كانَ سُكناي َفيكَ منقصةً

(٣٠)

«من المتقارب»

كتب إلى الوالي وهو في الاعتقال:

وَقَدْ قُدودُ الحِسانِ القُدودِ	أيا خدَّدَ اللهُ وَردَ الخُدودِ
وعَذَّبْنَ قلبي بطولِ الصُّدودِ	فهنَّ أسَلْنَ دمـاً مُقلتي
وكم للنَّوى من قتيلٍ شهيدِ	وكم للهوى من فتىً مُدْنَفٍ
وأعْلقَ نيرانَهُ بالكُبودِ	فوا حسرتا ما أمرَّ الفِراقَ
وأقْتَلَها للمُحِبِّ العميدِ	وأغرى الصَّبابةَ بالعاشقينَ
بحُبِّ ذواتِ اللَّمى النُّهودِ	وألْهجَ نفسي لغيرِ الخنا
ولا زالَ من نعمةٍ في مَزيدِ	فكانتْ وكنَّ فِداءَ الأميرِ
وحالَتْ عطاياهُ دونَ الوُعودِ	لقد حالَ بالسَّيفِ دونَ الوعيدِ
وأنجُمُ سؤَّالِهِ في السُّعودِ	فأنجُمُ أموالِهِ في النُّحوسِ
عليهِ لَبَشَّرتُهُ بالخُلودِ	ولو لم أخفْ غيرَ أعدائِهِ
وسُمْرٌ يُرِقْنَ دماً في الصَّعيدِ	رَمى حَلْباً بنواصي الخُيولِ
مَنْ لا في الرِّقابِ ولا في الغُمودِ	وبيضٌ مُسافرةٌ ما يُقِمْ
إلى كلِّ جيشٍ كثيرِ العديدِ	يَقُدْنَ الفَناءَ غداةَ اللِّقاءِ

Words wither unguarded by your poem
    Will what fades be kept by the inexhaustible?

29
He spoke about Abu Dulaf ibn Kundaj who visited him in prison. (Flowing fi)

I am used to long burial and wasting
    In this prison and the chains O Abu Dulaf
Nor by choice do I take your care for me
    Hunger makes lions content with the carrion
Be whatever you will O prison for truly
    I have become used to death in patient soul
If my stay with you were to decrease
    No pearl would grow in this oyster shell

30
He spoke in his youth and people had slandered him to the authority, and thus he was imprisoned. So he wrote to him in prison and praised him and declared himself innocent of what he was accused. (Tripping di)

O may God gouge the rosy cheeks
    And cut to shreds bodies of the beauties
They made my eyes flow with blood
    And punished my heart with long denial
How many youths are sick with love
    How many martyrs dead from separation
O alas how bitter is the parting
    That stokes its fires within the livers
Seducing the passions of lovers
    Killing them for the devoted beloved
But my soul was addicted to no evil
    In that love of red lips and those breasts
Let it and they be the Amir's ransom
    And may he not cease from greatest good
He set the sword between the threat
    And his gifts came before that promise
Stars of his wealth for bad times
    Stars to his clients for the good times
If I didn't fear another than his foe
    For him, I'd proclaim his immortality
He hit Aleppo by his horses' forelocks
    Many a lance dripped blood on the roads
The advancing swords did not stop
    On the necks nor yet in the scabbard
They led the field on battle morn
    Against every army in vast numbers

كَشاءَ أَحَسَّ بِزَّارِ الأُسُودِ	فَوَلَّى بِأَشْياعِهِ الخَرْشَيِّ
صَهيلَ الجِيادِ وخَفْقَ البُنُودِ	يُرَوْنَ مِنَ الذُّعْرِ صَوْتَ الرِّياحِ
أَوْ مَن كَآبائِهِ والجُدُودِ	فَمَنْ كالأَميرِ ابنِ بِنتِ الأَميـ
وسادوا وجادوا وهُم في المُهُودِ	سَعَوْا للمَعالي وهُم صِبْيَةٌ
هِباتُ اللُّجَينِ وعِتْقُ العَبيدِ	أَمالِكَ رِقّي ومَن شَأنُهُ
والمَوتُ مِنّي كحَبْلِ الوَريدِ	دَعَوْتُكَ عِنْدَ انقِطاعِ الرَّجا
وأَوْهَنَ رِجْلَيَّ ثِقْلُ الحَديدِ	دَعَوْتُكَ لَمّا بَراني البَلاءُ
فَقَد صارَ مَشْيُهُما في القُيُودِ	وقَدْ كانَ مَشْيُهُما في النِّعالِ
فَها أَنا في مَحْفِلٍ مِنْ قُرُودِ	وكُنتُ مِنَ النّاسِ في مَحْفِلٍ
وحَدّي قُبَيْلَ وُجُوبِ السُّجُودِ	تُعَجَّلُ في وُجُوبِ الحُدُودِ
بَينَ وِلادي وبَينَ القُعُودِ	وقيلَ: عَدَوْتَ على العالَمينَ
وقَدْرُ الشَّهادَةِ قَدْرُ الشُّهُودِ	فَما لَكَ تَقْبَلُ زُورَ الكَلامِ
ولا تَعْبَأَنَّ بعِجْلِ اليَهُودِ	فَلا تَسمَعَنَّ مِنَ الكاشِحينَ
ودَعْوى فَعَلْتُ بِشَأوٍ بَعيدِ	وكُنْ فارِقاً بَينَ دَعْوى أَرَدتُ
بنَفْسي ولَوْ كُنتُ أَشقى ثَمُودِ	وفي جُودِ كَفَّيكَ ما جُدْتَ لي

(٣١)

«من الوافر»

عذله أبو عبد الله معاذ بن إسماعيل اللاذقي على ما كان قد شاهد من تهوّر، فقال

خَفِيٌّ عَنكَ في الهَيْجا مَقامي	أَبا عَبْدِ الإِلَهِ مُعاذُ: إِنّي
نُخاطِرُ فيهِ بالمُهَجِ الجِسامِ	ذَكَرْتُ جَسيمَ ما طَلَبي وإِنا
ويَجْزَعُ مِن مُلاقاةِ الحِمامِ	أَمِثْلي تَأخُذُ النَّكَباتُ مِنْهُ
لَخَضَّبَ شَعرَ مَفرِقِهِ حُسامي	ولو بَرَزَ الزَّمانُ إِليَّ شَخصاً
ولا سارَتْ وفي يَدِها زِمامي	وما بَلَغَتْ مَشيئَتَها اللَّيالي
فَوَيلٌ في التَّيَقُّظِ والمَنامِ	إِذا امتَلأَتْ عُيُونُ الخَيْلِ مِني

The Kharshani and his flock turned
    Like sheep trembling at the lion's roar
They were shown terror in wind's cry
    The neighing horses and fluttering flags
Who like the Amir son of Amir's daughter
    Or who like his fathers and his grandfathers
Running to heights and they were youths
    Ruling and giving when they were cradled
O lord of my service whose affair is
    Gifts of silver and the freeing of slaves
I called to you when hope was lost
    My death was like a rope on the jugular
I called to you when grief thinned me
    And the weight of irons weakened my legs
Once their movement was in fine shoes
    But now their gait is held by these chains
I was one of the folk in assembly then
    But here I am in an assembly of monkeys!
Are duty's penalties forced upon me
    And my age a bit before prayer's duties?
They said: You offended the world
    Between my birth and learning to sit!
You should not accept false words
    Witness strength is in strong evidence
Don't listen to those who hide hate
    Don't worry about quarrels of the Jews
Separate the claim: You intended it
    From the claim: You did it without a doubt
In your hands' gift is what you give me
    Of myself, though I am more sad than Thamud

31
He spoke to Muadh
who blamed him
for his boldness in conflict.
(Exuberant mi)

O Abu Abdallah ibn Muadh for myself
    My stand in the conflict was hid from you
You thought my goal a great one so
    We risked the soul in the body for that
Can calamities seize on one like me
    Or he be anxious at meeting with death?
If fate were to appear to me as a man
    My sword would stain his hair's parting
Nights will not achieve their purpose
    Or pass with my bridle held in their hands
When horsemen's eyes are full of me
    Alas for them whether they wake or sleep

(٣٢)

«من الخفيف»

وقال في صباح وقد بلغ عن قوم كلامًا:

هَيَّجَتْنــي كِلابُكُـــمْ بالنَّبـــاحِ	أنــا عَيــنُ المُسَــوَّدِ الجَحْجَـاحِ
أمْ يكــونُ الصُّراحُ غَيــرَ صُـراحِ	أيكــونُ الهِجـانُ غَيــرَ هِجـانٍ
نَسَبَتْنـي لهُــمْ رؤوسُ الرِّمـاحِ	جَهِلونـي وإنْ عَمَـرْتُ قَليـلاً

(٣٣)

«من الوافر»

قال ارتجالًا وقد سأله صديق يعرف بأبي ضبيس الشقاب معه فامتنع:

وأحْلــى مِـن مُعاطـاةِ الكُـؤوسِ	ألَــذُّ مِـنَ المُـدامِ الخَنْدَريـسِ
وإقحامـي خَميسـاً في خَميسـي	مُعاطــاةُ الصَّفائِـح والعَوالـي
رأيـتُ العَيـشَ في أرَبِ النفُـوسِ	فَمَـوْتي في الوَغـى عَيشـي لأنّـي
أسَــرُّ بـهِ لكـانَ أبـا ضَبيـسِ	ولَـوْ سُـقِّيتُها بيَـدَيْ نَديـمٍ

(٣٤)

«من الطويل»

قال له بعض الكلابين: أشرب هذه الكأس سرورًا بك، فقال له ارتجالًا:

| شرِبنا الـذي مـن مثلـهِ شرِبَ الكَرْمُ | إذا مـا شرِبتَ الخَمـرَ صِرْفـاً مُهَنَّـأً |
| يُسَـقَونها ريّـاً وسـاقيهمِ العَـزْمُ | ألا حَبَّـذا قَـوْمٌ نُداماهُـمُ القَنـا |

(٣٥)

«من مجزوء الكامل»

وقال ارتجالًا:

بالصّافيــاتِ الأكْـوُبــا	لأحِبَّتــي أنْ يَمــلأوا
وعَلــيَّ أنْ لا أشْــرَبا	وعَلَيْهِــم أنْ يَبْذُلوا
تُ المُسْـمِعاتِ فأطْرَبـا	حتـى تكـونَ البَــاتِـرا

32
He said to someone who informed him of words that people spoke.
(Nimble hi)

I am source of rule for a great chief
    Though your dogs annoyed me by barking
Are nobly born other than nobly born
    Or those of pure race other than the pure?
They know me not, but if I live a bit
    Spearheads will tell them of my lineage

33
He spoke impromptu and Abu Dabis had just invited him to drink.
(Exuberant si)

More sweet than Khandarisan wine
    And sweeter than the cup's employment
Is the practice of blade and lance
    My rushing with a troop against troop
My dying in battle is my living
    And I see life as the need of souls
But if I drank from a pal's hand
    I would rejoice it was with Abu Dabis

34
One of the Kilab said to him: I drink this cup as a toast to you. So he answered him.
(Long si)

If you drink wine straight in joy
    We drink the like of the vine's liquor
O bravo men whose friends are lances
    They pour freely and the *saqi* is resolve

35
He spoke impromptu in his youth.
(Tripping ha)

It's my friends who fill
    The cup with this pure wine
It's for them to be lavish
    And yet for me not to drink
Until swords are heard
    And I am making the music

(٣٦)

«من البسيط»

قال لابن عبد الوهاب وقد جلس ابنه إلى جانب المصباح:

أَمـا تَـرى مـا أراهُ أَيُّهـا المَلِـكُ
كَأَنَّنـا فـي سَمـاءٍ مـا لَهـا حُبُـكُ

أَلفَرقَـدُ ابنُـكَ والمِصبـاحُ صاحِبُـه
وأَنـتَ بَـدرُ الدُّجـى والمَجلِـسُ الفَلَـكُ

(٣٧)

«من الكامل»

نام أبوبكر الطائي وهو ينشد، فقال:

إِنَّ القَوافـيَ لَـم تُنِمـكَ وإِنَّمـا
مَحَّقَتـكَ حتـى صِـرتَ مـا لا يُوجَـدُ

فَكَأَنَّ أُذنَـكَ فُـوكَ حيـنَ سَمِعتَهـا
وَكَأَنَّهـا مِمّـا سَكِـرتَ المُرقَـدُ

(٣٨)

«من البسيط»

كَتَمـتُ حُبَّـكِ حتـى مِنـكِ تَكرِمَـةً
ثُـمَّ استَـوى فيـهِ إِسـراري وإِعـلانـي

كَأَنَّـهُ زادَ حتـى فـاضَ عَـن جَسَـدي
فَصـارَ سُقمـي بِـهِ فـي جِسـمِ كِتمانـي

(٣٩)

«من الكامل»

حلف صديق له بالطلاق أن يشرب، فقال:

وَأَخٍ لَنـا بَعَـثَ الطَّـلاقَ أَلِيَّـةً
لَأَعَلَّـنَ بِهـذِهِ الخُرطُـمِ

فَجَعَلـتُ رَدِّي عِرسَـهُ كَفّـارَةً
مِـن شَربِهـا وشَرِبـتُ غَيـرَ أَثيـمِ

(٤٠)

«من البسيط»

وقال يمدحه:

أَظَبيَـةَ الوَحـشِ لَـولا ظَبيَـةُ الأَنَـسِ
لَمـا غَـدَوتُ بِجَـدٍّ فـي الهَـوى تَعِـسِ

وَلا سَقَيـتُ الثَّـرى والمُـزنُ مُخلِفَـةٌ
دَمعـاً يُنَشِّفُـهُ مِـن لَوعَـةٍ نَفَسـي

36
He spoke to
Ibn 'Abd al Wahhab
whose son was sitting beside
the lamp.
(Outspread ku)

Don't you see what I see O my lord?
    As if we were in the pathless heavens
Your son Farqad the lamp another
    You the night moon, the assembly the sky

37
He spoke
and Abu Bakr al Tai
fell asleep
while Abu Tayyib was reciting.
(Perfect du)

The rhymes don't make you sleep, they
    Efface you until you are what is not found
As if your ear was a mouth listening
    And they an opiate on which you got drunk

38
He spoke also in his youth.
(Outspread ni)

I hid your love since I honored you
    Then my secrecy and openness were one to you
It seemed to rise till it overflowed my body
    And the sickness in my body became my secrecy

39
He spoke
and a man offered him a cup
and swore he
would divorce if he did not drink.
(Perfect mi)

A brother lured us from a vow by divorce
    To drink again and again from this Khurtum
I made my denial of his wife a worse sin
    Than drinking it and I drank without the sin

40
He spoke praising
Ubaidallah ibn Khurasan al Trabulsi.
(Outspread si)

O wild fawn, but for a human fawn, I'd
    Never be in this pass of unlucky passion
Nor would I water earth as clouds deny
    The tears, and my soul is dry with sorrow

وَلا وَقَفْتُ بِجِسْمِ مُسْيٍ ثالِثَةٍ	ذي أرْسُمٍ دُرْسٍ في الأرْسُمِ الدُّرُسِ
صَريعَ مُقْلَتِها سَآلَ دِمْنَتِها	قَتيلَ تَكْسيرِ ذاكَ الجفنِ واللَّعَسِ
خَريدَةٌ لَوْ رَأتْها الشَّمسُ ما طَلَعَتْ	وَلَوْ رَآها قَضيبُ البانِ لَمْ يَمِسِ
ما ضاقَ قَبلكِ خَلخالٌ على رَشإٍ	وَلا سَمِعْتُ بِديباجٍ على كَنَسِ
إنْ تَرْمِنِي نَكَباتُ الدَّهرِ عَن كَثَبٍ	تَرِمْ امرَأ غيرَ رِعْديدٍ وَلا نَكِسِ
يَفْدي بَنيكَ عُبَيْدَ اللهِ حاسِدُهم	بِجَبْهَةِ العَيرِ يُفدى حافِرُ الفَرَسِ
أبا الغَطارِفَةِ الحامينَ جارَهُمُ	وتاركي الليثِ كَلْباً غيرَ مُفْترِسِ
مِن كلِّ أبيضَ وَضّاحٍ عِمامَتُهُ	كأنّما اشْتَمَلَتْ نُوراً عَلى قَبَسِ
دانٍ بَعيدٍ مُحِبٍّ مُبغِضٍ بَهِجٍ	أغَرَّ حُلوٍ مُمِرٍّ لَيَّنٍ شَرِسِ
نَدٍ أبيٍّ غَرٍ وافٍ أخي ثِقَةٍ	جَعْدِ سَريٍّ نَهْ نَدبٍ رَضٍ نَدُسِ
لَوْ كانَ فَيضٌ يَدَيْهِ ماءَ غادِيةٍ	عَزَّ القطا في الفيافي مَوضِعُ اليَبَسِ
أكارمٌ حَسَدَ الأرضَ السَّماءُ بِهمْ	وَقَصَّرَتْ كُلُّ مِصرٍ عن طَرابُلُسِ
أيُّ المُلوكِ وَهُمْ قَصْدي أحاذِرُهُ	وَأيُّ قِرنٍ وَهُمْ سَيْفي وَهُمْ تُرُسي

(٤١)

«من الكامل»

قال في صباه:

أحْبَبتُ بِرَّكَ إذْ أرَدْتَ رَحيلا	فَوَجَدْتُ أكثَرَ ما وَجَدْتُ قَليلا
وَعَلِمْتُ أنَّكَ في المكارمِ راغِبٌ	صَبٌّ إليها بُكْرَةً وأصيلا
فَجَعَلْتُ ما تُهدي إليَّ هَديَّةً	مِني إليكَ وَظَرْفَها التَّأميلا
بِرٌّ يَخِفُّ عَلى يَدَيْكَ قَبُولُهُ	وَيَكونُ مَحْمِلُهُ عَلَيَّ ثَقيلا

(٤٢)

«من الكامل»

يمدح محمد بن زريق الطرسومي:

هَذِهِ بَرَزْتِ لَنا فَهِجْتِ رَسيسا	ثمَّ انْثَنَيْتِ وما شَفَيْتِ نَسيسا

Nor stand three nights with this body
    Worn with grief near the worn camp traces
A murder of her eye inquiring of a camp
    Killed by languor of eyelids and the red lips
Virgin, if sun saw her it wouldn't rise
    If willow branch saw her it would not sway
Before you anklets were never tight on
    Fawns nor did I hear of damask on coverts
If fate's disasters strike near to me
    They strike a man not coward or weakling
Envious ransom your sons O 'Ubaidallah
    As the horse hoofs ransom the onager head
O father of chiefs who guard neighbors
    Leaving lions like dogs without their prey
His the whitest forehead so his turban
    Seems to cover the light in the live coal
Near and far, beloved, hated, joyous
    Elegant and sweet, biker, soft and hard
Generous, aloof, eager, true, trusty,
    Crisp, noble, wise, fine, content and witty
If his hands' bounty were morning rain
    Rare the dry place for desert sand grouse
Best men, heaven envied earth for them
    And every city has fallen short of Trabulsi
What kings do I fear if they are my goal
    What foes if they are my sword and shield

41
He spoke
also in his youth
to a friend
who was going on a journey.
(Perfect la)

I love your truth when you want to go
    And I find the greatest I had was small
I know you are desirous of noble acts
    Passionate for them morning and evening
So I make what you gave me a gift
    From me to you, and its cover is a hope
Truth finds its way easy to your hand
    But its bearing is the difficulty that I suffer

42
He spoke
praising
Muhammad ibn Zuraiq al Tarsusi.
(Perfect se)

O you who appeared and moved us deeply
    Then went away and did not heal the dying one

وَتَرَكْتِني لِلفَرْقَدَينِ جَليسا	وَجعلتِ حظّي منكِ حظّي في الكَرى
وأَدَرْتِ من خمرِ الفِراقِ كُؤوسا	قَطَعْتِ ذَيّاكِ الخُمارَ بسَكْرَةٍ
تَكفي مَزادَكُمُ وتُروي العِيسا	إنْ كُنتِ ظاعِنةً فإنَّ مَدامعي
ولِمِثْلِ وَجهكِ أَنْ يكونَ عَبُوسا	حاشى لِمِثْلِكِ أَنْ تكونَ بخيلةً
ولِمِثْلِ نَيْلِكِ أَنْ يكونَ خَسيسا	ولِمِثْلِ وَصْلِكِ أَنْ تكونَ مُمَنَّعاً
حَرْباً وغادَرَتِ الفُؤادَ وَطيسا	خَوْدٌ جَنَتْ بَيني وبَينَ عَواذِلي
تيهاً ويَمْنَعُهَا الحَياءُ تَميسا	بَيْضاءُ يَمْنَعُها تَكلُّمَ دَلُّها
هانَتْ علَيَّ صِفاتُ جالينوسا	لَمّا وَجَدْتُ دواءَ دائي عندها
أَبْقى نَفيسٌ لِلنَفيسِ نَفيسا	أَبْقى زُرَيْقٌ لِلثُغُورِ مُحَمَّداً
أو سار فارقَتِ الجُسُومُ الرُّؤوسا	إنْ حلَّ فارقَتِ الخَزائنُ مالَهُ
ورَضيتَ أوحَشَ ما كرِهتَ أَنيسا	مَلِكٌ إذا عاديْتَ نَفسَكَ عادِهِ
والشَّمَّرِيَّ المِطعَنَ الذَّعِيسا	الخائِضَ الغَمَراتِ غَيرَ مُدافَعٍ
إلَّا مَسْوداً جَنْبَهُ مَرؤوسا	كشَّفْتُ جَمْهَرَةَ العِبادِ فلَمْ أَجدْ
تَنفي الظُّنونَ وتُفسِدُ التَقييسا	بَشَرٌ تَصَوَّرَ غايةً في آيةٍ
وعَلَيْـهِ منها لا علَيها يُوسَى	وبهِ يُضَنَّ على البَرِيَّةِ لا بها
لَمَّا أَتى الظُّلُماتِ صِرْنَ شُموسا	لوْ كانَ ذو القَرْنَينِ أَعْمَلَ رأيَهُ
في يومِ مَعرَكَةٍ لأَعْيا عِيسى	أو كان صادَفَ رأسَ عازَرَ سَيفُهُ
ما انْشَقَّ حتى جازَ فيهِ مُوسى	أوْ كان لُجُّ البَحرِ مِثلَ يَمينِهِ
عُبِدَتْ فكانَ العالَمونَ مَجوسا	أوْ كان للنِّيرانِ ضَوءُ جَبينِهِ
ورأيْتُهُ فرأَيْتُ منهُ خميسا	لمّا سَمِعتُ بهِ سَمِعْتُ بواحدٍ
ولَسْتُ مُنْصُلَهُ فَسالَ نُفوسا	ولحَظْتُ أَنْمُلَهُ فسِلْنَ مَواهِباً
أَبداً ونَطْرُدُ باسمِهِ إبْليسا	يا مَنْ نَلوذُ مِنَ الزَمانِ بظلِّهِ
منْ في العِراقِ يراكَ في طَرَسُوسا	صَدَقَ المُخَبِّرُ عنكَ دونكَ وَصْفُهُ
يَشِنا المَقيلَ ويَكرَهُ التَعريسا	بَلَدٌ أَقَمْتُ بهِ وذِكْرُكَ سائِرٌ
وإذا خَدِرْتَ تَخِذْتَهُ عِرِّيسا	فإذا طَلَبْتَ فَريسةً فارَقْتَـهُ

You made my joy in you a joy in sleep
    And left me sitting beneath the Farqadain stars
You cut off a bit of drunkenness by pain
    To pass around the wine of parting's goblet
If you are of those departing, my tears
    Fill your water bag and the camel's thirst
Beware lest such as you become miserly
    Lest such a face as yours should try to frown
An embrace like yours lest it be forbid
    And such a gift as yours, if it be a small one
A woman exciting between me and critics
    A war while she left this heart as a furnace
Pure, her coquetry guards her from proud
    Talk, and shame protects her from swerving
When I found my sickness' cure with her
    The prescription of Galen was easy for me
Zuraiq stays on borders as Muhammad
    So precious he remains for precious souls
If he rests, hoards part with his wealth
    If he sallies, bodies part with their heads
A king who if you hate self you hate him
    And you prefer deserts if you hate friends
One who plunges into depths without aid
    Expeditions when the spears are thrusting
I examined all creation but I never yet
    Found any subjects beside him as leaders
A man who depicts the heights of miracle
    He baffles thought and corrupts comparison
A miser's in him for mankind, not to them
    He is sad for them and not because of them
If Dhu'l Qarnain made use of his wisdom
    When he came to the dark, suns had risen
If his sword had struck of Lazarus' head
    In a day's battle Jesus had been helpless
If the seas' waves were his right hand
    They'd not split when Moses crossed them
If sun and moon had his forehead's glow
    They'd be worshiped and the world Magian
When I heard of him I heard of one alone
    When I saw him I saw the battalion of him
I saw his fingers, they ran with gifts
    I touched his sword and souls ran from it
O him! in his shade we refuge from time
    Forever, by his name we drive off Iblis
Fame is true to you, its painting short
    One who is in Iraq can see you at Tarsus
You stay in a city, your memory travels
    It dislikes a siesta, hates a late sleep
If you seek your prey your depart from it
    When you withdraw you take it as your lair

كَثُرَ المُدَلِّسُ فاحْذَر التَّدلِيسَا	إنِّي نَثَرْتُ عَلَيكَ دُرّاً فانتَقِذْ
وجَلَوْتُها لكَ فاجتَلَيتَ عَرُوسَا	حَجَبْتُها عَنْ أهلِ إنْطاكِيَّةٍ
يَأوِي الخَرابَ ويَسكُنُ النّاؤُوسَا	خيرُ الطُّيورِ على القُصورِ وشَرُّها
أو جاهَدَت كَتَبَتْ عليكَ حَبِيسَا	لوْ جادَتِ الدُّنيا فَدَتكَ بأهلِها

(٤٣)

«من البسيط»

يمدحه أيضاً:

إذا فَقَدْناكَ يُعطي قبلَ أن يَعِدَا	مُحَمَّدَ بنَ زُرَيقٍ ما نَرى أحَداً
والدّارُ شاسِعَةٌ والزّادُ قد نَفِدَا	وقد قَصَدْتُكَ والتَّرْحالُ مُقتَرِبٌ
إذا اكتَفَيتُ وإلاّ أغرَقَ البَلَدَا	فَخَلِّ كَفَّكَ تَهمي واثِنِ وابِلَها

(٤٤)

«من البسيط»

يمدح عبد الله بن يحيى البحتري:

وجُدْتُ بي وبدَمعي في مَغانِيكا	بكَيتُ يا رَبعُ حتى كِدتُ أبكيكا
وارْدُدْ تَحِيَّتَنا إنّا مُحَيُّوكا	فعِمْ صَباحاً لقد هَيَّجْتَ لي طَرَباً
رِئمُ الفَلا بدَلاً مِن رِئمِ أهلِيكا	بأيِّ حُكمِ زَمانٍ صِرتُ مُتَّخِذاً
إلاّ ابتَعَثْنَ دماً باللَّحظِ مَسفوكا	أيّامَ فيكِ شُموسٌ ما انبَعَثْنَ لنا
كأنَّ نُورَ عُبَيدِ اللهِ يَعلُوكا	والعَيشُ أخضَرُ والأطلالُ مُشرِقَةٌ
وخابَ رَكبٌ رِكابٍ لم يُؤَمّوكا	نَجا امرُؤٌ يا ابنَ يَحيى كنتَ بُغيَتَهُ
جميعَ مَن مَدَحوهُ بالّذي فيكا	أحيَيتَ للشُّعَراءِ الشِّعرَ فامتَدَحوا
على دَقيقِ المعاني مِن مَعانيكا	وعَلَّموا النّاسَ مِنكَ المَجدَ واقتَدَروا
وكيفَ شِئتَ فما خَلقٌ يُدانيكا	فكُن كما شِئتَ يا مَن لا شَبيهَ لَهُ
إلى نَداكَ طَريقَ العُرفِ مَسلُوكا	شُكرُ العُفاةِ لِما أوْلَيتَ أوجَدَني
أنّي بقِلَّةِ ما أثنَيتُ أهجُوكا	وعُظمُ قَدرِكَ في الآفاقِ أوهَمَني
وإنْ فَخَرْتَ فكلٌّ مِن مَوالِيكا	كَفى بأنَّكَ مِنْ قَحطانَ في شَرَفٍ
على الوَرى لَرَأوْني مِثلَ شانِيكا	ولوْ نَقَصْتُ كما قد زِدْتَ مِن كَرَمٍ

I scatter pearls so take them as real
    The tricksters are many, beware of a fraud
I kept them veiled from Antakya's folk
    I show them so you appear as a bridegroom
Best of birds are in palaces, the worst
    Take shelter in ruins and roost in a tomb
If the world gives, it ransoms you by men
    If it battles it enlists anchorites for you

43
He also said about him.
(Outspread da)

Muhammad ibn Zuraiq we know of none who
    If we lost you would give before he vowed
I sought you out, the journey was short
    But the house was far and provision gone
Keep your hand from flow, stop its shower
    When I am content, or else the land drowns

44
He spoke praising Ubaidallah ibn Yahya.
(Outspread ka)

I wept O quarter till almost I was wept
    I, and my tears, gave myself in your abode
Be kind this morning for you stir my pain
    And return our greeting as we greeted you
By what rule of time can you be taken for
    A desert fawn, instead of maid of your clan?
Some days suns appear not with you except
    They draw blood for us, a glance's shedding
Life is green and ruins of a camp gleam
    As if light of Ubaidallah were over you
One is safe O Ibn Yahya if you are a goal
    Camel riders betrayed if not turning to you
You inspire poets to poetry, they praise
    All those they praise by what lies in you
They teach men glory by you, having power
    Over the finest meanings from your meaning
Be as you wish O you who are incomparable
    Or how you wish for no being approaches you
Suppliant's thanks to whom you give show
    the way to your bounty by well trodden paths
Your great power in the region tells me
    My little praise of you seems to mock you
It is enough eminence you are of Qahtan
    And if you boast then all are your clients
If I fall short as you exceed in bounty
    To men, they would know me as your enemy

لَبَّيْ نَداكَ لَقَدْ نادى فَأَسْمَعَني	يَفديكَ مِن رَجُلٍ صَحبي وَأَفديكا
ما زِلتَ تُتبِعُ ما تُولي يَداً بِيَدٍ	حَتّى ظَنَنتُ حَياتي مِن أَياديكا
فَإِن تَقُل هاءَ عاداتٌ عُرِفتَ بِها	أَو لا فَإِنَّكَ لا يَسخو بِلا فوكا

(٤٥)

«من الطويل»

يمدحه أيضًا:

أَريقُكِ أَم ماءُ الغَمامَةِ أَم خَمرُ	بِفيَّ بُرودٌ وَهوَ في كَبِدي جَمرُ
إِذا الغُصنُ أَم ذا الدِعصُ أَم أَنتِ فِتنَةٌ	وَذَيّا الَّذي قُلتُهُ البَرقُ أَم ثَغرُ
رَأَت وَجهَ مَن أَهوى بِلَيلٍ عَواذِلي	فَقُلنَ نَرى شَمساً وَما طَلَعَ الفَجرُ
رَأَينَ الَّتي لِلسِحرِ في لَحَظاتِها	سُيوفٌ ظُباها مِن دَمي أَبَداً حُمرُ
تَناهى سُكونُ الحُسنِ في حَرَكاتِها	فَلَيسَ لِرائي وَجهِها لَم يَمُتْ عُذرُ
إِلَيكَ اِبنَ يَحيى بنِ الوَليدِ تَجاوَزَت	بِيَ البيدَ عيسٌ عِظمُها وَالدَمُ الشَعرُ
نَضَحتُ بِذِكراكُم حَرارَةَ قَلبِها	فَسارَت وَطولُ الأَرضِ في عَينِها شِبرُ
إِلى لَيثِ حَربٍ يُلحِمُ اللَيثَ سَيفَهُ	وَبَحرِ نَدىً في مَوجِهِ يَغرَقُ البَحرُ
وَإِن كانَ يُبقي جودُهُ مِن تَليدِهِ	شَبيهاً بِما يُبقي مِنَ العاشِقِ الهَجرُ
فَتىً كُلَّ يَومٍ تَحتَوي نَفسُ مالِهِ	رِماحُ المَعالي لا الرُدَينِيَّةُ السُمرُ
تَباعَدَ ما بَينَ السَحابِ وَبَينَهُ	فَنائِلُها قَطرٌ وَنائِلُهُ غَمرُ
وَلَو تَنزِلُ الدُنيا عَلى حُكمِ كَفِّهِ	لَأَصبَحَتِ الدُنيا وَأَكثَرُها نَزرُ
أَراهُ صَغيراً قَدرُها عُظمُ قَدرِهِ	فَما لِعَظيمٍ قَدرُهُ عِندَهُ قَدرُ
مَتى ما يُشِرْ نَحوَ السَماءِ بِوَجهِهِ	تَخِرَّ لَهُ الشِعرى وَيَنخَسِفِ البَدرُ
تَرى القَمَرَ الأَرضِيَّ وَالمَلِكَ الَّذي	لَهُ المُلكُ بَعدَ اللَهِ وَالمَجدُ وَالذِكرُ
كَثيرُ سُهادِ العَينِ مِن غَيرِ عِلَّةٍ	يُوَرِّقُهُ في ما يُشَرِّفُهُ الفِكرُ
لَهُ مِنَنٌ تُفني الثَناءَ كَأَنَّما	بِهِ أَقسَمَت أَن لا يُؤَدّى لَها شُكرُ
أَبا أَحمَدٍ ما الفَخرُ إِلّا لِأَهلِهِ	وَما لِاِمرِئٍ لَم يُمسِ مِن بَحرِ فَخرِ
هُمُ الناسُ إِلّا أَنَّهُم مِن مَكارِمٍ	يُغَنّي بِهِم حَضَرٌ وَيَحدو بِهِم سَفرُ
بِمَن أَضرِبُ الأَمثالَ أَم مَن أَقيسُهُ	إِلَيكَ وَأَهلُ الدَهرِ دونَكَ وَالدَهرُ

Here at your word, it calls, makes me hear
    My friends your ransom as men, I ransom you
You still follow a last gift with another
    Until I think my life is among your gifts
If you say: Here! it's your known custom
    Or if: No but your mouth has never given No

45
He spoke praising Ubaidallah ibn Yahya.
(Long ru)

Is it your saliva, cloud water, or wine?
    In my mouth it is cool but on my liver coals
A bough on a sand hill, or a maiden, you
    And what I kissed, lightning or those teeth?
My critics saw the face I love at night
    They said: We see a sun but dawn rises not
They see what is magic in her glances
    Swords with edges ever red with my blood
Quiet beauty attains a climax in her gait
    No excuse for not dying at sight of her face
To you Ibn Yahya ibn Walid a camel runs
    In a desert with me, her flesh and blood poetry
With your memory I wet her burning heart
    She goes earth's length, a span in her eyes
To a lion of war whose sword feeds lions
    To a sea of bounty in whose wave seas drown
If his bounty leaves any of his heritage
    It is like what flight leaves to the beloved
A man, each day he gathers souls as store
    His lance is honor and not a brown Rudaini
One sees distance between him and clouds
    But their gifts are rain and his favors are a sea
If a world yields to his judgment's hand
    The world will discover its greatness small
His power's majesty makes her size little
    But his power is not power for the dreadful
If he turns his face toward the heavens
    The stars fall and the moon is in eclipse
You see an earthly moon and king with
    Dominion after God in glory and esteem
Much wakefulness of eye not illness
    Keeps him awake as thoughts ennoble him
His is a bounty destroying praise as if
    Thanks swore he could not be repaid for it
Abu Ahmad, no honor except in his clan
    Or boasting in affairs not touching Buhturi
They are men but belong to noble acts
    Cities enriched, travelers guided by them
By whom do I make proverbs or compare
    If the age and its men are now short of you?

(٤٦)

«من البسيط»

يمدح أخاه أبا عبادة:

حتى أكـونَ بــلا قَلْبٍ ولا كَبِدِ	ما الشَّوْقُ مُقْتِنِعاً منِّي بذا الكَمَدِ
تَشــكو إلَيّ ولا أشـكو إلى أحَــدِ	ولا الدِّيـارُ التـي كــانَ الحبيبُ بهــا
والسَّقمُ يُنحِلُني حتى حكـتْ جسدي	ما زالَ كـلُّ هزيمِ الـوَدْقِ يُنحِلُهــا
كأنّ ما سالَ من جَفنيّ من جَلَدي	وكلَّما فاضَ دمعي غاضَ مُصْطَبِري
وأينَ منكَ ابنَ يحيى صَوْلَةُ الأسَدِ	فأينَ من زفراتي مَنْ كَلِفْتُ بِهِ
وبالوَرى قَلَّ عِندي كـثرةُ العَـدَدِ	لَمَّـا وزَنتُ بكَ الدّنيـا فَمِلْـتُ بهـا
أبــا عُبــادَةَ حتــى دُرتَ في خلَدي	ما دار في خلَـدِ الأيّـامِ لي فَـرحٌ
أذاقَهـا طَعـمَ تُكْـلِ الأمَّ للوَلَـدِ	مَلِكٌ إذا امتـلأتْ مالاً خزائِنُـهُ
بقلبِهِ مـا تَرى عَيناهُ بَعْـدَ غَـدِ	ماضي الجَنانِ يُريهِ الحَزمُ قَبلَ غدٍ
ولا السَّماحُ الذي فيهِ سَمـاحُ يَـدِ	ما ذا البَهاءُ ولا ذا النُّورُ مِن بَشَـرٍ
حتى إذا افتَرَقـا عـادَتْ ولم يَعُـدِ	أيّ الأكُفِّ تُباري الغَيثَ ما اتَّفَقـا
حتى تَبَحْتَـرَ فهـوَ اليومَ مِـنْ أدَدِ	قد كنتُ أحْسَـبُ أنّ المجدَ من مُضَرٍ
حَسِبْتَها سُخباً جـادَتْ على بَلَـدِ	قـومٌ إذا أمْطَرتْ مَوْتـاً سُيوفُهُـمْ
إلّا وَجَــدْتُ مَداهـا غايةَ الأبَـدِ	لم أجرِ غايةً فكري منكَ في صِفةٍ

(٤٧)

«من الكامل»

يمدح مساور بن محمد الرومي:

أغِـذاءُ ذا الرَّشـاءِ الأغَنِّ الشَّيـحُ	جَلَـلاً كمـا بـي فَلْيَـكُ التَّبريـحُ
صَنَمـاً مـنَ الأصنـامِ لـولا الـرُّوحُ	لَعِبَتْ بِمِشْيَتِهِ الشَّمولُ وغـادَرَتْ
وجَنـاتُــهُ وفُــؤادِيَ المَجـروحُ	مـا بـالُـهُ لا حَظَّتُـهُ فتَضَـرَّجَـتْ
سَـهْمٌ يُعَـذِّبُ والسِّهـامُ تُريـحُ	ورَمـى ومـا رَمَتـا يَـداهُ فَصابَنـي
يَغدو الجَنانُ فَنَلْتَقـي ويَـروحُ	قَـرُبَ المَزارُ ولا مَـزارَ وإنّما
تَعريضُنـا فَبَـدا لـكَ التَّصريـحُ	وفَشَتْ سَرائِرُنـا إلَيـكَ وشَفَّنـا

46
He spoke
praising his brother
Abu Ubada Ubaidallah ibn Yahya al- Buhturi.
(Outspread di)

Passion is not content with me in this
    Grief, until I am without a heart and liver
Nor do campsites where the beloved is
    Complain to me nor do I complain to any
All the rumbling showers wear them down
    Illness thins me until my body discloses that
Each time my tears run, patience wanes
    As if my strength flowed from out my eyelids
Where are the sighs I was loaded with
    Where, Ibn Yahya, are your lionlike attacks?
I weigh the world with you, you exceed it
    So the large numbers of men seem few to me
Joy never settled in my soul for a day
    O Abu Ubada until you settled in my mind
A king, if his treasury is full of wealth
    He has it taste the mourning mother's food
An alert mind, troubles appear beforehand
    In his heart as his eyes see them afterward
This glory, this light is not of mankind
    Nor is generosity in it bounty of the hand
What a hand to rival rains in two seasons
    When they depart one returns, the other not
I had been thinking glory was of Mudar
    Until al Buhturi but now it appears in Udad
People who if their swords rain death
    You think a cloud is generous to the land
I find no end to my ideas of your traits
    Rather I find their end in eternity's goal

47
He spoke
praising
Musawar ibn Muhammad al Rumi.
(Perfect hu)

Bad as it is for me it may yet be worse
    Is wormwood a food for this singing fawn?
Drunkenness plays in his walk, makes him
    The statue among statues except for breath
He pays no mind, I look at him and his
    Cheeks blush but my heart feels the wound
He shoots but his hands aim not, arrows
    Hit me that still hurt but the arrows cease
The visit nears but no visiting occurs
    The heart is early as we meet and it rests
Our secret is disclosed to you, our hint
    Thins us so a declaration is plain to you

لَمـا تَقَطَّعَتِ الحُمـولُ تَقَطَّعَتْ	نَفْسـي أَسـىً وكـأنَّهـنَّ طُلُــوحُ
وَجَـلا الـوَداعُ مـن الحَبيـبِ مَحاسـناً	حُسْـنُ العَـزاءِ وقـد جُلِيـنَ قَبيـحُ
فَيَـدٌ مُسَـلَّمَةٌ وطَـرْفٌ شـاخِصٌ	وحَشًـاً يَـذوبُ ومَدْمَـعٌ مَسْـفُوحُ
يَجِدُ الحَمـامُ ولو كَوَحْـدي لانْبَرَى	شَجَـرُ الأراكِ مَـعَ الحَمـامِ يَنــوحُ
وأَمَـقَّ لـوْ خَـدَتِ الشِّمـالُ بِراكِبٍ	في عَرْضِـهِ لأنـاخَ وَهْـيَ طَليـحُ
نازَعْتُـهُ قُلُـصَ الرِّكـابِ ورَكْبُهــا	خَـوْفَ الهَـلاكِ حُداهُـمُ التَّسـبيحُ
لَـوْ لا الأميـرُ مُسـاوِرُ بـنُ مُحَمَّـدٍ	مـا جُشِّـمَتْ خَطَـراً وَرُدَّ نَصيــحُ
ومتى وَنَـتْ وأبـو المُظَفَّـرِ أُمُّهـا	فأتـاحَ لي ولَهـا الحِمـامَ مُتيــحُ
شِـمْنا وما حُجِبَ السَّمـاءُ بُروقَـهُ	وحَـرًى يَجُـودُ وما مَرَتْـهُ الرِّيــحُ
مَرْجُـوٌّ مَنْفَعَـةٍ مَخْـوفُ أَذِيَّــةٍ	مَغْبُـوقُ كَـأْسِ مَحامِـدٍ مَصبـوحُ
حَغِـقٌ على بَـدْرِ اللُّجَيـنِ وما أَتَـتْ	بإسـاءَةٍ وعَـنِ المُسـيءِ صَفُـوحُ
لَـوْ فُرِّقَ الكَـرَمُ المُفَـرَّقُ مالَـهُ	في النـاسِ لم يَكُ في الزَّمانِ شَحيحُ
أَلْغَـتْ مَسـامِعُهُ المَـلامَ وغـادَرَتْ	سِمَـةً على أنـفِ اللِّـئامِ تَلـوحُ
هـذا الـذي خَلَـتِ القُـرونُ وذِكْرُهُ	وحَديثُـهُ في كُتْبِهــا مَشْــروحُ
أَلْبأنـا بجَمالِــهِ مَبْهُــورَةً	وسَـحابُنا بنَوالِـهِ مَفْضُـوحُ
يَغْشَى الطِّعـانَ فَـلا يَـرُدُّ قَنـاتَـهُ	مكسـورَةً ومِـنَ الكُمـاةِ صَحيـحُ
وعلى التُّـرابِ مِـنَ الدِّمـاءِ مَجاسِدٌ	وعلى السَّمـاءِ مِـنَ العَجـاجِ مُسُـوحُ
يَخْطُـو التُّـرابَ إلى القَتيـلِ أمامَـهُ	رَبُّ الجَـوادِ وخَلْفَـهُ المَبْطُـوحُ
فمَقيـلُ حُبِّ مُحِبِّـهِ فَـرِحٌ بـهِ	ومَقيـلُ غَيْـظِ عَـدُوِّهِ مَقْـروحُ
يُخْفـي العَـداوَةَ وهـيَ غَيـرُ خَفِيَّـةٍ	نَظَـرُ العَـدُوِّ بما أَسَـرَّ يَبـوحُ
يـا ابنَ الذي مـا ضَـمَّ بُـرْدٌ كائِنِهِ	شَـرَفاً ولا كـالجَدِّ ضَـمَّ ضَريــحُ
نَفْديـكَ مـن سَـيّلٍ إذا سُـئِلَ النَّـدى	هَـوْلٌ إذا اخْتَلَـطَ دَمٌ ومَسيـحُ
لَـوْ كُنْـتَ بحـراً لم يكُـنْ بـكَ سـاحِلٌ	أو كُنـتَ غَيْثـاً ضـاقَ عنـكَ اللُّـوحُ
وخَشيـتُ مِنـكَ على البـلادِ وأهْلِهـا	ما كـانَ أنـذَرَ قَـوْمَ نُـوحٍ نُـوحُ
عَجَــزَّ بحُـرٌ فـاقَــةٌ وَوَراءَهُ	رِزْقُ الإلَـهِ وبـابُكَ المَفْتُـوحُ

When camels start away my soul is split
    With sorrow and they are like palm trees
Parting reveals the beloved's beauties
    Beauty of patience is ugly if she is away
A hand waving goodbye, glance lifted
    A heart that melts and tears that spread
The dove grieves, if it had my sorrow
    The thorn tree would aid a dove's lament
Such a length, if a north wind went with
    Rider on its back it would kneel exhausted
I strive with camel stirrups whose convoy
    For fear of death sings: Glory be to God!
But for Amir Masawar ibn Muhammad
    It would not tempt danger or reject advice
If she fails with Abu Muzaffar as a goal
    A fitting fate for her and me is our death
We see his flash but the sky has no cloud
    Freely he gives but winds do not milk him
Hope of some profit, fear of some evil
    Makes evening cup praised as morning
Raging at purses of silver as they bring
    Consolation and forgiveness for wrongdoers
If he shared his wealth in noble share
    With men there'd be no greed in the times
His ears disregard blame and tolerate
    The mark on the nose that you see as filth
One who if the age is forgot, his memory
    And his story are explained in their books
Our hearts overcome by his beauty
    Our clouds are disgraced by his kindness
He ruins by jousts, retrieves no spears
    Splintered to bits though armor is whole
That saffron on the dirt is from blood
    The hair cloth on the sky is battle dust
He steps from corpse to corpse before
    A lord of horses, behind him the prostrate
His beloved's heart rejoices in him
    The heart of hate in his foes is a wound
One veils enmity, it cannot be concealed
    The enemy glance reveals what is a secret
O son of him whom no robe shows as high
    As his son or any tomb covers like that father
We ransom your bounty if gifts are asked
    Your terror if blood and sweat are mingled
If you are a sea you will have no shore
    If you are a cloud, sky is too small for you
I fear for land and its folk due to you
    Since there's no Noah to warn Noah's folk
A free man is weak if poor, before him
    Is provision of God and your open door

مِنْ أَنْ يَكونَ سَواءَكَ المَمْدوحُ	إنَّ القَريضَ شَجٍ بِعِطْفي عائِذٌ
تَبْغي الثَّناءَ عَلى الحَيا فَتَفوحُ	وذَكِيُّ رائِحَةِ الرِّياضِ كَلامُها
تُولِيهِ خَيْراً واللِّسانُ فَصيحُ	جُهْدُ المُقِلِّ فَكَيْفَ بِابْنِ كَريمَةٍ

(٤٨)

«من الكامل»

يمدحه أيضًا:

أَمْ لَيْثُ غابٍ يَقْدُمُ الأُسْتاذا	أَمُساوِرٌ أَمْ قَرْنُ شَمْسٍ هَذا
قَطَعاً وقَدْ تَرَكَ العِبادَ جُذاذا	شِمْ ما انْتَضَيْتَ فَقَدْ تَرَكَتْ ذُبابَهُ
أَتَرى الوَرى أَضْحَوْا بَنيَ يَزْداذا	هَبَكَ ابْنَ يَزْداذٍ حَطَمْتَ وصَحْبَهُ
أَقْفاءَهُمْ وكُبودَهُمْ أَفْلاذا	غادَرْتَ أَوْجُهَهُمْ بِحَيْثُ لَقيتَهُمْ
في ضَنْكِهِ واسْتَحْوَذَ اسْتيحْواذا	في مَوْقِفٍ وَقَفَ الحِمامُ عَلَيْهِمْ
أَجْرَيْتَها وسَقَيْتَها الفولاذا	جَمَدَتْ نُفوسُهُمْ فَلَمّا جِئْتَها
في جَوْشَنٍ وأَخا أَبيكَ مُعاذا	لَمّا رَأَوْكَ رَأَوْا أَباكَ مُحَمَّداً
عَنْ قَوْلِهِمْ: لا فارِسٌ إلاّ ذا	أَعْجَلَتَ أَلْسُنَهُمْ بِضَرْبِ رِقابِهِمْ
مَطَرَ المَنايا وابِلاً ورَذاذا	غُرٌّ طَلَعَتْ عَلَيْهِ طَلْعَةَ عارِضٍ
بِدَمٍ وبَلَّ بِبَوْلِهِ الأَفْخاذا	فَغَدا أَسيراً قَدْ بَلَّلَتْ ثيابَهُ
فَانْصاعَ لا حَلَباً ولا بَغْذاذا	سَدَّتْ عَلَيْهِ المَشْرَقِيَّةُ طُرْقَةً
ما بَيْنَ كَرْخايا إلى كَلْواذا	طَلَبَ الإِمارَةَ في الثُّغورِ ونَشْوَةً
أَوْ ظَنَّهُ البَرْنيَّ والآزاذا	فَكَأَنَّهُ حَسِبَ الأَسِنَّةَ حُلْوَةً
جَعَلَ الطِّعانَ مِنَ الطِّعانِ مَلاذا	لَمْ يَلْقَ قَبْلَكَ مَنْ إذا اخْتَلَفَ القَنا
حَتّى يُوافِقَ عَزْمُهُ الإِنْفاذا	مَنْ لا تَوافِقُهُ الحَياةُ وطيبُها
في البَرْدِ خَزّاً والهَواجِرِ لاذا	مُتَعَوِّداً لُبْسَ الدُّروعِ يَخالُها
أَنْ لا تَكونَ لِمِثْلِهِ أَخَذاذا	أَعْجِبْ بِأَخْذِكَهُ وأَعْجَبُ مِنكُما

Verses blame my intent to take refuge
    With another than you as object of praise
Sweet garden perfumes are in the words
    As needing rain they see praise and spread
Need is small but what of bounty's son?
    If you do well by it a tongue will be eloquent

48
He spoke also praising Musawar ibn al Rumi.
(Perfect dha)

Is this Musawar, or the sun's horn, or
    The jungle lion who precedes the viceroy?
Sheathe what you unsheathed, you left its
    Blade broken and it left the people uprooted
Grant you broke Ibn Yazdadh and allies
    Don't you see that all men are Banu Yazdadh?
You left their faces where you met them
    In pieces as their necks and as their livers
In the battle death stood against them
    In its narrows, and then it gained the mastery
Their souls petrified as you approached
    You poured and gave to drink with the steel
They saw you, saw your father Muhammad
    In armor and your father's brother al Muadh
Striking off heads you urge their tongues
    To say: There is no horseman but this one!
You rose like a cloud on him heedless
    Raining death in storms and small showers
He was captive, you stained his clothes
    With blood, he wet his thighs with his urine
Against him the swords bar the ways
    He cannot turn to Aleppo not to Bagdadh
He sought border command but his root
    Was somewhere between Karkh and Kalwadha
As if he thought spearpoints sweet bits
    Or thought them dates of Barnia or Azadh
Before you one found when lances vary
    None who made joust refuge from jousting
One for whom life and its sweet is no
    Success until his forceful will succeeds
Used to wearing armor he thinks it
    In cold like silk, in noon heat, like cotton
Wonderful your taking him but how much
    More wonderful if there were not the taking!

(٤٩)

«من الكامل»

يرثي محمد بن إسحاق التنوخي:

أنَّ الحَيـاةَ وَإنْ حَرَصْتَ غُـرورُ	إنّي لأعْلَـمُ، واللَّبيـبُ خَبيــرُ،
بِتعلَّـةٍ وإلى الفَنـاءِ يَصيــرُ	ورَأيْتُ كُـلاً مـا يُعلَّـلُ نَفْسَـهُ
فيهـا الضِّيـاءُ بوَجْهِـهِ والنّـورُ	أمُجـاوِرَ الدَّيْمـاسِ رَهْـنَ قَـرارَةٍ
أنَّ الكَواكِـبَ في التُّرابِ تَغـورُ	مـا كنتُ أحسَـبُ قبلَ دفنكَ في الثَّرَى
رَضْـوَى على أيدي الرِّجـالِ تَسيـرُ	مـا كنتُ آمُلُ قبلَ أنْ أرَى نَعشَـكَ
صَعَقـاتُ موسَـى يَـوْمَ دُكَّ الطُّورُ	خَرَجُـوا بـهِ ولكُـلِّ بـاكٍ خَلْفَـهُ
والأرضُ واجفـةٌ تَكـادُ تَمـورُ	والشَّمسُ في كبِدِ السَّمـاءِ مريضةٌ
وعيـونُ أهـلِ اللاّذقيّـةِ صُـورُ	وحَفيـفُ أجنِحَـةِ المَلائـكِ حَوْلَـهُ
في قَلْبِ كُـلِّ مُوَحِّـدٍ مَحفـورُ	حتى أتَـوْا جَدَثـاً كَأنَّ ضَريحَـهُ
مُغْفٍ وإثمِـدُ عَيْنِـهِ الكـافورُ	تمزوَّدٍ كفَنَ البِلَـى مِـن مُلْكِـهِ
والبـأسُ أجمـعُ والحجَـى والخيـرُ	فيـهِ السَّماحـةُ والفَصاحـةُ والتّقَى
لمّـا انطـوَى فكأنَّـهُ مَنشـورُ	كفَلَ الثَّنـاءُ لـهُ بـرَدَّ حياتِـهِ
وكأنَّ عـازَرَ شَـخْصُهُ المَقبـورُ	وكأنّما عيسَـى بنتِ مَريَـمَ ذِكـرُهُ
وخَبَـتْ مَكـايِدُهُ وهُـنَّ سَعيـرُ	غاضَـتْ أنامِلُـهُ وهُـنَّ بُحُـورُ
في اللَّحـدِ حتى صافحَتْـهُ الحُورُ	يُبكَـى عَلَيْـهِ ومـا استَقَرَّ قَـرارُ
إنَّ العَظيـمَ على العَظيـمِ صَبُـورُ	صَبـراً بني إسحـقَ عَنْـهُ تَكَرُّمـاً
ولكُـلِّ مَفقـودٍ سِـواهُ نظيـرُ	فلكُـلِّ مَفجـوعٍ سِواكُـمْ مُشْبَـهٌ
يُمنَـى وَباعُ المَـوتِ عنـهُ قَصيـرُ	أيَّـامَ قائِـمُ سَيْفِـهِ في كَفِّـهِ الـ
في شَفْرَتَيْـهِ جَمـاجِمٌ ونحـورُ	ولَطـالَمـا انْهَمَلَـتْ بمـاءٍ أحمَـرَ
أنْ يَحزَنُـوا ومُحمَّـدٌ مَسـرورُ	فأعيـذُ إخوتَـهُ بـرَبّ مُحَمَّـدٍ
حَيـاهُ فيهـا مُنكَـرٌ ونكيـرُ	أو يَرغَبُـوا بقصورِهِـم عَـن حُفرَةٍ
عَنهـا فآجـالُ العِبـادِ حُضُـورُ	نَفَـرٌ إذا غابَـتْ غمـودُ سُيُوفِهِـمْ
مِـنْ بَطـنِ طَيـرٍ تنوفةٍ محشـورُ	وإذا لقُـوا جَيْشـاً تَيَقَّـنَ أنَّـهُ

49
He spoke
lamenting
Muhammad ibn Ishaq al Tanukhi.
(Perfect ru)

Indeed I know and the heart is aware
    That life, if you covet it, is only delusion
I see everyone is comforting himself
    With some excuse but moving toward death
Is not a tomb's vicinity pledge of rest
    In which rays and light are from his face?
I had not thought before your burial
    In earth the stars would descend to the dust
I did not hope before your bier I would
    See Radwa being borne by the hands of men
They went with him, each mourner behind
    Gave the cry of Moses when the Sinai shook
The sun in the sky's corner was sick
    The earth was disturbed and nearly quaked
A rustle of angel's wings was about him
    The eyes of Ladhakia's folk turned upward
When they brought the body its tomb was
    Dug in the hearts of all who knew the Unity
Ruin buried provisions from his wealth
    Asleep with camphor as collyrium for the eyes
In him was generosity, eloquence, piety
    Bravery complete, reason and all goodness
Praise sure for him at his life's turn
    When buried, and as it were resurrected
As if Jesus ibn Mary were his memorial
    And as if Lazarus had his shape in the grave
His fingers dried up and yet were seas
    His wiles quenched and they were flames
He was wept for but his rest was unquiet
    In the tomb until the houris came to greet him
Banu Ishaq's patience is liberal to him
    As great ones are patient in great matters
For every pain but yours a comparison
    For every loss but his there is an equal one
One day a sword hilt in his right hand
    The handclasp of death too short for him
Long did skulls flow with red liquor
    And the breast bones as his sword's lips
I free his brothers, by lord Muhammad
    Lest they grieve, for Muhammad is happy
Or lest they prefer palace to tomb
    Where angels, Munkar and Nakir, greet
A clan, if sheaths are free of swords
    Then the last day of the enemy is at hand
When they meet an army it's sure it
    Is resurrected from the desert bird bellies

لم تُثنَ في طَلَبٍ أعنّةَ خيلهمْ	إلّا وعُمرُ طَريدِها مَبتورُ
يَمَمتُ شاسعَ دارهمْ عَن نيّةٍ	إنّ المُحبَّ على البعادِ يَزورُ
وقَنِعتُ باللقيا وأوّلِ نَظرةٍ	إنّ القَليلَ منَ الحَبيبِ كَثيرُ

وسألوه أن ينفي الشماتة عنهم فقال:

إلآلِ إبراهيمَ بعدَ محمّدٍ	إلّا حَنينٌ دائمٌ وزَفيرُ
ما شَكَّ خابرُ أمرهمْ مِن بعدهِ	أنَّ العزاءَ عَليهمْ مَحظورُ
تُدمي خدودَهمُ الدموعُ وتَنقضي	ساعاتُ لَيلهمْ وهنَّ دُهورُ
أبناءُ عَمٍّ كلُّ ذَنبٍ لامرىءٍ	إلّا السِّعايةَ بَينَهمْ مَغفورُ
طارَ الوشاةُ على صَفاءِ ودادِهمْ	وكذا الذّبابُ على الطّعامِ يَطيرُ
ولقد مَنحتُ أبا الحُسينِ مَودّةً	جودي بها لعَدوّهِ تَبذيرُ
مَلِكٌ تَكوّنَ كيفَ شاءَ كأنّما	يَجري بفَضلِ قضائهِ المَقدورُ

(٥٠)

«من الطويل»

قال وقد سألوه زيادة في نفي الشماتة عنهم:

لأيّ صُروفِ الدهرِ فيهِ نُعاتِبُ	وأيَّ رَزاياهُ بوترٍ نُطالبُ
مَضى مَن فَقدنا صَبرَنا عندَ فَقدهِ	وقد كانَ يُعطي الصبرَ والصبرُ عازبُ
يَزورُ الأعادي في سَماءِ عَجاجةٍ	أسنّتُهُ في جانبَيها الكواكبُ
فتَسفِرُ عنهُ والسّيوفُ كأنّما	مَضاربُها ممّا انفَلَلنَ ضرائبُ
طَلَعنَ شُموساً والغُمودُ مَشارقٌ	لهنَّ وهاماتُ الرّجالِ مَغاربُ
مَصائبُ شتّى جُمِّعَت في مُصيبةٍ	ولم يَكفِها حتّى قَفَتها مَصائبُ
رَثى ابنَ أبينا غيرَ ذي رَحمٍ لَهُ	فَباعَدَنا عنهُ ونحنُ الأقاربُ
وعَرَّضَ أنا شامِتونَ بمَوتهِ	وإلّا فَزارَت عارضَيهِ القَواضبُ
أليسَ عَجيباً أنْ بَينَ بَني أبٍ	لنَجلِ يَهوديٍّ تَدِبُّ العَقاربُ
ألا إنّما كانتْ وفاةُ محمّدٍ	دَليلاً على أن ليسَ للهِ غالبُ

The horses' bridles turn not in pursuit
    Rather lives of those pursued are cut off
I sought their distant home as a goal
    Truly the beloved wants a visit from afar
I am content with meeting and a look
    Since a little bit of the beloved is much

The sons of the uncle of the dead man asked him to refute the gossips for them so he spoke impromptu.

Do Ibrahim's folk after Muhammad have
    Anything but an eternal longing and sighs?
A wise man in their affair has no doubt
    After him any comfort for them is forbidden
Tears make their cheeks bloody, his
    Of their nights pass but they are as ages
O uncle's sons every sin done by man
    Is pardoned except slanders against them
The gossips dart on the purity of their
    Loves like flies hovering over their food
I was lavish toward Abu Husayn in love
    My bounty to his enemies was squandering
A king who attained what he wanted as if
    Destiny came by decisions of his judgment

50
He spoke also to refute gossips for them.
(Long hu)

What changes of destiny do we criticize
    In which of its sorrows do we ask revenge?
Gone is he at whose loss we lost patience
    He gave us courage but patience was far off
He raided foes with dust clouds in heaven
    His spearheads on their flanks were as stars
The fled him and it's as if the swords
    Whose edges dulled were the broken ones
They rose like suns, scabbards were east
    For them, while skulls of men were the west
The scattered attacks unite as calamity
    He does not stop till other attacks follow
Ones not kin to him weep father's brother
    We were distant and yet nearest relatives
It's plain that gossips wanted his death
    If not, may the swords cut off his sideburns
Is it not wonderful among father's sons
    A Jew's child should creep as a scorpion
O indeed was not Muhammad's death
    A proof that he could not overcome God?

(٥١)

«من الطويل»

يمدح أخاء الحسين بن إسحق التنوخي:

ويا قَلبُ حتى أنتَ مِمَّن أُفارِقُ	هُوَ البَينَ حتى تَأنّى الخَزائِقُ
فَريقَيْ هَوىً مِنّا مَشوقٌ وشائِقُ	وضَقَفْنا ومِمّا زادَ بَثّاً وُقوفُنا
وصارَت بَهاراً في الخُدودِ الشَّقائِقُ	وقد صارَتِ الأجفانُ قَرْحى مِنَ البُكا
ومَيّتْ ومولودٌ وقالٍ ووامِقُ	على ذا مَضى النّاسُ اجتِماعٌ وفُرْقَةُ
وشِبْتُ وما شابَ الزَّمانُ الغَرانِقُ	تَغَيَّرَ حالي واللَّيالي بِحالِها
وعن ذي المَهاري أينَ مِنها النَّقانِقُ	سَلِ البِيدَ أينَ الجِنُّ مِنّا بِجَوْزِها
مُحَيّاكَ فيهِ فاهْتَدَيْنا السَّمالِقُ	ولَيْلٍ دَجوجِيٍّ كَأنّا جَلَتْ لنا
ولا خابَها الرُّكْبانُ لو لا الأيانِقُ	فما زالَ لَوْ لا نورُ وجهِكَ جنحُهُ
مِنَ السُّكْرِ في الغَرْزَينِ ثَوْبٌ شُبارِقُ	وهَزَّ أطارَ النَّومَ حتى كَأنّي
ذَفاريها كيرانُها والنَّمارِقُ	شَدّوا بِابنِ إسحقَ الحُسَينِ فَصافَحَتْ
عَلَيْها وتَرْتَجُّ الجِبالُ الشَّواهِقُ	مَنْ تَقْشَعِرُّ الأرضُ خوفاً إذا مَشى
يُرَجّى الحَيا مِنها وتُخْشى الصَّواعِقُ	فَتىً كالسَّحابِ الجُونِ يُخْشى ويُرْتَجى
وتَكذِبُ أحياناً وذا الدَّهرَ صادِقُ	ولكِنَّها تَمْضي وهذا مُخَيَّمٌ
مَغارِبُها مِنْ ذِكْرِهِ والمَشارِقُ	تَخَلّى مِنَ الدُّنْيا لِيُنْسى فَما خَلَتْ
فَهُنَّ مَدارِيها وهُنَّ المَخانِقُ	غَذا الهِنْدُوانِيّاتِ بِالهامِ والطُّلى
وتَخضَبُ مِنهُنَّ اللِّحى والمَفارِقُ	تَشَقَّقُ مِنهُنَّ الجُيوبُ إذا غَزا
ويُصلى بِها مَن نَفسُهُ مِنهُ طالِقُ	يُجَنِّبُها مَن حَتفُهُ عنه غافِلُ
يُرى ساكِتاً والسَّيفُ عن فيهِ ناطِقُ	يُحاجى بِهِ ما ناطِقٌ وهْوَ ساكِتٌ
ولا عَجَبٌ مِن حُسنِ ما اللهُ خالِقُ	نَكِرْتُكَ حتى طالَ مِنكَ تَعَجُّبي
وفي كُلِّ حَرْبٍ لِلمَنِيَّةِ عاشِقُ	كَأنَّكَ في الإعطاءِ لِلمالِ مُبغِضٌ
وحَلَّ بِها مِنكَ القَنا والسَّوابِقُ	ألا قَلَّما تَبقى على ما بَدا لَها
فإنْ لُحتَ ذابَتْ في الخُدورِ العَواتِقُ	الحَفرِ اللهُ واسْتُرْ ذا الجَمالَ بِبُرقعٍ
ويَحدو بِكَ السُّفّارُ ما ذَرَّ شارِقُ	سَيُحيي بِكَ السُّمّارَ ما لاحَ كَوْكَبٌ

51
He spoke praising Husayn ibn Ishaq al Tanukhi.
(Long qu)

This is parting when people won't delay
    When, O heart, you are among those I leave
We stopped, our stay increased the grief
    Two parts of love, each beloved and lover
The eyelids are made red with weeping
    And the roses became yellow on the cheeks
Due to this men perished, united, parted
    The dead and newborn, the hated and loved
My state changes as my nights their state
    I grow gray but youthful time will not be gray
Ask deserts: What are jinn to us in them
    What the male ostrich to one with the filly?
On many a dark night the desert seemed
    To show us your face and that was our guide
Its dusk endless but for your way's glow
    Nor would riding beasts go on except camels
Jogging made sleep flee till it seemed
    I was drunk in the stirrups like a torn cloak
They chant of Husayn ibn Ishaq, saddle
    And its pillow shake hands with their necks
Earth's hair stands if he walks on it
    The towering mountains are made to quake
A youth, a dark cloud feared, hoped for
    Its rain hoped for and the thunder feared
But these pass while his nature is true
    They betray at times and he's ever faithful
Aloof from worldly society, not absent
    From thought of him are its east and west
He feeds Indian swords on hands, necks
    These are their combs and those the collars
For them shirts tear when he is at war
    By them the beards and the hair are dyed
A death unneeded by him is far from them
    He burns for souls who are forced from him
One thinks by him, no talk if he's silent
    He is mute but a sword speaks for his mouth
I knew you not when my wonder lasted long
    But no wonder in beauty that God can create
It seemed in giving, you hated wealth
    And in every battle you were death's lover
O short their stay for what befalls
    The lance and war horse are loosed by you
Fear God and hide beauty in
    Veils for if seen it melts masked
Night is shamed by you while stars shine
    Caravans led by you as long as dawn glows

فَمـا تَـرزُقُ الأقـدارُ مَـن أنـتَ حـارِمٌ / ولا تَحـرِمُ الأقـدارُ مَـن أنـتَ رازِقُ
ولا تَفتُـقُ الأيّـامُ مـا أنـتَ راتِـقٌ / ولا تَرتُـقُ الأيّـامُ مـا أنـتَ فاتِـقُ
لَـكَ الخيرُ غَيري رامَ مـن غَيرِك الغِنى / وغَيري بغَيـرِ اللاذِقيّـةِ لا حِـقُّ
هـيَ الغـرَضُ الأقصَى ورُؤيَتُـكَ المنى / ومَنـزِلُكَ الدُنيـا وأنـتَ الخَلائِـقُ

(٥٢)

«من الوافر»

يمدح الحسين بن إسحق التنوخي، وكان قوم قد هجوه وظنوا الهجاء إلى أبي الطيب، فكتب اليـه بمابه فكتب أبـو الطيب إليه:

أتُنكِـرُ يـا ابـنَ إسـحَقَ إخائـي / وتَحسَـبُ مـاءَ غَيـري مِـن إنائـي؟
أأنطِـقُ فيكَ هُجـرا بعـدَ عِلمـي / بـأنّكَ خيـرُ مَـن تَحـتَ السَّمـاء
وأكرَهُ مِـن ذُبـابِ السَّيـفِ طَعمـاً / وأمضَى في الأمـور مِـنَ القَضـاء
ومـا أربَـتْ على العِشريـنَ سِنّـي / فكيـفَ مَلِلـتُ مِـنْ طـولِ البَقـاء؟
ومـا استَغرَقتْ وَصفَـكَ في مَديحـي / فأُنقِـصَ مِنـهُ شيئـاً بالهجَـاء
وهَبْنـي قلـتُ: هـذا الصُّبـحُ لَيـلٌ / أَيَعمَـى العالمـونَ عَـنِ الضِّيـاء؟
تُطيـعُ الحاسِديـنَ وأنـتَ مَـرءٌ / جُعِلـتُ فِـداءَهُ وهُـمْ فِدائـي
وهاجِي نَفسِـهِ مَـن لم يُمَيِّـز / كلامِـي مِـنْ كَلامِهِـمُ الهُـراء
وإنّ مِـنَ العَجائِـبِ أن تَرانـي / فتَعـدِلَ بـي أقـلَّ مِـنَ الهَبـاء
وتُنكِـرَ موتَهُـم وأنـا سُهَيـلٌ / طَلَعـتُ بمـوتِ أولادِ الزِّنـاء

(٥٣)

«من الطويل»

يمدحه أيضًا

مَلامـي النَّـوى في ظُلمِهـا غايةُ الظُّلـمِ / لَعَـلَّ بهـا مِثـلَ الـذي بـي مِن السُّقـمِ
فَلَـو لم تَغِـرْ لم تَـزوُ عنّـي لِقـاءَكُـم / ولَـو لم تُردكـم لم تكـن فيكـم خصمـي
أَمُنعِمَـةٌ بالعَـودَةِ الظَّبيـةُ التـي / بغَيـرِ وَلِيٍّ كـانَ نائِلُهـا الوَسمـي

Destiny supports none whom you forbid
    Nor do fates forbid those whom you support
Days do not break what you have joined
    Nor do the days join what you have broken
The best, I seek no wealth but yours
    Nor stay elsewhere than hen in Ladhaqia
This the farthest goal, your face reward
    Your house is the world, you all its people

52
Muhammad ibn Ishaq heard that Abu Tayyib had mocked him and it was only mockery by one who used his name but Muhammad ibn Ishaq blamed him and he spoke.
(Exuberant i)

Am I not your brother O Ibn Ishaq
    Do you think others water is from my jar?
Would I speak filth of you after I knew
    That you were best of those under heaven?
Most bitter to taste in the sword's edge
    And the sharpest in a matter of judgment?
My years do not reach more than twenty
    Why should I be weary of such a long life?
I drown your description in my praise
    And only to scant a bit of it by mockery?
But grant I said this dawn is night
    Are people who know blind to the light?
You subdued the jealous, you are a man
    For whom I am ransom, they are my ransom
My satire is for those who distinguish not
    Between my word and word of the worthless
Indeed it's surprising you have seen me
    And equated me with smallest dust specks
You ignore their death, I am Suhail
    Who brings death to these sons of whores

53
He spoke also praising Husayn ibn Ishaq al Tanukhi.
(Long mi)

Blame of distance, its evil great evil
    Perhaps it has some of the Illness I have
If not jealous could it block a meeting?
    If not desirous it would be a rival for me
Will the fawn be good enough to return?
    She gave her first shower without a second

تَرَشَّفْتُ فاها سُحْرَةً فكأنّي تَرَشَّفْتُ حرَّ الوَجدِ من باردِ الظَّلمِ
فَتاةٌ تَساوَى عِقدُها وكَلامُها ومَبسِمُها الدُّرِّيُّ في الحسنِ والنَّظمِ
ونَكهَتُها والمَنْدَلِيُّ وقَرقَفٌ مُعَتَّقَةٌ صَهباءُ في الرَّيحِ والطَّعمِ
جَفَتْني كأنّي لَستُ أَنْطَقَ قَومِها وأطعَنهم والشُّهبُ في صورةِ الدُّهمِ
يُحاذِرُني حَتْفي كأنّي حَتْفُهُ وتَنكُرُني الأفعَى فيقتُلُها سُمّي
طِوالُ الرُّدَينِيّاتِ يَقصِفُها دَمي وبيضُ السُّرَيجيّاتِ يقطَعُها لحمي
بَرَتْني السُّرَى بَرْيَ المُدَى فَرَدَدْنَني أخَفَّ على المركوبِ من نفسي جِرمي
وأبصَرَ من زرقاءَ جَوٍّ لأنَّني متى نَظَرَتْ عَينايَ ساواهما عِلمي
كأنّي دحوْتُ الأرضَ من خِبرتي بها كأنّي بنى الإسكندرُ السدَّ من عَزمي
لألقَى ابنَ إسحقَ الذي دقَّ فَهمُهُ فأبدعَ حتى جَلَّ عن دِقّةِ الفَهمِ
وأسمَعَ من ألفاظِهِ اللَّغَةَ التي يَلَذُّ بها سمعي ولَم ضُمّنتْ شَتمي
يَمينُ بَني قَحطانَ رأسُ قُضاعةٍ وعِرِّنينها بدرُ النجومِ بَني فَهمِ
إذا بَيَّتَ الأعداءَ كان سَماعُهُم صَريرَ العَوالي قَبلَ قَعقَعةِ اللُّجمِ
مُذِلُّ الأعِزَّاءِ المُعِزُّ وإنْ يَهِنْ بهِ يُتِمهُم فالمُوتِمُ الجابرُ اليُتمِ
وإنْ تُمْسِ داءً في القلوبِ قَناتُهُ فمُمسِكُها منهُ الشِّفاءُ من العُدمِ
مُقلَّدُ طاغي الشَّفرتَينِ مُحكَّمٍ على الهامِ إلَّا أنَّهُ جائرُ الحُكمِ
تَحَرَّجَ عن حَقْنِ الدِّماءِ كأنَّهُ يَرى قتلَ نفسٍ تركَ رأسٍ على جِسمِ
وَجدْنا ابنَ إسحقَ الحُسَينِ كجَدّهِ على كَثْرةِ القتلى بريئاً من الإثمِ
مَعَ الحزمِ حتى لو تَعَمَّدَ تَركَهُ لأَلْحَقَهُ تَضييعُهُ الحَزمَ بالحَزمِ
وفي الحَربِ حتى لو أرادَ تأخُّراً لأخَّرَهُ الطَّبعُ الكريمُ إلى القُدمِ
لهُ رَحمةٌ تُحيي العِظامَ وغَضْبةٌ بها فَضلَةٌ للجُرمِ عن صاحبِ الجُرمِ
ورِقَّةُ وجهٍ لو خَتَمتَ بنظرةٍ على وجنَتَيهِ ما انمَحى أثرُ الختمِ
إذاقَ الغواني حُسنُهُ ما أذَقنَني وعَفَّ فجازاهنَّ عنّي على الصَّرمِ
فِدىً مَن على الغَبراءِ أوَّلُهم أنا لهذا الأبيِّ الماجدِ الجائدِ القَرمِ
لقد حالَ بينَ الجِنِّ والأمنِ سيفُهُ فما الظنُّ بعدَ الجِنِّ بالعُربِ والعُجمِ
وأرهَبَ حتى لو تأمَّلَ دِرعَهُ جَرَتْ جَزَعاً من غيرِ نارٍ ولا فحمِ

I sucked her lips at dawn and it seemed
 I sucked warmth of love from cool saliva
A girl whose necklace was like her speech
 Her smile was pearls in beauty and harmony
The smell of her breath incense, Qarqafa
 Of aged vintage both in aroma and in taste
Rude to me her clan's most eloquent
 Bravest with a gray horse who seems black
My death was wary as if I were its death
 When the serpent stung me my poison killed
Length of Rudaini, my blood breaks it
 Brightness of Suraiji when my flesh cuts it
The night trip trims me thin as a knife
 My body lighter in saddle than breath jogs
More sharp sighted than Zarqa at night
 When my eyes look my feel equals them
As if I covered earth with my wisdom
 Or Alexander built the wall by my resolve
To meet Ibn Ishaq whose mind is keen
 Amazing as it glows with a fineness of wit
Listen to his words which are the speech
 Charming my ears even if it holds my blame
Banu Qahtan's right hand is Quda's head
 Their nose the moon of Banu Fahm's stars
When he meets a foe at night their ears
 Hear spears' whistle before bridles' jingle
Subduer of strength, comforter though he
 Destroys them, bereaver, helper of orphans
If his spear brings ills to hearts yet
 Those touched have a healing from poverty
Girded by despot's double edge he tries
 Skulls, except that it is an unfair judgment
He abstained from sparing blood as if
 He saw his own death in heads left on body
We saw Husayn ibn Ishaq as grandfather
 In the number of his battles free from blame
Resolved, until he intends to leave it
 Then his leaving makes resolve stick firm
So in war if he were to want a retreat
 His retreat has a noble nature's progress
His mercy brings bones to life as anger
 Has a surplus for sin, rather than sinner
A kindly face, if you fix a glance
 On his cheeks the print trace is not lost
His beauty attracts maids who avoid me
 But he is chaste and repays their shunning
Ransom are those in dust, first am I
 For this noble glory and excellent prince
His sword is between jinn and believers
 No fears of Arab or Persian after the jinn
He scares if they but look at his armor
 They melt in fear without a fire or a coal

وحَادَ فَلَوْلا جُودُهُ غيرَ شارِبِ … لقُلْنا كَريمٌ هَيَّجَتْهُ ابنـةُ الكَرمِ
أَطَعْناكَ طوعَ الدَّهرِ يا بنَ ابنِ يوسُفٍ … بشَهْوَتِنا والحاسِـدُو لكَ بـالرَّغمِ
وَيقنا بأَنْ تُعطي فَلَوْ لم تَجُدْ لنا … لَخلناكَ قد أعطَيتَ من قـوَّةِ الوَهمِ
دُعيتُ بتَقريظِيكَ في كـلّ مَجلِسٍ … فظَنَّ الذي يَدعو ثَنائي عليكَ اسمي
وأطْمَعتَـني في نَيـلِ مـا لا أنالُهُ … بِما نِلتُ حتى صِرتُ أطمَعُ في النجمِ
إذا ما ضَرَبْتَ القِرنَ ثمَّ أجَزتَنـي … فَكـلُّ ذَهَبٍ لي مَـرَّةً منـهُ بـالكَلمِ
أبَتْ لـكَ ذَمِّي نَخـوَةٌ يَمَنيَّـةٌ … ونَفسٌ بها في مَـأزقٍ أبَداً تَرْمي
فكَمْ قائِلٍ لو كـانَ ذا الشخصُ نفسَهُ … لكانَ قَراهُ مَكمَـنَ العَسكَرِ الدَّهمِ
وقائِلَـةٍ والأرضَ أعْنـي تَعَجُّبـاً … عليَّ امرُؤٌ يَمشي بوَقري مـن الحِلمِ
عَظُمْـتَ فَلَمـا لم تُكَلَّـمْ مَهابـةً … تواضَعْتَ وهو العُظْمُ عُظماً عن العُظمِ

(٥٤)

«من الوافر»

دخل على علي بن إبراهيم التنوخي، فعرض عليه كأساً بيده فيها شراب أسود فقال ارتجالاً:

إذا مـا الكـأسُ أرعَشَـتِ اليَديــنِ … صَحَـوْتُ فلـم تَحُـلْ بيــني وبَيـني
هجَرْتُ الخَمـرَ كالذهَبِ المُصَفّى … فخَمري مـاءُ مُـزنٍ كـاللُّجَينِ
أغـارُ مِـن الزجـاجـةِ وهيَ تجري … على شَفَـةِ الأمـيرِ أبــي الحُسَيـنِ
كـأنَّ بَياضَهـا والـرَّاحُ فيهـا … بَيـاضٌ مُحـدِقٌ بسَـوادِ عَيْـنِ
أتَيناهُ نُطـالِبُـهُ بِرفْـدٍ … فَطـالَبَ نفسَـهُ منـهُ ببدَيـنِ

(٥٥)

«من الطويل»

وشرب علي تلك الكأس فقال له ارتجالاً:

مَزَجْتَ ابنَ إبراهيـمَ صافيةَ الخَمـرِ … وهَنَّتْها مِن شارِبٍ مُسكِرِ السُّكرِ
رأَيتُ الحُمَيّا في الزجاجِ بكَفّـهِ … فشَبَّهْتُها بالشمسِ في البدرِ في البحرِ
إذا ما ذَكَرْنا جُودَهُ كـانَ حـاضِراً … نأَى أوْ دَنا يَسعى على قدَمِ الخِضْرِ

Bounteous! if his bounty were not sober
    We'd say: Noble! the vine's daughter gives
We obey you ever loyal Ibn Yusuf's son
    With our desires in spite of jealous beings
We trust what you give or if you do not
    We believe by force of habit you have given
I acclaim your praise in every assembly
    One wants to give my eulogy of you my name
You tempted me by gifts I had not taken
    The like of before, until I desired the stars
When you hit a warrior then you share
    Measure the gold for me once by his wound
A Yamani pride drives off my blame of you
    You yourself attack by it forever in the battle
How many talkers if they had such a form
    Would make its mask cover the largest army
Many a word sways earth in wonder at me
    A man who walks with my weight of thinking
Great when one won't address you in fear
    You are humble, greatness greater than pride

54
He came to Ali ibn Ibrahim al Tanukhi and he offered him a cup in his hand in which was a dark drink so he spoke impromptu.
(Exuberant ni)

When the cup makes the hands tremble
    I stop so it is not between me and myself
I flee wine that is like refined gold
    My wine is cloud water that is as silver
I'm jealous of the glass that pours
    Over the lips of the Amir Abu Husayn
As if its brightness and wine in it
    Were white of an eye with a dark pupil
We came to him seeking bounty when
    He sought the same himself as pay for it

55
So he drank it and said about him.
(Long ri)

Wine wishes health to you Ibn Ibrahim
    Enjoy it as a drinker among drunken topers
I saw the nectar in a glass in his hand
    I compared it to sun on the moon in the sea
If we think of his bounty it is present
    Far or near it runs on the feet of al Khidr

(٥٦)

«من الوافر»

يمدحه أيضًا:

لُيَيْلَتَنــا المَنوطَــةُ بالتَّنــادي	أحــادٌ أمْ سُــداسٌ في أُحــادِ
خَرائِــدُ سـافراتٌ في حِــدادِ	كــأنَّ بَنــاتِ نَعْــشٍ في دُجاهــا
وقَـوْدِ الخَيْـلِ مُشـرفةِ الهَــوادي	أُفَكِّــرُ في مُعــاقَرَةِ المنايــا
بسَـفْكِ دمِ الحَواضرِ والبَــوادي	زَعيـمٌ للقَنــا الخَطِّــيّ عَزْمــي
وكَــمْ هــذا التَّمــادي في التَّمــادي	إلى كَــمْ ذا التخلُّــفُ والتَّوانــي
بَبَيــعِ الشِّـعْرِ في سـوقِ الكَسـادِ	وشُغْــلُ النَّفسِ عــن طَلَــبِ المَعالي
ولا يَــوْمٌ يَمُــرُّ بمُسْــتَعادِ	ومــا مـاضي الشَّـبابِ بمُسْــتَرَدِّ
فقد وقَــعَ انْتِقــاصي في ازْدِيــادي	متى لَحظَــتْ بَيــاضَ الشَّيبِ عينــي
علــى مــا للأميـرِ مِــنَ الأيــادي	أأرْضَــى أنْ أعيــشَ ولا أُكــافي
وإنْ تَــرَكَ المَطايــا كالمَــزادِ	جَــزَى اللهُ المسيــرَ إليــهِ خَيــراً
وفيهــا قــوتُ يَــوْمٍ للقُــرادِ	فلَــمْ تلــقَ ابــنَ إبراهيــمَ عَنْســي
فصَيَّــرَ طولَــهُ عَــرْضَ النِّجــادِ	الَــمْ يَـكُ بينَنــا بَلَــدٌ بعيــدٌ
وقَــرَّبَ قُرْبَنــا قُــرْبَ البِعــادِ	وأبْعَــدَ بُعْدَنــا بُعْــدَ التَّدانــي
وأجْلَسَنــي على السَّــبْعِ الشِّــدادِ	فلَمّـا جِئْتُــهُ أعْلــى مَحَــلّــي
وألْقــى مالَــهُ قَبْــلَ الوِســادِ	تَهلَّــلَ قَبْــلَ تسـليمي عليــهِ
لأنَّــكَ قــد زَرَيْــتَ علــى العِبــادِ	نَلومُــكَ يــا عَلــيّ لغيــرِ ذَنْــبٍ
هِبــاتُكَ أنْ يُلَقَّــبَ بالجَــوادِ	وأنَّــكَ لا تَجــودُ علــى جَــوادِ
إذا مــا حُلّــتْ عاقِبَــةَ ارتِــدادِ	كــأنَّ سَــخاءَكَ الإسـلامَ تَخشـى
وقد طُبِعَــتْ سُــيوفُكَ مِن رُقــادِ	كــأنَّ الهــامَ في الهَيْجــا عُيــونٌ
فمــا يَخْطُــرْنَ إلّا في الفُــؤادِ	وقــد صُغَــتِ الأسِــنَّةُ مِن همــومٍ
مُعَقَّــدَةَ السَّـبائبِ للطِّــرادِ	ويــومٌ جَلَبْتَهـا شُــعْثَ النَّواصي
لَهُــمْ باللّاذِقيَّــةِ بَغْــيُ عــادِ	وحــامَ بهـا الهَــلاكُ علــى أُنــاسٍ

56
He spoke also praising
Ali ibn Ibrahim al Tanukhi.
(Exuberant di)

Is it single or is it six of them in one
    Our little night suspended till the trump?
As if Daughters of Rising in their dark
    Were virgins unveiled in mourning dress
I keep thinking about fate's tenacity
    And the reins of the horse high on the neck
My will is guarantee to Khatti spears
    For shedding blood of the city and desert
How long this failing off, falling short
    How long the stretching out of that goal?
Occupying a self in search of eminence
    By selling verses in this stagnant market
For youth's passing cannot be reclaimed
    Nor the day that is gone ever be retrieved
When the eyes see the white hair of age
    They find it in their pupils as a blindness
If I go on living after my extreme limit
    Then my decline coincides with increase
Shall I be content to live unsatisfied
    With what there is of favor with the Amir?
May God reward a trip to him with good
    Even if the camel is left like spent waterbag
My hardened beast meets not Ibn Ibrahim
    With blood in her to feed a tick for this day
Was there not between us a far desert
    Whose length was the width of a sword belt?
It pushed our distance as close as a span
    Kept near our closeness as near as removal
When I was nearby he raised my position
    And he seated me above the seven heavens
He rejoices before my greeting to him
    He gives gifts before a pillows is placed
O Ali we cannot blame you for any sin
    Except as you detract from all creatures
Your gifts are not offered to the good
    Lest some should call them only goodness
As if your bounty is Islam and you fear
    Penalty of renegades if you should change
It's as if skulls for battle were eyes
    And your swords sealed them with a sleep
You have bent the spearheads of desire
    They vibrated nowhere except in a heart
On the day you guided dusty maned
    With their tails knotted up for a pursuit

فَكانَ الغَربُ بَحراً مِن مِياهِ	وَكانَ الشَّرقُ بَحراً مِن جِيادِ
وَقَد خَفَقَت لَكَ الرّاياتُ فيهِ	فَظَلَّ يَموجُ بِالبيضِ الحِدادِ
لَقوكَ بِأَكبُدِ الإِبلِ الأَبايا	فَسُقتَهُم وَحَدُّ السَّيفِ حادِ
وَقَد مَزَّقتَ ثَوبَ الغَيِّ عَنهُم	وَقَد أَلبَستَهُم ثَوبَ الرَّشادِ
فَما تَرَكوا الإِمارَةَ لاِختِيارٍ	وَلا اِنتَحَلوا وَدادَكَ مِن وِدادِ
وَلا اِستَقَلّوا لِزُهدٍ في التَّعالي	وَلا اِنقادوا سُروراً بِاِنقِيادِ
وَلكِن هَبَّ خَوفُكَ في حَشاهُم	هُبوبَ الرّيحِ في رِجلِ الجَرادِ
وَماتوا قَبلَ مَوتِهِمُ فَلَمّا	مَنَنتَ أَعَدتَهُم قَبلَ المَعادِ
غَمَدتَ صَوارِماً لَو لَم يَتوبوا	مَحَوتَهُمُ بِها مَحوَ المِدادِ
وَما الغَضَبُ الطَّريفُ وَإِن تَقَوّى	بِمُنتَصِفٍ مِنَ الكَرَمِ التِّلادِ
فَلا تَغرُركَ أَلسِنَةٌ مَوالٍ	تَقَلُّبُهُنَّ أَفئِدَةٌ أَعادي
وَكُن كَالمَوتِ لا يَرثي لِباكٍ	بَكى مِنهُ وَيَروى وَهوَ صادي
فَإِنَّ الجُرحَ يَنفِرُ بَعدَ حينٍ	إِذا كانَ البِناءُ عَلى فَسادِ
وَإِنَّ الماءَ يَجري مِن جَمادٍ	وَإِنَّ النّارَ تَخرُجُ مِن زِنادِ
وَكَيفَ يَبيتُ مُضطَجِعاً جَبانٌ	فَرَشتَ لِجَنبِهِ شَوكَ القَتادِ
يَرى في النَّومِ رُمحَكَ في كُلاهُ	وَيَخشى أَن يَراهُ في السُّهادِ
أَشَرتُ أَبا الحُسَينِ بِمَدحِ قَومٍ	نَزَلتَ بِهِم فَسِرتَ بِغَيرِ زادِ
وَظَنّوني مَدَحتُهُمُ قَديماً	وَأَنتَ بِما مَدَحتُهُم مُرادي
وَأَنّي عَنكَ بَعدَ غَدٍ لَغادٍ	وَقَلبي عَن فِنائِكَ غَيرُ غادِ
مُحِبُّكَ حَيثُما اِتَّجَهَت رِكابي	وَضَيفُكَ حَيثُ كُنتَ مِنَ البِلادِ

(٥٧)

«من الوافر»

يمدحه ايضًا:

مُلِثَّ القَطرِ أَعطِشها رُبوعاً	وَإِلّا فَاِسقِها السَّمَّ النَّقيعا
أَسائِلُها عَنِ المُتَدَيِّريها	فَلا تَدري وَلا تُذري دُموعا

Destruction circled with them over men
    Among the wrongdoers of Ad at Ladhaqia
On the west there was its sea water
    And on the east was an ocean of horses
In it banners fluttered for you
    Perpetually foaming with swords of steel
They met you with stubborn camels
    You drove them as sword edge was singer
You tore rebellion's garment from them
    Dressed them with a garment of guidance
So they didn't leave command by choice
    Nor did they profess your love out of love
They submitted not to an Exalted rule
    Nor were they joyfully led by leadership
And yet your fear blew in their breasts
    Like a wind blowing in the legs of locusts
They died before their death's time
    Your favor returned them before judgment
You sheathe swords if they don't repent
    You erase them with them as ink is erased
This recent rage even if it is strong
    Cannot be equal to inherited generosity
Let no counselors' tongues deceive you
    Their hateful hearts can make them fickle
Be like death, mourn not the weeper
    He weeps due to that, waters and thirsts
For the wound will swell after the time
    When the scab has grown over a rawness
And water will flow from the rock
    And the fire will come out of the flint
How can a coward spend a night abed
    When you spread tragacanth thorns on it?
Asleep he sees your spears in his food
    So he fears that he will see them waking
I chose O Abu Husayn to laud the folk
    I came to them and left without the reward
Once they thought I was praising them
    You were my meaning if I spoke of them
As for me after tomorrow I go from you
    Yet my heart departs not from your court
Your lover where my steed turns itself
    And your guest wherever I am in any land

57
He spoke praising
Ali ibn Ibrahim al Tanukhi.
(Exuberant a)

O lasting rain make thirsty the quarters
    Or else pour on them these liquid poisons
I ask about their wandering inhabitants
    But they don't know and won't shed tears

زَمَانَ اللَّهْوِ والخَوْدَ الشَّمُوعَا	لَحاها اللهُ إلّا ماضِيَيْها
يُكَلِّفُ لَفظَها الطَّيْرَ الوُقُوعَا	مُنَعَّمَةٌ مُمَنَّعَةٌ رَداحٌ
فَيَبْقى مِنْ وِشاحَيْها شُسُوعا	تُرَفِّعُ ثَوْبَها الأرْدافُ عَنْها
لَهُ لَوْ لا سَواعِدُها نُزُوعا	إذا ما سَتَ رَأَيْتَ لَها ارْتِجاجاً
كَما تَتألَّمُ العَضْبَ الصَّنيعا	تَأَلَّمُ دَرْزَهُ والدَّرْزُ أَيْنٌ
يَظُنُّ ضَجيعُها الزَّنْدَ الضَّجيعا	ذِراعاها عَدُوًّا دُمْلُجَيْها
يُضِيءُ بمَنعِهِ البَدْرَ الطُّلُوعا	كَأَنَّ نِقابَها غَيْمٌ رَقيقٌ
بأكْثَرَ مِنْ تَدَلُّلِها خُضُوعا	أقُولُ لها اكشِفي ضُرِّي وقَوْلي
مَتى عُصِيَ الإلَهُ بأنْ أطيعا	أخِفتِ اللهَ في إحْياءِ نَفسٍ
وأَصْبَحَ كلُّ مَسْتُورٍ خَليعا	غَدا بِكِ كُلُّ خِلْوٍ مُسْتَهاماً
ثَبيرَ أوِ ابْنُ إبراهيمَ ريعا	أحِبَّكِ أوْ يَقولوا جَرَّ نَمْلٌ
يُشَيَّبُ ذِكْرُهُ الطّفْلَ الرَّضيعا	بَعيدُ الصِّيتِ مُنْبَتُّ السَّرايا
كأنَّ بهِ وليسَ بهِ خُشُوعا	يَعَضُّ الطَّرْفَ مِن مَكرٍ ودَهْيٍ
فَقَدْكَ سَألْتَ عن سِرٍّ مُذيعا	إذا اسْتَعْطَيْتَهُ ما في يَدَيْهِ
وإنْ لا يَبْتَدى يَرَهُ فَظيعا	قَبولُكَ مِنْهُ مَنٌّ عَلَيْهِ
ولِلتَّفريقِ يَكْرَهُ أنْ يَضيعا	لَهُونُ المالِ أفْرَشَهُ أديما
فَما لِكَرامَةٍ مَدَّ النُّطوعا	إذا ضَرَبَ الأميرُ رِقابَ قَوْمٍ
وليسَ بقاتِلٍ إلّا قَريعا	فَليسَ بواهِبٍ إلّا كَثيرا
كَفى الصَّمْصامَةُ التَّعَبَ القَطيعا	وليسَ مُؤدِّباً إلّا بنَصْلٍ
مُبارَزَهُ ويَمْنَعُهُ الرُّجُوعا	عَليٌّ ليسَ يَمْنَعُ مِنْ مَجيءٍ
ومُبْدِلُهُ مِنَ الزَّرَدِ النَّجيعا	عَليٌّ قاتِلُ البَطَلِ المُفَدَّى
وجازَ إلى ضُلوعِهمُ الضُّلوعا	إذا اعْوَجَّ القَنا في حامِليهِ
فأوْلَتْهُ انْدِقاقاً أوْ صُدُوعا	ونالَتْ ثَأرَها الأكْبادُ منْهُ
وإنْ كُنتَ الخُبَعْثِنَةَ الشَّجيعا	فَجِدْ في مُلْتَقى الخَيْلَيْنِ عَنْهُ
فأَنْتَ اسطَعْتَ شَيئاً ما استَطيعا	إنِ اسْتَجرأتْ تَرْمُقُهُ بَعيداً
ومَثَّلَهُ تَخِرَّ لَهُ صَريعا	وإنْ مارَيتَني فاركَبْ حِصاناً

O God curse them but for their poet
    And times of pleasure and playful girl
Gracious, inaccessible with heavy hips
    Her words would force the birds to cease
Her buttocks let her dress fall free
    Keeping space between her necklaces
When she sways you watch the motion
    If it were not for her arms they would fall
Stitches hurt her but stitching is soft
    Compared to the hurt of sharpened sword
Her arms are enemies to her bracelets
    Her bedmate thinks her forearm is a mate
It's as if her veil were a thin cloud
    That enhances a rising moon at the full
I say to her: Show me my distress
    My words more humble than her coquetry
Do you fear God resurrecting a soul?
    When does God rebel at any submission?
Each abandoned, mad lover comes to you
    Every shameless veiled one has appeared
I will love you till they say ants drag
    Mount Thabir or until Ibn Ibrahim dreads
Far famed are the sorties of cavalry
    At, his memory the suckling can grow gray
He casts down his eyes in art and craft
    As if he was and yet was not submissive
If you ask him to give you what he has
    In hand, you ask a secret and it is spoken
Your acceptance of his gift is a gift
    If it does not occur he sees it as rudeness
Scorning wealth he lays a leather mat
    And at a division he hates to put it away
If the Amir strikes off people's heads
    He spreads a carpet but not for bounty
He gives no gifts unless they are many
    Nor does he kill any but thoroughbreds
He teaches not except by sword edge
    The sword is enough for the whip's work
All is one who forbids no opponent
    To show himself, he only forbids return
Ali kills the champion, a ransomed one
    Exchanging his corselet for one of blood
He bends the lance against its bearers
    And it fastens their ribs to the other ribs
The livers take their revenge on it
    For they are burst or split when near to it
So avoid him in meetings of horsemen
    Unless you are of the fiercest of the lions
If you dare to look at him from afar
    You can do a thing no one else can do
If you disbelieve me get on a horse
    imagine for you will fall dead before him

غَمَامٌ رُبَّمَا مَطَرَ انْتِقَامَا	فَأَقْحَطَ وَدَقَّهُ البَلَدَ المَرِيعَا
رَآنِي بَعْدَ مَا قَطَعَ المَطَايَا	تَيَمُّمُهُ وَقَطَعَتِ القُطُوعَا
فَصَيَّرَ سَيْلُهُ بَلَدِي غَدِيراً	وَصَيَّرَ خَيْرَهُ سَنَتِي رَبِيعَا
وَجَاوَدَنِي بِأَنْ يُعْطَى وَأَحْوِي	فَأَغْرَقَ نَيْلُهُ أَخَذِي سَرِيعَا
أُمَنِّسِيَّ السَّكُونَ وَحَضْرَمَوْتاً	وَوالِدَتِي وَكِنْدَةَ والسَّبِيعَا
قَدِ اسْتَقْصَيْتَ فِي سَلَبِ الأَعَادِي	فَرُدَّ لَهُمْ مِنَ السَّلَبِ الهُجُوعَا
إِذَا مَا لَمْ تُسِرْ جَيْشاً إِلَيْهِمْ	أَسَرْتَ إِلَى قُلُوبِهِمُ الهُلُوعَا
رَضُوا بِكَ كَالرَّضِي بِالشَّيْبِ قَسْراً	وَقَدْ وَخَطَ النَّوَاصِيَ وَالفُرُوعَا
فَلَا عَزَلٌ وَأَنْتَ بِلَا سِلَاحٍ	لَحَاظُكَ مَا تَكُونُ بِهِ مَنِيعَا
لَوِ اسْتَبْدَلَتْ ذِهْنَكَ مِنْ حُسَامٍ	قَدَدْتَ بِهِ المَغَافِرَ وَالدُّرُوعَا
لَوِ اسْتَفْرَغْتَ جُهْدَكَ فِي قِتَالٍ	أَتَيْتَ بِهِ عَلَى الدُّنْيَا جَمِيعَا
سَمَوْتَ بِهِمَّةٍ تَسْمُو فَتَسْمُو	فَمَا تُلْفَى بِمَرْتَبَةٍ قَنُوعَا
وَهَبْكَ سَمَحْتَ حَتَّى لَا جَوَادٌ	فَكَيْفَ عَلَوْتَ حَتَّى لَا رَفِيعَا

(٥٨)

«من المنسرح»

يمدحه أيضًا:

أَحَقُّ عَافٍ بِدَمْعِكَ الهِمَمُ	أَحْدَثُ شَيْءٍ عَهْداً بِهَا القِدَمُ
وَإِنَّمَا النَّاسُ بِالمُلُوكِ وَمَا	تُفْلِحُ عُرْبٌ مُلُوكُهَا عَجَمُ
لَا أَدَبٌ عِنْدَهُمْ وَلَا حَسَبٌ	وَلَا عُهُودٌ لَهُمْ وَلَا ذِمَمُ
بِكُلِّ أَرْضٍ وَطِئْتَهَا أُمَمٌ	تُرْعَى بِعَبْدٍ كَأَنَّهَا غَنَمُ
يَسْتَخْشِنُ الخَزَّ حِينَ يَلْمُسُهُ	وَكَانَ يُبْرَى بِظُفْرِهِ القَلَمُ
إِنِّي وَإِنْ لُمْتُ حَاسِدِيَّ فَمَا	أُنْكِرُ أَنِّي عُقُوبَةٌ لَهُمُ
وَكَيْفَ لَا يُحْسَدُ امْرُؤٌ عَلَمٌ	لَهُ عَلَى كُلِّ هَامَةٍ قَدَمُ
يَهَابُهُ أَبْسَأُ الرِّجَالِ بِهِ	وَتَتَّقِي حَدَّ سَيْفِهِ البُهَمُ
كَفَانِي الذَّمَّ أَنَّنِي رَجُلٌ	أَكْرَمُ مَالٍ مَلَكْتُهُ الكَرَمُ

He is a cloud, often he rains revenge
    So his shower makes sterile fertile land
He saw me after a camel was exhausted
    Going to him with my broken saddle straps
His river flowed over my land in pools
    His goodness made all my year as spring
He aided me with what he gave as I took
    His gifts drowned my grasp with swiftness
Shall I forget Sukun and Hadramaut
    And my mother and the Kinda and Sabi'?
You went the limit in plunder of foes
    So return them their sleep from the loot
If you do not send an army against them
    You take captive their hearts with a fright
They accept you as one agrees to gray
    Compelled to the white tress and forelock
Not unarmed if you are without weapons
    Your glance has something which forbids
Or if you put in sword's place your mind
    You cut by it a breastplate and chain mail
If you exhausted your efforts in battle
    Yet you overcame all the world with them
You rose by ambition so rise, continue
    For you do not find content in any degree
Grant you give till none is generous
    How can you rise till there is no height?

58
He spoke
also praising
Ali ibn Ibrahim al Tanukhi.
(Flowing mu)

Aims: first traces erased by your tears
    The past most recent thing in their time
Yet folk must stay with their kings
    And Arabs are unlucky with foreign kings
No culture among them and no respect
    No covenants for them and no loyalties
In every land that you tread the folk
    Seem ruled by slaves as they are sheep
One thinks silk rough when he wears it
    But the rush was worn out by his toenails
As for me if I blame those who envy me
    I do not deny what a plague I was to them
Why can't a man be envied as a peak
    When his feet are above the heads of all?
The more polite sort of men fear him
    And heroes dread the edge of his sword
For I am a man who has enough blame
    And the noblest thing I own is generosity

94 Diwan al-Mutanabbi

مــا ليــسَ يَجــني عَلَيهـم العُــدَمُ	يَجْنـي الغِنـى للِّئـامِ لَـوْ عَقَلُــوا
والعـارُ يَبقــى والجُــرْحُ يَلْتَئِــمُ	هُـم لأَمْوالِهِـمْ ولَسْـنَ لَهُـمْ
ـيُّ يَهَـبُ الألـفَ وهْـوَ يَبْتَسِـمُ	مَـن طَلَـبَ المَجْـدَ فَلْيَكُـنْ كعَلِـ
ليــسَ لهــا مِــن وحائِهــا أَلَـمُ	ويَطْعَـنُ الخَيْـلَ كُـلَّ نافِـذَةٍ
فمـا لــهُ بعْــدَ فِعْلِــهِ نَــدَمُ	ويَعـرِفُ الأمــرَ قَبْـلَ مَوْقِعِــهِ
بيـضُ لَـهُ والعَبيــدُ والخَشَــمُ	والأمْــرُ والنَّهْــيُ والسَّـلاهِبُ وال
تَكــادُ منهــا الجِبــالُ تَنقَصِــمُ	والسَّطَواتُ التـي سَمِعْـتَ بهـا
دَّاعـي وفيـهِ عـن الخَنـى صَمَـمُ	يُرعيكَ سَمْعـاً فيـه اسْتِماعٌ إلى الـ
في مَجْـدِهِ كيـفَ تَخْلُـقُ النَّسَـمُ	يُريـكَ مِـنْ خَلْقِـه غَرائِبَــهُ
إنْ كُنتُمــا السَّــائِلَينِ يَنْقَسِــمُ	مِلْـتُ إلى مَــنْ يَكـادُ بَيْنَكُمـا
لَمَـنْ أَحَـبُّ الشُّنُـوفُ والخَدَمُ	مِـنْ بَعْـدِ مـا صِيـغَ مِـن مَواهِبِـهِ
ولا تَهَــدَّى لِمـا يَقــولُ فَـمُ	مـا بَذَلَـتْ مـا بــهِ يَجُـودُ يَــدٌ
أَسْـدٌ ولكِــنْ رِماحُهــا الأَجَـمُ	بَنُـو العَفَرْنَـى مَحَطَّـةُ الأسَـدِ الـ
طَعْــنُ نُحــورِ الكُمـاةِ لا الحُلَـمُ	قَـوْمٌ بُلُـوغُ الغُـلامِ عِنْدَهُـمْ
لا صِغَـرٌ عــاذِرٌ ولا هَــرَمُ	كأنّمـا يُولَـدُ النَّـدى مَعَهُـمْ
وإنْ تَولَّــوا صَنيعَــةً كَتَمُــوا	إذا تَولَّـوا عَـداوَةً كَشَفُــوا
أنَّهُـمْ أنْعَمُــوا ومــا عَلِمُـوا	تَظُـنّ مِــنْ فَقْـدِكَ اعْتِدادَهُـمْ
أو نَطَقُـوا فالصَّـوابُ والحِكَـمُ	إنْ بَرَقُــوا فالحُتُـوفُ حاضِـرَةٌ
فقَوْلُهُـمْ خــابَ سائِلــي القَسَـمُ	أو حَلَفُــوا بالغَمُـوسِ واجْتَهَـدُوا
فـإنّ أفخـاذَهُمْ لَهـا حُــزُمُ	أو رَكِبُــوا الخَيْـلَ غَيْــرَ مُسْرَجَـةٍ
مِن مُهَجِ الدَّارعيـنِ مـا احْتَكَمُوا	أوْ شَــهِدوا الحَــرْبَ لا قَحْـاً أخَـذُوا
كأنَّهــا في نُفوسِـهِـمْ شِـيَـمُ	تُشـرِقُ أعراضُهُــمْ وأوْجُهُــهُـ
غَــوْرُ ذَفِيءٌ ومـاؤهُ شَبِـمُ	لَــوْلاكَ لَـم أتْـرُكِ البُحَيْــرَةَ والـ
تَهْــدِرُ فيهــا ومـا بهـا قَطَـمُ	والمَـوْجُ مِثْـلُ الفُحـولِ مُزْبِـدَةً
فُرْســانَ بُلْــقٍ تَخونُهــا اللُّجُـمُ	والطَّيْــرُ فَـوْقَ الحَبـابِ تَحسَبُهـا
جيشــا وغَــى هــازِمٌ ومُنْهَــزِمُ	كأنَّهــا والرِّيـاحُ تَضْرِبُهــا

Wealth harms the greedy, if only they
    Knew it, as poverty can never harm them
They belong to **wealth**, not it to them
    And the shame remains while wounds heal
Whoever seeks glory let him be as 'Ali
    He gives a thousand while he is smiling
He jousts horsemen, all strokes pierce
    No pain is in them since they are swifter
He knows the event before it occurs
    Nor has he any regret after it happens
Command, denial, long tail horses, swords
    They are all his as well as slaves, and clients
Those attacks you have heard about
    The mountains almost are broken by them
He respects your word as he hears pleas
    And yet he is deaf to all the filthy language
He shows you his rarities in his nature
    How the spirit is created by means of glory
I went to one who, almost between two
    If you are his clients, would divide himself
After taking a gift from him there was
    For one I loved, earrings and bracelets
No hand so generous as when he gives
    And no mouth so guided to what he speaks
The tribe of bold Mahatta are irons
    And their spears are made into the lair
A people for whom maturity in boys is
    Thrusting at warrior breasts, not puberty
It seems as if bounty is born with them
    No little one is excused nor any old men
If they follow a foe they make it known
    If they do a good action they keep it hid
You'd think from your losing a count
    That they give gifts and do not know it
When they flash lightning death nears
    And if they reason it is correct and wise
Or swear a solemn oath and keep it
    They say, as an oath: May my client fail!
Or if they ride horses without saddle
    Truly their thighs have the determination
Or if present in fierce battle they take
    Of the souls in armor as they think best
Their ideals and goals shine like dawn
    As if their patterns were in their thoughts
But for you I'd not have left Buhaira
    For Gaur was hot and her waters cool
The waves were like foaming horses
    Plunging there with bridles unbroken
Birds above waves you thought them
    Piebald horses that the tides betrayed
As if they while winds drove them on
    Were an army in battle pursuing, pursued

كَأنَّها في نَهارِها قَمَرٌ	حَفَّ بِهِ مِنْ جنانِها ظُلَمُ
ناعِمَةُ الجِسْمِ لا عِظامَ لَها	لَها بَناتٌ وَما لَها رَخَمُ
يُقَرُّ عَنْهُنَّ بَطْنُها أبَداً	وَما تَشَكَّى وَلا يَسِيلُ دَمُ
تَغَنَّتِ الطَّيرُ في جَوانِبِها	وجادَتِ الأرْضُ حَوْلَها الدِّيَمُ
فَهْيَ كَماوِيَّةٍ مُطَوَّقَةٍ	جُرِّدَ عَنْها غِشاؤُها الأدَمُ
يَشينُها جَرْيُها عَلى بَلَدٍ	تَشينُهُ الأدْعِياءُ والقَزَمُ
أبا الحُسَيْنِ اسْتَمِعْ فَمَدْحُكُمُ	بالفِعْلِ قَبْلَ الكَلامِ مُنْتَظِمُ
وقَدْ تَوالى العِهادُ مِنْهُ لكُم	وجادَتِ المَطَرَةُ الَّتي تَسِمُ
أعيذُكُمْ مِنْ صُروفِ دَهْرِكُمُ	فإنَّهُ في الكِرامِ مُتَّهَمُ

(٥٩)

«من البسيط»

يمدح المغيث بن علي بن بشر العجلي:

دَمْعٌ جَرى فقَضى في الرَّبْعِ ما وَجَبا	لأهلِهِ وشَفى أنَّى ولا كَرَبا
عَجْنا فأذْهَبَ ما أبْقى الفِراقُ لنا	مِنَ العُقولِ وما رَدَّ الَّذي ذَهَبا
سَقَيْتُهُ عَبَراتٍ ظَنَّها مَطَراً	سَوائِلاً مِنْ جُفونٍ ظَنَّها سُحُبا
دارُ المُلِمِّ لها طَيفٌ تَهَدَّدَني	ليلاً فَما صَدَقَتْ عَيني ولا كَذَبا
أنَأيْتُهُ فَدَنا، أدْنَيْتُهُ فنَأى،	حَمَشْتُهُ فَنَبا، قَبَّلْتُهُ فأَبى
هامَ الفُؤادُ بأعرابِيَّةٍ سَكَنَتْ	بَيْتاً مِنَ القَلْبِ لَمْ تَمْدُدْ لَهُ طُنُبا
مَظْلومَةُ القَدِّ في تَشْبيهِهِ غُصُناً	مَظْلومَةُ الرِّيقِ في تَشْبيهِهِ ضَرَبا
بَيْضاءُ تُطمِعُ في ما تَحْتَ حُلَّتِها	وعَزَّ ذلِكَ مَطْلوباً إذا طُلِبا
كأنَّها الشَّمْسُ يُعْيي كَفَّ قابِضِهِ	شُعاعُها ويَراهُ الطَّرْفُ مُقْتَرِبا
مَرَّتْ بِنا بَينَ تِرْبَيْها فَقُلْتُ لَها	مِنْ أيْنَ جانَسَ هذا الشّادِنَ العَرَبا
فاسْتَضْحَكَتْ ثُمَّ قالَتْ كالمُغيثِ يُرى	ليْثُ الشَّرى وهوَ مِنْ عِجْلٍ إذا انْتَسَبا
جاءتْ بأشْجَعِ مَنْ يُسمى وأسْمَحِ مَنْ	أعْطى وأبْلَغِ مَنْ أمْلى ومَنْ كَتَبا
لَوْ حَلَّ خاطِرُهُ في مُقْعَدٍ لَمَشى	أوْ جاهِلٍ لَصَحا أوْ أخْرَسٍ خَطَبا

As if she in the daylight were a moon
    The darkness of gardens surrounding her
Soft is her body and no bones in it
    She has had daughters but has no womb
Her belly gives forth these eternally
    She does not complain and doesn't bleed
Always birds make music on her shores
    The showers enrich the gardens about her
So she is like a mirror encircled
    The top of her cover has been laid bare
But her waters disgrace her in a town
    Bastardy and vile origin are a disgrace
O Abu Husayn, hear, since your praise
    Is in acts before the words set in verse
First showers are friends to all of you
    And rains that impregnate are bounteous
I make you safe from time's changes
    They are what is ruinous to generosity

59
He spoke praising Mugith ibn All al Ijli.
(Outspread ba)

A tear flows to fulfill duty in an abode
    To its folk, can it heal without a sorrow?
We turn, for parting ruins what's left
    Of sanity and what is gone cannot return
I water it with tears, felt to be rain
    As their flow from eyes makes them clouds
A camp visited has a ghost to warn me
    Nightly, my eyes neither believe nor deny
I move, it comes, I pursue, it departs
    l warm and it rises, I kiss as it rejects
A heart longs for an Arab girl who is
    In a heart-tent with ropes she did not set
Crime against a waist to talk of sapling
    Wrong done to saliva compared to honey
White, one longs for that under a dress
    But it is hard to attain when it is attempted
She seems a sun whose beam eludes
    A grasper's hand though an eye sees it
She passed with maids as I said:
    Of what folk is this young bedouin deer?
She smiled and said: Of Mugith who is
    A thicket lion but his ancestry is of the ljli
She told of the brave name, generous
    As giver, finest of composers and writers
If his mind settles on cripples they walk
    On fools they know or the dumb they speak

وليسَ يحجبُهُ سِترٌ إذا احتجَبـا	إذا بَدا حجَبتْ عينيكَ هيبتُـهُ
ودُرُّ لفظٍ يُريكَ الدُّرَّ مخشَلَبا	بياضُ وجهٍ يُريكَ الشّمسَ حالكةً
رَطْبَ الغِرارِ مِنَ التأمُورِ مُختَضِبَا	وسيفُ عزمٍ تَرُدُّ السيفَ هيبتُـهُ
أقَلُّ مِنْ عُمرٍ ما يَحوي إذا وَهَبَا	عمرُ العدوِّ إذا لاقاهُ في رَهَجٍ
فكنْ مُعادِيَهُ أو كُنْ لهُ نَشَبَا	توقَّـهُ فمتى مـا شِـئْتَ تَبلُـوَهُ
حالتْ فلوْ قطرتْ في الماءِ ما شُرِبَا	تحلـو مَذاقتُـهُ حتـى إذا غَضِبَـا
وتَحسُدُ الخيلُ منها أيُّها رَكِبَـا	وتَغبِطُ الأرضُ منها حيثُ حَلَّ بـهِ
عن نفسِهِ ويَرُدُّ الجحفَلَ اللَّجِبَـا	ولا يَرُدُّ بفيهِ كـفُّ سـائلهِ
في مُلكِهِ افترقا مِـن قبلِ يصطَحِبَا	وكلّما لقِـيَ الدينـارُ صاحبَـهُ
فكلَّما قيلَ هذا مُجتَـدٍ نَعَبَـا	مالٌ كأنَّ غُرابَ البَينِ يَرقُبُـهُ
ولا عَجائِبِ بَحرٍ بعدَهـا عَجَبَـا	بَحرٌ عَجائِبُـهُ لم تُبْـقِ في سَمَـرٍ
يَشكـو مُحاولُها التقصيـرَ والتَّعَبَـا	لا يُقنِـعُ ابـنَ عليٍّ نَيْـلُ مَنزِلَـةٍ
رأساً لهمْ وغدا كـلُّ لهُـمْ ذَنَبَـا	هَزَّ اللِّـواءَ بنـو عِجْـلٍ بـهِ فغـدا
والرَّاكبيـنَ مِـنَ الأشياءِ ما صَعُبَـا	التـارِكينَ مِـنَ الأشيـاءِ أهْوَنَهـا
هامَ الكُمـاةِ على أرماحِهِمْ عَذَبَـا	مُـبَرقِعي خيلَهُـمْ بالبيضِ مُتَّخذي
خَرقـاءَ تتَّهِـمُ الإقدامَ والهَرَبَـا	إنَّ المنيَّـةَ لَـوْ لاقتهُـمْ وقَفَـتْ
فجازَ وهـوَ على آثارها الشُّـهُبَـا	مراتِـبٌ صعِـدَتْ والفكـرُ يَتبَعُهـا
فآلَ مـا امتلأتْ منـهُ ولا نَضَبَـا	محامِـدٌ نزَفَـتْ شِعـري ليَملأهـا
مَن يَستَطيعُ لأمرٍ فائتٍ طَلَبَـا	مكارمٌ لـكَ فُـتَّ العالمينَ بهـا
إليَّ بالخَبـرِ الرُّكبـانُ في حَلَبَـا	لمَّـا أقَمـتَ بإنطاكيَّـةَ اختَلَفَـتْ
أحُـثُّ راحلتـيَّ: الفقـرَ والأدَبَـا	فسِـرتُ نَحوَكَ لا أُلـوي على أحَـدٍ
لوْ ذاقهـا لبَكـى ما عـاشَ وانتَحَبَـا	أذاقَنـي زَمَنـي بَلـوَى شَرِقـتُ بهـا
والسَّمهَريَّ أخـاً والمَشرَفِيَّ أبَـا	وإنْ عَمَـرْتُ جَعَلـتُ الحـربَ والـدةً
حتـى كـأنَّ لـهُ في قَتْلِـهِ أرَبَـا	بكلِّ أشعثَ يَلقـى المـوتَ مُبتَسِمـاً
عن سرجِهِ مَرَحـاً بالعِزِّ أو طَرَبَـا	قُـحٍّ يكـادُ صَهيـلُ الخيـلِ يَقذِفُـهُ
والبَرُّ أوسَـعُ والدّنيـا لِمَـنْ غَلَبَـا	فالمَوتُ أعـذَرُ لي والصبـرُ أجمـلُ بـي

When he appears, respect veils your eyes
    But no curtain hides him if he draws a veil
A bright face makes the sun dark to you
    A jewel in a word seems like an egg pearl
Will's sword whose motion repels swords
    With dripping edge stained by heart's blood
The foe's life if he meets him in dust
    Is less than goods' life if he makes a gift
Watch out for him if you wish to test
    Become his enemy or some possession
His taste is sweet until he is angry
    It sours, if it drips in water do not drink
The earth covets a place where he stays
    As horses are jealous of those he rides on
He rejects by his mouth no suppliant
    From him yet he repels an army's uproar
When a diner meets its mate in his
    Purse they part before they are friends
Wealth, it's as if parting's raven saw
    Or shrieked each time one said: A client!
A sea with wonders untold at night
    No miracles in the sea after these marvels
Gaining a place won't satisfy Ibn Ljli
    If a seeker complains of effort or default
Banu Ljli unfurl a banner for him, he is
    Their chief and all become their followers
They are ones who abandon the easy
    They are ones who attempt the difficult
Their horses' armor is swords that take
    Skulls of warriors as gem for their spears
If the fates meet them they stand still
    Fearfully desiring to advance and retreat
The rank is high and thought follows
    On its trail as it goes beyond the stars
Praise exhausts my verses for them
    They return from filling it nor is it empty
Yours nobility to surpass the world's
    Who is able to attain that fleeting thing?
If you stay in Antakya riders come
    Again, again with news to me in Aleppo
I go to you, I turn not aside for anyone
    I whip my two camels: Poverty and Culture
My time made me savor grief, I choked
    If one tasted it he'd weep and howl lifelong
If I live I will make war my mother
    My spear a brother and my sword a father
Each unkempt one meets death smiling
    Until it is as if his dying were his reward
Sincere, almost a horse whinny hurls
    Him from saddle lively with joy or sorrow
Death more excused, courage finer to me
    The land wider, the world for one who wins

(٦٠)

«من الوافر»

يمدحه أيضًا:

وعُمْرٌ مِثلُ ما تَهَبُ اللِّئامُ	فُؤادٌ ما تُسَلِّيهِ المُدامُ
وإنْ كانَتْ لهُمْ جُثَثٌ ضِخامُ	ودَهْرٌ ناسُهُ ناسٌ صِغارٌ
ولكنْ مَعدِنُ الذَّهَبِ الرَّغامُ	وما أنا مِنْهُمُ بالعَيشِ فيهِمْ
مُفَتَّحَةٌ عُيونُهُمُ نِيامُ	أرانِبُ غَيرَ أنَّهُمُ مُلوكٌ
وما أقرانُها إلّا الطَّعامُ	بأجْسامٍ يَحَرُّ القَتلُ فيها
كأنَّ قَنا فَوارِسِها ثُمامُ	وخَيلٍ ما يخِرُّ لها طَعينٌ
وإنْ كَثُرَ التَّجَمُّلُ والكَلامُ	خَليلُكَ أنتَ لا مَنْ قُلتَ خِلّي
تَجَنَّبَ عُنقَ صَيقَلِهِ الحُسامُ	ولو حيزَ الحِفاظُ بغَيرِ عَقْلٍ
وأشْبَهُنا بدُنيانا الطَّغامُ	وشِبْهُ الشَّيءِ مُنجَذِبٌ إليهِ
تَعالى الجَيشُ وانحَطَّ القَتامُ	ولوْ لم يَعْلُ إلّا ذو مَحَلٍّ
لرُتْبَتِهِ أسامَهُمُ المُسامُ	ولوْ لم يَرْعَ إلّا مُستَحِقٌّ
ضِياءٌ في بَواطِنِهِ ظَلامُ	ومَنْ خَبَرَ الغَواني فالغَواني
بُ هَمّاً فالحَياةُ هيَ الحِمامُ	إذا كانَ الشَّبابُ السُّكرَ والشّي
ولا كُلٌّ على بُخلٍ يُلامُ	وما كُلٌّ بمَعذورٍ ببُخْلٍ
لمِثلي عندَ مِثلِهِمُ مُقامُ	ولم أرَ مِثلَ جيراني ومِثلي
فلَيسَ يَفوتُها إلّا الكِرامُ	بأرضٍ ما اشْتَهَيْتُ رأيتُ فيها
وكانَ لأهْلِها منها التَّمامُ	فهَلّا كانَ نَقْصُ الأهْلِ فيها
أنافا ذا المُغيثِ وذا اللُّكامُ	بها الجَبَلانِ مِنْ صَخرٍ وفَخرٍ
يَمُرُّ بها كَما مَرَّ الغَمامُ	ولَيسَتْ مِنْ مَواطِنِهِ ولكنْ
بَدرٌ ما لراضِعِهِ فِطامُ	سَقى اللهُ ابنَ مُنْجِبَةٍ سَقاني
ومَنْ إحدى عَطاياهُ الذِّمامُ	ومَنْ إحدى فَوائِدِهِ العَطايا
كَسِلْكِ الدُّرِّ يُخفيهِ النِّظامُ	وقد خَفِيَ الزَّمانُ بهِ عَلَينا
ومَنْ يَعشَقْ يَلَذَّ لهُ الغَرامُ	تَلَذَّ لهُ المُروءَةُ وهيَ تُؤذي

60
He spoke praising
al Mugith ibn Bishr al Ijli.
(Exuberant mu)

This is a heart wine cannot console
    And age such as avarice makes a gift of
This is a time whose men are small
    Even if their cadavers are monstrous
I live among them but am not of them
    And yet the gold mines are in the dirt
They are rabbits not kings who rule
    With their eyes open they are asleep
With bodies where a battle rages
    But competition there is only for food
Riders before whom jousters stay
    As if horsemen's lances were grasses
Your friend is you, not one you name
    Even if courtesies and words are many
If government is held without reason
    Yet a sword avoids the sharpener's neck
A thing's likeness is attracted to it
    Most like us in our world are the foolish
If only high rank elevates
    Then let armies rise and dust fall
If only the meritorious were to rule
    In their rank beasts would be herdsmen
He who tests women finds that they
    Have a brightness, but inside are dark
If youth is drunken and gray hair
    Is only care, then life is death itself
Not everyone is excused as a miser
    Nor is everyone blamed for stinginess
I see neither my friend's like or mine
    In my remaining with the likes of them
In a land where in all you want, you
    Find nothing is lacking except honor
O would the folk's faults were in it
    And would the perfection were in them!
You see two mountains of honor and rock
    The highest is Mugith and the other Lukam
That isn't his proper place, rather
    He passes over it as the clouds pass
God grant nobility's brother pours
    For me a drink, not weaning his suckling
A person, one of whose gifts is giving
    One of whose single gifts is that custom
Times have hidden him on our account
    As the necklace hides the pearls' thread
Manliness delights him even if it hurts
    As he who loves delights even in longing

وواصَلَها فَلَيسَ بِهِ سَقامُ	تَعَلَّقَها هَوى قَيسٍ لِلَيلى
فَما يُدرى أَشَيخٌ أَم غُلامُ	يَروعُ رَكانَةً وَيَذوبُ ظَرفاً
وَأَمّا في الجِدالِ فَلا يُرامُ	وَتَملِكُهُ المَسائِلُ في نَداهُ
وَقَبضُ نَوالِ بَعضِ القَومِ ذامُ	وَقَبضُ نَوالِهِ شَرَفٌ وَعِزٌّ
هِيَ الأَطواقُ وَالنّاسُ الحَمامُ	أَقامَت في الرِقابِ لَهُ أَيادٍ
كَما الأَنواءُ حينَ تُعَدُّ عامُ	إِذا عُدَّ الكِرامُ فَتِلكَ عِجلٌ
إِذا بِشِفارِها حَمِيَ اللِطامُ	تَقي جَبَهاتُهُم ما في ذَراهُم
لَأَعطَوكَ الَّذي صَلَّوا وَصاموا	وَلَو يَمَّمتُهُم في الحَشرِ تَجدو
خِفافٌ وَالرِماحَ بِها عُرامُ	فَإِن حَلَموا فَإِنَّ الخَيلَ فيهِم
وَشَزرُ الطَعنِ وَالضَربُ التُؤامُ	وَعِندَهُمُ الجِفانُ مُكَلَّلاتٌ
وَتَنبو عَن وُجوهِهِمُ السِهامُ	نَصَرَعُهُمُ بِأَعيُنِنا حَياءً
كَما حَمَلَت مِنَ الجَسَدِ العِظامُ	قَبيلٌ يَحمِلونَ مِنَ المَعالي
وَجَدُّكَ بِشرُ المَلِكُ الهُمامُ	قَبيلٌ أَنتَ أَنتَ وَأَنتَ مِنهُم
وَيُشرَكُ في رَغائِبِهِ الأَنامُ	لِمَن مالٌ تُمَزِّقُهُ العَطايا
لِأَنَّ بِصُحبَةٍ يَجِبُ الذَمامُ	وَلا نَدعوكَ صاحِبَهُ فَتَرضى
تُصافِحُهُ يَدٌ فيها جُذامُ	تَحايُدَهُ كَأَنَّكَ سامِرِيٌّ
أَفِدنا أَيُّها الحِبرُ الإِمامُ	إِذا ما العالِمونَ عَرَوكَ قالوا
بِهَذا يُعلَمُ الجَيشُ اللُهامُ	إِذا ما المُعَلِّمونَ رَأَوكَ قالوا
كَأَنَّكَ في فَمِ الزَمَنِ اِبتِسامُ	لَقَد حَسُنَت بِكَ الأَوقاتُ حَتّى
عَلَيكَ صَلاةُ رَبِّكَ وَالسَلامُ	وَأُعطيتَ الَّذي لَم يُعطَ خَلقٌ

(٦١)

«من الطويل»

يمدح أبا الفرج أحمد بن الحسين القاضي المالكي:

لِوَحشِيَّةٍ لا ما لِوَحشِيَّةٍ شَنفُ	لِجِنِّيَّةٍ أَم غادَةٍ رُفِعَ السَجفُ
سَوالِفُها وَالحَليُ وَالخَصرُ وَالرِدفُ	نَفورٌ عَرَّها نَفرَةً فَتَجاذَبَت
تَثَنّى لَنا خوطٌ وَلا حَظَنا خِشفُ	وَخيلَ مِنها مِرطُها فَكَأَنَّما

He loves with a love of Qais for Laila
    And embraces it but no sickness is in him
He scares the sedate and melts the brisk
    So one doesn't know is he elder or youth?
Problems possess him as to generosity
    But he does not succeed in this argument
Accepting his gifts is honor and glory
    But taking gifts of some people is blame
Many a gift of his stays on the necks
    They are the collar and men are the dove
The generous are counted, Ijil is thus
    Like stars that rise and set in a year's time
Their swords protect their foreheads
    When the blows grow hot on their edges
If you go to them on judgment day
    They give what they prayed and fasted for
Though clement the riders among them
    Are swift and their spears are contentious
With them the meat platters are crowned
    Jousting right and left and in double blows
We take them by blushes at our glances
    But the arrows are blunted with their faces
A tribe that bears the highest things
    Like the bony structure bears the body
A tribe you are part of yet you are you
    Your grandfather Bishr, royal and heroic
Giving his wealth tears it to pieces
    All creatures share in his huge bounty
We do not call you its lord to please
    For with lordship protection is a duty
Stripped off as if you were al Samari
    A hand with leprosy to be shaken by hand
When the learned come to you you say:
    You be ransom for us O instructed leader
When flag bearers see you they say:
    By this one the vast armies are guided
A season's made fine by you until it's
    As if you were the smile on time's mouth
Your gift is what creature never gave
    Your Lord's blessing is on you and peace

61
He spoke praising
Abu'l Faraj Ahmad ibn al Husayn
the Maliki Qadi. (Long fu)

Jinn or maid on whom a curtain is raised
    Or wild deer? no, the deer has no earrings
Shy one, soldiers scare her for her neck
    And beads, her waist and buttocks are heavy
Her silk dress makes one imagine that
    A sapling bent to us, gazelle looked at us

زِيَادَةَ شَيْبٍ وهيَ نَقصُ زِيادَتي	وقوَّةُ عِشقٍ وهيَ مِن قوَّتي ضُعْفُ
أراقَتْ دَمي مَن بي مِنَ الوَجدِ ما بها	من الوَجدِ بي والشَّوقُ لي ولها حِلْفُ
هَرَاقَتْ دَمي مَنْ بي مِنَ الْوَجْدِ مَابهَا	مِنَ الْوَجْدِ بي والشَّوْقُ لي وَلَهَا حِلْفُ
ومَن كلَّما جَرَّدتَها مِنْ ثِيابِها	كَساها ثِيابًا غَيرَها الشَّعرُ الوَحْفُ
وَقابَلَني رُمَّانَتا غُصنِ بانةٍ	يَميلُ به بَدرٌ ويُمسِكهُ حِقْفُ
أكيداً لَنا بَينٌ يا بَينُ واصَلتَ وَصْلَنا	فلا دارُنا تَدنو ولا عَيشُنا يَصفو
أرَدُّ وَيْلي لَوْ قَضَى الْوَيْلُ حاجةً	وأَكثرُ لَهفي لَوْ شَفى غُلَّةً لَهْفُ
ضَنى في الهَوى كالسَّمِّ في الشَّهدِ كامِناً	لَذِذْتُ به جَهلاً وفي اللَّذَّةِ الحتفُ
فأفْنى وما أفنَيتُهُ نَفسي كأنَّما	أبو الفَرَجِ القاضي له دونَها كَهفُ
قَليلُ الكَرَى لَوْ كانَتِ البيضُ والقَنا	كآرائهِ ما أَغنَتِ البيضُ والزَّغفُ
يَقومُ مَقامَ الجَيشِ تَقطيبُ وَجهِهِ	ويَستَغرِقُ الألفاظَ عن لَفظِهِ حرفُ
وإنْ فَقَدَ الإعطاءَ حنَّتْ يَمينُهُ	إليهِ حَنينَ الإلفِ فارَقهُ الإلفُ
أديبٌ رَسَتْ للعِلمِ في أرضِ صَدرِهِ	جِبالٌ جبالُ الأرضِ في جنبها قُفُّ
جَوادٌ سَمَتْ في الخَيرِ والشَّرِّ كفُّهُ	سُمُوًّا أوَدَّ الدَّهرَ أنَّ اسْمَهُ كَفُّ
وأضحى وبينَ النَّاسِ في كلِّ سَيِّدٍ	مِنَ النَّاسِ إلّا في سيادَتِهِ خُلفُ
يُفَقِّدونَهُ حتى كَأنَّ دِماءَهُمْ	لجاري هَواهُ في عُروقِهِمْ تَقفو
وُقوفينِ في وَقفَينِ شُكرٍ ونَائِلٍ	فنائلُهُ وَقفٌ وشُكرُهُمْ وَقْفُ
ولَمَّا فَقدناهُ مِثلَهُ دامَ كَشفُنا	عليهِ فدامَ الفَقدُ وانكشفَ الكَشْفُ
وما حارَتِ الأوْهامُ في عُظمِ شَأنِهِ	بأكثرَ مِمَّا حارَ في حُسنِهِ الطَّرْفُ
ولا نالَ مِنْ حسَّادِهِ الغَيظُ والأذى	بأعظَمَ مِمَّا نالَ من وَفرِهِ العُرْفُ
تَفكُّرُهُ عِلمٌ ومنطِقُهُ حُكمٌ	وباطِنُهُ دينٌ وظاهرُهُ ظَرْفُ
أماتَ رياحَ اللُّؤمِ وهيَ عَواصِفٌ	ومَغنى العُلى يودي ورَسْمُ النَّدى يعفو
فلَمْ نَرَ قَبلَ ابنِ الحُسَينِ أصابعاً	إذا ما هَطَلنَ استحيتِ الدِّيَمُ الوُطْفُ
ولا ساعِياً في قُلَّةِ المَجدِ مُدرِكاً	بأفعالِهِ ما ليسَ يُدرِكُهُ الوَصْفُ
ولم نَرَ شيئاً يَحمِلُ العِبءَ حَمَلهُ	ويَستَصغِرُ الدُّنيا ويَحمِلُهُ طِرْفُ
ولا جلَسَ البَحرَ المُحيطَ لقاصِدٍ	ومن تَحتِهِ فَرشٌ ومن فوقِهِ سَقفُ
فواعَجَباً منّى أحاولُ نَعْتَهُ	وقد فَنِيَتْ فيهِ القَراطيسُ والصُّحْفُ
ومن كَثرَةِ الأخبارِ عن مَكرُماتِهِ	يَمُرُّ لهُ صِنفٌ ويأتي لهُ صِنْفُ
وتَفتَرُّ منهُ عَنْ خِصالٍ كأنَّها	ثَنايا حَبيبٍ لا يُمَلُّ لَها رَشْفُ

White hair's growth is loss of my growth
    And the power of love weakens my strength
She who is my passion makes blood flow
    My passion and my love and hers are a bond
She, each time I strip her of her clothes
    Draws to herself another dress of soft hair
Buds of a willow branch come near to us
    A moon bends over and a sand hill restrains
A trick O parting that you persist still?
    Our homes not close as our lives not clear
I'd repeat alas if alas would ended a need
    I'd echo too bad if too bad healed the thirst
Love's illness is as poison hid in honey
    I, unwitting, enjoyed it and joy was death
It ruined, my soul could not avoid till
    Abu'l Faraj the judge was shelter from it
Little sleep is his, if sword and spear
    Are his ideas no helmet or armor will hold
A frown on his face takes an army's place
    A consonant in his word exceeds many words
If he loses a bestowal his right yearns
    For it as friend who goes longs for friend
Culture peaks root in his breast's wise
    Land, earth's mountains hills beside those
Liberal, his hand rises in good and evil
    On high, so fate wishes its name were hand
He appears, among men every ruler of
    Man finds opponents except in his ruling
They ransom him till it seems their blood
    Waits in their veins for his love's streams
Estate upon estate in thanks and gifts
    His gifts bequests, their thanks endowment
When we lost his like our search lasted
    For him but loss stayed and search removed
Fancy is no more excited by greatness
    Of such as him than eye is by his beauty
Rage and evil give no more envying him
    Than goodness will give out of his bounty
His thought knowledge, his talk wisdom
    Within religion and without, graciousness
He calms winds of blame that are storms
    A high camp lost and bounty's trace erased
We saw no such fingers before Ibn Husayn
    When they pour they shame thick rain clouds
Nor such a busy one reaching glory's peak
    With his deeds that description cannot reach
Nor any bearing a heavy load as he does
    He belittles the world yet a horse bears him
Never has deep sea sat still for clients
    Beneath it the carpet and above it the roof
O wonder for me to attempt description
    As the pages and writing wither before it
Profusion of stories about his good acts
    One kind passes away and another comes

كَثيرٌ ولكن ليسَ كالذَنبِ الأنفُ	قصَدتُكَ والرّاجونَ قصدي إليهمِ
تفوعانِ للمُكدي وبَينَهُما صَرفُ	ولا الفِضّةُ البَيضاءُ والتِبرُ واحداً
ولا مُنتَهى الجودِ الذي خلفَهُ خَلفُ	ولَستَ بدونِ يُرتَجى الغَيثُ دونَهُ
ولا البَعضُ من كلٍّ ولكنَّكَ الضِعفُ	ولا واحداً في ذا الورى من جَماعَةٍ
ولا ضِعفِ ضِعفِ الضِعفِ بل مثلَهُ ألفُ	ولا الضِعفَ حتى يَتبَعَ الضِعفَ ضِعفُهُ
غَلِطتُ ولا الثُلثانِ هذا ولا النِصفُ	أقاضينا هذا الذي أنتَ أهلُهُ
بذَنبي ولكنْ جئتُ أسألُ أن تَعفُو	وذَنبي تَقصيري وما جئتُ مادِحاً

(٦٢)

«من الكامل»

يمدح علي بن منصور الحاجب:

أللّابِساتُ مِنَ الحَريرِ جَلابِبا	بأبي الشُموسُ الجانِحاتُ غَوارِبا
وجَنّاتِهِنَّ النّاهِباتِ النّاهِبا	ألمُنهِباتُ عُقولَنا وقُلوبَنا
تُ المُبديّاتُ مِنَ الدَّلالِ عَرائِبا	ألنّاعِماتُ القاتِلاتُ المُحيِيا
فَوَضَعنَ أيدِيَهُنَّ فوقَ تَرائِبا	حاوَلنَ تَفديَتي وخِفنَ مُراقِبا
من حَرِّ أنفاسي فكُنتُ الذّائبا	وبَسَمنَ عَن بَردٍ خَشيتُ أذيبَهُ
وادٍ لَثَمتُ بهِ الغَزالَةَ كاعِبا	يا حَبَّذا المُتَحَمَّلونَ وحَبَّذا
مِن بَعدِ ما أنشَبنَ في مَخالِبا	كيفَ الرَجاءُ مِنَ الخُطوبِ تَخَلُّصاً
مُتَناهياً فَجَعَلنَهُ لي صاحِبا	أوحَدنَني ووَجَدنَ حُزناً واحِداً
مِحَنٌ أحَدُّ مِنَ السُيوفِ مَضارِبا	ونَصَبنَني غَرَضَ الرُماةِ تُصيبُني
مُستَسقياً مَطَرَت عليَّ مَصائِبا	أظَمَّتني الدُنيا فأمّا جئتُها
من دارشٍ فَغَدَوتُ أمشي راكِبا	وحُبيتُ من خُوصِ الرِكابِ بأسوَدٍ
جاءَ الزَمانُ إليَّ مِنها تائِبا	حالٍ متى عَلِمَ ابنُ مَنصورٍ بها
يَتَبارَيانِ دَماً وعُرفاً ساكِبا	مَلِكٌ سِنانُ قَناتِهِ وبَناتِهِ
ويَظُنّ دِجلَةَ ليسَ تَكفي شارِبا	يَستَصغِرُ الخَطَرَ الكَبيرَ لوَفدِهِ
بعَظيمِ ما صَنَعَت لظَنِّكَ كاذِبا	كَرَماً فلَو حدَّثتَهُ عن نَفسِهِ
وحَذارِ ثمّ حَذارِ مِنهُ مُحارِبا	سَل عَن شَجاعَتِهِ وزُرهُ مُسالِماً

They smile with traits that seem to be
    Teeth of a beloved whose saliva never tires
I made you my goal, those who wanted it
    Were many but the nose is not like the tail
Nor clear silver or pure gold the same in
    Their use to the poor, but both are expended
You're not small, showers fear smallness
    No end of the gift beyond which is another
You are not one among men in a group
    Nor one of all but rather you are double it
Nor yet double if double follows double
    Nor twice double double nor like a thousand
O our judge this is a family of which are
    I make a mistake, it is not a third nor a half
My sin is remissness, I offered no praise
    As my sin, rather I came to ask forgiveness

62
He spoke praising Ali ibn Mansur al Hajib.
(Perfect ba)

My father! the suns decline to the west
    And it is they who show their silken veiling
They who plunder our hearts and reason
    With those cheeks that sack the plunderers
Soft ones, killers, revivifies of the living
    Who put in force the tricks of the coquettes
They try to speak but they fear a guard
    So they put their hands above their breasts
They smile with coolness I fear to melt
    In the heat of my sighs, for I am melting
O well for those who saddle up, well
    For wadis where I veil myself from virgins
What hope to be free of these troubles
    After they have fixed their claws upon me?
They left me and united me to my grief
    Extreme for they made it alone my friend
They set me up as target for the arrows
    Suffering sharper than the sword's edges
The world made me thirsty as I came
    Seeking drink, she poured her grief on me
I was given in place of hollow eye camels
    Black soles to become a rider who walked
Such a state if Ibn Mansur knew of it
    Time would come to me repentant of it
A lord whose lance head and fingers
    Rival each other in blood or bounty's use
He makes big dangers small for his own
    And thinks the Dijla not enough to swallow
Noble and if you told him about himself
    And great things done he'd think you lied
Ask of his bravery, visit him in peace
    But beware, beware again of him in war

لَمْ تَلْقَ خَلْقاً ذاقَ مَوْتاً آئِبَا	فَالمَوْتُ تُعرَفُ بالصِّفاتِ طِباعُهُ
أَو قَسْطَلاً أَو طاعِناً أَو ضارِبَا	إِنْ تَلْقَهُ لا تَلْقَ إِلّا جَحْفَلاً
أَو راهِباً أَو هالِكاً أَو نادِبَا	أَو هارِباً أَو طالِباً أَو راغِبَا
فَوْقَ السُّهولِ عَواسِلاً وقَواضِبَا	وَإِذا نَظَرْتَ إِلى الجِبالِ رَأَيْتَها
تَحْتَ الجِبالِ فَوارِساً وجَنائِبَا	وَإِذا نَظَرْتَ إِلى السُّهولِ رَأَيْتَها
زِنْجاً تَبَسَّمَ أَوْ قَذالاً شائِبَا	وَعَجاجَةً تَرَكَ الحَديدُ سَوادَها
لَيْلاً وَأَطْلَعَتِ الرِّماحُ كَواكِبَا	فَكَأَنَّما كُسِيَ النَّهارُ بِها دُجى
وتَكَتَّبَتْ فيها الرِّجالُ كَتائِبَا	قَد عَسكَرَتْ مَعَها الرَّزايا عَسكَراً
أَسَدٌ تَصيرُ لَهُ الأَسودُ ثَعالِبَا	أَسَدٌ فَرائِسُها الأَسودُ يَقودُها
وعَلاً فَسَمَّوْهُ عَلِيَّ الحاجِبَا	في رُتْبَةٍ حَجَبَ الوَرى عَن نَيْلِها
ودَعْوَةً مِن غَضَبِ النُّفوسِ الغاصِبَا	ودَعْوَةً مِن فَرْطِ السَّخاءِ مُبَذِّراً
وعِداهُ قَتْلاً والزَّمانَ تَجارِبَا	هذا الَّذي أَفنى النُّضارَ مَواهِبَا
مِنهُ ولَيسَ يَرُدُّ كَفّاً خائِبَا	ومُخَيِّبُ العُذّالِ مِمّا أَمَّلوا
مِثلَ الَّذي أَبْصَرْتُ مِنهُ غائِبَا	هذا الَّذي أَبْصَرْتُ مِنهُ حاضِراً
يُهدي إِلى عَيْنَيكَ نوراً ثاقِبَا	كَالبَدرِ مِن حَيثُ التَفَتَّ رَأَيْتَهُ
جوداً ويَبْعَثُ للبَعيدِ سَحائِبَا	كَالبَحرِ يَقذِفُ للقَريبِ جَواهِراً
يَغْشى البِلادَ مَشارِقاً ومَغارِبَا	كَالشَّمسِ في كَبِدِ السَّماءِ وضَوْؤُها
وَتَروكَ كُلِّ كَريمِ قَومٍ عاتِبَا	أَمُهَجَّنَ الكُرَماءِ والمُزري بِهِم
وُجِدَتْ مَناقِبُهُم بِهِنَّ مَثالِبَا	شادوا مَناقِبَهُم وشِدْتَ مَناقِبا
إِنّا لَنُخبِرُ مِن يَدَيكَ عَجائِبَا	لَبَّيكَ غَيظَ الحاسِدينَ الرّاتِبَا
وهُجومَ غِرٍّ لا يَخافُ عَواقِبَا	تَدبيرَ ذي حُنكٍ يُفَكِّرُ في غَدٍ
أَنفَقْتَهُ في أَن تُلاقِيَ طالِبَا	وعَطاءَ مالٍ لَوْ عَداهُ طالِبٌ
لا تُلْزِمَنّي في الثَّناءِ الواجِبَا	خُذْ مِن ثَنائي عَلَيكَ ما أَسْطيعُهُ
ما يُدهِشُ المَلَكَ الحَفيظَ الكاتِبَا	فَلَقَدْ دَهِشْتُ لِما فَعَلْتَ ودونَهُ

(٦٣)

«من الطويل»

يمدح عمر بن سليمان الشرابي وهو يومئذ يتولى الفداء بين العرب والروم:

ونَتِّهِمُ الواشِينَ والدَّمعُ مِنهُمُ	نَرى عِظَماً بالبَينِ والصَّدُّ أَعظَمُ

So death's nature is known by feeling
    You'll find no creature tastes death twice
If you meet him you meet only an army
    Or the dust or a jousting or the slashing
Or fleeing or pursuing or desiring
    Or dreading or agonizing or the lament
When you look at the mountains see
    Them above plains as spears or swords
When you look at plains you see them
    Below mountains as riders and retainers
The steel stands out in darkest dust
    Like a black man smiling or locks of gray hair
If day is dressed with it the dark wins
    Night as the lances bring up the stars
Ruin makes an army by it for an army
    Men form battalions with it as conscripts
Lions their prey, a lion leads them
    He is a lion for whom the lions are foxes
Rank, men are kept from gaining it
    Eminent, so they call him Ali the keeper
They call him from excess bounty lavish
    The call him from anger at souls a robber
One who expends gold making gifts
    His enemies are dead, fate put to test
He denies critics in what they hope
    From him but disappoints none who ask
What you see of him when present
    Is like what you see of when he is absent
Like a moon wherever you turn, you see
    He guides to your eyes a penetrating beam
As a sea he yields gems for those nearby
    As bounty and raises up the distant clouds
Like sun at heaven's zenith, its light
    Overwhelming land in east and west
O degrader of their bounty, despiser
    Leaving all the liberal folk with censure
They show their virtues, you show honor
    Their virtue is found disgraceful with that
I'm here O lasting rage of the envious
    Truly we witness wonders from the bounty
Labor with prudence thinks of tomorrow
    But onslaughts of fools fear no outcomes
If a client turns from a rich gift
    You expend it searching for a recipient
Take my praise for what it is worth
    What is fit in praise is not expected of me
I marvel at what you do, less than it
    Astonishes the guardian angels who write

63
He spoke praising Umar ibn Sulayman. (Long mu)
We know parting grave but denial is more
    And we suspect gossips and tears from them

ومَنْ سِرُّهُ في جَفْنِهِ كيفَ يَكْتُمُ	ومَنْ لُبُّهُ مَعَ غَيرِهِ كَيفَ حالُهُ
غَفُولانِ عَنّا ظِلْتُ أبكي وتَبسِمُ	ولمّا التَقَيْنا والنَّوَى ورَقيبُنا
ولم تَرَ قَبْلي مَيِّتاً يَتَكَلَّمُ	فلَمْ أرَ بَدراً ضاحِكاً قبلَ وجْهِها
ضَعيفِ القُوَى مِن فِعلِها يَتَظَلَّمُ	ظَلومٌ كمَتَنَيها لِصَبٍّ كخَصْرِها
ووَجهٍ يُعيدُ الصُّبحَ واللَّيلُ مُظلِمُ	بفَرعٍ يُعيدُ اللَّيلَ والصّبحَ نَيِّرٌ
ولكِنّ جَيشَ الشَّوقِ فيهِ عَرَمرَمُ	فلَوْ كانَ قَلبي دارَها كانَ خالياً
ورَسْمٌ كجِسمي ناحِلٌ مُتَهدَّمُ	أثافٍ بِها ما بالفُؤادِ مِنَ الصَّلَى
وعَبرَتُهُ صِرْفٌ وفي عَبرَتي دَمُ	بَلَلْتُ بِها رُدنيّ والغَيمُ مُسعِدي
لما كانَ مُحمَرّاً يَسيلُ فأسْقَمُ	ولَوْ لم يكُنْ ما انهلَّ في الخدِّ من دمي
وقولْتُـهُ لي بَعدَنا الغُمضَ تطعَمُ	بنَفسي الخَيالُ الزّائِري بعد هجعَةٍ
لقُلتُ أبو حَفصٍ عَلَينا المُسَلَّمُ	سلامٌ فلَوْ لا الخَوفُ والبُخلُ عنْدَهُ
صَبوّاً كما يَصبُوا المُحِبُّ المُتَيَّمُ	مُجِبُّ النَّدَى الصّابي إلى بَذلِ مالِهِ
لَهُ ضَيغَماً قُلنا لَهُ أنتَ ضَيغَمُ	وأُقْسِمُ لَوْ لا أنَّ في كلِّ شَعرَةٍ
ونَبخَسُهُ والبَخسُ شيءٌ مُحرَّمُ	أَنقُصُهُ مِن حظِّهِ وهْوَ زائِدُ
ولا هوَ ضِرْغامٌ ولا الرَّأيُ مِخذَمُ	يَجِلّ عنِ التّشبيهِ لا الكَفُّ لَجَّةٌ
ولا حَدُّهُ يَنْبُو ولا يَتَثَلَّمُ	ولا جُرحُهُ يُؤسَى ولا غَورُهُ يُرَى
ولا يُحْلَلُ الأمرُ الذي هوَ مُبرَمُ	ولا يُبرَمُ الأمرُ الذي هوَ حالِلٌ
ولا يَخدُمُ الدّنيا وإيّاهُ تَخدُمُ	ولا يَرمَحُ الأذيالَ مِن جَبَريّةٍ
ولا تَسلَمُ الأعداءُ مِنهُ ويَسلَمُ	ولا يَشتَهي يَبقَى وتَفنَى هِباتُهُ
وأحسَنُ مِنْ يُسرٍ تَلقّاهُ مُعدِمُ	ألَذُّ مِنَ الصَّهباءِ بالماءِ ذِكرُهُ
وأعْوَزُ مِنْ مُستَرفِدٍ منهُ يُحرَمُ	وأغْرَبُ مِن عَنقاءَ في الطَّيرِ شَكلُهُ
مِنَ القَطرِ بعدَ القَطرِ والوَيلُ مُثجَمُ	وأكثرُ مِن بَعدِ الأيادي أياديا
مِنَ اللُّؤمِ آلى أنَّهُ لا يُهَوِّمُ	سَنِيُّ العَطايا لَوْ رَأى نَومَ عَينِهِ
على سائِلٍ أعْيا على النّاسِ دِرْهَمُ	ولو قالَ هاتوا دِرهَماً لم أجُدْ بهِ
لأَثَّرَ فيهِ بأسُهُ والتَّكَرُّمُ	ولَوْ ضَرَّ مَرٌّ قَبلَهُ ما يَسُرَّةُ
يَتامَى مِنَ الأغمادِ تُنضَى فتُوتَمُ	يُرَوِّي بكالفِرصادِ في كلِّ غارَةٍ

He whose heart is with another, how is he?
    Whose secret is in his eyes, how hide that?
When we met, distance and our guard
    Forgetful of us yet I wept and you smiled
I had seen no moon smile before her
    Before me you had not seen the dead talk
One hurt by love as her back by thighs
    With waning strength it complains of deeds
With hair returning night to dawn's glow
    A face bringing back dawn to dark night
My heart as her camp should be empty
    But yet the army of love there is immense
Hearthstones are fired like the heart
    And traces destroyed as my emaciate body
I wet my sleeve there with a shower
    Its tears were pure and my tears had blood
If what flows on my cheeks isn't blood
    That trickle wouldn't be red nor I be sick
By my soul a dream visits me in sleep
    Its word is: after us do you savor dozing?
Peace! if fear and greed were not here
    We'd say Abu Hafs had spoken the goodbye
A lover of bounty longs to give wealth
    Ardently as the enslaved lover makes love
I swear if each hair of him were not
    A lion we'd say of him: You are a lion
Don't we diminish his joy as he grows?
    We decry him and disparaging is forbid
He exceeds comparison, his hand no
    Sea, he's no lion, his wisdom no sword
Or his wounds healed, his holes seen
    Nor can his edges be dulled, or notched
Or anything be tied that he has untied
    Nor any matter loosed that he has knotted
Nor does he trail skirts in self conceit
    Nor does he serve the world as it serves
He wants no permanency, giving ruins
    Nor is a foe safe from him as he is safe
Sweeter than wine with water, his word
    Better than fortune if a poor man meets him
More rare then *anqa* bird is equal
    More scarce than one he denied as client
More supplied with gifts after a giving
    Than shower after shower in lasting rain
High in bounty, if he saw sleep as
    Avarice he'd swear he would not doze
If he said: bring a dirham not yet given
    To client he would get no such dirham
If what delights him worried men more
    His bravery and generosity affect him most
He pours mulberry juice in every raid
    With sheath's bright orphan as he orphans

112   Diwan al-Mutanabbi

مُذْ الغَزْوُ سارَ مُسَرَّجُ الخيلِ مُلجَمُ	إلى اليَوْمِ ما حَطَّ الفِداءُ سُروجَهُ
بأسيافِهِ والجَوُّ بالنَّقْعِ أدْهَمُ	يَشُقُّ بلادَ الرّومِ والنَّقْعُ أبْلَقُ
تُسايِرُ منهُ حَتْفَها وهيَ تَعْلَمُ	إلى المَلِكِ الطّاغي فكَمْ مِنْ كَتيبةٍ
أسيلةِ خَدٍّ عَنْ قَليلٍ سيُلْطَمُ	ومِنْ عاتِقٍ نَصْرانةٍ بَرَزَتْ لَهُ
مُتونُ المَذاكي والوَشيجُ المُقَوَّمُ	صُفوفاً لِليّثِ في لُيوثٍ حُصُونُها
وتَقَدَّمَ في ساحاتِهِمْ حينَ يَقدَمُ	تَغيبُ المَنايا عنهُمْ وهوَ غائِبٌ
عُمَ بنَ سُلَيْمانَ ومالٌ تُقَسَّمُ	أجِدَّكَ ما تَنفَكَّ عانَ تَفَكَّهُ
يداً لا تُؤَدّي شُكرَها اليَدُ والفَمُ	مُكافيكَ مَنْ أوْلَيْتَ دينَ رَسولِهِ
لِنَفسِكَ مِنْ جُودٍ فإنّكَ تُرْحَمُ	على مَهَلٍ إنْ كنتَ لستَ براحِمٍ
ومِثلُكَ مَفقودٌ ونَيلُكَ خِضرَمُ	مَحَلُّكَ مَقصودٌ وشانيكَ مُفحَمُ
إذا عَنَّ بَحْرٌ لم يَجُزْ لي التَّيَمُّمُ	وزارَكَ بي دونَ المُلوكِ تَحَرُّجٌ
مِنَ المَوتِ لم تُفقَدْ وفي الأرضِ مُسلِمُ	فعِشْ لَوْ فَدى المملوكُ رَبّاً بنفسِهِ

(٦٤)

«من الكامل»

يمدح عبد الواحد بن العباس بن أبي الإصبع الكاتب:

تَطِسُ الخُدودَ كما تَطِسْنَ اليَرْمَعا	أرَكائِبَ الأحبابِ إنّ الأدْمُعا
وامشينَ هَوْناً في الأزِمّةِ خُضَّعا	فاعْرِفْنَ مَن حَمَلَتْ عليكِنَّ النّوى
فاليَوْمَ يَمنَعُهُ البُكاءَ أنْ يَمنَعا	قد كانَ يَمنَعُني الحَياءُ مِنَ البُكا
في جِلدِهِ ولِكُلِّ عِرقٍ مَدْمَعا	حتى كأنَّ لِكُلِّ عَظمٍ رَنّةً
لِمُحِبِّهِ وبِمَصرَعي ذا مَصرَعا	وكَفى بِمَن فَضَحَ الجَدايةَ فاضِحا
سَتَرَتْ مَحاجِرَها ولم تَكُ تُرْقَعا	سَفَرَتْ وبَرْقَعَها الفِراقُ بصُفرَةٍ
ذَهَبٌ بِسِمطَيْ لُؤْلُؤٍ قد رُصِّعا	فكأنّها والدَّمعُ يَقْطُرُ فَوْقَها
في لَيْلةٍ فَأرَتْ لَيالي أرْبَعا	نَشَرَتْ ثَلاثَ ذَوائِبٍ من شَعرِها
فأرَتْنِيَ القَمَرَيْنِ في وقتٍ مَعا	واستَقبَلَتْ قَمَرَ السَّماءِ بوَجهِها
لو كانَ وَصلُكِ مِثلَهُ ما أقشَعا	رُدّي الوِصالَ سَقى طُلولَكِ عارِضٌ

Ransom price not from his saddle a day
    Saddle horse bridled after being on a raid
He crosses Rum lands, gloom is bright
    With his swords but air black with his dust
To king of tyrants, how many regiments
    Encounter him as death and know that?
How many virgin Christians show him
    The fair cheeks that soon will be clawed?
Rows for a lion among lions whose guard
    Is backs of stallions and the upright spears
Fate absent from them when he is gone
    It approaches their camps if he approaches
O good for you to free captives as you do
    May Ibn Sulayman live and wealth he shares!
He rewards one who gave his envoy's faith
    As gift, hand and mouth cannot give thanks
Be gentle, for if you show no mercy to
    Yourself in giving yet you are granted mercy
Your home the goal and your enemies
    Silent, your rivals lost, and your gifts myriad
Visiting you for me is leaving kings
    When the sea appears the dust is not for me
Live, if slaves are ransom for a lord from
    Death, you are not lost and earth is peaceful

64
He spoke praising Abd al Wahid ibn Abbas ibn Abu Asbai the Katib.
(Swift a)

O the camels of the beloved! true tears
    Beat the cheeks like they pound on stones
They know her whom parting loaded on you
    And they go softly with their obedient bridles
Once it was shame forbade me to weep
    But today weeping forbids that prohibition
Until it's as if a sob in every bone
    Is under the skin and in every vein tears
And enough shame to shame the fawn
    For his lover or my being slain in this way
She unveils as parting veils her pallor
    Veils her eye hollow though it has no veil
As if it with tears dripping over it
    Were gold, a double thread of pearls inset
She displays those three locks of hair
    To night and they show my night as fourth
She opposes a moon in a sky to a face
    And shows me two celestial lights at once
Return my embrace as clouds water
    A camp, if your caress is like it, it is endless

زَجَلٌ يُريكِ الجَوَّ ناراً والمَلا   كَالبَحرِ والتَلَعاتِ رَوضاً مُمرِعا
كَبَنانِ عَبدِ الواحِدِ الغَدِقِ الذي   أَروى وأَمَّنَ مَن يَشاءُ وأَجزَعا
أَلِفَ المُروءَةَ مُذْ نَشا فَكَأَنَّهُ   سُقِيَ اللِّبانَ بِها صَبيّاً مُرضَعا
نَظَمَت مَواهِبُهُ عَلَيهِ تَمائِماً   فاعتادَها فإذا سَقَطنَ تَفَزَّعا
تَرَكَ الصَنائِعَ كَالقَواطِعِ بارِقا   تٍ والمَعالِيَ كَالعَوالي شُرَّعا
مُتَبَسِّماً لُعُفاتِهِ عَن واضِحٍ   تَغشى لَوامِعُهُ البُروقَ اللُمَّعا
مُتَكَشِّفاً لُعُداتِهِ عَن سَطوَةٍ   لَو حَكَّ مَنكِبُها السَماءَ لَزَعزَعا
الحازِمِ اليَقِظِ الأَغَرِّ العالِمِ الـ   ـفَطِنِ الأَلَدِّ الأَريَحِيِّ الأَروَعا
الكاتِبِ اللَبِقِ الخَطيبِ الواهِبِ الـ   ـنَدُسَ اللَبيبَ الهِبرِزِيَّ المِصقَعا
نَفسٌ لَها خُلُقُ الزَمانِ لأَنَّهُ   يَسقي العِمارَةَ والمَكانَ البَلقَعا
وَيَدٌ لَها كَرَمُ الغَمامِ لأَنَّهُ   يَسقى العِمارَةَ والمَكانَ البَلقَعا
أَبَداً يُصَدَّعُ شَعبُ وَفرٍ وافِرٍ   ويَلَمَّ شَعبَ مَكارِمٍ مُتَصَدِّعا
يَهتَزُّ لِلجَدوى اهتِزازَ مُهَنَّدٍ   يَومَ الرَجاءِ هَزَزتَهُ يَومَ الوَغى
يا مُغنِياً أَمَلَ الفَقيرِ لِقاؤُهُ   ودُعاؤُهُ بَعدَ الصَلاةِ إذا دَعا
أَقصِر ولَستَ بِمُقصِرٍ جُزتَ المَدى   وبَلَغتَ حَيثُ النَجمُ تَحتَكَ فارِبَعا
وحَلَلتَ مِن شَرَفِ الفِعالِ مَواضِعاً   لَم يَحلُلِ الثَقَلانِ مِنها مَوضِعا
وحَوَيتَ فَضلَهُما وما طَمِعَ امرُؤٌ   فيهِ ولا طَمَعٌ لامرُؤٍ أَن يَطمَعا
نَفَذَ القَضاءُ بِما أَرَدتَ كَأَنَّهُ   لَكَ كُلَّما أَزمَعتَ أَمراً أَزمَعا
وأَطاعَكَ الدَهرُ العَصِيُّ كَأَنَّهُ   عَبدٌ إذا نادَيتَ لَبّى مُسرِعا
أَكَلَت مَفاخِرُكَ المَفاخِرَ وانثَنَت   عَن شَأوِهِنَّ مَطِيُّ وَصفي ظُلَّعا
وجَرَينَ جَريَ الشَمسِ في أَفلاكِها   فَقَطَعنَ مَغرِبَها وجُزنَ المَطلَعا
لَو نيطَتِ الدُنيا بِأُخرى مِثلِها   لَعَمَمنَها وخَشينَ أَن لا تَقنَعا
فَمَتى يُكَذَّبُ مُدَّعٍ لَكَ فَوقَ ذا   واللَهِ يَشهَدُ أَنَّ حَقّاً ما ادَّعى
ومَتى يُؤَدّي شَرحَ حالِكَ ناطِقٌ   حَفِظَ القَليلَ النَزرَ مِمّا ضَيَّعا
إن كانَ لا يُدعى الفَتى إلّا كَذا   رَجُلاً فَسَمِّ الناسَ طُرّاً إصبَعا
إن كانَ لا يَسعى لِجُودٍ ماجِدٌ   إلّا كَذا فالغَيثُ أَبخَلُ مَن سَعى

Thunder tells of sky lightning, a plain
    Like a sea, and the hills a fertile meadow
Like Abd al-Wahid's flowing finger to
    Gush and shelter one who years but fears
He was familiar to manliness from youth
    As if he had it with milk sucked in infancy
His gifts held charms on his account
    One is used to them and if lost one fears
He leaves good deeds like bight swords
    And the high acts like spears at the ready
Smiling to his clients a gracious smile
    Its flashes cover the blazing lightnings
Revealing to his foes impetuous pride
    If its shoulders touch sky it must shake
Determined, wakeful, strong in wit
    Prudent, warlike, generous and brilliant
A writer, brisk, persuasive, bounteous
    Intelligent, rational, elegant, and eloquent
A soul who owns the folk of the time
    Water of souls, separating the gathered
Gifts that have a rain cloud's bounty
    Poured out on settled land and desert
Every splitting huge masses collected
    Gathering masses of bounty to be split
He rejoices in gifts as a sword does
    On hope's day his joy is as on battle day
O riches, meeting him is poor man's hope
    His prayer after the service when he prays
Stop! But you do not stop till the goal
    You go with stars beneath as you succeed
You settle in places where acts are high
    Such a place where no man or jinn settle
You seize their good and what contents
    In it but no man joys in what pleases him
Judgment is done in what you want
    It is yours, if you judge a case so let it be
Stubborn fate submits as if it were
    A slave when you say: Come here quick!
Your honor devours a boaster, camels
    Of my art limp as they turn to their set goal
They run the sun's course in their sky
    Cross to their west and outpass the orient
If a world joined to another such as it
    They'd cover it and I fear not be content
If one denied claims for you beyond it
    God accepts the truth of what is claimed
A speaker gives proof of your condition
    He keeps little things among many states
If a hero claims to be no other than
    Such a limb then call other men toes
If glory did not achieve bounty except
    Thus, then rain would be the stingy gift

قَدْ خَلَّفَ العَبّاسُ غُرَّتَكَ ابْنَهُ   مَرْأًى لَنا وإلى القِيامةِ مَسْمَعا

(٦٥)

«من الطويل»

اجتاز بمكان يعرف بالفراديس من أرض قنسرين فسع زئير الأسد فقال:

أجارُكِ يا أَسَدَ الفَراديسِ مُكْرَمٌ   فَتَسْكُنَ نَفْسي أَمْ مُهانٌ فَمُسْلَمُ
ورائي وقُدّامي عُداةٌ كَثيرَةٌ   أُحاذِرُ مِنْ لِصٍّ ومِنكِ ومِنْهُمُ
فَهَلْ لَكِ في حِلْفي على ما أُريدُهُ   فَإِنِّي بِأَسْبابِ المَعيشَةِ أَعْلَمُ
إذاً لَأَتاكِ الرِّزْقُ مِنْ كُلِّ وِجْهَةٍ   وأَثْرَيْتِ مِمّا تَغْنَمينَ وأَغْنَمُ

(٦٦)

«من الخفيف»

يمدح عبد الرحمن بن المبارك الانطاكي:

صِلَةُ الهَجْرِ لي وهَجْرُ الوِصالِ   نَكَّساني في السُّقْمِ نُكْسَ الهِلالِ
فَغَدا الجِسْمُ ناقِصاً والذي يَنْـ   ـقُصُ مِنْهُ يَزيدُ في بَلْبالي
قِفْ على الدِّمْنَتَيْنِ بالدَّوِّ مِنْ رَيّـ   ـا كَخالٍ في وَجْنَةٍ جَنْبَ خالِ
بَطُلولٍ كَأَنَّهُنَّ نُجومٌ   في عِراصٍ كَأَنَّهُنَّ لَيالي
ونُؤيٌّ كَأَنَّهُنَّ عَلَيْها   نَّ خِدامٌ خُرْسٌ بِسوقِ خِدالِ
لا تَلُمْني فَإِنَّني أَعْشَقُ العُشّـ   ـاقَ فيها يا أَعْذَلَ العُذّالِ
ما تُريدُ النَّوى مِنَ الحَيَّةِ الذوّ   اقِ حَرَّ الفَلا وبَرْدَ الظِّلالِ
فَهْوَ أَمْضى في الرَّوْعِ مِنْ مَلَكِ المَوْ   تِ وأَسْرى في ظُلْمَةٍ مِنْ خَيالِ
والحَتْفِ في العِزِّ يَدْنو مُحِبٌّ   والعُمْرُ يَطولُ في الذُّلِّ قالِ
نَحْنُ رَكْبٌ مِلَجِنِّ في زِيِّ ناسٍ   فَوْقَ طَيْرٍ لَها شُخوصُ الجِمالِ
مِنْ بَناتِ الجَديلِ تَمْشي بِنا في الـ   بيدِ مَشْيَ الأَيّامِ في الآجالِ
كُلُّ هَوْجاءَ لِلدَّياميمِ فيها   أَثَرُ النّارِ في سَليطِ الذُّبالِ

Abbas made your splendor, O his son
    As a vision for us and until resurrection

65
He was traveling at a place known as Faradis in the region of Qannasrin and he heard the roaring of lions and spoke.
(Long mu)

Is your region honored O Faradis lioness?
    Then my soul rests or if it is mean then goodbye
Behind me and in front of me are many foes
    I am wary of thieves both among you and then
Do you agree with me in what I desire?
    For I know more about the ways of livelihood
So your food comes to you from each region
    When you are rich in your plunder and I share

66
He spoke praising Abd al-Rahman al-Mubarak al-Antakya
(Nible li)

Departure's bond and flight in embrace
    Returns me to illness like a waning moon
For the body suffers decrease as what
    Diminishes in it increases in its sorrow
Stop at traces in this plain of Rayya
    A beauty spot beside beauty spot on cheek
At the deserted mounds like the stars
    Near courtyards that are like the nights
And drain trenches as if they wore
    Ankle rings with no noise on plump legs
Blame me not, I'm most loving of lovers
    For her, O you the harshest of reprovers
What does distance want of a viper
    Tasting heat of deserts and cold of night?
He is sharper in fear than death's king
    Going longer in darkness than the dream
Toward a death in glory a lover bows
    Despising a life that is long in meanness
We are riders of jinn in human clothes
    On birds who have the camels' fine shape
From Jadila's daughters going with us
    The gait of days to death in a wasteland
All of a good she camel in the desert
    It leaves a fire track like a wick in its oil

118 Diwan al-Mutanabbi

عامِداتٍ لِلبَدْرِ وَالبَحْرِ وَالضِّرْ	غامَةِ ابنِ المُبارَكِ المِفْضال
مَنْ يَزُرْهُ يَزُرْ سُلَيْمانَ فِي المُلْـ	ـكِ جَلالاً ويُوسُفاً فِي الجَمال
وربيعاً يُضاحِكُ الغَيثُ فيهِ	زَهَرَ الشُّكْرُ مِن رياضِ المَعالي
نَفَحَتْنا مِنهُ الصَّبا بِنَسيمٍ	رَدَّ روحاً في مَيِّتِ الآمال
هَمُّ عَبدِ الرَّحمَنِ نَفعُ المَوالي	وبَوارُ الأعداءِ والأموال
أَكبَرُ العَيبِ عِندَهُ البُخلُ والطَّعْـ	ـنُ عَلَيهِ التَّشْبيهُ بِالرِّئبال
والجِراحاتُ عِندَهُ نَعَماتٌ	سُبِقَتْ قَبلَ سَيْبِهِ بِسُؤال
ذا السِّراجُ المُنيرُ هذا النَّقيُّ الـ	ـجَيْبُ هذا بَقِيَّةُ الأبْدال
فَخُذا ماءَ رِجْلِهِ وانْضِحا فِي الـ	ـمُدْنِ تَأمَنْ بَوائِقَ الزِّلْزال
وامْسَحا ثَوْبَهُ البَقيرَ عَلى دا	ئِكُما تُشْفَيا مِنَ الإعْلال
مالئاً مِنْ نَوالِهِ الشَّرقَ والغَرْ	بَ ومِن خَوْفِهِ قُلوبَ الرِّجال
قابِضاً كَفَّهُ اليَمينَ عَلى الدَّنْـ	ـيا ولَوْ شاءَ حازَها بِالشِّمال
نَفسُهُ جَيْشُهُ وتَدْبيرُهُ النَّصْـ	ـرُ وألحاظُهُ الظُّبى والعَوالي
ولَهُ فِي جَماجِمِ المالِ ضَربٌ	وَقْعُهُ فِي جَماجِمِ الأبطال
فَهُمُ لا تَقائِهِ الدَّهرَ فِي يَوْ	مِ نِزالٍ وليسَ يَوْمَ نِزال
رَجُلٌ طِينَةٌ مِنَ العَنْبَرِ الوَرْ	دِ وطينُ العِبادِ مِنْ صَلْصال
فَبَقِيّاتٌ طينِهِ لاقَتِ الما	ءَ فصارَتْ عُذوبَةً فِي الزُّلال
وبَقايا وَقارِهِ عافَتِ النا	سَ فَصارَتْ رَكانَةً فِي الجِبال
لَسْتُ مِمَّنْ يَغُرُّهُ حُبُّكَ السِّلْـ	ـمَ وَأَنْ لا تَرى شُهودَ القِتال
ذاكَ شَيءٌ كَفاكَهُ عَيْشُ شانيـ	ـكَ ذَليلاً وقِلَّةُ الأشْكال
واغْتِفارٌ لَوْ غَيَّرَ السُّخطُ مِنهُ	جُعِلَتْ هامَهُمْ نِعالَ النِّعال
لِجيادٍ بَدْخُلْنَ فِي الحَربِ أعرا	ءَ ويخرُجْنَ مِنْ دَمٍ فِي جَلال
واسْتَعارَ الحَديدُ لَوْناً وألْقى	لَوْنَهُ فِي ذَوائِبِ الأطْفال
أنتَ طَوْراً أَمَرُّ مِنْ ناقِعِ السِّمِّ	وطَوْراً أَحْلى مِنَ السَّلْسال
إنَّما النّاسُ حَيثُ أنتَ ومَا النّا	سُ بِناسٍ فِي مَوْضِعٍ مِنكَ خالِ

Aiming at full moon as sea and lion
    To Abu Mubarak who is most excellent
The visitor sees Sulayman in a famed
    Kingdom and Yusuf in all of his beauty
Like the spring a shower smiles in
    Flowers of thanks from gardens on high
From it east winds perfume with sighs
    Bringing back a soul to the dead hopes
Kind care is Abd al Rahman's wish
    And destruction of enemies of wealth
Greatest blame for him is stinginess
    Jousting for him is the lion's prototype
Wounds for him are calls for help
    That precede his gifts to his clients
This burning lamp, collar's purity
    This remnant of the prophetic deputies
Take water from his feet and sprinkle
    On cities to ward off dread earthquake
Rub cloth of his shirts, you two, on
    Your sores to heal them of sickness
Filling with his gifts east and west
    And with his terrors the hearts of men
He keeps his right hand from some
    If he desires them he takes with his left
Himself is his army, his acts victory
    Respect for him is in blades and spears
He strikes a blow at the head of wealth
    Whose impact is on the heads of heroes
They are always in fear of him, in time
    Of attack though it is not the battle day
A man whose clay is of red amber
    While the clay of men is earthenware
What is of his clay when it meets
    Water brings sweetness to cool liquid
His firm good judgment parts men
    But it has a steadiness of mountains
I am not one your love peace blinds
    Even if you seem not to witness battles
That is what life guards for you
    Your foes are vile and few are equals
He is forgiving but if rage turns him
    Their skulls are beaten by horse hoofs
Horses that enter into battle bare
    Come out having blood as horsecloths
Steel borrows its color as he casts
    Its color on the locks of the young men
At times more bitter than a poison
    You at times sweeter than fresh water
Humanity where you are men are not
    Men in the places where you are absent

(٦٧)

«من الكامل»

يمدح أبا علي هارون بن عبدالعزيز الأوراجي
الكاتب وكان يذهب إلى التصرف:

إذْ حَيْثُ كُنتِ مِنَ الظَّلامِ ضِياءُ	أمِنَ ازْدِيارِكِ في الدُّحى الرُّقَباءُ
وَمَسيرُها في اللَّيلِ وهيَ ذَكاءُ	قَلَقُ المَليحةِ وهيَ مِسكٌ هَتكُها
عَنْ عِلْمِهِ فَبِهِ عَلَيَّ خَفاءُ	أسَفي على أسَفي الذي دَلَّهْتِني
قَدْ كانَ لَمّا كانَ لي أعضاءُ	وَشَكِيَّتي فَقْدُ السَّقامِ لأنَّهُ
فَتَشابَها كِلْتاهُما نَجْلاءُ	مَثَلْتِ عَيْنُكِ في حَشايَ جِراحَةً
تَنْدَقُّ فيهِ الصَّعدَةُ السَّمْراءُ	نَفَذَتْ عَلَيَّ السّابِريَّ ورُبَّما
وإذا نَطَقْتُ فَإنَّني الجَوْزاءُ	أنا صَخرَةُ الوادي إذا ما زُوحِمَتْ
أنْ لا تَراني مُقْلَةٌ عَمْياءُ	وإذا خَفِيتُ على الغَبِيِّ فَعاذِرٌ
صَدْري بها أفضى أم البَيداءُ	شِيَمُ اللَّيالي أنْ تُشَكِّكَ ناقَتي
إسْآدَها في المَهْمَهِ الإنضاءُ	فَبِتُّ تُسْعِدُ مُسْعِداً في نَيِّها
مَنكوحَةٌ وَطَريقُها عَذْراءُ	أنْشاعُها مَمْغوطَةٌ وَخِفافُها
فيها كَما يَتَلَوَّنُ الحِرْباءُ	يَتَلَوَّنُ الخِرِّيتُ مِنْ خَوْفِ التَّوى
شُمُّ الجِبالِ ومِثْلُهُنَّ رَجاءُ	بَيْني وبَينَ أبي عَلِيٍّ مِثلُهُ
وهوَ الشِّتاءُ وصَيفُهُنَّ شِتاءُ	وعِقابُ لُبنانَ وكيفَ بِقَطْعِها
فَكَأنَّها بِبَياضِها سَوْداءُ	لَبِسَ التُّلوجُ بِها عَلَيَّ مَسالِكي
سالَ النُّضارُ بها وقامَ الماءُ	وكذا الكَريمُ إذا أقامَ بِبَلْدَةٍ
بُهِتَتْ فَلَمْ تَتَبَجَّسِ الأنواءُ	جَمَدَ القِطارُ ولوْ رَأَتْهُ كَما تَرى
حتّى كَأنَّ مِدادَهُ الأهواءُ	في خَطِّهِ مِن كُلِّ قَلْبٍ شَهْوَةٌ
حتّى كأنَّ مَغيبَهُ الأقذاءُ	ولكُلِّ عَيْنٍ قُرَّةٌ في قُرْبِهِ
في القَوْلِ حتى يَفعَلَ الشُّعَراءُ	مَنْ يَهتَدي في الفِعْلِ ما لا تَهتَدي
في قَلْبِهِ ولِأُذْنِهِ إصْغاءُ	في كُلِّ يَوْمٍ للقَوافي جَوْلَةٌ
في كُلِّ بَيْتٍ فَيْلَقٌ شَهْباءُ	وإغارَةٌ في ما احْتَواهُ كَأنَّما

67
He spoke praising Abu Ali Harun ibn Abdallah al-Awaraji the katib. (Perfect u)

Guards are safe from your visit at dusk
   Since where you are in the dark is light
Restless beauty unveils her for she is
   Musk, her moving in the night is the sun
I grieve for grief by which you derange
   Me knowing it since by it a veil covers me
My complaint is of the loss of illness
   Which existed when limbs were still mine
You put your eye in my mind as wound
   A wideness of both of them is copied there
It pierced my fine woven armor, seldom
   The brown shafted lance broke through it
I'm a wadi rock beaten on by floods
   When I speak I'm the bright Jauza star
If I hide from the simple my excuse is
   That the eyes of the blind will not see me
Habits of the night make my camel doubt
   Is my breast or the desert broader for her?
Going all night moving fast on her fat
   Emaciation speeds her through wasteland
Saddle straps slacken and her hoofs
   Are pierced though her path is a virgin
Gudes change color for fear of ruin
   There, like the chameleon changes color
Between me and Abu Ali stand like him
   Mountain peaks and like them are hopes
Heights of Lubnan, how to cross them
   For it is winter and summer is as winter
The snows have obscured my paths
   As if in their whiteness they were black
So a generous one who stays in town
   Makes silver flow and the water remain
Rains freeze and if rain stars knew him
   As now, they'd been amazed, not shone
Longing for his script in each heart
   Until it is as if his ink were an addiction
For every eye peace in his practice
   It's as if his absence were eye sickness
He's guided in action so poets can't
   Guide right in speech until he advises
Every day coming, going for rhymes
   In his heart and attention is to his ear
There are raids on what he gathers
   In each verse is a band of bright heroes

مَنْ يَظلِمُ اللَّؤماءَ في تكليفِهمْ ... أنْ يُصبِحُوا وَهُمْ لَـهُ أكفاءُ
ونَذيُهُمْ وبهمْ عَرَفْنا فَضْلَـهُ ... وبِضدِّها تَتَبَيَّنُ الأشياءُ
مَنْ نَفْعُهُ في أنْ يُهاجَ وضَرُّهُ ... في تَركِهِ لَوْ تَفطَنُ الأعداءُ
فالسِّلمُ يَكسِرُ مِن جَناحَيْ مالِهِ ... بِنوالِـهِ ما تَجبُرُ الهَيجاءُ
يُعطي فتعطى من لُهىً يدِهِ اللُّهى ... وتُرى برُؤيةِ رأيهِ الآراءُ
مُتَفَرِّقُ الطَّعمَينِ مُجتَمِعُ القُوى ... فكأنَّـهُ السَّـرَّاءُ والضَّرَّاءُ
وكأنَّـهُ مـا لا تَشاءُ عُداتُـهُ ... مُتَمَثِّـلاً لوُفُـودِهِ مـا شـاؤوا
يـا أيُّهـا الْمُجْدَى عَليـهِ روحُـهُ ... إذْ لَيْـسَ يأتيـهِ لهـا استِجـداءُ
إحْمَدْ عُفاتَكَ لا فَجِعْتَ بفَقدِهم ... فَلَتَرْكُ ما لم يأخُذوا إعْطاءُ
لا تَكثُـرُ الأمـواتُ كَـثرَةَ قِلَّـةٍ ... إلَّا إذا شَقِيَتْ بِـكَ الأحيـاءُ
والقَلْبُ لا يَنْشَـقُّ عَمَّـا تَحْتَـهُ ... حتَّـى تَحِلَّ بِـهِ لَـكَ الشَّحْنـاءُ
لم تُسْـمَ يا هَرونُ إلَّا بَعدَمـا أقْ ... تَـرَعَتْ ونازَعتِ اسمَـكَ الأسماءُ
فغَـدَوْتَ واسمُـكَ فيكَ غيـرُ مُشارَكٍ ... والنَّاسُ في مـا في يَدَيْـكَ سَواءُ
لَعَمَمْـتَ حتى المُـدْنُ مِنـكَ مِـلاءُ ... ولَفَتَّ حتى ذا الثَّناءِ لَفاءُ
وجُـدْتَ حتى كِـدْتَ تَبخَـلُ حائِـلاً ... للمُنْتَهـى ومِنَ السُّـرور بُكـاءُ
أبْـدَأتَ شيئاً ليسَ يُعـرَفُ بَـدؤُهُ ... وأعَـدْتَ حتى أنكَـرَ الإبْـداءُ
فالفَخرُ عَـن تَقصيرِهِ بِـكَ ناكِـبٌ ... والمَجْـدُ مِـنْ أنْ يُسْـتَزادَ بَـراءُ
فـإذا سُئِلْـتَ فَـلا لأنَّـكَ مُحـوِجٌ ... وإذا كُتِمْـتَ وشَـتْ بِـكَ الآلاءُ
وإذا مُدِحْـتَ فَـلا لتَكسِـبَ رفعَـةً ... للشَّاكِرينَ على الإلَـهِ ثَنـاءُ
وإذا مُطِـرْتَ فَـلا لأنَّـكَ مُجْـدِبٌ ... يُسقَى الخَصيبُ ويُمطَـرُ الدَّأماءُ
لم تَحْكِ نائِلَكَ السَّحابَ وإنَّما ... حُمَّـتْ بـهِ فَصَبيبُهـا الرُّحَضـاءُ
لست تَلْقَ هـذا الوَجْـهَ شَمسُ نَهارِنا ... إلَّا بوَجْـهٍ لَيـسَ فيـهِ حَيـاءُ
فَبأيِّمـا قَـدَمٍ سَـعَيْتَ إلى العُلـى ... أدُمُ الهِلال لأخْمَصَيـكَ حِـذاءُ
ولَـكَ الزَّمانُ مِـنَ الزَّمـانِ وقايَـةٌ ... ولَـكَ الحِمـامُ مِـنَ الحِمامِ فِداءُ
لوْ لم تكنْ من ذا الوَرى اللّذْ منكَ هُوَ ... عَقِمَـتْ بِمَوْلِـدِ نَسْلِهـا حَـوَّاءُ

He wrongs the stingy in charging them
    So they become, even they, equal to him
We blame yet by them we know virtue
    By their opposites things become known
One whose profit is attacked, his hurt
    Being left alone if only the enemy knew
For peace breaks wings of his wealth
    By his gifts and battle heals them again
He gives, huge gifts from his hand
    Wisdom is seen in a glance at his gift
Parting two tastes, uniting strength
    As if they were prosperity and misfortune
He seems what his foes don't want
    While showing partisans what they need
O one whose soul is generous gifts
    Even when no beggar comes for them
Thank the clients worry not at loss
    For a legacy they don't take as a gift
The dead count not as legions few
    Except as the living lament due to you
My heart splits from what is beneath
    Until some fear of you settles within it
O Harun unnamed till lots were drawn
    When names competed with your name
You came but others shared not yours
    Yet men are equal as to your generosity
True universal, cities filled with you
    You surpass ail so the eulogy is paltry
Generous till you are almost miserly
    Changing at the goal from joy to tears
You originate a thing as its source
    And add to it so the origin is denied
Honor deviates from shortcoming
    Glory free from asking an increase
If you are asked It's not your doing
    If you are hid your good deeds show
If you're praised it's not eminence
    Praise is for one who thanks God
If you have rain it's not you are dry
    Good land is watered, sea rained on
No clouds imitate your bounty but
    Are feverish for it so downpours sweat
Our day's sun confronts not his face
    Except her face has no shame upon it
With what foot did you run to heights?
    Surface of a moon is sole for your shoe
Yours a time of guarded times
    Yours a death of ransomed deaths
If you were not mankind which is of you
    Eve would be barren though bearing sons

(٦٨)

«من الرجز»

ولا لغَيرِ الغادِياتِ الهُطَّلِ	ومَنزِلٍ ليسَ لنا بِمَنزِلِ
مُحَلَّلٍ مِلْوَحْشٍ لم يُحَلَّلِ	نَدِيِّ الخُزامَى أذفَرِ القَرَنْفُلِ
مُحَيَّنُ النَّفسِ بعيدُ المَوئِلِ	عَنَّ لنا فيهِ مُراعِي مُغْزِلِ
وعادَةُ العُرْيِ عَنِ التَّفَضُّلِ	أغناهُ حُسنُ الجِيدِ عن لُبسِ الحَلي
مُعْتَرِضاً بِمثلِ قَرْنِ الأَيَّلِ	كأنَّهُ مُضَمَّخٌ بصَنْدَلِ
فَحَلَّ كَلَّابي وثاقَ الأَحْبُلِ	يَحُولُ بينَ الكَلْبِ والتَّأَمُّلِ
أقَبَّ سَاطٍ شَرِسٍ شَمَرْدَلِ	عن أشْدَقٍ مُسَوَّجَرٍ مُسَلْسَلِ
مُؤَجَّدِ الفِقْرَةِ رَخْوِ المَفصِلِ	مِنها إذا يُثْغَ لَهُ لا يُغْزَلِ
كأنَّما يَنظُرُ مِن سَجَنْجَلِ	لَهُ إذا أدْبَرَ لَحْظُ المُقْبِلِ
إذا تَلَا جاءَ المَدَى وقَدْ تَلِي	يَعْدُو إذا عَدَوُ المُسَهَّلِ
بأربَعٍ مَجْدُولَةٍ لَمْ تُجْدَلِ	يُقْعِي جُلُوسَ البَدَوِيِّ المُصْطَلِي
آثارُها أمْثالُها في الجَنْدَلِ	فَتْلَ الأيادِي رَبِذاتِ الأَرْجُلِ
يَجْمَعُ بينَ مَتْنِهِ والكَلْكَلِ	يَكَادُ في الوَثْبِ مِنَ التَّفَتُّلِ
شَبِيَّةٌ وسَمِيُّ الحِضارِ بالوَلِي	وبَينَ أعْلاهُ وبينَ الأَسْفَلِ
مُوَثَّقٌ على رِماحٍ ذُبَّلِ	كأنَّهُ مُضَبَّرٌ مِن جَرْوَلِ
يَخُطُّ في الأرضِ حِسابَ الجُمَّلِ	ذِي ذَنَبٍ أجْرَدَ غيرِ أعْزَلِ
لَوْ كانَ يُلِي السَّوْطَ تحريكٌ بَلِي	كأنَّهُ مِنْ جِسْمِهِ بِمَعْزِلِ
وعُقْلَةُ الظَّبْيِ وحَتْفُ التَّفِلِ	نَيلُ المُنَى وحُكْمُ نَفسِ المُرْسِلِ
قد ضَمِنَ الآخِرُ قَتْلَ الأوَّلِ	فانْبَرَيَا فَذَيْنِ تحتَ القَسْطَلِ
لا يأتَلِي في تَرْكِ أنْ لا يأتَلِي	في هَبْوَةٍ كِلاهُما لم يَذْهَلِ
يخالُ طُولَ البحرِ عَرْضَ الجَدْوَلِ	مُقْتَحِماً على المَكانِ الأهْوَلِ
إفتَرَّ عن مَذْرُوبَةٍ كالأَنْصُلِ	حتى إذا قِيلَ لهُ نِلْتَ افْعَلِ
مُرَكَّباتٍ في العَذابِ المُنْزَلِ	لا تَعْرِفُ العَهْدَ بصَقْلِ الصَّيْقَلِ
كأنَّها مِنْ ثِقَلٍ في يَذْبُلِ	كأنَّها مِنْ سُرْعَةٍ في الشَّمْأَلِ

68
He spoke describing a dog that Abu Ali al-Awaraji sent against a fawn and he chased it alone.
(Trembling li)

Many a campsite no campsite for us
    Nor for anything but the morning clouds
On dewy lavender odorous as clove
    Dwelling place of wild beasts not settled
Gazelle pastures revealed to us
    A doomed soul far from any shelter
His fine neck without any ornaments
    In the habit of nakedness without dress
As if daubed with sandalwood oil
    Confronting one with the horns of oryx
He comes between a dog and hope
    As the trainer loosens the tight leash Wide
Wide-jawed with collar and chain
    Thin, a leaper who is rough and fast
If they bleat he does not scare
    Strong backed with lithe muscles
His glance if he turns around
    As if he were looking in a mirror
He runs an easy gait in the rough
    He chases, reaches game, trailed
Sits like a bedouin warming
    Fine twisted legs without a flaw
Front wide set, back legs light
    Tracks held as copies on stones
He leaps almost folding them
    Joining the breast and haunches
Between top and bottom parts
    First run's shower is as a second
As if fashioned from a rock
    Fixed on the flexible lance
A stripped tail, not docked
    Traces on dust a florid writing
As if separate from his body
    Its feeble motion ruins a whip
Desire gained, hunter's rule
    Hobble for deer, death for foxes
Two opposed alone in dust
    One behind swears death to lead
Neither distracted in the dirt
    He avoids every mistake now
Running in the scene of fear
    A vast sea is a brook's width
One cries: You've got him!
    He bares fangs like swords
Not the smith's file work
    But pains of the Revelation
With a north wind's speed
    And Mount Yadhbul's weight

كَأَنَّهُ مِنْ عِلْمِهِ بِالمَقْتَلِ	كَأَنَّها مِنْ سَعَةٍ في هَوْجَلِ
فحالَ ما للقَفْزِ للتَجَدَّلِ	عَلَّمَ بُقْراطَ فِصادَ الأَكْحَلِ
فلم يَضِرْنا مَعَهُ فَقْدُ الأَجْدَلِ	وصارَ ما في جِلْدِهِ في المِرْجَلِ،
فالمُلْكُ لله العَزيزِ ثُمَّ لي	إذا بَقيتَ سالِماً أَبا عَلي

(٦٩)

«من المتقارب»

يمدح أبا الحسين بد بن عمار بن إسماعيل الأسدي الطبرستاني وهو يومئذ يتولى حرب طبرية من قبل أبي بكر محمد بن رائق سنة ٣٢٨هـ ٩٣٩م:

أَمِ الخَلْقُ في شَخْصِ حَيٍّ أُعيدا	أَحُلْماً نَرى أَمْ زَماناً جَديدا
كَأَنّا نُجومٌ لَقينَ سُعودا	تَجَلّى لَنا فَأَضَأنا بِهِ
لِبَدْرٍ وَلوداً وَبَدْراً وَليدا	رَأَيْنا بِبَدْرٍ وَآبائِهِ
رَضينا لَهُ فَتَرَكْنا السُّجودا	طَلَبْنا رِضاهُ بِتَرْكِ الَّذي
جَوادٌ بَخيلٌ بِأَنْ لا يَجودا	أَميرٌ أَميرٌ عَلَيْهِ النَّدى
كَأَنَّ لَهُ مِنْهُ قَلْباً حَسودا	يُحَدَّثُ عَنْ فَضْلِهِ مُكْرَهاً
وَيَقْدِرُ إِلّا عَلى أَنْ يَزيدا	وَيُقْدِمُ إِلّا عَلى أَنْ يَفِرَّ
فَما تُعْطِ مِنهُ نَجِدْهُ جُدودا	كَأَنَّ نَوالَكَ بَعْضُ القَضاءِ
رَدَدْتَ بِها الذُبَّلَ السُّمْرَ سودا	وَرُبَّما حَمْلَةٍ في الوَغى
وَرُمْحٍ تَرَكْتَ مُباداً مُبيدا	وَهَوْلٍ كَشَفْتَ وَنَصْلٍ قَصَفْتَ
وَقِرْنٍ سَبَقْتَ إِلَيْهِ الوَعيدا	وَمالٍ وَهَبْتَ بِلا مَوْعِدٍ
تَمَنّى الطُّلى أَنْ تَكونَ الغُمودا	بِهَجْرِ سُيوفِكَ أَغْمادَها
تَرى صَدَراً عَنْ وُرودٍ وُرودا	إِلى الهامِ تَصْدُرُ عَنْ مِثْلِهِ
دِ حتّى قَتَلْتَ بِهِنَّ الحَديدا	قَتَلْتَ نُفوسَ العِدى بِالحَدي
وَأَبْقَيْتَ مِمّا مَلَكْتَ النُفودا	فَأَنْفَدْتَ مِنْ عَيْشِهِنَّ البَقاءَ

As if the width of plains he
  Has knowledge of the killing
To teach Hippocrates veins
  Flow in a leap to make a fall
What is in skin comes in pot
  Unworried by falcon's lacking
If you remain in peace O Abu Ali
  Power is almighty God's, then mine

69
He spoke praising Abu Husayn Badr ibn Ammar ibn Ismail al Asadi al Tabarastani. (Trembling da)

Is it a dream or we see some new times
  Is creation renewed in this living shape?
He beams on us, makes us shine by him
  As if the stars had found us in the ascendant
We see by means of Badr and his fathers
  The moon has a birth, full moon has children
We seek his joy by leaving what pleases
  Us for him and so we abandon prostration
A prince, an who is ruled by bounty
  Generosity is stingy when he does not give
He speaks about his bounty with dislike
  As if he had some jealous person's heart
He goes on except in regard to fleeing
  He has power except in regard to profit
As if liberality were part of destiny
  For what you give is where we find joy
Many an attack in war you repelled
  With flexible spear brown with blood
Many a fear seen and blade broke
  Many a lance left splintered in the ruin
Many a gift given without a promise
  Many a hero outdistanced by a threat
In your swords' fright from sheaths
  Necks desired that they be scabbards
To skull they return from the likes of
  It in a return from the drink as a drink
You destroy enemies' souls by steel
  Until you ruin the steel with their souls
You consume what lasts in lives
  Make last what you own by consuming

وبِالمَوْتِ في الحَرْبِ تَبْغي الخُلودا	كَأَنَّكَ بِالفَقْرِ تَبْغي الغِنى
وآيَةُ مَجْدٍ أراها العَبيدا	خَلائِقُ تَهْدي إلى رَبِّها
حَقَرْنا البِحارَ بها والأُسودا	مُهَذَّبَةٌ حُلْوَةٌ مَرَّةٌ
تَغولُ الظُّنونَ وتُنضي القَصيدا	بَعيدٌ على قُرْبِها وَصْفُها
ولَسْتَ لفَقْدِ نَظيرٍ وَحيدا	فأنْتَ وَحيدُ بَني آدَمٍ

(٧٠)

«من المنسرح»

وقال فيه وقد فصده الطبيب فغاص المبضع فوق حقه فأضر به ذلك:

في البُعْدِ ما لا تُكَلِّفُ الإبِلُ	أبْعَدُ نأيَ المَليحَةِ البَخِلُ
مِنْ مَلَلٍ دائِمٍ بها مَلَلُ	مَلولَةٌ ما يَدومُ لَيْسَ لها
سَكْرانُ مِنْ خَمْرِ طَرْفِها ثَمِلُ	كَأَنَّما قَدُّها إذا انْفَتَلَتْ
كأَنَّهُ مِنْ فِراقِها وَجِلُ	يَجْذِبُها تَحْتَ خَصْرِها عَجُزٌ
يَنْفَصِلُ الصَّبْرُ حينَ يَتَّصِلُ	بي حَرُّ شَوْقٍ إلى تَرَشُّفِها
مِعْصَمٌ دائي والفاجِمُ الرَّجِلُ	الثَّغْرُ والنَّحْرُ والمُخَلْخَلُ والْـ
تَعْجِزُ عَنْهُ العَرامِسُ الذُّلُلُ	ومَهْمَهٍ جُبْتُهُ على قَدَمي
مُجْتَزِئٍ، بالظَّلامِ مُشْتَمِلُ	بِصارِمي مُرْتَدٍ، بمَخْبَرَتي
لَمْ تُعْيِني في فِراقِهِ الحِيَلُ	إذا صَديقٌ نَكِرْتُ جانِبَهُ
وفي بِلادٍ مِنْ أُخْتِها بَدَلُ	في سَعَةِ الخافِقينَ مُضْطَرَبٌ
ـارٌ عَنِ الشُّغْلِ بالوَرى شُغُلُ	وفي اعْتِمارِ الأميرِ بَدْرِ بنِ عَمّـ
حاجَةٍ لا يُبْتَدا ولا يُسَلُ	أصْبَحَ مالٌ كَمالِهِ لِذَوي الـ
يَبينُ فيهِ غَمٌّ ولا جَذَلُ	هانَ عَلى قَلْبِهِ الزَّمانُ فَما
يَقْتُلُ مَنْ ما دَنا لَهُ الأجَلُ	يَكادُ مِنْ طاعَةِ الحِمامِ لَهُ
يَفْعَلُ قَبْلَ الفِعالِ يَنْفَعِلُ	يَكادُ مِنْ صِحَّةِ العَزيمَةِ ما
كَأَنَّهُ بِالذَّكاءِ مُكْتَحِلُ	تُعْرَفُ في عَيْنِهِ حَقائِقُهُ

As if you want wealth from poverty
    Desired immortality from death in battle
A nature leading one to its Lord
    A sign of glory shown to the slaves
He is sincere, sweet and bitter
    We scorned the seas and lions in him
Description is far spite of nearness
    Thoughts bewildered, seeker worn out
For you are unique of Adam's sons
    But you are not lonely for loss of an equal

70
He spoke praising Badr ibn Ammar ibn Ismail and he had just been taken ill. So the surgeon bled but the scalpel went beyond its mark and he suffered from it.
(Flowing lu)

Farthest from beauty is stinginess
    In distance which no camel undertakes
Patient of what lasts but is not hers
    The weariness of lasting weariness in her
As if her outline as she turns were
    Drunk with her eye's intoxicating wine
Buttocks pull on her below the waist
    As if they were trembling at her going
I find love's heat sucking her lips
    Patience leaves me if it is lasting
Lips, breasts, ankles, wrists
    Are my sickness and the black curls
Many a desert I crossed on two feet
    A trained, strong camel perished in it
With my sword girded by experience
    Rewarding me enveloped in darkness
A friend whose favors I rejected
    Changes did not worry me at his loss
Coming, going at dawn and sunset
    Changes of cities from their kindred
Visiting the Amir Badr in Ammar
    Employment apart from work for men
Wealth himself, as his wealth is
    For one in need without hint or asking
The times are easy on his heart
    Neither grief nor frivolity show in it
Due to death's slavery to him he
    May destroy one whose end is not yet
Due to his will's power almost what
    He does is done before he finishes it
His qualities known by his eye
    As it he had anointed it with wisdom

عَلَيْهِ مِنها أخافُ يَشْتَعِلُ	أشْفِقُ عِنْدَ اتِّقادِ فِكرَتِهِ
بالهَرَبِ استَكْبَروا الذي فَعَلوا	أغَرُّ، أعْداؤهُ إذا سَلِموا
أرْبَعُها قَبلَ طَرْفِها تَصِلُ	يُقبِلُهُمْ وَجْهَ كُلِّ سابِحَةٍ
تَكونُ مِثْلَيْ عَسيبِها الخُصَلُ	جَرْداءَ مِلْءِ الحِزامِ مُجفِرَةٍ
أو أقبَلَتْ قلتَ ما لها كَفَلُ	إنْ أدْبَرَتْ قُلْتَ لا تَليلَ لها
كَأنّما في فُؤادِها وَهَلُ	والطَّعنُ شَزْرٌ والأرضُ واجِفَةٌ
يَصْبُغُ خَدَّ الخَريدَةِ الخَجَلُ	قَدْ صَبَغَتْ خَدَّها الدِّماءُ كما
بأدْمُعٍ ما تَسُحُّها مُقَلُ	والخَيْلُ تَبْكي جُلودُها عَرَقاً
كَأنّما كلُّ سَبْسَبٍ جَبَلُ	سارٍ ولا قَفْرَ مِنْ مَواكِبِهِ
شِدَّةُ ما قَدْ تَضايَقَ الأسَلُ	يَمْنَعُهُ أن يُصيبَها مَطَرُّ
لَيْثَ الشَّرى يا حِمامُ يا رَجُلُ	يا بَدْرُ يا بَحْرُ يا غَمامَةُ يا
عِندَكَ في كلِّ مَوْضِعٍ مَثَلُ	إنّ البَنانَ الذي تُقَبِّلُهُ
ما دونَ أعمارِهِمْ فَقَدْ بَخِلوا	إنّكَ مِنْ مَعْشَرٍ إذا وَهَبوا
قاماتُهُمْ في تَمامِ ما اعتَقَلوا	قُلوبُهُمْ في مَضاءِ ما امتَشَقوا
قَواضِبُ الهِنْدِ والقَنا الذُّبُلُ	أنتَ نَقيضُ اسمِهِ إذا اختَلَفَتْ
نَّكَ في حَوْمَةِ الوَغى زُحَلُ	أنتَ لَعَمري البَدْرُ المُنيرُ ولكِ
وبَلدَةٍ لَسْتَ حَلَّيها عُطُلُ	كَتيبَةٍ لَسْتَ رَبَّها نَفَلُ
حتى اشتَكَتْكَ الرِّكابُ والسُّبُلُ	قَصَدْتُ مِنْ شَرْقِها ومَغْرِبها
قدْ وَفَدَتْ تَجتَديكَها العِلَلُ	لم تُبقِ إلّا قَليلَ عافِيَةٍ
آسٍ جَبانٍ ومِبْضَعٌ بَطَلُ	عُذرُ المَلومينَ فيكَ أنّهُما
فَما دَرى كيفَ يُقطَعُ الأمَلُ	مَدَدْتَ في راحَةِ الطَّبيبِ يَداً
فَرُبَّما ضَرَّ ظَهْرَها القُبَلُ	إنْ يَكُنِ البَضْعُ ضَرَّ باطِنَها
يَشُقّ في عِرْقِ جَودِها العَذَلُ	يَشُقُّ في عِرْقِها الفِصادُ ولا
كَأنَّهُ مِنْ حَذاقَةٍ عَجِلُ	خامَرَهُ إذ مَدَدْتَها جَزَعٌ
غَيْرَ اجتِهادٍ، لأمِّهِ الهَبَلُ	جازَ حُدودَ اجتِهادِهِ فأتى
طَبْعٌ وعِندَ التَّعَمُّقِ الزَّلَلُ	أبْلَغُ ما يُطلَبُ النَّجاحُ بِهِ الـ

I tremble at kindling of his ideas
    For by it I fear he'll burst into flames
A noble chief, his foes yielding to
    Flight want to boast of what they do
He turns a fast horse toward them
    Its four legs appear before the eyes
Short hair, filling girth with belly
    The tail longer than the tail bone
She turns her back, no neck
    Faces forward, you'd say no rump
Lance thrusts twist, earth shakes
    Terror seems stricken in her heart
Blood already stains her cheek
    As shame stains a maiden's cheek
Horses weep, their skins sweat
    With tears the eyes do not let fail
He went, no plain left for army
    As if flat land were all mountains
Lest rain should touch an attack
    Will guard, so thick lances interlace
You are full moon, O sea, O cloud
    O lion of Shara, O a death, O a man!
Truly fingers are what ponder him
    By you proverbs grow in every place
You are of folks who making gifts
    Find all short of their life stinginess
Their hearts edges soon drawn
    Their body's height a couched lance
You disprove your name when
    Indian sword and pliant spear argue
You, by my life, shine as Badr yet
    In battles' uproar are dark as Zuhal
An army is booty if you rule not
    Land has no ornament without you
You are sought from east and west
    Till beasts and roads complain of you
You keep nothing but good health
    Illness would be sent if begged of you
Excuse for your two accidents is
    The coward doctor and brave lances
You offered gifts to leech's palm
    Hope did not know how to make cut
If treatment harms the inside of it
    Often kisses oppressed the outside
Bloodletting tore open a vein but
    Censure cannot split bounty's flow
Fear made him slip as you yield
    As if he hurried due to his training
He strove to a limit and arrived
    Without success:let his mother weep
Easy success is natural but
    In deep matters there's many a slip

(٧١)

«من الوافر»

يمدحه أيضًا:

بَقائي شاءَ لَيسَ هُمُ ارْتِحالا	وحُسْنَ الصَّبرِ زَمّوا لا الجِمالا
تَوَلَّوْا بَغْتَةً فكأنَّ بَيْناً	تَهَيَّبَني ففاجأني اغْتيالا
فكانَ مَسيرُ عيسِهمُ ذَميلاً	وسَيْرُ الدَّمعِ إثْرَهُمُ انهِمالا
كأنَّ العِيسَ كانتْ فَوْقَ جَفني	مُناخاتٍ فلمّا ثُرْنَ سالا
وحَجَّبتِ النَّوى الظَّبياتِ عَني	فَساعَدَتِ البَراقِعَ والحِجالا
لَبِسْنَ الوَشْيَ لا مُتَجَمِّلاتٍ	ولكنْ كَيْ يَصُنَّ بهِ الجَمالا
وضَفَّرْنَ الغَدائِرَ لا لحُسْنٍ	ولكنْ خِفْنَ في الشَّعرِ الضَّلالا
بجسمي مَنْ بَرَتْهُ فَلوْ أصارَتْ	وشاحي ثَقْبَ لُؤلُؤةٍ لجالا
ولوْ لا أنَّني في غَيرِ نَوْمٍ	لَكُنْتُ أظُنّني مِنّي خَيالا
بَدَتْ قَمَراً ومالَتْ خُوطَ بانٍ	وفاحَتْ عَنبَراً ورَنَتْ غَزالا
وحارَتْ في الحُكومَةِ ثمَّ أَبْدَتْ	لنا مِنْ حُسنِ قامَتِها اعتِدالا
كأنَّ الحُزنَ مَشغوفٌ بقَلبي	فَساعةَ هجرِها يَجِدُ الوِصالا
كذا الدُّنيا على مَن كانَ قَبْلي	صُروفٌ لم يُدِمْنَ عَلَيهِ حالا
أشدُّ الغَمِّ عندي في سُرورٍ	تَيَقَّنَ عَنهُ صاحِبُهُ انْتِقالا
ألِفْتُ تَرَحُّلي وجَعَلْتُ أرضي	قُوودي والعُزَيْرِيَّ الجِلالا
فما حاوَلْتُ في أرضٍ مُقاماً	ولا أزْمَعْتُ عَنْ أرضٍ زَوالا
على قَلَقٍ كأنَّ الرّيحَ تحتي	أُوَجِّهُها جَنوباً أو شَمالا
إلى البَدْرِ بنِ عَمّارِ الذي لَم	يكُنْ في غُرّةِ الشَّهرِ الهِلالا
ولم يَعْظُمْ لنَقْصٍ كانَ فيهِ	ولم يَزَلِ الأميرُ ولنْ يَزالا
بلا مِثْلٍ وإنْ أَبْصَرْتَ فيهِ	لكلِّ مُغَيَّبٍ حَسَنٍ مِثالا
إرِثٍ لَها إنَّها بِما مَلَكَتْ	وبالذي قَدْ أسَلْتَ تَنْهَمِلُ
مِثْلُكَ يا بَدْرُ لا يَكونُ ولا	تَصْلُحُ إلّا لِمِثلِكَ الدُّوَلُ

Weep for it since with what it had
    And what you shed came huge rain
You have no like O Badr nor is
    Rule sound except by such as you

71
He spoke also praising him.
(Exuberant la)

My survival wishes they'd not saddle
    But bridle painful beauty, not the camel.
They turned suddenly as if in parting
    Scared me surprised by that deception
Their camels' gait is easy paced
    But tears flow in their tracks strongly
As if the beast are upon my eyelids
    Kneeling, then they rise and tears flow
Parting screens gazelle maids from
    Me to assist the veil and the curtains
They wear brocade not to beautify
    But to protect their beauty with that
They plait braids not as ornament
    But for fear hair should go straying
By my body! someone wastes it as
    My sash holds pearl's string it's loose
If I were other than asleep I would
    Spend nights thinking I was a dream
She is a moon bent as willow to
    Spread amber, look with fawn's eyes
She came in the dark and showed
    To us an equal beauty in her light
Grief is madly in love with my heart
    As soon as she goes it finds embrace
So the world was for those before
    Misfortune did not last in mutability
Perplexity strongest for me in joy
    Its master was sure of this variability
I am used to travel and make earth
    My saddle, my Gurair camel is strong
I want no resting place on earth
    I have not decided to stop any place
On a swaying one as winds rush
    I steer to the south or to the north
To full moon Ibn 'Ammar who is
    No crescent for first of the month
He increases not from decrease
    He remains as Amir, will not cease
Without compare even if you see
    Him as model for every hid beauty

حُسامُ المُتَّقي أيّامَ صالا	حُسامٌ لابنِ رائِقٍ المُرَجّى
بَني أسَدٍ إذا دَعَـوا النِّزالا	سِنانٌ في قَناةِ بَني مَعَدٍّ
ومَقْـدِرَةً ومَحْمِيـةً وآلا	أعَزُّ مُغالِبٍ كفّاً وسَيفاً
وأكرَمُ مُنتَـمٍ عَمّـاً وخالا	وأشرَفُ فاخرٍ نَفساً وقَوماً
على الدّنيـا وأهْليها مُحـالا	يكونُ أخَفَّ إثناءٍ عَلَيـهِ
إذا لم يَتـرُكْ أحَدٌ مَقـالا	ويَبْقى ضِعْفُ ما قَد قيـلَ فيـهِ
مَواضِعَ يَشتَكي البَطَلُ السُّعالا	فيا ابنَ الطّاعِنينَ بكُلّ لَدْنٍ
منَ العَرَبِ الأسافِلِ والقِلالا	ويا ابنَ الضّارِبينَ بكُلّ عَضْبٍ
ومَن ذا يَحمَـدُ الـدّاءَ العُضـالا	أرى المُتَشاعِرينَ غَرُّوا بذَمّي
يَجِدْ مُـرّاً بـهِ المـاءَ الزُّلالا	ومَنْ يَكُ ذا فَمٍ مُـرٍّ مَريض
فقُلتُ نَعَمْ إذا شِئتُ استِفالا	وقالوا هَـلْ يُبَلِّغُكَ الثَّرَيّا؟
وبِيضَ الهِنـدِ والسُّمـرَ الطِّوالا	هـوَ المُفني المَذاكي والأعـادي
على حَـيٍّ تُصَبِّحُـهُ ثِقـالا	وقائدُهـا مُسَـوَّمَةً خِفافـاً
كأنّ على عَوامِلِها ذُبـالا	جَوائِـلَ بالقُنيّ مُثَقَّفـاتٍ
يَفِئْـنَ لِـوَطْءِ أرْجُلِهـا رِمـالا	إذا وَطِئَـتْ بأَيديها صُخـوراً
ولا لـكَ في سُـؤالِكَ لا ألَا لا	جَوابُ مُسائِلي ألَـهُ نَظيـرٌ؟
تَعُـدَّ رَجاءهـا إيّـاكَ مَـالا	لَقَـد أمِنَـتْ بـكَ الإعـدامَ نَفسٌ
غَدَتْ أوجالُها فيها وِجالا	وقد وَجِلَـتْ قُلوبٌ منكَ حتى
تُعَلِّمُهُـمْ عَلَيكَ بـهِ الدّلالا	سُرورُكَ أن تَسُرَّ النّـاسَ طُـرّاً
وإنْ سَكَتُوا سَألْتَهُمُ السُّؤالا	إذا سـألُوا شَكَـرْتَهُمْ عَلَيـهِ
يُنيـلُ المُسـتَماحَ بـأنْ يُنـالا	وأسعَدُ مَـنْ رأينا مُستَميـحٍ
فِراقَ القَوْسِ ما لا قَـى الرّجـالا	يُفارِقُ سَهمُكَ الرّجـلَ المُلاقـى
كأنّ الرّيشَ يَطْلِبُ النِّصـالا	فما تَقِـفُ السِّهـامُ على قَـرارٍ
وجـاوَزْتَ العُلـوَّ فَمـا تُعَـالى	سَبَقْـتَ السّابقِينَ فَما تُجارَى
لَما صَلَـحَ العِبـادُ لَـهُ شِمـالا	وأُقْسِـمُ لـوْ صَلَحْتَ يَميـنَ شَيءٍ
وإنْ طَلَعَـتْ كَواكِبُها خِصالا	أقَلِّبُ مِنـكَ طَرْفي في سَمـاءٍ

He is Ibn Raiq's sword who is hope
    For al Muttaqi's sword in day of battle
Head on Banu Maadd's spear he is
    Banu Asad's if they call for an attack
Strong victor in hand and sword
    Power in protection and family use
High in honor himself and his folk
    Noblest in father's and mother's line
Most worthy of praise that is for
    The world and its folk an absurdity
Double remains to be said of him
    When one omitted nothing to report
Son of thrusters by light lances
    In places where heroes feel a cough
Son of strikers by each sharp one
    Among Arabs both on high and low
I see would-be poets rage to blame me
    Who praises sickness and isn't cured?
With a mouth bitter with illness one
    Finds the sweetest water bitter for him
They: Has he put you on Thurayya?
    I say:Yes! if I want to come down there
He the destroyer, war horse, angry
    Indian steel and the long dark lances
Their leader who teaches briskness
    To the tribe he overwhelms at dawn
Horses roaming with upright spears
    On their shafts are the flaming wicks
If they tread rocks with forelegs
    They turn to sand with the hindlegs
Reply to one asking for an equal
    No! nor to you if you ask, not at all!
All are safe from poverty by you
    They count hope in you as wealth
Some hearts wary of you until
    Their fear becomes cowardice now
Your joy to make all men happy
    You teach familiarity with you by it
If they beg you thank them for it
    If they are silent you make them ask
Happiest he who sees us as seekers
    To gain a request he can nobly bestow
Your arrow dispatches one it meets
    As from bow released that hits no man
The arrows never remain at rest
    The feathers seem to seek the points
You get ahead of winners,no runner
    You cross the heights and don't climb
I swear if you were on the right
    Men would not be fit for the left of it
I am held by as my eye by heaven
    If it rises its stars are the influences

وأعجبُ كيفَ قَدَرْتَ تنشا وقد أُعطيتَ في المهدِ الكَمالا

(٧٢)

«من الرَّمل»

وقال فيه ارتجالاً وهو على الشراب وقد
صفت الفاكهة والنرجس:

إنّما بَدرُ بنُ عَمّارِ سَحابُ هَطِلٌ فيهِ ثَوابٌ وعِقابُ
إنّما بَدرٌ رَزايا وعَطايا ومَنايا وطِعانٌ وضِرابُ
ما يُجيلُ الطَّرفَ إلّا حَمِدَتْهُ جُهدَها الأيدي وذَمَّتْهُ الرِّقابُ
ما بهِ قَتلُ أعاديهِ ولكنْ يتَّقي إخلافَ ما ترجو الذئابُ
فَلَهُ هَيبَةُ مَن لا يُتَرَجَّى ولَهُ جُودٌ مُرَجَّى لا يُهابُ
طاعنُ الفرسانِ في الأحداقِ شزراً وعَجاجُ الحربِ للشمسِ نِقابُ
باعثُ النَّفسِ على الهَولِ الذي لَيْـ ـسَ لنَفسٍ وَقَعَتْ فيهِ إيابُ
بأبي ريحُكَ لا نَرْجِسُنا ذا وأحاديثُكَ لا هذا الشَّرابُ
ليسَ بالمُنكَرِ إنْ بَرَزْتَ سَبَقاً، غيرُ مدفوعٍ عن السَّبقِ العِرابُ

(٧٣)

«من الوافر»

خرج بدر بن عمار إلى أسد فهرب الأسد منه، وكان قد
خرج قبله إلى أسد آخر فهاجه عن بقرة افترسها بعد أن شبع
ونقل فوئب إلى كفل سرمه فأعجله عن استلال سيفه فضربه
بالسوط ودار به الجيش، فقال أبوالطيب:

في الخَدِّ أنْ عَزَمَ الخَليطُ رَحيلا مَطرٌ تَزيدُ بهِ الخُدودُ مُحولا
يا نَظرةً نَفَتِ الرُّقادَ وغادَرَتْ في حَدِّ قَلبي ما حَييتُ فُلولا
كانَتْ مِنَ الكَحلاءِ سُؤلي إنّما أجَلي تَمَثَّلَ في فُؤادي سُولا
أجدُ الجَفاءَ على سِواكِ مُروءةً والصَّبرَ إلّا في نَواكِ جَميلا

I am amazed, how could you grow
    You were given perfection in the cradle

72
He spoke about him impromptu while he was drinking and fruits were set and narcissus displayed.
(Exuberant bu)

Truly Badr ibn Ammar is a thundercloud
    A downpour of reward and of punishment
Truly Badr is misfortune and redress
    And the fates and thrusting and slashing
He gives no glances unless in praise
    In the huge gifts while the necks blame him
The death of his foes is not his worry
    He guards against chagrin for the wolves
He has fear for one who fears him not
    His bounty hoped for and never dreaded
He pierces horsemen's eyes right and
    Left, the battle dust is veil for the sunlight
Dispatcher of himself to terror with
    No return for a soul that falls therein
My father! your perfume not narcissus
    Your stories are not those of this drinking
No disapproval if you come out ahead
    No prohibition for the Arab horse to win

73
He spoke describing a lion hunt.
(Perfect la)

On cheeks as the tribe decides to go
    A rain by which cheeks increase sterility
O glance that destroys sleep, leaves
    On heart's edge what I feel as dullness
It had some collyrium of my need but
    My death depicted my heart's desire
I find avoiding others than you brave
    Patience fine except in your absence

وَأَرى تَدَلُّلَكِ الكَثيرَ مُحَبَّباً   وَأَرى قَليلَ تَدَلُّلٍ مَمْلولا
تَشْكو رَوادِفُكِ المَطِيَّةَ فَوْقَها   شَكْوى الَّتي وَجَدَتْ هَواكِ دَخيلا
وَيُعيرُني جَذْبُ الزِّمامِ لِقَلْبِها   فَمَها إِلَيْكِ كَطالِبٍ تَقْبيلا
حَدَقُ الحِسانِ مِنَ الغَواني هِجْنَ لي   يَوْمَ الفِراقِ صَبابَةً وَغَليلا
حَدَقٌ يُذِمَّ مِنَ القَواتِلِ غَيرَها   بَدْرُ بْنُ عَمّارِ بْنِ إِسْماعيلا
أَلفارِجُ الكَرْبَ العِظامَ بِمِثْلِها   وَالتّارِكُ المَلِكَ العَزيزَ ذَليلا
مَحِكٌ إِذا مَطَلَ الغَريمُ بِدَيْنِهِ   جَعَلَ الحُسامَ بِما أَرادَ كَفيلا
نَطِقٌ إِذا حَطَّ الكَلامُ لِثامَهُ   أَعْطى بِمَنْطِقِهِ القُلوبَ عُقولا
أَعْدى الزَّمانَ سَخاؤُهُ فَسَخا بِهِ   وَلَقَدْ يَكونُ بِهِ الزَّمانُ بَخيلا
وَكَأَنَّ بَرْقاً في مُتونِ غَمامَةٍ   هِنْدِيُّهُ في كَفِّهِ مَسْلولا
وَمَحَلُّ قائِمِهِ يَسيلُ مَواهِباً   لَوْ كُنَّ سَيْلاً ما وَجَدْنَ مَسيلا
رَقَّتْ مَضارِبُهُ فَهُنَّ كَأَنَّما   يُبْدينَ مِنْ عِشْقِ الرِّقابِ نُحولا
أُمُعَفِّرَ اللَّيْثِ الهِزَبْرِ بِسَوْطِهِ   لِمَنِ اِدَّخَرْتَ الصّارِمَ المَصْقولا
وَقَعَتْ عَلى الأُرْدُنَّ مِنْهُ بَلِيَّةٌ   نَضِّدَتْ بِها هامَ الرِّفاقِ تُلولا
وَرَدٌ إِذا وَرَدَ البُحَيْرَةَ شارِباً   وَرَدَ الفُراتَ زَئيرُهُ وَالنّيلا
مُتَخَضِّبٌ بِدَمِ الفَوارِسِ لابِسٌ   في غيلِهِ مِنْ لِبْدَتَيْهِ غيلا
ما قوبِلَتْ عَيْناهُ إِلّا ظُنَّتا   تَحْتَ الدُّجى نارَ الفَريقِ حُلولا
في وَحْدَةِ الرُّهْبانِ إِلّا أَنَّهُ   لا يَعْرِفُ التَّحْريمَ وَالتَّحْليلا
يَطَأُ الثَّرى مُتَرَفِّقاً مِنْ تيهِهِ   فَكَأَنَّهُ آسٍ يَجُسُّ عَليلا
وَيَرُدُّ عُفْرَتَهُ إِلى يافوخِهِ   حَتّى تَصيرَ لِرَأْسِهِ إِكْليلا
وَتَظُنُّهُ مِمّا يُزَمْجِرُ نَفْسُهُ   عَنْها لِشِدَّةِ غَيْظِهِ مَشْغولا
قَصَرَتْ مَخافَتُهُ الخُطى فَكَأَنَّما   رَكِبَ الكَمِيُّ جَوادَهُ مَشْكولا
أَلْقى فَريسَتَهُ وَبَرْبَرَ دونَها   وَقَرُبْتَ قُرْبَ خالِهِ تَطْفيلا
فَتَشابَهَ الخُلْقانِ في إِقْدامِهِ   وَتَخالَفا في بَذْلِكَ المَأْكولا
أَسَدٌ يَرى عُضْوَيْهِ فيكَ كِلَيْهِما   مَتْناً أَزَلَّ وَساعِداً مَفْتولا

I saw your many tricks as loveable
    And I saw a little coquetry as wearying
The camel groans at your buttocks
    Complaint that finds your love intrusive
A bridle on her head makes me
    Envy her mouth turning to you for a kiss
A kind eye among maids teases me
    On parting day with passion and thirst
He guards from killers other than her
    This eye, Badr ibn Ammar ibn Ismail
He dispels great care like she does
    And leaves greatest kingdoms abased
Steadfast if debtors delay his debt
    He has a sword to pledge his intent
Eloquent as speech puts down evil
    He gives a wise heart in his discourse
His bounty moves time so it gives
    Through him, yet time is stingy of him
As if lightning on cloud's back were
    Indian steel unsheathed in his hand
A place for its hilt flows with gifts
    If they were a stream it hasn't a bed
Its edges thin seem to display
    Emaciation by their love of necks
O a fierce lion hits dirt by his whip
    For whom do you keep a keen sword?
Misfortune befalls Jordan with it
    It piles a skull mound in a company
A red one reddens Buhaira sipping
    Its roar reaches Euphrates and the Nile
Stained with rider's blood, having
    In its lair dense thickets as its mane
Its eyes not met without seeming
    In darkness as part of a traveler's fire
In a monk's solitude except it does
    Not know what is lawful or forbidden
It trod earth confident in its pride
    Like the doctor probing an illness
It erects forelocks on its skulltop
    Till they become a crown for its head
You think since it echoes itself
    It attacks itself in its fierce rage
In fear they shorten step as if
    Armored warrior hobbled his horse
It throws down prey and roars
    You come near as it suspects you
For you are like in bold nature
    Different in lavishing nourishment
A lion sees his legs in you, both
    Slim at the back, muscled in front
In a fine limbed one's saddle
    Fast, unique rejecting comparison

في سَرْجٍ ظامِئَةِ الفُصوصِ طِمِرَّةٍ … يَأْبي تَفَرُّدُها لَها التَّمثيلا
نَيّالَةِ الطَّلِباتِ لَوْلا أنّها … تُعْطي مَكانَ لِجامِها ما نِيلا
تَنْدى سَوالِفُها إذا استَحْضَرْتَها … ويُظَنُّ عَقْدُ عِنانِها مَحْلولا
ما زالَ يَجْمَعُ نَفْسَهُ في زَوْرِهِ … حتى حَسِبْتَ العَرْضَ منهُ الطّولا
ويَدُقُّ بالصَّدْرِ الحِجارَ كَأنَّهُ … يَعْيا إلى ما في الحَضيضِ سَبيلا
وكَأَنَّهُ غَرَّتْهُ عَيْنٌ فادَّنى … لا يُبْصِرُ الخَطْبَ الجَليلَ جَليلا
أَنْفُ الكَريمِ مِنَ الدَّنِيئَةِ تارِكٌ … في عَيْنِهِ العَدَدَ الكَثيرَ قَليلا
والعارُ مَضَّاضٌ ولَيْسَ بِخائِفٍ … مِنْ حَتْفِهِ مَنْ خافَ مِمّا قيلا
سَبَقَ اللِّقاءَ كَهُ بوَثْبَةِ هاجِمٍ … لَوْ لَمْ تُصادِمْهُ لَجازَكَ مِيلا
خَذَلَتْهُ قُوَّتُهُ وقَدْ كافَحْتَهُ … فاسْتَنْصَرَ التَّسليمَ والتَّجْديلا
قَبَضَتْ مَنِيَّتُهُ يَدَيْهِ وعُنْقَهُ … فَكَأنَّما صادَفْتَهُ مَغْلولا
سَمِعَ ابنُ عَمَّتِهِ بهِ وبِحالِهِ … فَنَجا يُهَرْوِلُ أمسِ منكَ مَهولا
وأَمَرُّ مِمّا فَرَّ منهُ فِرارُهُ … وكَقَتْلِهِ أَنْ لا يَموتَ قَتيلا
تَلِفُ الذي اتَّخَذَ الجَراءَةَ خُلَّةً … وعَظَ الذي اتَّخَذَ الفِرارَ خَليلا
لَوْ كانَ عِلْمُكَ بالإلَهِ مُقَسَّماً … في النّاسِ ما بَعَثَ الإلَهُ رَسولا
لَوْ كانَ لَفْظُكَ فيهم ما أَنْزَلَ الـ … فُرْقانَ والتَّوْراةَ والإنْجيلا
لَوْ كانَ ما تُعْطيهِم من قبلِ أنْ … تُعْطِيَهِم لَمْ يَعْرِفوا التَّأْميلا
فَلَقَدْ عُرِفْتَ وما عُرِفَتْ حَقيقَةٌ … ولَقَدْ جُهِلْتَ وما جُهِلَتْ خُمولا
نَطَقَتْ بسُؤْدُدِكَ الحَمامُ تَغَنِّياً … وبما تُجَشِّمُها الجِيادُ صَهيلا
ما كلُّ مَنْ طَلَبَ المَعاليَ نافِذاً … فيها ولا كلُّ الرِّجالِ فُحولا

(٧٤)

«من الطويل»

ورد كتاب من ابن رائق على بدر بإضافة الساحل إلى عمله، فقال أبو الطيب:

تُهَنَّا بِصورٍ أمْ نُهَنِّئُها بِكا … وقُلْ للذي صُوِّرَ وأنْتَضَ لَهُ لَكا

She gets to a goal, if she won't
    Yield bridle's place it's untouched
Her neck sweats if you spur her
    The bridle's knot seems to be loose
The lion contracts to its chest
    Until you see its width is as its length
It beats on rock with its breast
    It wants a way into the mountain
As if its eye tricked as it came
    Not seeing great calamity near
Noble pride is prone to think
    The greatest numbers smallest
Shame is painful but no fear
    Of death for one dreading talk
It hopes to meet with a leap
    But if you don't hit it rushes past
Strength deserts as rise up
    It tries to win by swerving aside
Death grips by legs and neck
    As if it's caught in an iron collar
Its cousin hears of its fate and
    Escapes in flight afraid of you
Its rout more bitter than fear
    Of a death not dying fighting
Ruin with bravery as friend
    Exhorts one with flight as help
If your love of God were in
    Men, God had sent no Messenger
If your words were with them
    Then no Quran, Torah, Gospels
If your gifts existed before you
    Gave they'd not known a hope
You were known yet not so
    Unknown but yet not ignored
Fate speaks by your decree as
    A fine horse goes with a whinny
Not all who seek heights get up
    To them, not every man a stallion

74
**A letter came from
Ibn Raiq
authorizing Badr
to add the coastal regions
to his command.
So he spoke.
(Long ka)**

Do you take Tyre or do we for your sake?
    Tyre is small to you for you are one of his

حُبيتَ بِهِ إلّا إلى جَنبِ قَدرِكا	ومـا صَغُـرَ الأُردُنّ والسّاحِـلُ الّـذي
نُفوسٌ لَسارَ الشّرقُ والغَربُ نَحوَكا	تَحاسَـدَتِ البُلـدانُ حتى لَـو أنّها
ولَـوْ أنّـهُ ذو مُقْلَـةٍ وفَـمٍ بَكى	وأصْبَـحَ مِصْـرٌ لا تكـونُ أمـيـرَهُ

(٧٥)

«من الوافر»

نظر إلى ثياب مطوية فسأل عنها فقيل
هي خلع الولاية، وكان أبو الطيب
عند وصولها عليلا فقال:

عَدانـي أنْ أراكَ بهـا اعتِـلالي	أرَى حُلَـلاً مُطَـوَّاةً حِسَـانـاً
أتطـوي مـا عَلَيـكَ مِـن الجَمـالِ	وهَبْـكَ طَوَيتَها وخرَجـتَ عنها
مَـعَ الأولى بجسمِكَ في قِتالِ	لقَـدْ ظَلَّـتْ أواخِرُهـا الأعـالي
كـأنّ عَليـكَ أفئِـدَةَ الرّجـالِ	تلاحِظُـكَ العُيـونُ وأنـتَ فيهـا
فقَـدْ أحصَيْـتُ حَبّـاتِ الرّمـالِ	متـى أحصَيْـتُ فَضلَكَ في كَـلامٍ
وأنـتَ لهـا النّهايـةُ في الكَمـالِ	وإنّ بهـا وإنْ بـهِ لَنَقْصـاً

(٧٦)

«من الكامل»

سار بدر إلى الساحل ولم يسر أبو الطيب معه ثم
بلغه أن ابن كروس الأعور كتب إلى بدر يقول لـه:
إن أبا الطيب إنما تخلف عنك رغبة بنفسه عن المسير
معك. ولما عاد بدر إلى طبرية ضربت له قباب عليها
أمثلة من تصاوير، فقال أبو الطيب:

وألَـذُّ شَكْـوى عاشِـقٍ مـا أعْلَنـا	الحُـبُّ مـا مَنَـعَ الكَـلامَ الألْسُـنـا
من غيرِ جُـرمٍ واصِلـي صِلَـةَ الضّنى	ليـتَ الحَبيـبَ الهـاجـري هَجْـرَ الكَـرى

Not small are Jordan and the coasts
    Given by him except alongside your worth
Lands envy each other if they have souls
    The east and west would travel to you now
And if a city were to lose its prince
    It would lament as if it had eyes and mouth

75
**He came to him
and saw
an official robe
folded before him.
He had worn it
and put it aside
but Abu Tayyib
was not present
due to an illness
that befell him.
(Exuberant na)**

I see the fine garment folded up
    My ills kept me from seeing upon you
Granted you folded it and took it off
    Have you put away what is fine in you?
Is external honors are continually
    In conflict with what is near your body
Eyes look on you when you are in it
    As if the hearts of men were within you
When I told your virtue in words
    It is as if I counted them as sand grains

76
**He spoke
praising him.
And he had gone
to the coast
and then returned to Tiberias.
(Perfect na)**

Love is what denies words to the tongue
    Lover's sweetest sigh is what he declares
I wish a lover who fled with sleep, lost
    Without sin, would come as emaciation now

أَلْوانُنـــا مِمّــا اسْـتَفَعْنَ تَلَوُّنـــا	بِتْنـــا وَلَـوْ عَلِيتْنـــا لَـمْ تَضْـدُرْ مَـا
أَشْفَقْــتُ تَحْـتَــرِقُ الْعَــوَاذِلُ بَيْنَنـــا	وَتَوَقَّــدَتْ أَنْفاسُـــنا حَتـــى لَقَــدْ
نَظَـراً فُـرَادَى بَيْـنَ زَفَـراتٍ ثُنـا	أَفْــدي الْمُوَدَّعَــةَ الَّتــي أَتْبَعْتُهـا
ثُـمّ اعْــتَرَفْتُ بِهــا فَصــارَتْ دَيْدَنَــا	أَنْكَـرْتُ طارِقَـةَ الْحَــوادِثِ مَـرَّةً
فيهـا وَوَقْــتَيِ الضُّحَــى وَالْمَوْهِنــا	وَقَطَعْتُ في الدُّنْيـا الفَـلا وَرَكائِبي
وَبَلَغْـتُ مِــنْ بَــدْرِ بـنِ عَمّــارِ الْمُنَى	فَوَقَفْـتُ مِنْهـا حَيْـثُ أَوْقَفَنـي النَّـدَى
عَنْـهُ وَلَـوْ كَــانَ الوِعــاءُ الأَزْمُنــا	لأَبـي الْحُسَيْـنِ حَــدّاً يَضيـقُ وِعـاؤُهُ
وَنَهــى الجَبــانَ حَديثُهــا أَنْ يَجْبُنــا	وَشَجاعَـةً أَغْنــاهُ عَنْهــا ذِكْرُهــا
مــا كَــرَّ قَطُّ وَهَـلْ يَكُــرُّ وَما انْثَنى	نِيطَـتْ حَمائِلُــهُ بِعـاتِـقِ مِحْــرَبِ
مُتَخَــوِّفٍ مِــنْ خَلْفِــهِ أَنْ يُطْعَنــا	فَكَأنَّــهُ وَالطَّعْــنُ مِــنْ قُدّامِــهِ
فَقَضَــى عَلى غَيْـبِ الأُمــورِ تَيَقُّنــا	نَفَــتِ النَّوهَـمَ عَنْــهُ جِــدَّةُ ذِهْنِهِ
فَيَظَــلُّ في خَلَواتِـــهِ مُتَكَفِّنَــا	يَتَفَــزَّعُ الجَبّــارُ مِــنْ بَغَتاتِــهِ
واسْتَقْرَبَ الأَقْصَى فَثَـمَّ لَـهُ هُنَـا	أَمْضى إرادَتَـهُ فَسَـوْفَ لَــهُ قَــدْ
ثَوْبــاً أَخَــفَّ مِــنَ الْحَريــرِ وَأَلْيَنــا	يَجِـدُ الْحَديـدَ عَلى بَضاضَــةِ جِلْدِهِ
فَقْـدُ السُّيُوفِ الفاقِــداتِ الأَجْفُنــا	وَأَمَـرُّ مِــنْ فَقْــدِ الأَحِبَّــةِ عِنْــدَهُ
يَوْمــاً وَلا الإِحْسـانَ أَنْ لا يُحْسِنــا	لا يَسْتَكِــنَّ الرُّعْــبُ بَيْـنَ ضُلُوعِـهِ
فَكَأَنَّ مــا سَيَكُــونُ فيــهِ دُونـا	مُسْتَنْبِــطٌ مِــنْ عِلْمِــهِ مـا في غَــدِ
مِثْـلَ الَّــذي الأَفْــلاكُ فيــهِ وَالدُّنى	تَتَقــاصَــرُ الأَفْهــامُ عَــنْ إدْراكِــهِ
مَــنْ لَيْـسَ مِـنْ قَتْــلاهُ مِـنْ طُلَقائِـهِ	مَــنْ لَيْــسَ مِــنْ دانٍ مِمَّــنْ حَيَّنـا
قَفَلْـتَ إلَيْهـا وَحْشَـةً مِــنْ عِنْدِنـا	لَمَّـا قَفَلْــتَ مِــنَ السَّواحِــلِ نَحْوَنا
إلّا أَقــامَ بِــهِ الشَّــذا مُسْــتَوْطِنا	أَرِجَ الطَّريــقِ فَمــا مَــرَرْتَ بِمَوْضِعٍ
مَــدَّتْ مُحَيِّيَــةً إلَيْــكَ الأَغْصُنــا	لَــوْ تَعْقِــلُ الشَّجَــرُ الَّتــي قابَلْتَها
شَـوْقٌ بِهـا فَأَدَرْنَ فيــكَ الأَعْيُنــا	سَلَكَــتْ تَماثيــلُ القِبــابِ الجِــنَّ مِـن
لَــوْ لا حَيــاءٌ عاقَهــا رَقَصَــتْ بِنـا	طَرِبَــتْ مَراكِبُنــا فَخِلْنــا أَنَّهــا
يَخْبِبْـنَ بِالحَلَــقِ الْمُضاعَـفِ وَالقَنـا	أَقْبَلَــتْ تَبْسِــمُ وَالجِيــادُ عَوابِــسٌ
لَــوْ تَبْتَغــي عَنَقــاً عَلَيْــهِ لأَمْكَنــا	عَقَــدَتْ سَنابِكُهــا عَلَيْهــا عِثْيَــراً

We parted, if you see us you won't know
    Our color among those who have grown pale
Our souls are kindled so that indeed I
    Fear the gossips will burn up between us
I'm ransom for the departed as I follow
    With a single glance between double sighs
I knew not the bad event that one time
    But I recognized it as they did come often
I traveled world deserts and my camel
    Was there and my time dawn and midnight
I stayed where bounty made me stop
    I gained my reward from Badr ibn Ammar
Abu Husayn's vessel too small for gifts
    Even if the vessels are those of the times
Bravery! memory is content with him
    Its fame forbids cowards to be cowards
His sword hangs at his sturdy shoulder
    He never retakes, how return and not turn?
As if his thrusting on in front of him
    Were in fear lest he be hit from behind
His sharp wit cancels the uncertainty
    He judges hid matters with resoluteness
The strong fear his unforeseen attack
    He is ever in the shroud in his solitude
He steels his will, the future is past
    He reflects on what is far and it's near
He finds iron on his skin softness
    A garment lighter than silk and finer
More bitter than beloved's loss for him
    Loss of swords that have lost sheaths
Fear does not settle within his heart
    For the day, nor goodwill doing no good
The future flows from his knowledge
    As if what will be was recorded in that
Understanding falls short of his goal
    As it does what is in heaven and earth
He who is not killed by him is freed
    He who submits not is one he destroys
When you ride from the shore to us
    Desolation goes to it from among us
The way exhales for you pass no spot
    Except a perfume remains settled in it
If trees understood what you bring
    They'd bend their branches to obey
Jinn follow the awning paintings in
    Love of them, they turn an eye to them
Our wagons rejoice as we imagine
    A dance if shame did not hinder them
You come smiling but horses frown
    They trot in double ring mail and spears
The hoofs suspend dust around them
    If you want a fast pace they can do that

146 Diwan al-Mutanabbi

في مَوْقِفٍ بَيْنَ المَنِيَّةِ والمُنى	والأمْرُ أمْرُكَ والقُلُوبُ خَوافِقُ
ورَأيْتُ حتى ما رَأيْتُ مِنَ السَّنى	فَعَجِبْتُ حتى ما عَجِبْتُ مِنَ الظُّبى
في عَسْكَرٍ ومِنَ المَعالي مَعْدِنا	إنّي أراكَ مِنَ المَكارِمِ عَسْكَرا
ولِمَّا تَرَكْتُ مَخافَةَ أنْ تَفْطُنا	فَطَنَ الفُؤادُ لِمَّا أتَيْتُ على النَّوى
لَيْسَ الذي قاسَيْتُ مِنْهُ هَيِّنا	أضْحى فِراقُكَ لي عَلَيْهِ عُقُوبَةً
لِتَخَصَّني بِعَطِيَّةٍ مِنْها أنا	فاغْفِرْ فِدًى لكَ واحْبُني مِنْ بعدها
فالحُرُّ مُمْتَحَنٌ بأوْلادِ الزِّنى	وأنّهُ المُشيرُ عَلَيْكَ في بِضِلَّةٍ
في مجلسٍ أخَذَ الكَلامَ اللَّذْ عَنِّى	وإذا الفتى طَرَحَ الكَلامَ مُعَرِّضا
وعَداوَةُ الشُّعَراءِ بِئْسَ المُقْتَنى	ومَكايدُ السُّفَهاءِ واقِعَةٌ بِهمْ
ضَيْفٌ يَجُرُّ مِنَ النَّدامَةِ ضَيْفَنا	لُعِنَتْ مُقارَنَةُ اللَّئيمِ فإنّها
رُزْءٌ أخَفُّ عليَّ مِنْ أنْ يُوزَنا	غَضَبُ الحَسُودِ إذا لَقيتُكَ راضِيا
مِنْ غَيْرِنا مَعَنا بِفَضْلِكَ مُؤمِنا	أمْسَى الذي أمْسَى بِرَبِّكَ، كافِرا
فأعاضَهاكَ الله كَيْ لا تَحْزَنا	خَلَتِ البِلادُ مِنَ الغَزالةِ لَيْلَها

(٧٧)

«من الكامل»

دخل على بدر يوما فوجده خاليا وقد أمر الغلمان أن يحجبوا الناس عنه ليخلو للشرب، فقال ارتجالا:

هَيْهاتِ لَسْتَ على الحِجابِ بِقادِرِ	أصْبَحْتَ تَأمُرُ بالحِجابِ لِخَلْوَةٍ
لمْ يُحْجَبا لمْ يَحْتَجِبْ عَنْ ناظِرِ	مَنْ كانَ ضَوْءُ جَبينِهِ ونَوالُهُ
وإذا بَطَنْتَ فأنْتَ عَيْنُ الظاهِرِ	فإذا احْتَجَبْتَ فأنْتَ غيرُ مُحَجَّبِ

(٧٨)

«من السريع»

وسقاه بدر ولم يكن له رغبة في الشراب فقال:

لا لِسِوى وُدِّكَ لي ذاكا	لمْ تَرَ مَنْ نادَمْتُ إلاّ كا
أمْسَيْتُ أرْجُوكَ وأخْشاكا	ولا لحُبِّها ولكِنَّني

The command is yours as hearts thrill
　　In a battle between death and reward
Amazed till I wondered not at swords
　　I looked till I could not see the flashing
I see you as an army of generosity
　　Amidst an army and mine of eminence
The heart knows what I did in absence
　　And what I left in fear so you would know
Your departure clear to me as penalty
　　Nothing that I suffered by it was restful
Forgive as I'm ransom and grant me
　　To be chosen for a gift of which I'm part
Forget talk about me by those in error
　　A free man tormented by sons of whores
If a fellow flings out words in open
　　Court take his word for what it signifies
Fools' tricks return upon themselves
　　A poet's anger is an evil possession
A society of knaves is cursed for it
　　Like a guest telling regrets of the guests
Jealous hatred if I find you content
　　Is a misfortune too light for me to weigh
He who is an unbeliever in your Lord
　　Apart from us is safe in your favor to us
Lands lack a rising sun in their night
　　God atones with you so they are glad

77
Badr ordered
the people
to be kept from him.
(Perfect ri)

You order that screen for seclusion
　　Alas you have no power over the veil
One whose bright forehead and gifts
　　Are not hid cannot be hidden from sight
If you veil yourself you are not hid
　　If you in you have that outward vision

78
Badr poured wine
for him
but he had no desire
to drink so he spoke.
(Swift ki)

You know no one I drink with but you
　　And this is only due to your love for me
Not for the love of wine, and so I
　　Greet you as I hope and as I fear you

(٧٩)

«من الكامل»

وقال ايضًا:

في شُرْبِها وكَفَتْ جَوابَ السّائِلِ	عَذَلَتْ مُنادَمَةُ الأميرِ عَواذِلي
وحَملْتُ شكرَكَ واصطناعُك حاملي	مَطَرَتْ سَحابُ يَديكِ رِيَّ جَوانحي
والقَوْلُ فيكَ عُلُوُّ قَدْرِ القائِلِ	فمَتى أقومُ بشُكرِ ما أوْلَيْتَني

(٨٠)

«من الكامل»

وكان بدر قد تاب من الشراب مرة بعد أخرى ثم رآه أبو الطيب يشرب فقال ارتجالا:

شُرَكاؤُهُ في ملكِهِ لا مُلكِهِ	يا أيُّها المَلِكُ الذي نُدَماؤُهُ
لكَ توبةٌ من توبةٍ من سَفكِهِ	في كلِّ يَومٍ بَيننا دَمُ كَرمةٍ
أمنَ الشَّرابِ تَتوبُ أم مِن تَركِهِ؟	والصِّدقُ من شِيَمِ الكرامِ فقلْ لنا

(٨١)

«من الكامل»

فقال بدر: بل من تركه. فقال أبو الطيب:

يَوماً توَفَّرَ حَظُّهُ مِن مالِهِ	بدرُ فتىً لو كانَ مِن سؤالِهِ
ويَقِلُّ ما يأتيهِ في إقبالِهِ	تَتَحيَّرُ الأفعالُ في أفعالِهِ
مِنْ وَجهِهِ ويَمينِهِ وشِمالِهِ	قمراً تَرى وسَحابَتين بمَوضِعِ
كرَماً لأنَّ الطَّيرَ بعضُ عِيالِهِ	سَفكَ الدِّماءَ بجُودِهِ لا بأسِهِ
ذِكراً يَزولُ الدَّهرُ قَبلَ زَوالِهِ	إنْ يَفنَ ما بحَوي فقدْ أبقى لهُ

79
He said also.
(Perfect li)

Drinking with Amir blames one who blames
    Me for drinking—it is enough answer for spies
Your hand's cloud pours rain on my lands
    I give you thanks your kindness is my bearer
When I rise to praise you do not help me
    For words of you are a speaker's highest power

80
Badr had repented of drinking but he saw him drinking so he spoke.
(Perfect hi)

O king whose drinking companions are
    The partners of his rule without his power
Each day among us the grape's blood
    Makes you repent of repenting to shun it
Truth has the wine's nature so tell us
    Do you repent of the wine or of leaving it

81
And he said about trim also.
(Perfect hi)

Badr is a man, if he's his own client
    A day, his joy will outweigh the earth
One's acts are amazed at his actions
    He minimizes what he does by demands
We see a moon! two clouds in the place
    Of his countenance on the left and right
He sheds blood by bounty, not power
    Nobly, for the birds of prey are of his folk
If he destroys what he has, yet memory
    Holds and time will cease before its end

(٨٢)

«من السريع»

وسأله أبو الطيب حاجة فقضاها فنهض وقال:

| وعِفْـتُ في الجَلسَـةِ تَطويلَهـا | قَـدْ أَبَيْـتُ بالحاجَـةِ مَقضِيَّـةً |
| خَيرٌ لنَفسِـي مِـنْ بَقائـي لَهَـا | أنـتَ الـذي طُـولُ بَقـاءٍ لَـهُ |

(٨٣)

«من الكامل»

فسأله بدر الجلوس فقال:

مَـنْ لَـمْ يَكُـنْ لِمِثالِـهِ تَكوِيـنُ	يـا بَـدْرُ إنَّـكَ والحَديـثُ شُـجُونُ
مـا كـانَ مُؤتَمَنـاً بهـا جِبْريـنُ	لَعَظُمْـتُ حتـى لَـوْ تَكـونُ أمانـةً
فـإذا حضَـرْتَ فكُـلُّ فَـوْقٍ دُونُ	بَعـضُ البريَّـةِ فَـوْقَ بَعـضٍ خاليـاً

(٨٤)

«من الوافر»

قال فيه مرتجلا:

وبيـضُ الهِنْـدِ وهـيَ مُجَـرَّداتُ	فَدَتْـكَ الخَيْـلُ وهـيَ مُسَـوَّماتُ
وقَـدْ بَقيَـتْ وإنْ كَـثُرَتْ صِفـاتُ	وصَفْتُـكَ في قَـوافٍ سـائِراتٍ
وفِعْلُـكَ في فِعـالِهِم شِــياتُ	أقـاعِيلُ الـوَرى مِـنْ قَبْـلِ دُهْـمُ

(٨٥)

«من الطويل»

وقام منصرفا في الليل فقال:

ورُؤيـاكَ أحلى في العيـونِ مـنَ الغُمْـضِ	مضَى الليلُ والفضْلُ الذي لك لا يَمضي
شَهيدٌ بهـا بعضي لغيري على بَعضـي	على أنَّنـي طُوِّقْـتُ مِنْـكَ بِنعْمَـةٍ
تُخَـصُّ بـهِ يـا خيـرَ مـاشٍ علـى الأرْضْ	سَـلامُ الـذي فَـوْقَ السَّماواتِ عَرْشُـهُ

82
He asked a favor of him
and he granted it.
So he arose
and spoke.
(Swift ha)

I returned with a request granted
    I feared for its delay in this assembly
You are one who holds my life in his
    Better for my soul than my life in that.

83
Badr invited him
to sit with him so he spoke.
(Perfect nu)

O Badr if stories vary yet you are one
    For whom creation does not have an equal
You magnify it till if you were religion
    Angels would not have been trusted with it
Some of creation are set above others
    When you are present all above are below

84
He said about him also:
(Exuberant tu)

Horses are your ransom and are branded
    And Indian swords and they are unsheathed
I described you in verses that galloped
    But while they are many, adjectives remain
The actions of men of old are darkness
    Your deeds are bright spots on their deeds

85
And he rose as night
was coming to an end.
(Long di)

Night passes but good in you does not
    Your face is sweeter to eyes than clouds
Thus I am garlanded by you with favor
    Part of me showing to others a part of me
Peace in him whose throne is above sky
    Marked by it O best who tread on the earth

(٨٦)

«من الوافر»

جلس بدر يلعب بالشطرنج وقد كثر المطر فقال أبو الطيب:

عَجائِبَ ما رَأيتُ مِنَ السَّحابِ	أَلَمْ تَرَ أَيُّها المَلِكُ المُرَجّى
وتَرْشُفُ ماءَهُ رَشْفَ الرُّضابِ	تَشَكّى الأرضُ غَيبَتَهُ إلَيْهِ
وفيكَ تَأَمُّلي ولَكَ انْتِصابي	وأُوهِمُ أَنَّ في الشَّطْرَنْجِ هَمّي
مَغيبي لَيْلَتي وغَداً إيابي	سَأَمْضي والسَّلامُ عَلَيكَ مِنّي

(٨٧)

«من مخلع البسيط»

سقاه بدر ليلة فأخذ الشراب منه ثم أراد الانصراف فلم يقدر على الكلام فقال هذين البيتين وهو لا يدري فأنشده إياهما ابن الخراساني وهما قوله:

| لله ما تَصْنَعُ الخُمورُ | نالَ الَّذي نِلتُ مِنْهُ مِنّي |
| أآذِنٌ أَيُّها الأَميرُ؟ | وفي انصِرافي إلى مَحَلّي |

(٨٨)

«من المتقارب»

وعرض عليه الصبحة في غد فقال:

تُهَيِّجُ للقَلْبِ أَشْواقَهُ	وَجَدْتُ المُدامَةَ غَلّابَةً
ولَكِنْ تُحَسِّنُ أَخْلاقَهُ	تُسِيءُ مِنَ المَرءِ تَأدِيَهُ
وذو اللُّبِّ يَكْرَهُ إِنْفاقَهُ	وأَنْفَسُ ما لِلفَتى لُبُّهُ
ولا يَشْتَهي المَوْتَ مَنْ ذاقَهُ	وقَدْ مُتُّ أَمْسِ بها مَوْتَةً

86
He spoke
and he was playing chess
and it was raining hard
so he said:
(Exuberant bi)

Don't you see O king of things hoped for
    The wonders which I see now in that cloud?
Earth complains to it of its absence
    And sucks its drops of water as saliva
One fancies my desire is for chess
    But in you is my hope and in you my goal
I will go, peace be upon you from me
    My absence my night, morning my return

87
The drinking
got hold of Abu Tayyib
and he intended to depart
but he had no power
over his words.
Then he spoke
these two verses.
(Flowing ru)

It got of me what I got of it
    By God what drunkenness does!
As to my going to my quarters
    Is there a head steward O Amir?

88
The company met him
the following morning so he said:
(Tripping hu)

I found the wine overwhelming
    It stirred up the heart's passions
It spoiled the culture of a man
    However it adorned his character
The best of a man is his reason
    He who has reason hates its loss
Last night I died the death
    He wants no death who tastes it

(٨٩)

«من المتقارب»

كان لبدر بن عمار جليس أعور يعرف بابن كروس، وكان يحسد أبا الطيب لما كان يشاهده من سرعة خاطره لأنه لم يكن يجري في المجلس شيء إلا ارتجل فيه شعراً، فقال لبدر: أظنه يعمل هذا قبل حضوره ويعده. فقال له بدر: مثل هذا لا يجوز أن يكون وأنا أمتحنه بشيء أحضره للوقت. فلما كمل المجلس ودارت الكؤوس أخرج لعبة قد أعدها، لها شعر في طوها تدور على لولب وأحدى رجليها مرفوعة وفي يدها ريحان، وهي تدار على الجلاس فإذا وقفت حذاء الإنسا نقرها فدارت. فقال ابو الطيب فيها مرتجلاً:

وَجارِيَةٍ شَعرُها شَطرُها　　مُحَكَّمةٍ نافِذٍ أَمرُها
تَدورُ وَفي كَفِّها طاقةٌ　　تَضَمَّنَها مُكرَهاً شِبرُها
فَإِن أَسكَرَتنا فَفي جَهلِها　　بِما فَعَلَتهُ بِنا عُذرُها

(٩٠)

«من المنسرح»

وأديرت فوقفت حذاء أبي الطيب فقال:

جارِيَةٌ ما لِجِسمِها روحُ　　بِالقَلبِ مِن حُبِّها تَباريحُ
في كَفِّها طاقةٌ تُشيرُ بِها　　لِكُلِّ طيبٍ مِن طيبِها ريحُ
سَأَشرَبُ الكَأسَ عَن إِشارَتِها　　وَدَمعُ عَيني في الخَدِّ مَسفوحُ

(٩١)

«من المنسرح»

وشرب وأدارها فوقفت حذاء بدر فقال:

يا ذا المَعالي وَمَعدِنَ الأَدَبِ　　سَيِّدَنا وَأَبنَ سَيِّدِ العَرَبِ

89
He spoke describing an entertainer who was present in the shape of a maid.
(Flowing ha)

A girl whose hair is half her length
    Is being appointed to perform her task
She dances and in hand a nosegay
    But her gesture now implies dislike for it
If she makes us drunk her ignorance
    Of what she does to us is as her excuse

90
She came round and stopped in front of Abbu Tayyib so he said:
(Rowing hu)

A girl who has no spirit in her body
    In the heart of her lover as a passion
In her hand she waves a bouquet of
    Perfume in all of its sweet goodness
I will drink the cup that she offers
    As my eye's tears spread on cheeks

91
She went on around and stopped in front of Badr raising her leg so he spoke:
(Flowing bi)

O eminent one O mine of culture
    Our lord and son of a lord of the Arabs

أنْتَ عَلِيمٌ بِكُلِّ مُعْجِزَةٍ … وَلَوْ سَأَلْنَا سِواكَ لَمْ يُجِبِ
أهذِهِ قابَلْتَكَ راقِصَةً … أمْ رَفَعَتْ رِجْلَها مِنَ التَّعَبِ

(٩٢)

«من البسيط»

وقال أيضًا:

إنَّ الأمِيرَ أدامَ اللهُ دَوْلَتَهُ … لَفاخِرٌ كُسِيَتْ فَخْراً بِهِ مُضَرُ
في الشَّرْبِ جارِيَةٌ مِنْ تَحْتِها حَشَبٌ … ما كانَ والِدُها جِنٌّ ولا بَشَرُ
قامَتْ على فَرْدِ رِجْلٍ مِنْ مَهابَتِهِ … ولَيْسَ تَعْقِلُ ما تَأْتي وما تَذَرُ

(٩٣)

«من المنسرح»

وأديرت فسقطت فقال:

ما نَقَلَتْ عِنْدَ مَشْيَةٍ قَدَمَا … ولا اشْتَكَتْ مِنْ دُوارِها ألَمَا
لَمْ أرَ شَخْصاً مِنْ قَبْلِ رُؤْيَتِها … يَفْعَلُ أفْعالَها ومَا عَزَمَا
فَلا تَلُمْها على تواقُعِها … أطْرَبَها أنْ رَأتْكَ مُبْتَسِمَا

(٩٤)

«من الوافر»

ووصفها بشعر كثير وهجاها بمثله لم يحفظ فخجل ابن كروس وأمر بدر برفعها فرفعت فقال:

وذاتِ عَدائِرَ لا عَيْبَ فيها … سِوى أنْ لَيْسَ تَصْلُحُ للعِناقِ
إذا هَجَرَتْ فَعَنْ غَيرِ اخْتِيارٍ … وإنْ زارَتْ فَعَنْ غَيرِ اشْتِياقِ
أمَرْتَ بأنْ تُشالَ فَفارَقَتْنا … وما ألِمَتْ لحادِثَةِ الفِراقِ

You have knowledge of every wonder
    If we ask, aside from you is no answer
Is one who approaches you a dancer
    Or does she raise her foot in misfortune?

92
He said also about her:
(Outspread ru)

May God prolong the Amir's rule
    Excellent! Mudar puts on honor in him
A girl amid drinkers, under her a clog
    Her father was neither of jinn or mankind
She stood on one foot in fear of him
    She knew not what she did or she did not

93
And she turned
and fell so he said impromptu.
(Flowing ma)

She did not move her foot in going
    Nor complain of pain in her giddiness
I saw none with her face before now
    Do as she did with such determination
Do not blame her for her accident
    It pleased her that she saw you smiling

94
Badr commanded
that she be taken up
and it was done so he said:
(Tripping qi)

With braids having no fault in them
    Except they play not fair with the neck
If she flees it is without prejudice
    If she visits it is without any lustfulness
You had her raised so she left us
    She showed no pain in parting's calamity

(٩٥)

«من البسيط»

ثم التفت إلى بدر وقال: ما حملك أيها الأمير على ما فعلت؟ أردت نفي الظنة عن أدبك، فقال:

زَعَمْتَ أَنَّكَ تَنفي الظَّنَّ عَنْ أدبي　　　وأنتَ أعْظَمُ أهلِ الأرضِ مقدارا
إنّي أنا الذهبُ المعروفُ مَخْبَرُهُ　　　يزيدُ في السَّبكِ للدِّينارِ دينارا

(٩٦)

«من الكامل»

فقال بدر: بل للدينار قنطاراً، فقال:

برجاءِ جُودِكَ يُطْرَدُ الفَقْرُ　　　وبأنْ تُعادَى يَنْفَدُ العُمْرُ
فَخَرَ الزُّجاجُ بأنْ شَرِبْتَ بِهِ　　　وزَرَتْ على مَنْ عافَها الخمرُ
وسَلِمْتَ منها وهي تُسكِرُنا　　　حتى كأنَّكَ هابَكَ السُّكْرُ
ما يُرْتَجى أحدٌ لمكْرُمَةٍ　　　إلا الإلهُ وأنتَ يا بَدْرُ

(٩٧)

«من الخفيف»

خرج أبو الطيب إلى جبل جرش فنزل بأبي الحسين علي بن أحمد المري الخراساني وكان بينهما مودة بطبرية فقال يمدحه:

لا افتخارٌ إلا لمن لا يُضامُ　　　مُدْرِكٍ أو مُحاربٍ لا يَنامُ
ليسَ عزماً ما مرَّضَ المرءُ فيهِ　　　ليسَ هَمّاً ما عاقَ عنهُ الظَّلامُ
واحتمالُ الأذى ورؤيَةُ جانيـ　　　ـهِ غِذاءٌ تضْوَى بهِ الأجسامُ
ذلَّ مَنْ يغْبِطُ الذَّليلَ بعيشٍ　　　رُبَّ عيشٍ أخَفُّ منهُ الحِمامُ

95
He said to Badr:
What was your intent
in bringing in the entertainer.
He said: I wanted to quell
a suspicion
about your culture.
And Abu Tayyib said:
(Outspread ra)

You thought you'd dispel doubt of my art
    You are the greatest of the folk in this time
For I am gold well known whose imprint
    Increases in minting the diner to a diner

96
Badr said:
No, by God,
a bushel of dinars!
Abu Tayyib said:
(Perfect ru)

Hope of your bounty drives away poverty
    Insofar as you are hostile then life ceases
A glass boasts when you drink from it
    The wine chides the one who disliked it
You're safe from it as it inebriates us
    As if the drunkenness were in awe of you
No one has any hopes for liberality
    Except from God and so from you O Badr!

97
He spoke praising Abu Hasan
Ali ibn Ahmad al-Murri al-Khurasan.
(Nimble mu)

No honor for one unless he's unchecked
    By sleep in what he strives with or fights for
It's not purpose if a man is sick of it
    It is not desire if obscurity hinders one
Suffering evil and the tyrant's face
    Are the food that makes the body thin
He's base who competes with low life
    Many a life finds death easier than that

حُجَّةٌ لا جيءَ إليها اللِّئامُ	كُلُّ حِلْمٍ أتى بغَيرِ اقْتِدارِ
ما لجُرْحٍ بمَيِّتٍ إيلامُ	مَنْ يَهُنْ يَسْهُلِ الهَوانُ عَليهِ
عاً زَماني واستَكْرَمَتْني الكِرامُ	ضاقَ ذَرْعاً بأنْ أضيقَ بهِ ذَرْ
واقِفاً تحتَ أخمَصيَّ الأنامُ	واقِفاً تحتَ أخمَصَيْ قَدْرِ نفسي
ومَراماً أبْغي وظُلْمي يُرامُ	أقَراراً ألَذُّ فوقَ شَرارِ
والعِراقانِ بالقَنا والشَّآمُ	دونَ أنْ يَشرَقَ الحِجازُ ونَجْدٌ
رَ عَليُّ بنُ أحمَدَ القَمْقامُ	شَرِقَ الجَوُّ بالغُبارِ إذا سا
بُ الذَّكيُّ الجَعْدُ السَّريُّ الهُمامُ	الأديبُ المُهَذَّبُ الأصْيَدُ الضَّرْ
هُ ومِنْ حاسِدي يَديهِ الغَمامُ	والذي رَيبُ دَهرِهِ مِنْ أسارا
لالَ جُوداً كأنَّ مالاً سَقامُ	يَتَداوى مِنْ كَثرَةِ المالِ بالإقْـ
بَحُ مِنْ ضَيفِهِ رأتْهُ السَّوامُ	حَسَنٌ في عُيونِ أعدائِهِ أقْـ
لَحَماهُ الإحْلالُ والإعْظامُ	لَوْ حَمى سَيِّداً مِنَ المَوتِ حامٍ
لُّ ولكِنْ زَيُّها الإحْرامُ	وعَوارٍ لَوامِعٌ دينَها الجِـ
ثُمَّ قَيسٌ وبَعدَ قَيسٍ السَّلامُ	كُتِبَتْ في صَحائِفِ المَجدِ: بسْمِ
جَمَراتٌ لا تَشتَهيها النَّعامُ	إنَّما مُرَّةُ بنُ عَوفِ بنِ سَعدٍ
بّاحُ لَيلٍ مِنَ الدُّخانِ تِمامُ	لَيلُها صُبحُها مِنَ النَّارِ والأصْـ
قَصَرَتْ عَنْ بُلوغِها الأوْهامُ	هِمَمٌ بَلَّغَتْكُمُ رُتَبَاتٍ
نَفِدَتْ قَبْلَ يَنفَدُ الإقْدامُ	ونُفوسٌ إذا انْبَرَتْ لِقِتالٍ
عِ كأنَّ اقْتِحامَها اسْتِسْلامُ	وقُلوبٌ مُوَطَّناتٌ على الرَّوْ
قَدْ بَراها الإسْراجُ والإلْجامُ	قائِدو كُلِّ شَطْبَةٍ وحِصانٍ
بتَاءاتٍ نُطْقِهِ التَّمتَامُ	يَتَعَثَّرْنَ بالرُّؤوسِ كَما مَرَّ
قالَ فيكَ الذي أقولُ الحُسَامُ	طالَ غِشيانُكَ الكَريهةَ حتى
قَدْ كَفَتْكَ الصَّفائِحَ الأقْلامُ	وكَفَتْكَ الصَّفائِحُ النَّاسَ حتى
قَدْ كَفاكَ التَّجاربَ الألْهامُ	وكَفَتْكَ التَّجاربُ الفِكَرَ حتى
رِ بقَتْلٍ مُعَجَّلٍ لا يُلامُ	فارِسٌ يَشتَري بِرازَكَ للفَخْـ
رِ عَلَيهِ لفَقرِهِ إنْعامُ	نائِلٌ مِنكَ نَظْرَةً ساقَهُ الفَقْـ

All clemency one shows without power
    Is a pretext that the mean bring forward
The base man sees scorn easy to bear
    There is no pain in wounds for the dead
My time hampers my arm, I am curbed
    But the generous want to do good to me
Staying under my soul's hard feet
    With mankind waiting beneath my foot
Do I find joy in repose above sparks
    With a goal I covet, my foes on the run?
When Hijaz and Najd are choked by
    Those lances and two Iraqs and Syria?
And air chokes with dust as he goes
    That lord of vastness Ali ibn Ahmad
Cultured, trained, prince, lean one
    The sagacious, subtle, noble warrior
He has his time's doubts as captives
    Among those who envy his gifts clouds
He heals from great wealth by cutting
    With generosity, as if wealth were illness
Handsome but in foes' eyes uglier
    Than his guests a pasture camel sees
If anything guards a lord from death's
    Lion, majesty and grandeur protect you
Bright nudities whose faith is license
    But yet their dress is that of the pilgrim
Written on glory's page: In the name. . .
    And then Qais and after qais is peace!
Truly those of Murra ibn Auf ibn Sad
    Are the live coals ostriches won't savor
Their night is the dawn due to fires
    Their dawns due to smoke perfect night
Aspiration informs you of those ranks
    The imagination falls short of reaching
Souls who when they confront battle
    Are consumed before attack is finished
Hearts that are accustomed to terror
    As if their attacks were for a surrender
Leading on each rangy mare and stallion
    That the saddling and bridling wear down
They stumble over heads as a stutterer
    Will trip over the "t's" when he is speaking
Your overwhelmings lengthen calamity
    Till the sword tells about you what
I speak Swords have defended you from men
    As the pen has defended you from blades
Experience protected you from opinion
    Until inspiration reversed the experience
A knight in a duel with you for honor
    Is not to be blamed for his sudden death
One taking a glance from you as penury
    Drives him to it has a grace in his poverty

162   Diwan al-Mutanabbi

خَيْرُ أعضائِنا الرُّؤوسُ ولَكِنْ	فَضَّلَتْها بِقَصْدِكَ الأقْدامُ
قَد لَعَمري أقْصَرْتُ عَنـكَ وللوَفـ	ـدِ ازْدِحامٌ وللعَطايـا ازْدِحامُ
خِفْتُ أن صِرْتُ في يَمينكَ أن تأ	خُذَنـي في هِبـاتِكَ الأقْـوامُ
ومِنَ الرُّشْدِ لم أَزُرْكَ على القُرْ	بِ، علـى البُعْـدِ يُعـرَفُ الألْمامُ
ومِنَ الخَيرِ بُطْءُ سَعْيِكَ عَنـي	أسْـرَعُ السُّحْبِ في المَسيرِ الجَهامُ
قُـلْ فَكَـمْ مِـنْ جَواهـرٍ بِنظامٍ	وُدُّهـا أنّهـا بفيـكَ كَـلامُ
هابَكَ اللّيلُ والنّهارُ فَلَوْ تَنْـ	ـهاهُمـا لـم تَجُـزْ بِـكَ الأيّـامُ
حَسْبُكَ اللهُ ما تَضِلُّ عَن الحَـ	ـقِّ ولا يَهْتَدي إليـكَ أثامُ
لِمَ لا تَحْـذَرُ العَواقِـبَ في غَيْـ	ـرِ الدّنايا، أمّـا عَلَيْـكَ حَـرامُ
كَـمْ حَبيبٍ لا عُـذْرَ للَّـوْمِ فيـهِ	لَـكَ فيـهِ مِـنَ التُّقـى لُـوّامُ
رَفَعَـتْ قَـدْرَكَ النَزاهـةُ عَنْـهُ	وتَنَتْ قَلْبَكَ المَساعي الجِسامُ
إنّ بَعْضـاً مِـنَ القَريضِ هُـذاءٌ	لَيْسَ شَيْئاً وبَعضُـهُ أحْكـامُ
مِنْـهُ مـا يَجْـلِبُ البَراعـةَ والفَضْـ	ـلَ ومِنْـهُ مـا يَجْـلِبُ البِرْسـامُ

(٩٨)

«من البسيط»

قال فيه وقد أراد الأرتحال عنه:

لا تُنكِرَنّ رَحيلي عَنكَ في عَجَلٍ	فـإنّني لَرَحيلـي غَيْـرُ مُخْتـارِ
ورُبَّمـا فـارَقَ الإنْسـانُ مُهْجَتَـهُ	يَـوْمَ الوَغـى غَيْـرَ قـالٍ خَشْيَةَ العارِ
وقَـدْ مُنيـتُ بِحُسّـادٍ أحـارِبُهُمْ	فاجعَلْ نَـداكَ عليهـم بعضَ أنصاري

(٩٩)

«من الوافر»

يصف مسيره في البوادي وما لقي في أسفاره ويذم الأعور بن كروس:

عَذيـري مِـنْ عَـذارَى مِـنْ أمـورِ	سَكَـنَّ جَوانحـي بَـدَلَ الخُـدورِ

The best of our parts is the head but
    The feet are better still in seeking you
Yes, by my life, I was short of you
    In the crowd's push and press for gifts
I feared if I was at your right hand
    People would take me as a gift of you
I was told not to visit you when near
    Visits are praised when made from afar
Delay of your bounty to me was best
    The fastest clouds that move are empty
Speak, for many pearls on the string
    Wish that they were words in your mouth
Night and day fear you if you forbid
    Them, times would not pass for your sake
God defends you from missing truth
    And thus no sin attaches itself to you
Why are you not wary of results in
    Things other than the vile or the taboo?
Many a friend has no cause for blame
    Yet you can blame him respecting piety
Freedom from blame raised your worth
    Weighty business restrained your heart
Yes, some poetry is only nonsense talk
    Nothing at all, and some of it is wisdom
Excellence, generosity evoke some
    And some of it lung sickness draws out

98
He said also as he was intending to depart.
(Outspread ri)

Don't deny my leaving you in haste
    For I have no choice in this departure
Often a man parts from his own blood
    On battle day ungrudging, fearing shame
I was tested by the envious I opposed
    So give bounty to some who have aided me

99
He spoke describing his journey in the desert and in it he mocked Ibn Karawwus the One eye.
(Exuberant ri)

Who excuses me to these virgin events
    Dwelling in my breast instead of the tent?

164   Diwan al-Mutanabbi

عـــنِ الأســيافِ ليـــسَ عــنِ الثّغـــورِ	ومُبتَسِـــماتِ هَيجـــاواتِ عصــرٍ
وكُـــلَّ عُذافِـــرٍ قَلِـــقِ الضُّفـــورِ	رَكِبـــتُ مُشَـــمِّراً قَدَمـــي إليهـــا
وآونــةً علــى قَتَــدِ البَعيــرِ	أواناً في بُيــوتِ البَــدْوِ رَحْلــي
وأنصِـــبُ حُـــرَّ وَجْهــي للهَجيـرِ	أعَـــرِّضُ للرِّمـــاحِ الصُّـــمَّ نحـري
كـأنّي منْـــهُ فـي قَمَــرٍ مُنيــرِ	وأسري في ظَلامِ الليْــلِ وَحْــدي
على شَغَفي بها شَـــرْوَى نَقيــرِ	فَقُـــلْ في حاجـةٍ لم أقْـضِ منهـا
وعَيـنٍ لا تُـــدارُ علــى نَظيــرِ	ونَفْـــسٍ لا تُجيــبُ إلى خَسِيسٍ
يُنازِعُنـي ســوى شَرْفي وخيري	وكَفٍّ لا تُنـازِعُ مَـــنْ أتانـــي
بشَــرٍّ منــكَ يا شَــرَّ الدُّهـورِ	وقِلّــةِ ناصِــرٍ جُوزيـــتِ عـــني
لَخِلْتُ الأكْـــمَ موغِرَةَ الصُّـــدورِ	عَـــدُوّي كُــلُّ شــيءٍ فيــكَ حتـى
لَجُدْتُ بـهِ لِـــذي الجَـدِّ العَثـورِ	فلَــوْ أنّـي حُسِـــدْتُ علــى نَفيــسٍ
ومــا خَيْــرُ الحياةِ بــلا سُــرورِ	ولكِنّـــي حُسِـــدْتُ علــى حَياتـي
وإن تَفخـــرْ فيــا نِصْـــفَ البَصيرِ	فيــا ابـنَ كَــرّوسٍ يا نِصْــفَ اعمى
وتُبْغِضُنـا لأنّـــا غَيْــرُ عُـــورِ	تُعادينـا لأنّــا غَيْــرُ لُكْــنٍ
ولكِــنْ ضــاقَ فِتْــرٌ عَن مَسيرِ	فلَوْ كنتَ امرأً يُهْجـــى هَجَوْنـــا

(١٠٠)

«من البسيط»

يمدح أبا عبد الله محمد بن عبد الله بن محمد الخطيب الخصيبي وهو يومئذ يتقلد القضاء بانطاكية:

يَخلو مِــنَ الهَمّ أحلاهم مِنَ الفِطَنِ	أفاضِلُ النّــاسِ أغراضٌ لَــدى الزّمَنِ
شَــرٌّ على الحُــرِّ مِن سُــقْمٍ على بدَنِ	وإنّمـــا نَحــنُ في جيلٍ سَواسِــيَةٍ
تُخطي إذا جِئتَ في اســتفهامِها بِمَــنْ	حَــوْلي بكُلِّ مكانٍ منهـــم خِلَــقٌ
ولا أُمَــرُّ بخَلْــقٍ غيـرِ مُضْطَغَــنِ	لا أقْتَري بَلَــداً إلّا علـى غَــرَرٍ
إلّا أحَــقَّ بضَــرْبِ الــرّأسِ مِن وَثَنِ	ولا أُعاشِـــرُ مِن أملاكِهِــم مَلِكــاً

In smiles of battle that are wrung
    From the swords and not from the lips
I went toward them on my feet, girded
    And on every camel with restless tether
At times my saddle in bedouin tents
    At times on the thorn tree of the camel
I turned my breast to sharp spearheads
    And I set my face toward the heat of noon
I went through dark nights alone
    As if I had the moon's light out there
O tell of causes that end in nothing
    My effort like a crease on a date stone!
But soul responds not to the vile
    The eye that does not turn to any equal
A hand that opposes none coming
    To dispute except for honor and my good
Yet little help was given to me
    For evil from you O evil of the times!
All were hostile due to you till
    I thought the tells boiled in my breast
If I were envied for a precious thing
    I'd give it to one who must often stumble
But not if I were envied for my life
    For there is no good life without joy
O Ibn Karawwus, O half dim sighted
    Even if you boasted, yet O half
Seeing You hate us because we don't stammer
    Furious at us since we are not one-eyed
If you were a man to be mocked we'd
    Mock but thumb to index is a short trip!

100
He spoke praising Muhammad ibn Ubaidallah ibn Muhammad ibn al-Katib al Qadi al-Khasibi.
(Flowing ni)

The best men are targets for the time
    It frees from care one most free of wit
We are among a generation one, all
    Evil to noble souls as illness to body
About me in every place are shapes
    You'd offend if you asked them: Whose?
I never settle in a place without risk
    Nor pass among men without being hated
I associated with none of their kings
    Unworthy of head struck off like an idol

حتّى أُعَنِّفَ نفسي فيهم وأني	إنّي لأعْذِرُهُـــمْ مِمّـــا أَعَنَفَهُـــمْ
فَقْرُ الحِمارِ بلا رأسٍ إلى رَسَنِ	فَقْرُ الجَهولِ بِـلا قَلْبٍ إلى أدبٍ
عارِينَ مِن حُلَـلٍ كاسِينَ مِـن دَرَنِ	ومُدقِعِيـنَ بِسُبْـرُوتٍ صَحِبْتُهُـمْ
مَكْنُ الضِّبابِ لهُمْ زادٌ بـلا ثَمَنِ	خُرّابِ باديَـــةٍ غَرْثَــى بُطُونُهُــمْ
وما يَطيشُ لَهُمْ سَهْمٌ مِنَ الظَّنَنِ	يَسْــتَخبِرونَ فَــلا أعْطِيهِـم خَبَــري
كَيمــا يَـرى أنّنـا مِثْـلانِ في الوَهَنِ	وخَلَّـــةٍ في جَليسٍ ألْتَقِيــهِ بهـــا
فيُهْتَـدَى لي فَلَمْ أقدِرْ على اللَّحَنِ	وكِلْمَـةٍ في طَريـقٍ خِفْـتُ أعْرِبُهـا
ولكِـنَ العَـزْمُ حَـدُّ المَركَـبِ الخَشِنِ	قد هَـوَّنَ الصَّبـرُ عِندي كـلَّ نازلَـةٍ
وقَتْلَــةٍ قُرِنَــتْ بالــذَّمِّ في الجُبُنِ	كم مَخلَصٍ وعُلَّى في خوضِ مهلكةٍ
وهَـلْ تَـرُوقُ دَفينـاً جُـودَةُ الكَفَـنِ	لا يُعْجِبَــنَّ مُضيمـاً حُسْــنُ بِزَّتِــهِ
وأقْتَضِـي كَوْنَهـا دَهْـري ويَمْطُلُنـي	للهِ حَـــالٌ أُرَجِّيهــا وتُخلِفُنــــي
قصائداً مِـنْ إنـاثِ الخَيلِ والحُصُنِ	مَدَحْتُ قَومــاً وإنْ عِشنـا نَظمتُ لهم
إذا تُنوشِـــدْنَ لم يَدْخُلْـــنَ في أُذُنِ	تَحْــتَ العَجاج قَوافيها مُضَمَّــرَةً
ولا أُصالِــحُ مَغـروراً علـى دَخَـنِ	فــلا أُحـاربُ مَدفوعـاً إلى جُـدُرٍ
حَــرُّ الهَواجِـرِ في صُـمٍّ مِـنَ الفِتَـنِ	مُخَيَّــمُ الجَمْــعِ بالبَيداءِ يَصهَـرُهُ
على الخَصيصِيِّ عندَ الفَرضِ والسُّنَنِ	ألقَى الكِـرامُ الألَى بـادوا مكـارِمَهُمْ
لَـهُ اليَتامَــى بــدا بالمَجْدِ والمِنَنِ	فَهُنَّ في الحَجْرِ منــهُ كلَّمـا عَرَضَتْ
رأيٌ يُخَلِّــصُ بَيــنَ المــاءِ واللَّبَــنِ	قاضٍ إذا التَبَـسَ الأمرانِ عَــنْ لَــهُ
مُجـانِبُ العَيـنِ للفَحْشاءِ والوَسَنِ	عَــضُّ الشَّبـابِ بعيدٌ فَجْـرُ لَيْلَتِــهِ
وطَعْمُــهُ لقِــوامِ الجِسْـمِ لا السِّـمَنِ	شَـرابُهُ النَّشْــحُ لا للـرّيِّ يَطْلُبُــهُ
والواحِــدُ الحالَتيـنِ السِّـرِّ والعَلَـنِ	ألقائِـلُ الصِّـدْقَ فيــهِ مــا يُضِـرُّ بِــهِ
والمُظْهِرُ الحَقَّ للسَّاهي على الذَّهِنِ	ألفاصِـلُ الحُكْـمَ عَـيَّ الأوَّلـونَ بِـهِ
جَدّي الخَصيبُ عَرَفنا العِرْقَ بالغُصُنِ	أفعانَـهُ نَسَبـاً لَــوْ لَمْ يَقُــلْ مَعَهـا
نِ العارضِ الهَتِنِ ابنِ العارضِ الهَتِنِ	العارِضُ الهَتِنُ ابنُ العارِضِ الهَتِــنِ ابـ
آباؤُهُ مِــنْ مُغــارِ العِلْــمِ في قَرَنِ	قــد صَيَّــرَتْ أوَّلَ الدّنيـا وآخِرَهـا
أوْ كـانَ فَهْمُهُــمْ أيّــامَ لم يَكُـنِ	كأنَّهُـمْ وُلِــدوا مِــنْ قبلِ أنْ وُلِـدوا

I excuse them while I rebuke them for
    I upbraid myself about them and accept
A mindless fool's need for culture is
    The need of a heedless ass for a rope
I have been with desert beggars
    Bare of clothes and dressed in dirt
Sandy cattle thieves hungry bellies
    Lizard eggs were their no cost vittles
They asked but I gave them little
    The arrow of suspicion did miss them
Many a friend's trait imitated for them
    Thus we seemed alike in our ignorance
Many a phrase midway I fear too good
    They aid me but I can't master mistakes
Patience makes each attack easy
    Will softens every rough trip's edge
What purity, glory for a death seeker
    What a drubbing by blame for a coward!
Fine clothes don't awe a wronged one
    Does a splendid shroud delight a corpse?
By God I hope for a thing denied me
    My fate wants it to be and puts me off
I praised folk and if I live I'll make
    Qasidas of mares and stallions for them
Beneath the dust their rhymes are lean
    And if I recite they will not stop in an ear
I make no defensive war behind walls
    I make no peace deceitfully with mischief
Army tents are on a plain where heat
    Of noon fuses them with rebel's poison
Lost noble men cast their lot with
    Khasib according to justice and Sunna
They are in his care and when orphans
    Turn to him he rises in glory and bounty
A judge, if two matters tangle, wisdom
    Occurs to him to separate milk and water
Fresh youth far from gray night that
    Turns its eye to luxury and to dozing
He drinks little, seeks no drunkards
    Eating to preserve the body not to fatten
Truthful speaker even if it harms him
    Uniting kinds of secrecy and openness
He fixes judgment so ancients falter
    Showing justice to those lacking wisdom
His acts lineage even if he doesn't say
    Khasib my grandfather, we know the root
Rain cloud, rain cloud's son who was
    Son of rain cloud who was son of him
At world's origin and at its end his
    Fathers wisdom's ropes among cords
As if born before they were born
    Their wisdom in days they were not

الخاطِرينَ على أعدائِهِمْ أبداً ... مِنَ المَحامِدِ في أوفى مِنَ الجُنَنِ
للناظِرينَ إلى إقبالِهِ فَرَحٌ ... يُزيلُ ما بِجِباهِ القَوْمِ مِنْ غَضَنِ
كأنَّ مالَ ابنِ عبدِ اللهِ مُغْتَرَفٌ ... مِن راحَتَيْهِ بأرضِ الرومِ واليَمَنِ
لم نَفتَقِدْ بكَ مِن مُزْنٍ سِوى لَثَقٍ ... ولا مِنَ البَحرِ غيرَ الريحِ والسُفُنِ
ولا مِنَ الليثِ إلاّ قُبحَ مَنظَرِهِ ... ومِنْ سِواهُ سِوى ما ليسَ بالحَسَنِ
مُنذُ احتَبَيْتَ بإنطاكِيَةَ اعتَدَلَتْ ... حتى كأنَّ ذَوي الأوتارِ في هُدَنِ
ومُذْ مَرَرْتَ على أطوادِها قَرَعَتْ ... مِنَ السجودِ فلا نَبتٌ على القُنَنِ
أخلَتْ مَواهِبُكَ الأسواقَ مِن صَنَعٍ ... أغنى نَداكَ عنِ الأعمالِ والمِهَنِ
ذا جودُ مَن ليسَ مِن دَهرٍ على ثِقَةٍ ... وزُهدُ مَنْ ليسَ مِن دُنياهُ في وَطَنِ
وهذِهِ هِمّةٌ لم يُؤتَها بَشَرٌ ... وذا اقتِدارُ لِسانٍ ليسَ في المِنَنِ
فَمُرْ وأومِىء تُطَعْ قُدِّستَ مِن جبلٍ ... تَبارَكَ اللهُ مُجري الروحِ في حَضَنِ

(١٠١)

«من الطويل»

ورد على أبي الطيب كتاب من جدته لأمه تشكو شوقها إليه وطول غيبته عنها، فتوجه نحو العراق و لم يمكنه دخول الكوفة على حالته تلك فانحدر إلى بغداد. وكانت جدته قد يئست منه فكتب إليها كتابا يسألها المسير إليه فقبلت كتابه وحمت لوقتها سرورا به وغلب الفرح على قلبها فقتلها، فقال يرثيها:

ألا لا أرى الأحداثَ مَدحاً ولا ذَمّا ... فَما بَطشُها جَهلاً ولا كَفُّها حِلمَا
إلى مِثلِ ما كان الفتى مَرجِعُ الفتى ... يَعودُ كما أبدى ويُكري كما أرمى
لَكِ اللهُ مِنْ مَفجوعَةٍ بحَبيبِها ... قَتيلَةِ شَوقٍ غَيرَ مُلحِقِها وَصمَا
أحِنّ إلى الكأسِ التي شَرِبَتْ بها ... وأهوى لِمَثواها التُرابَ وما ضَمّا
بَكَيْتُ عَلَيها خيفةً في حَياتِها ... وذاقَ كِلانا صاحِبَهُ قِدَمَا
ولَو قَتَلَ الهَجرُ المُحِبّينَ كُلَّهُمْ ... مَضى بَلَدٌ باقٍ أجَدَّتْ لَهُ صَرْمَا

Ever walking proudly over foes
    Often praised as more guarded in war
Joy for those who await his coming
    He erases wrinkles on men's foreheads
As if Abdallah's wealth were taken
    By his hands in Rum and Yamani lands
We lose little in your rain but slime
    Nor yet of the sea but boats and wind
Nor yet of lion but his ugly look
    Nor yet of his likeness but his evil
When you gird Antakya it is safe
    It seems those who feud are at peace
If you cross their peaks they strive
    To lie flat without growth on their tops
Your gifts empty markets of labor
    Your bounty excludes work and skill
Kindness one trusts not to time
    Piety not yet at home in this world
Respect that men attain not to
    Control of speech not given in gifts
Go, nod, obey, revered as peak
    God bless spirit's way upon Hadani

101
He spoke
lamenting his grandmother
on his mother's side.
(Long ma)

O l know events aren't praised or blamed
    Their blows not folly as their truces not pity
To what a man was a man returns
    He ends as he began, loses as he profits
God for you! unfortunate in her lover
    A murder of love, no stain clings to her
I long for a cup from which she drank
    I love her dusty grave and what it holds
I wept for her in fear during her life
    Each tasted loss of his friend before
If lover's parting killed them all let
    The town go weep to renew parting

عَرَفْتُ اللّيالي قَبْلَ ما صَنَعَتْ بِنا   فَلَمّا دَهَتْني لم تَزِدْني بِها عِلْما
مَنافِعُها ما ضَرَّ في نَفْعِ غَيرِها   تَغَذّى وتَروى أن تَجوعَ وأن تَظْما
أتاها كِتابي بَعدَ يَأسٍ وتَرْحَةٍ   فَماتَتْ سُروراً بي فَمُتُّ بِها غَمّا
حَرامٌ على قَلبي السُّرورُ فَإِنّني   أَعُدُّ الذي ماتَتْ بِهِ بَعْدَها سُمّا
تَعَجَّبُ مِنْ لَفْظي وخَطّي كَأَنَّما   تَرى بِحُروفِ السَّطرِ أَغرِبَةً عُصْما
وتُلْثِمُهُ حتّى أَصارَ مِدادُهُ   مَحاجِرَ عَينَيْها وأنْيابَها سُحْما
رَقا دَمْعُها الجاري وجَفَّتْ جُفونُها   وفارَقَ حُبّي قَلْبَها بَعدَ ما أَدْمى
ولم يُسْلِها إلاّ المَنايا وإنَّما   أَشَدُّ مِنَ السُّقمِ الذي أَذهَبَ السُّقْما
طَلَبْتُ لها حَظّاً فَفاتَتْ وفاتَني   وقد رَضِيَتْ بي لَو رَضيتُ بها قِسْما
فَأَصْبَحتُ أَسْتَسقي الغَمامَ لِقَبرِها   وقد كنتُ أَسْتَسقي الوَغى والقَنا الصُّمّا
وكنتُ قُبَيلَ المَوتِ أَسْتَعظِمُ النَّوى   فقد صارَتِ الصُّغرى التي كانتِ العُظْمى
هَبيني أَخذتُ الثّارَ فيكِ مِنَ العِدى   فَكيفَ بأخذِ الثّارِ فيكِ مِنَ الحُمّى
وما انسَدَّتِ الدُّنيا عَلَيَّ لِضيقِها   ولكِنَّ طَرْفاً لا أَراكِ بِهِ أَعْمى
فَوا أَسَفا أَلاّ أُكِبَّ مُقَبِّلاً   لِرَأسِكِ والصَّدرِ اللَّذَيْ مُلِئا حَزْما
وأَلاّ أُلاقي روحَكِ الطَّيّبَ الذي   كَأَنَّ ذَكِيَّ المِسْكِ كان لَهُ جِسْما
ولَو لم تَكوني بِنْتَ أَكرَمِ والِدٍ   لَكانَ أَباكِ الضَّخمَ كَونُكِ لي أُمّا
لَئِنْ لَذَّ يَومُ الشّامِتينَ بِيَوْمِها   لَقَد وَلَدَتْ مِنّي لأنْفِهِمْ رَغْما
تَغَرَّبَ لا مُسْتَعظِماً غَيرَ نَفْسِهِ   ولا قابِلاً إلاّ لِخالِقِهِ حُكْما
ولا سالِكاً إلاّ فُؤادَ عَجاجَةٍ   ولا واحِداً إلاّ لِمَكْرُمَةٍ طَعْما
يَقولونَ لي ما أنتَ في كُلِّ بَلدَةٍ   وما تَبْتَغي؟ ما أَبْتَغي جَلَّ أن يُسَمّى
كَأَنَّ بَنيهِم عالِمونَ بِأَنَّني   جَلوبٌ إليهِم مِنْ مَعادِنِهِ اليُتْما
وما الجَمْعُ بَينَ الماءِ والنّارِ في يَدي   بِأَصْعَبَ مِنْ أن أَجْمَعَ الجَدَّ والفَهْما
ولكِنَّني مُسْتَنصِرٌ بِذُبابِهِ   ومُرْتَكِبٌ في كلِّ حالٍ بِهِ الغَشْما
وجاعِلُهُ يَومَ اللِّقاءِ تَحِيَّتي   وإلاّ فَلَسْتُ السَّيِّدَ البَطَلَ القَرْما
إذا فَلَّ عَزْمي عن مَدى خَوْفِ بُعْدِهِ   فَأَبْعَدُ شَيءٍ مُمكِنٍ لم يَجِدْ عَزْما
وإنّي لِمَنْ قَومٍ كَأَنَّ نُفوسَهُم   بِها أَنَفٌ أَن تَسكُنَ اللَّحمَ والعَظْما

I knew nights before they did this
    They hit me but gave none of their wit
Their profit lessened other's profit
    They fed, poured for hunger and thirst
My letter to her after despair, pain
    She died in joy of me, I wanting her
Joy is forbid to my heart for truly
    I count what died as poison after her
She wondered at my script, words
    She saw in lettered lines white ravens
She kissed it till its ink became
    Black on her eye sockets and her teeth
Her tear's flow thin, her eyelids dry
    My love left her heart after it was bled
Nothing but death consoled her, yet
    Worst illness is what drives off illness
I sought joy for her, she went, it left
    She was content I found a share in her
I wanted a cloud to water her grave
    I sought battle's flow and sharp lances
Before death I felt distance large
    But it became small which was great
Grant I took revenge for you on foes
    How could I find your revenge on fever?
A world didn't bar me with its limits
    But a blind eye couldn't show you there
O grief, shall I not fall down to kiss
    Your head and bosom filled with wisdom
Shall I not meet your sweet spirit that
    Has a body as it were of strongest musk?
If you weren't daughter of best father
    Your being mother to me is grandfather
If gloaters rejoice in her death day
    She bore me to rub their noses in dirt
An exile finds none great but himself
    And no way to wisdom but in his Creator
No path except that of a dusty heart
    Finding no nurture except in generosity
They say in every land: Who are you?
    What do you want? my desire unnamed
It's as if their sons knew what I was
    Bringing them orphanhood from its mine
Water and fire's union in my hand is not
    So hard as my uniting reward and reason
But I will seek victory with its edges
    Riding with it, spite of all, in darkness
On battle day its wielding my greeting
    Otherwise I'm no hero as warrior chief
When fear dulls my will to a far goal
    The farthest possible is finding no will
For I am of folk for whom our souls
    Seem to scorn dwelling in flesh or bone

كَذا أَنا يا دُنيا إِذا شِئتِ فاذهَبي … وَيا نَفسُ زيدي في كَرائِهِها قُدُمــا
فَـلا عَبَرَت بـي ساعَـةٌ لا تُعِزُّنــي … ولا صَحِبَتنـي مُهجَـةٌ تَقبَـلُ الظُّلمــا

(١٠٢)

وجعل قوم يستعظمون ما قاله في آخر هذه القصيدة فقال:

يَستَعظِمـونَ أَبياتــاً نِمـتُ بِهــا … لا تَحسُــدُنَّ عَلــى أَن يَنــامَ الأَســدا
لَو أَنَّ ثَمَّ قُلوبـاً يَعقِلــونَ بِهــا … أَنساهُـمُ الذُّعـرُ مِمّا تَحتَها الحَسَــدا

(١٠٣)

«من الكامل»

يمدح القاضي أبا الفضل بن عبد الله بن الحسين الأنطاكي:

لَكِ يا مَنازِلُ فِي القُلوبِ مَنازِلُ … أَقفَرتِ أَنتِ وَهُنَّ مِنكِ أَواهِـلُ
يَعلَمنَ ذاكِ وَما عَلِمتِ وَإِنَّما … أَولاكُما يَبكى عَلَيــهِ العاقِــلُ
وَأَنا الَّذي اِجتَلَبَ المَنِيَّةَ طَرفُــهُ … فَمَــنِ المُطالَـبُ وَالقَتيـلُ القاتِـلُ
تَخلو الدِّيارُ مِنَ الظِّباءِ وَعِندَهُ … مِن كُلِّ تابِعَـةٍ خَيـالٌ خاذِلُ
اللّاءِ أَفتَكَها الجَبانُ بِمُهجَتي … وَأَحَبُّها قُربـاً إِلَيَّ الباخِـلُ
الرّامِياتُ لَنا وَهُنَّ نَوافِـرٌ … وَالخاتِلاتُ لَنا وَهُنَّ غَوافِـلُ
كَأَنَّنا عَن شِبهِهِنَّ مِنَ المَها … فَلَهُنَّ فِي غَيرِ التُّرابِ حَبائِلُ
مِن طاعِني ثُغَرِ الرِّجالِ جَآذِرٌ … وَمِنَ الرِّماحِ دَمالِجٌ وَخَلاخِـلُ
وَلِذا اِسمُ أَغطِيَةِ العُيونِ جُفونُها … مِن أَنَّها عَمَلَ السُّيوفِ عَوامِـلُ
كَم وَقفَةٍ سَجَرَتكَ شَوقاً بَعدَ ما … غَرِيَ الرَّقيبُ بِنا وَلَجَّ العـاذِلُ
دونَ التَّعانُقِ ناحِلَينِ كَشَكلَي … نَصبٍ أَدَقُّهُما وَضَمَّ الشّاكِلُ
اِنعَم وَلَذَّ فَلِلأُمورِ أَواخِـرٌ … أَبَداً إِذا كانَت لَهُنَّ أَوائِـلُ
ما دُمتَ مِن أَرَبِ الحِسانِ فَإِنَّما … رَوقُ الشَّبابِ عَلَيكَ ظِلٌّ زائِلُ
لِلَّهوِ آوِنَةٌ تَمُرُّ كَأَنَّها … قُبَلٌ يُزَوِّدُها حَبيبٌ راحِـلُ
جَمَحَ الزَّمانُ فَلا لَذيذٌ خالِصٌ … مِمّا يَشوبُ وَلا سُرورٌ كامِلُ
حَتّى أَبو الفَضلِ اِبنُ عَبدِ اللَهِ رُؤ … يَتُهُ المُنى وَهِيَ المَقامُ الهائِلُ

Thus am 1, O world, if you wish depart
    But O my soul put me ahead of its hate
May no hour pass that won't harden me
    May no blood be mine that approaches evil

102
Some folk exaggerated
what he said in the last part of this qasida
so he said.
(Outspread da)

They exaggerate what I said in verses
    They should not be envious if a lion roars
If they had any heart they'd understand
    Fear makes them forget their jealousy in it

103
He spoke praising
the Qadi Abu Fadl ibn Abdallah
ibn al Hasan al-Antakya.
(Perfect lu)

For you O camp there are camps in hearts
    You are waste but they are peopled by you
You know this and you know it not
    Worthiest of you is a weeper who discerns
I'm one whose eye sought for death
    So who is avenger when a killer perishes?
Camps are empty of fawns but with him
    Is the stray ghost among all the weaklings
The boldest of them shy of my heart
    The most loving of them near me stingy
They shoot us though they are fleeing
    One trapped us though they did know it
They avoid us in their likeness to wild
    Cows for they have snares not set in dust
Oryx young, jousters at men's breasts
    The lances are bracelets and ankle rings
The eyelid's name for them is scabbard
    Since they wielders of the sword's work
How many watchings filled you with love
    As a guard wondered at us and gossip grew
Short of embrace, thin as vowel points
    In accusative as pointer scans and crowds
Be gracious and rejoice for things have
    Ends ever when they have their beginnings
You do not last as an object of beauty
    Youth's shade on you is a shade that fades
Pleasure has a flash that passes as if
    It were a kiss a departing lover bestows
Time runs away, no perfect pleasure
    Among those who grow gray, no full joy
Till we reach Abu Fadl ibn Abdallah
    Whose sight is reward in awesome union

مَمْطُورَةٌ طُرْقِي إِلَيْهَا دُونَهَا ... مِنْ جُودِهِ فِي كُلِّ فَجٍّ وَابِلِ
مَحْجُوبَةٌ بِسُرَادِقٍ مِنْ هَيْبَةٍ ... تَثْنِي الأَزِمَّةَ وَالمَطِيَّ ذَوَامِلِ
لِلشَّمْسِ فِيهِ وَلِلسَّحَابِ وَلِلبِحَا ... رِ وَلِلأُسْوَدِ وَلِلرِّيَاحِ شَمَائِلِ
وَلَدَيْهِ مِلْعَقَيَانِ وَالأَدَبِ المُفَا ... دِ وَمِلْحَيَاةٍ وَمِلْمَمَاتِ مَنَاهِلِ
لَوْ لَمْ يَهَبْ لِجَبِّ الوُفُودِ حَوَالَهُ ... لَسَرَى إِلَيْهِ قَطَا الفَلَاةِ النَّاهِلُ
يَدْرِي بِمَا بِكَ قَبْلَ تُظْهِرُهُ لَهُ ... مِنْ ذِهْنِهِ قَبْلَ تَسَائِلِ
وَتَرَاهُ مُعْتَرِضًا لَهَا وَمُوَالِيًا ... أَحْدَاقُنَا وَتَحَارُ حِينَ يُقَابِلُ
كَلِمَاتُهُ قُضُبٌ وَهُنَّ فَوَاصِلُ ... كُلُّ الضَّرَائِبِ تَحْتَهُنَّ مَفَاصِلُ
هَزَمَتْ مَكَارِمُهُ المَكَارِمَ كُلَّهَا ... حَتَّى كَأَنَّ المُكْرَمَاتِ قَنَابِلُ
وَقَتَلْنَ دَفْرًا وَالدُّهَيْمَ فَمَا تَرَى ... أُمَّ الدُّهَيْمِ وَأُمَّ دَفْرٍ ثَاكِلُ
عَلَّامَةُ العُلَمَاءِ وَلِلُّجِّ الَّذِي ... لَا يَنْتَهِي وَلِكُلِّ لُجٍّ سَاحِلُ
لَوْ طَابَ مَوْلِدُ كُلِّ حَيٍّ مِثْلَهُ ... وَلَدَا النِّسَاءُ وَمَا لَهُنَّ قَوَابِلُ
لَوْ بَانَ بِالكَرَمِ الجَنِينُ بَيَانَهُ ... لَدَرَتْ بِهِ ذَكَرٌ أَمْ أُنْثَى الحَامِلُ
لِيَزِدْ بَنُو الحَسَنِ الشِّرَافُ تَوَاضُعًا ... هَيْهَاتِ تُكْتَمُ فِي الظَّلَامِ مَشَاعِلُ
جَفَخَتْ وَهُمْ لَا يَجْفَخُونَ بِهَا بِهِمْ ... شِيَمٌ عَلَى الحَسَبِ الأَغَرِّ دَلَائِلُ
مُتَشَابِهُو وَرَعِ النُّفُوسِ كَبِيرُهُمْ ... وَصَغِيرُهُمْ عَفُّ الإِزَارِ حُلَاحِلُ
يَا افْخَرْ فَإِنَّ النَّاسَ فِيكَ ثَلَاثَةٌ ... مُسْتَعْظِمٌ أَوْ حَاسِدٌ أَوْ جَاهِلُ
وَلَقَدْ عَلَوْتَ فَمَا تُبَالِي بَعْدَ مَا ... عَرَفُوا أَيَحْمَدُ أَمْ يَذُمُّ القَائِلُ
أُثْنِي عَلَيْكَ وَلَوْ تَشَاءُ لَقُلْتَ لِي ... قَصَّرْتَ فَالإِمْسَاكُ عَنِّي نَائِلُ
لَا تَجْسُرُ الفُصَحَاءُ تُنْشِدُ هَهُنَا ... بَيْتًا وَلَكِنِّي الهِزَبْرُ البَاسِلُ
مَا نَالَ أَهْلُ الجَاهِلِيَّةِ كُلُّهُمْ ... شِعْرِي وَلَا سَمِعَتْ بِسِحْرِي بَابِلُ
وَإِذَا أَتَتْكَ مَذَمَّتِي مِنْ نَاقِصٍ ... فَهِيَ الشَّهَادَةُ لِي بِأَنِّي كَامِلُ
سَتَرُوا النَّدَى سَتْرًا الغُرَابِ سِفَادَهُ ... فَبَدَا وَهَلْ يَخْفَى الرَّبَابُ الهَاطِلُ
مَنْ لِي بِفَهْمِ أُهَيْلِ عَصْرٍ يَدَّعِي ... أَنْ يَحْسَبَ الهِنْدِيَّ فِيهِمْ بَاقِلُ
وَأَمَّا وَحَقَّكَ وَهْوَ غَايَةُ مُقْسِمٍ ... لَلْحَقُّ أَنْتَ وَمَا سِوَاكَ البَاطِلُ
الطِّيبُ أَنْتَ أَصَابَكَ طِيبَةٌ ... وَالمَاءُ أَنْتَ إِذَا اغْتَسَلْتَ الغَاسِلُ
مَا دَارَ فِي الحَنَكِ اللِّسَانُ وَقَلَّبَتْ ... قَلَمًا بِأَحْسَنَ مِنْ ثَنَاكَ أَنَامِلُ

Roads that lead to him are rained on
    Before him gifts shower in every pass
Hid by awnings in reverence to him
    It curbs bridles though camels are fast
In it a sun and clouds and ocean
    And the winds and the shape of lions
With him fine gold, culture redeemed
    In some of the sources of life and death
If he didn't fear noisy crowds about him
    Desert crowds would come to him as well
By quick wit he knows your need before
    It is shown, he responds before a request
Our eyes see him in front and they turn
    Away, but they return as he approaches
His words are swords, they divide
    All of the blows have muscle behind them
Generosity conquers all other bounty
    It's as if philanthropy were cavalry troops
They ruin stench and grief so you see
    No mother Duhaim or mother stink bereft
Most noted of the learned, this tide
    Won't end though all tides have shores
If birth in each tribe were pure as his
    Women would bear without midwives
If embryos appeared generous as he
    A bearer would know male from female
Noble Banu Hasan increase humility!
    Unlikely as a torch hid in the darkness
They veil gifts as ravens hide mating
    It appears, should the rain cloud hide?
Nature boasts of them, they do not
    As indication of their noble ancestry
Their elders alike soul's restraint
    Their youths wear simple chief's dress
O noble man, men: do three things
    They wonder at, envy, or ignore fame
You rose, but you did not worry if
    They knew a speaker praised, blamed
I praise you, if you wish then say:
    You're short but brevity is good for me
The eloquent dare not recite their
    Verses here but I am the fiercest lion
Not all the Jahiliya men could make
    My poems, nor Babylon hear my magic
If my faults come to you from a critic
    That is witness for me that I am worthy
Who credits small folk's wit who claim
    A grocer can appraise a sword for them?
O by your truth! the highest oath, you
    Are truth and another than you is false
Perfume when its odor comes to you
    You are water and you wash yourself
Tongue never moved in mouth or fingers
    Turned the pen better than in your praise

(١٠٤)

«من البسيط»

يمدح أخاه سهل سعيد بن عبيد الله بن الحسن الانطاكي:

تَدْمَى وألِّفَ في ذا القَلبِ أحزانَا	قَدْ عَلَّمَ البَينُ مِنّا البَينُ أجْفانَا
لَيْلَبَثَ الحَيُّ دونَ السَّيرِ حَيرانَا	أمَلْتُ ساعةَ كشفَ معصَمِها
صَوْنٌ عُقُولُهُمُ من لحظِها صَانَا	ولَوْ بَدَتْ لأتاهَتْهُم فَحَجَّبَها
يَظلُّ من وَخدِها في الخِدرِ خَشيانَا	بالواخِداتِ وحادِيها وبي قَمَرٌ
إذا نَضاها ويكسى الحُسنَ عُريانَا	أمّا الثِّيابُ فَتَعْرى مِن مَحاسِنِهِ
حتى يَصيرَ على الأعكانِ أعكانَا	يَضُمُّهُ المِسكُ ضَمَّ المُسْتَهامِ بهِ
فاليَوْمَ كلُّ عزيزٍ بَعدَكُم هَانَا	قد كنتُ أشفِقُ من دَمعي على بصري
وللمُحِبِّ مِنَ التَّذكارِ نِيرانَا	تُهدي البَوارقُ أخلافَ المِياهِ لكُمْ
قَلبٌ إذا شِئْتُ أنْ أسلاكُمْ خانَا	إذا قَدِمتُ على الأهوالِ شَيَّعَني
فَلا أعاتِبُهُ صَفْحاً وإهْوانَا	أبدو فيَسجُدُ مَن بالسَّوءِ يذكُرُني
إنَّ النَّفيسَ غَريبٌ حَيثُما كَانَا	وهكذا كنتُ في أهلي وفي وطَني
ألقى الكَمِيَّ ويلقاني إذا حَانَا	مَحسَّدُ الفَضلِ مكذوبٌ على أثَري
ولا أبيتُ على ما فاتَ حَسرَانَا	لا أشرَئِبُّ إلى ما لم يَفُتْ طَمَعاً
ولَوْ حَمَّلتَ إليَّ الدَّهرَ مَلآنَا	ولا أسَرُّ بما غَيري الحَميدُ بهِ
ما دُمتُ حَيّاً وما قَلقَلنَ كِيرانَا	لا يَجذِبَنَّ رِكابي نَحوَهُ أحَدٌ
إلى سَعيدِ بنِ عَبدِ اللهِ بُعْرانَا	لو استَطَعْتُ ركِبتُ النّاسَ كلَّهُمُ
عَمّا يَراهُ مِنَ الإحسانِ عُميانَا	فالعِيسُ أعقَلُ مِن قَومٍ رَأيتُهُم
ذاكَ الشُّجاعُ وإن لم يرضَ أقرانَا	ذاكَ الجَوادُ وإنْ قَلَّ الجَوادُ لَهُ
فَلَوْ أصيبَ بشيءٍ منهُ عَزّانَا	ذاكَ المُعَدُّ الذي تَقنو يَداهُ لنَا
حتى تُوهِّمَنَ للأزمانِ أزْمانَا	خَفَّ الزَّمانُ على أطرافِ أنْمُلِهِ
والسَّيفَ والضَّيفَ رَحبَ البالِ جَذلانَا	يَلقَى الوَغَى والقَنَا والنّازِلاتِ بهِ
ومن تَكَرُّمِهِ والبِشرُ نَشوانَا	تَخالُهُ من ذكاءِ القَلبِ مُحتَمِياً

104
He spoke praising his brother Abu Sahl Said
ibn Abdallah ibn al-Hasan al-Himsi.
(Outspread na)

Parting has taught our eyelids separation
    Bleeding, association of a heart and sorrow
I hoped when they went to see her wrist
    A tribe perplexed might stop before going
If she showed she'd divert them as one
    Drew curtains to keep wits from her glance
By the camel, a driver and myself! a moon
    Is panting in the curtains from her movement
As for the dress if one strips its beauty
    Undressed one clothes her in naked beauty
Musk embraces it with a lover's embrace
    Until that puts wrinkles on these belly folds
I was anxious in my tears for my sight
    But after you each dear thing is scorned
Clouds bring their watery breasts to you
    For me beloved memories come in flashes
If I met terrors a heart went with me
    When I wished solace from you it betrayed
I come and he who thinks ill of me bows
    I chide him not with forgiveness and scorn
So I am among my folk and in my land
    What is precious is alien wherever that is
I envy virtue, a liar about my mark casts
    Down a hero and meets me if his time nears
I'm not thirsty for what urges no need
    Nor do I reject whatever passes in regret
Nor am I happy when others are liked
    Even if you brought me. The time filled up
No one will attract my camel to him
    While I am alive or while the saddle rocks
But if I'd been able I'd have ridden
    All men as camels to Said ibn Abdallah
For a camel is wiser than folk I see
    As blind to what he sees as benevolence
It's bounty even if his gifts are small
    Bravery even if he's not content as hero
It's provision his hand gained for us
    If he gives some of it he glorifies us too
Time is light on his fingertips until
    They are imagined to be times for times
He meets battle, lances and attacks
    A sword and a guest's open hand gladly
You think from warm heart he's aflame
    From his joy and cheer that he is drunk

مِنْ جودِهِ وتَجُرّ الخيلَ أرسانا	وتَسحَبُ الحِبَرَ القَيناتُ رافِلَةً
كَمَنْ يُبَشِّرُهُ بالماءِ عَطشانا	يُعطي المُبَشِّرَ بالقُصّادِ قَبلَهُمُ
في قَومِهِم مِثلُهُم في الغُرِّ عَدنانا	حُزْتَ بَني الحَسَنِ الحُسنى فإنَّهُمُ
إلّا ونَحنُ نَراهُ فيهِمُ الآنا	ما شَيَّدَ اللهُ مِنْ مَجدٍ لسالِفِهِم
في الخَطِّ واللفظِ والهَيجاءِ فُرسانا	إنْ كوتِبوا أوْ لُقوا أو حوربوا وُجدوا
على رِماحِهِمِ في الطَّعنِ خِرْصانا	كأنَّ ألسُنَهُم في النُّطقِ قد جُعِلَتْ
أو يَنشَقونَ مِنَ الخَطِّيِّ رَيحانا	كأنَّهُم يَرِدونَ المَوتَ مِنْ ظَمإٍ
أعدى العِدى ولِمَن آخَيتُ إخوانا	الكائِنينَ لِمَنْ أبغي عَداوَتَهُ
ظُمْيَ الشِّفاهِ جِعادَ الشَّعرِ غُرّانا	خَلائِقٌ لَوْ حَواها الزِّنجُ لانقَلَبوا
لها اضطِراراً ولَوْ أقصَوكَ شَنآنا	وأنفُسٌ يَلمَعيّاتٌ تُحِبُّهُمُ
والِداتٍ وألباباً وأذهانا	الواضِحينَ أُبوّاتٍ وأجنِةً
إنَّ اللُّيوثَ تَصيدُ النّاسَ أحدانا	يا صائِدَ الجَحفَلِ المَرهوبِ جانِبُهُ
وإنَّما يَهَبُ الوَهّابُ أحيانا	وواهِباً، كلَّ وَقتٍ وقتُ نائِلِهِ
ثُمَّ اتَّخَذْتَ لها السُّؤّالَ خُزّانا	أنتَ الذي سَبَكَ الأموالَ مَكرُمَةً
لم تأتِ في السِّرِّ ما لم تأتِ إعلانا	عَلَيكَ مِنكَ إذا أخليتَ مُرتَقِبٌ
أنا الذي نامَ إنْ نَبَّهْتُ يَقظانا	لا أستَزيدُكَ فيما فيكَ مِن كَرَمٍ
ورَدَّ سُخطاً على الأيّامِ رِضوانا	فإنَّ مِثلَكَ باهَيْتُ الكِرامَ بِهِ
قَدراً وأرفَعُهُم في المَجدِ بُنيانا	وأنتَ أبعَدُهُم ذِكراً وأكبَرُهُمْ
وشَرّفَ النّاسَ إذ سَوّاكَ إنسانا	قد شَرَّفَ اللهُ أرضاً أنتَ ساكِنُها

(١٠٥)

«من الكامل»

يمدح أبا أيوب أحمد بن عمران:

داني الصِّفاتِ بَعيدٌ مَوصوفاتِها	سِرْبٌ مَحاسِنُهُ حُرِمَتْ ذَواتِها
بَشَراً رأيتُ أرَقَّ مِن عَبَراتِها	أوْفى فَكُنْتُ إذا رَمَيْتُ بمُقلَتي
تَوَهَّمُ الزَّفَراتِ زَجرَ حُداتِها	يَستاقُ عيسَهُمْ أنيني خَلفَها

Singing girls trail their dress skirts
    By his bounty, horses wear his halters
He gives a client welcome before
    As one does good to thirst with water
Beauty rewards the Banu Hasan they
    Among folk are as those in Eden's glory
God did not count glory lost in their
    Ancestors, indeed we find it in them now
If written to or met or warred on they
    In script and word and war are knights
As if their tongues in argument are
    As lanceheads on spears in jousting
As if they go to drink death thirsty
    Smell the Khatti spears as sweet herbs
Beings for whose hate desire worst
    Foes, for one I'm friendly with, brothers
Natures that if blacks had they'd try
    Thin lips, straight hair or white skins
Souls whose wit makes them loved
    Perforce even if far from you in hatred
From fathers with unclouded brows
    From mothers with minds and thought
O army hunter whose flanks are fear
    Whereas the lions must hunt men singly
Gifts, each hour is time for giving
    But donors dispense only now and then
You are one to pour wealth lavishly
    You accept clients for it as treasurers
Trusting yourself as guard if alone
    You do nothing secretly not done openly
I seek no increase of nobility in you
    I as sleeper would waken one who wakes
In such as you I glorify magnanimity
    Repelling what days hate by our content
You farthest in glory and greatest
    In power and highest in building fame
God honors earth in your dwelling
    He honors men since he made men as you

105
He spoke praising Abu Ayyub ibn Imran.
(Perfect ha)

A herd whose beauties I'm forbid to own
    Marks are nearby but portrayal is from afar
I paid for it when I shot my glances at
    White skin and I saw their thinnest tears
My groans urge their camels onward
    They fancy my sighs are the driver's cries

شَجَرٌ جَنَيتُ المَوْتَ مِنْ ثَمَراتِها	وكَأنَّها شَجَرٌ بَدَتْ لَكِنَّها
لَمَحَتْ حَرارَةَ مَدْمَعِيّ سِماتِها	لا سِرْتِ مِنْ إبِلٍ لَوْ أَنّي فَوقَها
وحَمَلْتِ ما حُمِّلْتِ مِنْ حَسَراتِها	وحَمَلْتُ ما حُمِّلْتِ مِنْ هذي المَها
لأَعِفُّ عَمّا في سَرابيلاتِها	إنّي على شَغَفي بِما في خَمرِها
فَيَّ كُلُّ مَليحَةٍ ضَرّاتِها	وتَرى المُروءَةَ الفُتُوَّةَ والأُبُوَّ
في خَلْوَتي لا الخَوْفُ مِنْ تَبِعاتِها	هُنَّ الثَّلاثُ المانِعاتي لَذَّتي
ثَبْتَ الجَنانِ كَأَنّني لَم آتِها	ومَطالِبٍ فيها الهَلاكُ أَتَيْتُها
أَقْواتَ وَحْشٍ كُنَّ مِنْ أَقْواتِها	ومَقانِبٍ بِمَقانِبٍ غادَرْتُها
أيدي بَني عِمرانَ في جَبهاتِها	أَقْبَلْتُها غُرَرَ الجِيادِ كَأنَّما
في ظَهرِها والطَّعنُ في لَبَّاتِها	الثّابِتينَ فُروسَةً كَجُلودِها
والرّاكِبينَ جُدودُهُمْ أَماتِها	ألعارِفينَ بِها كَما عَرَفَتْهُمُ
وكَأنَّهُمْ وُلِدوا على صَهَواتِها	فَكَأنَّها نُتِجَتْ قِياماً تَحْتَهُمْ
مِثْلُ القُلوبِ بِلا سُوَيداواتِها	إنَّ الكِرامَ بِلا كِرامٍ مِنْهُمُ
والمَجْدُ يَغْلِبُها على شَهَواتِها	تِلْكَ النُّفوسُ الغالِباتِ على العُلى
بِنَدى أَبي أيّوبَ خَيرِ نَباتِها	سُقيتِ مَنابِتَها التي سَقَتِ الوَرى
بَلْ مِنْ سَلامَتِها إلى أَوْقاتِها	لَيسَ التَّعَجُّبُ مِنْ مَواهِبِ مالِهِ
ما حِفْظُها الأشياءَ مِنْ عاداتِها	عَجَباً لَهُ حَفِظَ العِنانَ بأَنْمُلٍ
أَحْصى بِوافِرِ مُهْرِهِ ميماتِها	لَوْ مَرَّ يَركُضُ في سُطورِ كِتابَةٍ
حَتّى مِنَ الآذانِ في أَخراتِها	يَضَعُ السِّنانَ بحَيثُ شاءَ مُجاوِلاً
لَيسَتْ قَوائِمُهُنَّ مِنْ آلاتِها	تَكبو وراءَكَ يا ابنَ أَحْمَدَ قُرَّحٌ
أَجرى مِنَ العَسَلانِ في قَنَواتِها	رَعدُ الفَوارِسِ مِنكَ في أَبْدانِها
بِكَ راءَ نَفسَكَ لَم يَقُلْ لَكَ هاتِها	لا خَلْقَ أَسْمَحُ مِنكَ إلّا عارِفٌ
تَرتيلَكَ السُّوَراتِ مِنْ آياتِها	غَلِتَ الذي حَسَبَ العُشورَ بآيَةٍ
ويَبينُ عِتْقُ الخَيلِ في أَصْواتِها	كَرَماً تَبَيَّنَ في كَلامِكَ مائِلاً
لا تَخرُجُ الأقمارُ عَن هالاتِها	أَعيا زَوالُكَ عَنْ مَحَلٍّ نِلتَهُ
أَنتَ الرِّحالَ وشائِقٌ عِلّاتِها	لا نَعذُلُ المَرَضَ الذي بِكَ شائِقٌ

As if they were trees in a desert but
    Trees from which I pick death as fruit
Would you were not on a camel, if I
    Were my tears' treat would blot brands
I bore what you bore from wild cows
    You bore what I have borne of sorrow
I'm in love with what's under her veil
    But chaste as to what is under a dress
Every beauty knows manhood, soul
    And authority in me as check to them
These three forbid my pleasure in
    Private life, not fear of consequences
Among things wanted I face death
    With firm heart as if I had not come to it
Many a horse troop I left with troops
    As food for beasts who had been food
I came to them with one nobly marked
    On its forehead a grace of Banu Imran
Confident in horsemanship as skin
    On the back with thrust at the breast
Knowing it as they knew them since
    Ancestors were riders of their mothers
They gave birth standing beneath
    As if the men were born in the saddles
Noble things without their kindness
    Like hearts without their inner cores
Such conquering souls on heights
    Glory wins them spite of their passion
The growth that watered men came
    By gifts of Abu Ayyub, the best growth
No wonder in his giving flocks but
    Rather in their safety in these times
Wonder at his fingers' hold on reins
    Since their hold on things is unusual
If he spurs among army ranks he
    Prints their mim by his horse's hoofs
He puts lanceheads on any target
    He wants even to holes in the ears
Grown horses fall behind O Ibn Ahmad
    So their legs are no longer useful there
Knights bodies shudder due to you
    Running from points through the shafts
None more favored than you but he
    Knows you and does not say: Bestow!
You deceive those thinking of Tens
    Your chanting Surahs is as miracles
Nobility clearly shown in your words
    A horse's breeding is plain in whinnies
Your absence from a place unlikely
    Moons cannot escape the constellations
We don't blame your illnesses, you
    Magnet to men and to their ailments

182 Diwan al-Mutanabbi

فـإذا نَـوَتْ سَـفَراً إلَيْـكَ سَبَقْنَها … فَـأضَفْتَ قَبْـلَ مُضافِهَـا حالاتِهَـا
ومَنـازِلُ الحُمّـى الجُسـومُ فقُـلْ لنـا … مـا عُذرُهـا فـي تَركِهـا خيراتِهَـا
أعجَبتَهـا شَـرَفاً فَطـالَ وُقُوفُهـا … لِتـأمُّلِ الأعضـاءِ لا لأذاتِهَـا
وبَذَلْـتَ مـا عَشِقَتْهُ نَفسُـك كلَّـه … حتـى بَذَلْـتَ لِهَـذِهِ صِحّاتِهَـا
حـقُّ الكواكِبِ أن تعـودَك مِـن عَلٍ … وتَعـودُكَ الآسـادُ مِـنْ غاباتِهَـا
والجِـنُّ مِـن سُـتراتِها والوَحـشُ مِـن … فَلواتِهـا والطَّيـرُ مِـنْ وُكَناتِهـا
ذِكْـرَ الأنـامِ لَنـا فكانَ قصيـدَةً … كنـتَ البَديـعَ الفَرْدَ مِـنْ أبياتِهـا
في النّـاسِ أمثِلـةٌ تَـدورُ حَياتُهـا … كَمَماتِهـا ومَماتُهـا كَحَياتِهَـا
هِبْـتُ النّكَـاحَ حِـذارَ نَسْـلٍ مِثلهـا … حتّـى وَفَـرْتُ عَلَى النِّسَـاءِ بَناتِهـا
فـاليَوْمَ صِـرْتُ إلى الـذي لَـوْ أنَّـهُ … مَلِـكَ البَريَّـةِ لا سـتَقَلَّ هِباتِهَـا
مُسـتَرْخِصٌ نظَـرَّ إليـهِ بِمـا بِـهِ … نَظَـرَتْ وعَـثْـرَةَ رِجْلِـهِ بِدياتِهَـا

(١٠٦)

«من الطويل»

يمدح علي بن أحمد بن عامر الانطاكي:

أطـاوِعُ خيْـلاً مِـن فوارسِها الدَّهـرُ … وَحيداً ومـا قَـوْلِي كـذا ومَعِـيَ الصَّبْـرُ
وأشـجَعُ مِنـي كـلَّ يَـوْمٍ سَـلامَتي … ومـا ثَبَتَـتْ إلاّ وفـي نَفْسِـها أمْـرُ
تَمَرَّسْـتُ بالآفـاتِ حتـى تَركْتُهَـا … تقولُ أماتَ المَـوْتُ أم ذُعِـرَ الذُّعْـرُ
وأقْدَمْـتُ إقْـدامَ الأتـيِّ كـأنَّ لـي … سِوى مُهجَتي أو كـان لي عندهـا وِتْـرُ
ذُرى النَّفْـسِ تأخُـذُ وُسْـعَها قبـلَ بَينِها … فمُفْتَـرِقٌ جـاران دارُهُمـا العُمْـرُ
ولا تَحْسَـبَنَّ المجْـدَ زِقّـاً وقَيْنَـةً … فمـا المَجْـدُ إلاّ السَّيـفُ والفتكـةُ البِكـرُ
وتضريـبُ أعنـاقِ المُلـوكِ وأن تُـرَى … لـكَ الهَبَـواتُ السّـودُ والعسـكرُ المَجْـرُ
وترْكُـكَ فـي الدنْيـا دَوِيَّـاً كأنَّمـا … تَـداوَلَ سَـمعَ المَـرْءِ أنْمُلُـهُ العَشْـرُ
إذ الفضْلُ لم يَرْفَعْـكَ عن شُـكرِ ناقصٍ … على هِبَـةٍ فالفضْـلُ فيمَـن لـه الشّـكْرُ
ومَـنْ ينفـقُ السّـاعاتِ في جمـعِ مالِـهِ … مَخافـةَ فَقْـرٍ فالـذي فَعَـلَ الفقْـرُ
علـيَّ لأهـلِ الجَـوْرِ كـلُّ طِمِـرَّةٍ … عَلَيهـا غلامٌ مِلْـأُ حَيزومِـهِ غِمْـرُ
يُديـرُ بـأطْـرافِ الرِّمـاحِ عَلَيهِـمْ … كُـؤوسَ المَنايا حيـثُ لا تُشـتَهَى الخمـرُ

If they are far off you go ahead, you
    Meet before they tell of their incursions
Fever's dwelling is the body so tell
    What is its excuse in leaving its profit?
You surprised it by nobility, long stay
    To give hope to limbs, not to harm them
You lavished all your soul loved till
    You lavished for that its health itself
Stars duty to visit you from above
    Lions pay a call on you from their lair
Jinn from their hiding, wild beasts
    From deserts, birds from their nests
Humanity noted by us in a qasida
    You the unique image in all its verses
Men are examples whose life passes
    As their death and death is their living
I feared marriage due to such issue
    So I left the women with their daughters
Today I return to him who if he had
    Earth would think it small to give as gift
A look at him cheap for all who see
    As his stubbed toe is worth a bloodwit

106
He spoke praising
Ali ibn Ahmad ibn Amr al Antakya.
(Long ru)

I joust horses whose riders are time
    Alone, what do I say? patience is with me
Braver than myself, each day my bond
    It's not firm if it has no goal within itself
I wrestled with woes till I left them
    Saying: Has death died or fear afraid?
I went ahead in a rush as if I had
    Another soul or had a bloodprice on it
Let soul have its way before parting
    Neighbors whose camp is life separate
Don't think glory wineskin and singer
    Glory is only the sword and virgin fury
Cutting men's throats and watching
    Your black dust and streaming armies
Leaving in the world an uproar that
    One's ten fingers must stop his ears for
If worth barred not your faulty thanks
    For a gift merit is his who made the gift
One wastes time in amassing wealth
    For fear of want gathers only his penury
Every mare for me against tyrants
    On her a youth with breast full of hate
With spearpoint set he passes a cup
    Of death when the wine is not asked for

184 Diwan al-Mutanabbi

حِـبَـالٌ وبَحـرٌ شاهِـدٌ أنّـي البَحْـرُ	وكـم مِـن جِبـالٍ جُبْـتُ تَشهَـدُ أنّـي الـ
مِـن العيـسِ فيـهِ واسِـطُ الكـورِ والظَّهْـرُ	وخَـرقٍ مكـانٌ مِنـهُ مكانُنـا
عَلـى كُـرَةٍ أوْ أرْضُـهُ مَعَنـا سَـفْرُ	يَخِـدْنَ بِنـا فـي جَـوْزِهِ وكَأنّنـا
عَلـى أُفْقِـهِ مِـنْ بَرْقِـهِ حُلَـلٌ حُمْـرُ	ويَـومٌ وصَلَّنـاهُ بلَيْـلٍ كَأنّمـا
عَلـى مَتنِـهِ مِـنْ دَجنِـهِ حُلَـلٌ خُضْـرُ	ولَيْـلٍ وصَلَّنـاهُ بيَـومٍ كَأنّمـا
عَـلا لَـمْ يَمُـتْ أوْ في السَّحـابِ لَـهُ قَبْـرُ	وغَيْـثٍ ظَنَنّـا تَحتَـهُ أنَّ عامِـراً
يَجـودُ بِـهِ لَـوْ لَـمْ أُجِـزْ ويَـدي صِفْـرُ	أو ابْـنَ ابنِـهِ البـاقي عليَّ بـنَ أحمَـدٍ
سَحـابٌ عَلـى كلِّ السَّحـابِ لَـهُ فَخْـرُ	وإنَّ سَحـاباً جـودُهُ مِثـلُ جـودِهِ
ولَـوْ ضَمَّهَـا قَلْـبٌ لَمـا ضَمَّـهُ صَـدْرُ	فَتـىً لا يَضُـمُّ القَلْـبُ هِمّـاتِ قَلبِـهِ
وهَـلْ نافِـعٌ لَـوْ لا الأكُـفُّ القَنـا السُّمْـرُ	ولا يَنْفَـعُ الإمكـانُ لَـوْ لا سَخـاؤُهُ
كَمـا يَتلاقـى الهِنْدَوانِـيُّ والنَّصْـرُ	قِـرانٌ تَلاقـى الصَّلْـتُ فيـهِ وعامِـرٌ
تَـرى النـاسَ قُـلاًّ حَوْلَـهُ وهُـمْ كُثْـرُ	فَجـاءَ بـهِ صَلْـتُ الجَبيـنِ مُعَظَّمـاً
هُـوَ الكَـرَمُ المَـدُّ الـذي مـا لَـهُ جَـزْرُ	مُفَـدَّىً بآبـاءِ الرِّجـالِ سَمَيْـدَعـاً
يُسايِرُنـي في كلِّ رَكْـبٍ لَـهُ ذِكْـرُ	ومـا زِلْـتُ حتـى قـادَني الشَّـوْقُ نَحـوَهُ
فلَمّـا التَقَيْنـا صَغَّـرَ الخَبَـرَ الخُبْـرُ	وأسْتَكبِـرُ الأخبـارَ قَبْـلَ لِقائِـهِ
بكلِّ وآةٍ، كلُّ مـا لَقِيَـتْ نَحْـرُ	إليـكَ طَعَنّـا في مَـدَى كلِّ صَفْصَـفٍ
كَـأنَّ نَـوالاً صَـرَّ في جلدِهـا النِّبْـرُ	إذا ورَمَـتْ مِـن لَسعَـةٍ مَرَحَـتْ لَهـا
ودونَـكَ في أحوالِـكَ الشَّمـسُ والبَـدْرُ	فجِئنـاكَ دونَ الشَّمـسِ والبَـدرِ في النَّـوى
ولَـوْ كنـتَ بَـرْدَ المـاءِ لَـمْ يَكُـنِ العِشْـرُ	كَـأنَّـكَ بَـرْدُ المـاءِ لا عَيْـشَ دونَـهُ
وهـذا الكـلامُ النَّظـمُ والنّائِـلُ النَّثْـرُ	دَعـاني إليـكَ العِلْـمُ والحِلْـمُ والحِجـى
إذا كُتِبَـتْ يَبْيَـضُّ مِـن نورِهـا الحِبْـرُ	ومـا قُلـتُ مِـن شِعـرٍ تَكـادُ بُيوتُـهُ
نُجـومُ الثُّرَيّـا أو خَلائِقُـكَ الزُّهْـرُ	كَـأنَّ المَعانـي في فَصاحَـةِ لَفظِهـا
ومـا يَقْتَضينـي مِـن جَماجِمِهـا النَّسْـرُ	وجَنَّبَنـي قُـرْبَ السَّلاطيـنِ مَقْتُهـا
وأهـوَنُ مِـن مَـرْأىً صَغيـرٍ بِـهِ كِبْـرُ	وإنّـي رأيـتُ الضُّـرَّ أحسَـنَ مَنظَـراً
أوَدُّ اللَّواتـي ذا اسمُهـا منكَ والشَّطْـرُ	لِسانـي وعَيْنـي والفُـؤادُ وهِمَّتـي
ولكـنْ لِشِعـري فيـكَ مِـن نَفسِـه شِعْـرُ	ومـا أنـا وَحـدي قلـتُ ذا الشِّعـرَ كُلَّـهُ

Many a mountain I crossed to witness
    I was mountain, seas, I was the sea wave
Deserts where camel's place was ours
    Middle of the saddle on the camel back
Trotted with us amidst it as if we were
    On a ball or earth journeyed along side
Many a night we joined to day as if
    On its horizon red scarves were flying
Many a night we joined to day as if
    On darkness' back were green cloths
Many showers by which we felt 'Amr
    Would rise, not dead, or his cloud tomb
Or his son's son, 'Ali ibn Ahmad, who
    Gave so I would not pass empty handed
A cloud with bounty like his bounty
    A cloud with honor over every cloud
A man, no heart holds his desires
    If heart encloses them no breast covers
Goods of no use if not for his bounty
    What worth brown lances without hands?
Well joined as al Salt and Amr met
    As Indian sword and conquest embrace
They brought the broad revered brow
    You saw few men but they were much
Ransomed by fathers as noble chief
    The generous tide that had no ebbing
I did not stop till love led me to him
    His fame went with me in every convoy
I felt tales strained before meeting
    But when we did fact made story small
We drove through every desert place
    On each fast camel, all she met killing
If she swells from stings it rejoices
    As if ticks wrapped a gift in her skin
We came short of sun and moon
    Short of you in state are sun and moon
You were cool water no life without
    By your water there's no ten day thirst
Knowledge, clemency, wit called me
    Words composed, the gift that is prose
The lines I spoke as verses almost
    If written made ink white from a light
As if meanings in eloquent words
    Were Thurayya stars or a flower nature
Hate kept me from power's presence
    What eagles gave me from their skulls
I look on poverty as finer and easier
    Than sight of a small man who is proud
My tongue, heart, eye and ambition
    Are loves with names from you and more
Not I alone spoke the verses wholly
    My poem has a poem itself alive in you

وما ذا الــذي فيـهِ مــنَ الحُســنِ رَوْنَقـاً ولكـنْ بَـدا في وجهِـهِ نَحـوكَ البِشْــرُ
وإنّـي ولـوْ نِلْــتَ السَّمـاءَ لَعــالِمٌ بأنّكَ مــا نِلْــتَ الــذي يوجبُ القَــدْرُ
أزالَــتْ بِــكَ الأيّـامُ عَتْــبي كأنّمــا بَنُوهـا لَهـا ذَنْـبٌ وأنــتَ لَهـا عُـذْرُ

(١٠٧)

«من الوافر»

يمدح علي بن محمد بن سيار بن مكرم التميمي وكان يحب الرمي بالنشاب ويتعاطاه وكان لــه وكيـل يتعرض للشحر فأنفذه إلى أبي الطيب يناشده، فتلقاه وأجلسه في مجلسه و كتب إلى علي يقول:

ضُروبُ النّاسِ عُشّاقٌ ضُروبـا فـأعذَرُهُمْ أشَــفُّهُمْ حَبيبــا
ومـا سَكَني سِـوَى قَتْلِ الأعادي فهَــلْ مــنْ زَوْرَةٍ تَشفي القُلوبـا
تَظَـلُّ الطّيـرُ منهـا في حَديـثٍ تَــرُدّ بــهِ الصَّراصِــرَ والنّعيبــا
وقـد لَبِسَـتْ دِمـاءَهُمْ عَلَيهِــمْ جِـداداً لم تَشُـقَّ لَــهُ جُيُوبــا
أدَمْنــا طَعْنَهُـــمْ والقَتْــلَ حتّــى خَلَطْنــا في عِظامِهِمُ الكُعُوبــا
كـــأنّ خيولَنـا كـانَتْ قَديمـاً تُسَــقَّى في قُحوفِهِـمُ الحَليبــا
فَمَـرّتْ غَيْــرَ نـافِرَةٍ عَلَيهِــمْ تَــدوسُ بنــا الجَماجِـمَ والتَّريبــا
يُقَدّمُهـا وقـد خُضِبَـتْ شَـواها فَتـىً تَرمي الحُروبَ بــهِ الحُروبــا
شَــديدُ الخُنْزُوانَــةِ لا يُبــالي أصـابَ إذا تَنَمَّــرَ أمْ أصيبــا
أعَزْمـي طالَ هــذا اللّيــلُ فـانظُرْ أمِنْــكَ الصُّبْـحُ يَفْــرَقُ أنْ يَؤوبــا
كـأنّ الفَجْرَ حِــبٌّ مُسْــتَزار يُراعـي مِــنْ دُجُنَّـةِ رَقيبــا
كــأنّ نُجُومَــهُ حَلْـيٌ عَلَيْــهِ وقـد حُذِيَــتْ قَوائِمُــهُ الجَبوبــا
كــأنّ الجَـوّ قاسـى مـا أقاسـي فصـارَ سَـوادُهُ فيــهِ شُــحُوبــا
كــأنّ دُجـاهُ يَجْذِبُهــا سُـهادي فَليسَ تَغيـبُ إلّا أنْ يَغيبــا
أقَلِّــبُ فيــهِ أجْفـاني كـأنّي أعُــدّ بــهِ علــى الدّهـرِ الذّنوبــا

What is in it had no bright beauty but
    Cheerfulness came as it turned to you
If I get to heaven I know for sure you
    Will not get the degree proper to you
Days have stopped their reproach
    Their sons are sins and you their excuse

107
He spoke praising Ali ibn Muhammad ibn Sayyar ibn Mukarrim al Tamimi.
(Exuberant bi)

Various men are lovers of various types
    The most defensive are the best in passion
No peace for me but in the foe's death
    Where are the visits that can heal hearts?
The birds stay with them in this event
    Echoing it with a screaming and croaking
They have taken their blood upon them
    As mourning dress but not to tear clothes
We join their thrust and struggle until
    We mingle our spearheads with the bones
As if our horses from their youth on
    Were given milk drinks from their skulls
They rush upon them without any fear
    Trampling with us brainpans and breasts
They go with fetlocks stained with blood
    And youth, battles fling him into warfare
Pride's violent flea is never anxious
    If it strikes when it rages or is attacked
O my will! this night is long, so see
    If the dawn is afraid of you in returning
As if first light is the lover visiting
    Fearing a cloud's darkness like a guard
As if the stars were gold chains on it
    Its feet hobbled with the earth's surface
As if the air suffered what I suffered
    Its blackness became wan from fatigue
As if its dark captured my wakefulness
    And did not vanish till that vanished
I flutter my eyelids in it as if I were
    Counting with them the sins of time

يَظَلُّ بلَحظٍ حُسَّادي مَشوبا	ومــا لَيــلٌ بأَطْوَلَ مِــنْ نَهـارِ
أَرى لَهُـمْ مَعــي فيهـا نَصيبـا	ومــا مَــوْتٌ بـأَبْغَضَ مِــنْ حَيــاةٍ
لَــوِ انْتَسَـبَتْ لكُنـتُ هَـا نَقيبـا	عَرَفْتُ نَوائِبَ الحَدَثـانِ حتى
إلى ابـنِ سُــلَيْمانَ الخُطـوبا	ولَمّـا قَلَّتِ الإبـلُ امْتَطَيْنــا
ولا يَبْغــي لَهــا أَحَــدٌ رُكُوبــا	مَطايـا لا تَـذِلُّ لِمَـنْ عَلَيْهـا
فمـا فارَقْتُهــا إلّا جَديبــا	وتَرْتَــعُ دونَ نَبْــتِ الأرْضِ فينــا
فَلَـوْلاهُ لقُلْــتُ بهـا النَّسـيبا	إلى ذي شِـيمَةٍ شَــغَفَتْ فُـؤادي
وإنْ لم تُشــبِهِ الرَّشَــأَ الرَّبيبـا	تُنازِعُني هَواهـا كُلُّ نَفْـسٍ
أَتــى مِــنْ آلِ سَـيّارٍ عَجيبـا	عَجيــبٌ في الزَّمانِ وما عَجيــبٌ
يُسَــمّى كُلُّ مَــنْ بَلَــغَ المَشــيبا	وشَــيْخٌ في الشَّبابِ وليــسَ شَــيخاً
وَرَقَّ فنَحْــنُ نَفْــزَعُ أَن يَذوبَــا	قَسـا فالأسْـدُ تَفزَعُ مِـنْ يَدَيْـهِ
وأَسْــرَعُ في النَّـدى منهـا هُبُوبـا	أَشَــدُّ مِــنَ الرِّياحِ الهُـوجِ بَطشـاً
فقُلْــتُ رَأَيْتُــمُ الغَــرَضَ القَريبـا	وقالوا ذاكَ أَرْمـى مَــنْ رَأَيْنــا
ومـا يُخطي بمـا ظَنَّ الغُيُوبَـا	وهَـلْ يُخطي بأَسْــهُمِهِ الرَّمايـا
بأَنْصُلِهــا لأَنْصُلِهَــا نُدوبَــا	إذا نُكِبَــتْ كَنائنُــهُ اسْــتَبَّنا
فَلَـوْ لا الكَسْـرُ لا تَّصَلَتْ قَضيبَـا	يُصيبُ بِبَعْضِها أَفــواقَ بَعضٍ
لَــهُ حتى ظَنَنّـاهُ لَبيبَــا	بكُلِّ مُقَــوَّمٍ لم يَعصِ أَمْـراً
وبَيــنَ رَميْـهِ الهـدَفَ اللَّهيبـا	يُريـكَ النَّـزْعُ بَيـنَ القَــوْسِ منـهُ
ولم يَلِــدوا امـرأً إلّا نَجيبَـا	أَلَسْــتَ ابنَ الأُلى سَعِدوا وسـادوا
وصــادَ الوَحْـشَ نَمْلُهُــمْ دَبيبَـا	ونـالوا مـا اشْــتَهَوْا بـالحَزْمِ هَوْنـاً
كَسـاها دَفنُهُــمْ في التُّــرْبِ طيبــا	ومــا ريـحُ الرِّيـاضِ لَهـا ولكِـنْ
وصــارَ زَمانُــهُ البـالي قَشــيبا	أَيــا مَـنْ عـادَ رُوحُ المَجْــدِ فيـهِ
وأَنْشَــدَني مِــنَ الشِّــعرِ الغَريبَـا	تَيَمَّمَنــي وكيلُــكَ مادِحــاً لي
بَعَثْــتَ إلى المَســيحِ بــهِ طَبيبَــا	فـآجَرَكَ الألَـهُ عَلــى عَليــلٍ
ولَكِــنْ زِدْتَنــي فيهـا أَديبَــا	ولَسْـتُ بمُنكِــرٍ مِنْـكَ الهَدايــا
ولا دانَيْــتَ يــا شَــمسُ الغُروبَـا	فَــلا زالَــتْ دِيــارُكَ مُشْــرِقاتٍ

No night is so long as that day
    That is mixed with stares of jealousy
No death so hateful as that life
    Where I see them sharing with me in it
I knew a young man's misfortune till
    If any traced it I'd be the genealogist
If camels are found scarce we ride
    The beast calamity to ibn Abu Sulayman
A beast demeaning none who ride her
    Nor does one desire a convoy with her
It grazes earth's growth with us nor
    Have I failed her except by barrenness
To one with a nature my heart adores
    Except for him I'd sing her a love song
Each sigh puts me in love's agony
    But one can't compare her grown fawn
He is time's wonder but no wonder
    He comes from Sayyar's fine family
An elder in youth but not an elder
    As they call those who reach gray hair
He grows hard, lions fear his force
    He softens and we fear he will melt
More violent than strong wind's blow
    And swifter in giving than its calamity
They said: He hit what we looked at
    I said: You only saw a target close by
How could his arrow miss a target
    If he misses no hid thing he thinks about?
When his quiver is emptied it's clear
    Its arrowheads make wounds for arrows
He hits with one the notch of another
    If it won't break it will split the shaft of it
Each straight one follows his order
    Until we think that it has his thought
Drawn bowstring makes you see
    Flame between bow and its target hit
Aren't you son of those who thrive
    Beget no affairs without rule's goal?
They get their wish by easy vigor
    Their ants hunt wild beasts by need
Garden breezes are not theirs but
    Their graves clothe dust with perfume
O you to whom glory's breath returns
    Whose times return renewed from evil
Your manager came to me to praise
    He recited to me some strange verses
God rewards you with a troubled one
    You sent him to Messiah as physician
I refused no gifts from you but
    You added to them this cultured man
May your house never lack dawns
    O sun may you never approach the west

لأصْبَحَ آمِناً فيكَ الرَّزايا 	كمَا أنَا آمِنٌ فيكَ العُيوبَا

(١٠٨)

«من الطويل»

وقال يمدحه:

أقَلُّ فَعالِي بِلّةٌ أكْثَرُهُ مَجْدُ 	وذا الجِدُّ فيهِ نِلْتُ أم لم أنَلْ جَدُّ
سَأطْلُبُ حَقّي بالقَنَا ومَشايخٍ 	كأنَّهُمْ مِن طولِ ما الْتَثَمُوا مُرْدُ
ثِقالٍ إذا لاقَوْا خِفافٍ إذا دُعُوا 	كَثيرٍ إذا اشْتَدّوا قَليلٍ إذا عُدُّوا
وطَعْنٍ كأنَّ الطَّعنَ لا طَعنَ عِندَهُ 	وضَرْبٍ كأنَّ النّارَ مِن حَرِّهِ بَرْدُ
إذا شِئتُ حفّتْ بي على كلِّ سابحٍ 	رجالٌ كأنَّ المَوْتَ في فَمِها شَهْدُ
إذنّ إلى هذا الزَّمانِ أهَيْلَـهُ 	فأعْلَمُهُم فَدْمٌ وأحزَمُهُمْ وغْدُ
وأكرَمُهُمْ كَلْبٌ وأبصَرُهُـمْ عَمٍ 	وأسْهَدُهُمْ فَهْدٌ وأشجَعُهُمْ قِرْدُ
ومَن نَكَّدَ الدُّنيا على الحُرِّ أنْ يَرَى 	عَدُوّاً لَهُ ما مِن صَداقَتِهِ بُدُّ
فَيا نَكَدَ الدُّنيا متى أنْتَ مُقْصِرٌ 	عنِ الحُرِّ حتّى لا يكونَ لهُ ضِدُّ
يَروحُ ويَغدو كارِها لِوِصالِهِ 	وتَضْطَرُّهُ الأيّامُ والزَّمَنُ النَّكْدُ
بقَلبي وإنْ لم أرْوَ منها مَلالَةٌ 	وبي عن غَوانيها وإن وَصَلتْ صَدُّ
خَليلايَ دونَ النّاسِ حُزْنٌ وعَبرَةٌ 	على فَقْدِ مَن أحبَبْتُ ما لَهُما فَقْدُ
تَلِـجُّ دُموعي بالجُفونِ كأنَّما 	جُفوني لعَيْنَيْ كلِّ باكِيَةٍ خَدُّ
وإنّي لَتُغْنيني مِنَ الماءِ نُغْبَةٌ 	وأصْبِرُ عَنْهُ مِثلَما تَصْبِرُ الرُّبْدُ
وأمْضي كما يَمضي السِّنانُ لِطِيَّتي 	وأطْوى كما تُطوى المُجَلَّحَةُ العُقْدُ
وأكبِرُ نَفسي عَن جَزاءٍ بِغِيبَةٍ 	وكلُّ اغتِيابٍ جُهْدُ مَن مالَهُ جُهْدُ
وأرحَمُ أقواماً مِنَ العِيِّ والغَبَى 	وأعْذِرُ في بُغضي لأنَّهُمْ ضِدُّ
ويَمنَعُني مِمَّن سِوى ابنِ مُحَمَّدٍ 	أيادٍ لهُ عِندي تضيقُ بها عِندُ
تَوالى بلا وَعْدٍ ولكِنْ قَبْلَها 	شَمائِلُهُ مِن غيرِ وَعْدٍ بها وَعْدُ
سَرى السَّيفُ مِمّا تَطبَعُ الهِندُ صاحِبي 	إلى السَّيفِ مِمّا يَطبَعُ اللهُ لا الهِنْدُ
فَلَمَّا رَآني مُقبِلاً هَزَّ نَفسَهُ 	إليَّ حُسامٍ كلُّ صَفْحٍ لهُ حَدُّ
فَلم أرَ قَبلي مَن مَشى البَحرُ نَحوَهُ 	ولا رَجُلاً قامَتْ تُعانِقُهُ الأُسْدُ
كأنَّ القِسِيَّ العاصِيـاتِ تُطيعُهُ 	هَوىً أو بها في غيرِ أنْمُلِهِ زُهْدُ

May he be safe from misfortune as I
    Have immunity through you from reproach

108
He spoke praising him also.
(Long du)

My least acts, not the most, are glorious
    Diligence, whether I attain or not, is delight
I seek my right with spear and veterans
    Who seem beardless from long use of veil
Heavy when they attack, light if called
    Many when they are bold, few if counted
Jousting as if thrusts were not thrusts
    Blows as if fire were cold compared to them
I want around me on each swift horse
    Men in whose mouths death seems honey
I denounce little folk in these times
    Their wise men fools, their will weakness
Their nobles dogs, their vision blind
    Their guards cats, their braves monkeys
A worldly evil is a free man who sees
    His foe as needed due to his friendship
O harsh world why do you neglect
    The free man who has no adversary?
He goes, finds hated things on arrival
    And the days and hard times torment him
My heart, though I tell it not, is so
    I hate its women though they may yield
My two friends among men are sorrow
    And tears, no lack of them in lovers lost
My tears flow from eyes as if cheeks
    Of every weeper possessed my eyelids
A sip of water satisfies me altogether
    I restrain myself as an ostrich holds back
I go as spearpoint goes to target
    I hunger as one curly tailed feels hunger
My soul too large to reward backbiting
    Slander is power to one who is powerless
I pity folks who are weak and foolish
    I excuse hate since they are opponents
All but Ibn Muhammad's gifts deny me
    What I have of his has but a little room
They come without promises, before
    His nature without a promise is pledged
A sword Indians made went as friend
    To the sword God, not an Indian, made
When he saw me coming he moved
    To me, a sword whose sides had edges
No one before me saw a sea walk
    Nor any man stand as lions hugged him
As if enemy bows submitted to him
    In love, denying other fingers than his

وَيُمْكِنُهُ في سَهمِهِ المُرْسَلِ الرَدّ	يَكادُ يُصيبُ الشيءَ مِن قَبلِ رَمْيِهِ
مِنَ الشَعَرَةِ السَوداءِ والليلُ مُسوَدُ	وَيُنفِذُهُ في العَقدِ وَهوَ مُضَيَّقُ
وَإِن كَثُرَت فيها الذَرائِعُ والقَصدُ	بِنَفسي الذي لا يُزدَهى بِخَديعَةٍ
وَمَن عِرضُهُ حُرٌّ وَمَن مالُهُ عَبدُ	وَمَن بُعدُهُ فَقرٌ وَمَن قُربُهُ غِنى
وَيَمنَعُهُ مِن كُلِّ مَن ذَمُّهُ حَمدُ	وَيَصطَنِعُ المَعروفَ مُبتَدِئاً بِهِ
كَأَنَّهُمُ في الخَلقِ ما خُلِقوا بَعدُ	وَيَحتَقِرُ الحُسّادَ عَن ذِكرِهِ لَهُم
وَلَكِن عَلى قَدرِ الذي يُذنِبُ الحِقدُ	وَتَأَمَنُهُ الأَعداءُ مِن غَيرِ ذِلَّةٍ
فَإِنَّكَ ماءُ الوَردِ أَن ذَهَبَ الوَردُ	فَإِن يَكُ سَيّارُ بنُ مُكرَمٍ اِنقَضى
وَأَلفٌ إِذا ما جُمِّعَت واحِدٌ فَردُ	مَضى وَبَنوهُ وَاِنفَرَدَت بِفَضلِهِم
وَمَعرِفَةٌ عِدٌّ وَأَلسِنَةٌ لُدُّ	لَهُم أَوجُهٌ غُرٌّ وَأَيدٍ كَريمَةٌ
وَمَركوزَةٌ سُمرٌ وَمُقرَبَةٌ جُردُ	وَأَردِيَةٌ خُضرٌ وَمُلكٌ مُطاعَةٌ
تَميمُ بنُ مُرٍّ وَاِبنُ طابِخَةٍ أَدُّ	وَما عِشتَ ما ماتوا وَلا آباؤُهُم
وَبَعضُ الذي يَخفى عَلَيَّ الذي يَبدو	فَبَعضُ الذي يَبدو الذي أَنا ذاكِرٌ
وَحُقَّ لِخَيرِ الخَلقِ مِن خَيرِهِ الوُدُّ	أَلومُ بِهِ مَن لامَني في وِدادِهِ
بَني اللُؤمِ حَتّى يَعبُرَ المُلكُ الجَعدُ	كَذا فَتَنَحَّوا عَن عَلَيَّ وَطُرقِهِ
وَلا في طِباعِ التُربَةِ المِسكُ والنَدُّ	فَما في سَجاياكُم مُنازَعَةُ العُلى

(١٠٩)

«من الكامل»

أراد سفراً وودعه صديق له فقال ارتجالاً:

هُوَ تَوأَمي لَو أَنَّ بَينَنا يُولَدُ	أَمّا الفِراقُ فَإِنَّهُ ما أَعهَدُ
لَمّا عَلِمنا أَنَّنا لا نَخلُدُ	وَلَقَد عَلِمنا أَنَّنا سَنُطيعُهُ
عَنكُم فَأَردَأُ ما رَكِبتُ الأَجوَدُ	وَإِذا الجِيادُ أَبا البَهيِّ نَقَلنَنا
مَن لا يَرى في الدهرِ شَيئاً يُحمَدُ	مَن خَصَّ بِالذَمِّ الفِراقَ فَإِنَّني

He almost hits a thing before a shot
    So return is possible for an arrow shot
He hits a thing's center, narrower
    Than a black hair in the darkest night
My soul, he does not slight deceit
    Even if means and ends multiply in it
Those far from him poor, near rich
    His honor freedom, his wealth service
He does a good deed by his own will
    Denies it to all whom praise condemns
He scorns the envious in thoughts
    As if they were no part of the creation
His foes are sure he is not mean
    His hate is fitted to one who deserves
If Sayyar ibn Makarrim had an end
    He is rosewater when the rose is gone
He and his sons went, their virtue
    A thousand when collected in the one
Their handsome faces, kindly hands
    Have wisdom with sharpest tongues
Green garments, obedient subjects
    Spears on target, shorthaired horses
If they live, they die not, nor their
    Abu Tamim Murra or Ibn Tabikha Uddu
Some things appear, those I hint at
    Some that hide from me are what show
Today some blame me for loving him
    But love for best nature is due the best
So him, they stray from 'Ali in his way
    People of blame till a generous king dies
There is no retreat from your bounty
    Nor any musk and dew in dusty natures

109
He bid farewell to his friend and spoke impromptu.
(Perfect du)

As to parting, it is what am used to
    My twin if departure were something born
We knew we would have to submit to it
    When we knew that we were not immortal
When fine horses of Abu Bahlya took us
    From you the best I rode were most faulty
One points with blame to parting but I
    Am one who sees in these times no praise

(١١٠)

«من الخفيف»

وقال بدمشق يمدح أبا بكر علي بن صالح الروذباري الكاتب:

لَذَّةُ العَيــنِ عُـدَّةٌ للبِـراز	كَفِّرِ نَدى فِرِنْـدُ سَيْفِي الجُـراز
رّ أدِقَّ الخُطــوطِ في الأحْـراز	تَحْسَبُ المــاءَ خَطَّ في لَهَبِ النَّــا
ظِرَ مَـوْجٌ كَأنَّـهُ مِنكَ هـازي	كُلَّمــا رُمْتَ لَوْنَـهُ مَنـعَ النَّــا
مُتَـوالٍ في مُسْتَــوٍ هَزْهــازي	ودَقيـقٌ قَــذى الهَبــاءِ أنيــقٌ
شَــرِبَتْ والَّتـي تَليهــا جَـوازي	وَرَدَ المـاءَ فالجَوانِبَ قَــدْراً
هــيَ مُحتاجَــةٌ إلى خَــرّاز	حَمَلَـتْـهُ حَمــائِلُ الدّهــرِ حتى
ـهِ ولا عِــرْضَ مُنْتَضيهِ المَخـازي	وهْـوَ لا تَلْحَـقُ الدِّمــاءُ غِراَرَيْــ
يَــوْمَ شُــرْبي ومَعقِلي في البِــراز	يــا مُزيـلَ الظَّلامِ عَنّــي ورَوْضِي
مُقْلَـتي غِمْـدَهُ مِـنَ الإعْـزاز	واليَمــانيَ الذي لــو استَطَعْتُ كانَتْ
وصَليلي إذا صَلَلْـتَ ارْتِجــازي	إنَّ بَرْقــي إذا بَرَقْـتَ فَعَــالي
لا لِضَرْبِ الرِّقــابِ والأحْــواز	لَم أحَمِّلْـكَ مُعلِمــاً هَكَــذا!
فكِلانــا لجِنْسِــهِ اليَـوْمَ غــاز	ولِقَطْعي بِـكَ الحَديــدَ عَلَيْهــا
فتَصَـدَّى للغَيْـثِ أهْـلُ الحِجـاز	سَلَّـهُ الرَّكْـضُ بعــدَ وهْـنٍ بنَجْـدٍ
طالـبٌ لابنِ صالِحٍ مَـن يُـؤازي	وتَمَنَّيْــتُ مِثلَـــهُ فكَــأنِّي
ولا كُـلُّ مــا يَطِيــرُ بِبــاز	لَيـسَ كُـلُّ السَّراةِ بالرُّوذَبــارِيِّ
كــانَ مِــن جَوهَـرٍ على أبْــرَواز	فارسِـيٌّ لَــهُ مِــنَ المَجـدِ تــاجٌ
ولَــوْ أنّـي لَــهُ إلى الشَّمسِ عــازِ	نَفسُـهُ فَــوقَ كـلِّ أصْـلِ شَريــفٍ
عَـن حِسـانِ الوُجُــوهِ والأعجـازِ	شَـغَلَــتْ قَلْبَـهُ حِسـانُ المَعَــالي
قـوتَ مِـن لَفظِـهِ وَسامِ الرَّكـازِ	وكــأنَّ الفَريــدَ والــدُّرَّ واليـا
دونَـهُ قَضْـمَ سَـكَّـرِ الأهْــواز	تَقضَـمُ الجَمْــرَ والحديــدَ الأعادي
ونِــالَ الإسْـهابَ بالإيجــاز	بَلَغَتْــهُ البَلاغَــةُ الجَهْــدَ بالعَفْـ
مِ وثِقْـلِ الدُّيـونِ والأعْــوازِ	حامِــلُ الحَــرْبِ والدِّيــاتِ عَنِ القَـوْ

110
He spoke praising
Abu Bakr Ali ibn Sahl al Rudhbari.
(Nimble zi)

Like my outside my sharp sword's sheen
    A joy to the eye and a tool for these battles
You think water written in fire's flame
    The finest script on protective amulets
Each time you look at its color a wave
    Forbids the sight as it is shaken by you
Delicate bits of rays that are fine
    Repeating themselves in a long flow
It comes to water so the edges drink
    Perforce whoever follows them is sated
Time's hanger supports it until
    There is a need for the belt maker
For blood does not stick to its edges
    No; do affronts to the honor drawn forth
O you who keep dark from me, my joy
    On drinking day, my refuge in the desert
My Yamani who if I were able would see
    My eye as its scabbard due to these values
My lightning, when you flash my action
    My cadence when you clash as my rhymes
I do not wear it as ornament but rather
    To strike through the necks and midriffs
To cut with you through iron on them
    So each of us in his way wins this day
Drawing it going in midnight Najd
    So Folk in Hijaz clap hands for a shower
I longed for a thing like it as
    I sought Ibn Sahl who was its equal
Not every prince is from Rudhbar
    Not every thing that flies is a falcon
A Persian with a glorious crown
    One of the jewels in Parwiz' time
A soul better than any noble root
    If I traced a father for him to the sun
The love of high things in his heart
    Apart from beauty of face or buttocks
As if jewels, pearls and rubies,
    Were his words and veins of gold too
His foes gnaw in envy at coal and iron
    As if they were chewing on sugar canes
Eloquence makes the difficult easy
    As he achieves fullness with conciseness
Bearer of war and revenge for a folk
    And debtor's weight and the fainting
Why does he not accuse, why do they?
    For his, not the accusers, is the trouble
O you whose courts are wide yet have
    No lodging for a night for those who pass

كيـفَ لا يَشتَكـي وكيـفَ تَشَكّـوا	وبـهِ لا بَمَـنْ شَكاهـا المَـرازي
أيّهـا الواسِـعُ الفِنـاءِ ومـا فيـ	ـهِ مَبيـتٌ لِمالِـكَ المُجتـاز
بِــكَ أضْحَـى شَيّـا الأَسِنّـةِ عندي	كَشَبـا أسْـوُقِ الجَـرادِ النَّـوازي
وأَنْثَنـى عَنّـي الـرُّدَينيُّ حتـى	دارَ دَوْرَ الحُـروفِ في هَـوّاز
وبآبائِكَ الكِـرامِ التَّأَسّـي	والتَّسَلّـي عَمّـنْ مَضَـى والتَّعـازي
تَركـوا الأرْضَ بَعدَمـا ذَلَّلـوها	ومَشَـتْ تَحتَهُـمْ بـلا مِهْمـاز
وأعطاعَتْهُـمُ الجُيـوشُ وهِيبـوا	فكـلامُ الـوَرَى لهُـمْ كالنُّحـاز
وهِجـانٍ على هِجـانٍ تَأَبّـتْ	ـكَ عَديـدَ الحُبـوبِ في الأقْـواز
صَفّهـا السَّيـرُ في العَـراءِ فَكانَـتْ	فَـوْقَ مِثْـلِ المُـلاءِ مِثْـلَ الطَّـراز
وحَكَـى في اللُّحـومِ فِعلَـكَ في الوَفـ	ـرِ فـأوْدَى بـالعَنتـريسِ الكِنـاز
كُلَّمـا جـادَتِ الظُّنـونُ بوَعْـدٍ	عَنـكَ جـادَتْ يَـداكَ بالأنجـاز
مَلِـكٌ مُنشِـدُ القَريـضِ لَدَيـهِ	يَضَـعُ الثّـوْبَ في يَـدَيْ بَـزّاز
ولَنـا القَـوْلُ وهْـوَ أدْرَى بفَحْـوا	هُ وأهْـدَى فيـهِ إلى الإعجـاز
ومِـنَ النّـاسِ مَـنْ يَجـوزُ عَلَيْـهِ	شُعَـراءٌ كَأنّهـا الخازبـاز
ويضـرَى أنّـهُ البَصيـرُ بهـذا	وهْـوَ في العُمْـيِ ضائـعُ العُكّـاز
كُـلُّ شِعْـرٍ نَظيـرُ قائِلِـهِ فيـ	ـكَ وعَقْـلُ المُجيـزِ عَقْـلُ المُجـاز

(١١١)

«من الطويل»

يهجو قوما:

أماتكـمُ مـن قَبـلَ مَوْتِكُـمُ الجَهْـلُ	وجَرَّكُـمُ مـن خِفَّـةٍ بكُـمُ النَّمْـلُ
وُيَيْـدَ أبـيَّ الطَّيّـبِ الكَلْـبِ مـا لَكُـم	فَطِنْتُـمْ إلى الدعـوَى ومـا لكـم عَقْـلُ
ولـوْ ضَرَبَتْكُـم مَنجنيقـي وأصْلُكُـم	قَـويٌّ لَهَدَّتكُـم فكيـفَ ولا أصْـلُ
ولـوْ كُنتُـمْ مِمَّـنْ يُدَبِّـرُ أمْـرَهُ	لَمـا صِرْتُـمْ نَسْـلَ الـذي مـا لـهُ نَسْـلُ

For me points of your spears at dawn
    Are as ends of locust legs about to jump
Rudaini lances turn away from me
    They make loops of letters by quivering
By noble fathers, there is sympathy
    Consolation, strength for the departed
They left earth after subduing it
    And it ran under them without a spur
Armies yielded to them, they knew
    Words of men to them were only coughs
Fine camel after fine camel stayed
    With them in numbers like grains of sand
A trip through a plain ordered them
    As if they were embroidery on a garment
One sees your acts in abundant flesh
    They kill fine camels as their treasures
Each time thought grows rich in vows
    From you your hands reward by payment
A royal singer of verses before him
    Approving a garment in a seller's hands
Ours is speech, he knows ideas best
    Better guided toward an eloquent word
But some men are allowed around him
    Poetasters who seem to be buzzing flies
He thinks he is wise in this respect
    In blindness he throws away the bat
Each verse equal to one telling of you
    Mind of the praised is like the panegyrist

111
He spoke mocking some folk.
(Long lu)

Has folly killed you before your death
    Or ants run off with you light as straws?
Little brats of Ubayy Tayyib the dog,
    Why do you fancy a name without sense?
If my catapult hit you and your
    Root was deep yet gone! that root
If you were of one who rules his affair
    You'd not be offspring of one with no sons

(١١٢)

«من الطويل»

يمدح الحسين بن علي الهمذاني:

فَيـا لَيْتَنـي بُعْـدٌ ويـا لَيْتَـهُ وَجْـدُ	لقَـد حـازَني وَجْـدٌ بمَـن حـازَهُ بُعْـدُ
وإنْ كـانَ لـه يَبقى الحجـرُ الصّلـدُ	أسَرَّ بتَجديـدِ الهَـوى ذِكْـرُ مـا مضَـى
رُقـادٌ وقُـلّامٌ رَعَـى سَـرْبَكُم وَرْدُ	سُـهادٌ أتانـا منـكِ في العَيـن عِنْدَنـا
وحتى كـأنَّ اليَـأسَ مـن وَصْلِـكِ الوَعـدُ	مُمَثَّلَـةً حتَّـى كـأنْ لـم تُفـارقي
ويَعْبَـقُ في ثَوْبِـي مـن ريحِـكَ النَّـدُّ	وحتـى تَكـادي تمسَحيـن مَدامعـي
فمِـنْ عَهدِهـا أن لا يَـدومَ لهـا عَهـدُ	إذا غَـدَرَتْ حَسْنـاءُ وفَـتْ بعَهدِهـا
وإنْ فَركَـتْ فاذهَـبْ فمـا فِركُهـا قصـدُ	وإنْ عَشِـقَتْ كـانَت أشَـدَّ صَبابَـةً
وإنْ رَضِيَـتْ لـم يَبْـقَ في قَلبِهـا حِقـدُ	وإنْ حَقَـدَتْ لـم يَبْـقَ في قَلبِهـا رِضـى
يَضِـلُّ بهـا الهـادي ويَخفـى بهـا الرُّشـدُ	كذلـكَ أخـلاقُ النِّسـاء ورُبَّمـا
يَزيـدُ علـى مَـرِّ الزَّمـان ويَشتَـدُّ	ولكـنَّ حُبّـاً خامَـرَ القَلـبَ في الصِّبـا
مُكافـأةً يَغـدو إليهـا كمـا تَغـدو	سَقَـى ابنَ عليٍّ كـلَّ مُـزنٍ سقتكُـم
ويَنْبُـتَ فيهـا فَوقَـكِ الفَخـرُ والمجـدُ	لِتَـرْوى كمـا تُـروي بـلاداً سكَنْتِهـا
ويُخـرَقُ من زَحم على الرَّجـل البُـرْدُ	بمَـن تَشخَـصُ الأبصـارُ يـومَ رُكوبِـه
لكَثـرةِ إيمـاءٍ إليـهِ إذا يَبـدو	وتُلقِـي ومـا تَـدري البَنـانُ سِلاحَهـا
خَفيـفٌ إذا مـا أثقَـلَ الفَـرَسَ اللِّبْـدُ	ضَـروبٌ لهـام الضَّاربـي الهـام في الوَغى
ولَـوْ خَبَّأتْـهُ بَيـن أنيابِهـا الأُسْـدُ	بَصيـرٌ بأخـذِ الحَمـدِ مـن كـلِّ مَوضـعٍ
وبالذَّعـرِ مـن قِبَـل المهنَّـدِ يَنْقَـدُّ	بتأميلِـهِ يُغنـى الفتَـى قَبْـلَ نَيلِـه
لضَـربٍ وممَّـا السَّيـفُ منـهُ لـكَ الغِمدُ	وسَيْفـي لأنـتَ السَّيـفُ لا مـا تَسُـلُّـهُ
نَجيعـاً ولَـوْ لا القَـدحُ لـم يُثقِـب الزَّنْـدُ	ورُمْحـي لأنـتَ الرُّمـحُ لا مـا تُبِلُّـهُ
لأنَّهـم يُسْـدَى إليهـم بـأنْ يَسُـدوا	مِـن القاسِميـن الشُّكـرَ بَينـي وبَينَهـم
وشُكـرٌ على الشُّكـرِ الـذي وهَبـوا بَعـدُ	فشُكـري لهم شُكـران: شُكـرٌ على النَّـدى
وأشخاصُهـا في قَلـبِ خائفِهـم تَعـدو	صِيـامٌ بأبـوابِ القِبـابِ جِيادُهُـم
وأموالُهُـم في دارِ مَـنْ لـم يَفِـدْ وَفْـدُ	وأنفُسُـهُـم مَبـذولَـةٌ لـوُ فُودِهِـم

112
He spoke praising
al Husayn ibn Ali al Hamadani.
(Long du)

Passion holds me for one distance holds
    O would I were distance and he the passion
I'm captive to strong love's memory gone
    Even if the hard rock is no longer under it
Waking comes to our eye as sleep in you
    Bitterness as your wandering camels graze
Images until it's as if you had not gone
    As if despair of your embrace were promise
Till almost you brush away tears as
    Drops of your scent cling to my garments
If beauty tricks she's loyal to her vow
    Part of her vow is a vow not lasting in her
If she loves she is violent in passion
    If she's angry, away! her rage has no limit
If she hates no joy stays in heart
    If she's happy no hatred is in her breast
It is the nature of woman and often
    Her direction strays, her guidance hides
But loving veils the heart in youth
    Increasing time's loss intensifying it
May Ibn Ali pour from each cloud
    Sufficient for her what is enough for you
To water as it waters land you stay in
    To make honor and glory grow above you
For one eyes observe on parting day
    As a cloak is torn by the press of men
Fingers drop weapons unwittingly
    Due to much waving as he appears
Striker at head striker's head in war
    Light if a saddle pad is heavy on horse
Foresighted in taking praise in place
    Even if a lion hides between his teeth
By hope one is rich before his gift
    By fear he cuts through before a sword
My sword! the blade, not one you draw
    For blows, sword's metal is your sheath
My spear! lance, not one you wet
    With blood, without flint no spark spurts
They are the ones to share thanks
    They are benefited as they benefit
My grace double, thanks for gifts
    Thanks for thanks which they give later
Their horses standing at tent doors
    Their image in the hearts that fear them
Lavish of themselves for deputies
    Their own wealth envoy for that not sent
It's as if Husayn's gifts were armies
    Among them slaves and perfect horses

200   Diwan al-Mutanabbi

كَأَنَّ عَطِيّاتِ الحُسَيـنِ عَساكِرُ	فَفيها العِبْدى والمُطَهَّمةُ الجُرْدُ
أَرى القَمَرَ ابنَ الشَّمسِ قد لَبِسَ العُلى	رُوَيدَكَ حتى يَلبِسَ الشَّعرَ الخَدُّ
وغالَ فُضولَ الدِّرعِ مِن جَنَباتِها	على بَدَنٍ قَدِّ القَناةِ لَهُ قَدُّ
وباشَرَ أَبكارَ المَكارِمِ أَمرَدًا	وكانَ كَذا آباؤُهُ وهُمْ مُرْدُ
مَدَحْتُ أَباهُ قَبْلَهُ فَشَفى يَدي	مِنَ العُدمِ مَن تُشفى بِهِ الأَعيُنِ الرُّمْدُ
حَبَاني بِأَثمانِ السَّوابِقِ دونَها	مَخافةَ سَيري إنَّها لِلنَّوى جُنْدُ
وشَهوَةَ عَودٍ إنَّ جودَ يَمينِهِ	ثَناءٌ ثَناءٌ والجَوادُ بِها فَرْدُ
فَلا زِلتُ أَلقى الحاسِدينَ بِمِثلِها	وفي يَدِهِم غَيضٌ وفي يَدَيَّ الرِّفدُ
وعِندي قَباطِيُّ الهُمامِ ومالُهُ	وعِندَهُمُ مِمّا ظَفِرتُ بِهِ الجَحدُ
يَرومونَ شَأوي في الكَلامِ وإنَّما	يُحاكي الفَتى فيما خَلا المَنطِقَ القِردُ
فَهُم في جُموعٍ لا يَراها ابنُ دَأيةٍ	وهُم في ضَجيجٍ لا يُحَسُّ بِهِ الخُلدُ
ومِنّي استَفادَ النّاسُ كُلَّ غَريبةٍ	فَجازَوا بِتَركِ الذَّمِّ إِن لَم يَكُن حَمدُ
وجَدْتُ عَلِيّاً وابنَهُ خَيرَ قَومِهِ	وهُم خَيرُ قَومٍ واستَوى الحُرُّ والعَبدُ
وأَصبَحَ شِعري مِنهُما في مكانِهِ	وفي عُنُقِ الحَسناءِ يُستَحسَنُ العِقدُ

(١١٣)

«من الطويل»

يمدح الأمير أبا محمد الحسن بن عبيد الله بن طغج بالرملة:

أَنا لائِمي إِن كُنتُ وَقتَ اللَّوائِمِ	عَلِمتُ بِما بي بَينَ تِلكَ المَعالِمِ
وَلَكِنَّني مِمّا شَهِدتْ مُتَيَّمٌ	كَسالٍ وقَلبي بائِحٌ مِثلُ كاتِمِ
وقَفنا كأَنّا كُلَّ وَجدِ قُلوبِنا	تَمَكَّنَ مِن أَذوادِنا في القَوائِمِ
ودُسنا بِأَخفافِ المَطِيِّ تُرابَها	فَما زِلتُ أَستَشفي بِلَثمِ المَناسِمِ
دِيارُ اللَّواتي دارُهُنَّ عَزيزَةٌ	بِطولى القَنا يُحفَظنَ لا بِالتَّمائِمِ
حِسانُ التَّثَنّي يَنقُشُ الوَشيُ مِثلَهُ	إذا مِسْنَ في أَجسامِهِنَّ النَّواعِمِ
ويَسِمْنَ عَن دُرٍّ تَقَلَّدْنَ مِثلَهُ	كَأَنَّ التَّراقي وُشِّحَتْ بِالمَباسِمِ
فَما لي ولِلدُّنيا طِلابي نُجومُها	ومَسعايَ مِنها في شُدوقِ الأَراقِمِ
مِنَ الحِلمِ أَن تَستَعمِلَ الجَهلَ دونَهُ	إذا اتَّسَعَتْ في الحِلمِ طُرْقُ المَظالِمِ

I see a moon, son of sun in eminence
    Go slowly till the cheeks wear the beard
He expands the armor at its joints
    Over a body whose cut is like a spear's
Beardless he announced virgin bounty
    His fathers thus and they were beardless
I praised his father when he healed
    My hand of poverty as sick eyes are cured
He gave eight fast horses before which
    Fear of going but they were at the goals
Desire to return his right hand gift
    Double, double though bounty is unique
I cease not to foil the envious of them
    In their hands rage as in mine the gifts
A prince's Coptic robe and wealth
    They had disbelief which I overcame
They aim at the goal of speech but
    A monkey apes a man in foolishness
They in company a crow can't see
    They make noises a mole can't hear
Men hope to ransom my rare words
    They pay by not blaming if not by praise
I've found Ali and his son best folk
    Best even if free and slaves are equals
My poem becomes theirs in its setting
    On beauty's neck adorned with necklace

113
He spoke
praising
Abu Muhammad al-Hasan
ibn Abdallah ibn Tugj. (Long si)

I'm accuser, if I had time for blame I'd
    Know what's wrong with me by the traces
But I am one of the perplexed, enslaved
    As a river, my heart unveiled as a secret
He stopped as if all our heart's passion
    Had made the legs of our camels stubborn
We trod with soles of beasts the dust
    I sought healing from the kiss of the hoof
Camps that are their homes guarded
    By the long lances, not by the amulets
Adorable the brocade imprints its like
    When they sway, grace is in their bodies
Their smiles show pearly necklaces
    As if the breasts were adorned by teeth
What is world to me? my goal stars
    My course to them through snake's jaws
Rational you use ignorance against it
    When ways of evil are broad with reason

وأنْ تَرِدَ الماءَ الذي شَطرُهُ دَمُ / فَتُسقَى إذا لم يُسقَ مَنْ لم يُزاحِمِ
ومَنْ عَرَفَ الأيّامَ مَعرِفَتي بها / وبالنّاسِ رَوّى رُمحَهُ غيرَ راحِمِ
فَلَيسَ بِمَرحُومٍ إذا ظَفِروا بهِ / ولا في الرّدى الجاري عَلَيهِم بآثِمِ
إذا صُلْتُ لم أتْرُكْ مَصالاً لفاتِكٍ / وإنْ قُلْتُ لم أتْرُكْ مَقالاً لعالِمِ
وإلاّ فخانَتْني القَوافي وعاقَني / عَن ابنِ عُبَيدِ اللهِ ضُعْفُ العَزائِمِ
عَنِ المُقتَني بَذْلَ التِّلادِ تِلادَهُ / ومُجتَنِبِ البُخْلِ اجتِنابَ المَحارِمِ
تَمَنَّى أعاديهِ مَحَلَّ عُفاتِهِ / وتَحسُدُ كَفَّيهِ ثِقالُ الغَمائِمِ
ولا يَتَلَقَّى الحربَ إلاّ بمُهجَةٍ / مُعَظَّمَةٍ مَذْخورَةٍ للعَظائِمِ
وذي لَجَبٍ لا ذو الجَناحِ أمامَهُ / بناجٍ ولا الوَحْشُ المُثارُ بسالِمِ
تَمُرُّ عَلَيهِ الشَّمسُ وهيَ ضَعيفَةٌ / تُطالِعُهُ مِن بَينِ ريشِ القَشاعِمِ
إذا ضَوءُها لاقى مِنَ الطّيرِ فُرْجَةً / تَدَوَّرَ فَوقَ البَيضِ مثلَ الدراهِمِ
ويَخفى عَلَيكَ الرّعدُ والبَرْقُ فَوقَهُ / مِنَ اللَّمعِ في حافاتِهِ والهَماهِمِ
أرى دونَ ما بَينَ الفُراتِ وبَرْقَةٍ / ضِراباً يُمشّي الخَيلَ فَوقَ الجَماجِمِ
وطَعنَ غَطاريفٍ كأنَّ أكُفَّهُم / عَرَفنَ الرُّدَينيّاتِ قبلَ المَعاصِمِ
حَمَتْهُ على الأعداءِ مِن كلِّ جانبٍ / سُيوفُ بني طُغجَ بنِ جُفٍّ القَماقِمِ
هُمُ المُحسِنونَ الكَرَّ في حَومَةِ الوَغى / وأحسَنُ مِنهُ كُرُّهُم في المَكارِمِ
وهم يُحسِنونَ العَفْوَ عن كلِّ مُذنِبٍ / ويَحتَمِلونَ الغُرْمَ عن كلِّ غارِمِ
حَيِيّونَ إلاّ أنَّهُم في نِزالِهِمْ / أقَلُّ حَياءً مِنْ شِفارِ الصَّوارِمِ
ولَوْ لا احتِقارُ الأسْدِ شَبَّهتُهُم بها / ولكنَّها مَعدودَةٌ في البَهائِمِ
سَرَى النَّومُ عنّي في سُرايَ إلى الذي / صَنائِعُهُ تَسري إلى كلِّ نائِمِ
إلى مُطلِقِ الأسرى ومُختَرَمِ العِدى / ومُشكي ذَوي الشَّكوى ورَغمِ المَراغِمِ
كريمٌ لَفَظَتْهُ النّاسُ لَمّا بَلَغتَهُ / كأنَّهم ما جَفَّ مِن زادِ قادِمِ
وكادَ سُروري لا يَفي بنَدامَتي / على تَركِهِ في عُمْرِيَ المُتَقادِمِ
وفارَقْتُ شرَّ الأرضِ أهلاً وتُربَةً / بها عَلَوِيٌّ جَدُّهُ غيرُ هاشِمِ
بَلا اللهُ حُسّادَ الأميرِ بحِلمِهِ / وأجلَسَهُ مِنهُم مكانَ العَمائِمِ
فإنَّ لهم في سُرعَةِ المَوتِ راحَةً / وإنَّ لهمْ في العَيشِ حَزَّ الغَلاصِمِ
كأنّكَ ما جاوَدْتَ مَن بانَ جودُهُ / عَلَيكَ ولا قاوَمْتَ مَنْ لم تُقاوِمِ

If you drink water half of it bloody
    Drink where he won't who won't strive
He who knows days as I have known
    Among men waters his lance without pity
No pity when they overcome him nor
    Any evil for them in an unjust demise
If I attack I leave no reply to the bold
    If I speak I leave no response to the wise
Else my rhymes betray me, weakness
    Of will hinders me from Ibn Ubaidallah
From whose bounty is his heritage
    To put aside greed with sacred tabu
His foes desire the place of clients
    The weighty clouds envy his two hands
He meets no battle except with heart
    Magnified by the munition of greatness
Leading an army with no birds before
    To snatch, nor beasts urged by surrender
Sun rises over it but she is blinded
    Passing between great vulture feathers
When her rays strike between wings
    They whirl above helmets like dirhams
Thunder hides from you as lightning
    Flashes on its borders and its uproar
I see between Furat and the wasteland
    An attack that leads horses over the skulls
A jousting chief as he restrains them
    They know Rudaini lances before the wrists
They guard him from foes everywhere
    Swords of a prince of Banu Tugj ibn Juff
They return to attack in thick of battle
    Better than that their return to generosity
They do best in forgiving every sin
    Are angry at the debts of every debtor
Modest except in their onslaughts
    Less modest there than the sword edges
But for scorn of lions I'd compare you
    After all they are counted among beasts
Sleep left me due to my travel to him
    Whose good deeds travel to the sleeper
Freeing captives and destroying foes
    Rescuing those who weep in the dust
Noble, I shook off men reaching him
    As if they were dry scraps after journey
Almost my joy equaled my regret
    For my absence from him in my past life
I left earth's evil, people and land
    For Alids whose kin weren't Hashimi
God's army beset envy of the Amir
    Set him among them in place of turban
For in swift death they found a peace
    In life they had only the throat slashing
You subdued one whose gift rivaled
    Yours and fought none who was not strong

(١١٤)

«من الوافر»

وساله أبو محمد أن يشرب فامتنع، فقال له: بحقي عليك إلا شربت، فقال:

| وَوُدٌّ لَمْ تُشَبِّهْهُ لي بِمَـــذقِ | سَقاني الخَمرَ قَولُكَ لي بِحَقّي |
| على قَتلي بها لَضَرَبتُ عُنقي | يَميناً لَو حَلَفتَ وَأَنتَ تَأتي |

(١١٥)

«من الكامل»

ثم أخذ الكأس منه وقال:

| أَمسى الأَنامُ لَهُ مُجِلّاً مُعظِمَا | حُيّيتَ مِن قَسَمٍ وَأَفدي مُقسِمَا |
| وَأَخَذتُها فَلَقَد تَرَكتُ الأَحرَمَا | وَإِذا طَلَبتُ رِضى الأَميرِ بِشُربِها |

(١١٦)

«من مخلع البسيط»

وغنى المغني فقال:

| يا خَيرَ مَن تَحتَ ذي السَّماءِ | ماذا يَقولُ الَّذي يُغَنّي |
| إِلَيكَ عَن حُسنِ ذا الغِناءِ | شَغَلتَ قَلبي بِلَحظِ عَيني |

(١١٧)

«من المتقارب»

وعرض عليه سيفا فأشار به إلى بعض من حضر وقال:

| وَبابَةَ كُلَّ غُلامٍ عَتا | أَرى مُرهَفاً مُدهِشَ الصَّيقَلينَ |
| أَجَرِّبُهُ لَكَ في ذا الفَتى | أَتَأذَنُ لي وَلَكَ السّابِقاتُ |

114
Abu Muhammad
invited him to drink
and he refused.
So he said to him:
But I have a claim over you!
(Exuberant ql)

Your words were: Pour me wine! My rights!
    However love for me doesn't mix with insincerity
If you swore by the right hand, insisted
    On my death with it, I'd strike off my head!

115
Then he took
the cup and said:
(Perfect ma)

You greet with an oath, I ransom a witness
    Mankind is existing for his glorious greatness
I seek the Amir's pleasure by drinking
    I take it and avoid the greatest prohibition

116
A singer sang
so he spoke addressing
Abu Muhammad.
(Outspread i)

What is it that he who sings is saying?
    O best of those who are under the heavens
You turn my heart with an eye's glance
    To you, away from the beauty of the song

117
He showed him a sword
and pointed with it to one
who was nearby,
(Tripping ta)

I see the smith's dazzling thin edges
    And they are what suit every proud youth
If you allow it as you have beforehand
    I will test it for you with this warrior's arm

(١١٨)

«من الوافر»

ثم أراد الانصراف فقال:

| وَمُنصَرَفي لَــهُ أمضَى السِّــلاحِ | يُقــاتِلُني عَلَيــكَ اللّيــلُ جِــدّاً |
| بَعيــدٌ بَــينَ جَفــني والصّبــاحِ | لأنّــي كلّمــا فــارَقتُ طَــرفي |

(١١٩)

«من مجزو، الكامل»

وسايره وهو لا يدري أين يريد به، فلما دخل كفرديس قال:

كــالغُمصِ في الجفــنِ المُســهَّدْ	وزيــارَةٍ عَــن غَــيرِ مَوعِــدْ
دُ مَــعَ الأمــيرِ أبــي مُحَمَّــدْ	مَعَجَــتْ بنــا فيهــا الجيــا
لَــوْ أنَّ ســاكِنَها مُخَلَّــدْ	حَتّــى دَخَلنــا جَنَّــةً
بٍ كأنَّهــا في خَــدِّ أغيَــدْ	خَضــراءَ حَمــراءَ التُّــرا
فَوَجَدتُــهُ مــا ليــسَ يُوجَــدْ	أحبَبــتُ تَشــبيهاً لَهــا
ئِــقِ فَهْــيَ واحِــدَةٌ لأوحَــدْ	وإذا رَجَعــتَ إلى الحَقــا

(١٢٠)

«من الطويل»

وقال فيه:

وَفَــى لي بأهليــهِ وزادَ كَثيــرا	ووَقــتٍ وَفَــى بالدَّهــرِ لي عنــدَ سَيّــدٍ
وزَهــرٍ تَــرى للمــاءِ فيــهِ خَريــرا	شَــربتُ على اســتِحسانِ ضَــوءِ جَبينِــهِ
وأصبَــحَ دَهــري في ذُراهُ دُهــورا	غَــدا النّــاسُ مِثلَيهِــم بــهِ لا عدمتُــه

118
He intended to depart so he said,
(Perfect hi)

Night strives with me competing for you
    My departure is the sharpest weapon for it
Since each time I go, my eye finds
    Distance between my eyelids and that dawn

119
He went on a journey
and did not know where
he had gotten to
when he entered
what seemed to be a garden.
So he spoke:
(Perfect d)

But many an unexpected visit
    Is like a sleep to waking eyelid
Horses ambled with us here
    Along with Amir Abu Muhammad
Until we entered the garden
    Would its dwellers were immortal
Both green and read is the earth
    As if it were on a youth's cheek
I wanted some comparison for it
    But I found that nothing existed
Then you had recourse to truths
    Single for the one who is unique

120
He said about him also:
(Long ra)

Many times are an age for me with my lord
    He outweighs his folk with me and much more
I drink in beautiful light from his brow
    The blossoms you see in murmuring waters
Folk make him a model and I do not lack
    My times in his court in becoming immortal

(١٢١)

«من البسيط»

قال يصف مجلسين له قد انزوى أحدهما عـن الآخر ليرى من كل واحد منهما ما لا يرى من صاحبه:

مُقَـابِلانِ ولَكِـنْ أحْسَـنَـا الأدَبَـا	ألمَجلِسانِ على التَّمْييـزِ بَيْنَهُـمَـا
وإنْ صَعِـدْتَ إلى ذا مَـالَ ذا رَهَبَـا	إذا صَعِـدْتَ إلى ذا مَــالَ ذا رَهَبَــا
إنّـي لأبْصِـرُ مِـنْ فِعْلَيْهِمَـا عَجَبَـا	فَلِـمْ يَهَـابُكَ مـا لا حِـسَّ يَرْدَعُـهُ

(١٢٢)

«من البسيط»

وأقبل الليل وهما في بستان فقال:

| أنْ لم يَـزُلْ ولجنْـحِ الليّـلِ إجْنَـانُ | زالَ النّهَـارُ ونُــورٌ مِنْـكَ يُوهِمُنَـا |
| فَـرُحْ فَكُـلُّ مَكَـانٍ مِنْـكَ بُسْتَـانُ | فإنْ يَكُـنْ طَلَـبُ البُسْتَـانِ يُمسِكُنَا |

(١٢٣)

«من الوافر»

ولما استقل في القبة نظر إلى السحاب فقال:

| فقُلْـتُ إليْـكَ إنّ مَعـي السَّـحَابَا | تَعَـرَّضَ لي السَّـحَابُ وقـد قَفَلْنَـا |
| فأمْسَـكَ بعدَمَـا عَـزَمَ انسِـكَابَا | فَشِـمْ في القُبَّـةِ المَلِكَ المُرَجَّـى، |

(١٢٤)

«من المتقارب»

قال وقد كره الشرب وكثر البخور وارتفعت رائحة الند بمجلسه:

| وحُسْـنُ الغِنـاءِ وصافـي الخُمُـورِ | أنْشُـرُ الكِبـاءِ وَوَجْـهُ الأميـرِ |
| فـإنّي سَكِـرْتُ بشُـرْبِ السّـرورِ | فَـداءٌ خُمـاري بِشُـرْبي لَهَـا |

121
He spoke describing two courtiers
who met each other like two buffaloes held by ropes.
(Outspread ba)

Two courtiers differ from each other
    They are opposed though of fine culture
If you go to one the other turns in fear
    You go to the other and the first turns shyly
Why does he fear who sees no bridle
    As I see the strangeness in their behavior?

122
Night approached and the two were in a garden
alone, so he said:
(Outspread nu)

Day ends but light from you reminds us
    It does not end if night's wing makes a cover
If desire for a garden could hold us
    Stay, for every place with you is a garden

123
When he went from the garden
he looked at the clouds
and said:
(Exuberant ba)

A cloud shone for me as we returned
    So I said: Be off! the true cloud is with me
See the king's tent who is our hope
    And hold off until he decides to pour out
Till we entered a garden
    Would its men were immortal
Bright red its dust
    It seemed on fine cheeks
I wanted likeness for it
    And found it incomparable
If you return to reality
    It is unique in its leading

124
The drinking disgusted him when there was much incense
and the odor of musk in the majlis. So he said:
(Tripping ri)

O stick of aloes and the prince's face
    And beauty of a singer: the purity of wine
Cure my drunkenness in drink of them
    For I am drunk with the drink of happiness

(١٢٥)

«من مخلّع البسيط»

وأشار إليه طاهر العلوي بمسك وأبو محمد حاضر فقال:

| كَفَى بِقُرْبِ الأَميرِ طِيبَا | أَلطَّيِّبُ مِمَّا غَنِيتُ عَنْهُ |
| كَمَا بِكُمْ يَغْفِرُ الذُّنُوبَا | يُحْيِينِي بِهِ رَبُّنَا المَعَالي |

(١٢٦)

«من مخلّع البسيط»

وجعل الأمير يضرب البخور بكمه ويقول سوقاً إلى أبي الطيب فقال:

| وأفْصَحَ النَّاسِ في المَقَالِ | يا أكْرَمَ النَّاسِ في الفَعَالِ |
| فَهَكَذَا قُلْتَ في النَّوالِ | إنْ قُلْتَ في ذا البَخُورِ سَوْقاً |

(١٢٧)

«من الخفيف»

وحدث أبو محمد عن مسيرهم بالليل لكبس بادية وأن المطر أصابهم فقال أبو الطيب:

| فَلِمَنْ ذا الحَديثُ والإعْلامُ | غَيرُ مُسْتَنْكَرٍ لَكَ الأَقْدامُ |
| يَمْنَعُ اللَّيلُ هَمَّهُ والغَمَامُ | قَد عَلِمنا مِن قَبْلُ أنَّكَ مَن لا |

(١٢٨)

«من الخفيف»

وقال فيه وهو عند طاهر العلوي:

| ومِنْ حَقِّ ذا الشَّريفِ عَلَيكَا | قَدْ بَلَغْتَ الَّذي أرَدْتَ مِنَ البِرِّ |
| تِلكَ ذا خِفْتُ أنْ تَسيرَ إلَيكَا | وإذا لَم تَسِرْ إلى الدَّارِ في وَقْـ |

125
Tahir the Alid
remarked on his being absent
when Abu Muhammad
was present so he said.
(Outspread li)

Is not the goodness I did without
    Supplied by nearness to the prince?
Our exalted lord set me up with him
    Just as He forgives those sins of yours

126
Abu Muhammad
ordered some musk
to be scattered
on his sleeve
and sent him some of it.
(Outspread li)

O most generous of men in deed
    Most eloquent of men in speaking
If you said by scattered perfume:
    Pour, then you spoke by way of gift

127
Abu Muhammad
told about his journey
on a night attack
in the desert
when the rain overtook them
so he said:
(Nimble wu)

Courage asks not in vain of you
    So whose the story and distinction?
We knew before you were one
    Whom no night or rain could bar in a wish

128
He spoke also
and he was with Tahir the 'Alid.
(Nimble ka)

You achieved your wish for virtue
    And true is that nobility that is yours
If you travel not to your home now
    I fear that it will journey toward you

(١٢٩)

«من مخلّع البسيط»

وهم بالنوض فأقعده أبو محمد فقال:

بِهِ وحُرَّ المُلوكِ عَبْدَا	يا مَنْ رَأَيْتُ الحَليمَ وَغْدا
وأَنْتَ للمَكْرُماتِ أُهْدَى	مالَ عَلَيَّ الشَّرابُ جِدَّا
عَدَدْتُهُ مِنْ لَدُنْكَ رَفْدَا	فَإِنْ تَفَضَّلْتَ بِانْصِرافي

(١٣٠)

«من الرمل»

وحدث أبو محمد أن أباه استخفى مرة فعرفه رجل يهودي فقال أبو الطيب:

| أَنْ يَرى الشَّمْسَ فلا يُنكِرُهَا | لا تَلومَنَّ اليَهودِيَّ عَلى |
| ظُلْمَةً مِنْ بَعْدِ ما يُبصِرُهَا | إنَّما اللَّوْمُ على حاسِبِها |

(١٣١)

«من الخفيف»

وسئل عمّا ارتجله: فيه من الشعر فأعاده فتعجب قوم من حفظه إياه فقال:

| لا بقَلْبي لِمَا أَرى في الأميرِ | إنَّما أَحْفَظُ المَديحَ بعَيْني |
| نَظَمَتْ لي غَرائِبَ المَنْثورِ | مِنْ خِصالٍ إذا نَظَرْتُ إليها |

(١٣٢)

«من الوافر»

وجرى حديث وقعة أبي الساج مع أبي طاهر صاحب الأحساء فذكر أبو الطيب ما كان فيها من القتل فهال بعض الجلساء ذلك وجزع منه فقال أبو الطيب لأبي محمد ارتجالا:

| وفَارِسَ كُلِّ سَلْهَبَةٍ سَبوحِ | أَباعِثَ كُلِّ مَكْرُمَةٍ طَمُوحِ |

129
He wanted to rise
but he was made
to sit so he said:
(Swift da)

O you in whom I see pliancy as folly
    Or the freedom of the king as slavery
The drinking leans heavy on me
    While you are guided to generosity
If you favor me with my dismissal
    I'll count it as a kindness on your part

130
Abu Muhammad
recalled that his father
was drunk one time
and a Jew saw him.
So he said:
(Extended ha)

Don't blame the Jew because
    He saw the sun and didn't deny it
Because blame is for reckoning
    Her darkness after one has seen her

131
He was asked for
an impromptu poem
and he gave it.
And they were amazed
at his memory
and he said:
(Nimble ri)

I hold the goal of praise in my eye
    Not in memory when I look at the Amir
Many qualities as I look at them
    Are composed into the rare embroidery

132
He spoke
and a friend of his
had just told
Abu Muhammad ibn Ubaidallah
about a skirmish
whose cause
and sight had frightened him.
(Exuberant hi)

O reviver of every rare generosity
    And rider of every swift, strong horse

وطــاعِـنِ كـلّ نَجْــلاءَ غَمُــوس   وعــاصِيَ كـلّ عَــذّالٍ نَصِيــح
سَـقاني اللهُ قبـلَ المَــوْتِ يَوْمــاً   دَمَ الأعــداءِ مـن جــوْفِ الخُــرُوح

(١٣٣)

«من المتقارب»

وأطلق الباشق على سماناة فأخذها فقال:

أمِــنْ كُــلّ شيء بَلَغْــتَ المُــرادَا   وفي كـلّ شــأو شـأوْتَ العِبَــادَا
فَمــاذا تَرَكْــتَ لِمَــنْ لم يَسُــدْ   ومــاذا تركْــتَ لمَنْ كــانَ سَــادَا
كــأنّ السُّمــانى إذا مــا رَأتْــكَ   تَصَيَّدُهــا تَشْــتَهي أنْ تُصَــادَا

(١٣٤)

«من الرّجز»

واجتاز أبو محمد ببعض الجبال فأثارت الغلمان خشفاً فتلقفته الكلاب فقال أبو الطيب مرتجلاً:

وشــامِخٍ مِــنَ الجبــالِ أقْــوَدِ   فَــرْدٍ كيـأفُوخِ البَعــيرِ الأصْيَـدِ
يُســارُ مِــنْ مَضيِقِــه والجَلْمَــدِ   في مِثْـلِ مَتْــنِ المَسَــدِ المُعَقَّــدِ
زُرنــاهُ للأمـرِ الــذي لم يُعْهَــدِ   للصيْــدِ والنزهَــةِ والتمَــرّدِ
بكــلّ مَسْقــيّ الدّمــاءِ أسْــوَدِ   مُعَــاوِدٍ مُقَــوَّدٍ مُقَلَّــدِ
بكــلّ نــابٍ ذرِبٍ مُحَــدَّدِ   علــى حِفــافَيْ حَنَــكٍ كالمِبْرَدِ
كطــالِبِ الثّــأرِ وإنْ لم يَحْقِــدِ   يَقْتُــلُ مــا يَقْتُلُــهُ ولا يَــدي
يَنْشُـدُ مــن ذا الخِشْــفِ ما لم يَفقِدِ   فَثــارَ مِــن أخضرَ مَمْطُــورٍ نَــدِ
كأنّــهُ بَــدْءُ عِــذارِ الأمْــرَدِ   فلَــمْ يكـدْ إلّا لَحَتْــفٍ يَهتَــدي
ولم يَقَــعْ إلّا عَلـى بَطْــنِ يَــدِ   فلَــمْ يَــدَعْ للشّاعِرِ المُجَــوِّدِ
وَصفــاً لَــهُ عِنــدَ الأميـرِ الأمْجَـدِ   المَلِــكِ القَــرْمِ أبــي مُحَمَّــدِ
القانِــصِ الأبْطـالَ بــالمُهَنَّــدِ   ذي النِّعَــمِ الغُــرِّ البَـوادي العُــوَّدِ
إذا أرَدْتُ عَدَّهــا لم تُعْــدَدِ   وإنْ ذكَــرْتُ فَضْلَــهُ لم يَنْفَــدِ

Thruster in each broad bloody wound
    Opponent of every slanderer of sincerity
May God pour me before death's day
    The blood of a foe from the wound's depth

133
He released a falcon against the quails and took them and he spoke. (Tripping da)

Have you found meaning in all things
    And outdistanced the world at every goal?
What do you give him who hasn't ruled
    What do you have left for him who has ruled?
It is as if the quail, when they saw you
    Pursuing them, also wanted to be pursued

134
Abu Muhammad crossed through some mountains and the slaves tracked a fawn and the dogs took it so Abu Tayyib spoke. (Exuberant di)

Many a peak on this long mountain
    Is remote, like the sick camel's neck
One goes on narrow ways and rocks
    As if the road's middle is knotted rope
We visit for things unaccustomed
    For hunting and pleasure and the play
With each shedder of black blood
    Trained with the leash and the collar
And all the sharpened curved teeth
    Like files on both edges of the mouth
Seeker of revenge without any hate
    He takes what he kills without quarter
He pursues a fawn and won't lose it
    It starts from the bushes wet with dew
Like beard's growth on hairless cheek
    It wants to follow nothing but its own ruin
It cannot fall except within claws
    It doesn't leave any plunder to the poet
I describe it to a glorious prince
    King Abu Muhammad the tribe's chief
Hunter of warriors with Indian sword
    Showing bright graces, appearing again
If I want their number it won't come
    I think of his bounty and it has no end

(١٣٥)

«من المتقارب»

قال وقد استحسن عين باز في مجلسه:

وَلَوْ لا المَلاحَةُ لم أعْجَبِ	أيا ما أُحَيْسِنَها مُقْلَةً
سُوَيْداءُ مِنْ عِنَبِ الثَّعْلَبِ	خَلوقِيَّةٌ في خَلوقَيْها
كَسَتْهُ شُعاعاً على المَنكِبِ	إذا نَظَرَ البازُ في عِطْفِهِ

(١٣٦)

«من الخفيف»

وعاتبه على تركه مديحه فقال:

وقَليلٌ لَكَ المَديحُ الكَثيرُ	تَرْكُ مدحيكَ كالهِجاءِ لِنَفْسي
ـرِ لأمْرٍ مِثلي بِهِ مَعْذورُ	غَيرَ أنّي تَرَكْتُ مُقْتَضَبَ الشِّعْـ
ظي وَجُودٌ على كَلامي يُغيرُ	وسَجاياكَ مادِحاتُكَ لا لَفْـ
ـكَ وأسْقاكَ أيُّها الأميرُ	فَسَقى اللهُ مَنْ أحَبُّ بكَفّيْـ

(١٣٧)

«من البسيط»

وقال يودعه:

هذا الوَداعُ وَداعُ الروح للجَسَدِ	ما ذا الوَداعُ وَداعُ الوامِقِ الكَمِدِ
فَلا عَدا الرَّمْلَةَ البَيضاءَ مِنْ بَلَدِ	إذا السَّحابُ زَفَتْهُ الرِّيحُ مُرْتَفِعاً
إنْ أنْتَ فارَقْتَنا يَوْماً فَلا تَعُدِ	ويا فِراقَ الأميرِ الرَّحْبِ مَنْزِلُهُ

(١٣٨)

«من الطويل»

يمدح أبا القاسم طاهر بن الحسين بن طاهر العلوي:

| ورُدّوا رُقادي فَهوَ لَحظُ الحَبائبِ | أعيدوا صَباحي فَهوَ عِندَ الكَواعِبِ |

135
He admired the eye of a falcon in his court so he spoke.
(Tripping bi)

O how should I prettify her eye
    If only beauty were not surprising
With is spicy yellow saffron
    A small black grape of nightshade
When a falcon looks at his side
    It dresses a shoulder in light rays

136
He complained to him about leaving off praising him so he said:
(Nimble ru)

Leaving your praise is satire on myself
    If the praise for you is short it is still much
I have not left off cuffings of verse
    In affairs such as mine there are excuses
Your nature is your praise not my words
    And the bounty is envied due to my eulogy
God bless one loving me by your hand
    May he pour out the drink for you O prince

137
He spoke bidding him farewell.
(Outspread di)

The farewell is no sad lover's goodbye
    This parting is parting of the soul and body
As for cloud, the wind drives it high
    May it not come near to Ramla, gem of cities
O farewell to a prince whose house is wide
    If you leave us this day may you not be angry

138
He spoke praising Abu Qasim Tahir ibn al-Husayn ibn Tahir the 'Alawi.
(Long bi)

Return my morning for it is with virgins
    Restore my sleep that has love's vision

عَلَى مُقْلَةٍ مِنْ بَعْدِكُمْ فِى غَيَاهِبِ	فَإِنَّ نَهَارِى لَيْلَةٌ مُدْلَهِمَّةٌ
عَقَدْتُمْ أَعَالِي كُلِّ هُدْبٍ بِحَاجِبِ	بَعِيدَةُ مَا بَيْنَ الْجُفُونِ كَأَنَّمَا
لَفَارَقْتُهُ وَالدَّهْرُ أَخْبَثُ صَاحِبِ	وَأَحْسَبُ أَنِّى لَوْ هَوِيتُ فِرَاقَكُمْ
مِنَ البُعْدِ مَا بَيْنِي وَبَيْنَ المَصَائِبِ	فَيَا لَيْتَ مَا بَيْنِي وَبَيْنَ أَحِبَّتِي
عَلَيْكِ بِبَدْرٍ عَنْ لِقَاءِ التَّرَائِبِ	أَرَاكِ ظَنَنْتِ السِّلْكَ جِسْمِي فَعُقْتِهِ
مِنَ السُّقْمِ مَا غَيَّرْتُ مِنْ خَطِّ كَاتِبِ	وَلَوْ قَلَمٌ أُلْفِيتُ فِي شَقِّ رَأْسِهِ
وَلَمْ تَدْرِ أَنَّ العَارَ شَرُّ العَوَاقِبِ	تَخَوِّفِنِي دُونَ الَّذِي أَمَرَتْ بِهِ
يَطُولُ اسْتِمَاعِى بَعْدَهُ لِلنَّوَادِبِ	وَلَا بُدَّ مِنْ يَوْمٍ أَخَرَّ مُحَجَّلٍ
وَقُوعُ العَوَالِي دُونَهَا وَالْقَوَاضِبِ	يَهُونُ عَلَى مِثْلِي إِذَا رَامَ حَاجَةً
يَزُولُ وَبَاقِى عَيْشِهِ مِثْلُ ذَاهِبِ	كَثِيرٌ حَيَاةُ المَرْءِ مِثْلُ قَلِيلِهَا
عِضَاضُ الأَفَاعِي نَامَ فَوْقَ العَقَارِبِ	إِلَيْكِ فَإِنِّي لَسْتُ مِمَّنْ إِذَا اتَّقَى
أَعَدُّوا لِيَ السُّودَانَ فِي كَفْرِ عَاقِبِ	أَتَانِي وَعِيدُ الأَدْعِيَاءِ وَأَنَّهُمْ
فَهَلْ فِي وَحْدِي قَوْلُهُمْ غَيْرُ كَاذِبِ	وَلَوْ صَدَقُوا فِي جَدِّهِمْ لَحَذِرْتُهُمْ
كَأَنِّي عَجِيبٌ فِي عُيُونِ العَجَائِبِ	إِلَيَّ لَعَمْرِي قَصْدُ كُلِّ عَجِيبَةٍ
وَأَيُّ مَكَانٍ لَمْ تَطَأْهُ رَكَائِبِي	بِأَيِّ بِلَادٍ لَمْ أَجُرَّ ذَوَائِبِي
فَأَثْبَتَ كُورِي فِي ظُهُورِ المَوَاهِبِ	كَأَنَّ رَحِيلِي كَانَ مِنْ كَفِّ طَاهِرٍ
وَهُنَّ لَهُ شِرْبٌ وُرُودُ المَشَارِبِ	فَلَمْ يَبْقَ خَلْقٌ لَمْ يَرِدْنَ فِنَاءَهُ
قِرَاعُ العَوَالِي وَابْتِذَالُ الرَّغَائِبِ	فَتًى عَلَّمَتْهُ نَفْسُهُ وَجُدُودُهُ
وَرَدَّ إِلَى أَوْطَانِهِ كُلَّ غَائِبِ	فَقَدْ غَيَّبَ الشُّهَّادَ عَنْ كُلِّ مَوْطِنٍ
أَعَزُّ امْتِحَاءً مِنْ خُطُوطِ الرَّوَاجِبِ	كَذَا الفَاطِمِيُّونَ النَّدَى فِي بَنَانِهِمْ
سِلَاحُ الَّذِي لَاقَوْا غُبَارُ السَّلَاهِبِ	أُنَاسٌ إِذَا لَاقَوْا عِدِّي فَكَأَنَّمَا
دَوَامِي الهَوَادِي سَالِمَاتِ الجَوَانِبِ	رَمَوْا بِنَوَاصِيهَا القَسِيَّ فَجِئْنَهَا
وَأَكْثَرُ ذِكْراً مِنْ دُهُورِ الشَّبَائِبِ	أُولَئِكَ أَحْلَى مِنْ حَيَاةٍ مُعَادَةٍ
مِنَ الفِعْلِ لَا فَلَّ لَهَا فِي المَضَارِبِ	نَصَرْتَ عَلِيّاً يَا ابْنَةَ بَوَاتِرٍ
أَبُوكَ وَأَجْدَى مَا لَكُمْ مِنْ مَنَاقِبِ	وَأَبْهَرُ آيَاتِ التِّهَامِي أَنَّهُ
فَمَاذَا الَّذِي تُغْنِي كِرَامُ المَنَاصِبِ	إِذَا لَمْ تَكُنْ نَفْسُ النَّسِيبِ كَأَصْلِهِ

My day is night that is intensely dark
    To the eyes that due to your loss are weak
To distance between eyelids it's as if
    You hooked each eyelash end to eyebrow
I think if I wanted parting from you
    I'd lose it for time is the foulest of friends
O would what is between me and my
    Lover afar were between me and sorrow
You knew my body a thread so you
    Kept it off by a pearl lest it touch a breast
If I were thrown in a pen's tip cut by
    Illness I'd not alter the writer's strokes
She scares me with less than she asks
    She doesn't know shame as the worst end
A sure day, bright as a white leg horse
    After which the wailing is heard for long
Easy for one like me if he aims at goals
    The clash of swords and spears before it
Much life for a man is like a little, it
    Ends and life's scrap is as what passed
Be off! I'm not one who when on guard
    Against a snake bite sleeps on scorpions
Threats of claimants reached me they
    Brought Sudanese for me to Kafr Aqib
If they spoke true of kin I'd beware
    But are their words about me not lies?
By my life! every surprise end is mine
    As if I were a marvel in eyes of wonder
In what land did I not trail my braids
    What place have my camels not trod?
My departure was from Tahir's hand
    My saddle was fixed on the back of gifts
All who live have come to his court
    They are drink to him coming to a pool
A youth whose soul and kin teach him
    Beating the foe and scattering huge gifts
He draws courtiers from every home
    Sends back to his homeland every exile
So the Fatimids their fingers' bounty
    Is harder to erase than wrinkles in joints
Men who if they meet a foe it seems
    Spears they oppose are only horse dust
They toss the forelocks as if from bows
    Come bloody necked but flanks unharmed
They are sweeter than life renewed
    More often recalled than times of youth
You added Ali, O his son by swords
    In deeds, no dullness in that striking
Brightest of Tihami's signs is this
    He was your father as your rich merit
If traditions way is not as its stock
    What use is that precious thing a root?

وَمـا قَرُّبَتْ أَشْبـاهُ قَـوْمٍ أَبـاعِـدٍ | وَلا بَعَّدَتْ أَشْبـاهُ قَـوْمٌ أَقـارِبِ
إذا عَلَـوِيٌّ لم يكـنْ مِثْـلَ طـاهرٍ | فَمـا هُـوَ إلّا حُجَّـةٌ للنّـواصِـبِ
يَقولـونَ تأثيـرُ الكَواكـبِ في الـوَرَى | فَمـا بـالُـهُ تأْثيـرُهُ في الكَواكِـبِ
عَـلا كَتَـدَ الدّنيـا إلى كـلِّ غايـةٍ | تَسيـرُ بـهِ سَيْـرَ الذَّلـولِ بَراكِـبِ
وَحُـقَّ لَـهُ أن يَسبِـقَ النّـاسَ جالِسـاً | ويُـدْرِكَ مـا لم يُدْرِكـوا غيـرَ طـالِبِ
ويُحْـذَى عَرانيـنَ المُلـوكِ وإنّهـا | لِمَـنْ قَدَمَيْـهِ في أَجَـلِّ المَراتِـبِ
يَـدٌ للزّمـانِ الجَمْـعُ بَيْنـي وبَيْنَـهُ | لَتَفْريقِـهِ بَيْنـي وبَيْـنَ النّوائـبِ
هُـوَ ابنُ رَسـولِ اللهِ وابنُ وَصِيِّـهِ | وشِبْهُهُما شَبَّهْـتُ بعـدَ التّجـارِبِ
يَـرَى أنّ مـا بـانَ مِنـكَ لِضارِبٍ | بِأَقتَـلَ مِمّـا بـانَ منـكَ لِعائِـبِ
ألا أيّهـا المـالُ الذي قـد أَسـادَهُ | تَعَـزَّ فَهَـذا فِعْلُـهُ بالكَتائِـبِ
لَعَلَّـكَ في وَقْـتٍ شَغَلْـتَ فُـؤادَهُ | عـن الجُـودِ أو كَثَّـرْتَ جيـشَ مُحـارِبِ
حَمَلْـتُ إليـهِ مِـنْ لِسانـي حديقـةً | سقاهـا الحِجـى سقـيَ الرّيـاضَ السّحائِـبَ
فَحُيّيْـتَ خيـرَ ابـنٍ لخيـرِ أبٍ بهـا | لأشـرفِ بَيْـتٍ في لُـؤَيّ بنِ غـالِبِ

(١٣٩)

«من الرجز»

كان لأبي الطيب حجرة تسمى الجهامة ولها مهر يسمى الطخرور، فأقام الثلج على الأرض بانطاكية وتعذر المرعى على المهر فقال:

مـا للمُـروجِ الخُضـرِ والحَدائِـقِ | يَشكـو خَلاهـا كَثـرَةَ العَوائِـقِ
أقـامَ فيهـا الثّلـجُ كالمُرافِـقِ | يَعقِـدُ فـوقَ السِّـنّ ريـقَ الباصِـقِ
ثـمّ مَضَـى لا عـادَ مِـنْ مُفـارِقِ | بقـائِـدٍ مِـنْ ذَوْبِـهِ وسـائِـقِ
كأنّمـا الطّخـرورُ بـاغي آبِـقِ | يـأكُـلُ مـن نَبْـتٍ قصيـرٍ لاصِـقِ
كَقَشـرِكَ الحِبَـرَ عـنِ المَهـارِقِ | أرودُهُ مِنّـهُ بكـالشّـوذانِـقِ
بُمُطلَـقِ اليُمنـى طويـلِ الفـائِـقِ | عَبْـلِ الشَّـوَى مُقـارِبِ المَرافِـقِ
رَحْـبِ اللَّبـانِ نائِـهِ الطّرائِـقِ | ذي مَنخِـرٍ رَحْـبٍ وإطْـلٍ لاحِـقِ

Comparison of unlike folk unequal
    As comparison of similar folk never far
If an Alid is not like Tahir, he is
    Nothing but argument for the rebels
They say the stars influence men
    But what of his influence on the stars?
He rides the world's back to a goal
    The gait of one obedient to its rider
Good he outpaces men as he sits
    To reach what they gain not by search
He makes shoes of men's noses
    On his feet they find their high rank
Time's gift, between him and me
    Separation between us misfortune
God's rasul's son, executor's son
    Comparison for them matched to fact
He knows what in you is attacked
    Is no worse than that for backbiters
O wealth that is now destroyed
    Take courage, it is his way for armies
Maybe you distracted his heart
    From generosity or increased an army
I brought him gardens on my tongue
    My wit watered like clouds on meadows
May you be greeted by best son of best
    Abu Luayy ibn Galib of the noblest house

139
Abu Tayyib spoke describing his horse and commemorating the lack of fodder for him. (Trembling qi)

Nothing green in fields or in gardens
    Their herbage complains of the harshness
Snow had stayed there like a friend
    Freezing on the teeth the film of saliva
But it left, not returning after parting
    With captains in its thaw and followers
As if Tukhrur is seeking a fugitive as
    He eats the grass that is short and close
Like your peelings of ink from a sheet
    I seek it like a kestrel falcon for his sake
Right leg different in color, long
    Necked, aligned joints firm at the knees
A broad chest with strong muscles
    Showing wide nostrils and lean belly

222 Diwan al-Mutanabbi

شادِخَةٍ غُرَّتُهُ كالشّارِقِ	مُحَجَّــلٍ نَهْدٍ كُمَيْتٍ زاهِــقِ
باقٍ على البَوْغاءِ والشّقائِقِ	كأنَّهــا مِــنْ لَوْنِـهِ في بــارِقِ
للفارِسِ الرّاكِضِ مِنهُ والواثِــقِ	والأبْرَدَيْــنِ والهَجيــرِ الماحِــقِ
كأنّـهُ في رَيْدِ طَــوْدٍ شاهِقِ	خَــوْفُ الجَبــانِ في فُـؤادِ العاشِــقِ
لَــوْ سابَقَ الشّمسَ مِن المَشارِقِ	يَشْــأى إلى المِسْمَـعِ صَوْتَ النّــاطِقِ
يَـتْــرُكُ في حِجــارَةِ الأبــارِقِ	جــاءَ إلى الغَــرْبِ مَجيــءَ السّابِقِ
مَشياً وإنْ يَعْــدُ فكالخَنــادِقِ	آثــارَ قَلْــعِ الحَلْــي في المَناطِقِ
لأحْسَــبَتْ خَوامِــسَ الأيانِــقِ	لَــوْ أوردَتْ غِــبَّ سَحــابٍ صادِقِ
شَحـا لَـهُ شَحْوَ الغُرابِ النّاعِقِ	إذا اللّجــامُ جــاءَهُ لِطــارِقِ
مُنحَــدِرٌ عَــنْ سِــيَّيْ جُلاهِـقِ	كأنّمــا الجِلْــدُ لِعُرْيِ النّــاهِقِ
وزادَ في السّاقِ على النّقائِقِ	بَــزَّ المَذاكي وهْــوَ في العَقائِـقِ
وزادَ في الأذْنِ علــى الخَزائِــقِ	وزادَ في الوَقْــعِ علــى الصّواعِـقِ
يُمَيِّــزُ الهَــزْلَ مِــنَ الحَقائِقِ	وزادَ في الحَــذَرِ على العَقاعِــقِ
يُريـكَ خُرْقــاً وهْـوَ عَيْنُ الحاذِقِ	ويُنــذِرُ الرَّكْــبَ بكُــلِّ سارِقٍ
قُوبِــلَ مِــنْ آفِــقَةٍ وآفِــقِ	يَحُــكُّ أنّى شــاءَ حَكَّ الباشِقِ
فَعُنْقُــهُ يُرْبــي علــى البَواسِـقِ	بَيــنَ عِتــاقِ الخَيْــلِ والعَتائِقِ
أعِــدُّهُ للطّعــنِ في الفَيــالِقِ	وحَلْقُــهُ يُمْكِــنُ فِــتْرَ الخانِقِ
والسَّيْــرِ في ظِــلِّ اللِّواءِ الخافِقِ	والضَّــرْبِ في الأوْجُهِ والمَفارِقِ
يَقطُــرُ في كُمَّــي إلى البَنــائِقِ	يحمِلُنــي والنَّصْـلُ ذو السَّفاسِــقِ
ولا أُبالــي قِلَّــةَ المُوافِــقِ	لا ألحَــظُ الدّنيــا بعَيْنـي وامِـقِ
أنْــتَ لَنــا وكُلُّنــا للخالِــقِ	أيْ كَبْــتَ كُــلِّ حاسِــدٍ مُنــافِقِ

(١٤٠)

«من الوافر»

كبست انطاكية وهو فيها فقتل الطخرور وأمه فقال:

فَــلا تَقنَــعْ بِمــا دونَ النّجــومِ	إذا غــامَرْتَ في شَــرَفٍ مَــرُومِ

White legs, large, reddish, sturdy
    Ample his blaze like the rising sun
As if with its lightning colors it
    Hovered over the dust and desert rock
Cool at morn, hottest noon and eve
    For the horseman riding him steadily
A coward's fear in a lover's heart
    As if he were on a high mountain side
Ahead of speaker's voice in an ear
    To outdistance the sun in eastern lands
He goes west with a winner's gait
    As he leaves the stones of a sandy hill
With imprint of gems set in a belt
    As he trots, H he runs they are trenches
If they drink from the faithful clouds
    There is enough for the five day camel
A bridle comes to him on a night trip
    He opens his mouth as a croaking raven
As if the hide on bare face bones
    Stretched from the curve of a crossbow
In first hair he beat a mature horse
    His legs faster than those of an ostrich
Hoofs louder than than thunderclaps
    His ears more sensitive than the rabbits
More alert to danger than the raven
    Distinguishing between jest and earnest
He warns the rider of every thief
    Seems stupid, is cleverness itself
Grooms himself as falcons preen
    Derived from fine mother and father
Among noblest stallions and mares
    His neck has grown like the palm tree
A throat held by a strangler's hand
    Counts in the thrusting as a battalion
A blow in the face in the parting
    Running in shadows of fluttering flags
He bears me and double edge blade
    It drips on the armor down to the shirt
I see the world with no lover's eye
    I do not bother with small successes
You strike down an envious hypocrite
    You are ours, all of us are the Creator's

140
He spoke when Antioch was besieged
and the foal and mare were killed so he spoke.
(Exuberant mi)

When you strive madly for some high goal
    Be not content with what is short of the stars

كَطَعْمِ المَوْتِ في أمرٍ عَظيمِ	فَطَعْمُ المَوْتِ في أمرٍ حَقيرٍ
صَفائِحُ دَمْعُها ماءُ الجُسومِ	سَتَبكي شَجوَها فَرَسي ومُهري
كَما نَشَأ العَذاري في النَعيمِ	قَرينُ النارِ ثمَّ نَشَأنَ فيها
وأيدِيها كَثيراتُ الكُلومِ	وفارَقنَ الصَياقِلَ مُخلِصاتٍ
وتِلكَ خَديعَةُ الطَبعِ اللَئيمِ	يَرى الجُبَناءُ أنَّ العَجزَ عَقلٌ
ولا مِثلُ الشَجاعَةِ في الحَكيمِ	وكلُّ شَجاعَةٍ في المَرءِ تُغني
وآفَتُهُ مِنَ الفَهمِ السَقيمِ	وكَم مِن عائِبٍ قَولاً صَحيحاً
على قَدَرِ القَرائِحِ والعُلومِ	ولكِن تأخُذُ الآذانُ مِنهُ

(١٤١)

عَرَضاً نَظَرتُ وَخِلتُ أنّي أسلَمُ	لِهَوى النُفوسِ سَريرَةٌ لا تُعلَمُ
لَأخوكَ ثَمَّ أرَقُّ مِنكِ وأرحَمُ	يا أُختَ مُعتَنِقِ الفَوارِسِ في الوَغى
أنَّ المَجوسَ تُصيبُ فيما تَحكُمُ	يَرنو إليكِ مَعَ العَفافِ وَعِندَهُ
وَلَوْ أنَّها الأولى لَراعَ الأسحَمُ	راعَتكِ رائِعَةُ البَياضِ بعارِضي
فالشَيبُ مِن قِبَلِ الأوانِ تَلَثُّمُ	لَو كانَ يُمكِنُني سَفَرتُ عَنِ الصِبا
يَقَقاً يَميتُ ولا سَوداً يَعصِمُ	وَلَقَد رَأيتُ الحادِثاتِ فَلا أَرى
ويَشيبُ ناصِيَةَ الصَبيِّ ويَهرَمُ	والهَمُّ يَختَرِمُ الجَسيمَ نَحافَةً
وَأخو الجَهالَةِ في الشَقاوَةِ يَنعَمُ	ذو العَقلِ يَشقى في النَعيمِ بِعَقلِهِ
يَنسى الَذي يُولى وَعافٍ يَندَمُ	والناسُ قَد نَبَذوا الحِفاظَ فَمُطلَقٌ
وَأرحَم شَبابَكَ مِن عَدُوٍّ تَرحَمُ	لا يَخدَعَنَّكَ مِن عَدُوٍّ دَمعُهُ
حَتّى يُراقَ عَلى جَوانِبِهِ الدَمُ	لا يَسلَمُ الشَرَفُ الرَفيعُ مِنَ الأذى
مَن لا يَقِلُّ كَما يَقِلُّ ويَلؤُمُ	يُؤذى القَليلُ مِنَ اللِئامِ بِطَبعِهِ
ذا عِفَّةٍ فَلَعَلَّهُ لا يَظلِمُ	الظُلمُ مِن شِيَمِ النُفوسِ فَإنْ تَجِدْ
ما بَينَ رِحلَيها الطَريقُ الأعظَمُ	يَحمى ابنُ كَيغَلَغَ الطَريقَ وَعِرسُهُ
إنَّ المَنِيَّ بِحَلقَتَيها خِضرِمُ	أقِمِ المَسالِحَ فَوقَ شُفرِ سَكينَةٍ
واستُر أباكَ فَإنَّ أصلَكَ مُظلِمُ	وَأرفُقْ بِنَفسِكَ إنَّ خَلقَكَ ناقِصٌ

For death's taste in the little things
    Is like the taste of death in the great things
You will weep my mare and colt's grief
    As swords whose tears are blood of bodies
They approached the fire and grew in it
    Like the virgins who grow in a tranquillity
They left the sword polishers perfect
    And the hands of men had many a wound
A coward thinks weakness reasonable
    But that is the trick of some sordid nature
Each brave act for a man is worthwhile
    Nothing is like bravery for the wise man
How many who complain of a true word
    When the lack is in the sickness of mind
For the ears seize on that which is
    According to insights and experiences

141
He spoke mocking Ishaq ibn Ibrahim ibn Kaigalag. (Perfect mu)

Hearts' love has a secret not understood
    As suddenly I look when I think
I am secure O sister of riders eager in the battle
    Your brother has more pity, mercy than you
He looks long at you shyly for he knows
    Magians died for what they thought good
Elegant white in sideburns charms you
    If it were first then the black would delight
If possible then I'd unveil youth since
    Gray hairs before their time are as a veil
I've seen misfortune but I've not seen
    Snowy hair die nor black hair protected
Desire weakens lust with emaciation
    Whitens the forelock of youth and he ages
Rational man's bliss grieves due to his
    Reason and foolish man prefers his misery.
Men cast off restraints and the one set
    Free forgets a friend and regrets pardon
Let not tears of a friend deceive you
    Pity your youth instead of a foe you pity
High noble nature yields not to evil:
    Until the blood trickles from its sides
A little vileness harms by its nature
    One not small as it belittles and ruins
Wrong is souls' nature and if you find
    One pure he is weak if he does not wrong
Ibn Kaigalag bars the way, his wife too
    The biggest road is that between her legs
So set a guard over the she ass cunt
    For death is in her womb like a huge sea
Be gentle for your nature is waning
    Conceal your father for your root is evil

وَرِضَاكَ فَيْشَلَةٌ وَرَبُّكَ دِرْهَمُ	وَغِنَاكَ مَسْـأَلَةٌ وَطَيْشُكَ نَفْخَةٌ
تَقْـوَى عَلَى كَمَـرِ الْعَبِيـدِ وَتُقْـدِمُ	وَاحْـذَرْ مُنَـاوَاةَ الرِّجَـالِ فَإِنَّمَـا
عَـنْ غَيِّـهِ وَخِطَـابُ مَـنْ لاَ يَفْهَـمُ	وَمِـنَ الْبَلِيَّـةِ عَـذْلُ مَـنْ لاَ يَرْعَـوِى
تَحْـتَ الْعُلُـوجِ وَمِـنْ وَرَاءِ يُلْجَـمُ	يَمْشـى بِأَرْبَعَـةٍ عَلَـى أَعْقَابِـهِ
مَطْرُوفَةٌ أُوقِتَّ فِيهَـا حِصْرِمُ	وَجُفُونُـهُ مَـا تَسْتَقِـرُّ كَأَنَّهَـا
قِـرْدٌ يُقَهْقِـهُ أَوْ عَجُـوزٌ تَلْطِـمُ	وَإِذَا أَشَـارَ مُحَدِّثًـا فَكَأَنَّـهُ
حَتَّـى يَكَـادَ عَلَـى يَـدٍ يَتَعَمَّـمُ	يَقْلِـى مُفَارَقَـةَ الْـكَاكُفِّ قَذَالُـهُ
وَيَكُـونُ أَكْـذَبَ مَـا يَكُـونُ وَيُقْسِـمُ	وَتَـرَاهُ أَصْغَـرَ مَـا تَـرَاهُ نَاطِقًـا
وَأَوَدُّ مِنْـهُ لِمَـنْ يَـوَدُّ الأَرْقَـمُ	وَالـذُّلُّ يُظْهِـرُ فِـى الذَّلِيـلِ مَـوَدَّةً
صَفْـرَاءُ أَضْيَـقُ مِنْـكَ مَـاذَا أَزْعُـمُ	وَمِـنَ الْعَـدَاوَةِ مَـا يَنَـالُكَ نَفْعُـهُ
يَـا ابْـنَ الأَعَيِّـرِ وَهْـىَ فِيـكَ تَكَـرُّمُ	أَرْسَـلْتَ تَسْأَلُنِـى الْمَدِيـحَ سَفَاهَـةً
وَلَشَـدَّ مَـا قَرُبَـتْ عَلَيْـكَ الأَنْجُـمُ	أَتَـرَى الْقِيَـادَةَ فِـى سِـوَاكَ تَكَسُّـبًا
إِنَّ الثَّنَـاءَ لِمَـنْ يُـزَارُ فَيُنْعِـمُ	فَلَشَـدَّ مَـا جَـاوَزْتَ قَـدْرَكَ صَاعِـدًا
تَـدْنُو فَيُوحَـأُ أَخْدَعَـاكَ وَتَنْهَـمُ	وَأَرْغَـتَ مَـا لِأَبِـى الْعَشَـائِرِ خَالِصـاً
وَلِمَـنْ يَجُـرُّ الْجَيْـشَ وَهْـوَ عَرَمْـرَمُ	وَلِمَـنْ أَقَمْـتَ عَلَـى الْهَـوَانِ بِبَابِـهِ
فَتُصِيبُـهُ مِنْهَـا الْكَمِـىُّ الْمُعْلَـمُ	وَلِمَـنْ يُهِيـنُ الْمَـالَ وَهْـوَ مُكَـرَّمُ
وَثَنَـى فَقَوَّمَهَـا بِآخَـرَ مِنْهُـمُ	وَلِمَـنْ إِذَا الْتَقَـتِ الْكُمَـاةُ بِمَـازِقٍ
وَالرُّمْـحُ أَسْمَـرُ وَالْحُسَـامُ مُصَمِّـمُ	وَلَرُبَّمَـا أَطَـرَ الْقَنَـاةَ بِفَـارِسٍ
وَفَعَـالُ مَـنْ تَلِـدُ الأَعَـاجِمُ أَعْجَـمُ	وَالْوَجْـهُ أَزْهَـرُ وَالْفُـؤَادُ مُشَـيَّعٌ
	أَفْعَـالُ مَـنْ تَسِـلْدُ الْكِـرَامُ كَرِيمَـةٌ

Your wealth doubtful, your jest a fart
    Your pleasure a cock, your master a dirham,
Beware of men's hostility for you are
    Hard on a slave's penis and often fucked
Slander by one with no respect is trial
    In error, pleas from one who knows nothing
He walks on all fours to the rear among
    The unbelievers bridled from the behind
His eyelids winking as if they watered
    Or unripe fruit had been crushed in them
If his gestures tell a story it's like
    A monkey chatters or an old woman slaps
Back of his head fears a rising hand
    Till he almost wears turbans for the fists
He seems smaller when he talks
    Most of all false when swearing an oath
Baseness shows itself by being base
    More loveable than he as lover a snake
His good deeds only stir your enmity
    His friendship only bothers and troubles
You foolishly sent to ask my praise
    Safra more urgent than you, what gall!
Don't you see guidance earned still
    O son of little one-eye, your only desire
How much you exceeded your power
    How terribly the stars came close to you
You sought what belongs to Abu Ashair
    Praise is only for one visited and gracious
For one at whose gates you are denied
    You approach, one hits your neck, rebuked
One who scorns wealth and is generous
    One who leads armies that are immense
He who if warriors meet in battle
    Has his part in it as a master warrior
Often he turns a lance against knights
    It bends and then stands firm behind them
His face is shining, his heart is bold
    His lance brown and his sword hardened
Deeds of one nobly born are noble
    Deeds of one stranger born are barbarian

(١٤٢)

«من الطويل»

بلغه وهو بدمشق أنّ إسحاق بن كيغلغ
يتوعّده في بلاد الروم فقال:

يَجُوبُ حُزُوناً بَيْنَنا وسُهُولا	أتاني كلامُ الجاهلِ ابنِ كَيْغَلْغِ
وبَيْـني سِوى رُمْحي لكانَ طَويلا	ولوْ لم يكُنْ بينَ ابنِ صَفراءَ حائلٌ
ولكنْ تَسَلَّى بالبُكاءِ قَليلا	وإسْحاقُ مأمونٌ على مَنْ أهانَهُ
وليسَ جميلاً أن يكونَ جَميلا	وليسَ جميلاً عِرْضُهُ فيَصُونَهُ
لقدْ كانَ مِن قبلِ الهِجاءِ ذَليلا	ويكـذِبُ مـا أذْلَلْتُـهُ بهِجائـهِ

(١٤٣)

«من البسيط»

وورد الخبر بأنّ غلمان ابن كيغلغ قتلوه فقال:

هذا الدَّواءُ الذي يَشفي مِنَ الحُمُقِ	قالوا لَنا: ماتَ إسحَقْ! فقلتُ لهمْ:
أو عاشَ عاشَ بلا خَلْـقٍ ولا خُلُـقِ	إنْ ماتَ ماتَ بلا فَقْـدٍ ولا أسَـفٍ
خوْنَ الصَّديقِ ودَسَّ الغَدرَ في المَلَقِ	مِنـهُ تَعَلَّـمَ عبْـدٌ شَـقَّ هامَتَـهُ
مَطرودَةٍ ككعُوبِ الرَّمحِ في نَسَـقِ	وحَلفَ ألْفَ يَمينٍ غَيـرَ صادِقـةٍ
خِلْـواً مِنَ البـأسِ مَمْلوءاً مِنَ النَّزَقِ	ما زِلـتُ أعرفُـهُ قِـرْداً بـلا ذَنَـبٍ
لا تَسْـتَقِرُّ على حـالٍ مِنَ القَلَـقِ	كريشـةٍ في مَهَـبِّ الرّيـحِ ساقِطَةٍ
فتَكتَسي منـهُ ريحَ الجَـوْرَبِ العَـرِقِ	تَستَغرقُ الكَفَّ فَوْديـهِ ومُنكَبـهُ
موتاً من الضّربِ أمْ موتاً من الفَـرَقِ	فسائِلوا قاتِليـهِ كَيفَ ماتَ لَهُـمْ
بغَيـرِ جسْـمٍ ولا رأسٍ ولا عُنُـقِ	وأيـنَ مَوقِـعُ حَـدّ السَّيفِ مِن شَبَحٍ
لكـانَ الأمَ طِفْـلٍ لُـفَّ في خِـرَقِ	لَـوْ لا اللِّئـامُ وشيءٌ مِـنْ مُشابَهَةٍ
مِمـا يَشُـقّ علـى الآذانِ والحَـدَقِ	كـلامُ أكـثرِ مَـنْ تَلقَـى ومَنظَـرُهُ

142
A rumor came to him that Ibn Kaigalag had threatened him so he said.
(Long la)

News of fool Ibn Kaigalag came to me
    It crossed rough and smooth between us
If between Safra's son and me no bar
    Other than my lance then it's long enough
Ishaq is safe from one who scorns him
    Yet he amuses himself with weeping a bit
His honor is not good so he guards it
    He'd not be pretty even if that were pure
He lies if he says I shame him by jest
    Indeed he was base before the satires

143
The news came that Ibn Kaigalag's slaves had killed him so he spoke.
(Outspread qi)

They said to us: Ishaq died. So I said
    This medicine cures him of foolishness
If he died he died without loss or grief
    Or lived he lived without good or grace
By him a slave learned how to split
    A skull, betray friend, hide fraud in guile
Not true to a crony's right hand vow
    Cast off like spearpoints one after other
I always knew him an ape without tail
    Zero of misery filled with his stupidities
Falling like a feather in windy gusts
    Never stable in turbulent circumstance
A hand engulfs his temples and neck
    Clothes him in a cloak of sweaty fumes
Ask those who hit him what death
    Came to him, beating or frightening?
Had a sword's edge place for him
    Who had neither body, head or neck?
But for vile ones and some of his likes
    He's the ugliest brat ever wrapped in rags
Most of the words one hears and his face
    Are such as split the ears and one's vision

(١٤٤)

«من الوافر»

نزل على علي بن عسكر ببعلبك فخلع عليه
وحمله وسأله أن يقيم عنده وكان يريد السفر
إلى أنطاكية فقال يستأذنه:

روينـــا يــا ابـــن عســـكر الهُمَامَـــا   ولـم يتـــرُكْ نـــداكَ لنـــا هُيَامَـــا
وصــار أحــبَّ مـا تُهـدِّي إلينـا   لغَيــر قِلَــى وَداعَــكَ والسَّــلامَا
ولـم نمـلَـلْ تفقُّـدَكَ المَـوالي   ولــم نـذمُـــمْ أيــادِيَـكَ الجسـامَا
ولكـــنّ الغيـــوثَ إذا توالَـــتْ   بـأرضٍ مُســافِرٍ كَــرِهَ الغَمامَـا

(١٤٥)

«من البسيط»

قال في صباه:

وشــادنٍ روحُ مَــن يهــواهُ فــي يَــدِهِ   سَــيفُ الصُّــدودِ علــى أعْلــى مُقَلَّـدِهِ
مــا اهتَــزَّ مِنــهُ علــى عُضْـوٍ لِيَبْتُـرَهُ   إلّا اتَّقــاهُ بتُــرْسٍ مِــن تَجَلّــدِهِ
ذَمَّ الزَّمـانَ إليــهِ مِــنْ أَحِبَّتِــهِ   مـا ذَمَّ مـن بَـدرِهِ فـي حَمـدِ أحمـدِهِ
شمـسٌ إذا الشَّمـسُ لاقتـهُ علـى فـرسٍ   تَــرَدَّدَ النّــورُ فيهــا مِــنْ تَــرَدُّدِهِ
إن يقبُـحُ الحُسْـنُ إلّا عنـدَ طَلعتِـهِ   والعَبــدُ يَقبُــحُ إلّا عنــدَ سَــيِّدِهِ
قالـت عـنِ الرُّفْـدِ طِـبْ نفسـاً فقلـتُ لهـا   لا يَصْــدُرُ الحُــرُّ إلّا بعْــدَ مَــوْرِدِهِ
لــم أعــرفِ الخيــرَ إلّا مُــذْ عَرَفْــتُ فتــىً   لـم يُولَـدِ الجُـودُ إلّا عنـدَ مَوْلِـدِهِ
نفــسٌ تُصَغِّــرُ نفــسَ الدّهــرِ مــن كِبَــرٍ   لهـا نُهًـى كَهْلِـهِ فـي سِـنِّ أمْرَدِهِ

(١٤٦)

«من الخفيف»

يمدح أبا العشائر الحسن بن علي بن الحسن
ابن الحسين بن حمدان العدوي:

أتـراهــا لكـــثـــرة العشّــاق   تحســبُ الدّمــعَ خِلقـةً فـي المـآقـي

144
He stayed with
Ali ibn Asker at Baalbak
and he honored him.
So he said
as he intended to depart.
(Exuberant ma)

Pour out for us O magnanimous Ibn Asker
    So do not end your bounty to those who thirst
It would be best to make no gifts to us
    Your farewell and goobye without rancor
We do not worry about your coming loss
    Nor condemn the large favors in your bounty
But yet the shower when it comes near
    The traveler's earth will reject in a cloud

145
He spoke a qasida
which he composed
in his youth.
(Long hi)

The sword of removal is on his neck as
    It cuts the throat of his beloved when drawn
Not shaking it against a limb to sever
    Rather protecting with the shield of patience
The time blames him, for those he loves
    Not blaming its moon for praise as I praise
He is a sun and when the sun strikes him
    Riding its light glitters on it as he moves on
Beauty is only ugly when he appears, no
    Slave is base except before him as master
She said: help your self with gifts, but
    I: A free man won't return till after drinking
I knew no good until I knew the truth
    Generosity wasn't born except at his birth
A soul belittles the soul's age by pride
    Its mature wisdom is in its beardless years

146
He spoke
praising
Abu Ashair al Husayn
ibn Ali ibn al-Husayn ibn Hamdan.
(Nimble qi)

Do you think that due to many lovers
    She reckons tears are natural to eyes?

راعِها غَيرَ جَفنِها غَيرَ راقي	كَيفَ تَرثي الَّتي تَرى كُلَّ جَفنٍ
كِ عُوفِيَتِ مِن ضَنىً واشتِياقِ	أَنتِ مِنّا فَتَنتِ نَفسَكِ لَكِنَّ
تِ لَحالَ النُحولُ دونَ العِناقِ	حُلتِ دونَ المَزارِ فاليَومَ لَو زُر
كانَ عَمداً لَنا وحَتفَ اتِّفاقِ	إِنَّ لَحظاً أَدمَيتِهِ وأَدمَنا
لِأَرارِ الرَّسيمِ مُخَّ المَناقي	لَو عَدا عَنكِ غَيرَ هَجرِكَ بُعدٌ
مِثلَ أَنفاسِنا عَلى الأَرماقِ	ولَسِرنا ولَو وَصَلنا عَلَيها
لَونُ أَشفارِهِنَّ لَونُ الحِداقِ	ما بِنا مِن هَوى العُيونِ اللَواتي
فَأَطالَت بِها اللَيالي البَواقي	قَصَّرَت مُدَّةَ اللَيالي المَواضي
لِ بِما نَوَّلَت مِنَ الإيراقِ	كاثَرَت نائِلَ الأَميرِ مِنَ الما
سادَ هَذا الأَنامَ بِاستِحقاقِ	لَيسَ إلّا أَبا العَشائِرِ خَلقٌ
لَقَ بِالذُعرِ والدَمِ المُهراقِ	طاعِنُ الطَعنَةِ الَّتي تَطعَنُ الفي
سَبَرَ عَنها مِن شِدَّةِ الإِطراقِ	ذاتُ فَرغٍ كَأَنَّها في حَشا المُخ
هَبْ أَن يَشرَبَ الَّذي هُوَ ساقِ	ضارِبُ الهامِ في الغُبارِ وما يَر
بَينَ أَرساغِها وبَينَ الصِفاقِ	فَوقَ شَقّاءَ لِلأَشَقِّ مَجالٌ
صَدَقَ القَولَ في صِفاتِ البُراقِ	ما رَآها مُكَذِّبُ الرُسلِ إلّا
ها وأَطرافُها لَهُ كالنِطاقِ	هَمُّهُ في ذَوي الأَسِنَّةِ لا فيـ
دِرُ أَمرٌ لَهُ عَلى إِقلاقِ	ثاقِبُ الرَأيِ ثابِتُ الحِلمِ لا يَق
دَمكُم في الوَغى مُتونُ العِتاقِ	يا بَني الحارِثِ بنِ لُقمانَ لا تَعـ
يٍ فَكانَ القِتالُ قَبلَ التَلاقي	بَعَثوا الرُعبَ في قُلوبِ الأَعادي
تَنتَضيها نَفسُها إلى الأَعناقِ	وتَكادُ الظُبى لِما عَوَّدوها
عَ القَنا أَشفَقوا مِنَ الإِشفاقِ	وإذا أَشفَقَ الفَوارِسُ مِن وَق
كَبُدورِ تَمامِها في المُحاقِ	كُلُّ ذِمرٍ يَزدادُ في المَوتِ حُسناً
لَم يَكُن دونَها مِنَ العارِ واقي	جاعِلٍ دِرعَهُ مَنِيَّتَهُ إِن
فَهوَ كالماءِ في الشِفارِ الرِقاقِ	كَرَمٌ خَشَّنَ الجَوانِبَ مِنهُم
لَزِمَتهُ جِنايَةُ السُرّاقِ	ومَعالٍ إِذا ادَّعاها سِواهُم
غائِبُ الشَخصِ حاضِرُ الأَخلاقِ	يا ابنَ مَن كُلَّما بَدَوتَ بَدا لي

How can she weep who thinks each eye
    But her own sees her with tears stopped?
You were ours in seducing yourself but
    You stayed free of emaciation and grief
You forbade a visit so now if you want
    This emaciation could forbid the embrace
The glance you prolonged and we fixed
    Was intended by us but death intervened
If distance, not your flight, forbade
    The fast gait would melt the camel's fat
We would travel and if we came to her
    We'd find our souls were at a last breath
What is for us in love of eyes whose
    Eyelash color is the color of the pupils?
They shorten the passing night's time
    And the lingering nights grow long by it
They increase gifts of the Amir's flock
    When they bring the hunter's empty bag
No creature other than Abu Ashair
    Can deserve to rule over these people
A jouster with thrusts to hit an army
    With terror and the blood gushes forth
Endowed with a flood as if in heart
    He hears it as perforce he looks down
One who strikes heads in dust and
    Has no fear lest he drink what he pours
On a mare that's ecstacy for stallion
    Between her pasterns and inner skin
No prophet's disbeliever sees unless
    He finds Buraq's description spoken true
His goal those holding lances, not them
    Their points like a waistband around him
Piercing intellect and firm clemency
    Man has no power over him through fear
O Banu Harith ibn Luqman let no backs
    Of fine horses be lacking to you in battle
They send terror into enemy hearts
    It's as if death comes before the attack
Almost when they make use of a blade
    It makes a sheath for itself in the throat
When horsemen tremble from a shock
    Of spears they quake because of horror
Each brave man adds to his beauty in
    Death as a moon at full moves to the dark
He's one to make armor death itself
    If no shelter from shame is short of that
Generosity to roughen sides of foes
    It is like water to polish the thin edges
As to heights when others claim them
    The crime of the theft will be inescapable
O son of him who when you appear
    Is present in nature but absent in person

لَوْ تَنَكَّرْتَ في المَكَرِّ لِقَوْمٍ   حَلَفُوا أَنَّكَ ابنُهُ بِالطَّلاقِ
كيفَ يَقوَى بِكَفِّكَ الزَّنْدُ والآ   فاقُ فيها كَالكفِّ في الآفاقِ
قَلَّ نَفْعُ الحَديدِ فيكَ فَما يَلـ   ـقاكَ إلَّا مَنْ سَيْفُهُ مِنْ نِفاقِ
إلْفُ هذا الهَواءِ أَوْقَعَ في الأَنْـ   ـفُسِ أَنَّ الحِمامَ مُرُّ المَذاقِ
والأَسى قبلَ فُرْقَةِ الرّوحِ عجزٌ   والأَسى لا يَكونُ بَعدَ الفِراقِ
كمْ ثَراءٍ فَرِحتَ بِالرّمْحِ عنهُ   كانَ مِن بَخلِ أَهلِهِ في وِثاقِ
والغِنى في يَدِ اللّئيمِ قَبيحٌ   قَدْرَ قُبْحَ الكَريمِ في الإِمْلاقِ
ليس قَولي في شَمسٍ فِعلكَ كالشَّمْـ   ـسِ ولكِن كَالشّمسِ في الإِشراقِ
شاعِرُ المَجْدِ خِدْنُهُ شاعِرُ اللّفْـ   ـظِ كِلانا رَبُّ المَعاني الدِّقاقِ
لَمْ تَزَلْ تَسمَعُ المَديحَ ولكِنْ   صَهيلَ الجِيادِ غَيرُ النّهاقِ
لَيتْ لي مِثلَ جَدِّ ذا الدَّهرِ في الأَدْ   ـهُرِ أَوْ رِزقِهِ مِنَ الأرزاقِ
أَنْتَ فيهِ وكَانَ كُلُّ زَمانٍ   يَشتَهي بَعضَ ذا على الخَلَّاقِ

(١٤٧)

«من الكامل»

ودخل عليه يوماً فوجده على الشراب وفي يده بطيخة من الند في غشاء من خيزران عليها قلادة لؤلؤ وعلى رأسها عنبر قد أدير حولها فحياه بها وقال: أي شيء تشبه هذه؟ فقال ارتجالاً:

وبُنَيَّةٍ مِنْ خَيْزُرانٍ ضُمِّنَتْ   بَطّيخَةً نَبَتَتْ بِنارٍ في يَدِ
نَظَمَ الأَميرُ لها قِلادَةَ لُؤلُؤٍ   كَفِعالِهِ وكَلامِهِ في المَشْهَدِ
كالكَأسِ باشَرَها المِزاجُ فَأَبرَزَتْ   زَبَداً يَدورُ على شَرابٍ أَسْوَدِ

If you veil yourself in attacks on men
 They swear you are his son indubitably
How shall an arm empower a hand
 If the world in it has the span of fingers?
Steel has little use for you because
 None meet you but with useless sword
This breath's friend is more vital in
 A soul since death has its bitter taste
Grief before soul departs is feeble
 There is no sorrow after the departure
How much wealth relieved by a lance
 That was in chains to the stingy people
Riches.in a base man's hand are ugly
 As the bane of the generous is poverty
My word of your sunny act is no sun
 But rather like the dawning of that sun
Poet of glory and friend to word poet
 Both of us masters of the finest meaning
You cease not to listen to praises but
 The whinny of a fine horse is no heehaw
Would I had the luck of this time
 Among ages or its ration among rations
You are of it and every time yearns
 For some of this time from its Creator

147
**He came to him
one day
and he was drinking
and before him
was a melon
with musk and amber
in a basket
on top of which was a fish
surrounded by a necklace of pearls.
So he greeted him and said:
With what would you compare this?
And he spoke:
(Perfect di)**

Many a basket of bamboo conceals
 A melon growing in the heat as a favor
The Amir made a pearl necklace for it
 Witnessing like his actions and his words
Like a cup a mix greets by showing
 Some of the whirling in the dark of a drink

(١٤٨)

«من الطويل»

وقال فيها:

وسَوْداءَ مَنظومٍ عَلَيها لآلِئٌ   لها صُورةُ البِطّيخِ وهيَ مِنَ النَّدِّ
كَأنَّ بَقايا عَنبَرٍ فَوْقَ رَأسِها   طلوعُ رَواعي الشّيبِ في الشّعرِ الجَعدِ

(١٤٩)

«من السريع»

وعرض عليه الشراب فأبى وقال:

ما أنا والخَمرَ وبطّيخةً   سَوْداءَ في قِشرٍ مِنَ الخَيْزُرانْ
يَشغَلُني عَنها وعَنْ غَيْرِها   تُوطّيني النَّفسَ لِيَوْمِ الطِّعانْ
وكُلِّ نَجْلاءَ لها صائِكٌ   يَخضِبُ ما بَينَ يَدي والسِّنانْ

(١٥٠)

«من الوافر»

وقال يمدحه ويذكر إيقاعه بأصحاب باقيس ومسيره من دمشق:

مَبيتي مِنْ دِمَشقَ على فِراشٍ   حَشاهُ لي بَحَرِّ حَشايَ حاشِ
لَقى لَيلٍ كَعَينِ الظَّبيِ لَوْناً   وهَمٌّ كالحُمَيّا في المُشاشِ
وشَوْقٌ كالتَوَقّدِ في فُؤادٍ   كَجَمرٍ في جَوانحَ كالمُحاشِ
سَقى الدَّمُّ كُلَّ نَصلٍ غَيرِ نابٍ   ورَوّى كُلَّ رُمحٍ غَيرَ راشِ
فإنَّ الفارسَ المَنعوتَ خَفَّتْ   لمُنصِلِهِ الفَوارسُ كالرّياشِ
فقد أضحى أبا الغَمراتِ يُكنى   كَأنَّ أبا العَشائِرِ غَيرُ فاشِ
وقد نُسِيَ الحُسَينُ بما يُسَمّى   رَدى الأبطالِ أو غَيْثُ العِطاشِ
لَقوهُ حاسِراً في دِرْعِ ضَرْبٍ   دَقيقِ النّسْجِ مُلتَهِبِ الحَواشي

148
He said about it also.
(Long di)

A black girl with pearl string on her
    It has the shape of a melon but is musky
As if a bit of ambergris on her head
    Is a dawning glint of gray in kinky hair

149
He said about it also.
(Swift ni)

I want none of the wine or melon
    Black in the rind of that bamboo shell
My soul habit keeps me from it
    And from others on jousting days
But every wide thrust is sticky
    Staining me from hand to spearhead

150
He spoke also praising Abu Ashair al-Husayn ibn Ali ibn Hamdan.
(Exuberant shi)

My shelter was the lapwing's on the bed
    Whose stuffing had for me my heart's warmth
Tossed by a night of fawn's eye color
    And by a desire like night in these bones
And by love burning in this heart
    Like coals in ribs that seem to flame
May blood flow over every blade not dull
    And pour from all the lances not awakened
For the rider is far famed and riders
    Fly far from his sword like the feathers
He is called Father of Fierceness
    As if Abu Ashair were not as obvious
Husayn is forgotten since he is named
    Death to Heroes or Shower to the Thirsty
They meet him unclad in sword armor
    Fine of weave with border flame tested

وأيدي القَوْمِ أجنحةُ الفَراشِ	كأنّ على الجَماجمِ منهُ ناراً
يُعاوِدُها المُهنَّدُ مِنْ عُطاشِ	كأنّ جَواريَ المُهَجاتِ ماءُ
وذي رَمَقٍ وذي عَقلٍ مُطاشِ	فَوَلَّوْا بَينَ روحٍ مُفلتاتٍ
تَواري الضَبّ خافَ مِنَ احتِراشِ	ومُنعَفِرٍ لنَصلِ السّيفِ فيهِ
وما بعُجايةٍ أثرُ ارْتِهاشِ	يُدمّي بعضُ أيدي الخيلِ بعضاً
تَباعَدُ جَيْشِهِ والمُسْتَجاشي	ورائعُها وحيدٌ لم يُرَعْ
تَلوي الخوصِ في سَعَفِ العِشاشِ	كأنّ تَلوّيَ النُّشّابِ فيهِ
بأهلِ المجدِ مِن نَهبِ القُماشِ	ونَهبُ نفوسِ أهلِ النّهبِ أولى
بطانٌ لا تُشارِكُ في الجِحاشِ	تَشارِث في النّدامِ إذا نَزَلْنا
تَبينُ لَكَ النّعاجُ مِنَ الكِباشِ	ومن قَبلِ النّطاحِ وقبلِ يأني
ويا مَلِكَ المُلوكِ ولا أحاشي	فَيا بَحرَ البُحورِ ولا أوَرّي
فما يَخفى عَليكَ مَحلُّ غاشِ	كأنّكَ ناظِرٌ في كلّ قلبٍ
ولم تَقبّل عليّ كلامَ واشِ	أأصبرُ عنكَ لم تَبخلْ بشيءٍ
عَتيقُ الطّيرِ ما بينَ الخِشاشِ	وكيفَ وأنتَ في الرّؤساءِ عِندي
ولا راجيكَ للتّخييبِ خاشِ	فما خاشيكَ للتّكذيبِ راجٍ
ولَوْ كانوا النّبيطَ على الجِحاشِ	تُطاعِنُ كلّ خيلٍ كنتَ فيها
وإنّي مِنْهُم لألَيكَ عاشِ	أرى النّاسَ الظّلامَ وأنتَ نورٌ
أنوفاً هُنّ أولى بالخِشاشِ	بُليتَ بهم بَلاءَ الوَرْدِ يَلْقى
وحَوْلَكَ حينَ تَسمَنُ في هِراشِ	عَليكَ إذا هُزِلْتَ مَعَ اللّيالي
فقلتُ نَعَمْ ولو لَحِقوا بشاشِ	أتى خبرُ الأميرِ فقيلَ كَرّوا
يَسيرٌ قِتالُهُ والكَرُّ ناشي	يقودُهُمْ إلى الهيجا لجُوجٌ
على إعقاقِها وعلى غِشاشي	وأسرَجْتُ الكُميتَ فناقَلَتْ بي
بِرمحي كلّ طائِرةِ الرّشاشِ	مِنَ المُتمرّداتِ تُذَبُّ عنها
حديثٌ عنهُ يحمِلُ كلّ ماشِ	ولَوْ عُقِرَتْ لَبَلّغَني إليْهِ
وَشيكٌ فما يُنَكِّسُ لانتِقاشِ	إذا ذُكِرَتْ مَواقِفُهُ لحَافٍ
وتُلهي ذا الفِياشِ عنِ الفِياشِ	تُزيلُ مَخافةَ المَصبورِ عنهُ

As if a fire from it were on skulls
    And hands of folk were wings of moths
As if heart's blood flowing were water
    From thirst the sword becomes used to it
They fled among those whose souls go
    Those at last gasp and with reason lost
Dust flecked by the sword edge like
    A lizard who hides in fear of the hunter
Horses bloody each other's front legs
    And what is on ankles comes further up
He is their unique fear, not feared
    His distant army, not a seeker of armies
As if a quivering arrow was for him
    Like a trembling palm leaf on thin stem
Soul plunder of warlike men worthier
    Of men of glory than plunder of property
Big bellied ones shared their drink
    When we attacked but not the defense
Before growth of horn or maturity for
    You the sheep is known from the ram
O ocean of seas I cannot hide it
    O Full moon among full moons bar none
As if you had insight into all hearts
    No camps of those you seek avoid you
Shall I shun you if you aren't stingy
    Or don't accept gossip's words about me?
But why? for you among princes for me
    Are noblest of birds and no little creature
One fears you not with false faith nor
    Does one hope in you with vain worry
You are in all horsemen who joust
    Even if Iraqi peasants upon young asses
I see men as darkness, you as light
    I travel among them all night to the dawn
With them I suffer the grief of a rose
    Before noses fitted with the wooden bit
Against you as you grow thin in nights
    Around you as you grow fat into uproar
Amir's news comes to say: They attack!
    I say: Yes, may they pursue to Shawsh!
Stubbornly he leads them on to battle
    His battles prolong life in youthful wars
I saddle a bay horse, it carries me
    On its pregnant belly and at my speed
The ungovernable one guarded
    With my lance in all the flying blood
If hamstrung it is reported for me
    To him, the news carried on a trotter
When his station is seen by a barefoot
    Thorn stung, no flinching as it's drawn
He ends fears of being taken captive
    Is diverted from boasting due to honor

وما وُجدَ اشتياقٌ كاشتياقي ولا عُرفَ انكماشٌ كانكماشي
فسِرْتُ إليكَ في طَلَبِ المَعالي وسارَ سِوايَ في طَلَبِ المَعاشِ

(١٥١)

«من الوافر»

وأرسل أبو العشائر بازياً على حجلة
فأخذها فقال أبو الطيب:

وطائرةٍ تَتبَّعُها المَنايا على آثارِها زَجِلُ الجَناحِ
كأنَّ الرّيشَ منه في سِهامٍ على جَسَدٍ تَجَسَّمَ من رياحِ
كأنَّ رُؤوسَ أقلامٍ غِلاظٍ مُسِحْنَ بريش جُؤجُوهِ الصَّفَّاحِ
فأقعَصَها بحُجْنٍ تَحْتَ صُفْرٍ لَها فِعْلُ الأَسِنَّةِ والصِّفَاحِ
فقلتُ لكلَّ حَيٍّ يَوْمُ سُوءٍ وإنْ حَرَصَ النُّفوسُ على الفَلاحِ

(١٥٢)

«من الوافر»

فقال: أوفي وقتك قلت هذا؟ فقال:

أتنكرُ ما نَطَقْتُ به بَديهاً وليسَ بمنكَرٍ سَبْقُ الجَوادِ
أراكِضُ مُعوصاتِ الشِّعرِ قسراً فأقتُلُها وغَيري في الطِّرادِ

(١٥٣)

«من المتقارب»

ودخل على أبي العشائر وعنده رجل ينشده
شعراً في بركة في داره فقال:

لئِنْ كانَ أحْسَنَ في وَصفِها لقد فاتَهُ الحسنُ في الوَصْفِ لكْ
لأنَّكِ بَحْرٌ وإنَّ البِحارَ لتأنَفُ مِنْ حالِ هذي البِرَكْ

No love is found like to my passion
> No eagerness known like my enthusiasm

I came to you seeking high values
> Others beside me went in search of life

151
He sent out
a falcon for a partridge
and he took it,
So he said.
(Exuberant di)

Many a bird that fate follows
> With whirring wings on its trail

As if its feathers were arrows
> With a body as bulky as the wind

As if heads of pens were thick
> Anointed with fine breast feathers

He kills with claws on his feet
> That do the blades' and spears' work I say:

Any living thing has doomsday
> Even if souls guard against the villains

152
Abu 'Ashair
said to him:
How quickly you spoke it!
So he said.
(Exuberant di)

Do you deny what I said was impromptu?
> But there's no denying this winning horse

I hunt difficult verses by compulsion
> I make a kill and none but me is hunting

153
He came to him
and with him was a man
reciting poetry
describing a pool of his
but he did not mention him
in this poem,
So Abu Tayyib spoke.
(Tripping k)

If he did well in describing it yet
> He left out beauty in describing you

For you are a sea, and as a sea
> Cancel out in every respect the pool

كـأنَّـكَ سَـيْفُـكَ لا مـا مَلَـكْ   تَ يَبْقَى لَدَيْكَ ولا ما مَلَكْ
فـأكثـرُ مـن جَرْيهـا مـا وَهَبْـتَ   وأكـثـرُ مِـن مائِهـا مـا سَفَـكْ
أسـأتَ وأحْسَـنْـتَ عَـن قُـدْرَةٍ   ودُرْتَ على النّـاسِ دَوْرَ الفَلَكْ

(١٥٤)

«من المنسرح»

وقال يمدحه:

لا تَحْسَـبـوا رَبْعَكُـمْ ولا طَلَلَـهْ   أوَّلَ حَـيٍّ فِراقُكُـمْ قَتَلَـهْ
قـد تَلِفَـتْ قَبْلَـهُ النّفوسُ بكُـمْ   وأكـثـرْتِ في هواكُـمُ العَذَلَـهْ
خَـلا وفيـهِ أهْـلٌ وأوْحَشَـنـا   وفيـهِ صِـرْمٌ مُـرَوَّحٌ إبِلَـهْ
لـوْ سـارَ ذاكَ الحَبيـبُ عـن فَلَـكٍ   مـا رضِيَ الشّمسُ بُرْجَـهُ بَدَلَـهْ
أحِـبُّـهُ والهَـوَى وأدُوْرَهُ   وكُـلُّ حُـبٍّ صَبـابَـةٌ ووَلَـهْ
يَنصُـرُها الغَيْـثُ وهـيَ ظامِئَـةٌ   إلى سِـواهُ وسُحْبُهـا هَطِلَـهْ
وا حَـرَبـا منـكِ يـا جَدايَتَهـا   مُقيمَـةً، فـاعلَمـي، ومُرْتَحِلَـهْ
لـوْ خُلِـطَ المِسْـكُ والعَبيـرُ بهـا   ولَسْـتِ فيهـا لَخِلْتُهـا تَفِلَـهْ
أنا ابنُ مَن بعضُهُ يَفـوقُ أبـا الـ   ـباحِـثِ والنّجلُ بعضُ مـن نَخَلَـهْ
وإنَّما يَذكُـرُ الجُـدودَ لَهُـمْ   مَـنْ نَفَـرُوهُ وأنفَـدوا حِيَلَـهْ
فَخْـراً لعَضْـبٍ أروحُ مُشْتَـمِلَهْ   وسَـمْهَريٍّ أروحُ مُعْتَقِلَـهْ
وليَفخـر والفخـرُ إذ غـدَوْتُ بـه   مُرْتَديـاً خِـيْرَةً ومُنتَعِـلَـهْ
أنـا الـذي بيَّـنَ الإلَـهُ بـه الـ   ـأقـدارَ والمَـرْءُ حَيْثُمـا جَعَلَـهْ
جَوْهَـرَةٌ تَفْـرَحُ الشِّـرافُ بهـا   وغُصَّـةٌ لا تُسيـغُها السَّفَلَـهْ
إنَّ الكِـذابَ الـذي أكـادُ بِـهِ   أهْـوَنُ عِنـدي مِـنَ الـذي نَقَلَـهْ
فَـلا مُبّـالٍ ولا مُـدّاجٍ ولا   وانٍ ولا عاجِـزٍ ولا تُكَلَـهْ
ودارعٍ سِـيْفـتُهُ فَخَـرَّ لَقَـىً   في المُلْتَقى والعَجـاجِ والعَجَلَـهْ
وسـامعٍ رُعْتُـهُ بقافِيَـةٍ   يَحـارُ فيها المُنَقَّـحُ القُوَلَـهْ

You are a sword, nothing you own
  Stays with you nor what it possesses
More than what it pours you give
  More than its water is what it sheds
You do evil and good with power
  You whirl over men as the turning sky

154
He spoke also praising Abu Ashair al Husayn ibn Ali al-Hamdan.
(Flowing h)

Think not your quarter or its tell is
  First of living things parting killed
Souls perished before it through you
  As by your love they increased its blame
Empty, waste for us but folk are there
  And tents and camels resting from grazing
If that lover traveled through the sky
  His stars wouldn't want sun in his place
I love him and passion and campsites
  For every lover is tender hearted and mad
A shower succors them but they thirst
  For something else though the clouds pour
But O your destruction, O her fawn!
  Whether staying or going recognize me!
If musk and perfume were mingled and
  You not there I'd think it smelled fearfully
I'm son of one greater than a father
  As genealogist, child is part of the father
He reminds ancestors that they are
  Those who honor him and exhaust his art
Honor to a sword, I rejoice to wear it
  And to the lance, I rejoice to grasp that
Honor did me honor when I came to it
  With its best garment and with its shoes
I am he by whom God reveals what is
  Fate and manhood wherever He placed it
I am a jewel that nobility rejoices in
  Obstruction not swallowed by baseness
As for a falsehood he is tricked by
  I will scorn those who carry it to him
Not bothered or hypocritical nor
  Shortcoming, or wearied or impotent
Many an armed one I hit and he fell
  In dust and battle in those onslaughts
Many a listener I scared with rhymes
  Excited him with them in choice speech

مَنْ لا يُساوي الخبزَ الذي أكَلَهْ	وربَّما أشْهَدُ الطَّعامَ مَعي
والدُّرُّ دُرٌّ برغْمِ مَنْ جَهِلَهْ	ويُظْهِرُ الجَهْلَ بي وأعْرِفُهُ
أسْحَبَ في غَيرِ أرْضِهِ حُلَلَهْ	مُستَحيياً مِن أبي العَشائِرِ أنْ
ثِيابَهُ مِنْ جَليسِهِ وجَلهْ	أسحَبُها عنْدَهُ لَدَى مَلِكٍ
أوَّلَ مَحْمُولِ سَيْبِهِ الجَمَلَهْ	وبيضُ غِلمْانِهِ كنائِلِهِ
أبْذُلُ مِثلَ الوُدِّ الذي بذلَهْ	ما لِيَ لا أمْدَحُ الحُسَيْنَ ولا
أمْ بَلَغَ الكَيْذُبانُ ما أمَلَهْ	أأخفَتِ العَيْنُ عندَهُ أثَراً
مَنخُوَّةٍ ساعةَ الوَغَى زَهِلَهْ	أم لَيْسَ ضَرَّابَ كلِّ جُمجُمَةٍ
لَوْ كانَ للجُودِ مَنْطِقٌ عَذَلَهْ	وصاحِبُ الجُودِ ما يُفارِقُهُ
لَوْ كانَ للهَوْلِ مُحْرِمٌ هَزَلَهْ	وراكِبَ الهَوْلِ لا يُفتَرُّهْ
طَيِّءَ المُشرَعَ القَنا قِبَلَهْ	وفارِسَ الأحْمَرِ المُكلَّلِ في
أقسَمَ باللهِ لا رأتْ كفَلَهْ	لَمَّا رأتْ وجْهَهُ خُيولُهُمْ
أكبَرُ مِنْ فِعْلِهِ الذي فعَلَهْ	فأكْبَروا فِعْلَهُ وأصْغَرَهُ،
بعضُ جَميلٍ عن بَعضِهِ شَغَلَهْ	القاطِعُ الواصِلُ الكميلُ فَلا
وطاعِنٍ واهِباتٌ مُتَّصِلَهْ	فواهِبٌ والرِّماحُ تَشجُرُهْ
وكلَّما خِيفَ منزِلٌ نَزَلَهْ	وكلَّما أمِنَ البِلادَ سَرَى
أمكَنَ حتى كأنَّهُ خَتَلَهْ	وكلَّما جاهَرَ العَدوَّ ضُحىً
سَنَّ عليهِ الدِّلاصَ أو نَثَلَهْ	يحتَقِرُ البيضَ واللُّدانَ إذا
وهَذَّبتْ شِعرِيَ الفَصاحَةُ لَهْ	قد هَذَّبتْ فَهمَهُ الفِقاهةُ لي
لا يَحمَدُ السَّيفُ كلَّ مَن حمَلَهْ	فصِرْتُ كالسَّيفِ حامِداً يدَهْ

(١٥٥)

«من الوافر»

أراد أبو الطيب الانصراف من عنده في بعض الليالي فقال له إجلس فأمر له بجارية ثم نهض فقال له إجلس فجلس فأمر له لمهر فقال له الخصي تمدح الليلة يا أبا الطيب فقال:

ويَسري كُلَّما شِئتُ الغَمامُ	أعَنْ إذني تَمُرُّ الرِّيحُ رَهْواً
تَبَجَّسُهُ بها وكذا الكِرامُ	ولكِنَّ الغَمامَ لَهُ طِباعٌ

Often I have been present at a meal
    With me one not worth the bread he ate
He showed ignorance to me as I said:
    Pearl is pearl spite of one's not knowing
It's a shame for Abu 'Ashair that I
    Should trail his garments in other lands
I dragged them there with the kings
    His robes honored him as his proxies
His slaves' swords are like his gifts
    His bounty's first load is the rain cloud
Not for me to refuse to praise Husayn
    For I cannot lavish love as he lavishes
Do watchmen at his fear the news
    Or a slanderer achieve what he desired?
Was there no striking off every head
    That is proud in furious battle's hour?
Bounty's master cannot say farewell
    Even if bounty has a slanderous tongue
A rider on terror that does not weaken
    Even if the terror is girded by exhaustion
A rider on a red one moving forward
    Among the Tai with lance in rest ahead
If their horsemen look on his face he
    Swears by God they'll not see his back
They magnify his deed, he belittles
    Greater than his act is he who does it
A killer, persevering, perfect one
    No part of beauty separate from his way
Giver while his spears pierce for him
    As jousting and generosity are joined
Ever he makes safe the land by raids
    All the while the camps fear his attacks
If he appears to a foe in the morning
    His strength makes it seem an ambush
He scorns a sword and light lance as
    He puts on chain mail or allows it to flow
Understanding educates his mind
    As his eloquence enhances my word
I was like a sword praising his hand
    A sword does not praise all who bear it

155

He was with him at night drinking and each time he intended to depart he gave him something until he gave him a robe and a maid and a colt. So he spoke. (Exuberant mu)

Does wind blow softly on my order
    The cloud come each time I desire it?
No indeed a cloud has its own nature
    Which flows from it and thus the presents

(١٥٦)

«من المنسرح»

وأراد أبو العشائر سفراً فقال يودعه:

والدَّهْرُ لَفْظٌ وأنتَ مَعناهُ	أَلناسُ ما لم يَرَوْكَ أشْباهُ
والبَأْسُ باعٌ وأنتَ يُمناهُ	والجُودُ عَيْنٌ وأنتَ ناظِرُها
أغْبَرَ فُرْسانُهُ تَحاماهُ	أفْدي الذي كلُّ مَأْزِقٍ حَرِجٍ
فيهِ وأَعْلى الكَمِيِّ رِجْلاهُ	أَعْلى قَناةِ الحُسَيْنِ أَوْسَطُها
بأَلْسُنٍ ما لَهُنَّ أفْواهُ	تُنْشِدُ أثْوابُنا مَدائِحَهُ
أغْنَتْهُ عَنْ مِسْمَعَيْهِ عَيْناهُ	إذا مَرَرْنا على الأَصَمِّ بها
بُعْدِ ولَوْ نُلْنَ كُنَّ جَدْواهُ	سُبْحانَ مَنْ خارَ للكَواكِبِ بالْـ
لَصاعَ جُودُهُ وأفْناهُ	لَوْ كانَ ضَوْءُ الشُّموسِ في يَدِهِ
مُوَدِّعٌ دينَهُ ودُنْياهُ	يا راحِلاً كلُّ مَنْ يُوَدِّعُهُ
فيكَ مَزيدٌ فَزادَكَ اللهُ	إنْ كانَ فيما نَراهُ مِنْ كَرَمٍ

(١٥٧)

«من المنسرح»

وقال قوم: لم يكنك يا أبا التشائر، فقال:

ذلِكَ عِيٌّ إذا وَصَفْناهُ	قالوا أَلَمْ تَكْنِهِ فقُلْتُ لَهُمْ
لَبْسٍ مَعاني الوَرى بمَعْناهُ	لا يَتَوَقَّى أبو العَشائِرِ مِنْ
ولَيْسَ إلاَّ الحَديدَ أمْواهُ	أفْرَسُ مَنْ تَسْبَحُ الجِيادُ بِهِ

(١٥٨)

«من الوافر»

وأخرج إليه أبو العشائر جوشناً حسناً أراه إياه في ميا فارقين فقال مرتجلاً:

وزَلَّتْ عَنْ مُباشِرِها الحُتوفُ	بِهِ وبمِثْلِهِ شُقَّ الصُّفوفُ
جَواشِنُها الأَسِنَّةُ والسُّيوفُ	فَدَعْهُ لَقىً فإنَّكَ مِنْ كِرامٍ

156
Abu Ashair
decided to go on a journey
so he spoke bidding him farewell.
(Flowing hu)

Men who have not seen you are alike
    Time is a word and you are its meaning
Bounty an eye and its vision in you
    A hero shakes hands, you the right one
I ransom all the hard pressed men
    In battle dust as his knights guard him
Husayn's lance tip is in his middle
    And the warrior's head is at his feet
Our garments sing praises for him
    With the tongues that have no mouths
When we pass a deaf man with them
    His eyes have no use for his two ears
Glory to Him who made stars distant
    For otherwise they would be his bounty
If the sun's light were in his hands
    His generosity and art would diffuse it
O rider, all who say goodbye to him
    Say farewell to his religion and world
If what we see of generosity has any
    Growth in you, may God increase that

157
One said to Abu Ashair:
You are only known by your surname
but Abu Tayyib does not use it.
(Outspread hu)

They: Don't you use his surname? And I
    That is impossible when we describe him
Abu Ashair is not given his due by
    Using the meanings of men as his meaning
Most knightly is one whose horse swims
    Even when the waves are nothing but iron

158
Abu Ashair
brought a fine breastplate for him
so he spoke impromptu.
(Exuberant fu)

With this and its like ranks are split
    And the last gasp ceases in greeting it
Throw it away for you, due to nobility
    Are its breastplate and sword and spear

(١٥٩)
«من المنسرح»

ضرب أبو العشائر مضربه على الطريق وكثرت سؤاله فقال أبو الطيب:

لامَ أُناسٌ أبا العَشائِرِ في	جُودِ يَدَيهِ بِالعَينِ وَالوَرَقِ
وَإِنَّما قيلَ لِمْ خُلِقْتَ كَذا	وَخالِقُ الخَلْقِ خالِقُ الخُلُقِ
قالوا: أَلَمْ تَكفِهِ سَماحَتُهُ	بَنى بَيتَهُ عَلى الطُّرُقِ
فَقُلتُ: إِنَّ الفَتى شَجاعَتُهُ	تُريهِ في الشُّحِّ صورَةَ الفَرَقِ
الشَّمسُ قَد حَلَّتِ السَّماءَ وَما	يَحجُبُها بُعدُها عَنِ الحَدَقِ
بِضَربِ هامِ الكُماةِ تَمَّ لَهُ	كَسبُ الَّذي يَكسِبونَ بِالمَلَقِ
كُن لُجَّةً أَيُّها السِّماحُ فَقَد	أَمِنَهُ سَيفُهُ مِنَ الغَرَقِ

(١٦٠)
«من الطويل»

كان أبو العشائر قد غضب على أبي الطيب فأرسل غلمانا له ليوقعوا به فلحقوه بظاهر حلب ليلا فرماه أحدهم بسهم وقال: خذه وأنا غلام أبي العشائر. فقال أبو الطيب:

وَمُنْتَسِبٍ عِندي إلى مَن أُحِبُّهُ	وَلِلنَّبْلِ حَوْلي مِن يَدَيهِ حَفيفُ
فَهَيَّجَ مِن شَوقي وَما مِن مَذَلَّةٍ	حَنَنتُ وَلكِنَّ الكَريمَ أَلوفُ
وَكُلُّ وِدادٍ لا يَدومُ عَلى الأَذى	دَوامَ وِدادي لِلحُسَينِ ضَعيفُ
فَإِن يَكُن الفِعلُ الَّذي ساءَ واحِداً	فَأَفعالُهُ اللّائي سَرَرْنَ أُلوفُ
وَنَفسي لَهُ نَفْسي الفِداءُ لِنَفسِهِ،	وَلكِنَّ بَعضَ المالِكينَ عَنيفُ
فَإِن كانَ يَبغي قَتلَها يَكُ قاتِلاً	بِكَفَّيهِ فَالقَتلُ الشَّريفُ شَريفُ

(١٦١)
«من الطويل»

وَفاؤُكُما كَالرَّبعِ أَشجاهُ طاسِمُهْ	بِأَن تُسعِدا وَالدَّمعُ أَشفاهُ ساجِمُهْ
وَما أَنا إِلّا عاشِقٌ كُلِّ عاشِقٍ	أَعَقُّ خَليلَيهِ الصَّفِيَّينِ لائِمُهْ
وَقَد يَتَزَيّا بِالهَوى غَيرُ أَهلِهِ	وَيَستَصحِبُ الإِنسانُ مَن لا يُلائِمُهْ
بَليتُ بِلى الأَطلالِ إِن لَم أَقِفْ بِها	وُقوفَ شَحيحٍ ضاعَ في التُّربِ خاتَمُهْ
كَئيباً تَوَقّاني العَواذِلُ في الهَوى	كَما يَتَوَقّى رَيِّضَ الخَيلِ حازِمُهْ
قِفي تَغرَمِ الأولى مِنَ اللَّحظِ مُهجَتي	بِثانِيَةٍ وَالمُتلِفُ الشَّيءَ غارِمُهْ

159
An awning was set up for Abu Ashairy. So he spoke.
(Flowing qi)
Folk blame Abu Ashair on account of
    His hand's bounty with gold and silver
One says: Who made you this way?
    The Maker of men is maker of character
They say: Cannot kindness cure him
    From setting up his tent on this roadway?
I say: Because a young man's bravery
    Shows him in stinginess a kind of dread
The sun inhabits the heavens but her
    Distance does not veil her from the eye
By striking warriors' heads reward
    Is earned, others gain it by their flattery
Be an ocean O magnanimous one!
    His sword makes him safe from drowning

160
He spoke and he recalled that he shot at him by his order.
(Long fu)
I have a champion for one I love and
    Whir of arrows about me from his hand
He attacks in love, not in baseness
    Do I love, rather my nobility is devoted
No friendship can endure with injury
    Weakness prolongs my love for Husayn
If there is an act which harms one
    Yet his acts that rejoiced are myriad
My soul is his, may it ransom his soul
    But some of these kings are too severe
If he wants to kill let it be
    By his hand who kills as nobleman

II: *al-Saifyat*: Poems for Saif al-Daula
161
He spoke praising Saif al Daula on his going to Antakya and capturing the fortress of Barzuia, Jumadi, 337. (Long h)
Your two vows, quarter whose traces pine
    Are your solace with tears whose flow heals
I am nothing but a lover and every lover
    The more steady of two good friends blames
They use love's dress who aren't his folk
    A man takes as friend one not equal to him
I waste with the tells if I do not stand
    As a miser who loses his ring in this dust
Morose, censurers warn me against love
    As a saddle girth warns a new-broken colt
Stop, the first glance must pay my heart
    With a second as destroyers of a thing pay

سَقاكِ وحَيّانَا بـكِ اللهُ إنّمـا على العيسِ نَورٌ والخُدورُ كمائمُهْ
وما حاجةُ الأظعانِ حَوْلَكِ في الدّجى إلى قَمَرٍ ما واجدٌ لكِ عادِمُهْ
إذا ظَفِرَتْ منـكِ العُيـونُ بنظرَةٍ أثابَ بها مُعيي المَطيّ ورازِمُهْ
حَبيبٌ كـأنّ الحُسـنَ كـانَ يُجِبُّـهُ فآثَرهُ أوْ جـارَ في الحُسـنِ قاسِمُهْ
تحُولُ رمـاحُ الخَطّ دونَ سِبائِهِ وتُسبَى لَه مِنْ كلّ حَيٍّ كرائمُهْ
ويُضحى غُبارُ الخَيلِ أدنى سُتورِهِ وآخِرُهـا نَشـرُ البكـاءِ المُلازِمُـهْ
وما اسْتَغْرَبَتْ عَيني فِراقاً رأيْتُهُ ولا عَلَّمَتْـني غَيـرَ ما القَلبُ عالمُهْ
فَـلا يَتّهِمْـني الكاشِـحونَ فـإنّني رَعيتُ الرّدى حتى حَلَتْ لي علاقِمُهْ
مُشيّبُ الـذي يَبكـي الشّبـابَ مُشيبُهْ فكَيـفَ تَوَقّيـهِ وبانيـهِ هادِمُـهْ
وتَكْمِلـةُ العَيـشِ الصّبـا وعَقيبُـهُ وغائِبُ لَـونِ العارِضَيـنِ وقادِمُـهْ
وما خَضَبَ النّاسُ البَياضَ لأنّـهُ قَبيحٌ ولكـنْ أحسـنُ الشّعَرِ فاحِمُهْ
وأحسَـنُ مِـنْ مـاءِ الشّبيبةِ كُلّـهِ حَيا بارِقٍ في فازَةٍ أنا شـائِمُهْ
عَلَيها رياضٌ لـم تحُكْهـا سَحابَةٌ وأغصانُ دَوْحٍ لم تُغَنِّ حَمائِمُهْ
وفوقَ حَواشي كـلّ ثَـوبٍ مُوَجَّـهٍ مـن الـدُّرّ سِمطٌ لم يُثَقّبْهُ ناظِمُهْ
تَـرى حَيَـوانَ البَـرّ مُصطَلِحـاً بـهِ يُحاربُ ضِدٌّ ضِدَّهُ ويُسالِمُهْ
إذا ضَرَبَتْـهُ الرّيـحُ مـاجَ كَأنّـهُ تجـولُ مَذاكيـهِ وتَدأى ضَراغِمُـهْ
وفي صورةِ الرّوميّ ذي التّـاجِ ذِلّـةٌ لأبْلَـجَ لا تيجانَ إلاّ عَمائِمُـهْ
تُقَبِّلُ أفْـواهُ المُلـوكِ بسـاطَهُ ويَكْبُـرُ عَنهـا كُمُّـهُ وبَراجِمُـهْ
قيامـاً لِمَـنْ يَشـفي مِـنَ الـدّاءِ كيُّـهُ ومَـنْ بَيـنَ أُذنَيْ كـلّ قَـرمٍ مَواسِمُهْ
قَبائِعُهـا تحْـتَ المَرافِـقِ هَيْبَـةً وأنْفَـذُ مِمّا في الجُفـونِ عَزائِمُهْ
لَـهُ عَسَكَرا خَيْلٍ وطَيرٍ إذا رَمَى بها عَسـكَراً لم يَبقَ إلاّ جماجُمـهْ
أجَلّتْهـا مِـنْ كـلّ طـاغٍ ثيابُـهُ ومَوْطِئِها مِن كـلّ باغٍ مَلاغِمُهْ
فَقـدْ مَلّ ضَـوْءُ الصّبْـحِ مِمّا تغيرُهُ ومَلّ سَوادُ اللّيـلِ ممّا تزاجِمُهْ
ومَلّ القَنـا مِمّا تَـدُقّ صُـدورَهُ ومَلّ حَديـدُ الهنـدِ ممّا تلاطِمُهْ
سَحابٌ مِنَ العِقبانِ يزْحَـفُ تحتَها سحابٌ إذا استسقتْ سقتها صَوارِمُهْ
سلَكتْ صـروفَ الدّهـرِ حتى لقيتُـهُ على ظَهرِ عَـزْمٍ مؤيَّداتٍ قوائِمُهْ

God pour out for you, revive us by you
    A flower on the camel, its petals curtains
Women near you at dark have no need
    For a moon, they lack it not who love you
When eyes obtain a glance from you
    They spur a weary camel by it, nourish it
A lover who seems beloved by beauty
    Chose him or was unjust in sharing traits
Khatti lances forbid taking him captive
    His generosity takes pledges in the tribes
Horses' dust makes his nearest curtain
    The farthest spreading is clinging incense
My eye felt no parting strange if I looked
    Then taught me only what the heart knew
He who knew hate did not suspect me
    I fed on death till colocynth was sweeter
A fool is he whose gray weeps for youth
    Why dread that when the builder is wrecker?
Perfect life is youth and its conclusion
    Lost color in sideburns and what precedes
A man doesn't dye white hair because
    It's ugly but rather because black hair is fine
More handsome than all youth's juices
    A shower flashing awning and my forecast
On it meadows that clouds do not water
    High branched trees whose doves don't coo
On a border of each double edged strip
    A thread of pearls, no composer threaded it
You see animals of the land reconciled
    Contrary wars on contrary and makes peace
If the wind blows, it billows as if it
    Made the horse prance and the lion crouch
Among images a Rumi with crown kneels
    To a dawn who has no crown but a turban
It's lips of kings that kiss his carpet
    His sleeve and fingers too great for them
Waiting for him whose fire cures ills
    Whose brand is between each hero's ears
Their sword hilts at the elbows in fear
    Pierced by one whose will is in a sheath
An army of horses and birds if he hits
    An army with them only their skulls remain
Their horsecloths every tyrant's robe
    Their treading on mouths of each despot
Dawn's light pales as as they raid with
    Him black night yields as they press round
Spears tire as they strike his breast
    Indian steel is weary as it pounds on him
A cloud of eagles moves on, under
    A cloud whose swords pour as they thirst
I followed time's changes till I met him
    On the back of resolve its legs firmly set

ولا حَمَلَتْ فيها الغُرابَ قَوادِمُهْ	مَهالِكَ لم تَصْحَبْ بها الذئبَ نَفسُهْ
وخاطَبْتُ بُحْراً لا يَرى العِبْرَ عائِمُهْ	فأبصَرْتُ بَدراً لا يَرى البَدرُ مِثلَهْ
بلا واصِفٍ والشِعْرُ تَهْذي طَماطِمُهْ	غَضِبْتُ لَهُ لَمّا رَأيْتُ صِفاتِهِ
سَرَيْتُ فكنتُ السِرَّ والليلُ كاتِمُهْ	وكنتُ إذا يَمّمْتُ أرضاً بَعيدةً
فلا المَجدُ مخفيه ولا الضَربُ ثالِمُهْ	لقد سَلّ سيفَ الدَولةِ المَجدُ مُعلِماً
وفي يَدِ جَبّارِ السَماواتِ قائِمُهْ	على عاتِقِ المَلْكِ الأغَرِّ نِجادُهْ
وتَدَّخِرُ الأموالَ وهيَ غَنائِمُهْ	تُحارِبُهُ الأعداءُ وهيَ عَبيدُهْ
ويَستعظِمونَ المَوتَ والمَوتُ خادِمُهْ	يَستَكبِرونَ الدَهْرَ والدَهرُ دونَهُ
وإنّ الذي سَمّاهُ سَيفاً لَظالِمُهْ	وإنَّ الذي سَمّى عَلِيّاً لَمُنصِفٌ
وتَقطَعُ لَزَباتِ الزَمانِ مَكارِمُهْ	وما كلُّ سَيفٍ يَقطَعُ الهامَ حَدُّهْ

(١٦٢)

«من الخفيف»

يمدحه وقد عزم على الرحيل عن أنطاكية:

نَحْنُ نَبْتُ الرُبى وأنتَ الغَمامُ	أينَ أزمَعْتَ أيّهذا الهُمامُ؟
لكَ وخانَتْهُ قُربَكَ الأيّامُ	نحنُ مَن ضايَقَ الزَمانُ له فيـ
ـمُ وهذا المُقامُ والأجْذامُ	في سَبيلِ العُلى قِتالُكَ والسِّلْـ
ـلُ وأنّا إذا نَزَلْتَ الخِيامُ	ليتَ أنّا إذا ارتَحَلْتَ لكَ الخَيْـ
ومَسيرٌ للمَجدِ فيه مُقامُ	كلُّ يَومٍ لكَ احتِمالٌ جَديدٌ
تَعِبَتْ في مُرادِها الأجسامُ	وإذا كانتِ النُفوسُ كِباراً
وكذا تَقلَقُ البُحورُ العِظامُ	وكذا تَطلُعُ البُدورُ عَلَينا
رَ لَوَ أنّا سِوى نَواكَ نَسامُ	ولَنا عادةُ الجَميلِ من الصَبْـ
كلُّ شَمسٍ ما لم تَكُنْها ظَلامُ	كلُّ عَيشٍ ما لم تَطيبُهُ حِمامُ
مَن به يَأنَسُ الخَميسُ اللُهامُ	أزِلِ الوَحْشَةَ التي عِندَنا يا
ـبِ كأنَّ القِتالَ فيها ذِمامُ	والذي يَشهَدُ الوَغى ساكِنَ القَلْـ
تَلاقى الفِهاقُ والأقدامُ	والذي يَضرِبُ الكَتائِبَ حتى

Deserts where his soul would not allow
    The wolf and wings would not bear a raven
I saw a moon no moon saw its like I
    Went to a sea whose swimmer saw no shore
I raged for him when I saw his picture
    Without a poet, a poem whose babbler raved
When I was crossing distant lands I
    Went at night and was a secret night hid
Glory draws the Sword of State as sign
    For majesty cannot hide nor blows dull it
His sword belt on nobility's shoulder
    His hilt in the hand of heaven's strength
Foes war on him but they are his slaves
    They heap up wealth but they are plunder
They magnify time but it is less than he
    They wonder at death but it is his servant
He who named him Ali was fair in it
    He who named him sword was not just
Not every sword is keen to take heads
    His bounty breaks the drought of the time

162
He spoke
praising
Saif al Daula
and he had decided
on a journey from Antakya.
(Nimble mu)

Where are you going O great prince?
    We are plants on hills and you the cloud
We are ones time oppressed due to you
    And the days cheated it of your presence
On the high road your struggle and rest
    And this the place to stand and hasten on
Would we were your horse and saddle
    And when you dismount we were the tent
Every day a new departure for you
    An expedition to glory where a home is
But when the souls are of high rank
    Bodies are exhausted by their intentions
Thus the full moons rise above us
    Thus the mighty oceans are disturbed
A beautiful habit of patience is ours
    If only the burden is not your distance
Each life you do not sweeten is dead
    Every sun that is not you is a darkness
Make an end to the loneliness we feel
    O you with whom a huge army is intimate
Who witness the battle with calm heart
    As it a struggle was all taken for granted
You who are striking battalions until
    The neck's vertebrae and the feet meet

فــأذاهُ عَلــى الزَّمــانِ حَــرامُ	وإذا حَــلَّ ســاعةً بمَكــانِ
والـذي تَمطُـرُ السَّـحابُ مُـدامُ	والـذي تُنبـتُ البـلادُ سُـرورٌ
كَرَمــاً مــا اهتَــدَتْ إليــهِ الكِــرامُ	كلَّمــا قيــلَ قــد تناهــى أرانــا
وارتِياحــاً تَحــارُ فيــهِ الأنــامُ	وكِفاحــاً تكِــعُ عنــهُ الأعــادي
دولــةِ المَلْــكِ في القلــوبِ حُســامُ	إنَّمــا هَيْبــةُ المُؤَمَّــلِ سَــيْفِ الــ
وكثيــرٌ مِــنَ البليـــغِ السَّــلامُ	فكثيــرٌ مِــنَ الشّــجاعِ التَّوقّــي

(١٦٣)

«من الوافر»

وقال عند رحيله من أنطاكية وقد كثر المطر:

تَــأنَّ وعُــدَّةُ ممّــا تُنيــلُ	رُوَيْــدَكَ أيُّهــا المَلِــكُ الجَليــلُ
فمـا فيمـا تَجـودُ بـهِ قَليــلُ	وَجــودُكَ بالمُقــامِ ولَــوْ قَليــلاً
كأنَّهُمــا وَداعُــكَ والرَّحيــلُ	لأَكْبَــتَ حاسِــداً وأرى عَــدُوّاً
أتَغلِــبُ أم حَيــاهُ لكُــم قَبيــلُ	ويَهْــدَأُ ذا السَّــحابُ فقــد شكَكْنــا
فهـا أنـا في السَّـماحِ لـهُ عَــذولُ	وكنْــتُ أعيــبُ عَــذلاً في سَــماحٍ
وسَــيْفُ الدَّولــةِ الماضي الصَّقيلُ	ومــا أخشــى نُبــوَّكَ عــن طَريــقٍ
لسَــيْرِكَ أنَّ مَفرِقَهــا السَّــبيلُ	وكــلُّ شَــواةِ غِطْريــفٍ تَمنَّــى
جَــرَتْ بــكَ في بجاريــهِ الخُيــولُ	ومِثــلُ العَمْــقِ مَمْلــوءٍ دِمــاءً
فأَهْــوَنُ مــا يَمُــرُّ بــهِ الوُحــولُ	إذا اعتــادَ الفتــى خــوضَ المَنايــا
أطاعَتْــهُ الحُزونــةُ والسُّــهولُ	ومَــن أمضــرَ الحُصــونَ فمــا عَصَتْــه
وتُنشِــرُ كُــلَّ مَــن دَفَــنَ الخُمــولُ	أتَخفِــرُ كُــلَّ مَــنْ رَمَــتِ اللَّيــالي
يَعيــشُ بــهِ مِــنَ المــوتِ القَتيــلُ	ونَدعــوكَ الحُســامَ وهــلْ حُســامٌ
وأنــتَ القاطِــعُ البَــرُّ الوَصــولُ	ومــا للسَّــيفِ إلَّا القَطْــعَ فِعْــلٌ
وقــد فَنِــيَ التكلُّــمُ والصَّهيــلُ	وأنــتَ الفــارسُ القَــوَّالُ صَبْــراً
ويَقصُــرُ أنْ ينــالَ وفيــهِ طُــولُ	يَحيــدُ الرُّمــحُ عنــكَ وفيــهِ قَصْــدٌ
لقــالَ لــكَ السِّــنانُ كمــا أقــولُ	فلــوْ قَــدَرَ السِّــنانُ علــى لِســانٍ
ولكِــنْ ليــسَ للدّنيــا خَليــلُ	ولــوْ جــازَ الخُلــودُ خَلَــدْتَ فَــرْداً

When he camps for an hour at a place
    It is forbidden for time to make or lay it waste
So whatever a land grows is happiness
    And that which the clouds rain down is wine
If one says: There's an end! he shows
    Bounty such as generosity never attained
And striking before which the foes faint
    Cheerful giving at which men are amazed
Respect Saif al-Daula, the hoped for
    He in our hearts as a king is a scimitar
Much for the brave to be on their guard
    It's time for the eloquent to announce: Peace!

163
He spoke at the departure of Saif al-Daula and there was much rain.
(Exuberant lu)

Be easy with your self O splendid king
    Delay and count it with what you bestow
Your bounty is in staying if only a bit
    But it is not small insofar as you give it
Put down the envious for I see foes
    As if they were your farewell and going
The cloud appeased as we doubted
    If Taglib's clan or its rain were your tribe
I blamed those who censure bounty
    But here am I censuring his generosity
I fear no misfortune for you on the way
    For Saif al Daula is sharp and burnished
Every head among chiefs hopes that
    The path of your journey is his hair part
It seems the hollows are full of blood
    And the horses run with you in its flow
When a hero is used to wading death
    He scorns the filth that he passes there
He commands forts so they don't bully
    Rough and smooth places yield to him
Do you protect all whom nights attack
    Can you revive all whom obscurity buries?
We call you sword but is there a sword
    That the bodies of the dead must live by?
The only action for a sword is cutting
    But you are the just slasher that unites
You the knight who cries: Courage!
    When sword and whinny dwindle away
The well aimed spear swerves from you
    It is short of the striking though it is lengthy
Or if the lance had the tongue's power
    It would say to you as a spear what I speak
If eternity exists you alone are immortal
    But there is no true friendship in the world

(١٦٤)

«من الوافر»

يرثي والدة سيف الدولة وعزيه بها في سنة سبع وثلاثين وثلاث مئة (٩٤٨م):

وَتَقتُلُنـا المَنونُ بِلا قِتـالِ	نَعِـدُّ المَشرَفيَّـةَ وَالعَوالــي
وَما يُنجينَ مِـن حَبَبِ اللَّيالي	وَنَرتَبِـطُ السَّوابِـقَ مُقرَبّـاتٍ
وَلكِـن لا سَبيـلَ إِلى الوِصـالِ	وَمَـن لَم يَعشَـقِ الدُّنيـا قَديمـاً
نَصيبُـكَ في مَنامِكَ مِن خَيـالِ	نَصيبُـكَ في حَياتِـكَ مِـن حَبيـبٍ
فُـؤادي في غِشاءٍ مِـن نِبـالِ	رَمانـي الدَّهـرُ بِالأَرزاءِ حَتّـى
تَكَسَّـرَتِ النِّصالُ عَلـى النِّصـالِ	فَصِـرتُ إِذا أَصابَتنـي سِهـامٌ
لِأَنّـي مـا اِنتَفَعـتُ بِأَن أُبالـي	وَهانَ فَمـا أُبالـي بِالرَّزايـا
لِأَوَّلِ مَيتَـةٍ في ذا الجَـلالِ	وَهَـذا أَوَّلُ النّاعيـنَ طُـرّاً
وَلَم يَخطُر لِمَخلـوقٍ بِبـالِ	كَأَنَّ المَـوتَ لَم يَفجَع بِنَفسٍ
عَلى الوَجـهِ المُكَفَّـنِ بِالجَمـالِ	صَـلاةُ اللَهِ خالِقِنـا حَنـوطٌ
وَقَبَّـلَ اللَحـدِ في كَرَمِ الخِـلالِ	عَلى المَدفونِ قَبلَ التُّربِ صَوناً
جَديـداً ذِكرُنـاهُ وَهـوَ بـالِ	فَإِنَّ لَـهُ بِبَطـنِ الأَرضِ شَخصـاً
بَـلِ الدُّنيـا تَـؤولُ إِلى زَوالِ	وَما أَحَـدٌ يُخَلَّـدُ في البَرايـا
تَمَنَّتـهُ البَواقـي الخَوالـي	أَطابَ النَّفسَ أَنَّـكِ مُتِّ مَوتـاً
تُسَـرُّ النَفـسُ فيـهِ الـزَّوالُ	وَزُلتِ وَلَم تَرَي يَومـاً كَريهـاً
وَمُلـكُ عَلـيٍّ اِبنِـكِ في كَمـالِ	رِواقُ العِـزِّ فَوقَـكِ مُسبَطِـرٌّ
نَظيـرَ نَـوالِ كَفِّـكِ في النَّـوالِ	سَقـى مَثـواكِ غادٍ في الغَـوادي
كَأَيـدي الخَيـلِ أَبصَرَتِ المَخالي	لِساحيـهِ عَلـى الأَجداثِ حَفشٌ
وَما عَهدي بِمَجـدٍ عَنـكِ خـالِ	أُسائِـلُ عَنـكِ بَعدَكِ كُـلَّ مَجدٍ
وَيَشغَلُـهُ البُكـاءُ عَـنِ السُّـؤالِ	يَمُـرُّ بِقَبـرِكِ العافـي فَيَبكـي
لَـوَ اَنَّـكِ تَقدِريـنَ عَلى فَعـالِ	وَمـا أَهـداكِ لِلجَـدوى عَلَيـهِ
وَإِن جانَبـتُ أَرضَـكِ غَيرُ سـالِ	بِعَيشِـكِ هَـل سَلَـوتِ فَإِنَّ قَلبي
بَعُـدتِ عَـنِ النُّعامـى وَالشَّمالِ	نَزَلـتِ عَلـى الكَراهَـةِ في مَكانٍ

164
He spoke an elegy for the mother of Saif al-Daula and consoled him in the year 337
(Exuberant li)

We prepare the swords and long lances
    But death beats us without the contention
We tether the swift horses close by
    But they do not escape the prowling night
Who has not loved the world gone on
    But yet there is no way to rejoin what it was
Your share in a loved one during life
    Is a share you have in the dream in sleep
The times hit me with misfortunes till
    My heart was fainting with the missiles
I had a feeling when arrows struck me
    The head of one broke on another's head.
It was easy so I didn't fret about loss
    For I could find no use in being anxious
This is the first of all death notices
    For the first dead lady with such glory
As if death had never surprised a soul
    Nor shaken a creature with any anxiety
God our maker's grace is burial spice
    For the face of one shrouded in splendor
For one buried safely before the dust
    Or before the tomb in generous qualities
In it, in earth's womb, a person is
    Renewed so we remember what decays
No one is immortal among earthlings
    No, the world is in pursuit of cessation
It's food for the soul you died a death
    Survivors and deceased would desire
You ended but you never saw evil days
    So that the spirit rejoiced in its stopping
A canopy of glory was stretched above
    Your son Ali's kingdom in its perfection
May he water your house by early rain
    Equal to the gifts of your hand in bounty
A sweeping downpour on the grave as
    Horse's hoofs that see the bags of feed
After you I asked every glory about you
    No thought of fame is free of you for me
A beggar sees a tomb shedding tears
    As the weeping keeps from the begging
He cannot guide you to gifts for him
    Would that you had the power of acting
By your life! do you forget if my heart
    Though far from your land has no solace?

وتَمْنَعُ منكِ أنداءُ الطِّلالِ	تُحَجَّبُ عنكِ رائحةُ الخُزامَى
بَعيدُ الدَّارِ مُنْبَتُّ الحِبالِ	بِدارِ كلِّ ساكِنِها غَريبٌ
كَتومُ السِّرَّ صادِقةُ المَقالِ	حَصانٌ مثلُ ماءِ المُزْنِ فيهِ
وواحِدُها نِطاسِيُّ المَعالي	يُعَلِّلُها نِطاسِيُّ الشَّكايا
سَقاهُ أسِنَّةَ الأسَلِ الطِّوالِ	إذا وَصَفوا لهُ داءً بِثَغْرٍ
تَعُدُّ لها القُبورُ مِنَ الحِجالِ	ولَيسَتْ كالإناثِ ولا اللَّواتي
يكونُ وَداعُها نَفضَ النِّعالِ	ولا مَنْ في جَنازَتِها تِجارٌ
كأنَّ المَروَ مِن زِفِّ الرِّئالِ	مَشَى الأمَراءُ حَوْلَيها حُفاةً
يَضَعْنَ النَّقْسَ أمكِنَةَ الغَوالي	وأبْرَزَتِ الخُدورُ مُخبَّآتٍ
فَدَمْعُ الحُزْنِ في دَمعِ الدَّلالِ	أَتَتْهُنَّ المُصيبةُ غافِلاتٍ
لفُضِّلَتِ النِّساءُ على الرِّجالِ	ولوْ كانَ النِّساءُ كَمَنْ فَقَدْنا
ولا التَّذكيرُ فَخرٌ للهِلالِ	وما التَّأنيثُ لاسمِ الشَّمسِ عَيبٌ
قُبَيلَ الفَقدِ مَفقودُ المِثالِ	وأفجَعُ مَنْ فَقَدْنا مَن وَجَدْنا
أواخِرُنا على هامِ الأوالي	يُدَفِّنُ بَعضُنا بَعضاً وتَمْشي
كَحيلٍ بالجَنادِلِ والرِّمالِ	وكَمْ عَينٍ مُقَبَّلةِ النَّواحي
وبالٍ كانَ يَفكُرُ في الهُزالِ	ومُغْضٍ كانَ لا يُغْضي لَخَطبٍ
وكيفَ بِمثلِ صَبرِكَ للجِبالِ	أَسَيفَ الدَّوْلةِ اسْتَنجِدْ بِصَبرٍ
وخَوضَ المَوتِ في الحَربِ السِّجالِ	وأنتَ تُعَلِّمُ النَّاسَ التَّعَزِّي
وحالُكَ واحدٌ في كلِّ حالِ	وحالاتُ الزَّمانِ عَليكَ شَتَّى
على عَللِ الغَرائبِ والدَّخالِ	فلا غِيضَتْ بِحارُكَ يا جَموماً
كأنَّكَ مُسْتَقيمٌ في مُحالِ	رَأيتُكَ في الَّذينَ أرَى مُلوكاً
فإنَّ المِسكَ بَعضُ دَمِ الغَزالِ	فإنْ تَفُقِ الأنامَ وأنْتَ مِنهُمْ

You went down to that hateful place
  Removed yourself from south and north
Veiled from you is lavender's perfume
  Forbidden to you the smell of a shower
In camps where folk are all strangers
  Long the flight and broken these ropes
Pure as water of a rain cloud in which
  A secret was hidden, a word was faithful
One skilled in complaint attended her
  Her only one, a physician of the heights
When one told him of a border disease
  He poured in the points of long lances
She was not like a woman nor those
  For whom a bride chamber tomb is made
Nor were those at her funeral hirelings
  Whose farewell is dust shaken from shoes
Commanders walked barefoot about her
  As if the stones were fluff of the ostriches
The veiled one's curtains were opened
  They had applied soot in place of perfume
The calamity came to them unexpected
  Tears of grief instead of the tears of joy
If some women were like one we lost
  Then women would be superior to men
Nor would sun's femininity be shame
  Nor the masculine be boast of crescents
Our most painful losses come before
  We know a loss whose pattern we lost
Some of us bury others and the last
  Of us tramples on the skulls of the first
How many eyes with eyebrows kissed
  Now have the collyrium of pebbles and sand
Many a downcast eye blinks not at fate
  Many a decayed now ponders weight loss
Saif al Daula ask aid of patience, how
  Can mountains have patience like yours?
For you are one to teach men courage
  And a death plunge in the battle stream
Time's changes are various for you
  But your condition one in every change
May your seas never be empty O full
  For watering the strangers and strays
I see you among those I know as kings
  As if you were straight among the crooked
You surpass mankind yet you are of them
  For the musk is part of the gazelle's blood

(١٦٥)

«من المتقارب»

يمدحه ويذكر استنقاذه أبا وائل تغلب بــن داود بن حمدان العدوي من أسر الخارجي سنة سبع وثلاثين وثلاث مئة (٩٤٨م):

إلامَ طَماعِيَةُ العــاذِلِ	ولا رأيَ في الحُبّ للعـاقِلِ
يُرادُ مِــنَ القَلْبِ نِسْيانُكُمْ	وتأبَى الطِّبــاعُ علـى النَّاقِلِ
وإنِّي لأعْشَقُ مِــنْ أجْلِكُمْ	نُحُولي وكــلَّ امرىءٍ ناحِلِ
ولَـوْ زُرْتُـمْ ثُـمَّ لَمْ أبْكِكُمْ	بكَيْتُ على حُبِّيَ الزَّائِلِ
أتُنكِرُ خَدّي دُموعي وقَدْ	جَرَتْ منهُ في مَسلَكٍ سابِلِ
أأوَّلُ دَمــعٍ جـرَى فَوْقَهُ	وأوَّلُ حُــزْنٍ علــى راحِلِ
وهَبْتُ السَّلُوَّ لِمَنْ لامَني	وبِتُّ مِــنَّ الشَّـوقِ في شاغِلِ
كأنَّ الجُفــونَ على مُقْلَتي	ثِيابٌ شُقِقْنَ على ثاكِلِ
ولَوْ كنتُ في أسْرِ غَـيرِ الهَوَى	ضَمِنْتُ ضَمــانَ أبــي وائِلِ
فَـدَى نَفسَـهُ بضَمانِ النُّضارِ	وأعطى صُدورَ القَنـا الذَّابِلِ
ومَنْـاهُمُ الخَيْـلَ مَجْنُونَـةً	فَجِئنَ بكُـلِّ فَتــى باسِلِ
كأنَّ خَلاصَ أبـي وائِلِ	مُعــاوَدَةُ القَمَــرِ الآفِلِ
دَعـا فسَــمِعتَ وكمْ ساكِتٍ	على البُعـدِ عندَكَ كالقائِلِ
فَبِيَّتَــهُ بِكَ في جَحْفَلٍ	لَــهُ ضامِنٍ وبِــهِ كـافِلِ
خَرَجْـنَ مِــنَ النَّقْعِ في عارِضٍ	ومِنْ عَـرَقِ الرَّكضِ في وابِلِ
فَلَمّا نَشِـفْنَ لَقِينَ السِّياطَ	بمِثْـلِ صَفــا البَلَـدِ الماحِلِ
شَفَـنَّ لخَمْـسٍ إلى مَــنْ طَلَــبْنَ	قُبَيْــلَ الشُّفــوفِ إلى نــازِلِ
فَدانَــتْ مَرافِقُهُــنَّ الثَّـرى	على ثِقَّــةٍ بِالـدَّمِ الغاسِلِ
ومـا بَــينَ كـاذَتَي المُسْتَغيرِ	كَمَـا بَــينَ كـاذَتَي البـائِلِ
فَلَقِّــينَ كُـلَّ رُدَيْنِيَّــةٍ	ومَصْبوحَــةٍ لَبَــنَ الشَّــائِلِ
وجيشَ إمَامٍ على ناقَـةٍ	صَحيـحِ الإمامَــةِ في الباطِلِ

165
He spoke praising him and recalled his rescue of Abu Wail Taglib ibn Dawud when the Kharajites took him captive. And the Kharajite was killed in Shaban in the year 337:
(Tripping li)

How long this eagerness for censure?
    Love makes no sense for a rational man
He wants the forgetful heart for you
    But it is nature that rejects such change
Indeed I am in love through love of you
    With emaciation and each emaciate boy
If you ceased to be I'd not weep for you
    I would weep for my love that ceased to be
Can my cheek deny tears when in fact
    They flow from it in well traveled paths?
Is it the first tear that flows over it?
    Is this the first grief for the departure?
I leave solace to one who blames me
    To spend the night in the work of love
As if the eyelids over my eyes were
    Garments rent due their bereavement
If I were prisoner of any but passion
    I would become a hostage for Abu Wail
He was ransomed by a pledge of gold
    But they got those flexible lance nipple
He endowed them with war horses
    They came with all those brave youths
It was as if Abu Wail's liberation
    Meant the return of the darkened moor
He called, you heard, how many silent
    Though far away seem to speak to you
You came to him with a great troop
    As pledge for him, as surety with him
They came from dust in high clouds
    And with their sweat running in torrents
If they dried they felt the whips as if
    They were rocks in the rainless land
They took five days for the search
    Before the sight of place to descend
Their legs sank in dirt to ankles
    Trusting they'd be washed in blood
What was between avengers' thighs
    Was like that between pisser's thighs
They confronted each Rudaini lance
    They drank the dry camel's early milk
The army of a leader on a camel is
    Perfected in leadership to falsehood

262 *Diwan al-Mutanabbi*

نَوافِرَ كالنَّحلِ والعاسِلِ	فَأَقبَلنَ يَنحَزنَ قُدّامَهُ
رَأَت أُسدُها آكِلَ الآكِلِ	فَلَمّا بَدَوتُ لِأَصحابِهِ
لَهُ فيهِم قِسمَةُ العادِلِ	بِضَربٍ يَعُمُّهُمُ جائِرٍ
كَما اِجتَمَعَت دِرَّةُ الحافِلِ	وَطَعنٍ يُجَمِّعُ شُذّانَهُم
تَحَيَّرَ عَن مَذهَبِ الراجِلِ	إِذا ما نَظَرتَ إِلى فارِسٍ
فَتىً لا يُعيدُ عَلى الناصِلِ	فَظَلَّ يُخَضِّبُ مِنها اللِحى
وَلا يَتَضَعضَعُ مِن خاذِلِ	وَلا يَستَغيثُ إِلى ناصِرٍ
وَلا يَرجِعُ الطَرفَ عَن هائِلِ	وَلا يَزَغُ الطَرفَ عَن مُقدَمِ
وَإِن كانَ دَيناً عَلى ماطِلِ	إِذا طَلَبَ التَبلَ لَم يَشأَهُ
فَإِنَّ الغَنيمَةَ في العاجِلِ	خُذوا ما أَتاكُم بِهِ واعذِروا
فَعودوا إِلى حِمصَ في القابِلِ	وَإِن كانَ أَعجَبَكُم عامُكُم
قَتَلتُم بِهِ في يَدِ القاتِلِ	فَإِنَّ الحُسامَ الخَضيبَ الَّذي
فَلَم تُدرِكوهُ عَلى السائِلِ	يَجودُ بِمِثلِ الَّذي رُمتُم
مَكانَ السِنانِ مِنَ العامِلِ	أَمامَ الكَتيبَةِ تُزهى بِهِ
قِتالاً بِكُم عَلى بازِلِ	وَإِنّي لَأَعجَبُ مِن آمِلٍ
بِغاضٍ عَلى فَرَسٍ حائِلِ	أَقالَ لَهُ اللَهُ لا تَلقَهُم
بَراها وَغَنّاكَ في الكاهِلِ	إِذا ما ضَرَبتَ بِهِ هامَةً
دَعَتهُ لِما لَيسَ بِالنائِلِ	وَلَيسَ بِأَوَّلِ ذي هِمَّةٍ
وَيَغمُرُهُ المَوجُ في الساحِلِ	يُشَمِّرُ لِلُجِّ عَن ساقِهِ
عَلى سَيفِ دَولَتِها الفاصِلِ	أَمّا لِلخِلافَةِ مِن مُشفِقٍ
وَيَسري إِلَيهِم بِلا حامِلِ	يَقُدُّ عِداها بِلا ضارِبٍ
وَما يَتَحَصَّلنَ لِلناحِلِ	تَرَكتَ جَماجِمَهُم في النَقا
فَأَنتَ بِإِحسانِكَ الشامِلِ	وَأَنبَتَّ مِنهُم رَبيعَ السِباعِ
كَعَودِ الحُلِيِّ إِلى العاطِلِ	وَعُدتَ إِلى حَلَبٍ ظافِراً
يُؤَثِّرُ في قَدَمِ الناعِلِ	وَمِثلُ الَّذي دُستَهُ حافِياً
لَهُ شِيَةُ الأَبلَقِ الجائِلِ	وَكَم لَكَ مِن خَبَرٍ شائِعٍ

They turned, were outflanked by him
    Like the frightened bees and beeman
So when you appeared to his cohort
    The lions saw a devourer and his prey
In blows he shared to them unequally
    From him the portion was just for them
By strokes he pulled a scattered mob
    As a stream from an udder holds itself
Whenever you looked at horsemen
    You perplexed the legs into the flight
So he continued to dye their beards
    As hero he did not count on the fading
He asks no help from his allies
    Nor is he routed but by being forsaken
He can't keep his horse from the front
    Nor can he keep his eye from the terror
If he seeks revenge it won't escape
    Even though the debt is now deferred
Take what he brings you and excuse
    For the loot is for those who are swifter
If this your year has confused you
    Then return to Hims in the next one
For a sword stained with blood that
    Beat you is now in the hand of a killer
He makes a gift with what you saw
    But you didn't attain it as suppliant
At the army's head he will shine
    In place of spearpoint for the rider
Indeed I'm amazed at expectations
    Of a victory with an old camel or a cuff
Did not God not tell him not to meet
    Those with swords on spirited horses?
If you strike the skulls with them they
    Split and sing for you on the shoulders
He's not the first gripped by ambition
    To attract him to what cannot be gained
He girded skirts at his feet for deeps
    But the waves engulfed him on the shore
Do none in the caliphate have concern
    For the sword of state that brings order?
He cuts off foes without a stroke and
    Travels to them without being carried
You leave their skulls in sandy hills
    They cannot be retrieved with a sieve
You make them grow in beasts' fields
    They praise your universal good qualities
You return to Aleppo as conqueror like
    A jewel returns to an unadorned woman

بَغِيضُ الحُضورِ إلى الواغِلِ	ويَوْمٌ شَرابٌ بَنيهِ الرَّدَى
وتَغفِرُ للمُذنِبِ الجاهِلِ	تَفُكُّ العُناةَ وتُغْني العُقاةَ
وأرضاهُ سَعْيُكَ في الآجِلِ	فَهَنَّاكَ النَّصرَ مُعطيكَهُ
وأخدَعُ مِن كِفَّةِ الحابِلِ	فَذي الدّارُ أخوَنُ مِن مُومِسٍ
وما يَحْصُلُونَ على طائِلِ	تَفانى الرِّجالُ على حُبِّها

(١٦٦)

«من البسيط»

قال عند مسيره لنصرة أخيه ناصر الدولة لما قصده معز الدولة بن الحسين (الديلمي) إلى الموصل، وذلك سنة سبع وثلاثين وثلاث مئة (٩٤٨م):

والطَّعْنُ عِندَ مُجيبيهِنَّ كالقُبَلِ	أغلَى المَمالِكِ ما يُبنَى على الأسَلِ
حتى تُقلقِلَ دَهراً قبلُ في القُلَلِ	وما تَقِرُّ سُيوفٌ في مَمالِكِها
طولُ الرِّماحِ وأيدي الخيلِ والإبِلِ	مِثلُ الأميرِ بَغَى أمراً فَقَرَّبَهُ
من تَحتِها بمَكانِ التُّربِ من زُحَلِ	وعَزْمَةٍ بَعَثَتْها هِمَّةٌ زُحَلٌ
توَحَّشٌ لمُلَقَّى النَّصرِ مُقتَبَلِ	على الفُراتِ أعاصيرٌ وفي حَلَبٍ
ويَجعَلُ الخيلَ أبدالاً مِنَ الرُّسُلِ	تضِلُّ أسِنَّتُهُ الكُتبَ التي نَفَذَتْ
وما أعَدُّوا فَلا يَلقَى سِوَى نَفَلِ	يَلقَى المُلوكَ فلا يَلقَى سِوَى جَزَرٍ
صِيانَةَ الذَّكَرِ الهِنديِّ بالخَلَلِ	صانَ الخليفةُ بالأبطالِ مُهْجَتَهُ
والقائِلُ القَوْلَ لم يُترَكْ ولم يُقَلِ	الفاعِلُ الفِعلَ لم يُفعَلْ لِشِدَّتِهِ
ضَوءَ النَّهارِ فصارَ الظُّهرُ كالطَّفَلِ	والباعِثُ الجيشَ قد غالَتْ عَجاجَتُهُ
ومُقلَةُ الشَّمسِ فيها أحيَرُ المُقَلِ	الجَوُّ أضيَقُ ما لاقاهُ ساطِعُها
فَما تُقابِلُهُ إلاّ على وَجَلِ	يَنالُ أبعَدَ مِنها وهيَ ناظِرَةٌ
وظاهِرَ الحَزْمِ بينَ النَّفسِ والغِيَلِ	قد عَرَّضَ السَّيفَ دونَ النَّازِلاتِ بِهِ
لَهُ ضَمائِرُ أهلِ السَّهلِ والجَبَلِ	ووُكِّلَ الظَّنُّ بالأسرارِ فانكَشَفَتْ

Such a matter you trod barefoot that
    Would have torn the feet wearing shoes
Many a story about you is published
    That has the piebald of a pinto shining
Many a drinking day with death's folk
    The most hated presence as the intruder
You end slavery, enrich the beggar
    And you forgive the sins of the ignorant
May he who gives victory bless you
    May your work please him at life's end
A world has more deceit than a whore
    Trickier than the snares of the trapper
Men wither away with infatuation for
    Her and do not achieve anything lasting

166
He spoke concerning his journey to his brother Nasir al-Daula when Mutizz al-Daula threatened him in the year 337.
(Outspread li)

A kingdom's height is built on spears
    Their rovers' jousting is like kissing
Swords do not ensure their royalty
    Until they strike a time before at heads
Thus a prince seeking power takes
    Long lances, gifts of horses, camels
Determination, desire moves, Zuhal
    Below it in the place of earth to Zuhal
Over Furat a whirlwind, in Aleppo
    Desolation due to meeting young Nasir
His glances follow letters that pierce
    He has cavalry substitute for messages
He sees kings only as sheep to kill
    They don't defy him, he leaves, only loot
A caliph guards his blood with heroes
    Cherishing Indian steel with a scabbard
He does deeds undone in difficulty
    He speaks words unknown, never said
He sends armies whose dust destroys
    The daylight at noon becomes a twilight
A plain narrows as its clouds meet it
    The sun's eye there is most confused
He shines further, it is an eye that
    Does not approach him except in fear
He opposed a sword to his attackers
    Put resolution between him and deceit
He suspects secrets, they are known
    His the hid things of plain and hill folk

وهْوَ الجَوادُ يَعُدُّ الجُبْنَ مِنْ بَخَلِ	هُوَ الشّجاعُ يَعُدُّ البُخْلَ مِنْ جُبْنِ
وقَدْ أغَذَّ إليْهِ غيرَ مُحْتَفِلِ	يَعودُ مِنْ كُلِّ فَتْحٍ غَيرَ مُفْتَضِحِ
ولا تُحَصِّنُ دِرْعٌ مُهْجَةَ البَطَلِ	ولا يُجيرُ عَلَيْهِ الدّهْرُ بُغْيَتَهُ
وجَدْتُها مِنهُ في أبْهَى مِنَ الحُلَلِ	إذا خَلَعْتُ على عِرْضٍ لَهُ حُلَلاً
كَما تُضِيرُ رِياحُ الوَرْدِ بالجُعَلِ	بذي الغَباوَةِ مِنْ أنْشادِهِ ضَرَرٌ
وجَرَّدَتْ خيرَ سَيفٍ خِيرَةَ الدّوَلِ	لَقَدْ رَأتْ كلُّ عَينٍ مِنكَ مالِئَها
مِنَ الحُروبِ ولا الآراءُ عَنْ زَلَلِ	فَما تُكَشِّفُكَ الأعداءُ عَنْ مَلَلِ
تَرَكْتَ جَمْعَهُمُ أرْضاً بِلا رَجُلِ	وكَمْ رِجالٍ بِلا أرْضٍ لكَثرَتِهِمْ
حتى مَشَى بكَ مَشْيَ الشّارِبِ الثَّمِلِ	ما زالَ طِرْفُكَ يَجري في دِمائِهِم
فيما يَراهُ وحُكْمُ القَلْبِ في الجَدَلِ	يا مَنْ يَسيرُ وحُكْمُ النّاظِرينَ لَهُ
وُفِّقْتَ مُرْتَحِلاً أوْ غَيرَ مُرْتَحِلِ	إنَّ السّعادَةَ فيما أنْتَ فاعِلُهُ
وخُذْ بِنَفْسِكَ في أخْلاقِكَ الأُوَلِ	أجْرِ الجِيادَ على ما كنتَ مُجريها
قَرْعُ الفَوارِسِ بالعَسّالَةِ الذُّبُلِ	يَنْظُرْنَ مِنْ مُقَلٍ أدْمَى أحِجَّتَها
ولا وَصَلْتَ بِها إلَّا إلى أمَلِ	فَلا هَجَمْتَ بِها إلّا على ظَفَرِ

(١٦٧)

«من الكامل»

يمدحه وقد سأله المسير معه لما سار لنصرة أخيه ناصر الدولة:

وأرادَ فيكَ مُرادَكَ المِقْدارُ	سِرْ! حَلَّ حَيْثُ تَحَلَّهُ النُّوّارُ
حَيْثُ اتّجَهْتَ وديمَةٌ مِدْرارُ	وإذا ارْتَحَلْتَ فشَيَّعَتكَ سَلامَةٌ
مَرْفوعَةٌ لِقُدومِكَ الأبْصارُ	وصَدَرْتَ أغْنَمَ صادِرٍ عَنْ مَوْرِدٍ
حتى كأنَّ صُروفَهُ أنْصارُ	وأراكَ دهرُكَ ما تُحاوِلُ في العِدَى
وتَزَيَّنَتْ بِحَديثِهِ الأسْمارُ	أنتَ الذي بَجَحَ الزّمانُ بذِكْرِهِ
وإذا عَفا فَعَطاؤهُ الأعْمارُ	وإذا تَنَكَّرَ فالفَناءُ عِقابُهُ
دَرُّ المُلوكِ لدَرِّها أغْبارُ	ولَهُ وإنْ وَهَبَ المُلوكُ مَواهِبٌ

Brave, he thinks avarice dastardly
    Bounteous, he finds a faint heart stingy
He returns from a win without boasts
    He hurries to it without the rendezvous
Destiny denies him none of his wishes
    No armor can protect the warrior's blood
I put a robe on him for honor's sake
    I find it more fine on him than any robe
For the ignorant reciting it is wrong
    Like rose perfume is harmful to beetles
Every eye looks its fill of you indeed
    Best of the state draws the best sword
The foe discovers in you no fatigue
    In warring, nor counselors find faults
How many men without land you left
    In all their numbers without any land
Your horse runs ever in their gore
    Until it goes a drunkard's gait for you
O he goes forth, Byes' judgment his
    What one sees is heart's judgment joy
Happiness exists as you create it
    You succeed whether in saddle or out
Make horses run as you lead them
    Take for yourself in your nature's prime
They stare from eyes whose sockets
    Bleed with hits by the dripping lances
You attack none with them only to win
    You arrive with them only at your desire

167
He spoke
praising him
and he asked for permission
to go along with him on this journey.
(Perfect ru)

Go! may flowers grow where you settle
    Destiny intends in you what you intend
If you saddle up peace goes with you
    Wherever you go continuous showers go
Your fate shows what it wants for foes
    Until it seems its calamities aid as allies
You return richest coming from water
    The eyes are raised to your approach
You're one whose memory rejoices
    Evening talk adorned with its stories
If he refuses, ruin is the end of it
    When he forgives then his gift is life
Even if kings give, his is beneficent
    The kings' stream to that stream dregs

وتَخافُ أنْ يَدنُو إليكَ العارُ	لله قلبُكَ ما تخافُ مِنَ الرَّدى
ويَحيدُ عَنكَ الجَحفَلُ الجَرّارُ	وتَحيدُ عَنْ طَبعِ الخَلائِقِ كُلِّهِ
ويَذِلُّ مِنْ سَطَواتِهِ الجَبّارُ	يا مَنْ يَعِزُّ على الأعِزَّةِ جارُهُ
دونَ اللِّقاءِ ولا يَثيطُ مَزارُ	كُنْ حيثُ شِئتَ فما تحولُ تَنوفَةٌ
يُنضَى المَطِيُّ ويَقرُبُ المُستارُ	وبدونِ ما أنا مِنْ ودادِكَ مُضمِرٌ
ما لي على قَلَقي إلَيْهِ خِيارُ	إنَّ الذي خَلَّفتُ خَلْفي ضائِعٌ
لَوْ لا العِيالُ وكلُّ أرضٍ دارُ	وإذا صُحِبْتَ فكلُّ ماءٍ مَشرَبٌ
صِلَةٌ تَسيرُ بِذِكرِها الأشعارُ	إذِنُ الأميرِ بأَنْ أعُودَ إلَيهِمُ

(١٦٨)

«من الطويل»

يرثي أبا الهيجاء عبد الله بن سيف الدولة بحلب وقد توفي بميا فارقين في صفر سنة ثمان وثلاثين وثلاث مئة (٩٤٩م):

وهذا الذي يُضنِي كذاكَ الذي يُبلي	بنا مِنكَ فوقَ الرَّملِ ما بكَ في الرَّملِ
إذا عِشتَ فاخترتَ الحِمامَ على الثُّكلِ	كأنَّكَ أبصرتَ الذي بي وخِفتَهُ
دموعٌ تُذيبُ الحُسنَ في الأعيُنِ النُّجلِ	تركتَ خدودَ الغانياتِ وفَوقَها
وقد قَطَرَتْ حُمراً على الشَّعَرِ الجَثلِ	نَبلُ الثَّرى سوداً مِنَ المِسكِ وحدَه
وإنْ تَكُ طفلاً فالأسى ليسَ بالطفلِ	فإنْ تَكُ في قبرٍ فإنَّكَ في الحَشا
ولكنْ على قدرِ المخيلةِ والأصلِ	ومِثلُكَ لا يُبكَى على قدرِ سِنِّهِ
نَداهُم ومِن قَتلاهُمُ مُهجَةُ البخلِ	ألستَ مِنَ القومِ الأُلى مِن رِماحِهِم
ولكنَّ في أعطافِهِ مَنطِقَ الفضلِ	بمَولودِهِم صَمَتَ اللِّسانَ كغَيرِهِ
ويَشغَلُهُمْ كسبُ الثَّناءِ عَنِ الشُّغلِ	تُسَلِّيهِم عَلياؤُهُم عَن مُصابِهِم
وأقدَمَ بَينَ الجَحفَلَينِ مِنَ النَّبلِ	أقلّ بلاءً بالرَّزايا مِنَ القَنا
فإنَّكَ نَصلٌ والشَّدائِدُ للنَّصلِ	عَزاءَكَ سَيفَ الدَّولةِ المُقتَدى بهِ
كأنَّكَ مِن كلِّ الصَّوارِمِ في أهلِ	مُقيمٌ مِنَ الهَيجاءِ في كلِّ مَنزِلِ

By God your heart can fear no death
    It only fears lest some shame come to you
You flee from whims of human nature
    And so a numerous army flees from you
O he is hard on neighbors' hardness
    The strong one subdued in his assaults
Be where you like no desert intervenes
    Between the meeting nor is the visit far
Least emaciation I have in your love
    Makes a camel thin as journey shortens
Truly what I left behind me is lost
    Not by choice but by my passion for him
If you are there every water is sweet
    Though not familiar every land is home
Princely permission as I return to them
    Is the gift poetry will carry in its memory

168
He spoke lamenting the son of Saif al-Daula who died at Mayyfariqin in the year 338.
(Long li)

We above sand have what you have below
    This wastes one just as that consumes another
As if you saw what I have and feared when
    Alive to take your death over the bereavement
You left a singing girl's cheek when over it
    The tears melted the beauty in the wide eyes
She wet black musk unmingled on earth
    And she dripped crimson on the thick hair
If you are entombed, it is in the heart
    If you were a child, grief is not for children
Such as you are not wept for his years
    Rather for his chivalry and his lineage
Are you not of folk who hold a lance
    As their bounty, the foes in greedy souls?
In infancy silent tongued as others
    Yet in their faces speaking excellence
Their ideals console them in a mishap
    Earning praise keeps them from all labor
Less concerned in war than the lances
    More forward between armies than arrows
Your patience Saif al Daula is a model
    You the blade and hardship is for blades
Staying in the conflict at every stage
    As if you were relative of every sword

وأَثْبَتَ عَقْلاً والقُلوبُ بِلا عَقلِ	ولم أرَ أعصى منكَ للحُزْنِ عَبرَةً
وتنصُرُهُ بَينَ الفَوارسِ والرَّجلِ	تخونُ المنايـا عَهْدَهُ في سَليلِهِ
ويَبدو كما يَبدو الفِرنْدُ على الصَّقلِ	ويَبقى على مَرِّ الحَوادِثِ صَبْرُهُ
فَفيهِ لها مُغْنٍ وفيها لَهُ مُسْلِ	ومَنْ كانَ ذا نَفسٍ كنَفسِكَ حرَّةٍ
يَصولُ بِلا كَفٍّ ويَسعى بِلا رِجلِ	وما الموتُ إلا سارِقٌ دَقَّ شَخْصُهُ
ويُسْلِمُهُ عِنـدَ الوِلادَةِ للنَّملِ	يَـرُدُّ أبـو الشِّبْلِ الخَميسَ عن ابْنِهِ
إلى بَطنِ أُمٍّ لا تُطـرَّقُ بـالحَملِ	بنفسي وَليـدٌ عادَ مِن بَعدِ حَمْلِـهِ
وصَدَّ وفينـا غُلَّـةَ البَلَدِ المَحْلِ	بَدا ولَـهُ وَعْـدُ السَّـحابَةِ بـالرِّوى
إلى وَقتِ تَبديلِ الرِّكابِ مِن النَّعلِ	وقد مَـدَّتِ الخَيلُ العِتاقُ عُيونَها
وجاشَتْ له الحَرْبُ الضَّروسُ وما تَغلي	ورِيعَ لَهُ جَيشُ العَدوِّ ما مَشى
ويَأكُلُـهُ قبلَ البُلـوغِ إلى الأكلِ	أَيُفْطِمُـهُ التَّوارِبُ قَبـلَ فِطامِهِ
ويَسمَعُ فيهِ ما سمعتَ مِن العَذلِ	وقبلَ يَرى من جُودِهِ ما رأيتَهُ
ويُمسي كما تُمسي مَليكاً بِلا مِثلِ	ويَلقى كما تَلقى مِن السِّلمِ والوَغى
وتَمْنَعُـهُ أَطرافُـهُنَّ من العَـزلِ	تُوَلّيـهِ أوساطَ البـلادِ رِماحُـهُ
تَفوتُ مِـنَ الدُّنيا ولا مَوهِبٍ جَـزلِ	أَنَبْكي لِمَوتانا عَلـى غَيرِ رَغبَـةٍ
تَيقَّنـتَ أنَّ المـوتَ ضَـربٌ مِن القَتلِ	إذا مـا تأمَّلـتَ الزَّمانَ وصَرْفَـهُ
وهَل خَلْوَةُ الحَسْنـاءِ إلا أَذى البَعلِ	هَلِ الوَلَدُ المَحْبـوبُ إلّا تَعِلَّـةٌ،
فَلا تَحسَبَنّي قُلتُ ما قُلتُ عَن جَهـلِ	وَقَد ذُقْتُ حُلْواءَ البَنيـنَ عَلى الصِّبـا،
ولا تُحسِنُ الأيّامُ تَكتُبُ ما أُمْلـى	وَمـا تَسَـعُ الأزمـانُ عِلمـي بِأمرِهـا
حَياةً وأن يُشتاقَ فيهِ إلى النَّسلِ	ومـا الدّهـرُ أهـلٌ أن تُؤمَّـلَ عِنـدَهُ

(١٦٩)

«من الخفيف»

وسأله سيف الدولة عن صفة فرس يرسله إليه فقال ارتجالاً:

ولَـوَ أَنَّ الجِيـادَ فيهـا أُلـوفُ	مَوقِـعُ الخَيـلِ مِـنْ نَـداكَ طَفيـفُ

I see none more brave in grief's tears
    Firmer in reason when heart has none
Death betrayed trust to his offspring
    It aided him among knights and soldiers
His courage holds in lapse of events
    He shows like a sword shines in burnish
One owning soul like your free soul
    Is self-sufficient due to it and consoled
Death is only a thief with airy shape
    It attacks without hands, runs without feet
Cub's father repels spearmen from a son
    But yet he yields at its birth to the tiny ants
By my soul a child returns after birth
    To a mother's womb with no labor pains
He appeared, had a rain cloud's promise
    He died leaving us the thirsty barren land
A thoroughbred horse turned its eyes
    To a time of change from shoe to stirrup
Foe's army fears him before he walks
    War's teeth gnash for him without biting
Has dust weaned him before weaning
    And eaten him before he got to his food?
Before he saw nobility as you see it
    And hear what you hear from the critic?
He finds as you some peace and war
    Grasps as you do a realm without equal
His lances see the center of the land
    The points protect him from withdrawal
We weep for our dead who lack desire
    Pass from a world that has no great gift
If you reflect on time and its change
    You are sure a death is a kind of murder
Is loved child anything but diversion
    Solitude with beauty only evil to spouse?
I tasted sweetness with some in youth
    Don't think I said what I did in ignorance
Fate isn't wider than my knowing it
    Nor the days write better than my hopes
The age isn't worthy one should hope
    For life though one longs for offspring now

169
He spoke impromptu when he was asked to describe a horse that was set to him.
(Nimble fu)

Place for horses in your bounty is small
    Even if there were a thousand steeds in that

وَمِنَ اللَّفْظِ لَفْظَةٌ تَجْمَعُ الوَصْـــــفَ وذاكَ المُطَهَّمُ المَعْرُوفُ
مَا لَنَا فِي النَّدَى عَلَيْكَ اختيارٌ كُلُّ مَا يَمْنَحُ الشَّرِيفُ شَرِيفُ

(١٧٠)

«من المنسرح»

قال وقد خيره في حجرتين أحداهما دهماء والأخرى كميت:

أخْتَرْتُ دَهْمَاءَ تَيْنِ يَا مَطَرُ وَمَنْ لَهُ فِي الفَضَائِلِ الخِيَرُ
وَرُبَّمَا فَالَتِ العُيُونُ وَقَدْ يَصْدُقُ فِيهَا وَيَكْذِبُ النَّظَرُ
أنْتَ الَّذِي لَوْ يُعَابُ فِي مَلَإٍ مَا عِيبَ إلَّا بِأَنَّهُ بَشَرُ
وَإنَّ إعْطَاءَهُ الصَّوَارِمَ وَالْـــــ خَيْلَ وَسُمْرَ الرِّمَاحِ وَالعَكَرُ
فَاضِحُ أعْدَائِهِ كَأَنَّهُمُ لَهُ يَقِلُّونَ كُلَّمَا كَثُرُوا
أعَاذَكَ اللهُ مِنْ سِهَامِهِمُ وَمُخْطِىءٌ مَنْ رَمِيَّةُ القَمَرُ

(١٧١)

«من الكامل»

وأنفذ إليه خلعاً فقال:

فَعَلَتْ بِنَا فِعْلَ السَّمَاءِ بِأَرْضِهِ خِلَعُ الأمِيرِ وَحَقُّهُ لَمْ نَقْضِهِ
فَكَأَنَّ صِحَّةَ نَسْجِهَا مِنْ لَفْظِهِ وَكَأَنَّ حُسْنَ نَقَائِهَا مِنْ عِرْضِهِ
وَإذا وَكَلْتَ إلى كَرِيمٍ رَأَيْهُ فِي الجُودِ بَانَ مَذِيقُهُ مِنْ مَحْضِهِ

(١٧٢)

«من الكامل»

قال يمدحه:

لا الحُلْمُ جَادَ بِهِ وَلا بِمِثَالِهِ لَوْ لا اذِّكَارُ وَدَاعِهِ وَزِيَالِهِ
إنَّ المُعِيدَ لَنَا المَنَامَ خَيَالَهُ كَانَتْ إعَادَتُهُ خَيَالَ خَيَالِهِ

In words one word sums up a description
    And that is: Perfection, and this is well known
We have no choice in bounty from you
    Everything which a noble man gives is noble

170
He spoke
and he had him
choose between two
horses,
a black and a roan:
(Flowing ru)

I take the black of these two O rain
    O you the choicest among the virtues
For often the eyes are speaking
    But vision both tricks and tells true
You are one who if one blamed
    Has blame only because he's human
And his gifts swords and horses
    Brown lances and whole camel herds
Who shames his enemies as if they
    Decreased each time they increased
God guard you from their arrows
    For he fails whose target is the moon

171
Saif al-Daula
ordered a robe
sent to Abu Tayyib
so he spoke:
(Perfect hi)

It was for us heaven's act for its earth
    A princely robe and his right not annulled
As if weave's fineness were in his word
    The beauty of its brightness from his honor
If you rely on the nobility of his ideas
    In bounty, the purity of his taste is clear

172
He spoke
praising him
(Perfect hi)

No dream brings him or his image but
    A memory of his farewell and of his loss
Sleep brought back his ghost to us
    His return was the dream of his ghost

بِتْنَا يُناوِلُنَا المُدامَ بِكَفِّهِ	مَنْ لَيسَ يَخْطُرُ أَنْ نَراهُ بِبَالِهِ
نَجْني الكَواكِبَ مِن قَلائِدِ جيدِهِ	ونَنالُ عَينَ الشَمسِ مِن خَلخالِهِ
بِنْتُم عَنِ العَينِ القَريحَةِ فيكُمُ	وَسَكَنْتُمُ طَيَّ الفُؤادِ الوالِهِ
فَدَنَوْتُمُ وَدُنُوُّكُمْ مِن عِنْدِهِ	وَسَمِعْتُمُ وسَماعُكُم مِن مالِهِ
إنّي لَأبغَضُ طَيفَ مَن أَحبَبْتُهُ	إذْ كانَ يَهجُرُنا زَمانَ وِصالِهِ
مِثلُ الصَبابَةِ والكَآبَةِ والأَسى	فارَقْتُهُ فَحَدَثْنَ مِن تَضْرحالِهِ
وَقَدِ استَقَدتُ مِنَ الهَوى وأَذَقْتُهُ	مِن عِفَّتي ما ذُقتُ مِنْ بَلبالِهِ
ولَقَدْ خَبَأْتُ مِنَ الكَلامِ سُلافَةً	وسَقَيتُ مِن نادَمتُ مِن جِرْيالِهِ
وَإذا تَعَثَّرَتِ الجِيادُ بِسَهلِهِ	بَرَّزْتُ غَيرَ مُعَثَّرٍ بِجِبالِهِ
وحَكَمْتُ في البَلَدِ العَراءِ بِناعِجٍ	مُعتادِهِ مُجتابِهِ مُغتالِهِ
يَمشي كَما عَدَتِ المَطِيّ وَراءَهُ	ويَزيدُ وَقتَ حَمامِها وكَلالِهِ
وتُراعُ غَيرَ مُعَقَّلاتٍ حَولَهُ	فَيَفوتُها مُتَضَحْجِفاً بِعِقالِهِ
فَغَدا النَجاحُ وراحَ في أخفافِهِ	وَغَدا المِراحُ وراحَ في إرْقالِهِ
وَشَرِكْتُ دَولَةَ هاشِمٍ في سَيفِها	وشَقَقتُ خيسَ المُلكِ عن رِئْبالِهِ
عَن ذا الَذي حُرِمَ اللُيوثُ كَمالَهُ	يُنسي الفَريسَةَ خَوْفَهُ بِجَمالِهِ
وَتَواضُعُ الأُمَراءُ حَوْلَ سَريرِهِ	وتُري المَحَبَّةَ وَهيَ مِن آكالِهِ
وَيَميتُ قَبلَ قِتالِهِ ويَعِشُّ قَبـ	ـلَ نَوالِهِ ويُنيلُ قَبلَ سُؤالِهِ
إنَّ الرِيَاحَ إذا عَمَدْنَ لِناظِرٍ	أغناهُ مُقبِلُها عَنِ استِعجالِهِ
أعطى ومَنَّ على المُلُوكِ بِعَفوِهِ	حتى تَساوى النَاسُ في إفضالِهِ
وإذا غَنوا بِعَطائِهِ عَن هَزِّهِ	وَالى فَأَغنى أن يَقولوا وَالِهِ
وكَأنَّما جَدْواهُ مِن إكْثارِهِ	حَسَدٌ لِسائِلِهِ على إقْلالِهِ
غَرَبَ النُجومُ فَغُرنَ دُونَ هُمومِهِ	وطَلَعنَ حينَ طَلَعنَ دُونَ مَنالِهِ
واللهُ يُسْعِدُ كُلَّ يَومٍ جَدَّهُ	ويَزيدُ مِن أعدائِهِ في آلِهِ
لَوْ لَمْ تَكُنْ تَجري على أسيافِهِ	مُهَجاتُهُمْ لَجَرَتْ على إقْبالِهِ

In our night he gave wine by a hand
    Did not think in his heart we saw him
We took stars from his neck's jewels
    We got a sun's eye from his ankle ring
You parted from an eye wounded by
    You held in a dejected heart's thought
You were close and your coming was
    Kindly and your bounty was its wealth
Yes, I hate a phantom of him I love
    For he fled at the time of its embrace
Like passion, grief and sorrow when
    I parted from him they told of his going
I took revenge on love, made it taste
    My virtue what I tasted of his sorrow
Indeed I keep for every land a time
    To scare the lion away from his cub
Then front will meet front, between
    Will be blows as death roams the field
I hid the fine wine of my words but
    Shared the red with one I drank with
When coursers stumbled on a plain
    I crossed its mountains without a fall
I ruled a vast desert on a white camel
    Used to it, exploring it, destroyed by it
He goes his gait as if nags ran behind
    In their strength as he won in his fatigue
They without hobbles are scared of him
    But he passes them speeding with a clog
Success appears, he exults in his legs
    Gaiety comes and he rejoices in his gait
I share the Hashimi rule in their sword
    And so I entered the royal lair of their lion
One whose perfection is forbid to lions
    The prey forgets fear due to his bravery
Princes are humbled about his throne
    He looks at his clients and it is his food
He kills before his war and sends joy
    Before his gifts and gives before asked
Winds that come to one who hopes
    Find their coming eases a need for haste
He gives and endows kings with pardon
    Until mankind are equal in his generosity
If enriched by his gift on his initiative
    He repeats and thwarts the word: Repeat
As if his bounty in its frequency were
    Jealous of his clients in their fewness
Stars set and fall short of his plan
    They rise, if they, short of his giving
God prospers his fortunes every day
    He increases his family with his enemy
If their heart's blood does not flow
    On his swords it flows with their fortune
They leave no imprint on him from battle
    Except for the bloodstains on his armor

لـم يَتْرُكـوا أَثَـراً عَلَيـهِ مـن الوَغَـى	إلّـا دِمـاءَهُـمْ علـى سِـرْبـالِـهِ
فَلِمِثْلِـهِ جَمَـعَ العَرَمْـرَمُ نَفْسَـهُ	وبِمِثْلِـهِ انفصَمَـتْ عُـرَى أقتـالِـهِ
يـا أَيُّهـا القضمَـرُ المُبـاهـي وجهَـهُ	لا تُكَذَّبَـنّ فلسـتَ مـن أشـكـالِـهِ
وإذا طَمَـى البحـرُ المحيـطُ فقُـلْ لَـهُ	دَعْ ذا فإنّـكَ عـاجِـزٌ عَـن حـالِـهِ
وَهـبَ الـذي وَرِثَ الجـدودَ ومـا رأى	أفعـالَهُـم لابـنٍ بــلا أفعـالِـهِ
حتى إذا فـي التّـراثِ سِـوَى العُلـى	قَصَـدَ العُـداةَ مِـنَ القنـا بطِوالِـهِ
وبـأرْعَـنَ لَبِـسَ العجـاجَ إليهِـمْ	فـوقَ الحديـدِ وجَـرَّ مِـن أذيـالِـهِ
فكَأنّمـا قَـذِي النّهـارُ بنَقْعِـهِ	أو غَـضَّ عنـهُ الطَّـرفَ مـن إجلـالِـهِ
الجيـشُ جيشُـكَ غيـرَ أنّـكَ جيشَـةٌ	فـي قَلبِـهِ ويَمينِـهِ وشِـمـالِـهِ
تَـرِدُ الطِّعـانَ المُـرَّ عـنْ فُرسـانِهِ	وتُنـازِلُ الأبطـالَ عَـن أبطـالِـهِ
كُـلٌّ يُريـدُ رجـالَـهُ لحَيـاتِـهِ	يـا مَـنْ يُريـدُ حياتَـهُ لِرِجـالِـهِ
دونَ الحـلاوَةِ في الزّمـانِ مَـرارَةٌ	لا تُختَطَـى إلّا علـى أهْوالِـهِ
فلـذاكَ جاوَزَهـا عَلـيٌّ وَحْـدَهُ	وسَعـى بمُنصُلِـهِ إلى آمـالِـهِ

(١٧٣)

«من الكامل»

قال يمدحه:

أنـا مِنـكَ بَيـنَ فضـائـلٍ ومَكـارِمٍ	وَمِـنِ ارتيـاحِـكَ فـي غَمـامٍ دائِـمِ
ومِـنِ احتِقـارِكَ كـلَّ مـا تحبُـو بـهِ	فيمـا ألا حِظُّـه بعَينَـيْ حـالِـمِ
إنّ الخليفـةَ لـم يُسَمِّـكَ سيفَهـا	حتـى بَـلاكَ فكُنْـتَ عَيـنَ الصّـارِمِ
فـإذا تَـتَـوَّجَ كنـتَ دُرَّةَ تـاجِـهِ	وإذا تَخَتَّـمَ كنـتَ فَصَّ الخـاتِـمِ
وإذا انتَضـاكَ علـى العِـدَى في مَعرَكٍ	هَلَكـوا وضـاقَـتْ كفُّـهُ بالقـائِـمِ
أبـدَى سَخـاؤكَ عَجـزَ كـلِّ مُشَمَّـرٍ	في وَصْفِـهِ وأضـافَ ذَرعَ الكـاتِـمِ

For him a huge host unites itself, by
    Such as him his foes' straps are broken
Attend O moon whose face is shining
    Do not tell lies for you are not his kind
When the deep sea swells admonish it:
    Leave it, you are weak compared to him!
He gives what he got of kin and feels
    Their acts not his unless by his endeavor
Inheritance is lost but for high ideas as
    He seeks the enemy with the long lances
With an army that wears dust about them
    Over their armor and trails it as a skirt
As if day were blinded by its gloom
    Or cast down its eyes from his glory
An army your army but you are its
    And its heart and its right and its left
You drink bitter drafts by its knights
    You bring down warriors with its men
All want his soldiers for his life's sake,
    O he desires his life for his son
Bitter comes before sweet in a time
    You cannot reach it except after terror
For this only 'Ali is able to gain and
    Acquire by his sword what he hopes for

173
He spoke also praising him.
(Perfect)

I am amidst benefits and noble acts
    In a steady shower by your good wishes
Things you scorn are those you lavish
    I look at them with the dreamer's vision
The caliph did not name you his sword
    Until he tested you and found you sharp
When he was crowned you were a gem
    When he sealed, you were the ring jewel
When you unsheathed for foes in war
    Who perished, his hand held onto the hilt
Your bounty shows weakness in all who
    Describe it and hinders the arm that hides

(١٧٤)

«من الوافر»

قال يمدحه وقد أمر له بفرس وجارية:

وَأَيُّ قُلُوبِ هذا الرَّكْبِ شاقا	أيَدْري الرَّبعُ أيَّ دَمٍ أراقا
تَلاقى في جُسُومٍ ما تَلاقى	لَنا ولِأَهْلِهِ أَبَداً قُلُوبُ
عَفاهُ مَنْ حَدا بِهِم وَساقا	ومَا عَفَتِ الرِّياحُ لَهُ مَحَلاّ
فَحَمَّلَ كُلَّ قَلْبٍ ما أَطاقا	فَلَيْتَ هَوى الأحبَّةِ كانَ عَدْلاً
فَصارَتْ كُلُّها للدَّمْعِ ماقا	نَظَرْتُ إلَيْهِم والعَيْنُ شَكْرَى
وَأعْطاني مِنَ السَّقَمِ المُحاقا	وقَدْ أخَذَ التَّمامَ البَدْرُ فيهِم
يَقُودُ بِلا أزمَّتِها النِّياقا	وبَيْنَ الفَرْعِ والقَدَمَيْنِ نُورٌ
بِها نَقْصٌ سَقانِيها دِهاقا	وطَرْفٌ إنْ سَقى العُشّاقَ كأساً
كأنَّ عَلَيْهِ مِنْ حَدَقٍ نِطاقا	وَخَضَّرَ تَثْبُتُ الأبصارُ فيهِ
وَسَيْفي والهَمَلَّعَةَ الدَّفاقا	سَلي عَنْ سيرَتي فَرَسي ورُمْحي
وَنَكَّبْنَا السَّماوَةَ والعِراقا	تَرَكْنا مِنْ وَراءِ العيسِ نَجْداً
لِسَيْفِ الدَّوْلَةِ المَلِكِ ائتِلاقا	فَما زالَتْ تَرى واللَّيلُ داجٍ
إذا فَتَحَتْ مَناخِرَها انتِشاقا	أدَلَّتْها رِياحُ المِسْكِ مِنْهُ
فَلَمْ تَعْتَرِضيْنَ لَهُ الرَّفاقا	أَباحَكِ أيَّها الوَحْشُ الأَعادي
لِضَحْكِكِ عَنْ رَذاياناً وَعاقا	ولَوْ تَبِعَتْ ما طَرَحَتْ قَناهُ
مِنَ النِّيرانِ لَمْ نَخْفِ احتِراقا	ولَوْ سِرْنا إلَيْهِ في طَريقٍ
إلى مَنْ يَتَّقُونَ لَهُ شِقاقا	إماماً للأئمَّةِ مِنْ قُرَيْشٍ
وللهَيْجاءِ حينَ تَقومُ ساقا	يَكونُ لَهُم إذا غَضِبوا حُساماً
إذا فَهِقَ المَكَرُّ دَماً وَضاقا	فَلا تَسْتَنْكِرَنَّ لَهُ ابْتِساماً
وَحَمَّلَ هَمَّهُ الخَيْلَ العِتاقا	فَقَدْ ضَمِنَتْ لَهُ المُهَجَ العَوالي
وإنْ بَعُدُوا جَعَلْنَهُمُ طِراقا	إذا أَنْعَلْنَ في آثارِ قَوْمٍ
نَصَبْنَ لَهُ مُؤَلَّلَةً دِقاقا	وإنْ نَقَعَ الصَّريخُ إلى مَكانٍ
وَكانَ اللَّبْثُ بَيْنَهُما فُواقا	فَكانَ الطَّعْنُ بَيْنَهُما جَواباً
مُعاوِدَةً فَوارِسُها العِناقا	مُلاقِيَةً نَواصيَها المَنايا

174
He spoke praising Saif al-Daula and he had ordered for him a maid and a black horse.
(Exuberant qi)

Does the area know whose blood is shed
    And what hearts in these riders must suffer?
For us and for its folk hearts always exist
    To meet in the bodies that cannot embrace
Winds do not sweep the campsite for him
    He who drives them and guides it defaces
Would that the beloved's love were just
    So as to load each heart as it could bear
I watched them, the eye was overfull
    And all of it was a duct for these showers
The moon reached its full among them
    And it gave me the sickness of its waning
Between head and feet there was light
    That guided the camels without the bridle
An eye, if one poured the beloved a cup
    Loss would give me a drink to overflowing
A waist that vision fixed itself upon
    As if there were a belt of eyes upon it
My horse and sword console me for my
    Life as my spear and swift, rangy camel
We left Najd behind on the white camel
    We turned aside from Samawa and Iraq
She did not stop looking in dark night
    For Saif al-Daula king of the lightning
Her guide a musky wind from him
    She opened her nostrils to sniff at it
He leaves the foe, O beast, to beasts
    Why do you confront his traveling party?
If you follow what his spear attacks
    It will keep you from our poor camels
If we journeyed to him on high ways
    Of sun and moon we'd not fear burning
He is a leader of leaders of Quraysh
    Against those who menace with schism
A sword against them if they rage
    A driver in battle if they are rebels
They can't be ignorant of his smiles
    When attacks bloody mouths and press
The lances have guaranteed blood
    He loads his will on the fine horses
If they are shoe'd for tracking folk
    Though they are far the foe is the sole
If a cry for help is faint from a place
    They prick the fine ears for his sake
Jousting between them as a reply
    Comes after a bit as between milkings
So they toss the forelocks at death
    Accustoming the riders to catastrophe

وَقَدْ ضَرَبَ العَجاجُ لَها رِواقا	تَبيتُ رِماحُهُ فَوقَ الهَوادي
عُلِلْنَ بِها اصْطِباحاً واغْتِباقا	تَميلُ كَأنَّ في الأَبْطالِ خَمراً
فَلَمْ يَسكَرْ وَجادَ فَما أَفاقا	تَعَجَّبَتِ المُدامُ وَقَدْ حَساها
فَلَمّا فاقَتِ الأَمْطارَ فاقا	أَقامَ الشِّعْرُ يَنتَظِرُ العَطايا
وَوَفَّينا القِيانَ بِهِ الصَّداقا	وَزَنّا قيمَةَ الدَّهْماءِ مِنهُ
وَلِلكَرَمِ الذي لَكَ أَنْ يُباقى	وَحاشا لارْتِياحِكَ أَنْ يُبارى
تَراجَعَتِ القُرومُ لَهُ حِقاقا	وَلَكِنّا نُداعِبُ مِنكَ قَرْماً
وَيَسلُبُ عَفْوُهُ الأَسْرى الوِثاقا	فَتىً لا تَسلُبُ القَتْلى يَداهُ
وَلَمْ أَظْفَرْ بِهِ مِنكَ استِراقا	وَلَمْ تَأتِ الجَميلَ إِليَّ سَهْواً
كَبا بَرْقٌ يُحاوِلُ بي لَحاقا	فَأَبلِغْ حاسِدِيَّ عَلَيكَ أَنّي
إذا ما لَمْ يَكُنَّ ظُبىً رِقاقا	وَهَلْ تُغْني الرَّسائِلُ في عَدُوٍّ
فَإنّي قَدْ أَكَلْتُهُمُ وَذاقا	إذا ما النّاسُ جَرَّبَهُمْ لَبيبٌ
وَلَمْ أَرَ دينَهُمْ إلّا نِفاقا	فَلَمْ أَرَ وُدَّهُمْ إلّا خِداعاً
وَعَمّا لَمْ تُلِقْهُ مَا أَلاقا	يُقَصِّرُ عَنْ يَمينِكَ كُلُّ بَحْرٍ
أَعَمْداً كانَ خَلْقُكَ أَمْ وِفاقا	وَلَوْ لا قُدْرَةُ الخَلّاقِ قُلْنا
وَلا ذاقَتْ لَكَ الدُّنيا فِراقا	فَلا حَطَّتْ لَكَ الهَيْجاءُ سَرْجاً

(١٧٥)

«من المنسرح»

يمدحه أيضاً ويرثي أبا وائل تغلب بن داود ابن حمدان وقد توفي في حمص سنة ثمان وثلاثين وثلاث مئة (٩٤٩م):

أَكرَمَ مِنْ تَغلِبَ بنِ داودِ	ما سَدِكَتْ عِلَّةٌ بِمَورودِ
حَلَّ بِهِ أَصدَقُ المَواعيدِ	يَأنَفُ مِنْ ميتَةِ الفِراشِ وَقَدْ
غَيرِ سُروجِ السَّوابِحِ القُودِ	وَمِثلُهُ أَنكَرَ المَماتَ عَلى

His lances spend night above necks
    The dust is set up for them like a tent
They bend as if wine from warriors
    Repeated the morning and evening cups
The wine wonders, he has drunk it but
    Is not drunk, is generous and recovers
Poetry stands by awaiting the giving
    As it exceeds in a shower that surpasses
We pay the black horse's price from it
    We promise to pay for the girl with dowry
God forbid your mercy be imitated or
    Your generosity need be immortalized
We were only joking with you as chief
    Old camels yield to him as in their prime
He a hero whose hand loots no corpse
    His pardon plunders prisoners of chains
You do not come with gifts by chance
    Nor do I gain them from you as in theft
Tell them who stir envy of me with you
    Lightning misses that tries to destroy me
For about what are those letters
    To foes if one has no fine edged sword?
As for mankind that wisdom tests
    They have tasted but I have eaten them
I find their love not other than tricks
    I see their belief only as their hypocrisy
Each sea falls short of your right hand
    And what you do not hold, of that
I take But for the power of creation we'd say
    Is your character in intention or chance?
May war not alight from saddle for you
    Nor world ever give the taste of farewell

175
He spoke praising him and lamenting Abu Wail Taglib the first of Jumadi in 333.
(Flowing di)

Illness never clung to any mortal
    More nobly than to Taglib ibn Dawud
He was one to scorn a death in bed
    If the moisture promise was to be held
Such as he refused a death which was
    Without a saddle on the fast long horse

282 Diwan al-Mutanabbi

بَعْدَ عِثَارِ القَنَـا بلَبَّتِـهِ	وَضَرْبِـهِ أرؤسَ الصَّنـاديدِ
وَخَوْضِـهِ غَمْـرَ كـلِّ مَهْلَكَـةٍ	للذَّمِّ فيهـا فُـؤادُ رعْديدِ
فـإنْ صَبَرْنَـا فإنَّنـا صُبُـرٌ	وَإنْ بَكَيْنَـا فَغَيْـرُ مَـرْدودِ
وَإنْ جَزِعْنـا لَـهُ فَـلا عَجَـبٌ	ذا الجَـزْرُ في البَحْرِ غَيْـرُ مَعْهـودِ
أيـنَ الهِبـاتُ الَّتـي يُفَرِّقُهَـا	علـى الزَّرَافَـاتِ وَالمَواجِيـدِ
سالِمُ أهْـلِ الـوِدادِ بَعْدَهُـمْ	يَسْـلَمُ للحُـزْنِ لا لَتخْلِيـدِ
فَمَـا تَرَجَّـى النُّفوسُ مِـنْ زَمَـنٍ	أحْمَـدُ حالَيْـهِ غَـيْرُ مَحْمـودِ
إنْ نُيُـوبَ الزَّمـانِ تَعْرِفُنـي	أنَـا الَّذي طـالَ عَجْمُهـا عُودي
وَفِيَّ مَـا قَـارَعَ الخُطُـوبَ ومَـا	آنَسَـني بالمَصائِـبِ السُّـودِ
مَـا كُنْـتَ عَنْـهُ إذِ اسْتَغَاثَـكَ يَـا	سَيْفَ بَنـي هاشِـمٍ بَمَغْمـودِ
يَا أكْـرَمَ الأكْرَمِيـنَ يَا مَلِـكَ الـ	أمْلاكِ طُـرّاً يَـا أصْيَـدَ الصِّيـدِ
قَـدْ ماتَ مِـنْ قَبْلِهـا فَأنْشَـرَهُ	وَقْـعُ قَنَـا الخَـطّ في اللَّغادِيدِ
وَرَمْيُـكَ اللَّيْـلَ بـالجُنـودِ وَقَـدْ	رَمَيْـتَ أجْفـانَهُـمْ بتَسْـهيدِ
فَصَبَّحْتَهُـمْ رِعالُهَـا شُـزَّبـاً	بَـيْـنَ ثُبـاتٍ إلى عَبَـاديـدِ
تَحْمِـلُ أغْمادُهَـا الفِـداءَ لَهُـمْ	فانْتَقَدُوا الضَّـرْبَ كالأخاديـدِ
مَوْقِعُـهُ في فِـراشِ هَامِهـم	وَرِيحُـهُ في مَنَـاخِرِ السَّيِّـدِ
أفْنـى الحَيَـاةَ الَّتـي وَهَبْـتَ لَـهُ	في شَـرَفٍ شَاكِـراً وَتَسْـويـدِ
سَقيمَ جِسْـمٍ صَحيـحَ مَكْرُمَـةٍ	مَنجُـودَ كَـرْبٍ غِيـاثَ مَنجُـودِ
ثُـمَّ غـدَا قَيْـدُهُ الحِمَـامَ وَمَـا	تَخْلُـصُ مِنْـهُ يَمِيـنُ مَصْفُـودِ
لا يَنْقُـصُ الهالِكُـونَ مِـنْ عَـدَدٍ	مِنْـهُ عَلـيٌّ مُضَيِّـقُ البِيـدِ
تَهُـبُّ في ظَهْرِهَـا كَتَائِبُـهُ	هُبُـوبَ أرْواحِـهِ المَراويـدِ
أوَّلَ حَـرْفٍ مِـنْ اسمِـهِ كَتَبَـتْ	سَنَـابِكِ الخَيْـلِ في الجَلاميـدِ
مَهْمَـا يُعَـزِّ الفَتـى الأميـرَ بـهِ	فَـلا بإقْدامِـهِ وَلا الجُـرودِ
وَمِـنْ مُنَانَـا بَقـاؤهُ أبَـداً	حتَّـى يُعَـزَّى بكُـلِّ مَوْلـودِ

After the lance imprint on his breast
    And his cutting off the heads of chiefs
His plunge into ruin's deepest hole
    Where the heart of a brave man trembles
If we are patient then we are flinty
    And if we weep that is no reproach to us
If we grieve for him it is no wonder
    Such an ebb tide in a sea is unforeseen
Where are the gifts to be distributed
    To the assemblies and the individuals?
Good folks' safety after their parting
    Escapes from grief but not from eternity
What can souls hope for from time
    Whose best condition is without praise?
Misfortunes of time know me well
    Long their teeth have tested my wood
I have what strikes back at calamity
    Makes me friends with black disaster
When he asked aid you didn't stay
    In sheath O sword of the Hashimi clan
O noblest of nobles O king of kings
    O hunter of all the hunters everywhere
He died once before this and blows
    Of Khatti lances on the throat freed him
Your attack was at night with heroes
    You struck their eyelids with waking
Their lean riders came at them near
    Morning among troops up to the folk
Their scabbards bore ransom for one
    They paid the cash in blows like furrows
His stroke was on their skull bones
    Its scent was in the nostrils of a beast
He lost the life that you gave to him
    With nobility he was grateful and loyal
Sick in body, young in goodness
    Plagued with evil as aid to affliction
Then death appeared with his chains
    The hand with shackles loosed him not
The dying diminished not in numbers
    For him, 'Ali made the deserts too small
His troops go up and down its flats
    With blasts of winds that come and go
The hoofs of horses write his fame's
    First letter on the wasteland's stones
One consoles the young prince for him
    Let it not be for his boldness and bounty
It is our wish he endure so forever so
    He may be consoled by all who are born

(١٧٦)

«من الرّجز»

قال وقد ركب سيف الدولة في تشييع عبد يماك لما أنفذه في المقدمة إلى الرقة وهاجت ريح شديدة:

لَيْتَ الرِّيـاحَ صُنْـعَ مـا تَصنَــعُ	لاعَـدِمَ المُشَيِّعُ المُشَيَّــعُ
وَسَجْسَـجٌ أنْـتَ وَهُـنَّ زَعْـزَعُ	بَكَـرْنَ ضَـرّاً وبكَـرْتَ تَنْفَــعُ
وَأنْـتَ نَبْـعٌ والمُلُـوكُ خِـرْوَعُ	وواحِـدٌ أنْـتَ وهُـنَّ أربَــعُ

(١٧٧)

«من الوافر»

قال وهو يسايره إلى الرقة وقد اشتد المطر بموضع يعرف بالثدين:

تَحَيَّـرُ مِنْـهُ فـي أمْـرٍ عُجـابِ	لِعَيْنـي كُـلَّ يَوْمٍ مِنْـكَ حَـظٌّ
وَمَوْقِـعُ ذا السَّحـاب عَلـى سَحـابِ	حِمَالَـةُ ذا الحُسـامِ عَلـى حُسـامٍ
وَيَخْلُـقُ مَـا كَسَاهَـا مِـنْ ثِيـابِ	تَجِـفّ الأرْضُ مـن هـذا الرَّبـابِ
وَلا يَنفَـكّ غَيْثُـكَ فـي انْسِـحابِ	وَمَـا يَنفَـكّ مِنْـكَ الدَّهْـرُ رَطْبـاً
مُسَايَـرَةَ الأحِبّـاءِ الطّـرابِ	تُسايِـركَ السَّـواري والغَـوادي
وَتَعجِـزُ عَـنْ خَلائِقِـكَ العِـذابِ	تُفيـدُ الجُـودَ مِنْـكَ فَتَحْتَذيـهِ

(١٧٨)

«من الكامل»

وأجل سيف الدولة ذكره وهو يسايره فقال:

| تَأتي النَّـدى ويُـذاعُ عَنْـكَ فَتَكْـرَهُ | أنـا بالوُشـاةِ إذا ذَكَرْتُـكَ أشْبَـهُ |
| أيْقَنْـتُ أنَّ اللهَ يَبْغـي نَصْـرَهُ | وَإذا رَأيْتُـكَ دونَ عِـرْضٍ عـارِضـاً |

176
He spoke
when Saif al-Daula
was escorting his servant
Yamak when they drove
to Raqqa in the vanguard.
And the wind was blowing hard.
(Trembling u)

The escorted one is not lacking escort
    I would the winds did what you are doing
They are early perforce but you for use
    You are the smooth plain, they the rough
You are only one and they are four
    You the hard wood and the kings the soft

177
He spoke
and he was on the road
to Raqqa in heavy rain
in a place known as Thadiin
(Exuberant bi)

To my eye each day with you is lucky
    You amaze it by some wonderful thing
The clash of sword against sword is
    The downpour of this cloud on a cloud
The earth will dry after the shower
    What clothes it as a dress wears out
But moisture from you never ceases
    And your shower will continue to pour
Evening and early clouds escort
    You in the journey of a joyful lover
As ransom for your bounty they copy
    But yet fall short of your sweet person

178
He spoke
as Saif al-Daula
praised his ideas
as he traveled with him.
(Perfect hu)

I slander when I think of you in metaphor
    Bounty comes, one talks of you, you demur
But when I see you opposed to honor
    I am sure God wishes to increase that

(١٧٩)

«من البسيط»

وزاد سيف الدولة في وصفه فقال:

وَرُبَّ قافِيَةٍ غاظَتْ بِهِ مَلِكا	رُبَّ نَجيعٍ بِسَيفِ الدَّوْلَةِ انْسَفَكا
وَيُصَيِّرِ الخَيلَ لا يَستَكرِمُ الرَّمَكا	مَن يَعرِفِ الشَّمسَ لَم يُنكِرْ مَطالِعَها
إنَّ البِلادَ وإنَّ العالَمينَ لَكا	تَسُرُّ بِالمالِ بَعضَ المالِ تَملِكُهُ

(١٨٠)

«من المتقارب»

وتوسط سيف الدولة في الطريق فرأى جبلاً فقال:

وَلا يَفعَلُ السَّيفُ أفعالَهُ	يَؤُمُّ ذا السَّيفُ آمالَهُ
وَإِنْ سارَ في جَبَلٍ طالَهُ	إذا سارَ في مَهمَهٍ عَمَّهُ
يُثَمِّرُ مِنْ مالِهِ مالَهُ	وَأنتَ بِما نُلتَنا مالِكٌ
يُرَشِّحُ للفَرسِ أشبالَهُ	كَأنَّكَ ما بَينَنا ضَيغَمٌ

(١٨١)

«من الوافر»

عاب قوم عليه علو الخيام فقال:

أبَيتُ قَبُولَهُ كُلَّ الإباءِ	لَقَدْ نَسَبُوا الخِيامَ إلى عَلاءِ
وَلا سَلَّمْتُ فَوقَكَ للسَّماءِ	وَما سَلَّمْتُ فَوقَكَ لِلثُّرَيّا
سَلَبْتَ رُبُوعَها ثَوبَ البَهاءِ	وَقَدْ أوحَشتَ أرضَ الشّامِ حَتّى
فَتَعرِفُ طِيبَ ذَلِكَ في الهَواءِ	تَنَفَّسُ والعَواصِمُ مِنكَ عَشرٌ

179
He spoke
and Saif al-Daula
had just admired his description.
(Outspread ka)

Much blood was shed by Saif al-Daula
    And many a poem has made a king envious
He who sees the sun won't want her dawn
    Or knows a horse won't admire pregnant mares
You endow with wealth the flock you own
    For the land and all the world that you observe

180
He spoke
and they were passing
through mountains
on the way to Amid.
(Tripping hu)

This sword moves forward to his hopes
    But the blade does not achieve his deeds
As he crosses a plain he spreads far
    If he goes on a mountain he elevates it
You by what you give us are a king
    In multiplying his wealth by his flocks
As if you among us were the lion
    Who accustoms his cubs to hunt the prey

181
One of the men
blamed him for his saying:
Would that we when you
went were your horse /
And that we when you settled
were the tent.
He said: You are the tent
that is above him!
So he spoke.
(Exuberant i)

They have elevated a tent to nobility
    I reject that interpretation absolutely
I grant no place above you to stars
    I do not grant a place above you to sky
You laid waste the Syrian land until
    You looted its quarters of bright ideas
You sigh, cities ten nights from you
    Yet they know the sweetness in the air

(١٨٢)

وذكر سيف الدولة جد أبي التشائر وأباه فقال:

وَوَلِيُّ النَّمَاءِ مَــنْ تَنْمِيهِ	أَغْلَبُ الحَيِّزَيْنِ مَـا كُنْتَ فيهِ
دِنْيَةً دُونَ جَدِّهِ وَأَبِيهِ	ذَا الَّــذي أَنْــتَ جَــدُّهُ وَأَبُــوهُ

(١٨٣)

«من الوافر»

قال وقد أذن المؤذن فرفع سيف الدولة الكأس من يده:

وَلا لَيَّنْتَ قَلْبـاً وَهْــوَ قَـاسِ	ألا أذّن فَمَـا أذكَــرتَ نَاسِــي
وَلا عَــنْ حَــقِّ خَالِقِــهِ بِكَــاسِ	وَلا شُــغِلَ الأميــرُ عَــنِ المَعَالي

(١٨٤)

«من الطويل»

فقال:

وَأَقْتَلَهُم للدّارعِينَ بِــلا حَـربِ	فَدَيناكَ أهدى النّـاسِ سَهماً إلى قَلبي
فأنتَ جميلُ الخُلفِ مستحسَنُ الكِذبِ	تَفَرَّدَ في الأحكامِ في أهلِــهِ الهَوَى
وإن كُنتُ مَبـذولَ المَقاتِلِ في الحبّ	وإنّي لَممنـوعُ المَقاتِــلِ في الوَغَى
أصابَ الحُدورَ السهلَ في المرتقى الصَّعبِ	وَمَـن خُلِقَـت عَيناكَ بَــينَ جُفونِــهِ

(١٨٥)

«من الطويل»

أمر سيف الدولة غلمانه أن يلبسوا وقصد ميا فارقين في خمسة آلاف من الجند وألفين من غلمانه ليزور قبر والدته وذلك في شوال سنة ثمان وثلاثين وثلاث مئة (٩٤٩م) فقال:

| أكُلَّ فصيحٍ قــالَ شِــعراً مُتَيَّـمُ | إذا كـانَ مَــدحٌ فالنَّسِــيبُ المُقَــدَّمُ |

182
Saif al-Daula mentioned his father
and grandfather to Abu Ashair.
So Abu Tayyib spoke.
(Flowing hi)

The best of two sides is where you are
    The lord of lineage is he who makes it grow
One whose grandfather and father you are
    Is nearer than to his grandfather or his father

183
He spoke and the muezzin
was calling to prayers so Saif al-Daula
put aside the cup in his hand.
(Exuberant si)

Do not call, you recall no absent one
    Nor do you soften one with a hard heart
A prince is not turned from heights
    Nor from his Creator's claims by a cup

184
Saif al-Daula recited a verse
that he wanted some additions to.
So he spoke adding to it. The verse was:
I went, going early, to meet a beauty /
I saw nothing sweeter than your eye or heart.
(Long bi)

We ransom you, best man to share my heart
    Most deadly for the armored ones not in battle
Love is unique in its rule over its folk
    You are fine in obstinacy, fair in falsehood
I am indeed guarded from death in war
    Even though I am devoted to death in love
He whom your eyes created between lids
    Finds the plain's slope on the steep ascent

185
He spoke also praising
Saif al-Daula at Mayyafariqin
and he had ordered the army to horse and armor and
weapons and provisions.
his was in Shawwal of the year 338.

If one praised, a love prelude was first
    Do all the eloquent speak as love's slaves?

290 Diwan al-Mutanabbi

بِهِ يُبدأُ الذِّكرُ الجَميلُ ويُختَمُ	لَحُبُّ ابنِ عَبدِ اللهِ أَولى فإنَّهُ
إلى مَنظَرٍ يَصغُرنَ عَنهُ ويَعظُمُ	أَطَعتُ الغَواني قَبلَ مَطمَحِ ناظِري
يُطَبَّقُ في أوصالِهِ ويُصَمِّمُ	تَعَرَّضَ سَيفُ الدَّولَةِ الدَّهرَ كُلَّهُ
وَبانَ لَهُ حتّى على البَدرِ مِيسَمُ	فَجازَلَهُ حتّى على الشَّمسِ حِكمَةً
فإن شاءَ حازُوها وإن شاءَ سَلَّمُوا	كَأَنَّ العِدى في أَرضِهِم خُلَفاؤُهُ
ولا رُسُلٌ إلّا الخَميسُ العَرَمرَمُ	ولا كُتبَ إلّا المَشرَفيّةُ عِندَهُ
وَلَم يَخلُ مِن شُكرٍ لَهُ مَن لَهُ فَمُ	فَلَم يَخلُ مِن نَصرٍ لَهُ مَن لَهُ يَدٌ
وَلَم يَخلُ دينارٌ وَلَم يَخلُ دِرهَمُ	ولَم يَخلُ مِن أَسمائِهِ عُودُ مِنبَرِ
بَصيرٌ وَما بَينَ الشُّجاعَينِ مُظلِمُ	ضُروبٌ وَما بَينَ الحُسامَينِ ضَيِّقٌ
نُجومٌ لَهُ مِنهُنَّ وَردٌ وَأَدهَمُ	تُباري نُجومَ القَذفِ في كُلِّ لَيلَةٍ
وَمِن قَصدِ المُرّانِ ما لا يُقَوَّمُ	يَطَأنَ مِنَ الأَبطالِ مَن لا حَمَلنَهُ
وَهُنَّ مَعَ النّينانِ في الماءِ عُوَّمُ	فَهُنَّ مَعَ السِّيدانِ في البَرِّ عُسَّلٌ
وَهُنَّ مَعَ العِقبانِ في النِّيقِ حُوَّمُ	وَهُنَّ مَعَ الغِزلانِ في الوادِ كُمَّنُ
بِهِنَّ وفي لَبّاتِهِنَّ يُحَطَّمُ	إذا حَلَبَ النّاسَ الوَشيجَ فإنَّهُ
وَبَذلِ اللُّهى والحَمدِ والمَجدِ مُعلَمُ	بِغُرَّتِهِ في الحَربِ والسِّلمِ والحِجى
ويَقضي لَهُ بالسَّعدِ مَن لا يُنَجِّمُ	يُقِرُّ لَهُ بالفَضلِ مَن لا يَوَدُّهُ
يُطالِبُهُ بالرَّدِّ عادَ وجُرحُهُ	أَجارَ على الأَيّامِ حتّى ظَنَنتُهُ
وَهَديِاً لِهذا السَّيلِ ماذا يُؤَمِّمُ	ضَلالاً لِهذِي الرّيحِ ماذا تُريدُهُ
فَيُخبِرَهُ عَنكَ الحَديدُ المُثَلَّمُ	أَلَم يَسأَلِ الوَبلُ الَّذي رامَ ثِنيَنا
تَلَقّاهُ أَعلى مِنهُ كَعباً وَأَكرَمُ	ولَمّا تَلَقّاكَ السَّحابُ بِصَوبِهِ
وَبَلَّ ثِياباً طالَما بَلَّها الدَّمُ	فَباشَرَ وَجهاً طالَما باشَرَ القَنا
مِنَ الشَّأمِ يَتلُو الحاذِقَ المُتَعَلِّمُ	تَلاكَ وَبَعضُ الغَيثِ يَتبَعُ بَعضَهُ
وَجَشَّمَهُ الشَّوقُ الَّذي تَتَجَشَّمُ	فَزارَ الَّتي زارَت بِكَ الخَيلُ قَبرَها
على الفارِسِ المُرخى الذَّوابَةِ مِنهُمُ	وَلَمّا عَرَضتَ الجَيشَ كانَ بَهاؤُهُ
يَسيرُ بِهِ طَودٌ مِنَ الخَيلِ أَيهَمُ	حَوالَيهِ بَحرٌ لِلتَّجافيفِ مائِجٌ
يُجَمِّعُ أَشتاتَ الجِبالِ ويَنظِمُ	تَساوَت بِهِ الأَقطارُ حتّى كَأنَّهُ

Ibn Abdallah's love is nearer for by it
    A beautiful memory begins and ends in him
I yielded to maids before my eyes' desire
    Was a vision to dwarf others and to enhance
Saif al Daula confronts an entire age
    He strikes at its limbs and he penetrates
His rule rises until it is above the sun
    His beauty shines until it is above the moon
As if his foes in the lands were his vicars
    When he desires they hold them or yield
No letters but the Mashrafi for him, no
    Messengers but battalions of huge armies
Not lacking in aid from any with a hand
    Or lacking in thanks from any with a mouth
Nor does the pulpit wood lack his names
    Nor do the dinars or dirhams fail for them
Striker if what between swords is thin
    Foresighted when darkness hits the brave
His comets compete as shooting stars
    Every night the red and black among them
They trample heroes they did not bear
    Spear fragments that could not withstand
They are running with wolves on land
    They swim width the big fish in the ocean
They are hid with gazelles in a valley
    They hover with eagles among the peaks
When men obtain the ashwood then he
    With them and their breasts smashes out
By his eminence in war, peace, word
    Lavish giving, praise and known glory
He who won't love him grants his good
    He who knows no stars allots blessings
He guards against days till I think
    Aad and Jurham will seek their return
Confusion on the wind that desires
    Guidance for a shower that it intends
Did not the flood try to stop us
    And a blunted sword informed of you?
When a cloud meets you in downpour
    It meets higher than it in nobler breast
It works on roads when he bears lance
    It wets clothes soon as blood wets them
It hits you as shower follows shower
    From Syria like student follows teacher
It visits her tomb that the horse visits
    Love burdens him she was burdened by
If you lead an army its pride is for them
    In a rider with those floating turban ends
Around him a sea of undulating water
    A mountain of horse goes raging along
All regions equal to him so he must
    Gather jumbled peaks to give them order

مِنَ الضَّربِ سَطرٌ بِالأَسِنَّةِ مُعجَمُ	وَكُلُّ فَتىً لِلحَربِ فَوقَ جَبينِهِ
وَعَينيهِ مِن تَحتِ التَّريكَةِ أَرقَمُ	يَمُدُّ يَدَيهِ في المُفاضَةِ ضَيغَمُ
وَما لَبِسَتهُ وَالسِّلاحُ المُسَمَّمُ	كَأَجناسِها راياتُها وَشِعارُها
يُشيرُ إِلَيها مِن بَعيدٍ فَتَفهَمُ	وَأَدَّبَها طولُ القِتالِ فَطَرفُهُ
وَيُسمِعُها لَحظاً وَما يَتَكَلَّمُ	تُجاوِبُهُ فِعلاً وَما تَسمَعُ الوَحى
تَرِقُّ لِمَيِّ فارِقينَ وَتَرحَمُ	تُجانِفُ عَن ذاتِ اليَمينِ كَأَنَّها
دَرَت أَيَّ سورَيها الضَّعيفُ المُهَدَّمُ	وَلَو زَحَمَتها بِالمَناكِبِ زَحمَةً
مِنَ الدَّمِ يُسقى أَو مِنَ اللَّحمِ يُطعَمُ	عَلى كُلِّ طاوٍ تَحتَ طاوٍ كَأَنَّهُ
فَكُلُّ حِصانٍ دارِعٌ مُتَلَثِّمُ	لَها في الوَغى زِيُّ الفَوارِسِ فَوقَها
وَلَكِنَّ صَدمَ الشَّرِّ بِالشَّرِّ أَحزَمُ	وَما ذاكَ بُخلاً بِالنُّفوسِ عَلى القَنا
وَأَنَّكَ مِنها؟ ساءَ ما تَتَوَهَّمُ	أَتَحسَبُ بيضَ الهِندِ أَصلَكَ أَصلُها
مِنَ التِّيهِ في أَغمادِها تَتَبَسَّمُ	إِذا نَحنُ سَمَّيناكَ خِلنا سُيوفَنا
فَيَرضى وَلَكِن يَجهَلونَ وَتَحلُمُ	وَلَم نَرَ مَلكاً قَطُّ يُدعى بِدونِهِ
مِنَ العَيشِ تُعطي مَن تَشاءُ وَتَحرِمُ	أَخَذتَ عَلى الأَرواحِ كُلَّ ثَنِيَّةٍ
وَلا رِزقَ إِلّا مِن يَمينِكَ يُقسَمُ	فَلا مَوتَ إِلّا مِن سِنانِكَ يُتَّقى

(١٨٦)

«من المتقارب»

ضربت لسيف الدولة خيمة عظيمة فهبّت ريح شديدة فسقطت فقال:

وَتَشمَلُ مَن دَهرَها يَشمَلُ	أَيَقدَحُ في الخَيمَةِ العُذَّلُ
مُحالٌ لَعَمرُكَ ما تَسأَلُ	وَتَعلو الَّذي زُحَلٌ تَحتَهُ
وَما فَصُّ خاتَمِهِ يَذبُلُ	فَلِمْ لا تَلومُ الَّذي لامَها
وَيَركُضُ في الواحِدِ الجَحفَلُ	تَضيقُ بِشَخصِكَ أَرجاؤُها
وَيُركَزُ فيها القَنا الذُبَّلُ	وَتَقصُرُ ما كُنتَ في جَوفِها
كَأَنَّ البِحارَ لَها أَنمُلُ	وَكَيفَ تَقومُ عَلى راحَةٍ
وَحَمَّلتَ أَرضَكَ ما تَحمِلُ	فَلَيتَ وَقارَكَ فَرَّقتَهُ

Each youthful warrior has on his brow
    A writing of blows spelled with spears
A lion extends his arm in chain mail
    His eyes beneath a visor are as snakes
As their races their flags and the hair
    What they wear and poisoned weapons
Long wars taught them and his glance
    Signals to them and they understand it
They respond by acts but hear nothing
    They hear a look but he does not speak
They shun the right hand as H they
    Pitied Mayyafariqin and felt sympathy
If they shove others with shoulders
    They know which of two walls is weakest
For each thin belly under thin belly
    He pours bloody drink, feeds with flesh
Rider's dress in war is theirs and
    Every war horse has armor to veil it
It's no greed of soul faced by lance
    Rather firmest push to evil with an evil
Do Indian swords feel your root theirs?
    You from them? wrong what they fancy
If we name you we think our swords
    Due to pride smile in their scabbards
We see no king claim anything near him
    He's happy and pities but they are witless
You take from these souls every path
    To give what you please and you refuse
No death except what your spear sends
    No provision but what your hand shares

186
A large tent was set up for Saif al Daula at Mayyafariqin and the folk gathered in the places nearby. But a violent wind came up and the tent fell and the folk talked about the fall of it.
(Tripping lu)

Is blame any use with respect to a tent
    Could she cover one who guarded her fate?
Was she above one who has Zuhal below
    A place, by your life, she never has asked for!
Why didn't she rebuke him who blamed her
    The stone of his seal ring wasn't like Yadhbul
Her space too narrow for your person
    Though a huge army lined up alongside it
She was too low when you were inside
    Though pliant lances were upright within her
And how could she stand over a hand
    Whose fingers are as it were the ocean?
Would you could part with your dignity
    And load your land with what you now carry

فَصارَ الأَنامُ بِهِ سادَةً	وَسُدْتَهُمْ بِالَّذي يَفْضُلُ
رَأَت لَوْنَ نورِكَ في لَونِها	كَلَونِ الغَزالَةِ لا يُغْسَلُ
وَأَنَّ لَها شَرَفاً باذِخاً	وَأَنَّ الخِيامَ بِها تَخجَلُ
فَلا تُنكِرَنَّ لَها صَرعَةً	فَمِن فَرَحِ النَفسِ ما يَقتُلُ
وَلَو بُلِّغَ النّاسُ ما بُلِّغَت	لَخانَتهُمْ حَولَكَ الأَرجُلُ
وَلَمّا أَمَرتَ بِتَطنيبِها	أَشيعَ بِأَنَّكَ لا تَرحَلُ
فَما اعتَمَدَ اللهُ تَقويضَها	وَلَكِنْ أَشارَ بِما تَفعَلُ
وَعَرَّفَ أَنَّكَ مِنْ هَمِّهِ	وَأَنَّكَ في نَصْرِهِ تَرفُلُ
فَما العانِدونَ وَما أَتْلَوا	وَمَا الحاسِدونَ وما قَوْلُوا
هُمْ يَطلُبونَ فَما أَدرَكوا	وَهُمْ يَكْذِبونَ فَمَنْ يَقبَلُ
وَهُمْ يَتَمَنَّونَ ما يَشتَهونَ	وَمَن دونِهِ حَدُّكَ المُقبِلُ
وَمَلْمومَةً زَرَدٌ ثَوبُها	وَلَكِنَّهُ بِالقَنا مُخمَلُ
يُفاجِئُ جَيشاً بِها حَيْنُهُ	وَيُنْذِرُ جَيشاً بِها القَسطَلُ
جَعَلتُكَ في القَلْبِ لي عُدَّةً	لِأَنَّكَ في اليَدِ لا تُجعَلُ
لَقَد رَفَعَ اللهُ مِن دَولَةٍ	لَها مِنكَ يا سَيفَها مُنصُلُ
فَإِن طُبِعَت قَبلَكَ المُرهَفاتُ	فَإِنَّكَ مِن قَبْلِها المِقصَلُ
وَإِن جادَ قَبلَكَ قَومٌ مَضَوا	فَإِنَّكَ في الكَرَمِ الأَوَّلُ
وَكَيْفَ تُقَصِّرُ عَنْ غايَةٍ	وَأُمُّكَ مِن لَيْثِها مُشْبِلُ
وَقَدْ وَلَدَتْكَ فَقالَ الوَرى	أَلَم تَكُنِ الشَّمسُ لا تُنجَلُ
فَتَبّاً لِدينِ عَبيدِ النُجومِ	وَمَن يَدَّعي أَنَّها تَعْقِلُ
وَقَدْ عَضَرَفَتْكَ فَما بالُها	تَراكَ تَراها وَلا تَنزِلُ
وَلَو بِتِّما عِندَ قَدْرَيْكُما	لَضَبَّت وَأَعلاكُما الأَسْفَلُ
أَنَلْتَ عِبادَكَ ما أَمَّلَت	أَنالَكَ رَبُّكَ ما تَأمُلُ

Men would become princes with that
    And you rule them with what you had left of it
She sees her color's hue in her light
    Which the sun's color does not wash away
She had such a tremendous height
    That other tents were ashamed to compare
They should not repudiate her fall
    For some joys exist that kill the soul
If men attain what she attained
    Legs would betray them as they go to you
When you gave order for her pitching
    The news spread that you were not going
God did not intend her to collapse
    But he gave the hint what you should do
He revealed you as of his persuasion
    That you in his aid were trailing the skirt
Who are these strays who have no root
    Who are the jealous ones with their gossip?
They are seeking but do not attain
    They are telling lies but who believes?
They imagine what they are greedy for
    But your gracious bounty is beyond that
A squadron in chain mail is your dress
    Even when the velvet is made of spears
With them his ruin surprises one army
    And the dust of them warns yet another
I made provision for you in my heart
    But you did not take it with any hand
God indeed raised up the kingdom
    From you, O her sword, who is its point
If the edges were shaped before you
    Yet you before them were one who cut
If folk now gone excelled before you
    Yet you were the first in all generosity
How could come short of any goal?
    Your mother bore a cub from the lion
She bore you indeed and men said:
    Isn't the sun incapable of any bearing?
Woe to a slave's faith in the stars
    And he who claims they are rational
They know you but have no minds
    They see you see them but do not bow
If you spend night in your places
    The highest of you spends it as lowest
You give your servants what they want
    May your Lord give you what you hope

(١٨٧)

«من الوافر»

قال وقد صف سيف الدولة الجيش في منزل يعرف بالسنبوس:

وَنارٌ في العَدُوِّ لَها أجيجُ	لهذا اليَومِ بَعدَ غدٍ أريجُ
وَتَسلَمُ في مَسالِكِها الحَجيجُ	تَبيتُ بها الحَواضِنُ آمِناتٍ
فَرائِسَ أيُّها الأَسَدُ المَهيجُ	فلا زالَت عُداتُكَ حيثُ كانَت
وَأنتَ بِغَيرِ سَيفِكَ لا تَعيجُ	عَرَفتُكَ والصُّفوفُ مُعَبَّآتٌ
إذا يَسجُو فكَيفَ إذا يَموجُ	وَوَجهُ البَحرِ يُعرَفُ مِن بَعيدٍ
إذا مُلِئَت مِنَ الرَّكضِ الفُروجُ	بِأرضٍ تَهلِكُ الأَشواطُ فيها
فَتَفديهِ رَعيَّتُهُ العُلوجُ	تُحاوِلُ نَفسَ مَلكِ الرّومِ فيها
وَنحنُ نُجومُها وَهيَ البُروجُ	أَبِالغَمَراتِ تُوعِدُنا النَّصارى
إذا لاقى وَعارَتُهُ لَجوجُ	وَفينا السَّيفُ حَملَتهُ صَدوقٌ
وَيَكثُرُ بِالدُّعاءِ لَهُ الضَّجيجُ	نَعَوِّذُهُ مِنَ الأَعيانِ بَأساً
بِما حَكَمَ القَواضِبُ الوَشيجُ	رَضينا والدُّمُستُقُ غَيرُ راضٍ
وَإن يُحجِم فَموعِدُنا الخَليجُ	فَإِن يُقدِم فَقَد زُرنا سَمَندو

(١٨٨)

«من البسيط»

قال وقد ظفر بسيف الدولة في هذه الغزوة:

إن قاتَلوا جَبُنوا أو حدَّثوا شَجُعوا	غَيري بِأكثرِ هذا النّاسِ يَنخَدِعُ
وَفي التَّجارِبِ بَعدَ الغَيِّ ما يَزَعُ	أَهلُ الحَفيظَةِ إلّا أن تُجَرِّبَهُم
أنّ الحَياةَ كَما لا تَشتَهي طَبَعُ	وَما الحَياةُ ونفسي بَعدَما عَلِمَت
أَنفُ العَزيزِ بِقَطعِ العِزِّ يُجتَدَعُ	لَيسَ الجَمالُ لِوَجهٍ صَحَّ مازِنُهُ
وَأَترُكُ الغَيثَ في غِمدي وَأَنتَجِعُ	أَأَطرَحُ المَجدَ عَن كِتفي وأَطلُبُهُ
دَواءُ كُلِّ كَريمٍ أو هيَ الوَجَعُ	وَالمَشرَفِيَّةُ لا زالَت مُشَرَّفَةً

187
He spoke and Saif al Daula rode from a place known as Sanbus in the direction of Samandu in the year 339.
(Exuberant ju)

Today after a time perfumes will rise
    And fires against the enemy in flames
Chaste women safe at night from them
    And pilgrims with peace in their paths
Your rage did not cease wherever you
    Saw prey O lion who has been stirred up
I knew you, ranks were set in order
    You had no care except for your sword
The sea's ways are known from afar
    If it is quiet but how if the waves surge?
In lands where weary travel ruins
    When the crotches fester from running
They seek the king of Rum himself
    His foreign troops are ransom for him
Do Christians threaten us with war'
    We are their stars in the constellation
With us a sword whose edge is true
    Whose war is resolute when he moves
We seek safety in him from evil eyes
    Uproar increases with prayers for him
Domesticus pleases us without joy
    Where the sword and ash wood judge
If he comes we visit him at Samandu
    If he flees our bond is at the Khalij sea

188
He spoke praising him and recalling the battle in which the Muslims suffered a reverse near the Lake of al-Hadath. He described the event little by little and in detail.
(Outspread u)

I am not deceived by most of these men
    If they fight they run, if they talk they boast
Brave folk except when one tests them
    In the test after mistakes they do not hold
Life, my soul, is nothing after it knows
    That is foul in a way that you don't want
Beauty of face is not in straight noses
    A proud nose cut off from honor is mangled
Do I toss glory away and yet want it
    Can I leave help in sheath and seek food?
A Mashrafi sword ceases not from honor
    A cure for every noble man or a disease

في الـدَّرْبِ والـدَّمُ في أعطافِـهِ دُفَـعُ	وفارسُ الخَيْلِ مَنْ خفَّتْ فوقَرَها
وأغضَبْتُـهُ وَمَـا في لَفْظِـهِ قَـذَعُ	فأَوْحَدَتْـهُ وما في قلْبِـهِ قَلَـقٌ
والجَيْـشُ بـابنِ أبي الهَيْجاءِ يمتنـعُ	بالجَيْشِ تَمْنَـعُ السَّاداتُ كلُّهُـمُ
على الشَّكيمِ وأَدْنى سَيْرِها سَرَعُ	قـادَ المَقانِبَ أقصَى شُرْبِها نَهَـلٌ
كالمَوْتِ ليسَ لَـهُ رِيٌّ وَلا شِبَـعُ	لا يَعْتَقي بَلَـدٌ مَسْراهُ عَـنْ بَلَـدٍ
تَشْقَى بـهِ الـرُّومُ والصُّلْبانُ والبِيَـعُ	حتى أقـامَ على أرْباضِ خَرْشَنَةٍ
والنَّهْبِ مَـا جَمَعُـوا والنَّارِ مَا زَرَعُـوا	للسَّبْيِ مَـا نَكَحُـوا والقَتْلِ مَا وَلَـدُوا
لَـهُ المَنابِـرِ مَشْهُـوداً بهـا الجُمَـعُ	مُخَلًّـى لَـهُ المَـرْجُ مَنْصُوباً بصارِخَـةٍ
حتى تَكـادُ على أحْيائِهِـمْ تَقَـعُ	يُطَمِّـعُ الطَّيـرَ فيهِـمْ طُـولُ أكْلِهِـمُ
على مَحَبَّتِـهِ الشَّرْعُ الـذي شَرَعُـوا	وَلَـوْ رآهُ حَوارِيُوهُـمْ لَبَنَـوْا
سُـودُ الغَمامِ فَظَنّـوا أنَّهـا قَـزَعُ	لامَ الدُّمُسْتُقُ عَيْنَيْـهِ وقَـدْ طَلَعَـتْ
على الجِيـادِ الّتي حَوْلَيْهَـا جَـذَعُ	فيها الكُمـاةُ الّتـي مَفطومُها رَجُـلٌ
وفي حَناجِرِها مِـن آلِـسٍ جُـرَعُ	يَـذْري اللُّقانُ غُبـاراً في مَناخِرِهـا
فالطَّعْنُ يَفْتَـحُ في الأجْـوافِ مـا يَسَعُ	كأنَّهـا تَتَلَقَّـاهُـمْ لِتَسْلُكَهُـمْ
مِـنَ الأسِنَّـةِ نـارٌ والقَنـا شَمَـعُ	تَهْـدي نَواظِرَهـا والحَـرْبُ مُظْلِمَـةٌ
على نُفوسِـهِمُ المُقْـوَرَّةِ المُـزَعُ	دونَ السِّهـامِ ودُونَ القِـرنِ طافحَـةٌ
أظْمَى تُفارِقُ مِنْـهُ أُخْتَهـا الضِّلَـعُ	إذا دعـا العِلْجُ عِلْجـاً حالَ بَيْنَهُمَـا
إذ فاتَهُـنَّ وأمضَـى منـهُ مُنْصَـرَعُ	أحَـلُّ مِـنْ وَلَـدِ الفُقَّـاسِ مُنْكَتِـفٌ
نَجـا ومِنْهُـنَّ في أحْشـائِهِ فَـزَعُ	وَمَـا نَجـا مِنْ شِفـارِ البِيضِ مُنْفَلِـتٌ
ويَشْرَبُ الخَمْـرَ حَـوْلاً وهوَ مُمْتَقـعُ	يُمـاشِـرُ الأمْـنَ دَهْـراً وَهـوَ مُخْتَبَـلُ
للبـاتِراتِ أميـنٌ مَـا لَـهُ وَرَعُ	كَـمْ مِنْ حُشاشَـةٍ بطريـقٍ تضَمَّنَهـا
ويَطـرُدُ النَّـوْمَ عَنْـهُ حيـنَ يَضْطَجِـعُ	يُقاتِـلُ الخَطْـوَ عنْـهُ حيـنَ يَطْلُبُـهُ
حتى يَقـولَ لها عُـودي فَتَنْدَفِـعُ	تَغْـدو المَنايـا فَـلا تَنْفَـكُّ واقِفَـةً
خانوا الأميـرَ فجازاهُـمْ بما صَنَعُـوا	قَـلْ للدُّمُسْتُـقِ إنَّ المُسْـلمينَ لَكُـمْ
كـأنَّ قَتْلاكُـمْ إيّـاهُـمْ فجَعُـوا	وَجَدْتُمُوهُـمْ نِيامـاً في دِمـائِكُمْ
مِنَ الأعادي وإنْ هَمّـوا بهِمْ نَزَعُـوا	ضَعْفـى تَعِـفُّ الأيـادي عَـنْ مِثالِهِـم
فَلَيْـسَ يأكُـلُ إلَّا المَيْتَـةَ الضَّبُـعُ	لا تَحسَبـوا مَنْ أسَرْتُم كـانَ ذا رَمَـقٍ

A horseman as she rushes, steadies her
    In glens, and blood on her side in showers
She leaves him but no fear in his heart
    She riles him but no baseness in his word
Princes defend themselves by armies
    But the army is defended by Ibn Abu Haija
One drink leads troops to farther drink
    Speed on the bit but the reins held tight
No town hinders his journey to another
    Like death no water and no fodder are his
Till he comes to walls of Kharshana
    Rum and crosses and churches regret it
The married as slaves, the babes dead
    The savings plunder and the harvest fire
Marj is left to him setting up pulpits
    At Sarikha for his witnessing on Friday
He feeds birds with them, long the meal
    Until they almost fall upon the living ones
If the disciples saw him they'd set up
    For love of him a sect that would be legal
Domesticus blames his eyes, clouds
    Appear, they think of dark rain clouds
In them warrior weanlings and men
    As palm trunks on two year old horses
Luqan winnowed dust in their noses
    In their throats the swallowed Halys
They met them as roads to tread on
    Jousting opened bellies they widened
They guided eyes in a dark battle
    Points were fires and lances candles
Before summer heat, before the cold
    The swift lean ones overrun their souls
When pagan calls to pagan a lance
    Intervenes as a rib parts from its sister
The best sons of Phocas shackled
    He passes them, braver than he dead
What escaped from bright swords
    Flight saved, terror is in their hearts
He took sanctuary a while, went mad
    Drank wine for a year but still was pale
Many a patrician soul was pledged
    To a sword secured while he abstained
It hindered his waking if he tried it
    It drove off sleep if he attempted to lie
Death appears forever waiting till
    He says: Return! then it moves away
Tell Domesticus: One who yielded
    Betrayed the Amir who repays the deed
You found them sleeping in your blood
    As if their violent defeat distressed them
Feeble, foes abstain from their likes
    As foes, if they want them they retreat

أَسْدٌ تَمُرُّ فُرادَى لَيسَ تَجْتَمِعُ	هَلّا عَلى عَقِبِ الوادي وَقَد طَلَعَت
وَالضَّرْبُ يَأخُذُ فَوقَ مَا يَدَعُ	تَشُقُّكُم بِفَتاها كُلُّ سَلْهَبَةٍ
لِكَي يَكونوا بِلا فَسْلٍ إذا رَجَعوا	وَإنَّما عَرَّضَ اللهُ الجُنودَ بِكُم
وَكُلُّ غازٍ لِسَيفِ الدَّولَةِ التَّبَعُ	فَكُلُّ غَزوٍ إلَيْكُم بَعدَ ذا فَلَهُ
وَأَنتَ تَخْلُقُ ما تَأتي وَتَبْتَدِعُ	تَمْشِي الكِرامُ عَلى آثارِ غَيرِهِمِ
وَكانَ غَيرُكَ فيهِ العاجِزُ الضَّرَعُ	وَهَل يَشينُكَ وَقتٌ كُنتَ فارِسَهُ
فَلَيسَ يَرفَعُهُ شَيءٌ وَلا يَضَعُ	مَن كانَ فَوقَ مَحَلِّ الشَّمسِ موضِعُهُ
إنْ كانَ أَسْلَمَها الأَصحابُ وَالشِّيَعُ	لَم يُسلِمِ الكَرَّ في الأَعقابِ مُهْجَتَهُ
فَلَم يَكُنْ لِدَنيءٍ عِندَها طَمَعُ	لَيْتَ المُلوكَ عَلى الأَقدارِ مُعْطِيَةٌ
وَأَنْ قَرَعْتَ حَبيبَكَ البيضُ فَاسْتَمِعوا	رَضِيَتَ مِنهُم بِأَن زُرْتَ الوَغى فَرَأَوا
مَن كُنتَ بِغَيرِ الصِّدقِ تَنتَفِعُ	لَقَد أَباحَكَ غِشّاً في مُعامَلَةٍ
وَأَرضُهُم لَكَ مُصطافٌ وَمُرتَبَعُ	الدَّهرُ مُعتَذِرٌ وَالسَّيفُ مُنتَظِرٌ
وَلَو تَنَصَّرَ فيها الأَعصَمُ الصَّدَعُ	وَما الجِبالُ لِنَصرانٍ بِحامِيَةٍ
حَتّى بَلَوْتُكَ وَالأَبطالُ تَمتَصِعُ	وَما حَمِدتُكَ في هَولٍ ثَبَتَّ بِهِ
وَقَد يُظَنُّ جَباناً مَنْ بِهِ زَمَعُ	فَقَد يُظَنُّ شُجاعاً مَن بِهِ خَرَقٌ
وَلَيسَ كُلُّ ذَواتِ المِخْلَبِ السَّبُعُ	إنَّ السِّلاحَ جَميعُ النّاسِ تَحمِلُهُ

(١٨٩)

«من الطويل»

عزم سيف الدولة على لقاء الروم في النبوس سنة أربعين وثلاث مئة (٩٥١م) وبلغه أن العدو في أربعين ألفاً فتهيبهم أصحابه فأنشد أبو الطيب:

وَنَسأَلُ فيها غَيرَ ساكِنِها الإذْنا	نَزورُ دياراً ما نُحِبُّ لَها مَغنى
عَلَيها الكُماةُ المُحسِنونَ بِها ظَنّا	نَقودُ إلَيها الآخِذاتِ لَنا المَدى
وَنُرضِي الَّذي يُسَمّى الإلَهَ وَلا يُكْنى	وَنُصفي الَّذي يُكْنى أَبا الحَسَنِ الهَوى

Think not those you took have breath
    For the jackal will eat only carcasses
Halloo on the wadi banks where lions
    Come and pass one by one, not prides
Each long horse splits you with lances
    A blow takes more of you than it leaves
God sets soldiers over against you
    They are without stain when they return
Every attack on you after this is his
    Every attacker Saif al Daula's follower
Nobles walk in footsteps not their own
    You created what comes as originator
Can time harm you if you are the hero?
    In it others are weaklings and suckers
His place is above the sun's orbit
    Nothing new exalts or abases him
Often attacked in mountains his blood
    Not betrayed though allies do surrender
Would kings were donors, knew good
    So there were no temptation to the evil
You prize those who watch as you strike
    And strike with lucid sword as they listen
Some show you frauds in a province
    Without veracity if you make use of that
Fate makes excuses but sword waits
    Their lands yours in summer and spring
Nazarene hills cannot protect them
    Even if sturdy goats become Christians
I praise you not for dread you endure
    Until I prove you and the heroes fight
Some think ibn every is reckless
    Some see cowardice if one shudders
As for armor all mankind can wear it
    But not everyone with claws is a lion

189

He spoke and Saif al-Daula had just made an attack on the Domesticus in the year 340.
(Long na)

We visit camps and homes we don't love
    We ask permission of no inhabitants here
We lead those who take us to this goal
    Upon them warriors who approve of them
We cherish him called Abu Hasan Hawa
    We accept him called God, no other name

إذا ما تَرَكْنا أَرْضَهُمْ خلفَنا عُدْنا	وَقَدْ عَلِمَ الرُّومُ الشَّقِيّونَ أَنَّـا
لِيسنا إلى حاجاتِنا الضَّربَ والطَّعنا	وأَنّا إذا ما المَوتُ صَرَّحَ في الوَغى
إلَيْنا وقُلْنا للسُّيوفِ هَلُمّنا	قَصَدنا لَهُ قَصْدَ الحَبيبِ لِقاءَهُ
تَكدَّسنَ من هَنّا عَلَينا ومَن هَنّا	وَخَيلٍ حَشَوْناها الأسِنَّةَ بَعدَما
فَلَمّا تَعارَفْنا ضُرِبنَ بِها عَنّا	ضُرِبنَ إِلَيْنا بالسِّياطِ جَهالَةً
نُبارِ إلى ما تَشتَهي يَدَكَ اليُمنى	تَعَدَّ القُرى والمَسُّ بِنا الجَيشَ لَمسَةً
ونَحنُ أُناسٌ نُتبِعُ البارِدَ السُّخنا	فَقَد بَرَدَت فَوقَ اللُّقانِ دِماؤُهم
فَدَعنا نَكُن قَبلَ الضِّرابِ القَنا اللُّدنا	وَإن كُنتَ سَيفَ الدَّولَةِ العَضبَ فيهِمِ
وأَنتَ الَّذي لَو أَنَّهُ وَحدَهُ أَغنى	فَنَحنُ الأُلى لا نَأتَلي لَكَ نُصرَةً
ومَن قال لا أَرْضى من العَيشِ بِالأَدنى	يَقيكَ الرَّدى مَن يَبتَغي عِندَ العُلى
ولَم يَكُ لِلدُّنيا ولا أَهلِها مَعنى	فَلَو لاكَ لَم تَجرِ الدِّماءُ وَلا اللُّهى
ومَا الأَمنُ إِلّا ما رَآهُ الفَتى أَمنا	ومَا الخَوفُ إِلّا مَا تَخَوَّفَهُ الفَتى

(١٩٠)

«من الطويل»

قال وقد أراد سيف الدولة قصد خرشنة
فعاقه الثلج عن ذلك:

وَإِنَّ ضَجيعَ الخَودِ مِنّي لَماجِدُ	عَواذِلُ ذاتِ الخالِ في حَواسِدُ
وَيَعصي الهَوى في طَيفِها وَهوَ راقِدُ	يَرُدُّ يَداً عَن ثَوبِها وَهوَ قادِرُ
مُحِبٌّ لَها في قُربِهِ مُتَباعِدُ	مَتى يَشتَفي مِن لاعِجِ الشَّوقِ في الحَشا
فَلِمَ تَتَصَبّاكَ الحِسانُ الخَرائِدُ	إذا كُنتَ تَخشى العارَ في كُلِّ خَلوَةٍ
ومَلَّ طَبيبي جانِبي والعَوائِدُ	أَلَحَّ عَلَيَّ السُّقمُ حَتّى أَلِفتُهُ
جَوادي وهَل تَشجي الجِيادَ المَعاهِدُ	مَرَرتُ عَلى دارِ الحَبيبِ فَحَمحَمَت
سَقَتها ضَريبَ الشَّولِ فيهِ الوَلائِدُ	وَما تُنكِرُ الدَّهماءُ مِن رَسمِ مَنزِلٍ
تُطارِدُني عَن كَونِهِ وَأُطارِدُ	أَهُمُّ بِشَيءٍ والَّلَيالي كَأَنَّها

The Rum, schismatics, know that we
    As we leave their land behind will return
When death lets down its veil in war
    We take up our cause in blow and thrust
We go to it with lover's aim whose tryst
    Is with us as we say to swords: Onward!
Many a home we strike with spears as
    They come from hither and yon against us
Beaten to us with whips unwitting when
    They know us they are whipped from us
Go past towns and take an army for us
    You arrive at what your right hand wants
Indeed their blood cools above Luqan
    We are men who follow the cool with heat
If you are Saif al-Daula keen for them
    Allow us to be light lances before the cut
We are ones who won't withhold aid
    You are one who alone has no need of it
He keeps you from death wanting glory
    And says: I'm not content with a base life
But for you no blood flows or bounty
    Nor in world or its people any meaning
For dread is nothing but what one fears
    Safety only what a hero knows as secure

190
He spoke and Saif al Daula intended to attack Kharshana but the snow kept him from it.
(Long du)

Critics of one who has a mole envy me
    Indeed my fine bedfellow is most noble
His hand kept from her dress and yet
    He denied her love's dream when asleep
If a lover recovers from burning love
    Within, parting is in his nearness to her
Since you feared shame in solitude
    Why would the pretty woman beguile you?
Illness stays with me till we are pals
    My doctor and nurse are bored at my side
I pass the beloved's camp and my horse
    Whinnies, why does the place grieve her?
A black isn't ignorant of camp traces
    The girls poured camel's crabber for her
I long for something, it seems my nights
    Drive me from its essence and I feel this

وَحيدٌ مِنَ الخُلّانِ في كُلّ بَلْدَةٍ	إذا عَظُمَ المَطْلوبُ قَلَّ المُساعِدُ
وَتُسْعِدُني في غَمْرَةٍ بَعدَ غَمْرَةٍ	سَبوحٌ لَها مِنها عَلَيْها شَواهِدُ
تَثَنّى عَلى قَدْرِ الطِّعانِ كَأَنَّما	مَفاصِلُها تَحْتَ الرِّماحِ مَراوِدُ
وَأُورِدُ نَفْسي وَالمُهَنَّدَ في يَدي	مَوارِدَ لا يُصْدِرْنَ مَنْ لا يُجالِدُ
وَلَكِنْ إذا لَمْ يَحْمِلِ القَلْبُ كَفَّهُ	عَلى حالَةٍ لَمْ يَحْمِلِ الكَفَّ ساعِدُ
خَليلَيَّ إنّي لا أَرى غَيْرَ شاعِرٍ	فَلِمْ مِنْهُمُ الدَّعْوى وَمِنّي القَصائِدُ
فَلا تَعْجَبا إنَّ السُّيوفَ كَثيرَةٌ	وَلَكِنَّ سَيْفَ الدَّوْلَةِ اليَوْمَ واحِدُ
لَهُ مِنْ كَريمِ الطَّبْعِ في الحَرْبِ مُنْتَضٍ	وَمِنْ عادَةِ الإحْسانِ وَالصَّفْحِ غامِدُ
وَلَمّا رَأَيْتُ النّاسَ دونَ مَحَلِّهِ	تَيَقَّنْتُ أَنَّ الدَّهْرَ لِلنّاسِ ناقِدُ
أَحَقَّهُمْ بِالسَّيْفِ مَنْ ضَرَبَ الطُّلى	وَبِالأَمْنِ مَنْ هانَتْ عَلَيْهِ الشَّدائِدُ
وَأَشْقى بِلادِ اللهِ ما الرّومُ أَهْلُها	بِهذا وَما فيها لِمَجْدِكَ جاحِدُ
شَنَنْتُ بِها الغاراتِ حَتّى تَرَكْتُها	وَجَفْنُ الَّذي خَلْفَ الفُرَنْجَةِ ساهِدُ
مُخَضَّبَةً وَالقَوْمُ صَرْعى كَأَنَّها	وَإنْ لَمْ يَكونوا ساجِدينَ مَساجِدُ
تَنَكَّسُهُمْ وَالسّابِقاتُ جِبالُهُمْ	وَتَطْعَنُ فيهِمْ وَالرِّماحُ المَكايِدُ
وَتَضْرِبُهُمْ هيبًا وَقَدْ سَكَنوا الكُدى	كَما سَكَنَتْ بَطْنَ التُّرابِ الأَساوِدُ
وَتُضْحي الحُصونُ المُشْمَخِرّاتُ في الذُّرى	وَخَيْلُكَ في أَعْناقِهِنَّ قَلائِدُ
عَصَفْنَ بِهِمْ يَوْمَ اللُّقانِ وَسُقْنَهُمْ	بِهَنْريطَ حَتّى ابْيَضَّ بِالسَّبْيِ آمِدُ
وَأَلْحَقْنَ بِالصَّفْصافِ سابورَ فَانْهَوى	وَذاقَ الرَّدى أَهْلاهُما وَالجَلامِدُ
وَغَلَّسَ في الوادي بِهِنَّ مُشَيَّعٌ	مُبارَكُ ما تَحْتَ اللِّثامَيْنِ عابِدُ
فَتًى يَشْتَهي طولَ البِلادِ وَوَقْتُهُ	تَضيقُ بِهِ أَوْقاتُهُ وَالمَقاصِدُ
أَخو غَزَواتٍ ما تَغِبُّ سُيوفُهُ	رِقابَهُمْ إلّا وَسَيْحانُ حامِدُ
فَلَمْ يَبْقَ إلّا مَنْ حَماها مِنَ الظِّبى	لَمى شَفَتَيْها وَالثُّدِيُّ النَّواهِدُ
تُبَكّي عَلَيْهِنَّ البَطاريقُ في الدُّجى	وَهُنَّ لَدَيْنا مُلْقَياتٌ كَواسِدُ
بِذا قَضَتِ الأَيّامُ ما بَيْنَ أَهْلِها	مَصائِبُ قَوْمٍ عِنْدَ قَوْمٍ فَوائِدُ
وَمِنْ شَرَفِ الإقْدامِ أَنَّكَ فيهِمِ	عَلى القَتْلِ مَوْموقٌ كَأَنَّكَ شاكِدُ
وَأَنَّ دَمًا أَجْرَيْتَهُ بِكَ فاخِرٌ	وَأَنَّ فُؤادًا رُعْتَهُ لَكَ حامِدُ

I'm alone among friends in every land
    When a goal is great the helpers are few
A fast swimmer aids me in the deeps
    These things witness she has the power
She bends in the direction of a joust
    As if her joints were bridled to a lance
I bring my soul and sword in hand to
    Water with no return to one who fears
If the heart does not bear its hand in
    An affair, the arm will not bear a hand
My two friends I see only non-poets
    Why do they make claims, I qasidas?
Be not amazed, swords are many
    But Saif al-Daula only rules these days
His noble nature unsheathed in war
    Used to goodness and mercy sheathed
When I saw men short of his rank
    I was sure time had high standards
Worthiest of swords to beat heads
    Of rule that troubles are easy to solve
He plagues God's lands the Rum hold
    By this and those who disown his glories
You set cavalry on them till you leave
    The eyelids beyond Franja are sleepless
Dyed with blood folk are prostrate as if
    They are in a mosque but not praying
You overturn them, horses their hills
    You transfix them with spear stratagems
You cut them apart, they flee to rocks
    Like big snakes live in the dusty hollows
High forts appear on peaks early
    Your horsemen necklaces for the necks
They stormed them at Luqan, drove
    To Hinzit until Amid shone with slaves
They got to Salsaf after Sabur, it fell
    The people tasted death after the stones
A hero went with them late in a valley
    Blessed servant not under a double veil
The youth wanted wider land and time
    His hour and goals are too small for him
War's brother his swords are not slow
    On their necks unless Saihan is frozen
Only those saved from swords remain
    Red were the lips and high their breasts
Patricians weep for them in the dusk
    They are thrown like pillows among us
War for these as with other folk is
    Misfortune to some`, benefit to others
It shows nobility that you by them
    Are beloved in spite of the beating
Blood you made flow is honor to you
    The heart you made fearful praises you

وَلكِنَّ طَبعَ النَفسِ لِلنَفسِ قائِدُ	وَكُلٌّ يَرى طُرقَ الشَجاعَةِ وَالنَدى
لَهَنَّتِ الدُنيا بِأَنَّكَ خالِدُ	نَهَبتَ مِنَ الأَعمارِ ما لَو حَوَيتَهُ
وَأَنتَ لِواءُ الدينِ وَاللَهُ عاقِدُ	فَأَنتَ حُسامُ المُلكِ وَاللَهُ ضارِبُ
تَشابَةَ مَولودٌ كَريمٌ وَوالِدُ	وَأَنتَ أَبو الهَيجاءِ بنُ حَمدانَ يا اِبنَهُ
وَحارِثُ لُقمانٍ وَلُقمانُ راشِدُ	وَحَمدانُ حَمدونٌ وَحَمدونُ حارِثٌ
وَسائِرُ أَملاكِ البِلادِ الزَوائِدُ	أُولَئِكَ أَنيابُ الخِلافَةِ كُلُّها
وَإِن لامَني فيكَ السُهى وَالفَراقِدُ	أُحِبُّكَ يا شَمسَ الزَمانِ وَبَدرَهُ
وَلَيسَ لِأَنَّ العَيشَ عِندَكَ بارِدُ	وَذاكَ لِأَنَّ الفَضلَ عِندَكَ باهِرٌ
وَإِنَّ كَثيرَ الحُبِّ بِالجَهلِ فاسِدُ	فَإِنَّ قَليلَ الحُبِّ بِالعَقلِ صالِحٌ

(١٩١)

«من الطويل»

قال يعزيه بعبده بمال وقد توفي في شهر رمضان سنة أربعين وثلاث مئة:

لَآخُذُ مِن حالاتِهِ بِنَصيبِ	لا يُحزِنِ اللَهُ الأَميرَ فَإِنَّني
بَكى بِعُيونٍ سِرَّها وَقُلوبِ	وَمَن سَرَّ أَهلَ الأَرضِ ثُمَّ بَكى أَسىً
حَبيبٌ إِلى قَلبي حَبيبُ حَبيبي	وَإِنّي وَإِن كانَ الدَفينُ حَبيبَهُ
وَأَعيا دَواءُ المَوتِ كُلَّ طَبيبِ	وَقَد فارَقَ الناسَ الأَحِبَّةُ قَبلَنا
مُنِعنا بِها مِن جيفَةٍ وَذُهوبِ	سُبِقنا إِلى الدُنيا فَلَو عاشَ أَهلُها
وَفارَقَها الماضي فِراقَ سَليبِ	تَمَلَّكَها الآتي تَمَلُّكَ سالِبٍ
وَصَبرِ الفَتى لَو لا لِقاءُ شَعوبِ	وَلا فَضلَ فيها لِلشَجاعَةِ وَالنَدى
حَياةُ أَميرِءٍ خانَتهُ بَعدَ مَشيبِ	وَأَوفى حَياةِ الغابِرينَ لِصاحِبٍ
إِلى كُلِّ تُركِيِّ النِجارِ جَليبِ	لَأَبقى يَماكٌ في حَشاىَ صَبابَةً
وَلا كُلُّ جَفنٍ ضَيِّقٍ بِنَحيبِ	وَما كُلُّ وَجهٍ اِبيَضَّ بِمُبارَكٍ
لَقَد ظَهَرَت في حَدِّ كُلِّ قَضيبِ	لَئِن ظَهَرَت فينا عَلَيهِ كَآبَةٌ
وَفي كُلِّ طِرفٍ كُلَّ يَومٍ رُكوبِ	وَفي كُلِّ قَوسٍ كُلَّ يَومٍ تَناضُلٍ

Everyone sees bravery and bounty
    But a soul's nature is to have a leader
You rob those of life who if spared
    The world would greet with your fame
You are sword's rule, God strikes
    Religion's banner, God the standard
Abu Haija ibn Hamdan O his son
    Best of children and fathers alike
Hamdan is praised, praised al Harith
    Harith is of Luqman who is the guided
All of these were the caliph's teeth
    Other kings of the land were excess
I love you O sun of time and its moon
    Even Suha and Farqad blame me for you
For virtue in you is shining clear
    Not because life with you is untroubled
For a little love to the wise is health
    As much love to the ignorant is corruption

191
He consoled
Saif al-Daula for his slave Yamak
and he died
in the month of Ramadan in the year 340.
(Perfect bi)

May God not grieve the Amir for I
    Must have some share in his condition
He who elated earth's folk wept in pain
    Wept with the eyes and heart he rejoiced
As for me if the dead man was his friend
    A friend of my friend is my heart's friend
Folk before this have parted from lovers
    Death's illness exhausts every physician
We are preceded here, if its folk had
    Lived we would be unable to come or go
An heir seizes with a looter's grip
    Inheritance departs as the plunder goes
No virtue here for brave or bounteous
    No courage for youth without death's face
Complete mortal life for a friend is life
    For a man broken off after the graying
May Yamak remain in my heart as passion
    For every Turk whose root is transplanted
But not every white face has a blessing
    Not every narrow eyelid has an excellence
If sorrow for him shows itself in us
    It also appears in the edge of every sword
In every bow each day it vies in archery
    And in every horse every day it is pressed

وَتَدْعُو لِأَمْرٍ وَهْوَ غَيْرُ مُجيبِ	يَعِزُّ عَلَيْهِ أَنْ يُخِلَّ بِعادَةٍ
نَظَرْتَ إلى ذي لِبْدَتَيْنِ أديبِ	وَكُنتَ إذا أَبْصَرْتَهُ لَكَ قائِماً
فَمِنْ كَفِّ مِتْلافٍ أَغَرَّ وَهُوبِ	فَإِنْ يَكُنِ العِلْقُ النَّفيسُ فَقَدْتَهُ
إذا لَمْ يُعَوَّذْ مَجْدَهُ بِعُيوبِ	كَأَنَّ الرَّدى عادٍ عَلى كُلِّ ماجِدٍ
غَفَلْنا فَلَمْ نَشْعُرْ لَهُ بِذُنوبِ	وَلَوْ لا أَيادي الدَّهْرِ في الجَمْعِ بَيْنَنا
إذا جَعَلَ الإحْسانَ غَيْرَ رَبيبِ	وَلِلتَّرْكُ لِلْأَحْسانِ خَيْرٌ لِمُحْسِنٍ
غَنِيٌّ عَنِ اسْتِعْبادِهِ لِغَريبِ	وَإِنَّ الَّذي أَمْسَتْ نِزارٌ عَبيدَهُ
وَبِالقُرْبِ مِنْهُ مَفْخَراً لِلَبيبِ	كَفى بِصَفاءِ الوُدِّ رِقّاً لِمِثْلِهِ
أَجَلُّ مُثابٍ مِنْ أَجَلِّ مُثيبِ	فَعُوِّضَ سَيْفُ الدَّوْلَةِ الأَجْرَ إِنَّهُ
يُطاعِنُ في ضَنْكِ المَقامِ عَصيبِ	فَتى الخَيْلِ قَدْ بَلَّ النَّجيعُ نُحورَها
فَما خَيْمُهُ إلا غُبارُ حُروبِ	يَعافُ خِيامَ الرَّيْطِ في غَزَواتِهِ
بِشَقِّ قُلوبٍ لا بِشَقِّ جُيوبِ	عَلَيْنا لَكَ الإسْعادُ إِنْ كانَ نافِعاً
وَرُبَّ نَدِيِّ الجَفْنِ غَيْرَ كَئيبِ	فَرُبَّ كَئيبٍ لَيْسَ تَنْدى جُفونُهُ
بَكَيْتَ فَكانَ الضَّحْكُ بَعْدَ قَريبِ	تَسَلَّ بِفِكْرٍ في أَبيكَ فَإِنَّما
بِخُبْثٍ ثَنَتْ فَاسْتَدْبَرَتْهُ بِطيبِ	إذا اسْتَقْبَلَتْ نَفْسُ الكَريمِ مُصابَها
سُكونُ عَزاءٍ أَوْ سُكونُ لُغوبِ	وَلِلواحِدِ المَكْروبِ مِنْ زَفَراتِهِ
فَلَمْ تَجْرِ في آثارِهِ بِغُروبِ	وَكَمْ لَكَ جَدّاً لَمْ تَرَ العَيْنُ وَجْهَهُ
مُعَذَّبَةٌ في حَضْرَةٍ وَمَغيبِ	فَدَتْكَ نُفوسُ الحاسِدينَ فَإِنَّها
وَيَجْهَدُ أَنْ يَأْتي لَها بِضَريبِ	وَفي تَعَبٍ مَنْ يَحْسُدُ الشَّمْسَ نُورَها

(١٩٢)

«من الطويل»

يمدحه ويذكر بناءه مرعش في المحرم سنة ٣٤١ (٩٥٢م)

فَإِنَّكَ كُنْتَ الشَّرْقَ لِلشَّمْسِ وَالغَرْبا	فَدَيْناكَ مِنْ رَبْعٍ وَإِنْ زِدْتَنا كَرْبا
فُؤاداً لِعِرْفانِ الرُّسومِ وَلا لُبّا	وَكَيْفَ عَرَفْنا رَسْمَ مَنْ لَمْ يَدَعْ لَنا

It was hard on him to leave his habit
    If you call for a thing and he can't reply
As I looked at him standing with you
    I saw one with the double mane of skill
He was a rich jewel but you lost him
    From a lavish hand generous in giving
As if death was hostile to each glory
    If he didn't refuge from blame in fame
If it weren't time's gift uniting us we
    Would forget and not feel its crimes
Gifts refused are best for takers if
    One makes a gift without perfection
He for whom Nizar is a servant
    Can do without making slaves of others
He satisfies pure love as slave to him
    And nearness to him by honor of kinship
May Saif al-Daula's loss be repaid
    The best reward for the best rewarder
Hero to horses with gory chests, he
    Jousts in tight spots with a violence
He loathes broad tents in his wars
    His only tent the dust of the battle
Joy for us is duty if useful to you
    In hitting hearts not in rending clothes
Many a grieving one has dry eyes
    Many with copious tears have no grief
Be consoled with thoughts of your kin
    You wept but smiles came soon after
If a noble soul approaches calamity
    In fear it turns and changes to patience
One who finds affliction in his sighs
    Has peace in strength and in fatigue
Many of your kin whom we never saw
    You did not weep by tears in their tracks
Souls of the envious ransom you
    Tortured in both presence and absence
In fatigue one envies the sun's light
    Only strives to attain it by the imitation

192
He spoke
praising Saif al-Daula
and commemorating the building
of Mariash in Mirram in 341.
(Long ba)

We ransom you as camp as agony grows
    For you are dawn to a sun and to its sun and its setting
Can we recall traces of one who left
    Neither heart nor mind to know the traces

نَزَلْنا عَنِ الأكوارِ نَمشي كَرامَةً // لِمَنْ بانَ عَنهُ أنْ نُلِمَّ بِهِ رَكْبا
نَذُمُّ السَّحابَ الغُرَّ في فِعلِهَا بِهِ // وَنُعرِضُ عَنها كُلَّما طَلَعَتْ عَتْبا
وَمَن صَحِبَ الدُّنيا طَويلاً تَقَلَّبَتْ // على عَينِهِ حتى يَرى صِدْقَها كِذبا
وكَيفَ التَذاذي بالأصائِلِ والضُّحى // إذا لم يَعُدْ ذلكَ النَّسيمُ الذي هَبَّا
ذَكَرتُ بِهِ وَصلاً كأنْ لم أفُزْ بِهِ // وَعَيشاً كَأنّي كُنتُ أقطَعُهُ وَثْبا
وفَتّانَةَ العَينَينِ قَتّالَةَ الهَوى // إذا نَفَحَتْ شَيخاً رَوائِحُها شَبّا
لها بَشَرُ الدُّرِّ الذي قُلِّدَتْ بِهِ // ولم أرَ بَدراً قَبْلَها قُلِّدَ الشُّهْبا
فَيا شَوقُ ما أبْقى ويا لي مِنَ النَّوى // ويا دَمْعُ ما أجْرى ويا قلبُ ما أصْبى
لَقَد لَعِبَ البَيْنُ المُشِتُّ بها وَبي // وزَوَّدَني في السَّيرِ ما زَوَّدَ الظَّبّا
ومَن تَكُنِ الأُسْدُ الضَّواري جُدودَهُ // يَكُنْ لَيلُهُ صُبحاً وَمَطعَمُهُ غَصْبا
ولَستُ أُبالي بَعدَ إدراكِيَ العُلى // أكانَ تُراثاً ما تَناوَلْتُ أمْ كَسْبا
فَرُبَّ غُلامٍ عَلَّمَ المَجدَ نَفْسَهُ // كَتعليمِ سَيفِ الدَّولَةِ الطَّعنَ والضَّرْبا
إذا الدَّولَةُ استَكفَتْ بِهِ في مُلِمَّةٍ // كَفاها فكانَ السَّيفَ والكَفَّ والقَلْبا
تُهابُ سُيوفُ الهِندِ وَهْيَ حَدائِدٌ // فَكَيفَ إذا كانَتْ نِزارِيَّةً عُرْبا
وَيُرْهَبُ نابُ اللَّيثِ واللَّيثُ وَحْدَهُ // فَكَيفَ إذا كانَ اللُّيوثُ لَهُ صَحْبا
وَيُخشى عُبابُ البَحرِ وهوَ مَكانَهُ // فَكَيفَ بِمَن يَغشى البِلادَ إذا عَبّا
عَليمٌ بأسرارِ الدِّياناتِ واللُّغى // لَهُ خَطَراتٌ تَفضَحُ النَّاسَ والكُتْبا
فَبورِكتَ مِن غَيْثٍ كأنَّ جُلودَنا // بِهِ تُنبِتُ الدِّيباجَ والوَشْيَ والعَصْبا
ومَن واهِبٍ حَزْلاً ومَن زاجِرٍ هَلا // ومَن هاتِكٍ دِرْعاً ومَن ناثِرٍ قَصْبا
هَنيئاً لأهلِ الثَّغرِ رَأيُكَ فيهِمُ // وأنَّكَ حَزبُ اللهِ صِرتَ لهم حِزبا
وأنَّكَ رُعْتَ الدَّهرَ فيها ورَيبَهُ // فإنْ شَكَّ فَلْيُحدِثْ بِساحَتِها خَطْبا
فَيوماً بِخَيلٍ تَطرُدُ الرّومَ عَنهُمُ // وَيَوماً بِجودٍ تَطرُدُ الفَقرَ والجَدْبا
سَراياكَ تَتْرى والمُستُقُّ هارِبٌ // وأصحابُهُ قَتْلى وأموالُهُ نُهْبى
أتى مُرعَشاً يَستَقرِبُ البُعدَ مُقبِلاً // وأدبَرَ إذ أقبَلتَ يَستَبعِدُ القُربا
كَذا يَترُكُ الأعداءَ مَن يَكرَهُ القَنا // وَيُقفِلُ مَن كانَتْ غَنيمَتُهُ رُعْبا
وهَل رَدَّ عَنهُ باللُّقانِ وُقوفُهُ // صُدورَ العَوالي والمُطَهَّمَةَ القُبّا

We got down from saddles to walk in honor
    Of him who went on lest we approach rudely
We blame high clouds for their acts there
    Turning from them reproaching as they come
If one is in a world for long it changes
    In his eyes until he sees its faith as lies
What is my joy in evenings or mornings
    Since the wind that blew does not return
I think of union I seem not to have won
    And life which I seem to pass in one jump
One charms by eyes fatal to love
    If her smell comes to a shaikh he's young
Her skin is pearl which was a necklace
    None saw a moon before ringed by stars
O desire how lasting, O the separation
    O what tears flow, O heart overwhelmed!
Parting that scatters played with her
    Fed me on a journey what it fed a lizard
But he whose forbears were fierce lions
    Finds night as day and his food by force
I don't worry after attaining heights
    Whether I inherit what I gain or earn it
For many a youth taught himself glory
    As Saif al-Daula learned by push and cut
When a state in trouble conquers by him
    He suffices and is sword, hand and heart
Indian swords are feared as steel
    But how if they are an Arab of Nizar?
Lion's fangs are dreaded if alone
    How when lions are companions to him?
Sea surge is frightful in one place
    How with him who covers land in a flow?
Knowing religion's secrets and tongues
    He has ideas which shame men and books
Blessed by showers so our skins seem
    To grow brocades and silks and fine cloth
Among liberal givers, pushers forward
    Those who tear off armor, scatter bones
Your wisdom for them joy to border folk
    You are God's party and so theirs also
One day your horsemen drive off Rum
    Then by gifts you drive off want and need
Your sorties continue, Domesticus flees
    His lieutenants dead, his wealth plundered
Nearing he thought far Marash close by
    He turned as you came, thought near far
He hated lances, abandoned the foe
    He journeys whose plunder is a terror
Did his stand at Luqan ward off keen
    Breasts of lances and strong lean horses?
He went on after spears tangled a bit
    As one eyelid meets another when dozing

كَما يَتَلَقَّى الهُدْبُ في الرَّقدةِ الهُدَبا	مَضى بَعدَ ما التَفَّ الرِّماحانِ ساعةً
إذا ذَكَرَتْها نَفْسُهُ لَمَسَ الجَنَبا	وَلَكِنَّهُ وَلَّى وَلِلطَّعنِ سَورَةٌ
وَشَعَّثَ النَّصارى والقَرابينَ والصُّلْبا	وَخَلَّى العَذارى والبَطاريقَ والقُرى
حَريصاً عَلَيها مُستَهاماً بِها صَبّا	أَرى كُلَّنا يَبغي الحَياةَ لِنَفسِهِ
وَحُبُّ الشُّجاعِ الحَربَ أَورَدَهُ الحَرْبا	فَحُبُّ الجَبانِ النَّفْسَ أَورَدَهُ البَقا
إلى أَنْ تَرى أَحسانَ هذا لِذا ذَنْبا	وَيَختَلِفُ الرِّزقانِ والفِعلُ واحِدٌ
إلى الأَرضِ قد شَقَّ الكَواكِبَ والتُّرْبا	فَأَضحَتْ كَأَنَّ السُّورَ مِن فَوقِ بدئهِ
وَتَفزَعُ فيها الطَّيرُ أَن تَلقُطَ الحَبّا	تَصُدُّ الرِّياحُ الهُوجُ عَنها مَخافةً
وَقد نَدَفَ الصِّنَّبرُ في طُرقِها العُطْبا	وَتَرَدى الجِيادُ الجُرْدُ فَوقَ جِبالِها
بَنى مَرعَشاً؛ تَبّاً لآرائِهِم تَبّا	كَفى عَجَباً أَن يَعجَبَ النّاسُ أَنّهُ
إذا حَذِرَ المَحذورَ واستَصعَبَ الصَّعْبا	وَما الفَرقُ ما بَينَ الأَنامِ وَبَينَهُ
وَلَم تَترُكِ الشَّأمَ الأَعادي لَهُ حُبّا	وَلَم تَفتَرِقْ عَنهُ الأَسِنّةُ رَحمةً
كَريمُ الثَّنا ما سُبَّ قَطُّ وَلا سَبّا	وَلَكِنْ نَفاها عَنهُ غَيرَ كَريمةٍ
خَريقُ رِياحٍ واجَهَتْ غُصُناً رَطْبا	وَجَيشٍ يُثَنّي كُلَّ طَودٍ كَأَنَّهُ
فَمَدَّتْ عَلَيها مِن عَجاجَتِهِ حُجْبا	كَأَنَّ نُجومَ اللَّيلِ خافَتْ مُغارَهُ
فَهذا الَّذي يُرضي المَكارِمَ وَالرَّبّا	فَمَن كانَ يُرضي اللُّؤمَ والكُفرَ مُلكُهُ

(١٩٣)

«من الطويل»

قال وقد أهدى إليه سيف الدولة ثياب ديباج ورمحا وفرسا معها مهرها وكان المهر أحسن:

إذا نُشِرَتْ كانَ الهِباتُ صِوانَها	ثِيابٌ كَريمٌ ما يَصونُ حِسانَها
وَتَجلو عَلَينا نَفسَها وَقِيانَها	تُرينا صَنّاعُ الرّومِ فيها مُلوكَها
فَصَوَّرَتِ الأَشياءَ إلّا زَمانَها	وَلَم يَكفِها تَصويرُها الخَيلَ وَحدَها

He turned away when jousting was hot
    As his soul recalled it he felt at his sides
He left virgins, patricians, estates and
    Wild haired Nazarenes, courtiers, crosses
I know each of us wants life for himself
    Coveting it and hoping for it passionately
A coward's love of self brings him fear
    A brave man's self-love brings him battle
If two decisions differ the act is one so
    What seems a good for one is sin to another
It shines as if a wall from its top stone
    Down to earth must split the stars and dust
Bustling winds are stopped by it in fear
    Birds are scared by it from gleaming grain
Short hair horses pound to its mountain
    A north wind sends down cotton on it ways
Enough of a wonder that men marvel he
    Built Marash, fie on their notions, shame!
What difference between men and him
    If he fears the feared, finds the hard hard
The caliph readied him to work on foes
    Named him before the world a Keen Sword
Spears did not scatter from him in pity
    Nor did an enemy leave Syria for love of him
But he bans them from him without honor
    Noble in praise, never cursing nor cursed
An army to split each mountain as if it
    Were searing wind aimed at tender stalks
As if night stars feared his attack and
    Stretched over it a veil of his dark dust
Whoever asking wants blame and doubt
    Yet he is pleased with nobility and a Lord

193
Saif al-Daula presented him with gifts among which were a Rumi robe, a spear and a mare along with her colt, and the colt was the better one.
(Long hi)

Noble robes do not keep their beauty
    But if given the giver is their wardrobe
A Rum weaver shows their kings in it
    She reveals herself and her slaves to us
Her design was not content with riders
    For she painted all things except her time

وَمَا ادَّخَرْتَها قُدْرَةً في مُصَوِّرِ	سِوى أنَّها ما أنْطَقَتْ حَيَوانَها
وَسَمْراءُ يَسْتَغْوي الفَوارِسَ قَدُّها	وَيُذْكِرُها كَرّاتِها وَطِعانَها
رُدَيْنِيَّةٌ تَمَّتْ وَكادَ نَباتُها	يُرَكَّبُ فيها زُجُّها وَسِنانَها
وَأُمُّ عَتيقٍ خالُهُ دونَ عَمِّهِ	رَأى خَلْقَها مَنْ أعْجَبَتْهُ فعانَها
إذا سايَرَتْهُ بايَنَتْهُ وَبانَها	وَشانَتْهُ في عَينِ البَصيرِ وَزانَها
فأينَ التي لا تأمَنُ الخَيلُ شَرَّها	وَشَرِّيَ لا تُعْطي سِوايَ أمانَها
وأينَ التي لا تَرْجِعُ الرُّمْحَ خائِباً	إذا خَفَضَتْ يُسْرى يَدَيَّ عِنانَها
وَما لي ثَناءٌ لا أَراكَ مَكانَهُ	فَهَلْ لَكَ نُعْمى لا تَراني مَكانَها

(١٩٤)

«من البسيط»

قال وقد جرى له خطاب مع قوم متشاعرين وظن الحيف عليه والتحامل:

وا حَرَّ قَلْباهُ مِمَّنْ قَلْبُهُ شَبِمُ	وَمَنْ بِجِسْمي وَحالي عِنْدَهُ سَقَمُ
ما لي أكتُمُ حُبّاً قد بَرى جَسَدي	وَتَدَّعي حُبَّ سَيفِ الدَّوْلَةِ الأُمَمُ
إنْ كانَ يَجْمَعُنا حُبٌّ لِغُرَّتِهِ	فَلَيْتَ أنّا بِقَدْرِ الحُبِّ نَقْتَسِمُ
قد زُرْتُهُ وَسُيوفُ الهِندِ مُغْمَدَةٌ	وَقد نَظَرْتُ إلَيهِ وَالسُّيوفُ دَمُ
فكانَ أحسَنَ خَلْقِ اللهِ كُلِّهِمِ	وَكانَ أحسَنَ ما في الأحسَنِ الشِّيَمُ
فَوْتُ العَدوِّ الذي يَمَّمْتَهُ ظَفَرٌ	في طَيِّهِ أسَفٌ في طَيِّهِ نِعَمُ
قد نابَ عنكَ شديدُ الخَوفِ واصطَنَعَتْ	لَكَ المَهابَةُ ما لا تَصنَعُ البُهَمُ
ألزَمْتَ نَفْسَكَ شَيئاً لَيسَ يَلزَمُها	أنْ لا يُوارِيَهُمْ أرْضٌ وَلا عَلَمُ
أكُلَّما رُمْتَ جَيْشاً فانْثَنى هَرَباً	تَصَرَّفَتْ بِكَ في آثارِهِ الهِمَمُ
عَلَيكَ هَزْمُهُمُ في كُلِّ مُعْتَرَكٍ	وَما عَلَيكَ بِهِمْ عارٌ إذا انْهَزَموا
أما تَرى ظَفَراً حُلْواً سِوى ظَفَرٍ	تَصافَحَتْ فيهِ بيضُ الهِندِ وَاللِّمَمُ
يا أعْدَلَ النّاسِ إلّا في مُعامَلَتي	فيكَ الخِصامُ وأنتَ الخَصْمُ وَالحَكَمُ
أُعيذُها نَظَراتٍ مِنكَ صادِقَةً	أنْ تحسَبَ الشَّحمَ فيمن شَحمُهُ وَرَمُ

Unrestrained in her power of form
    She could not make her creatures talk
A lance whose length seduces a rider
    Who recalls repeated attacks and jousts
Rudaini perfected almost its growth
    Fitted it with its iron foot and its point
Noble's dam had kin less than stud's
    He saw her beauty noted, glared at her
Who is she whose evil riders doubt
    Or my evil, or her safety given only to me?
She goes with him to show him, he her
    Keen eyed she blames him as he adorns
Who is she who shies not slyly at spear
    As it lowers and my hand pulls on reins?
No praise by me if I see not you in him
    Or favor in you not seeing me in her place

194
He spoke
praising Saif al-Daula
and complaining to him.
(Outspread mu)

O hot is his heart for the cold hearted
    One with whom my body and state is sick
Why do I hide love emaciating my flesh
    When nations claim love for Saif al-Daula?
If love united us in his bright, brow
    Would we might share by decree of love
I came to him with Indian swords sheathed
    I watched him and those swords were bloody
All in our majlis will know that
    I am the best whose foot moves there
He, God's handsomest in all creation,
    Finest among the fine things his character
Missing the foe you pursue is a victory
    In part of it pain and in part an excellence
Violent fear is your lieutenant, for your
    Terror did the work warriors could not do
You demanded what there was no need for
    That no land or mountain be cover for them
If you beat an army and it turns to flee
    Will ambition aid you in the pursuit of it?
It's your duty to rout them in every war
    But not to put shame on them when they run
Do you see victory sweet only as prize
    Where Indian steel and a neck curl clasp?
O most just of men except in my affairs
    The feud is yours who both plead and judge

إِذا اسْتَوَتْ عِنْدَهُ الأنْوارُ وَالظُّلَمُ	وَما انْتِفاعُ أخي الدُّنْيا بِناظِرِهِ
بِأنَّني خَيْرُ مَنْ تَسْعَى بِهِ قَدَمُ	سَيَعْلَمُ الجَمْعُ مِمَّنْ ضَمَّ مَجْلِسُنا
وَأسْمَعَتْ كَلِماتي مَنْ بِهِ صَمَمُ	أنا الَّذي نَظَرَ الأعْمَى إلى أَدَبي
وَيَسْهَرُ الخَلْقُ جَرَّاها وَيَخْتَصِمُ	أنامُ مِلْءَ جُفوني عَنْ شَوارِدِها
حَتَّى أَتَتْهُ يَدٌ فَراسَةٌ وَفَمُ	وَجاهِلٍ مَدَّهُ في جَهْلِهِ ضَحِكي
فَلا تَظُنَّنَّ أنَّ اللَّيْثَ يَبْتَسِمُ	إذا رَأَيْتَ نُيوبَ اللَّيْثِ بارِزَةً
أدْرَكْتُها بِجَوادٍ ظَهْرُهُ حَرَمُ	وَمُهْجَةٍ مُهْجَتي مِنْ هَمِّ صاحِبِها
وَفِعْلُهُ ما تُريدُ الكَفُّ وَالقَدَمُ	رِجْلاهُ في الرَّكْضِ رِجْلٌ وَاليَدانِ يَدُ
حَتَّى ضَرَبْتُ وَمَوْجُ المَوْتِ يَلْتَطِمُ	وَمُرْهَفٍ سِرْتُ بَيْنَ الجَحْفَلَيْنِ بِهِ
وَالسَّيْفُ وَالرُّمْحُ وَالقِرْطاسُ وَالقَلَمُ	الخَيْلُ وَاللَّيْلُ وَالبَيْداءُ تَعْرِفُني
حَتَّى تَعَجَّبَ مِنِّي القورُ وَالأَكَمُ	صَحِبْتُ في الفَلَواتِ الوَحْشَ مُنْفَرِداً
وِجْدانُنا كُلَّ شَيْءٍ بَعْدَكُمْ عَدَمُ	يا مَنْ يَعِزُّ عَلَيْنا أنْ نُفارِقَهُمْ
لَوْ أنَّ أمْرَكُمْ مِنْ أمْرِنا أمَمُ	ما كانَ أخْلَقَنا مِنْكُمْ بِتَكْرِمَةٍ
فَما لِجُرْحٍ إذا أرْضاكُمُ ألَمُ	إنْ كانَ سَرَّكُمْ ما قالَ حاسِدُنا
إنَّ المَعارِفَ في أهْلِ النُّهَى ذِمَمُ	وَبَيْنَنا لَوْ رَعَيْتُمْ ذاكَ مَعْرِفَةٌ
وَيَكْرَهُهُ اللهُ ما تَأْتونَ وَالكَرَمُ	كَمْ تَطْلُبونَ لَنا عَيْباً فَيُعْجِزُكُمْ
أنا الثُّرَيَّا وَذانِ الشَّيْبُ وَالهَرَمُ	ما أبْعَدَ العَيْبَ وَالنُّقْصانَ مِنْ شَرَفي
يُزيلُهُنَّ إلى مَنْ عِنْدَهُ الدِّيَمُ	لَيْتَ الغَمامَ الَّذي عِنْدي صَواعِقُهُ
لا تَسْتَقِلَّنَّ بِها الوَخّادَةَ الرُّسُمُ	أرى النَّوَى يَقْتَضيني كُلَّ مَرْحَلَةٍ
لَيَحْدُثَنَّ لِمَنْ وَدَّعْتُهُمْ نَدَمُ	لَئِنْ تَرَكْنَ ضَميراً عَنْ مَيامِنِنا
أنْ لا تُفارِقَهُمْ فَالرَّاحِلونَ هُمُ	إذا تَرَحَّلْتَ عَنْ قَوْمٍ وَقَدْ قَدَروا
وَشَرُّ ما يَكْسِبُ الإنْسانُ ما يَصِمُ	شَرُّ البِلادِ مَكانٌ لا صَديقَ بِهِ
شُهْبُ البُزاةِ سَواءٌ فيهِ وَالرَّخَمُ	وَشَرُّ ما قَنَصَتْهُ راحَتي قَنَصٌ
تَجوزُ عِنْدَكَ لا عُرْبٌ وَلا عَجَمُ	بِأَيِّ لَفْظٍ تَقولُ الشِّعْرَ زِعْنِفَةٌ
قَدْ ضُمِّنَ الدُّرَّ إلَّا أنَّهُ كَلِمُ	هَذا عِتابُكَ إلَّا أنَّهُ مِقَةٌ

I took refuge in your trusted glances
    Not to think fat one whose fat is a tumor
What use to a worldly brother is an eye
    If the light and dark are the same to him
I am he whose culture the blind look to
    And my words have made the deaf to hear
I sleep quiet eyed apart from any roving
    But men wake to their courses and contend
My smile allows many a fool his folly
    Until the ferocious paw and mouth hit him
If you see the fangs of the lion bared
    You should not think the lion is smiling
Many a heart with huge lust for blood
    I hit from a horse with an inviolate back
Back feet and front feet moving as one
    His action is what hand and foot desire
Many a keen sword I took to armies
    Until I hit as death's waves pounded up
Horsemen, night and desert know me
    And battle and blows, paper and the pen
I was with beasts in wasteland alone
    When slopes and hills were amazed at me
O you whose parting was hard on us
    Our feeling for all after you is empty now
What honor for us from you in bounty
    If your concern is near to our concern?
If what those who envy us say pleases
    Then no wound for me if pain delights you
Between us if you respect it is wisdom
    Knowledge that for wise men is loyalty
Often you sought faults in us, tired
    But God and nobility hated what you did
How far is blame and loss from my peak
    I am Thurayya and they gray hair and age
Would the cloud whose lightning hit
    Had sent them to one who got the shower
I see distance allots me all journeys
    That strong striding camels cannot reduce
So I will leave Dumair on our right hand
    Sorrow for those to whom I say: Goodbye
If you go from folk and they are able
    To not let you go, it is they who depart
Worst land a place with no friend
    The worst one can earn is what dishonors,
Worst game my hand hunts is where
    The gray falcon is equal to the vulture
Whatever words rascals speak in verse
    They aren't either Arab or Persian for you
This is reproach to you but it is love
    Enclosed in pearls except they are words

(١٩٥)

«من الوافر»

ولما أنشد هذه القصيدة وانصرف اضطرب المجلس وكان نبطي من كبراء كتابه يقال له أبو الفرج السامري فقال له: دعني أسعى في دمه، فرخص له في ذلك وفيه يقول أبو الطيب:

فَطِنْتَ وَكُنْتَ أَغْبَى الأَغْبِيَاءِ	أَسَامَرِّيُّ ضُحْكَةَ كُلِّ رَاءٍ
كَأَنَّكَ مَا صَغُرْتَ عَنِ الهِجَاءِ	صَغُرْتَ عَنِ المَدِيحِ فقلتَ أَهْجَى
وَلَا جَرَّبْتُ سَيْفِي فِي هَبَاءِ	وَمَا فَكَّرْ مُقْبَلَكَ فِي مُحَالٍ

(١٩٦)

«من الطويل»

قال فيما كان يجري بينهما من معاتبة مستعتباً من القصيدة الميمية:

فَدَاهُ الوَرَى أَمْضَى السُّيُوفِ مَضَارِبَا	أَلَا مَا لِسَيْفِ الدَّوْلَةِ اليَوْمَ عَاتِبَا
تَنَائِفَ لَا أَشْتَاقُهَا وَسَبَاسِبَا	وَمَا لِي إِذَا مَا اشْتَقْتُ أَبْصَرْتُ دُونَهُ
أَحَادِيثُ فِيهَا بَدْرُهَا وَالكَوَاكِبَا	وَقَدْ كَانَ يُدْنِي مَجْلِسِي مِنْ سَمَائِهِ
وَحَسْبِيَ مَوْهُوبًا وَحَسْبُكَ وَاهِبَا	حَنَانَيْكَ مَسْؤُولًا وَلَبَّيْكَ دَاعِيًا
أَهَذَا جَزَاءُ الكَذِبِ إِنْ كُنْتُ كَاذِبَا	أَهَذَا جَزَاءُ الصِّدْقِ إِنْ كُنْتُ صَادِقًا
مَجَا الذَّنْبَ كُلَّ المَحْوِ مَنْ جَاءَ تَائِبَا	وَإِنْ كَانَ ذَنْبِي كُلَّ ذَنْبٍ فَإِنَّهُ

(١٩٧)

«من البسيط»

يمدحه لما رضي عنه:

دَعَا فَلَبَّاهُ قَبْلَ الرَّكْبِ وَالإِبِلِ	أَجَابَ دَمْعِي وَمَا الدَّاعِي سِوَى طَلَلِ
وَظَلَّ يَسْفَحُ بَيْنَ العُذْرِ وَالعَذَلِ	ظَلِلْتُ بَيْنَ أُصَيْحَابِي أَكَفْكِفُهُ

195
**When he had recited
this qasida and departed,
the majlis was in an uproar.
And a Nabataean
who was in the majlis
said to him:
Let me go after him
and draw blood.
But he kept him from it.
The Nabataean was al Samarri
who was proud of his writings.
About him Abu Tayyib spoke.
(Exuberant i)**

O Samarri, laughing stock of all wits, do
    You understand it? you dullest of all fools!
Too small to see, you said I mocked
    As if you were not too little for a satire
I paid no attention to folly before it
    So I will not test my sword on dust motes

196
**He spoke also
about what had happened
between them by way of complaint
concerning the mim qasida.
(Long ha)**

O let Saif al-Daula not complain today
    Men ransom him, keenest of swords in edge
What's for me if I stray, see after him
    Deserts I do not desire and the wasteland?
He brought my meeting near his heaven
    I spoke in it with its moon and its high stars
Have pity on a beggar, be near a suitor
    I have had enough of gifts and you of giving
Is this truth's reward if I am truthful?
    Or is it the reward of falsehood if I am false?
If my sin was worst of sins yet he who
    Comes repentant wipes out the worst faults

197
**He spoke also excusing himself
for what he said to him in his mim qasida.
(Outspread li)**

My tears respond, the caller only a tell
    Crying, one answers before rider and camel
I tried to stop it among my dear friends
    But it flowed between excuse and censure

كذاكَ كنتُ وما أشكو سوى الكِلَلِ	أشكو النَّوى ولهُمْ من عَبْرتي عجبٌ
مِنَ اللِّقاءِ كمُشْتاقٍ بلا أَمَلِ	وَمَا صَبابَةُ مُشْتاقٍ على أَمَلِ
لا يُتحِفُوكَ بغَيرِ البِيضِ والأَسَلِ	متى تَزُرْ قَوْمَ مَنْ تَهْوَى زيارَتَها
أنا الغَريقُ فما خَوْفي مِنَ البَلَلِ	والهَجْرُ أَقْتَلُ لي مِمَّا أراقِبُهُ
بِهِ الذي بي وما بي غَيرُ مُنْتَقِلِ	ما بالُ كُلِّ فُؤادٍ في عَشِيرَتِها
لُمُقْلَتَيْها عَظيمُ المُلْكِ في المُقَلِ	مُطاعَةُ اللَّحْظِ في الأَلْحاظِ مالِكَةٌ
في مَشْيِها فيَنلْنَ الحُسْنَ بالحِيَلِ	تشَبَّهُ الخَفِراتُ الآنساتُ بها
فَما حَصَلْتُ على صابٍ ولا عَسَلِ	قدْ ذُقْتُ شِدَّةَ أَيَّامي ولَذَّتَها
وقدْ أراني المَشيبُ الرَّوحَ في بَدَلي	وقدْ أراني الشَّبابُ الرَّوحَ في بَدَني
بصاحِبٍ غَيرَ عِزْهاةٍ ولا غَزِلِ	وقدْ طَرَقْتُ فَتاةَ الحَيِّ مُرْتَدِياً
وليسَ يَعلَمُ بالشَّكوى ولا القُبَلِ	فَباتَ بَينَ تَراقِينا نُدافِعُهُ
على ذَوائِبِهِ والجَفْنِ والخِلَلِ	ثم اغْتَدى وبِهِ مِنْ دِرْعِها أَثَرُ
أَوْ مِنْ سِنانِ أَصَمِّ الكَعْبِ مُعتَدِلِ	لا أَكْسِبُ الذِّكرَ إلاَّ مِنْ مَضارِبِهِ
فَزانَها وكَساني الدَّرْعَ في الحُلَلِ	جادَ الأَميرُ بِهِ لي في مَواهِبِهِ
بِحَمْلِهِ، مَنْ كَعَبْدِ اللهِ أَوْ كَعَلي	ومِنْ عَليِّ بنِ عَبْدِ اللهِ مَعْرِفَتي
بِيضِ القَواضِبِ والعَسَّالَةِ الذُّبُلِ	مُعطي الكواعِبِ والجُرْدِ السَّلاهِبِ والـ
مِلءَ الزَّمانِ ومِلءَ السَّهْلِ والجَبَلِ	ضاقَ الزَّمانُ ووَجْهُ الأرضِ عن مَلِكٍ
والبَرُّ في شُغُلٍ والبَحْرُ في خَجَلِ	فنَحنُ في جَذَلٍ والرُّومُ في وَجَلٍ
ومِنْ عَدِيٍّ أَعادي الجُبنِ والبَخَلِ	مَن تَغلِبَ الغالِبينَ النَّاسَ مَنْصِبُهُ
بالجاهِلِيَّةِ عَينُ العِيِّ والخَطَلِ	والمَدْحُ لابنِ أبي الهَيْجاءِ تُنْجِدُهُ
فَما كُلَيْبٌ وأَهلُ الأَعصُرِ الأُوَلِ	لَيْتَ المَدائِحَ تَسْتَوْفي مَناقِبَهُ
في طَلْعَةِ البَدرِ ما يُغنِيكَ عن زُحَلِ	خُذْ ما تَراهُ ودَعْ شَيْئاً سَمِعْتَ بِهِ
فإنْ وَجَدْتَ لِساناً قائِلاً فقُلْ	وقَدْ وَجَدتَ مَكانَ القَوْلِ ذا سَعَةٍ
خَيرُ السُّيوفِ بكَفَّيْ خَيرَةِ الدُّوَلِ	إنَّ الهُمامَ الذي فَخرُ الأنامِ بهِ
فَما يَقُولُ لِشَيءٍ لَيْتَ ذلِكَ لي	تُمسِي الأمانيُّ صَرْعَى دونَ مَبْلَغِهِ

I weep for absence, they stare at my tears
    But so I was when I fretted only for the veil
No, passion of a lover who has hope of
    Meeting is like a lover who is without hope
If you visit the people of one you love
    They make no gift without sword and spear
Flight is more deadly than my watching
    I am drowning but my fear is not of wetness
No thought in any of her folk of what
    Troubles me, my trouble will not change
She conquers glances like a queen
    By her two eyes, great power in her eyes
Bashful companions are imitating her
    In her walk to acquire beauty by her art
I tasted need in my days and sweets
    But I stayed not with colocynth or honey
Youth surely showed me body's spirit
    Gray hair showed me a soul in my change
I came at night to a maid returned with
    A friend neither continent nor amorous
That night we put it between our breasts
    It knew nothing of complaint or of kisses
It went early with a bit of her perfume
    On its hanger, sheath and sheath cover
I am recognized only by striking or
    By the hard tip of the shaft's breast
The Amir gave it to me among gifts
    Adorned it, dressed me in armored suit
From Ali ibn Abdallah is my skill in
    Bearing it, who is as Abdallah or Ali
Giver of high breasted ones, shorthairs
    Longbacked, bright edges, tough pliant
Time and earth's face are too narrow
    A king who fills time, shore and mountain
We in exultation, the Rum in terror
    The land is busy and the sea is shamed
From Taglib, victors of men, his origin
    From Aad the foes of cravens and misers
Praise for Ibn Haija, tracing him to
    The Ignorance is truly weak sophistry
Would that praises equaled his virtue
    Not as Kulaib or people of early times
Take what you see, leave the heard
    Full moon rising dispenses with Zuhal
You found a wide way with speech
    If you find a tongue to speak then speak
A hero has humanity's pride in him
    Best sword in the best state's hands
Desires bow down to his perfection
    He says to nothing: Would it were mine
Observe as two swords unite in dust
    A difference in their nature and action

إلى اخْتِلافِهِمـا في الخَلْـقِ وَالعَمَـلِ	أُنظُـرْ إذا اجْتَمَـعَ السَّيْفانِ في رَهَـجٍ
أَعَـدَّ هَـذا لِـرَأْسِ الفارِسِ البَطَـلِ	هَذا المُعَـدُّ لِرَيْـبِ الدَّهْـرِ مُنْصَلِتَـاً
وَالـرّومُ طائِـرَةٌ مِنْـهُ مَـعَ الحَجَـلِ	فَالعُرْبُ مِنْـهُ مَـعَ الكُـدْرِيِّ طائِـرَةٌ
تَمْشِـي النَّعامُ بِـهِ في مَعْقِلِ الوَعِـلِ	وَمـا الفِـرارُ إلى الأجْبـالِ مِـنْ أسَـدٍ
وَزالَ عَنْها وَذاكَ الـرَّوْعُ لَـمْ يَـزُلِ	جـازَ الـدُّروبَ إلى مـا خَلْـفَ خَرْشَنَـةٍ
فَإنَّمـا حَلَمَـتْ بِالسَّبْي وَالجَمَـلِ	فَكُلَّمـا حَلَمَـتْ عَـذْراءُ عِنْدَهُـمْ
مِنها رِضاكَ وَمَن لِلعُورِ بِالحَـوَلِ	إن كنتَ تَرْضَى بِـأَنْ يُعطُوا الجِزَى بَدَلَو
يـا غَيْـرَ مُنْتَحِـلٍ في غَيْـرِ مُنْتَحَـلِ	نادَيْـتُ مَجْدَكَ في شِعْري وَقَـدْ صَدَرَا
فَطالِعاهُـمْ وَكُونـا أبْلَـغَ الرُّسُـلِ	بِالشَّـرْقِ وَالغَـرْبِ أقْـوامٌ نُحِبُّهُـمُ
أُقَلِّـبُ الطَّـرْفَ بَيْـنَ الخَيْلِ وَالخَوَلِ	وَعَرَّفـاهُـمْ بِأنّـي في مَكارِمِـهِ
وَالشُّكرُ مِن قِبَلِ الأحْسـانِ لا قِبَلـي	يا أيُّهـا المُحْسِـنُ المَشْكـورُ مِن جِهَتـي
بِـأَنَّ رَأْيَـكَ لا يُؤتَى مِـنَ الزَّلَـلِ	ما كـانَ نَوْمـي إلاَّ فَـوْقَ مَعْرِفَتـي
زِد هَـشَّ بِشٍّ تَفَضَّـلْ أدْنِ سُـرَّ صِـلِ	أقِلْ أنِـلْ أقطِـعْ احمِلْ عَـلِّ سَـلِّ أعِـدْ
فَرُبَّمـا صَحَّـتِ الأجْسـامُ بِالعِلَـلِ	لَعَـلَّ عَتْبَـكَ مَحْمُـودٌ عَواقِبُـهُ
أذُبُّ مِنـكَ لِـزُورِ القَـوْلِ عَن رَجُـلٍ	وَمـا سَمِعْـتُ وَلا غَيـرِي بِمُقْتَـدِرٍ
لَيْسَ التَكَحُّـلُ في العَيْنَيـنِ كَالكَحَـلِ	لِأَنْ حِلْمَـكَ حِلْـمٌ لا تَكَلَّفُـهُ
وَمَـنْ يَسُـدَّ طَريـقَ العارِضِ الهَطِلِ	وَمَـا ثَنـاكَ كَـلامُ النّـاسِ عَـن كَـرَمٍ
وَلا مِطـالٌ وَلا وَعْـدٍ وَلا مَـذَلِ	أنتَ الجَـوادُ بِـلا مَـنٍّ وَلا كَـدَرٍ
غَيْـرَ السَّنَّـورِ وَالأشْـلاءِ وَالقُلَـلِ	أنتَ الشُّجـاعُ إذا ما لَـم يَطَـأْ فَـرَسٌ
كَأنَّهـا مِـنْ نُفـوسِ القَـوْمِ في جَـدَلِ	وَرَدَّ بَعْـضُ القَنـا بَعضـاً مُقارَعَـةً
بِعاجِـلِ النَّصْـرِ في مُسْتَأْخِـرِ الأجَـلِ	لا زِلْـتَ تَضرِبُ مِن عاداكَ عَن عُـرُضٍ

(١٩٨)

«من الرمل»

وقال وقد استحسنت هذه القصيدة:

سـارَ فَهْـوَ الشَّمْـسُ وَالدُّنيا فَلَـكْ	إنَّ هَـذا الشِّعـرَ في الشِّعـرِ مَلَـكْ

Ready to be drawn against fate's evil
    Prepared as leader of the brave knights
Arabs flee from him like sand grouse
    The Rum flee from him like partridges
But no flight to hills from the lions
    Ostriches run with him to goat's refuge
He crosses passes behind Kharshana
    Retires from it but fear does not retreat
Each time the virgins dream at home
    They will dream of captivity and camels
If you wish they pay tax giving just as
    You want, for one eye prefers a squint
I tell your glory in verses that travel O
    No presence for what is no false claim
To east and west are folk we love
    Who study both in the noblest envoys
They tell them, due to his noble act,
    Hold the eye among knights and slaves
O most gracious goodness in my behalf
    Thanks come from a gift and not from me
My sleep was only upon my knowledge
    That your thought cannot come to error
Aid, get, cross, rush, raise, cheer, teach
    Add, smile, laugh, please, come, joy, give
Maybe your hardness is good at last
    Often health of body comes with illness
I know not, nor others, of one in power
    Better shield for me against false speech
Your clemency is not false clemency
    Using eyeshadow is not having fine eyes
Generous without reproach or fatigue
    Without delay or promises or annoyance
Men's words don't turn you from honor
    Who can block the path of a rain cloud?
Brave when a horse no longer steps
    On anything but armor, limbs and heads
Some lances return blows of others
    As if they argued with souls of warriors
You do not stop striking all your foes
    Hastening aid while holding back death

198
When he recited this qasida they thought well of it and he said.
(Tripping k)

A poem among verses is indeed an angel
    It moves and is the sun, the world is its sky

عَدَلَ الرَّحْمَنُ فيهِ بَيْنَنا	فَقَضَى باللَّفْظِ لي والحَمْدِ لكْ
فَإذا مَرَّ بِأُذْنَيْ حاسِدٍ	صارَ مِمَّنْ كانَ حَيّاً فَهَلَكْ

(١٩٩)

ولما أنشد أقل أنل رآهم يعدون ألفاظه فقال وزاد فيه:

أقِلْ أنِلْ أُنْ صُنْ أحْمِلْ عَلَّ سَلَّ أَعِدْ	زِدْهَشَّ بَشَّ هَبْ اغْفِرْ أَذْنْ سُرَّ صِلِ

(٢٠٠)

«من الطويل»

وقال وقد سئل بيتاً يتضمن أكثر ما يمكن من الحروف:

عِشْ ابْقَ اسْمُ سُدْ جُدْ قُدْ مُرانَهَ اسْرُفْهُ تَسَلْ	غِطِ ارْمِ صِبِ احْمِ اغْزُ اسْبِ رُغْ زَعْ دِلِ اثْنِ نَلْ
وَهَــذا دُعــاءٌ لَــوْ سَكَتَّ كَفِيتَـهُ	لأنّـي سـأَلْتُ اللهَ فيكَ وقَدْ فَعَلْ

(٢٠١)

«من الوافر»

وحضر مجلس سيف الدولة وبين يديه اترج وطلع وهو يمتحن الفرسان وعندي ابن حبش شيخ المصيصة فقال له: لا تتوهم هذا للشرب، فقال أبو الطيب:

شَديدُ البُعْدِ مِن شُرْبِ الشَّمولِ	تُرُنْجُ الهِنْدِ أَوْ طَلْعُ النَّخيلِ
ولكِنْ كُلَّ شيءٍ فيهِ طِيبٌ	لَدَيكَ مِنَ الدَّقيقِ إلى الجَليلِ
ومَيْدانُ الفَصاحَةِ والقَوافي	ومُمْتَحَنُ الفَوارِسِ والخُيولِ

May mercy be just between it and us
    Credit the words to me, the praise to you
If it passes the ears of the envious
    It goes as one that lives and is a destroyer

199
He recited verse 40
"Aid, get. . ."
and saw them counting
the words so he said.
(Outspread li)

Raise, get, aid, guard, rush, rise, cheer, teach
    Add, speed, smile, grant, forgive, come, laugh, give

200
And he knew they wanted
to increase the letters
so he said.
(Trembling li)

Live, stay, rise, do, give, go, bid, deny, cry, be, say, ask
    Rage, fix, hit, put, war, take, end, cut, pay, set, dam, get

201
He was present
in the majlis
of Saif al Daula
in Shawwal
of the year 341
and before him
was orange and date juice.
And he was testing horses
so he said:
Doesn't this tempt you to drink?
So he spoke.
(Exuberant li)

A long way from intoxicating drink
    Is Indian orange or fruit of the palm
On the contrary everything is sweet
    With you and from smallest to greatest
The field of eloquence and rhymes
    And the testing of horsemen and horses

(٢٠٢)

«من الوافر»

وَكَانَ بِقَدْرِ مَا عَايَنْتُ قِيلي	أَتَيْتُ بِمَنْطِقِ العَرَبِ الأَصيلِ
بِمَنْزِلَةِ النِّسَاءِ مِنَ البُعُولِ	فَعَارَضَهُ كَلامٌ كَانَ مِنْهُ
وَأَنْتَ السَّيْفُ مَأْمُونُ الفُلُولِ	وَهذا الدُّرُّ مَأْمُونُ التَّشَظِّي
إِذا احْتاجَ النَّهارُ إِلى دَليلِ	وَلَيْسَ يَصِحُّ في الأَفْهامِ شَيْءٌ

(٢٠٣)

«من المتقارب»

ودخل عليه في ذي القعدة سنة إحدى وأربعين وثلاث مئة (٩٥٢م) وقد جلس لرسول ملك الروم وهو قد ورد يلتمس الفداء وركب الغلمان بالتجافيف وأحضروا لبؤة مقتولة ومعها ثلاثة أشبال أحياء وألقوها بين يديه فقال أبو الطيب ارتجالاً:

وَزُرْتَ العُداةَ بِآجالِها	لَقِيتَ العُفاةَ بِآمالِها
كَ بَيْنَ اللُّيوثِ وَأَشْبالِها	وَأَقْبَلَتِ الرّومُ تَمْشي إِلَيْ
فَأَيْنَ تَفِرُّ بِأَطْفالِها	إِذا رَأَتِ الأَسْدَ مَسْبِيَّةً

(٢٠٤)

«من الطويل»

وقال بعد ذلك إنشاداً:

وَلِلحُبِّ ما لَمْ يَبْقَ مِنّي وَما بَقي	لِعَيْنَيْكِ ما يَلْقى الفُؤادُ وَما لَقي
وَلكِنَّ مَنْ يُبْصِرْ جُفونَكِ يَعْشَقِ	وَما كُنْتُ مِمَّنْ يَدْخُلُ العِشْقُ قَلْبَهُ
مَجالٌ لِدَمْعِ المُقْلَةِ المُتَرَقْرِقِ	وَبَيْنَ الرِّضى وَالسُّخْطِ وَالقُرْبِ وَالنَّوى
وَفي الهَجْرِ فَهوَ الدَّهْرَ يَرْجو وَيَتَّقي	وَأَحْلى الهَوى ما شَكَّ في الوَصْلِ رَبُّهُ
شَفَعْتُ إِلَيْها مِنْ شَبابي بِرَيِّقِ	وَغَضْبى مِنَ الإِدْلالِ سَكْرى مِنَ الصِّبى
سَتَرْتُ فَمي عَنْهُ فَقَبَّلَ مَفْرِقي	وَأَشْنَبَ مَعْسولِ الثَّنِيَّاتِ واضِحٍ
فَلَمْ أُبَيِّنْ عاطِلاً مِنْ مُطَوَّقِ	وَأَجْيادِ غِزْلانٍ كَجيدِكِ زُرَّنِي

202
One of those present opposed al Mutanabbi in these verses.
And he said it was his right to say: You are far from drinking
wine / With orange or date juice/ To urge you to heights and
lances / And earning praise and fine memories./ And eloquent
sparks of scholars' thoughts / And testing of horses and
horsemen. So Abu Tayyib spoke.
(Trembling li)
I brought clear rooted reasoning
   My speech was according to my intent
A word was opposed to it which was
   As the woman in respect to her husband
But a pearl is safe from the boring
   As you are a sword safe from dullness
Nothing is sound to understanding
   When the daylight has need of a guide

203
He spoke in Dhu Qada when the messenger of the king
of Rome arrived to arrange for ransom. The slaves rode in
armor and set out weapons of war and displayed a dead
lioness, and with her three live cubs
and brought them before him.
(Tripping ha)
You gave the suppliants their hopes
   You have visited the enemy with death
The Rum come walking on foot to you
   Between that lioness and her young ones
When they see lions held prisoner
   Where do they go with their children?

204
He spoke praising him
and recalling the letter of the king of Rome that came to him.
(Long qi)
Your eyes are what love finds and found
   In love things don't stay for me yet continue
I wasn't one into whose heart love came
   But he who sees your eyelids is the lover
In joy and anger, nearness, distance
   The range of the Byes' tears is glittering
Sweetest his lord doubts in embrace
   And flight, for he always hopes and fears
Many a coquette's rage, drunk in youth
   I interceded with due to my tender years
Many a cool toothed, sweet, bright one
   I veiled my mouth from as he kissed my hair
Gazelles with fine necks as they visit
   But I cannot tell adorned from unadorned

328 Diwan al-Mutanabbi

وَمَــا كُـلُّ مَــنْ يَهْــوَى يَعِـفُّ إذا خَـلا   عَفَـافي وَيُرْضـي الحُـبَّ وَالخَيـلُ تلتقـي

سَـقَى اللهُ أَيَّـامَ الصِّبَـى مـا يَسُـرُّهَا   وَيَفْعَـلُ فِعْـلَ البَابِلـيّ المُعَتَّـقِ

إذا مـا لَبِسْـتَ الدَّهْـرَ مُسْتَمْتِعـاً بِـهِ   تَخَـرَّقْــتَ والمَلْبُــوسُ لَـمْ يَتَخَـرَّقِ

وَلَـمْ أَرَ كالأَلْحَــاظِ يَـوْمَ رَحيلِهِـمْ   بَعَثْــنَ بكـلِّ القتـلِ مـن كـلِّ مُشْفِـقِ

أَدَرْنَ عُيونـاً حائِـراتٍ كأَنَّهَـا   مُرَكَّبَــةٌ أَحداقُهَــا فَـوْقَ زِئْبَـقِ

عَشِيَّـةً يَعْدُونَـا عَـن النَّظَـرِ البُكَـا   وَعـن لـذَّةِ التَّوْديـعِ خـوفُ التَّفَـرُّقِ

نُوَدِّعُهُــمْ والبَيْــنَ فينَــا كأنَّـهُ   قَنَـا ابـنِ أبـي الهَيْجـاءِ فـي قلبِ فَيلَـقِ

قَـوَاضٍ مَـوَاضٍ نَسْــجُ داوُدَ عندَهـا   إذا وَقَعَـتْ فيـهِ كَنَسْـجِ الخَدَرْنَـقِ

هَـوَادٍ لأَمْلاكِ الجُيُـوشِ كأَنَّهَـا   تَخَــيَّرُ أَرْوَاحِ الكُمَــاةِ وتَنْتَقِــي

تَقُــدُّ عَلَيْهِــمْ كـلَّ دِرْعٍ وَجَوْشَـنٍ   وتَفـري إليهـم كـلَّ سُـورٍ وَخَنْـدَقِ

يُغِــيرُ بهَــا بَيــنَ اللُّقَـانِ وَوَاسِـطٍ   وَيَـرْكُزُهَـا بَيْـنَ الفُـرَاتِ وَجِلَّـقِ

وَيُرْجِعُهَـا حُمْـراً كـأنَّ صَحيحَهَـا   يُبَكّــى دَمـاً مِـن رَحْمَـةِ المُتَدَقَّـقِ

فَـلا تُبْلِغَـاهُ مَـا أقــولُ فإِنَّـهُ   شُـجَاعٌ متى يُذْكَـرْ لـهُ الطَّعْـنُ يشتـقِ

ضَــروبٌ بأَطْـرَافِ السُّيُـوفِ بَنانُـهُ   لَعُـوبٌ بأَطْـرَافِ الكَـلامِ المُشَــقَّقِ

كسَـائِلِهِ مَـنْ يَسْـألُ الغيْـثَ قَطْـرَةً   كعَاذِلِـهِ مَـنْ قـالَ لِلفَلَـكِ ارْفُـقِ

لقـدْ جُـدْتَ حتـى جُـدْتَ فـي كـلِّ مِلَّـةٍ   وحتـى أَتـاكَ الحَمْـدُ مـن كـلِّ مَنْطِـقِ

رأى مَلِـكُ الـرُّومِ ارْتِياحَـكَ للنَّـدَى   فَقَــامَ مَقــامَ المُجْتَـدي المُتَمَلِّـقِ

وَخَلَّـى الرِّمَـاحَ السَّـمْهَرِيَّةَ صاغِـراً   لأَدْرَبَ منــهُ بالطِّعَــانِ وَأَحْـذَقِ

وكــاتَبَ مِـن أرضٍ بعيـدٍ مَرامُهَـا   قريـبٍ علـى خيـلٍ حَوالَيْـكَ سُــبَّقِ

وقَـدْ سـارَ فـي مَسْـراكَ منهـا رَسُـولُهُ   فَمَــا سَــارَ إلاَّ فَـوْقَ هَـامٍ مُفَلَّـقِ

فَلَمَّــا دَنَــا أخْفَـى عَلَيْـهِ مَكانَـهُ   شُــعَاعُ الحَديـدِ البارِقِ المُتَألِّـقِ

وأَقْبَــلَ يَمْشــي فـي البِسَـاطِ فمـا دَرَى   إلى البَحْـرِ يَسْـعى أمْ إلـى البَـدْرِ يَرْتَقِـي

وَلَـمْ يُثْنِـكَ الأَعْـدَاءُ عَـنْ مُهَجَاتِهِـمْ   بِمثْـلِ خُضُــوعٍ فـي كَـلامٍ مُنَمَّـقِ

وكُنْــتَ إذا كاتَبْتَــهُ قَبْـلَ هـذِهِ   كَتَبْــتَ إليْـهِ فـي قَـذالِ الدُّمُسْــتُقِ

فـإنْ تُعْطِـهِ مِنْـكَ الأَمَـانَ فَسَـائِلٌ   وإنْ تُعْطِـهِ حَـدَّ الحُسَـامِ فَأَخْلِـقِ

وهَـلْ تَـرَكَ البِيضُ الصَّوارِمُ منهُـمْ   حَبيسـاً لِفــؤادٍ أوْ رَقيقـاً لِمُعْتِـقِ

Not all who love are chaste, lacking my
    Purity, or please love as riders met in war
May God rain on youth's happy days
    And work the work of old Babylonian wine
When you wore the time with joy in it
    You were pierced but the dress not torn
I never saw the glances on parting day
    That search out every murder full of pity
They turn their eyes in perplexity as if
    They mixed their looks with quicksilver
At eve tears prevent us from seeing
    The fear of parting from farewell's needs
We say goodbye to them and absence
    Is Abu Haija's spear in an army's heart
With deadly point, even David's web
    When it hits is like the spider's weave
Guided to kings with armies as if it
    Selected warrior souls and took them
It strips them of armor and shield
    And crosses every wall and moat
Jealous of those from Luqan and was it
    It is set between the Furat and the Jilliq
He returns it crimon as if its sheath
    Wept blood in pity for the broken bones
What I say attains not to him, brave
    When joust is noted, its name is his
A striker with fingers in sword tips
    A player with delicacy in the word edges
As his client one has showers in drops
    As his blame one says to this sky: Gently
You give till you are good to all faiths
    And praise reaches you from every tongue
A Rum king sees your joy in generosity
    So he takes the stance of a humble beggar
He leaves Samhari lances as one abased
    As one more apt in joust and more skilled
He wrote from a far land whose targets
    Are near to fast horses surrounding you
His messenger traveled your route
    He did not go except over the split skulls
As he neared the light of flashing steel
    Glittered and veiled for him his station
He came walking on rugs but knew not
    If he went to a sea or climbed to the moon
A foe cannot turn you from their blood
    With seeming humility in affected words
When you wrote him before you were
    Writing on the skull of the Domesticus
If you gave immunity, he asked for it
    If you gave sword's edge, it was his due
How can cutting steel keep from them
    Captive as hostage or slave as freeman?

وَمَرّوا عَلَيْها رَزْدَقاً بَعْدَ رَزْدَقِ	لَقَدْ وَرَدوا وِرْدَ القَطا شَفَراتِها
أنَرْتُ بها ما بَينَ غَرْبٍ وَمَشْرِقِ	بَلَغْتُ بِسَيفِ الدَّوْلَةِ النُّورَ رُتْبَةً
أراهُ غُباري ثُمّ قالَ لَهُ الحَقِ	إذا شاءَ أنْ يَلْهُو بِلِحْيَةِ أحْمَقِ
وَلَكِنّهُ مَنْ يَزْحَمِ البَحرَ يَغرَقِ	وَما كَمَدُ الحُسّادِ شيءٌ قَصَدْتُهُ
وَيُغْضي عَلى عِلْمٍ بِكُلِّ مُخَرِّقِ	وَيَمْتَحِنُ النّاسَ الأميرُ بِرَأيِهِ
إذا كانَ طَرْفُ القَلْبِ لَيسَ بِمُطرِقِ	وَإطْراقُ طَرْفِ العَينِ لَيسَ بِنافِعٍ
وَيا أيّها المَحْرومُ يَمّمْهُ تُرْزَقِ	فَيا أيّها المَطْلوبُ جاوِرْهُ تَمْتَنِعْ
وَيا أشْجَعَ الشُّجْعانِ فارِقْهُ تَفْرَقِ	وَيا أجْبَنَ الفُرْسانِ صاحِبْهُ تَجتَرِىء
سَعى جَدُّهُ في كَيدِهم سَعيَ مُخنِقِ	إذا سَعَتِ الأعْداءُ في كَيدٍ بِجَدِّهِ
إذا لَمْ يَكُنْ فَضْلَ السَّعيدِ المُوَفَّقِ	وَما يَنْصُرُ الفَضْلُ المُبينُ عَلى العِدى

«من الوافر»

(٢٠٥)

ودخل عليه ليلاً وهو يصف سلاحاً كان بين يديه فرفع فقال:

كَأَنّكَ واصِفٌ وَقْتَ النِّزالِ	وَصَفْتَ لَنا، وَلَمْ نَرَهُ، سِلاحاً
فَشَوَّقَ مَنْ رَآهُ إلى القِتالِ	وَأنّ البَيْضَ صُفَّ عَلى دُروعِ
قَرَأتَ الخَطَّ في سُودِ اللَّيالي	وَلَوْ أطْفَأتَ نارَكَ تا لَدَيْهِ
لَقَلَّبَ رَأيَهُ حالاً لِحالِ	وَلَوْ لَحَظَ الدُّمُسْتُقُ حافَتَيْهِ
فأحْسَنُ ما يَكونُ عَلى الرِّجالِ	إنِ اسْتَحْسَنْتَ وَهْوَ عَلى بِساطٍ
لَقَلَّبَ رَأيَهُ حالاً لِحالِ	وَلَوْ لَحَظَ الدُّمُسْتُقُ جانِبَيْهِ

«من المنسرح»

(٢٠٦)

وقال وقد عرض على الأمير سيوف فيها واحد غير مذهب فأمر بإذهابه:

وَخاضِبَيْهِ النَّجيعُ وَالغَضَبُ	أحْسَنُ ما يُخْضَبُ الحَديدُ بِهِ
يَجْتَمِعُ الماءُ فيهِ وَالذَّهَبُ	فَلا تَشينَنَّهُ بِالنُّضارِ فَما

They drink at its edges like sand grouse
    They pass before them in rank after rank
I reach with Saif al Daula's light such
    Heights I shine for those in east and west
If he likes to play with a fool's beard
    He shows him my dust, tells him truth
Jealousy's grief is not what I want
    But he who fights the sea will be drowned
The Amir tests common men by wisdom
    Closes his eyes to stupidity, recognizing
Turning away eye's glance is useless
    When the looks of eyes can't be downcast
O sought after as nearness is denied
    O you forbid to those seeking a support
O cowardly knights who attend, take
    Heart, the bravest who quit are fearful
If the foe runs into his glory's trap
    His glory enraged is busy with fortune
Evident excellence conquers no foe
    If there is no excess of joyful success

205
**He came to him at night
as he was examining some weapons
and he had one in his hand.
So he raised it and he said.
(Exuberant li)**

You told us of it but saw no blade
    As if you feigned the moment of attack
When helmets are arrayed over armor
    So one who sees it longs for the battle
If you put out your fire you'd read
    From the script in the darkest night
If the Domesticus saw its edges
    He'd roll his eyes from flash to flash
You approved it here on the carpet
    But it is better when girded on a man
In it and in him something's missing
    For you are perfection's goal in these

206
**Some swords were set out
for Saif al Daula
and he had one that was not gilded
so he ordered that it be gilded.
And Abu Tayyib spoke.
(Flowing bu)**

The steel is best colored if
    Its double dye is bloodied anger
Do not deface it with gold for
    Temper and gilt do not mix in it

(٢٠٧)

«من الخفيف»

أرسل شاعر إلى الأمير أبياناً يذكر فيها فقره ويزعم أنه رآها في النوم، فقال أبو الطيب:

وَأَنَلْنَاكَ بَــدْرَةً فِي المَنَامِ	قَدْ سَمِعْنَضا مَا قُلْتَ فِي الأَحْلَامِ
فَكَانَ النَّوَالُ قَدْرَ الكَلَامِ	وَانْتَبَهْنَا كَمَا انْتَبَهْتَ بِلَا شَيْءٍ
فَهَلْ كُنْتَ نَائِمَ الأَقْلَامِ	كُنْتَ فِيمَا كَتَبْتَهُ نَائِمَ العَيْنِ
هَلْ رَقْدَةٌ مَعَ الإِعْدَامِ	أَيُّهَا المُشْتَكِي، إِذَا رَقَدَ الإِعْدَامُ
وَمُمَيِّزْ خِطَابَ سَيْفِ الأَنَامِ	إفْتَحِ الجَفْنَ وَاتْرُكِ القَوْلَ فِي النَّوْمِ
بَدِيلٌ وَلَا لِمَا رَامَ حَامِ	الَّذِي لَيْسَ عَنْهُ مُغْنٍ وَلَا مِنْهُ
وَلَكِنَّهُ كَرِيمُ الكِرَامِ	كُلُّ آبَائِهِ كِرَامُ بَنِي الدُّنْيَا

(٢٠٨)

«من الكامل»

واستزاده سيف الدولة أيضاً فقال:

وَهَوَى الأَحِبَّةِ مِنْهُ فِي سَوْدَائِهِ	عَذَلُ العَوَاذِلِ حَوْلَ قَلْبِي التَّائِهِ
وَيَصُدُّ حِينَ يَلُمْنَ عَنْ بُرَحَائِهِ	يَشْكُو المَلَامَ إِلَى اللَّوَائِمِ حَزَّةً
أَسْخَطْتُ أَعْذَلَ مِنْكَ فِي إِرْضَائِهِ	وَمُهْجَتِي يَا عَاذِلِي المَلِكُ الَّذِي
مَلَكَ الزَّمَانَ بِأَرْضِهِ وَسَمَائِهِ	إِنْ كَانَ قَدْ مَلَكَ القُلُوبَ فَإِنَّهُ

207
He spoke and a man
from the astrologers of Rahb
who had just sent Saif al-Daula some verses
in which he complained of poverty
and mentioned that he had seen the verses
in a dream.
(Nimble mi)

We heard what you spoke in a dream
   So we got you the thousand in a sleep
We woke as you woke without a coin
   So the gift is according to your saying
The eye was asleep as you wrote it
   And why were you sleeping at the pen?
O complainer of poverty in your sleep
   Sleep cannot exist along with poverty
Open eyes and leave talk in dreams
   Prefer the words of humanity's sword
No one can now do without or find
   Substitute or guard for it if it is cutting
All his fathers were noble sons in
   The world, he is the noblest of nobles

208
Saif al-Daula asked for an addition to some verses
of Abu Dharr Sahl ibn Muhammad the katib
in the same meter and rhyme.
These are the verses: O censurer leave the words from one whom / Length of illness and trouble wastes / If you can aid him then cure his ills / And help him to find the source of his grief Until he tells you of a friend who / Hopes in his violent and tender times Or do not and leave him for he has no defense against / The constant blame where you can advise 1 am ransom for I wronged by criticism / Of his love and did not fear his guard/ The sun rises from his forehead lines / The full moon from his shirt collar.
(Perfect hi)

Blame of censurers in my puzzled heart
   Love of a darling is part of it in that center
Grief complains in its heat of reprovers
   And is frustrated when they oppose its pain
By my heart of blame the king is one for
   Whom I am angry at all men if pleasing him
If he did not own hearts yet he would
   Possess the time in heaven and his earth

ألشَّمسُ مِن حُسَّادِهِ والنَّصرُ مِن	قُرَنَائِهِ والسَّيفُ مِن أَسمَائِهِ
أينَ الثَّلاثَةُ مِن ثَلاثِ خِلالِهِ	مِن حُسنِهِ وإبَائِهِ ومَضَائِهِ
مَضَتِ الدُّهُورُ ومَا أَتَينَ بِمِثلِهِ	وَلَقَد أَتَى فَعَجَزنَ عَن نُظَرَائِهِ

(٢٠٩)

«من الكامل»

وأمره بإجازة أبيات فقال:

ألقَلبُ أَعلَمُ يا عَذُولُ بِدَائِهِ	وَأَحَقُّ مِنكَ بِجَفنِهِ وبِمَائِهِ
فَوَمَن أُحِبُّ لأُعصِيَنَّكَ في الهَوَى	قَسَماً بِهِ وبِحُسنِهِ وبَهَائِهِ
أَأُحِبُّهُ وَأُحِبُّ فيهِ مَلامَةً؟	إنَّ المَلامَةَ فيهِ مِن أَعدَائِهِ
عَجِبَ الوُشاةُ مِنَ اللِّحاةِ وقَولُهُم	دَع ما نَراكَ ضَعُفتَ عَن أخفَائِهِ
ما الخِلُّ إلَّا مَن أَوَدُّ بِقَلبِهِ	وأَرَى بِطَرفٍ لا يَرَى بِسِوَائِهِ
إنَّ المُعِينَ عَلى الصَّبابَةِ بالأَسَى	أَولَى بِرَحمَةِ رَبِّها وإخَائِهِ
مَهلاً فَإنَّ العَذلَ مِن أَسقَامِهِ	وتَرَفُّقاً فالسَّمعُ مِن أَعضَائِهِ
وهَبِ المَلامَةَ في اللَّذاذَةِ الكَرَى	مَطرُودَةً بِسُهادِهِ وبُكائِهِ
لا تَعذُلِ المُشتاقَ في أَشوَاقِهِ	حتَّى يَكونَ حَشاكَ في أَحشَائِهِ
إنَّ القَتيلَ مُضَرَّجاً بِدُموعِهِ	مِثلُ القَتيلِ مُضَرَّجاً بِدِمائِهِ
والعِشقُ كالمَعشُوقِ يَعذُبُ قُربُهُ	للمُبتَلَى ويَنالُ مِن حَوبَائِهِ
لَو قُلتَ للدَّنِفِ الحَزينِ فَدَيتُهُ	ممَّا بِهِ لأَغرَيتَهُ بِفِدَائِهِ
وُقِيَ الأَميرُ هَوَى العُيونِ فإنَّهُ	ما لا يَزُولُ بِبَأسِهِ وسَخَائِهِ
يَستَأسِرُ البَطَلَ الكَمِيَّ بِنَظرَةٍ	ويَحُولُ بَينَ فُؤادِهِ وعَزَائِهِ
إنِّي دَعَوتُكَ للنَّوائِبِ دَعوَةً	لَم يُدعَ سامِعُها إلى أَكفَائِهِ
فَأَتَيتَ مِن فَوقِ الزَّمانِ وتَحتِهِ	مُتَصَلصِلاً وأَمامِهِ ووَرائِهِ
مَن للسُّيوفِ بأَن يَكونَ سَمِيَّها	في أَصلِهِ وفِرِندِهِ ووَفَائِهِ
طُبِعَ الحَديدُ فكانَ مِن أَجناسِهِ	وعَلِيٌّ المَطبُوعُ مِن آبائِهِ

The sun envies him, victory is one of
    His associates, the sword among his names
Where are three like is three qualities
    His beauty, his ancestors and his keenness
Ages passed and brought none as his like
    They run and are exhausted by watching him

209
Saif al-Daula asked him for more so he said.]
(Perfect hi)

A heart O censurer knows its ills best
    More worthy than you of its eyelid and tear
By one I love I'm no rebel to your love
    Swearing by him and beauty and elegance
Shall love him and love rebuke for him?
    Indeed rebuke for him is from his enemies
Gossips are amazed at blame and say:
    Leave what we see you are too weak to hide
A friend is one I love only for his soul
    I see with an eye seeing none as his equal
He who aids a passionate one in grief
    Is worthy of mercy's Lord and brotherhood
Go slowly for censure is in joy as sleep
    Be kindly for the ear is one of his members
Grant censure is in its joy like slumber
    That is driven off by waking and weeping
Don't excuse a lover in his passion so
    Far as to find your heart within his heart
For a stricken one is stained by tears
    Like a corpse is sprinkled with his blood
Love is like the beloved whose presence
    Is sweet to one testing and taking his spirit
If you said to one very ill: I'm ransom
    For it, you'd make him jealous of a ransom
May the Amir be guarded by loving eyes
    As one who has no end of bravery and gifts
He captures armed warriors by a glance
    Intervenes between his heart and his glory
Often I called on you for aid in trouble
    Some who heard were not called to equals
You came from above the time, beneath
    Clashing, and from in front and from behind
He belongs to swords for he is so named
    By his source, his temper and trustinesss
The steel was shaped, it was his nature
    And Ali was of the nature of his ancestors

(٢١٠)

«من المتقارب»

وَسِرُّكَ سِرِّي فَما أُظهِرُ	رِضاكَ رِضايَ الَّذي أُوثِرُ
وَآمَنَكَ الوُدُّ ما تَحذَرُ	كَفَتكَ المُروءَةُ ما تَتَّقي
إِذا أُنشِرَ السِّرُّ لا يُنشَرُ	وَسِرُّكُمُ في الحَشا مَيِّتٌ
وَكاتَمَتِ القَلبَ ما تُبصِرُ	كَأَنّي عَصَت مُقلَتي فيكُمُ
مِنَ الغَدرِ وَالحُرُّ لا يَغدِرُ	وَإِفشاءُ ما أَنا مُستَودَعٌ
فَإِنّي عَلى تَركِها أَقدَرُ	إِذا ما قَدَرتُ عَلى نَطقَةٍ
وَأَملِكُها وَالقَنا أَحمَرُ	أَصَرِّفُ نَفسي كَما أَشتَهي
وَأَمرُكَ يا خَيرَ مَن يَأمُرُ	دَوالَيكَ يا سَيفَها دَولَةً
فَلَبّاهُ شِعري الَّذي أَذخَرُ	أَتاني رَسولُكَ مُستَعجِلاً
لَبّاهُ سَيفِيَ وَالأَشقَرُ	وَلَو كانَ يَومَ وَغىً قاتِماً
فَإِنَّكَ عَينٌ بِها يَنظُرُ	فَلا غَفَلَ الدَهرُ عَن أَهلِهِ

(٢١١)

«من المتقارب»

قال وقد استبطأ سيف الدولة مدحه وتنكر لذلك:

وَصارَ طَويلُ السَلامِ اِختِصارا	أَرى ذَلِكَ القُربَ صارَ اِزوِرارا
أَموتُ مِراراً وَأَحيا مِرارا	تَرَكتَني اليَومَ في خَجلَةٍ
وَأَزجُرُ في الخَيلِ مُهري سِرارا	أُسارِقُكَ اللَحظَ مُستَحيِياً
إِلَيكَ أَرادَ اِعتِذاري اِعتِذارا	وَأَعلَمُ أَنّي إِذا ما اِعتَذَرتُ
تِ إِن كانَ ذَلِكَ مِنّي اِختِيارا	كَفَرتُ مَكارِمَكَ الباهِرا
لَ هَمٌّ حَمى النَومَ إِلّا غِرارا	وَلَكِن حَمى الشِعرَ إِلّا القَلي
وَلا أَنا أَضرَمتُ في القَلبِ نارا	وَما أَنا أَسقَمتُ جِسمي بِهِ
إِلَيَّ أَساءَ وَإِيّايَ ضارا	فَلا تُلزِمَنّي ذُنوبَ الزَمانِ

210

A messenger from Saif al-Daula came in haste with a note in which were two verses about hiding a secret and they were: Do you fear that I will tell the story / When my joy in hiding it is great? If I did not keep it to stay with you / I'd see myself as you see me. And they are Abbas ibn al Ahnaf. So Abu Tayyib spoke.
(Tripping ru)

Your pleasure is the joy that I chose
    Your secret my secret so why reveal it?
Manliness that guards is enough for you
    The love which takes heed makes you safe
Your secret in my heart is as a corpse
    If the secret revives it will not be related
As if my eyes transgressed with you
    As they hid from the heart what they saw
Telling what I am entrusted with
    Is fraud and the noble man is not fraud
Since I have power over articulation
    I have even more power over not speaking
I give my soul a free hand as I wish
    I control it when the lance grows crimson States,
O their sword, come by turns
    Yours the command O best of commanders
Your messenger came to me in haste
    So I answered him with my stored verses
If it had been a dark day of battle
    My sword and the red horse had met him
Destiny is not forgetful of its men
    For you are the eye by which that sees

221

He spoke and Saif al Daula thought he was slow in his praise but he denied it.
(Tripping ra)

I see this closeness can be withdrawn
    And the long peace is now abbreviated
Today you abandoned me to shame and
    I died once but at other times I was revived
I stole a glance from you, was ashamed
    I rebuked the mare of my colt in solitude
I see that when I make excuse to you
    I must intend it as my excuse for excuse
I'd deny your splendid generosity
    If this were a matter for my volition
Care stops the verses but for a few
    Prevents my sleep except for dozing
I do not make my body sick over it
    I will not light that fire in this heart
Do not afflict me with time's sins
    To me it is evil and pressed hard on me

تُ لا يَختَصِصنَ مِنَ الأرضِ دارَا	وَعِندي لَكَ الشُّرُدُ السَّائِرا
وَنَبنَ الجِبالَ وَخُضنَ البِحارَا	قَوافٍ إذا سِرنَ عَن مَقوَلي
وَما لَم يَسِر قَمَرٌ حَيثُ سارَا	وَلي فيكَ ما لَم يَقُل قائِلٌ
لَكانوا الظَّلامَ وَكُنتَ النَّهارَا	فَلَو خُلِقَ النَّاسُ مِن دَهرِهِم
وَأَبعَدُهُم في عَدُوٍّ مُغارَا	أَشَدُّهُم في النَّدى هِزَّةً
فَلَستُ أَعُدُّ يَساراً يَسارَا	سَما بِكَ هَمّي فَوقَ الهُمومِ
لَم يَقبَلِ الدُّرُّ إلّا كِبارَا	وَمَن كُنتَ بَحراً لَهُ يا عَلي

(٢١٢)

«من الطويل»

يمدحه أيضاً:

طِوالٌ وَلَيلُ العاشِقينَ طَويلُ	لَيالِيَّ بَعدَ الظَّاعِنينَ شُكولُ
وَيُخفينَ بَدراً ما إلَيهِ سَبيلُ	يَبِنَّ لِيَ البَدرُ الَّذي لا أُريدُهُ
وَلَكِنَّني لِلنَّائِباتِ حَمولُ	وَما عِشتُ مِن بَعدِ الأَحِبَّةِ سَلوَةً
وَفي المَوتِ مِن بَعدِ الرَّحيلِ رَحيلُ	وَإنَّ رَحيلاً واحِداً حالَ بَينَنا
فَلا بَرِحَتني رَوضَةٌ وَقَبولُ	إذا كانَ شَمُّ الرَّوحِ أدنى إلَيكُمُ
لِماءٍ بِهِ أَهلُ الحَبيبِ نُزولُ	وَما شَرِقي بِالماءِ إلّا تَذَكُّراً
فَلَيسَ لِظَمآنٍ إلَيهِ وُصولُ	يُحَرِّمُهُ لَمعُ الأَسِنَّةِ فَوقَهُ
لِعَيني عَلى ضَوءِ الصَّباحِ دَليلُ	أَما في النُّجومِ السَّائِراتِ وَغَيرِها
فَتَظهَرَ فيهِ رِقَّةٌ وَنُحولُ	ألم يَرَ هذا اللَّيلُ عَينَيكِ رُؤيَتي
شَفَت كَبِدي وَاللَّيلُ فيهِ قَتيلُ	لَقيتُ بِدَربِ القُلَّةِ الفَجرَ لَقيَةً

So my scattered movings lead to you
    They find no special home upon the earth
Many a rhyme as it moved from my mouth
    Sprang over mountains and waded the sea
If men were created from their times
    They would be the dark and you the light
I feel for you what no poet ever said
    And what no moon enjoys when it shines
Most eager of those rejoicing in bounty
    Most wide ranging of those raiding a foe
My ambition rises by you above heroes
    And I do not count good fortune as luck
He who has had you as the sea O 'Ali
    Will accept only pearls that are egg size

212

Saif al Daula
journeyed from Aleppo to Dyar Mudar
to stir up the bedouin there
and he stopped at Harran
and took pledges from the Banu Utail
and Qushair and Ajalon.
An idea came to him there to make a raid
so he crossed the Furat to Daluk.
Abu Tayyib spoke recalling his route
and his deeds in Jumadi in the year 342.
(Tripping lu)

My nights after the girls going are as
    The long ones and rovers' eights are long
They show me a moon I do not desire
    They hide the moon which has no way to it
After the beloved I do not live in
    Solace, but I must beat the calamities
One journey changed things between us
    And death after that trip is another journey
If the perfumed breeze was nearest you
    May neither gardens nor south wind depart
I do not choke on water but to remember
    Water where the clan of the beloved settle
Flashing spearpoints defend it above
    There is no approach to it for the thirsty
Only in wandering stars and the others
    Are the guides for my eyes to dawn's light
Doesn't night see your eyes in my face
    Where weakness and emaciation appear?
I met splendid dawn at Darb al Qulla
    My sorrow healed and night was a corpse

بَعَثْتِ بِهَا وَالشَّمْسُ مِنْكِ رَسُولُ	وَيَوْماً كَأَنَّ الحُسْنَ فِيهِ عَلَامَةٌ
وَلَا طُلِبَتْ عِنْدَ الظَّلَامِ ذُحُولُ	وَمَا قَبْلَ سَيْفِ الدَّوْلَةِ أثَارَ عَاشِقٌ
تَرُوقُ عَلَى استِغْرَابِهَا وتَهُولُ	وَلَكِنَّهُ يَأْتِي بِكُلِّ غَرِيبَةٍ
وَمَا عَلِمُوا أنَّ السِّهَامَ خُيُولُ	رَمَى الدَّرْبَ بالجُرْدِ الجِيَادِ إلى العِدَى
لَهَا مَرَحٌ مِنْ تَحْتِهِ وصَهِيلُ	شَوَائِلَ تَشْوَالَ العَقَارِبِ بِالقَنَا
بَحْرَانِ لَبَّتهَا قَنَاً وَنُصُولُ	وَمَا هِيَ إلَّا خَطْرَةٌ عَرَضَتْ لَهُ
بِأَرْعَنَ وَطْءُ المَوْتِ فِيهِ ثَقِيلُ	هُمَامٌ إذا مَا هَمَّ أمْضَى هُمُومَهُ
إذا عَرَّسَتْ فِيهَا فَلَيْسَ تَقِيلُ	وَخَيْلٍ بَرَاهَا الرَّكْضُ فِي كُلِّ بَلْدَةٍ
عَلَتْ كُلَّ طَوْدٍ رَايَةً وَرَعِيلُ	فَلَمَّا تَجَلَّى مِنْ دُلُوكٍ وصَنْجَةٍ
وَفِي ذِكرِهَا عِنْدَ الأَنِيسِ خُمُولُ	عَلَى طُرُقٍ فِيهَا عَلَى الطُّرْقِ رِفْعَةٌ
قِبَاحاً وَأَمَّا خَلْقُهَا فَجَمِيلُ	فَمَا شَعَرُوا حَتَّى رَأَوْهَا مُغِيرَةً
فَكُلُّ مَكَانٍ بِالسُّيُوفِ غَسِيلُ	سَحَائِبُ يَمْطُرْنَ الحَدِيدَ عَلَيْهِمْ
كَأَنَّ جُيُوبَ الشَّاكِلَاتِ ذُيُولُ	وَأَمْسَى السَّبَايَا يَنْتَحِبْنَ بِعِرْقَةٍ
وَلَيْسَ لَهَا إلَّا الدُّخُولَ قُفُولُ	وَعَادَتْ فَظُنُوهَا بَمَوْزَارٍ قُفَّلَا
بِكُلِّ نَجِيعٍ لَمْ تَخُضْهُ كَفِيلُ	فَخَاضَتْ نَجِيعَ القَوْمِ خَوْضاً كَأَنَّهُ
بِهِ القَوْمُ صَرْعَى والدِّيَارُ طُلُولُ	تُسَايِرُهَا النِّيرَانُ فِي كُلِّ مَنْزِلٍ
مَلَطْيَةُ أُمُّ لِلْبَنِينَ ثَكُولُ	وَكَرَّتْ فَمَرَّتْ فِي دِمَاءِ مَلَطْيَةٍ
فَأَضْحَى كَأَنَّ المَاءَ فِيهِ عَلِيلُ	وَأَضْعَفْنَ مَا كَلَّفْنَهُ مِنْ قُبَاقِبٍ
تَخِرُّ عَلَيْهِ بالرِّجَالِ سُيُولُ	وَرُعْنَ بِنَا قَلْبَ الفُرَاتِ كَأَنَّمَا
سَوَاءٌ عَلَيْهِ غَمْرَةٌ ومَسِيلُ	يُطَارِدُ فِيهِ مَوْجَهُ كُلُّ سَابِحٍ
وَأَقْبَلَ رَأْسٌ وَحْدَهُ وَتَلِيلُ	تَرَاهُ كَأَنَّ المَاءَ مَرَّ بِجِسْمِهِ
وَصُمَّ القَنَا مِمَّنْ أَبَدْنَ بَدِيلُ	وَفِي بَطْنِ هِنْرِيطٍ وسِمْنِينَ لِلظُّبَى
لَهَا غُرَرٌ مَا تَنْقَضِي وحُجُولُ	طَلَعْنَ عَلَيْهِمْ طَلْعَةً يَعْرِفُونَهَا
فَتُلْقِي إلَيْنَا أَهْلَهَا وَتَزُولُ	تَمَلُّ الحُصُونُ الشُّمُّ طُولَ نِزَالِنَا
وَكُلُّ عَزِيزٍ لِلأمِيرِ ذَلِيلُ	وَبِتْنَ بِحِصْنِ الرَّانِ رَزْحَى مِنَ الوَجَى

It was a day as if beauty was its token
    You sent out, the sun was your messenger
No lover before Saif al Daula had revenge
    Nor was vengeance taken on the darkness
But he has brought all those rare things
    To amaze with their rarity and to overcome
He hits a foe's pass on short hair horses
    And they do not know the arrows are riders
Tail high they go with scorpion lances
    They are happy beneath them in a whinny
This is only a hunch that occurs to him
    At Harran, answered with spears and blades
Hero, if need be he executes his will
    With an army, death's heavy tread in that
Horses whose gait thins them in every
    Land, after the late night stop is no siesta
As they fan from Rum Daluk and Sanja
    Pennants and troops scale every mountain
Over ways with peaks above the paths
    Among gentle folk whose memory is faint
They do not know until they see them
    Hatefully yet their nature seems handsome
Like clouds they rain iron upon them
    For every place is washed by the sword
Women captives lament in Arqa at eve
    As if bodices of the bereft were the skirts
They return and Mauzar thinks it a rout
    But not them, rather an attack's approach
They plunge into blood of all wading
    They seem surety for blood not stepped in
The flames accompany them on all ways
    Where people are slain and homes in ruin
They attack again, pass Malatia's dead
    Malatia the mother bereft of her children
They double Qubaqib's taken share
    And it seems its water is all drunk up
They scare Furat's water with us as if
    The torrents fell on it due to the waders
Each swimmer drives back the waves
    Equally, whether in depths or the rain
It seems water flows over its body
    And its head and neck alone approach
In Hinzit valley and Sumnin by sword
    And lance head, substitutes for the dead
They come among them, recognized
    Theirs a blaze unfading and leg markers
Towering forts yield to our attacks
    Cast out to us their folk and perish
They spend night Hisn Ran, hoof pain
    All proud weary ones beside their Amir

وَفي كُلِّ سَيفٍ ما خَلاهُ فُلولُ	وَفي كُلِّ نَفسٍ ما خَلاهُ مَلالَةٌ
وَأَودِيَةٌ مَجهولَةٌ وَهُجولُ	وَدونَ سُمَيساطَ المَطاميرُ وَالمَلا
وَلِلرّومِ خَطبٌ في البِلادِ جَليلُ	لَبِسنَ الدُّجى فيها إِلى أَرضِ مَرعَشٍ
دَرَوا أَنَّ كُلَّ العالَمينَ فَضولُ	فَلَمّا رَأَوهُ وَحدَهُ قَبلَ جَيشِهِ
وَأَنَّ حَديدَ الهِندِ عَنهُ كَليلُ	وَأَنَّ رِماحَ الخَطِّ عَنهُ قَصيرَةٌ
فَتىً بَأسُهُ مِثلُ العَطاءِ جَزيلُ	فَأَورَدَهُم صَدرَ الحِصانِ وَسَيفَهُ
وَلَكِنَّهُ بِالدّارِعينَ بَخيلُ	جَوادٌ عَلى العِلّاتِ بِالمالِ كُلِّهِ
بِضَربٍ حُزونُ البيضِ فيهِ سُهولُ	فَوَدَّعَ قَتلاهُم وَشَيَّعَ فَلَّهُم
وَإِن كانَ في ساقَيهِ مِنهُ كُبولُ	عَلى قَلبِ قُسطَنطينَ مِنهُ تَعَجُّبٌ
فَكَم هارِبٍ مِمّا إِلَيهِ يَؤولُ	لَعَلَّكَ يَوماً يا دُمُستُقُ عائِدٌ
وَخَلَّفتَ إِحدى مُهجَتَيكَ تَسيلُ	نَحَوتَ بِإِحدى مُهجَتَيكَ جَريحَةً
وَيَسكُنُ في الدُنيا إِلَيكَ خَليلُ	أَتُسلِمُ لِلخَطّيَّةِ اِبنَكَ هارِباً
نَصيرُكَ مِنها رَنَّةٌ وَعَويلُ	بِوَجهِكَ ما أَنساكَهُ مِن مُرشَّةٍ
عَلِيٌّ شَروبٌ لِلجُيوشِ أَكولُ	أَغَرَّكُم طولُ الجُيوشِ وَعَرضُها
غَذاهُ وَلَم يَنفَعكَ أَنَّكَ فيلُ	إِذا لَم تَكُن لِلَّيثِ إِلّا فَريسَةً
هِيَ الطَعنُ لَم يُدخِلكَ فيهِ عَذولُ	إِذا الطَعنُ لَم تُدخِلكَ فيهِ شَجاعَةٌ
فَقَد عَلَّمَ الأَيّامَ كَيفَ تَصولُ	وَإِن تَكُنِ الأَيّامُ أَبصَرنَ صَولَهُ
فَإِنَّكَ ماضي الشَفرَتَينِ صَقيلُ	فَدَتكَ مُلوكٌ لَم تُسَمَّ مَواضِياً
فَفي النّاسِ بوقاتٌ لَها وَطُبولُ	إِذا كانَ بَعضُ النّاسِ سَيفاً لِدَولَةٍ
إِذِ القَولُ قَبلَ القائِلينَ مَقولُ	أَنا السّابِقُ الهادي إِلى ما أَقولُهُ
أُصولٌ وَلا لِلقائِليهِ أُصولُ	وَما لِكَلامِ النّاسِ فيما يُريدُني
وَأَهدَأُ وَالأَفكارُ في تَجولُ	أَعادى عَلى ما يوجِبُ الحُبَّ لِلفَتى
إِذا حَلَّ في قَلبٍ فَلَيسَ يَحولُ	سِوى وَجَعِ الحُسّادِ داوِ فَإِنَّهُ
وَإِن كُنتَ تُبديها لَهُ وَتُنيلُ	وَلا تَطمَعَن مِن حاسِدٍ في مَوَدَّةٍ
كَثيرُ الزَرايا عِندَهُنَّ قَليلُ	وَأَنّا لَنَلقى الحادِثاتِ بِأَنفُسٍ
وَتَسلَمَ أَعراضٌ لَنا وَعُقولُ	يَهونُ عَلَينا أَن تُصابَ جُسومُنا

In every soul but his fatigue grips
    In each sword but him dullness holds
Before Sumaisat gorges and deserts
    The unexplored ravines and the valleys
They saw darkness near Mar'ash
    A long search for Rum lost in the land
They saw him alone before his men
    They knew all the world was redundant
Khatti lances were short for him
    As Indian steel was dull against him
He slakes by steed's breast swords
    Hero whose courage is bounteous gifts
Generous in any case with wealth
    Yet he is grudging to those in armor
He leaves the dead to chase fugitives
    By blows so the round helmets are flat
In Constantine's heart is admiration
    Though on its legs are his heavy chains
Maybe some day O Domesticus you
    Return, many a fugitive returns to him
You ran with one of your souls hurt
    Left behind the other soul bleeding
You left to Khatti your son in flight
    Can any friend rely on you in time?
By your face, blood made you forget
    Your help for it weeping and wailing
Did army size and front meet you?
    Ali drinks armies and then eats them
When the lion has no prey but one
    He feeds no matter if you're elephant
If jousting doesn't engage you keen
    As jousting, then blame can't hold you
If the days had watched the attack
    He would teach days how to skirmish
Kings not named sharp your ransom
    For you are keen, polished on edges
If any exist as half Saif al Daula
    Then horns and drums are so also
I'm winner guided as I speak of him
    When bombast forces before speech
Nothing to words of men who doubt
    By way of root, nor root to speakers
Hated for love that is owed a hero
    I rest but thoughts against me roam
You heal all but the pain of envy
    When it settles in a heart it endures
Expect no friendship from jealousy
    Even if you show it and make, gifts
Yes we met misfortunes alone
    Many raids for them, such small things
No matter to us our bodies attacked
    If only our honor and reason are safe

فَتيهاً وفَخراً تَغلِبُ ابنَةَ وائِلِ ... فَأَنتِ لِخَيرِ الفاخِرينَ قَبيلُ
يَغُمُّ عَلَيها أَن يَموتَ عَدُوُّهُ ... إِذا لَم تَغُلهُ بِالأَسِنَّةِ غولُ
شَريكُ المَنايا وَالنُفوسُ غَنيمَةٌ ... فَكُلُّ مَماتٍ لَم يُمِتهُ غُلولُ
فَإِن تَكُنِ الدَولاتُ قِسماً فَإِنَّها ... لِمَن وَرَدَ المَوتَ الزُؤامَ تَدولُ
لِمَن هَوَّنَ الدُنيا عَلى النَفسِ ساعَةً ... وَلِلبيضِ في هامِ الكُماةِ صَليلُ

(٢١٣)

«من الطويل»

قال وقد تأخر مدحه عنه فظن أنه عاتب عليه:

بِأَدنى اِبتِسامٍ مِنكَ تَحيا القَرائِحُ ... وَتَقوى مِنَ الجِسمِ الضَعيفِ الجَوارِحُ
وَمَن ذا الَّذي يَقضي حُقوقَكَ كُلَّها ... وَمَن ذا الَّذي يُرضي سِوى مَن تُسامِحُ
وَقَد تَقبَلُ العُذرَ الخَفِيَّ تَكَرُّماً ... فَما بالُ عُذري واقِفاً وَهوَ واضِحُ
وَإِن مُحالاً إِذ بِكَ العَيشُ أَن أَرى ... وَجِسمُكَ مُعتَلٌّ وَجِسمِيَ صالِحُ
وَما كانَ تَركُ الشِعرِ إِلّا لِأَنَّهُ ... تُقَصِّرُ عَن وَصفِ الأَميرِ المَدائِحُ

(٢١٤)

«من الوافر»

قال فيه يعوده من دمل كان به:

أَيَدري ما أَرابَكَ مَن يُريبُ ... وَهَل تَرقى إِلى الفَلَكِ الخُطوبُ
وَجِسمُكَ فَوقَ هِمَّةِ كُلِّ داءٍ ... فَقُربُ أَقَلِّها مِنهُ عَجيبُ
يُحَمِّشُكَ الزَمانُ هَوىً وَحُبّاً ... وَقَد يُؤذى مِنَ المُقَةِ الحَبيبُ
وَكَيفَ تُعِلُّكَ الدُنيا بِشَيءٍ ... وَأَنتَ لِعِلَّةِ الدُنيا طَبيبُ
وَكَيفَ تَنوبُكَ الشَكوى بِداءٍ ... وَأَنتَ المُستَغاثُ لِما يَنوبُ
مَلِلتَ مُقامَ يَومٍ لَيسَ فيهِ ... طِعانٌ صادِقٌ وَدَمٌ صَبيبُ
وَأَنتَ المَرءُ تُمرِضُهُ الحَشايا ... هِمَّتِهِ وَتَشفيهِ الحُروبُ
وَما بِكَ غَيرُ حُبِّكَ أَن تَراها ... وَعِثيَرُها لِأَرجُلِها جَنيبُ
مُجَلَّحَةً لَها أَرضُ الأَعادي ... وَلِلسُمرِ المَناحِرُ وَالجُنوبُ

O pride and honor of Taglib's Wail
    You finest tribe of those who boast
It grieves Ali his foe must die
    If ruin does not seize him on a lance
Partner of death when souls are loot
    So every death he forfeits is a fraud
If victory were given by lot it would
    Be for him death's swift drink to win
For him who scorns a world now
    Making a sword ring on warrior skull

213
He was slow in his praise so a complaint was made to him and he excused himself.
(Long hu)

The least smile from you revives nature
    The limbs of the weak body grow stronger
Who can pay your worth in its entirety
    Who can be content but he who is lenient?
You accepted an easy excuse cordially
    No matter urging my excuse though plain
Impossible, if life is with you, that
    I see your body sick and my body healthy
Neglecting the verses is only because
    Praise is short of the Amir's description

214
He spoke and Saif al Daula suffered from an ulcer in they year 342.
(Exuberant bu)

Does what pierces you know who is hurt
    Or why misfortune ascends to this heaven?
Your body is above the aim of any ill
    Nearness to the least of it is the wonder
Time gave kisses in love and passion
    But the beloved suffered from that caress
How could a world make you sick now
    When you are doctor to the world's ills?
How could grief afflict you with pain
    If you are savior when affliction comes?
You wearied of living a day by having
    No strong jousting and no blood flowing
You are a king whose heart is sick
    With his ambition but you can heal it
Only your love can display it and
    Its little tracks make the leg shadows
White legged it takes the enemy land
    The nose and the sides are for a spear

فَقَرَّطَهَا الأَعِنَّةِ راجِعاتٍ	فَإِنَّ بَعيدَ ما طَلَبَتْ قَريبُ
إذا داءٌ بُقراطَ هَفا عَنْهُ	فَلَمْ يُعْرَفْ لِصاحِبِهِ ضَريبُ
بِسَيْفِ الدَّوْلَةِ الوُضَّاءِ تُمْسي	جُفوني تَحْتَ شَمْسٍ ما تَغيبُ
فَأَغْزُو مَنْ غَزا وَبِهِ اقْتِداري	وَأَرْمي مَنْ رَمى وَبِهِ أُصيبُ
وَلِلحُسَّادِ عُذْرٌ أَنْ يَشِحُّوا	عَلى نَظَري إِلَيْهِ وَأَنْ يَذوبوا
فَإِنّي قَدْ وَصَلْتُ إِلى مَكانٍ	عَلَيْهِ تَحْسُدُ الحَدَقَ القُلوبُ

(٢١٥)

«من المتقارب»

لما وافى رسول ملك الروم رأى سيف الدولة يتشكى فقال: أتراه يفرح بعلتنا؟ فقال أبو الطيب:

فُديتَ بِماذا يُسَرُّ الرَّسولُ	وَأَنْتَ الصَّحيحُ بِذا لا العَليلُ
عَواقِبُ هَذا تَسوءُ العَدُوَّ	وَتَثْبُتُ فيهِمْ وَهَذا يَزولُ

(٢١٦)

«من الطويل»

قال فيه يعوده من مرض:

إذا اعتَلَّ سَيْفُ الدَّوْلَةِ اعتَلَّتِ الأَرْضُ	وَمَنْ فَوْقَها وَالبَأْسُ وَالكَرَمُ المَحْضُ
وَكَيْفَ انْتِفاعي بِالرُّقادِ وَإِنَّما	بِعِلَّتِهِ يَعْتَلُّ في الأَعْيُنِ الغُمْضُ
شَفاكَ الَّذي يَشْفي بِجودِكَ خَلْقَهُ	فَإِنَّكَ بَحْرٌ كُلُّ بَحْرٍ لَهُ بَعْضُ

(٢١٧)

«من البسيط»

قال وقد عوفي سيف الدولة مما كان به:

المَجْدُ عوفِيَ إِذْ عوفيتَ وَالكَرَمُ	وَزالَ عَنْكَ إِلى أَعدائِكَ الأَلَمُ
صَحَّتْ بِصِحَّتِكَ الغاراتُ وَابتَهَجَتْ	بِها المَكارِمُ وَانهَلَّتْ بِها الدِّيَمُ

Loosen reins on those wanting return
    For the distant which they seek is near
It is an ill Hippocrates erred about
    The like was not known to his disciples
By Saif al-Daula's gleam my eyelids
    Are struck under a sun that is not hid
He wars on him who wars, he my power
    He aims at attackers and by him I am hit
The envious are excused in their envy
    Of my sight of him even though they melt
For I have come to a place where
    The hearts envy the apple of the eye

215
Saif al-Daula said that the messenger of the king of Rome rejoiced at his illness. So Abu Tayyib spoke.
(. . . lu)

Ransomed by what pleases an envoy
    For you are healthy in that and not ailing
The end of this is you grieve the foe
    And are firm against them and so it ceases

216
He spoke about him when he was complaining about the ulcer that afflicted him.
(Long du)

If Saif al-Daula is ill the land is sick
    And what is on it, the men and bounty
How shall I make any use of sleep?
    By his illness, sleep is the eyes' own ill
He heals who heals his folk by gifts
    You are the sea that every sea is part of

217
He spoke and Saif al Daula was healed.
(Outspread mu)

Glory and nobility recover as you heal
    Grief ceases from you and goes to the foe
War is whole in your health, and bounty
    Rejoices in it, continuous showers pour

وَرَاجِعَ الشَّمسَ نوراً كانَ فارَقَها ... كَأَنَّما فَقدُهُ في جِسمِها سَقَمُ
وَلاحَ بَرقُكَ لي مِن عارِضَي مَلِكٍ ... ما يَسقُطُ الغَيثُ إِلّا حينَ يَبتَسِمُ
يُسَمّى الحُسامَ وَلَيسَت مِن مُشابَهَةٍ ... وَكَيفَ يَشتَبِهُ المَخدومُ وَالخَدَمُ
تَفَرَّدَ العُربُ في الدُنيا بِمَحتِدِهِ ... وَشارَكَ العُربَ في أَحسانِهِ العَجَمُ
وَأَخلَصَ اللَهُ لِلإِسلامِ نُصرَتَهُ ... وَإِن تَقَلَّبَ في آلائِهِ الأُمَمُ
وَما أَخَصُّكَ في بُرءٍ بِتَهنِئَةٍ، ... إِذا سَلِمتَ فَكُلُّ النّاسِ قَد سَلِموا

(٢١٨)

«من البسيط»

يهننه بعيد الفطر:

أَلصَومُ وَالفِطرُ وَالأَعيادُ وَالعُصُرُ ... مُنيرَةٌ بِكَ حَتّى الشَمسُ وَالقَمَرُ
تُري الأَهِلَّةَ وَجهاً عَمَّ نائِلُهُ ... فَما يُخَصُّ بِهِ مِن دونِها البَشَرُ
ما الدَهرُ عِندَكَ إِلّا رَوضَةٌ أُنُفٌ ... يا مَن شَمائِلُهُ في دَهرِهِ زَهَرُ
ما يَنتَهي لَكَ في أَيّامِهِ كَرَمٌ ... فَلا اِنتَهى لَكَ في أَعوامِهِ عُمُرُ
فَإِنَّ حَظَّكَ مِن تَكرارِها شَرَفٌ ... وَحَظُّ غَيرِكَ مِنها الشَيبُ وَالكِبَرُ

(٢١٩)

«من الرّجز»

مد نهر قويق فأحاط بدار سيف الدولة وخرج أبو الطيب من عنده فبلغ الماء إلى صدر فرسه فقال:

حَجَّبَ ذا البَحرَ بِحارٌ دونَهُ ... يَذُمُّها النّاسُ وَيَحمَدونَهُ
يا ماءُ هَل حَسَدتَنا مَعينَهُ ... أَم اِشتَهَيتَ أَن تَرى قَرينَهُ
أَم اِنتَجَعتَ لِلغِنى يَمينَهُ ... أَم زُرتَهُ مُكَثِّراً قَطينَهُ
أَم جِئتَهُ مُخَندِقاً حُصونَهُ ... إِنَّ الجِيادَ وَالقَنا يَكفينَهُ
يا رُبَّ لُجٍّ جُعِلَت سَفينَهُ ... وَعازِبِ الرَوضِ تَوَفَّت عونَهُ

Departed light returns to the sun
    As if its loss were sickness to her body
Your lightning gleams from royal lips
    Showers do not fall except as he smiles
Called a sword but it is no comparison
    How can a slave be compared to the master?
Arabs are unique in time by his race
    Arab shares with Persian in his goodness
God is sincere in peace with his help
    Even if the nations change by his grace
I do not say joy in health is yours only
    For if you are safe then all men are safe

218
He spoke praising him at the end of the month of Ramadan in the year 342.
(Outspread ru)

Fasting, breaking fast, holidays, times
    Find their light in you as do sun and moon
His gifts seem a crescent turned to all
    Nor is any man favored by them beyond it
Times with you are only ungrazed fields
    O you whose character blossoms in the age
In its days bounty will not end for you
    So may life not end for you in its years
Your joy in their return is unrivaled
    But others' joy in them: gray hair, old age

219
He spoke and the river Quwaiq at Aleppo had overflowed and surrounded the palace of Saif al Daula.
(Trembling hu)

Floods, less than he covers his sea
    Men disapprove it and pay homage to him
O water why do you envy us his flowing
    Or do you want to appear to be his equal?
Do you seek his right hand's wealth
    Visit him to increases his folk's numbers?
Do you come as moat for his fortress?
    But lance and horse are enough for him
O many a tide they used for his boats
    Many a far field is wasted for his asses

وَشَرْبِ كَأْسٍ أَكْثَرَتْ رَنِينَه	وَذي جُنُونٍ أَذْهَبَتْ جُنُونَه
وَضَيْغَمٍ أَوْلَجَهَا عَرينَه	وَأَبْدَلَتْ غِنَاءَهُ أَنِينَه
يَقُودُهَا مُسَهَّداً جُفُونَه	وَمَلِكٍ أَوْطَأَهَا جَبِينَه
مُشَرِّفاً بِطَعْنِهِ طَعِينَه	مُبَاشِراً بِنَفْسِهِ شُؤُونَه
شَمْسٌ تَمَنَّى الشَّمْسَ أَنْ تَكُونَه	بَحْرٌ يَكُونُ كُلَّ بَحْرٍ نُونَه
مُشَرِّفاً بِطَعْنِهِ طَعِينَه	مُبَاشِراً بِنَفْسِهِ شُؤُونَه
أَبْيَضَ مَا فِي تاجِهِ مَيْمُونَه	عَفِيفَ مَا فِي ثَوْبِهِ مَأْمُونَه
يُجِبْكَ قَبْلَ أَنْ تُتِمَّ سِينَه	إِنْ تَدْعُ يَا سَيْفُ لِتَسْتَعِينَه
مَنْ صَانَ مِنْهُمْ نَفْسَهُ وَدِينَه	أَدَامَ مِنْ أَعْدَائِهِ تَمْكِينَه

(٢٢٠)

«من الطويل»

يمدحه ويهنئه بعيد الأضحى سنة اثنتين وأربعين وثلاث مئة (٩٥٣م) أنشده إياها في ميدانه بحلب وهما على فرسيهما:

وَعَادَةُ سَيْفِ الدَّوْلَةِ الطَّعْنُ فِي العِدَى	لِكُلِّ امْرِئٍ مِنْ دَهْرِهِ مَا تَعَوَّدَا
وَيُمْسِي بِمَا تَنْوِي أَعَادِيهِ أَسْعَدَا	وَإِنْ يُكَذِّبِ الإِرْجَافَ عَنْهُ بِضِدِّهِ
وَهَادٍ إِلَيْهِ الجَيْشَ أَهْدَى وَمَا هَدَى	وَرُبَّ مُرِيدٍ ضَرَّةً ضَرَّ نَفْسَهُ
رَأَى سَيْفَهُ فِي كَفِّهِ فَتَشَهَّدَا	وَمُسْتَكْبِرٍ لَمْ يَعْرِفِ اللهَ سَاعَةً
عَلَى الدُّرِّ وَاحْذَرْهُ إِذَا كَانَ مُزْبِدَا	هُوَ البَحْرُ غُصْ فِيهِ إِذَا كَانَ سَاكِناً
وَهَذَا الَّذِي يَأْتِي الفَتَى مُتَعَمِّدَا	فَإِنِّي رَأَيْتُ البَحْرَ يَعْثُرُ بِالفَتَى
تُفَارِقُهُ هَلْكَى وَتَلْقَاهُ سُجَّدَا	تَظَلُّ مُلُوكُ الأَرْضِ خَاشِعَةً لَهُ
وَيَقْتُلُ مَا تُحْيِي التَّبَسُّمَ وَالجَدَا	وَتُحْيِي لَهُ المَالَ الصَّوَارِمَ وَالقَنَا
يَرَى قَلْبُهُ فِي يَوْمِهِ مَا تَرَى غَدَا	ذَكِيٌّ تَظَنِّيهِ طَلِيعَةَ عَيْنِهِ
فَلَوْ كَانَ قَرْنُ الشَّمْسِ مَاءً لَأَوْرَدَا	وَصُولٌ إِلَى المُسْتَصْعَبَاتِ بِخَيْلِهِ

Many a fool driven off in his madness
    Many a drinker of a cup screamed twice
They have changed his song to groans
    Many a lion whose lair he has entered
Many a king whose forehead he trod
    Leading them to the sleepless eyelids
Giving news of his affairs in person
    Overcoming his enemies by jousting
Chaste in what his garments keep safe
    Bright as to what he entrusts to a turban
An ocean, all seas only fish to him
    And a sun, the sun wishes she were him
O sword if you claim to help him
    He answers before you finish letter sin
May his power outlast his enemies
    Who guards himself and faith from them

220
He spoke praising him and congratulating him on the feast of sacrifices in the year 342.
(Long da)

To every man in his time a skill he uses
    Jousting the foe is Saif al-Daula's mastery
Refuting rumors against him with deeds
    And being happier than his foes intended
Many hoping to hurt him hurt themselves
    Army leaders make gifts to him unwittingly
Many a proud one not knowing God
    Saw his sword in his hand and converted
He is a sea, dive there when it is quiet
    For pearls but beware when the surf is up
I've known a sea overwhelm young men
    But this one coming to a man has purpose
Earth's kings remain submissive to him
    They go from him to ruin or meet him prone
The sword and spear revive his wealth
    A smile and generosity kill what revives
Astute, his eye's vanguard suspects it
    His heart knows now what he sees later
He gets riders past difficult places
    If the sun's horn had water he'd reach it

352 Diwan al-Mutanabbi

لذلـك سـمّى ابـن الدُّمُسْتُـق يومَـهُ	مَمـاتـاً وسَـمّاهُ الدُّمُسْتُـقُ مولِـدا
سَـرَيْتَ إلى جَيحـانَ مـن أرْضِ آمِـدٍ	ثَلاثـاً، لقـد أدنـاكَ ركـضٌ وأبْعَـدا
فَـوَلّى وأعطـاكَ ابْنَـهُ وَجيوشَـهُ	جَميعـاً وَلم يُعـطِ الجَميـعَ ليُحْمَـدا
عَرَضْـتَ لَـهُ دونَ الحَيـاةِ وَطَرْفِـهِ	وأبْصَـرَ سَيـفَ اللهِ منـكَ مُجَـرَّدا
وَمـا طَلَبَـتْ زُرْقُ الأسِنّـةِ غَـيرَهُ	ولكِـنّ قُسْطَنطينَ كـانَ لَـهُ الفِـدى
فأصْبَـحَ يَجْتـابُ المُسـوحَ مَخـافـةً	وقـد كـان يَجتـابُ الـدَّلاصَ المُسَرَّدا
وَيَمْشِـي بـه العُكّـازَ في الدّيـر تائبـاً	وَمـا كـان يَرْضى مشـيَ أشقَـرَ أجرَدا
وَمـا تـابَ حتـى غـادَرَ الكَـرُّ وَجْهَـهُ	جَريحـاً وَخلّـى جَفنَـهُ النقـعُ أرْمَـدا
فَلَـوْ كـانَ يُنجـي مـن عَلِّـي تَرَهُّـبٌ	تَرَهبّـتِ الأمـلاكُ مَثنـى وَمَوْحَـدا
وكـلُّ امـرىءٍ في الشّـرقِ وَالغـرْبِ بعـدَه	يُعِـدُّ لَـهُ ثَوبـاً مِـن الشَّعـرِ أسْـوَدا
هَنيئـاً لَـكَ العيـدُ الـذي أنـتَ عيـدُهُ	وَعيـدٌ لِمَـنْ سَمّـى وَضَحّـى وَعَيَّـدا
وَلا زَالَـتِ الأعيـادُ لُبْسَـكَ بَعْـدَهُ	تُسَـلِّـمُ مخْروقـاً وَتُعْطـى مُجَـدَّدا
فَـذا اليَـوْمُ في الأيـامِ مثلُـكَ في الـوَرى	كمـا كنـتَ فيهـم أوْحَـداً كـانَ أوْحَـدا
هـوَ الجِـدّ حتـى تَفْضُـلُ العَيـنُ أُخْتَهـا	وَحتـى يكـونُ اليَـوْمُ لليَـوْمِ سَيِّـدا
فَيـا عَجَبـاً مِـنْ دائِـلٍ أنـتَ سَيْفُـهُ	أمـا يَتَوَقّـى شَفـرَتَيْ مـا تَقَلَّـدا
وَمَـنْ يَجعـلُ الضِّرْغـامَ للصّيْـدِ بـازَهُ	تَصَيَّـدَهُ الضِّرْغـامُ فيمـا تَصَيَّـدا
رَأيْتُـكَ مَحْـضَ الحِلْـمِ في مَحْـضِ قُـدرَةٍ	وَلَـوْ شئـتَ كـانَ الحِلْـمُ منـكَ المُهَنَّـدا
وَمـا قَتْـلُ الأحـرارِ كالعَفـوِ عَنْهُـم	وَمَـنْ لـكَ بالحُـرِّ الـذي يَحفَـظُ اليَـدا
إذا أنـتَ أكْرَمْـتَ الكَريـمَ مَلَكْتَـهُ	وَإنْ أنـتَ أكْرَمْـتَ اللئيـمَ تَمَـرَّدا
وَوَضْـعُ النَّـدى في موضـعِ السَّيفِ بالعُلـى	مُضِـرٌّ كوضْـعِ السيفِ في موضـعِ النَّـدى
ولكِـنّ تَفـوقُ النّـاسِ رَأيـاً وَحِكمـةً	كمـا فُقْتَهُـم حـالاً وَنَفسـاً وَمَحْتِـدا
يَـدِقّ علـى الأفكـارِ مـا أنـتَ فـاعِـلٌ	فيُتـرَكُ مـا يَخفـى وَيؤخَـذُ مـا بَـدا
أزِلْ حَسَـدَ الحُسّـادِ عَنّـي بِكبتِهـم	فـأنتَ الـذي صَيَّرْتَهُـمْ لِيَ حُسَّـدا
إذا شَـدَّ زَنْـدي حُسْـنُ رأيِـكَ فيهـم	ضَرَبْـتُ بسَيـفٍ يَقطَـعُ الهـامَ مُغْمَـدا
وَمـا أنـا إلاّ سَمْهَـرِيٌّ حَمَلْتَـهُ	فَزَيَّـنَ مَعْروضـاً وَراعَ مُسَـدَّدا
وَمَـا الدّهـرُ إلاّ مِـنْ رُواةِ قَصائـدي	إذا قُلـتُ شِعـراً أصبَـحَ الدّهـرُ مُنشِـدا

Thus a son of Domesticus called his day
    Dying, and the Domesticus called it birth
He traveled to Jaihan from Amid lands
    Three nights riding took you near and far
He turned and gave his son and army
    All, but he did not give it all for praise
You rose between his life and vision
    He saw God's sword in you unsheathed
The blue lance sought none but him
    When Constantine was ransom for him
He put on a monk's robe out of fear
    Once he put on the linked coat of mail
Canes helped his monastery penance
    Not content to go no shorthaired sorrel
He repented, not till war left his face
    Wounded as dust left his eyelids rheumy
If he could escape Ali as a monk
    Kings would be monks in pairs or singly
Every man in east or west after this
    Would have a black hair robe himself
A feast whose festival you are honors
    A rite for all who pray, sacrifice, rejoice
May feasts be as robes for you after
    ou return them worn to be given new
This day among days is like you
    You are sole among men, it is unique
It is chance if an eye is favored over
    Its sister as one day is lord over others
O wonder, a ruler whose sword is you
    Does he not fear edges he has girded?
He who makes a lion hunt has a hawk
    The lion will hunt as he hunts the others
I know you as pure clemency in power
    If you wish your clemency can be steel
Nothing kills free men like forgiving
    But which of your free men remember?
If you honor a good man you own him
    If you are good to the vile one he rebels
Putting bounty in sword's high place
    Harms like setting sword in gifts' place
You excel men in wisdom and wit
    As you excel in nobility, soul, lineage
What you do is too subtle to think
    One leaves the hid to take the obvious
End jealous envy by crushing them
    You are one who made them envy me
If your good idea nerves my arm I'll
    Beat with sheathed blade their heads
I'm only a strong spear you carry
    Adorning upright but feared if leveled
Time is only one reciter of my jewels
    If I speak verse the age comes to sing it

وَغَنّى بِهِ مَن لا يُغَنّي مُغَرِّدَا	فَسارَ بِهِ مَن لا يَسيرُ مُشَمِّراً
بِشِعري أَتاكَ المادِحونَ مُرَدَّدَا	أَجِزني إِذا أَنشَدتَ شِعراً فَإِنَّما
أَنا الطائِرُ المَحكِيُّ وَالآخَرُ الصَدى	وَدَع كُلَّ صَوتٍ غَيرَ صَوتي فَإِنَّني
وَأَنعَلتُ أَفراسي بِنُعماكَ عَسجَدَا	تَرَكتُ السُرى خَلقي لِمَن قَلَّ مالُهُ
وَمَن وَجَدَ الإِحسانَ قَيداً تَقَيَّدَا	وَقَيَّدتُ نَفسي في ذَراكَ مَحَبَّةً
وَكُنتَ عَلى بُعدٍ جَعَلناكَ مَوعِدَا	إِذا سَأَلَ الإِنسانُ أَيّامَهُ الغِنى

(٢٢١)

«من الرّجز»

وجرى ذكر ما بين العرب والأكراد من الفضل فقال سيف الدولة: ما تقول في هذا يا أبا الطيب؟ فقال:

فَخَيرُهُم أَكثَرُهُم فَضائِلا	إِن كُنتَ عَن خَيرِ الأَنامِ سائِلا
اَلطاعِنينَ في الوَغى أَوائِلا	مَن كُنتَ مِنهُم يا هُمامُ وائِلا
قَد فَضَلوا بِفَضلِكَ القَبائِلا	وَالعاذِلينَ في النَدى العَواذِلا

(٢٢٢)

«من البسيط»

قال وقد دخل عليه رسول ملك الروم سنة ثلاث وأربعين وثلاث مئة (٩٥٤م):

لا يَصدُقُ الوَصفُ حَتّى يَصدُقَ النَظَرُ	ظُلمٌ لِذا اليَومِ وَصفٌ قَبلَ رُؤيَتِهِ
إِلى بِساطِكَ لي سَمعٌ وَلا بَصَرُ	تَزاحَمَ الجَيشُ حَتّى لَم يَجِد سَبَباً
مُعايِناً وَعِياني كُلُّهُ خَبَرُ	فَكُنتُ أَشهَدُ مُختَصّاً وَأَغيَبُهُ
لِأَنَّ عَفوَكَ عَنهُ عِندَهُ ظَفَرُ	أَليَومَ يَرفَعُ مَلكُ الرومِ ناظِرَهُ
فَما يَزالُ عَلى الأَملاكِ يَفتَخِرُ	وَإِن أَجَبتَ بِشَيءٍ عَن رَسائِلِهِ
مِنَ السُيوفِ وَباقي القَومِ يَنتَظِرُ	قَدِ اِستَراحَت إِلى وَقتٍ رِقابُهُم

He runs by it who goes with ungirt loins
    He sings with it who has never sung songs
Pay men who hear my verses recited
    By my poetry eulogists come in crowds
Disregard each voice but my voice
    I'm the speaker told about as others echo
I left night trips to one of small good
    Shod my horse with gifts of purest gold
I chained myself to your shield in love
    He who finds a chain good, is now bound
When a man asks his times for wealth
    And you are absent makes a date with you

221

There was talk about the virtues of the Arabs and the Kurds so Saif al Daula said: What do you say about this, your judgment, Abu Tayyib. So he spoke.
(Trembling la)

If you ask about the best of men
    The best of them has the most virtue
Such as you are O hero of Wail
    The first of the jousters in a battle
Censurers of those who blame gifts
    Have preferred tribes by your merit

222

He spoke and the envoy of the king of Rome had just come to Saif al- Daula in Safar of the year 340.
(Outspread ru)

Day's evil has a name before it's seen
    But a word is not true until vision tests it
The army pushed till it found no way but
    To your carpet, as I heard but did not see
I was present as chosen yet was absent
    As to seeing, my eyes reported all of this
Today the king of Rum raises his vision
    Since your pardon to him is victory for him
If you answer anything to his letter
    There will be no end to the kings' boasting
His guards think of resting a bit now
    From swords, but other peoples expect them

(٢٢٣)

«من الطويل»

قال يمدحه بعد دخول رسول الروم عليه:

دُرُوعٌ لِمَلْكِ الرُّومِ هذي الرَّسائِلُ	يَرُدُّ بها عَنْ نَفْسِهِ وَيُشاغِلُ
هيَ الزَّرَدُ الضّافي عليهِ وَلَفْظُها	عَلَيْكَ ثَناءٌ سابغٌ وَفَضائِلُ
وأَنَّى اهْتَدى هذا الرَّسُولُ بأرْضِهِ	وما سكَنَتْ مذْ سرْتَ فيها القَساطِلُ
وَمِنْ أيِّ ماءٍ كانَ يَسقي جِيادَهُ	ولَمْ تَصْفُ مِنْ مَزْجِ الدِّماءِ المَناهِلُ
أتاكَ يكادُ الرَّأسُ يَجحَدُ عُنقَهُ	وتَنقَدُّ تحتَ الدِّرْعِ منهُ المَفاصِلُ
يُقَوِّمُ تَقويمُ السِّماطَينِ مِشْيَهُ	إلَيكَ إذا ما عَوَّجَتْهُ الأفاكِلُ
فَقاسَمَكَ العَينَينِ منهُ وَلَحظَهُ	سَمِيُّكَ والخَيلُ الذي لا تُزايِلُ
وأَبصَرَ منكَ الرِّزْقَ والرِّزْقُ مُطمِعٌ	وأَبصَرَ منهُ المَوْتَ والمَوْتُ هائِلُ
وَقَبَّلَ كُمّاً قبَّلَ التُّرْبَ قَبْلَهُ	وَكُلَّ كَمِيٍّ واقِفٍ مُتَضائِلُ
وأَسْعَدُ مُشتاقٍ وأَظْفَرُ طالِبٍ	هُمامٌ إلى تَقبيلِ كَمِّكَ واصِلُ
مَكانٌ تَمَنَّاهُ الشِّفاهُ ودُونَهُ	صُدورُ المَذاكي والرِّماحُ الذَّوابِلُ
فَما بَلَّغَتْهُ ما أرادَ كَرامَةٌ	عَلَيكَ ولكِنْ لم يَخِبْ لكَ سائِلُ
وأَكبَرَ مِنهُ هِمَّةً بَعَثَتْ بهِ	إلَيكَ العِدى واستَنظَرَتْهُ الجَحافِلُ
فأَقْبَلَ مِنْ أَصْحابِهِ وهوَ مُرْسَلٌ	وعادَ إلى أصحابِهِ وهوَ عاذِلُ
تَحَيَّرَ في سَيْفٍ رَبيعَةَ أصْلُهُ	وطابعُهُ الرَّحمَنُ والمَجدُ صاقِلُ
وَما لَوْنُهُ مِمّا تُحَصِّلُ مُقْلَةٌ	ولا حَدُّهُ مِمّا تَجُسُّ الأنامِلُ
إذا عايَنَتْكَ الرُّسْلُ هانَتْ نُفُوسُها	عَلَيها وَما جاءَتْ بهِ والمَراسِلُ
رَجا الرُّومُ مَنْ تُرْجى النَّوافِلُ كلُّها	لَدَيهِ ولا تُرْجى لدَيهِ الطَّوائِلُ
فإنْ كانَ خَوْفُ القَتلِ والأَسْرِ ساقَهُمْ	فقد فَعَلوا ما القَتلُ والأَسْرُ فاعِلُ

You exchanged them for other nations
    So people's heads and necks may multiply
Your bounty's likeness to morning rain
    Is your hand's second bounty as rain takes
The sun receives rising light from you
    As the moon receives its light from hers

223
He spoke also praising him after the arrival of the envoy of the king of Rum. (Long lu)

The letters are hauberks for the Rum king
    He defends himself by them as he struggles
Thick chain mail for him and their swords
    Fulsome praise for you and an attainment
How could this envoy cross his land
    When dust you stirred up hasn't settled?
From which pools did he water horses?
    None of the springs are free of bloody mix
He comes to you, almost the head fears
    The neck with muscles cut due to fleeing
He has a soldier's stance in his walk
    To you, except when trembling distorts it
He shares eyes and vision with you
    Your name and the friend that endures
He sees in you his life and he wants it
    He sees death in it and death is dreadful
He kisses a sleeve, kisses dust before
    While the warriors stand all insignificant
Happiest of lovers, luckiest of clients
    Is a hero who attains to kiss your sleeve
A place his lips long for but in front
    Breasts of war horses and pliant spears
Nobility won't get what it wants of you
    And yet a client is not rejected by you
Greater ones than him the eager foe
    Has sent you, armies have waited on it
He moves from his friends as envoy
    Returns to his companions to complain
Rabita's offspring worries by a sword
    The Merciful formed and glory polished
The eye cannot attain to such a color
    Not can the fingers test the edge of it
If messengers see you their souls are
    Scorned as is the message sent by them
The Rum beg of one who gives gifts
    They do not seek his hatred from him
If fear of death and capture drove them
    They act now as dead men and prisoners

وَجاؤوكَ حتى ما تُرادُ السَّلاسِلُ	فخافوكَ حتى ما لِقَتلِ زيادَةُ
كأنَّكَ بَحرٌ والمُلوكُ جَداوِلُ	أرى كُلَّ ذي مُلْكٍ إلَيكَ مَصيرُهُ
فَوابِلُهُم طَلٌّ وطَلُّكَ وابِلُ	إذا مَطَرَتْ مِنهُم ومنكَ سَحائِبُ
وقَد لَقِحَتْ حَربٌ فإنَّكَ نازِلُ	كريمٌ متى استُوهِبْتَ ما أنتَ راكِبٌ
ولا تُعطِيَنَّ النّاسَ ما أنا قائِلُ	أذا الجُودِ أعْطِ النّاسَ ما أنتَ مالكٌ
ضَعيفٌ يُقاويني قَصيرٌ يُطاوِلُ	أفي كُلِّ يَومٍ تَحتَ ضِبْني شُوَيْعِرٌ
وقَلبي بصَمتي ضاحِكٌ مِنهُ هازِلُ	لِساني بنُطقي صامِتٌ عنهُ عادِلٌ
وأغيَظُ مَن عاداكَ مَن لا تُشاكِلُ	وأَعْجَبُ مَن ناداكَ مَن لا تُجيبُهُ
بَغيضٌ إليَّ الجاهِلُ المُتَعاقِلُ	وما التّيهُ طِبّي فيهم غَيرَ أنّني
وأكثَرُ مالي أنّني لَكَ آمِلُ	وأكبَرُ تِيهي أنّني بِكَ واثِقٌ
يَعيشُ بها حَقٌّ ويَهلِكُ باطِلُ	لَعَلَّ لسَيفِ الدَّولَةِ القَرْمِ هَبَّةً
وهُنَّ الغَوازي السّالِماتُ القَواتِلُ	رَمَيتُ عِداهُ بالقَوافي وفَضلِهِ
ولَو حارَبَتهُ ناحَ فيها الثَّواكِلُ	وقَد زَعَموا أنَّ النُّجومَ خَوالِدٌ
وألطَفُها لَو أنَّهُ المُتَناوِلُ	وَما كانَ أدناها لَهُ لَو أرادَها
إذا لَثَمَتْهُ بالغُبارِ القَنابِلُ	قَريبٌ عَلَيهِ كُلُّ ناءٍ على الوَرى
ولَيسَ لها وَقتاً عن الجُودِ شاغِلُ	تُدَبِّرُ شَرْقَ الأرضِ والغَرْبَ كَفُّهُ
فَمَن فَرَّ حَرباً عارَضَتهُ الغَوائِلُ	يُتَبِّعُ هُرّابَ الرِّجالِ مُرادَهُ
تَلقّاهُ مِنهُ حَيثُما سارَ نائِلُ	ومَن فَرَّ مِن إحسانِهِ حَسَداً لَهُ
لَهُ كامِلاً حتى يُرى وهوَ شامِلُ	فَتًى لا يَرى أحسانَهُ وهوَ كامِلٌ
فأنتَ فتاها والمَليكُ الحُلاحِلُ	إذا العَرَبُ العَرْباءُ رازَتْ نُفوسَها
بأمرِكَ والتَفَّتْ عَلَيكَ القَبائِلُ	أطاعَتْكَ في أرواحِها وتَصَرَّفَت
وَما يَنكُتُ الفُرسانَ إلَّا العَوامِلُ	وكُلَّ أنابيبِ القَنا مَدَدٌ لَهُ
إلَيكَ أنقِياداً لاقتَضَتهُ الشَّمائِلُ	رَأيتُكَ لَو لَم يَقتَضِ الطَّعنَ في الوَغى
مِنَ النّاسِ طُرّاً عَلَّمَتهُ المَناصِلُ	ومَن لَم تُعَلِّمهُ لَكَ الذُّلَّ نَفسُهُ

They fear you so death is no reward
    They come to you so chains add nothing
So I see all royalty coming to you as
    If you were the sea and the kings rivers
If clouds give rain from you and them
    Their showers are dew, your dew showers
Noble man who gives what you ride on
    War rages for you and you the attacker
O give bounty to men whom you own
    Never give to men what I am speaker of
Every day under my armpit a little poet
    A weakling heartens me, short in stretch
My speaking tongue is quiet to avoid
    My heart silently laughs, jesting with him
I tire of one talks if you don't answer
    I detest one who offends if you aren't him
Pride is not my habit with them, but
    Hateful to me is the fool and a sophist
My greatest joy is I can trust you
    My greatest wealth is I can hope in you
Maybe noble Saif al-Daula will allow
    Truth to come alive and vanity to perish
I hit his foes by my verse and his merit
    They were raided and yielded as beaten
They think the stars are immortal but
    If they make war on him the bereft wail
Nor would the near be his if he wished
    Or the easiest if he wanted to hold them
All things far for men are near for him
    If the herd of horses are veiled in dust
His hand rules earth east and west
    And has only time to bestow his bounty
His will follows the flight of men
    He who flees in war has ruin facing him
He who flees good work envious of him
    Meets some of it where his gifts appear
Hero whose good though perfect he feels
    Imperfect till it's seen as enveloping all
When the Arabs of the Arabs consider
    You are their hero and greatest of kings
They submit to you in their souls, obey
    Your command as the tribes gather round
All of the lance joints support it
    Yet only the point can pierce the knight
I see you, if jousting wins no war for
    You, yielding as good qualities gain it
He who does not learn surrender
    Swords will teach him with all mankind

(٢٢٤)

«من الطويل»

رَأى خَلَّتي مِن حَيثُ يَخفى مكانُها ** فكانَتْ قَذَى عَينَيهِ حتى تَجَلَّتِ

وسأله إجازته فكتب تحته ورسوله واقف:

لَنا مَلِكٌ لا يَطعَمُ النَّومَ هَمُّهُ ** مَمَاتٌ لِحَيٍّ أوْ حَياةٌ لِمَيِّتِ

ويَكبُرُ أنْ تَقذَى بِشَيْءٍ جُفُونُهُ ** إذا ما رَأتْهُ خَلَّةً بِكَ فَرَّتِ

جَزَى اللهُ عَنِّي سَيْفَ دَوْلَةِ هاشِمٍ ** فإنَّ نَداهُ الغَمرَ سَيْفي ودَوْلَتي

(٢٢٥)

«من الوافر»

أحدث بنو كلاب حدثاً بنواحي بالس وسار سيف الدولة خلفهم وأبو الطيب معه فأدركهم بعد ليلة بين ماءين يعرفان بالغبارات والخزارات فأوقع بهم وملك الحريم فأبقى عليه فقال أبو الطيب بعد رجوعه من هذه الغزوة وأنشده إياها في جمادى الأخرى سنة ثلاث وأربعين وثلاث مئة (٩٥٤م):

بِغَيرِكَ راعِياً عَبِثَتْ الذِّئابُ ** وَغَيرَكَ صارِماً ثَلَّمَ الضِّرابُ

وَتَمْلِكُ أنْفُسَ الثَّقَلَينِ طُرّاً ** فكَيفَ تَحُوزُ أنْفُسَها كِلابُ

وَما تَرَكُوكَ مَعْصِيَةً وَلَكِنْ ** يُعافُ الوَرْدُ والمَوْتُ الشَّرابُ

طَلَبْتَهُمْ عَلى الأمْواهِ حَتَّى ** تَخَوَّفَ أنْ تُفَتِّشَهُ السَّحابُ

فَبِتَّ لَيالِياً لا نَومَ فِيها ** تَخُبُّ بِكَ المُسَوَّمَةُ العِرابُ

يَهُزُّ الجَيشُ حَوْلَكَ جانِبَيهِ ** كَما نَفَضَتْ جَناحَيها العُقابُ

وَتَسْألُ عَنهُمُ الفَلَواتُ حتى ** أجابَكَ بَعضُها وَهُمُ الجَوابُ

فَقاتَلَ عَنْ حَريمِهِمْ وَفَرّوا ** نَدى كَفَّيكَ والنَّسَبُ القُرابُ

وَحِفْظُكَ فيهِمْ سَلَفَيْ مَعَدٍّ ** وَأنَّهُمُ العَشائِرُ والصِّحابُ

224
**Saif al-Daula sent Abu Tayyib
the words of the poet:
I'll thank life if it softens by death /
My hands give nothing even if strong*
A man not hiding wealth from his friend /
Nor making complaint when the shoe is worn out*
He sees poverty in the place where it hides /
It was a mote in his eye until it was glorified
And he asked him to add to it
so he spoke and the messenger stood by waiting.
(Long li)**

Our king savors no sleep but his will
    Is death to the living, life to the dead
His eyes too great to feel any motes
    When poverty sees him with you it cools
God reward Saif al Daula al Hashimi
    His great bounty is my sword and state

225
**He spoke commemorating
his battle with the Banu
Kilab in Jumadi
in the year 343.
(Exuberant bu)**

If others than you rule wolves will play
    When others strike the sword will be dull
You possess jinn and men's souls all
    How should the Kilab hold on to their souls
They do not leave you to rebel but still
    The drinker must loathe a drink of death
You sought them at water holes until
    The cloud feared you were seeking itself
You spent the nights without any sleep
    The marked Arab steed trotted with you
The army shook its flanks around you
    Like the eagle that ruffles its wing span
You asked the desert about them till
    Some responded to you and were replies
Some took sacred things as they fled
    Your hand's bounty, near relationship
Your care for them as descendants
    Of Maadd who were kin and so friends

وَقَدْ شَرِقَتْ بِظُعْنِهِم الشِّعَابُ	تُكَفْكِفُ عَنْهُمْ صُمَّ العَوَالِي
وَأَجْهَضَتِ الحَوائِلُ وَالسِّقَابُ	وَأَسْقَطَتِ الأَجِنَّةُ فِي الوَلَايَا
وَكَعْبٌ فِي مَيَاسِرِهِمْ كِعَابُ	وَعَمْرٌو فِي مَيَامِنِهِمْ عُمُورُ
وَخَاذَلَهَا قُرَيْطٌ وَالضِّبَابُ	وَقَدْ خَذَلَتْ أَبُو بَكْرٍ بَنِيهَا
تَخَاذَلَتِ الجَمَاجِمُ وَالرِّقَابُ	إِذَا مَا سِرْتُ فِي آثَارِ قَوْمٍ
عَلَيْهِنَّ القَلائِدُ وَالمَلَابُ	فَعُدْنَ كَمَا أُخِذْنَ مُكَرَّمَاتٍ
وَأَيْنَ مِنَ الَّذِي تُوَلِّي الثَّوَابُ	يُثِيبُكَ بِالَّذِي أَوْلَيْتَ شُكْرًا
وَلَا فِي صَوْنِهِنَّ لَدَيْكَ عَابُ	وَلَيْسَ مَصِيرُهُنَّ إِلَيْكَ شَيْنًا
إِذَا أَبْصَرْنَ غُرَّتَكَ اغْتِرَابُ	وَلَا فِي فَقْدِهِنَّ بَنِي كِلَابٍ
تُصِيبُهُمُ فَيُؤْلِمُكَ المُصَابُ	وَكَيْفَ يَتِمُّ بَأْسُكَ فِي أُنَاسٍ
فَإِنَّ الرَّفْقَ بِالجَانِي عِتَابُ	تَرَفَّقْ أَيُّهَا المَوْلَى عَلَيْهِمْ
إِذَا تَدْعُو لِحَادِثَةٍ أَجَابُوا	وَإِنَّهُمْ عَبِيدُكَ حَيْثُ كَانُوا
بِأَوَّلِ مَعْشَرٍ خَطِئُوا فَتَابُوا	وَعَيْنُ المُخْطِئِينَ هُمْ وَلَيْسُوا
وَهَجْرُ حَيَاتِهِمْ لَهُمُ عِقَابُ	وَأَنْتَ حَيَاتُهُمْ غَضِبَتْ عَلَيْهِم
وَلَكِنْ رُبَّمَا خَفِيَ الصَّوَابُ	وَمَا جَهِلَتْ أَيَادِيكَ البَوَادِي
وَكَمْ بُعْدٍ مُوَلَّدُهُ اقْتِرَابُ	وَكَمْ ذَنْبٍ مُوَلَّدُهُ دَلَالٌ
وَحَلَّ بِغَيْرِ جَارِمِهِ العَذَابُ	وَجُرْمٍ جَرَّهُ سُفَهَاءُ قَوْمٍ
فَقَدْ يَرْجُو عَلَيًّا مَنْ يَهَابُ	فَإِنْ هَابُوا بِجُرْمِهِم عَلِيًّا
فَمِنْهُ جُلُودُ قَيْسٍ وَالثِّيَابُ	وَإِنْ يَكُ سَيْفَ دَوْلَةٍ غَيْرَ قَيْسٍ
وَفِي أَيَّامِهِ كَثُرُوا وَطَابُوا	وَتَحْتَ رَبَابِهِ نَبَتُوا وَأَثْرُوا
وَذَلَّ لَهُمْ مِنَ العَرَبِ الصِّعَابُ	وَتَحْتَ لِوَائِهِ ضَرَبُوا الأَعَادِي
تَنَاهَى عَنْ شُمُوسِهِمِ ضَبَابُ	وَلَوْ غَيْرُ الأَمِيرِ غَزَا كِلَابًا
يُلَاقِي عِنْدَهُ الذِّئْبَ الغُرَابُ	وَلَاقَى دُونَ ثَنَايَاهُم طِعَانًا
وَيَكْفِيهَا مِنَ المَاءِ السَّرَابُ	وَخَيْلًا تَغْتَذِي رِيحَ المَوَامِي
فَمَا نَفَعَ الوُقُوفُ وَلَا الذَّهَابُ	وَلَكِنْ رَبُّهُمْ أَسْرَى إِلَيْهِمْ
وَلَا خَيْلٌ حَمَلْنَ وَلَا رِكَابُ	وَلَا لَيْلٌ أَجَنَّ وَلَا نَهَارُ

You turned the lance point as the hill
    Passes choked with women on camels
Babes were let fall on camel rugs
    Male and female camel colts dropped
Amr was an emigrant on the right
    And Ka'b a bone's joint on the left
Abu Bakr was ashamed of her sons
    Quraitza and Dibab blushing for them
If you follow tracks of the people
    The skulls and heads are left behind
Women return as if in reverence
    ith the necklaces and charms held
Firm in thanks for what you gave
    ut where is a reward for what he did?
Their journey was no disgrace nor
    Their protection by you any censure
Nor their loss of the Banu Kilab
    Any forsaking when they saw you
How could your valor to men end
    In subduing them if victory pained you?
You are friendly, O lord, to them
    But pity for culprits is blameworthy
They your servants where you are
    When you call in trouble they answer
They are true wrongdoers but are
    Not the first folk to err and repent
You are their life, angry at them
    Losing life for them is destruction
Your gifts not unknown to bedouin
    But yet many times the effect is hidden
Many a sin has a misguided birth
    Often distance is due to being close
Many a crime men's folly attracts
    Penalty falls on another than the doer
If they fear Ali in their crimes
    Those who fear must trust Ali truly
If Saif al-Daula is not of Qais yet
    From him Qais has courage and cover
In his shade they grow and flower
    In his days they multiply and sweeten
Under his banner they beat the foe
    And the fiercest Arabs submit to them
If another than Amir wars on Kilab
    The mists will turn him from their suns
He met the foe outside the guard
    Stones, where ravens meet the wolf
Horses that feed on desert winds
    The mirage is enough water for them
But their lord comes at night
    No use in waiting and escaping
No night can cover them nor day
    No horses take them off nor camels

لَـهُ فـي البَــرِّ خَلفَهُــمُ عُبــابُ	رَمَيتَهُــمُ بِبَحــرٍ مِــن حَديــدٍ
وَصَبَّحَهُــمْ وَبَسْــطُهُمُ تُــرابُ	فَمَسَّــاهُمْ وَبَسْــطُهُمْ حَريــرٌ
كَمَــنْ فــي كَفِّــهِ مِنهُــمْ خِضــابُ	وَمَــنْ فـي كَفِّــهِ مِنهُــمْ قَنــاةٌ
زَمــنٌ أَبْقــى وَأَبْقَتْــهُ الحِــرابُ	بَنــو قَتْلــي أَبيــكَ بِــأَرْضِ نَجــدٍ
وَفي أَعْنــاقِ أَكثَرِهِــمْ سِــخابُ	عَفــا عَنهُــمْ وَأَعْتَقَهُــمْ صِغــاراً
وَكُــلِّ فَعــالِ كُلِّكُــمُ عُجــابُ	وَكُلُّكُــمْ أَتـــى مَــأْتــى أَبيــهِ
وَمِثْــلَ سُــرَاكَ فَلْيَكُــنِ الطِّــلابُ	كَـذا فَلْيَسْــرِ مَــن طَلَــبَ الأَعــادي

(٢٢٦)

«من الطويل»

يمدحه ويذكر بناءه ثغر الحدث سنة ثلاث
وأربعين وثلاث مئة (٩٥٤م):

وَتَــأْتي عَلــى قَــدْرِ الكِــرامِ المَكــارِمُ	عَلــى قَــدْرِ أَهْــلِ العَــزْمِ تَــأْتي العَزائِــمُ
وَتَصْغُــرُ فــي عَيْــنِ العَظيــمِ العَظائِــمُ	وَتَعْظُــمُ فـي عَيْــنِ الصَّغيــرِ صِغارُهــا
وَقَــدْ عَجَــزَتْ عَنـهُ الجُيــوشُ الخَضــارِمُ	يُكَلَّــفُ سَيْــفُ الدَّوْلَــةِ الجَيْشَ هَمَّــهُ
وَذَلِــكَ مــا لا تَدَّعيــهِ الضَّراغِــمُ	وَيَطلُــبُ عِنــدَ النّـاسِ ما عِنــدَ نَفْسِــهِ
نُســورُ الفَــلا أَحْداثُهــا وَالقَشــاعِمُ	يُفَــدّي أَتَــمُّ الطَّيْــرِ عُمْــراً سِلاحَــهُ
وَقَــدْ خُلِقَــتْ أَسْيافُــهُ وَالقَوائِــمُ	وَمــا ضَرَّهــا خَلْــقٌ بِغَيْــرِ مَخالِــبٍ
وَتَعْلَــمُ أَيُّ السَّــاقِيَيْنِ الغَمائِــمُ	هَلِ الحَــدَثُ الحَمْــراءُ تَعــرِفُ لَوْنَهــا
فَلَمّــا دَنــا مِنهــا سَقَتْهــا الجَماجِــمُ	سَقَتْهــا الغَمــامُ الغُــرُّ قَبْــلَ نُزولِــهِ
وَمَــوْجُ المَنايــا حَوْلَهــا مُتَلاطِــمُ	بَناهــا فَأَعْلــى وَالقَنــا يَقْــرَعُ القَنــا
وَمِــنْ جُثَــثِ القَتْلــى عَلَيْهــا تَمائِــمُ	وَكــانَ بِهــا مِثْــلُ الجُنــونِ فَأَصْبَحَــتْ
عَلــى الدّيْــنِ بِالخَطِّــيِّ وَالدَّهْــرُ راغِــمُ	طَريــدَةَ دَهْــرٍ ساقَهــا فَرَدَدْتَهــا
وَهُــنَّ لِمــا يَأْخُــذْنَ مِنــكَ غَــوارِمُ	تُفيــتُ اللَّيــالي كُــلَّ شَــيْءٍ أَخَذْتَــهُ
مَضــى قَبْــلَ أَنْ تُلقــى عَلَيْــهِ الجَوازِمُ	إِذا كــانَ مــا تَنْويــهِ فِعْــلاً مُضارِعــاً
وَذا الطَّعْــنُ آســاسٌ لَهــا وَدَعائِــمُ	وَكَيْــفَ تُرَجّــي الــرّومُ وَالــرّوسُ هَدْمَهــا

You charge on them with an iron sea
    It leaves behind them waves on land
Evening comes, their carpets silk
    With the dawn the carpets are dust
What he has in his hand is a spear
    As the color on his hands is of them
Of those your father killed in Najd
    One yet remains, a short spear saved
He forgave them, spared little ones
    Amulets on the necks of most of them
All of you did what his father did
    All of your acts just as astonishing
So may it be if one seeks the foe
    Likewise your joy in the attainment

226
He spoke praising him and commemorating the building of the border fort of al Hadath and its siege by the mercenary army of Rome in the year 343.
(Long mu)

According to men's wills strength comes
    Noble acts come in respect to their bounty
Small seems great to little folk's eyes
    Greatness seems small to eyes of the great
Saif al-Daula loads an army with his plan
    And these vast forces are exhausted by him
He seeks from men what he is himself, it
    Is something which even lions do not demand
Longest lived birds ransom his weapons
    The young and old eagles of the wasteland
Born with no claws is no worry to them
    For his swords and their hilts are created
Does red al Hadath understand her color
    She know which of two cupbearers is cloud?
Fine mists flowed on her before his blow
    When he neared her, skulls poured for her
He founded, raised her, spear met spear
    And the waves of death pounded about her
She seemed insane but she would endure
    Corpses of the dead were amulets upon her
Time's beast took her but you turned her
    To faith with Khatti lances spite of the fates
You made the nights lose all they took
    If they took from you they were the debtors
When you intend a verb in jussive form
    It is past before you put the jazm to its end
Can Rum and Russians hope to destroy
    If such strokes are her base and her pillars?

فَما ماتَ مَظلومٌ وَلا عاشَ ظالِمُ	وَقَد حاكَموها وَالمَنايا حَواكِمُ
سَرَوا بِجيادٍ ما لَهُنَّ قَوائِمُ	أَتَوكَ يَجُرّونَ الحَديدَ كَأَنَّما
ثِيابُهُمُ مِن مِثلِها وَالعَمائِمُ	إِذا بَرَقوا لَم تُعرَفِ البيضُ مِنهُمْ
وَفي أُذُنِ الجَوزاءِ مِنهُ زَمازِمُ	خَميسٌ بِشَرقِ الأَرضِ وَالغَربِ زَحفُهُ
فَما يُفهَمُ الحَدَّاثُ إِلّا التَراجِمُ	تَجَمَّعَ فيهِ كُلُّ لِسنٍ وَأُمَّةٍ
فَلَم يَبقَ إِلّا صارِمٌ أَو ضُبارِمُ	فَلِلَّهِ وَقتٌ ذَوَّبَ الغِشَّ نارُهُ
وَفَرَّ مِنَ الفُرسانِ مَن لا يُصادِمُ	تَقَطَّعَ ما لا يَقطَعُ الدِرعَ وَالقَنا
كَأَنَّكَ في جَفنِ الرَدى وَهوَ نائِمُ	وَقَفتَ وَما في المَوتِ شَكٌّ لِواقِفٍ
وَوَجهُكَ وَضّاحٌ وَثَغرُكَ باسِمُ	تَمُرُّ بِكَ الأَبطالُ كَلمى هَزيعةً
إِلى قَولِ قَومٍ أَنتَ بِالغَيبِ عالِمُ	تَجاوَزتَ مِقدارَ الشَجاعَةِ وَالنُهى
تَموتُ الخَوافي تَحتَها وَالقَوادِمُ	ضَمَمتَ جَناحَيهِم عَلى القَلبِ ضَمّةً
وَصارَ إِلى اللَبَّاتِ وَالنَصرُ قادِمُ	بِضَربٍ أَتى الهاماتِ وَالنَصرُ غائِبٌ
وَحَتّى كَأَنَّ السَيفَ لِلرُمحِ شاتِمُ	حَقَرتَ الرُدَينِيَّاتِ حَتّى طَرَحتَها
مَفاتيحُهُ البيضُ الخِفافُ الصَوارِمُ	وَمَن طَلَبَ الفَتحَ الجَليلَ فَإِنَّما
كَما نُثِرَت فَوقَ العَروسِ الدَراهِمُ	نَثَرتُهُم فَوقَ الأُحَيدِبِ كُلِّهِ
وَقَد كَثُرَت حَولَ الوُكورِ المَطاعِمُ	تَدوسُ بِكَ الخَيلُ الوُكورَ عَلى الذُرى
بِأُمَّاتِها وَهيَ العِتاقُ الصَلادِمُ	تَظُنُّ فِراخُ الفَتخِ أَنَّكَ زُرتَها
كَما تَتَمَشّى في الصَعيدِ الأَراقِمُ	إِذا زَلِقَت مَشَّيتَها بِبُطونِها
قَفاهُ عَلى الإِقدامِ لِلوَجهِ لائِمُ	أَفي كُلِّ يَومٍ ذا الدُمُستُقُ مُقدِمٌ
وَقَد عَرَفَت ريحَ اللُيوثِ البَهائِمُ	أَيُنكِرُ ريحَ اللَيثِ حَتّى يَذوقَهُ
وَبِالصَهرِ حَمَلاتُ الأَميرِ الغَواشِمُ	وَقَد فَجَعَتهُ بِاِبنِهِ وَاِبنِ صِهرِهِ
لِما شَغَلَتها هامُهُم وَالمَعاصِمُ	مَضى يَشكُرُ الأَصحابَ في فَوتِهِ الظُبى
عَلى أَنَّ أَصواتَ السُيوفِ أَعاجِمُ	وَيَفهَمُ صَوتَ المَشرَفِيَّةِ فيهِمُ
وَلَكِن مَغنوماً نَجا مِنكَ غانِمُ	يُسَرُّ بِما أَعطاكَ لا عَن جَهالَةٍ
وَلَكِنَّكَ التَوحيدُ لِلشِركِ هازِمُ	وَلَستَ مَليكاً هازِماً لِنَظيرِهِ
وَتَفتَخِرُ الدُنيا بِهِ لا العَواصِمُ	تَشَرَّفُ عَدنانٌ بِهِ لا رَبيعَةُ

They summoned her but the fates judged
  No wronged one died nor a criminal lived
They came to you dragging chain mail as
  If they went at night on horses without feet
If they flashed, the swords not seen
  For the armor and helmets were alike
A host, it came from lands east, west
  In the ears of the Jauza a humming now
Each nation and tongue gathered there
  Only interpreters understood the speaker
By God, a time for fire to melt sword
  Nothing remains but the lion's blades
What did not cut armor or spear broke
  Those who did not strike fled from knights
You stood, ruin undoubted for the firm
  Like you on an eyelid of death that dozed
Heroes passed you wounded fleeing
  Your face was clear, your lips smiling
You exceeded bravery, reason's limit
  The folk said: You must know the unseen!
You pressed two wings hard on heart
  As pinfeathers died and pinions beneath
A blow at the skull, victory is absent
  He goes to the breast, victory advances
You scorned the Rudaini, dropped it
  So the sword was abusing the spear
He who seeks glorious victory had
  His keys in bright, light sword blades
You scattered them over Uhaidab
  As dirhams are scattered over a bride
Your horses trample on nests on peaks
  And carrion increases around the nests
Eagle nestlings think you visit them
  With the mothers, but they are steeds
When they slip you make them go
  On bellies like snakes slither on slopes
Is Domesticus advancing every day
  His neck blaming face for a progress?
Does he deny lion odor till he tastes?
  Even beasts know that smell of a lion
In his son, brother in law and his son
  The fearful attack of an Amir pained him
He thanked friends for escape from him
  As the skulls and wrists kept them busy
He knows sounds of scimitars' work
  But the sword's ring is foreign speech
Happy, not ignorant, in what he gave
  Though plundered, he shunned a spoiler
You are no kinglet routing your equal
  But monotheism pursuing a polytheism
Adnan excels in this, not just Rabi'a
  A world honored by it, not just capitals

فَإِنَّكَ مُعْطِيهِ وَإِنّي نَاظِمُ	لَكَ الحَمدُ في الدُّرِّ الذي لِيَ لَفظُهُ
فَلا أَنا مَذمومٌ وَلا أَنتَ نادِمُ	وَإِنّي لَتَعدو بي عَطاياكَ في الوَغى
إِذا وَقَعَت في مِسمَعَيهِ الغَماغِمُ	عَلى كُلِّ طَيّارٍ إِلَيها بِرِجلِهِ
وَلا فيهِ مُرتابٌ وَلا مِنهُ عاصِمُ	أَلا أَيُّها السَيفُ الذي لَيسَ مُغمَداً
وَراجيكَ وَالإِسلامُ أَنَّكَ سالِمُ	هَنيئاً لِضَربِ الهامِ وَالمَجدِ وَالعُلى
وَتَفليقُهُ هامَ العِدى بِكَ دائِمُ	وَلَم يا الرَحمَنُ حَدَّيكَ ما وَقى

(٢٢٧)

«من الطويل»

قال وقد ورد فرمان الثغور ومعهم رسول ملك الروم يطلب الهدنة وأنشده إياها بحضرتهم وقت دخولهم لثلاث عشرة بقين من محرم افتتاح سنة أربع وأربعين وثلاث مئة (٩٥٥م):

وَسَحَّ لَهُ رُسلَ المُلوكِ غَمامُ	أَراعٍ كَذا كُلَّ الأَنامِ هُمامُ
وَأَيّامُها فيما يُريدُ قِيامُ	وَدانَت لَهُ الدُنيا فَأَصبَحَ جالِساً
كَفاها لِمامٍ لَو كَفاهُ لِمامُ	إِذا زارَ سَيفُ الدَولَةِ الرومَ غازِياً
لِكُلِّ زَمانٍ في يَدَيهِ زِمامُ	فَتىً تَتبَعُ الأَزمانِ في الناسِ خَطوَهُ
وَأَجفانَ رَبِّ الرُسلِ لَيسَ تَنامُ	تَنامُ لَدَيكَ الرُسلُ أَمناً وَغِبطَةً
إِلى الطَعنِ قُبلاً ما لَهُنَّ لِجامُ	جِذاراً لِمَعروري الجِيادِ فُجاءَةً
وَتُضرَبُ فيهِ وَالسِياطُ كَلامُ	تَعَطَّفُ فيهِ الأَعِنَّةُ شَعرُها
إِذا لَم يَكُن فَوقَ الكِرامِ كِرامُ	وَما تَنفَعُ الخَيلُ الكِرامُ وَلا القَنا
كَأَنَّهُم فيما وَهَبتَ مَلامُ	إِلى كَم تَرُدُّ الرُسلَ عَمّا أَتَوا لَهُ
فَعَوذُ الأَعادي بِالكَريمِ ذِمامُ	فَإِن كُنتَ لا تُعطي الذِمامَ طَواعَةً
وَإِن دِماءً أَملَّتكَ حَرامُ	وَإِنَّ نُفوساً أَممَّتكَ مَنيعَةٌ
وَسَيفُكَ خافوا وَالجِوارَ تُسامُ	إِذا خافَ مَلكٌ مِن مَليكٍ أَجَرتَهُ
وَحَولَكَ بِالكُتبِ اللِطافِ زِحامُ	لَهُم عَنكَ بِالبيضِ الخِفافِ تَفَرُّقٌ
فَتَختارُ بَعضَ العَيشِ وَهوَ حِمامُ	تَغُرُّ حَلاواتُ النُفوسِ قُلوبَها
يُذِلُّ الَّذي يَختارُها وَيُضامُ	وَشَرُّ الحِمامَينِ الزَوامَينِ عيشَةٌ
وَلَكِنَّهُ ذُلٌّ لَهُم وَغَرامُ	فَلَو كانَ صُلحاً لَم يَكُن بِشَفاعَةٍ
بِتَبليغِهِم ما لا يَكادُ يُرامُ	وَمَن لِفُرسانِ الثُغورِ عَلَيهِم

Your praise in a pearl, mine in a word
    For your are the giver and I the arranger
Your gift runs with me in the battle
    I can not be criticized nor you be sorry
On every sortie there with his legs
    When the war cries strike in his ears
O sword which hasn't been sheathed O
    No doubt in that nor safeguard against it
Rejoice striking skulls, glory and rank
    Your devotees and Islam make you safe
Why would not Mercy guard your edges?
    His splitting foes' skulls by you moves on

227
He spoke and the border knights had arrived and with the envoy of the king of Rum seeking a truce.
(Long mu)

Can a hero inspire fear thus in all men
    The cloud rain kings' messengers for him?
A world submit to him and be sedentary
    While its days stand by as he desires them?
If Saif al-Daula visits the Rum in war
    A sally is enough for them if it is for him
A man, times follow his steps among men
    At every moment the reins are in his hands
Messengers sleep safe, content with him
    But eyes of a messenger's lord do not sleep
Wary of unexpected bare backed horses
    Heading to jousting without their bridles
They turn and their manes are as reins
    Whipped on there, and the lash is a word
Noble horses are no use nor the lances
    If no nobility is seated on the nobleness
How long deny envoys what they want
    As if they were blamed insofar as you give?
If you are not given vows of submission
    Yet the foe's refuge with bounty is fealty
Some souls come to you protected
    The blood that hopes in you is sacred
If a king fears a king you stand by him
    They fear your sword as you offer to help
A rout for them is in your light swords
    Press about you with flattering letters
Sweets of life confuse their hearts
    They choose part of life that is death
Worst of two swift deaths is a life that
    Demeans one who chose to be cheated
If any peace exists without intercession
    Yet it is humiliation for them and shame
A favor to border knights to do for
    Them what they could hardly expect

وَلَوْ لم يكونوا خاضِعينَ لَحامُوا	كَتائِبُ جَاؤوا خاضِعينَ فَأقْدَمُوا
وَعَزّوا وَعَامَتْ في نَداكَ وَعَامُوا	وَعَزّتْ قَديماً في ذَراكَ خُيُولُهُمْ
صَلاةٌ تَوَالى مِنْهُمُ وَسَلامُ	على وَجْهِكَ المَيمونِ في كلّ غارَةٍ
وَأنتَ لأهلِ المَكْرُماتِ إمَامُ	وَكُلَّ أُناسٍ يَتْبَعُونَ إمَامَهُمْ
وَعُنْوَانُهُ للنّاظِرينَ قَتَامُ	وَرُبّ جَوابٍ عَنْ كتابٍ بَعَثْتَهُ
وَمَا فُضّ بالبَيْداءِ عَنهُ خِتَامُ	تَضيقُ بهِ البَيْداءُ من قَبْلِ نَشرِهِ
جَوَادٌ وَرُمْحٌ ذابِلٌ وَحُسَامُ	حُرُوفُ هِجَاءِ النّاسِ في ثَلاثَةٍ:
لِيُغْمَدَ نَصْلٌ أوْ يُحَلّ حِزَامُ	أخا الحَرْبِ قدْ أتْعَبْتَها فَألَهْ ساعَةً
فإنّ الذي يَعْمُرْنَ عِندَكَ عَامُ	وَإنْ طَالَ أعمَارُ الرّماحِ بهُدْنَةٍ
وَتُفْني بهنّ الجَيْشَ وَهوَ لُهَامُ	وَمَا زِلْتَ تُفني السُّمْرَ وَهْيَ كَثيرَةٌ
وَفيهَا رِقَابٌ للسّيُوفِ وَهَامُ	مَتى عَاوَدَ الجَالُونَ عَاوَدْتَ أرْضَهُمْ
وَقَدْ كَعَّبَتْ بنْتٌ وَشَبّ غُلامُ	وَرَبّوْا لَكَ الأوْلادَ حتى تُصيبَها
إلى الغايَةِ القُصْوَى جَرَيْتَ وَقَامُوا	جَرَى مَعَكَ الجَارُونَ حتى إذا انتَهَوْا
وَلَيسَ لبَدْرٍ مُذْ تَمَمْتَ تَمَامُ	فَلَيسَ لشَمسٍ مُذْ أنَرْتَ إنَارَةٌ

Horsemen approach humbly close
    If they didn't fear they'd be cowardly
Their horses fed in your courts and
    Swam as men did in your good bounty
At your blessed appearance in war
    Prayers were sent by them as greeting
All men followed their leadership
    You were leader of folk of noble deeds
Many an answer to letters you sent
    Their title for readers was dust clouds
Deserts too narrow before unfolding
    The seal was unbroken in wastelands
Alphabet letters in men were three:
    Fine steeds, supple lances and swords
The war you suffer O now has time
    For sheathed blade, loose saddle girth
If lance life is lengthened by truce
    Those who live with you have a year
You destroy dark ones that are many
    And ruin them with armies that are huge
If roamers turn, you bend to the land
    In it are necks for a sword, and skulls
They have boys for you till you attack
    Daughters high breasted, grown youths
Rivals contend with you till they reach
    The utmost goal as you run, they stand
For no light is in sun if you shine, no
    Fullness in the moon when you are full

(٢٢٨)

«من الطويل»

يمدحه ويذكر قصة حرب جرت:

مَجَرَّ عَوالِينـا وَمَجْرَى السَّـوابِقِ	تَذَكَّـرْتُ مـا بَـيـنَ العُذَيـبِ وَبـارِقِ
بِفَضْلَةِ مـا قَـدْ كَسَّـرُوا فـي المَفارِقِ	وَصُحْبَـةَ قَـوْمٍ يَذبَحُـونَ قَنيصَهُـمْ
كَـأَنَّ ثَراهـا عَنْبَـرٌ فـي المَرافِـقِ	وَلَيْـلاً تَوَسَّـدْنا الثَّوِيَّـةَ تَحْتَـهُ
حَصـىً تُربُهـا ثَقْبْنَـهُ لِلْمَخانِـقِ	بِلادٌ إِذا زارَ الحِسـانَ بِغَيْرِهـا
عَلى كـاذِبٍ مِنْ وَعدِها ضَوْءُ صـادِقِ	سَقَتْنـي بِهـا القُطْرُبُّلِـيَّ مَليحَـةٌ
وَسُقْمٌ لِأَبْـدانٍ وَمِسْكٌ لِناشِـقِ	سُهادٌ لِأَجْفـانٍ وَشَمْسٌ لَنـاظِرِ
عَفيـفٍ وَيَهـوى جِسمَـهُ كُـلُّ فاسِـقِ	وَأَغْيَـدَ يَهْـوى نَفْسَـهُ كُـلُّ عـاقِلٍ
بَـلا كُلُّ سَمْـعٍ عَـنْ سِواها بِعائِـقِ	أَديـبٌ إِذا مـا جَسَّ أَوْتـارَ مِزْهَـرٍ
وَصُدْغـاهُ فـي خَدَّيْ غُـلامٍ مُراهِـقِ	يُحَـدِّثُ عَمَّـا بَيْـنَ عـادٍ وَبَيْنَـهُ
إِذا لَم يَكُـنْ فـي فِعْلِـهِ وَالخَلائِـقِ	وَمَا الحُسْنُ في وَجْهِ الفَتى شَرَفاً لَـهُ
وَلا أَهْلُـهُ الأَدنَـوْنَ غَيـرُ الأَصـادِقِ	وَمَـا بَلَـدُ الإِنْسـانِ غَيـرُ المُوافِـقِ
وَإِنْ كـانَ لا يَخْفـى كَـلامُ المُنافِـقِ	وَجـائِـزَةٌ دَعْـوَى المَحَبَّـةِ وَالهَـوى
وَإِشْمـاتِ مَخْلـوقٍ وَإِسْخـاطِ خـالِقِ	بِـرَأْيِ مَـنْ اِنْقـادَتْ عُقَيْـلٌ إِلى الرَّدى
وَيُوسِـعُ قَتْـلَ الجَحْفَـلِ المُتَضـايِقِ	أَرادوا عَلِيّـاً بِالَّـذي يُعجِـزُ الـوَرى
وَلا حَمَلُـوا رَأْسـاً إِلى غَيـرِ فـالِقِ	فَمَـا بَسَطـوا كَفّـاً إِلى غَيـرِ قـاطِعِ
وَقَـدْ هَرَبـوا لَـوْ صَادَفـوا غَيـرَ لاحِـقِ	لَقَـدْ أَقْدَمـوا لَـوْ صـادَفـوا غَيـرَ آخِـذٍ
رَمَـى كُلَّ ثَـوْبٍ مِـنْ سِنـانٍ بِخـارِقِ	وَلَمّـا كَسـا كَعْبـاً ثِيابـاً طَغَـوْا بِهـا
سَقـى غَيـرَهُ فـي غَيـرِ تِلْكَ البَـوارِقِ	وَلَمّا سَقـى الغَيْثَ الَّـذي كَفَـروا بِـهِ
كَمـا يوجِـعُ الحِرْمـانُ مِـنْ كَـفِّ رازِقِ	وَما يوجِـعُ الحِرْمـانُ مِـنْ كَـفِّ حـارِمٍ
سَنـابِكُهـا تَحْشـو بُطـونَ الحَمـالِقِ	أَتَاهُـم بِهـا حَشْـوَ العَجـاجَـةِ وَالقَنـا
فَهُنَّ عَلـى أَوْسـاطِها كَالمَنـاطِقِ	عَوابِـسَ حَلَّـى يابِـسُ المـاءِ حُزْمَهـا
طِوالَ العَوالـي فـي طِـوالِ السَّمـالِقِ	فَلَيْـتَ أَبـا الهَيْجـا يَـرى خَلْـفَ تَدْمُـرَ
قَبـائِـلَ لا تُعْطـي القَفِيَّ لِسـائِـقِ	وَسَـوْقَ عَلِـيٍّ مِـنْ مَعَـدٍّ وَغَيْرِهـا

228
On the attack of Saif al-Daula on the Banu Utail, Qushair, Ajlan and Kilab in 344.
(Long qi)

I recall what was at Udhaib and Bariq
  Jousting our lances and running winners
Groups of men who sacrificed their prey
  With fragments they broke on hair partings
Nights as we slept with Thawiya below
  As if its dust were amber on the cushions
A land, if its dust as pebbles were taken
  Beauties elsewhere would shine in collars
A pretty girl poured Qutrubbal for me
  Faith's glow over her deceitful promise
Drowsy eyes, sunlight in a glance
  Illness for a body and musk for the nose
A slender youth, the wise loved him
  Chastely as all the lewd loved his body
Educated, when he touched the lute
  He made each ear deaf except for one
He tells of Ad times and his own
  His curls are on an adolescent cheek
No beauty of face to mark a youth
  If it is not in his acts and character
No city for man except what suits
  Nor any family closeness but as friends
A gift, the call of beloved and lover
  If not, hypocrite words are not hidden
My truth! who led Utail to ruin, to
  The foe's joy and Creator's wrath?
They enticed Ali with men's trials
  Spread out the death of a vast army
They put no hand on any dull thing
  Nor bear a head that will not split
They'd have gone if none stopped
  They'd have fled if none had pursued
If he honors Kab with robes they rebel
  He tears the robes to shreds with spears
If he sent showers they rejected so
  He poured other things, other flashes
Want gave no pain in interdiction
  As deprivation of the giver's hand
He came amid dust and lances
  Hooves filled hollows of the eyes
Dark dried sweat on the girths as
  Gems that were belts on the middles
Would Abu Haija could see far
  Tadmur, long lances on a broad plain
Ali's driving the Maadd and other
  Tribes who never turned neck in fear

قُشَيْرٌ وَبَلْعَجْـلانِ فيهـا خَفِيّـةٌ	كَراءَيْـنِ في ألْفـاظِ ألثَـغَ نَـاطِقِ
تُخَلِّيهـمِ النِّسْوانَ غَـيرَ فَـوَارِكٍ	وَهُـمْ خَلَّـوُا النِّسْوانَ غَيـرَ طَوالِـقِ
يُفَـرِّقُ مـا بَـينَ الكُمـاةِ وَبَيْنَهـا	بِطَعْـنٍ يُسَـلّي حَـرُّهُ كُـلَّ عاشِـقِ
أتَـى الظُّعْـنَ حتى ما تَطيـرُ رَشاشَـةٌ	مِـنَ الخيـلِ إلاّ في نُحـورِ العَواتِـقِ
بكُـلّ فَـلاةٍ تُنكِـرُ الإنْـسَ أرْضُهـا	ظَعائـنُ حُمـرُ الحَلـي حمـرُ الأيانِـقِ
وَمَلْمومَـــةٌ سَـــيْفِيَّةٌ رَبَعِيَّـــةٌ	تَصيحُ الحَصَى فيها صِيـاحَ اللَّقالِـقِ
بَعيـدَةُ أطْـرافِ القَنـا مِـنْ أُصُولِـهِ	قَريبَـةُ بَـينَ البَيـضِ غَـيرُ البَلامِـقِ
نَهاهَـا وَأغْناهَـا عَـنِ النَّهـبِ جُـودُه	فَمـا تَبْتَغـي إلاّ حُمـاةَ الحَقائِـقِ
تَوَهَّمَهَـا الأعْـرابُ سَـورَةَ مُـتْرَفٍ	تُذَكِّـرُهُ البَيْـداءُ ظِـلَّ السُّـرادِقِ
فَذَكَّـرْتَهُـمْ بِالمـاءِ سـاعةَ غَبَّـرَتْ	سَماوَةُ كَلبٍ في أنوفِ الخَزائِـقِ
وكانـوا يَـرَوْعونَ المُلـوكَ بِـأنْ بَـدَوْا	وَأنْ نَبَتَـتْ في المـاءِ نَبْـتَ الغَلافِـقِ
فهاجُـوكَ أهْـدَى في الفَـلا مِـن نُجُومـه	وَأبْـدَى بُيُوتـاً مِـن أداحـى النَّقانِـقِ
وَأصْبَـرَ عَـن أمْواهِـهِ مِـن ضِبابِـه	وَآلَـفَ مِنهـا مُقْلَـةً للوَدائِـقِ
وَكـانَ هَديـراً مِـنْ فُحُـولٍ تَرَكْتَهـا	مُهَلَّبَـةَ الأذنـابِ خُـرْسَ الشَّقاشِـقِ
فَمـا حَرَمُـوا بالرَّكـضِ خَيلَـكَ راحَـةً	وَلكـنْ كَفاهـا البَـرُّ قَطْـعُ الشَّواهِـقِ
وَلا شَـغَلُوا صُـمَّ القَنـا بقُلُوبِهِـمْ	عَنِ الرَّكْزِ لكـنْ عـن قلـوبِ الدَماسِـقِ
ألَـمْ يَحذَرُوا مَسْـخَ الذي يَمسَـخُ العِـدَى	ويَجعَـلُ أيـدي الأُسْـدِ أيْـدي الخَرانِـقِ
وَقَـد عايَنُـوه في سِـواهُم وَرُبَّمـا	أرَى مارِقـاً في الحَـربِ مَصـرَعَ مـارِقِ
تَعَـوَّدَ أنْ لا تَقْضَـمَ الحَـبَّ خَيْلُـهُ	إذا الهـامُ لـم تَرْفَـعْ جُنُـوبَ العَلائِـقِ
وَلا تَـرِدَ الغُـدْرانَ إلاّ وَمَاؤُهـا	مِـنَ الـدَّمِ كالرَّيحـانِ فَـوقَ الشَّقائِـقِ
لَوَفْـدُ نُمَيـرٍ كـانَ أرْشَـدَ مِنْهُـمْ	وَقَـد طَـرَدُوا الأظعـانَ طَـرْدَ الوَسائِـقِ
أعَـدُّوا رِماحـاً مِـنْ خُضُـوعٍ فَطَاعَنُـوا	بهـا الجَيـشَ حتـى رَدَّ غَـرْبَ الفَيالِـقِ
فَلَـمْ أرَ أرْمَـى مِنـهُ غَيـرَ مُخاتِـلٍ	وأسْـرَى إلى الأعْـداءِ غَيـرَ مُسـارِقِ
تُصيـبُ المَجانيـقُ العِظـامُ بكَفِّـهِ	دَقائِـقَ قَـد أعْيَـتْ قِسِـيَّ البَنادِقِ

Qushair and Ajalon in small bits
    Like r's in a word mispronounced
Women let them alone in parting
    They let women alone not divorced
He cuts between warrior and them
    Thrusting, his heat diverts the lovers
He goes to women as blood ends
    On horses but stays on girls' breasts
On every desert free of mankind
    Women in red dress on red camels
Squadrons of Rabi'a's sword as
    Pebbles cry the cry of the cranes
Far the spearheads from the butts
    hick under helmets the collar dust
Bounty forbids, enriched by booty
    They want in defense of their own
An Arab imagines an easy result
    Desert reminds him of awning shade
You remind them of water when
    Kalb's Samawa is a dusty pride
They feared kings coming here
    For green scum grew in water holes
They roused you, guided by stars
    They made tents of the ostrich nests
More patient of water than lizards
    More used than they to heat on eyes
Camels grumbled as you left them
    Tail hair cut, the uvula made silent
They offer horses no rest on a run
    The deserts forbid crossing peaks
Spearhead in their hearts don't
    Shun the earth or the Rumi breasts
Won't they fear deforming a foe by
    Making lion paws into rabbit's feet?
They saw him with others often
    He showed rebels in war destroyed
His horses unused to eating barley
    If skulls rise not to feed bag mouths
They relish no pools but their water
    Has blood like myrtles under roses
Numair's tribe more guided they
    Drove howdahs as wild ass herds
The used submissive lances to
    Joust an army, turn aside blades
I saw none shoot better in tricks
    Nor luckier unless by foe's deceit
Huge catapults broke by a hand
    Lightly as he wears out a crossbow

(٢٢٩)

«من الوافر»

يصف إيقاعه بهذه القبائل وكان أبو الطيب لم يحضر الواقعة فشرحها له سيف الدولة:

طِوالُ قَنـاً تُطاعِنُها قِصارُ	وَقَطرُكَ في نَدىً وَوَغىً بِحارُ
وَفيكَ إِذا جَنى الجاني أَناةٌ	تَظُنّ كَرامَةً وَهيَ احتِقارُ
وَأَخذٌ لِلحَواضِرِ وَالبَوادي	بِضَبطٍ لَم تُعَوَّدهُ نِزارُ
تَشَمَّمهُ شَميمَ الوَحشِ إِنساً	وَتُنكِرهُ فَيَعروها نِفارُ
وَمَا انقادَت لِغَيرِكَ في زَمانٍ	فَتَدري ما المَقادَةُ وَالصِّغارُ
فَقَرَّحَتِ المَقاوِدُ ذِفرَيَيها	وَصَعَّرَ خَدَّها هذا العِذارُ
وَأَطمَعَ عامِرَ البُقيا عَلَيها	وَنَزَّقَها احتِمالُكَ وَالوَقارُ
وَغَيَّرَها التَّراسُلُ وَالتَّشاكي	وَأَعجَبَها التَّلَبُّبُ وَالمُغارُ
جِيادٌ تَعجَزُ الأَرسانُ عَنها	وَفُرسانٌ تَضيقُ بِها الدِّيارُ
وَكانَت بِالتَّوَقُّفِ عَن رَداها	نُفوساً في رَداها تُستَشارُ
وَكُنتَ السَّيفَ قائِمُهُ إِلَيهِم	وَفي الأَعداءِ حَدُّكَ وَالغِرارُ
فَأَمسَت بِالبَدِيَّةِ شَفرَتاهُ	وَأَمسى خَلفَ قائِمِهِ الخِيارُ
وَكانَ بَنو كِلابٍ حَيثُ كَعبٌ	فَخافوا أَن يَصيروا حَيثُ صاروا
تَلَقَّوا عِزَّ مَولاهُم بِذُلٍّ	وَسارَ إِلى بَني كَعبٍ وَساروا
فَأَقبَلَها المُروجَ مُسَوَّماتٍ	ضَوامِرَ لا هُزالٌ وَلا شِيارُ
تُثيرُ عَلى سَلَمِيَّةَ مُسبَطِرّاً	تَناكَرَ تَحتَهُ لَو لا الشِّعارُ
عَجاجاً تَعثُرُ العِقبانُ فيهِ	كَأَنَّ الجَوَّ وَعثٌ أَو حَبارُ
وَظَلَّ الطَّعنُ في الخَيلَينِ خَلساً	كَأَنَّ المَوتَ بَينَهُما اختِصارُ
فَلَزَّهُمُ الطِّرادُ إِلى قِتالٍ	أَحَدُّ سِلاحِهِم فيهِ الفِرارُ
مَضَوا مُتَسابِقي الأَعضاءِ فيهِ	لِأَرؤُسِهِم بِأَرجُلِهِم عِثارُ
يَشُلُّهُمُ بِكُلِّ أَقَبَّ نَهدٍ	لِفارِسِهِ عَلى الخَيلِ الخِيارُ
وَكُلِّ أَصَمَّ يَعسِلُ جانِباهُ	عَلى الكَعبَينِ مِنهُ دَمٌ مُمارُ

229
He spoke describing his attack on these tribes.
(Exuberant ru)

The long lances you thrust are too short
    Your drops in bounty or battle are oceans
You are clement if a felon does evil
    They think it generosity but it is scorn
Firm to townsfolk and the bedouin
    With restraint that Nizar is not used to
They sniff men's smell like beasts
    Reject it and timidity disgraces them
Always they are led by you alone
    hey know no yielding or submission
Because the lead rope galls a neck
    And then a bridle pulls at the cheeks
Restraint to them encouraged Amr
    Your patience and reserve spurred
Messages and complaints shamed
    Preparations and raids amaze them
Horses for whom bridles are weak
    Riders for whom the camp is narrow
They are expecting their death
    Souls whose ruin you will advise
Your sword had a hilt for them
    Your edge and point against the foe
Its double edge was on Badiya
    After that Hiyar behind that hilt
Banu Kilab in Kab's territory
    They were afraid in such a place
They met his power by yielding
    Joined Banu Kilab who came along
He pens them in the high fields
    Lean, they aren't skinny or heavy
They climb to Salamiya in dust
    Only landmarks tell what is under
What a dust! eagles struggle in it
    As if the air were sandy desert dirt
Jousting for pairs of fast horses
    As if death were rushing between
Urgency presses them to fight
    Their only defense is in fleeing
They run, legs try to surpass
    Their heads with fatigue to limbs
He drives them on lean horses
    To his knights on the choice steeds
Each hard one quivers, long on
    Its double edge the blood flows

وَلَبَّتْــهُ لِتَغْلِبــهِ وجَـــارِ	يُغـادِرُ كُـلَّ مُلْتَفِـتٍ إلَيْـهِ
دَجَـا لَيْـلانِ لَيْــلٌ وَالغُبَـــارُ	إذا صَرَفَ النّهارُ الضَّوْءَ عَنْهُمْ
أضَـاءَ المَشْـرَفِيَّةُ وَالنَّهَــارُ	وَإِنْ جَنَـحَ الظَّلامُ انْجـابَ عَنْهُمْ
رُغَـاءٌ أَوْ ثُــؤَاجٌ أَوْ يُعَــارُ	وَيَبْكـي خَلفَهُــمْ دَثْـرٌ بُكَـاهُ
تَحَــيَّرَتِ المَتَــالي وَالعِشَـارُ	غَطـا بالعِثْيَـرِ البَيْـدَاءَ حتـى
كِـلا الجَيْشَـيْنِ مِـنْ نَقْـعٍ إزَارُ	وَمَـرّوا بالجَبـاةِ يَضُــمُّ فيهـا
وَقَـدْ سَقَـطَ العِمَامـةُ وَالخِمـارُ	وَجـاؤوا الصَّحْصَحـانَ بِـلا سُـرُوجٍ
وَأُوطِئَــتِ الأصَيْبِيَــةُ الصِّغَــارُ	وَأُرْهِقَـتِ العَـذَارَى مُرْدَفـاتٍ
وَنَهْيـا وَالبُيَيْضَـةُ وَالجِفَــارُ	وَقَـدْ نَـزَحَ الغُوَيْـرُ فَـلا غُوَيْـرٌ
وَتَدْمُــرُ كاسِمَهـا لَهُــمْ دَمَــارُ	وَلَيْـسَ بِغَيْـرِ تَدْمُــرَ مُسْتَغَـاثٌ
فصَبَّحَهُــمْ بـرَأيٍ لا يُــدارَى	أرادوا أنْ يُدِيــرُوا الـرَّأيَ فيهـا
وَأَقْبَــلَ أَقْبَلَــتْ فيـهِ تَحَــارُ	وَجَيْـشٍ كُلَّمــا حـارُوا بأرْضٍ
وَلا دِيَــةٌ تُسَــاقُ وَلا اعْتِــذارُ	يَحُـفُّ أَغَـرُّ لا قَـوَدٌ عَلَيْــهِ
وَكُــلُّ دَمٍ أَرَاقَتْــهُ جُبَـــارُ	تُريـقُ سُيُوفُـهُ مُهَـجَ الأعـادي
عَلَــى طَيْـرٍ وَلَيْـسَ لَهــا مَطَـارُ	فَكـانوا الأُسْـدَ لَيْـسَ لَهــا مَصَـالٌ
بأرْمَـاحٍ مِـنَ العَطَـشِ القِفَـارُ	إذا فـاتُوا الرِّمـاحَ تَنـاوَلَتْهُمْ
فَيَخْتـارُونَ وَالمَـوْتُ اضْطِـرارُ	يَـرَوْنَ المَـوْتَ قُدَّامـاً وَخَلْفـاً
فَقَتْلاهُــمْ لِعَيْنَيْــهِ مَنَــارُ	إذا سَلَـكَ السَّمَـاوَةَ غَيْـرُ هـادٍ
وَفي المَاضي لِمَـنْ بقِـيَ اعْتِبَـارُ	وَلَـوْ لَمْ يُبْـقِ لَمْ تَعِـشْ البَقَايـا
فَمَـنْ يُرْعِـي عَلَيْهِـمْ أَوْ يَغَـارُ	إذا لَمْ يُـرْعِ سَيِّدُهُـمْ عَلَيْهِـمْ
وَيَجْمَعُــهُمْ وَإيّـاهُ النَّجَــارُ	تَفَرَّقُهُــمْ وَإيّـاهُ السَّجَايَــا
وَأَهْلُ الرَّقَّتَيْـنِ لَهــا مَـزَارُ	وَمَـالَ بهـا عَلـى أَرَاكٍ وَعُـرْضٍ
وَزَارُهُــمْ الـذي زَارُوا خُـوَارُ	وَأَجْفَـلَ بالفُـرَاتِ بَنُـو نُمَيْــرٍ
بهِـمْ مِـنْ شُـرْبِ غَيْرِهِمْ خُمـارُ	فَهُــمْ حِـزَقٌ عَلـى الخَابُـورِ صَرْعَـى
وَلَـمْ تُوقَـدْ لَهُـمْ بالليـلِ نَـارُ	فَلَـمْ يَسْـرَحْ لَهُـمْ في الصُّبْـحِ مـالٌ
فَلَيْـسَ بنـافِـعٍ لَهُـمُ الحِـذارُ	حِـذارَ فَتـىً إذا لَمْ يَرْضَـى عَنْهُـمْ

It leaves everything coiled upon
    It as the breast makes a fox hole
When day drives light from them
    Night darkens doubly in dusty sun
If darkness' wing swept from them
    The day and the Mashrafi flashed out
Behind them flocks weep their wail
    With grumbling, bleating, bellowing
Covering desert with dust until
    Nursing dams and pregnant fear
They pass Jaba and a dust cloak
    Envelopes both armies roundabout
They reach Sahsan without saddles
    And the turbans and the veils fall off
They load young fillies behind but
    The little girls are trampled underfoot
Guwaira drunk dry, so no Guwaira
    Also Nihya and Buyaida and Jifar
They sought no refuge but Tadmur
    Tadmur like its name was ruins then
They intend to change a plan there
    Dawn came with the plan unchanged
Army everywhere they turn now
    It came as they came confounded
He took them nobly, no reprisals
    No blood money paid, no excuses
His swords dripped foe's blood
    All the blood was free of revenge
They were lions without strength
    To fly, but even so they had no wings
If they escaped spears a desert
    Took them with the spears of thirst
They saw death before and behind
    They chose and death is necessary
He goes in Samawa unguided
    Their dead signposts to his eyes
He won't stop, the remnant dies
    A lesson of the past for the living
If their lord takes no care of them
    Who is for them, jealous for them?
His character differs from them
    But one ancestry unites him to them
So he turned to Arak and 'Urdi
    The folk of the Raqqas had a visit
Banu Numair feared at the Furat
    The roar they roared was a billow
A herd on the Khabur prostrate
    Drunk with drink that was for others
They sent out no flocks at morn
    Nor was any fire lit in their night
Wary of the man, discontented
    But there was no need for caution

وَجَدْواهُ الَّتــي سَـأَلوا اغْتِفــارُ	تَبيتُ وُفودُهُـمْ تَسْـري إِلَيْـهِ
وَهامُهُــمْ لَــهُ مَعَهُــمْ مُعـارُ	فَخَلَفَهُـمْ بِـرَدِّ البيـضِ عَنْهُـمْ
كَريـمُ العِـرْقِ وَالحَسَـبُ النُّضـارُ	هُـمْ مِمَّـنْ أَذَمَّ لَهُـمْ عَلَيْـهِ
وَلَيْـسَ لَبَحْـرِ نائِلِـهِ قَـرارُ	فَأَصْبَـحَ بِالعَواصِـمِ مُسْتَقِـرّاً
تُدارُ عَلـى الغَنـاءِ بِـهِ العُقـارُ	وَأَضْحـى ذِكْـرُهُ فـي كُلِّ قُطْرٍ
وَتَحْمَـدُهُ الأَسِنَّـةُ وَالشِّفـارُ	تَخِـرُّ لَـهُ القَبائِـلُ ساجِداتٍ
فَفـي أَبْصارِنـا مِنْـهُ انْكِسـارُ	كَأَنَّ شُعـاعَ عَيْـنِ الشَّمـسِ فيهِ
وَخَيْـلُ اللهِ وَالأَسَـلُ الحِـرارُ	فَمَـنْ طَلَـبَ الطِّعـانَ فَـذا عَلَيٌّ
بِأَرْضٍ مـا لِنازِلِهـا اسْتِتـارُ	يَـراهُ النـاسُ حَيْـثُ رَأَتْـهُ كَعْبٌ
طِـلابٌ الطّالِبيـنَ لا الانْتِظـارُ	يُوَسِّـطُهُ المَفـاوِزَ كُلَّ يَـوْمٍ
وَمـا مِـنْ عـادَةِ الخَيْـلِ السِّـرارُ	تَصاهَـلُ خَيْلُـهُ مُتَجاوِبـاتٍ
يَـدٌ لَـمْ يُدْمِهـا إِلّا السِّـوارُ	بَنــو كَعْـبٍ وَمـا أَثَّـرْتَ فيهِـمْ
وَفيها مِـنْ جَلالَتِـهِ افْتِخـارُ	بِهـا مِـنْ قَطْعِـهِ أَلَـمٌ وَنَقْـصٌ
وَأَدْنـى الشِّـرْكِ فـي أَصْـلٍ حِـوارُ	لَهُـمْ حَـقٌّ بِشِـرْكِكَ فـي نِـزارٍ
فَأَوَّلُ قُـرْحِ الخَيْـلِ المِهـارُ	لَعَـلَّ بَنيهِـمْ لِبَنيـكَ جُنْـدٌ
وَأَعْفـى مَـنْ عُقوبَتُـهُ البَـوارُ	وَأَنْـتَ أَبَـرُّ مَـنْ لَـوْ عُـقَّ أَفْنى
وَأَحْلَـمُ مَـنْ يُحَلِّمُـهُ اقْتِـدارُ	وَأَقْـدَرُ مَـنْ يُهَيِّجُـهُ انْتِصـارُ
وَلا فـي ذِلَّـةِ العُبْـدانِ عـارُ	وَمــا فـي سَطْـوَةِ الأَرْبـابِ عَيْـبٌ

(٢٣٠)

«من الطويل»

قال يودعه وقد خرج إلى إقطاع أقطعه إياه بناحية معرة النعمان:

تُرَبّـي عِـداهُ ريشَهـا لِسِهامِـهِ	أَيـا رامِيـاً يُصْمـي فُـؤادَ مَرامِـهِ
عَلـى طِرْفِـهِ مِـنْ دارِهِ بِحُسامِـهِ	أَسيـرٌ إِلـى إِقْطاعِـهِ فـي ثِيابِـهِ

The chiefs went at night to him
> Found him indulgent to pleading
He granted life returning swords
> Their heads were his though bare
They swore their fealty to him
> Of noblest stock counted the best
Thus dawn was quiet in 'Awasim
> But no stagnation in a sea of giving
His memory shone in all the land
> And wine was sent round with song
Tribes fell down prostrate to him
> The spears and blades praised him
An eye of sun's rays shone in him
> In our eyes we knew defeat by him
He who seeks jousting is 'Ali only
> So horses are God's, lances thirsty
Men see him where Kab saw him
> In a land where attacks had no veil
He was in a wasteland every day
> Seeking jousting, not waiting for it
His horses whinny to each other
> Yet it is horse's nature to be secret
Kab and impressions you made
> Is a hand only a bracelet bloodies
For them rain and loss from him
> For them in his glory there is honor
Theirs a right in sharing Nizar as
> Close as in sharing neighborhood
Their sons and yours are soldiers
> As the first five year olds are foals
Best of those who if thwarted ruin
> Most forgiving to those who must die
Strongest of those victory spurs
> Most patient in clemency's power
No blame in the attack of a lord
> No shame in submission of servant

230
He spoke bidding farewell to him and he went to the estate which he had granted him.
(Long hi)

O archer who hits the heart aimed at
> You increase wealth by feathered arrows
I travel to his estate in his garments
> His horse from his palace with his sword

وَرُومُ العِبَدّى هَاطِلَاتُ غَمَامِهِ	وَمَا مَطَرَتْنِيهِ مِنَ البِيضِ وَالقَنَا
وَمَنْ فِيهِ مِنْ فُرْسَانِهِ وَكِرَامِهِ	فَتًى يَهَبُ الإِقْلِيمَ بِالمَالِ وَالقُرَى
جَزَاءً لِمَا خَوَّلْتُهُ مِنْ كَلَامِهِ	وَيَجْعَلُ مَا خَوَّلْتُهُ مِنْ نَوَالِهِ
مُطَالِعَةَ الشَّمْسِ الَّتِي فِي لِثَامِهِ	فَلَا زَالَتِ الشَّمْسُ الَّتِي فِي سَمَائِهِ
فَتَعْجَبُ مِنْ نُقْصَانِهَا وَتَمَامِهِ	وَلَا زَالَ تَجْتَازُ البُدُورُ بِوَجْهِهِ

(٢٣١)

«من الخفيف»

يرثي أخت سيف الدولة الصغرى ويسليه ببقاء الكبرى، أنشده إياها يوم الأربعاء النصف من شهر رمضان سنة أربع وأربعين وثلاث مئة (٩٥٥م):

تَكُنِ الأَفْضَلَ الأَعَزَّ الأَجَلَّاء	إِنْ يَكُنْ صَبْرُ ذِي الرَّزِيَّةِ فَضْلَا
بابَ فَوْقَ الَّذِي يُعَزِّيكَ عَقْلَا	أَنْتَ يَا فَوْقَ أَنْ تُعَزَّى عَنِ الأَحْـ
اكَ قَالَ الَّذِي لَهُ قُلْتَ قَبْلَا	وَبِأَلْفَاظِكَ اهْتَدَى فَإِذَا عَزَّ
وَسَلَكْتَ الأَيَّامَ حَزْنًا وَسَهْلَا	قَدْ بَلَوْتَ الخُطُوبَ مُرًّا وَحُلْـوًا
ـرِبَ قَوْلًا وَلَا يُجَدِّدُ فِعْلَا	وَقَتَلْتَ الزَّمَانَ عِلْمًا فَمَا يُغْـ
وَأَرَاهُ فِي النَّاسِ ذُعْرًا وَجَهْلَا	أَجِدُ الحُزْنَ فِيكَ حِفْظًا وَعَقْلَا
كَرُمَ الأَصْلُ كَانَ لِلْإِلْفِ أَصْلَا	لَكَ إِلْفٌ يَجُرُّهُ وَإِذَا مَا
لَمْ يَزَلْ لِلوَفَاءِ أَهْلُكَ أَهْلَا	وَوَفَاءٌ نَبَتَّ فِيهِ وَلَكِنْ
بَعَثَتْهُ رِعَايَةً فَاسْتَهَلَّا	إِنَّ خَيْرَ الدُّمُوعِ عَوْنًا لِدَمْعٍ
بِ إِذَا اسْتَكْرَهَ الحَدِيدُ وَصَلَّا	أَيْنَ ذِي الرِّقَّةُ الَّتِي لَكَ فِي الحَرْ
رُومَ وَالهَامَ بِالصَّوَارِمِ تُفْلَى	أَيْنَ خَلَّفْتَهَا غَدَاةَ لَقِيتَ الـ
جَعَلَ القِسْمُ نَفْسَهُ فِيهِ عَدْلَا	قَاسَمَتْكَ المَنُونُ شَخْصَيْنِ جَوْرًا
دَرَنٍ سَرَى عَنِ الفُؤَادِ وَسَلَّى	فَإِذَا قِسْتَ مَا أَخَذْنَ بِمَا غَا
وَتَبَيَّنْتَ أَنَّ جَدَّكَ أَعْلَى	وَتَيَقَّنْتَ أَنَّ حَظَّكَ أَوْفَى
بِالأَعَادِي فَكَيْفَ يَطْلُبْنَ شُغْلَا	وَلَعَمْرِي لَقَدْ شَغَلْتَ المَنَايَا
ـرًا أَسِيرًا وَبِالنَّوَالِ مُقِلَّا	وَكَمْ انْتَشْتَ بِالسُّيُوفِ مِنَ الدَّهْـ
صَالَ خَتْلًا رَآهُ أَدْرَكَ تَبْلَا	عَدَهَا نُصْرَةً عَلَيْهِ فَلَمَّا
ـهِ وَتَبْقَى فِي نِعْمَةٍ لَيْسَ تَبْلَى	كَذَبَتْهُ ظُنُونُهُ، أَنْتَ تُبْلِيـ

He gives showers of swords and spears
    And Rumi slaves are in his cloud's pouring
A man giving fields of flocks and towns
    His horsemen and his fine things in them
He makes his gifts from what I fancy
    As payment when I see some of his words
May the sun in his heaven not cease
    With the rising sun now under his veil
May moons not cease to grow in his face
    Amazed at their waning and at his fullness

231
He spoke at Aleppo consoling him for his younger sister and urging him to take solace in the elder in the month of Ramadan in the year 344.
(Nimble la)

If patience in one who sorrows is good
    You are most virtuous, strong and glorious
O you are superior to a lover's solace
    And above one who encourages by reason
By your words he is guided to console
    Speaking what you spoke to him before
You bore things both bitter and sweet
    Trod paths of the days rough and smooth
You strove with time in wisdom, there
    Were no strange words and no new deeds
I find grief in you patient and rational
    I see it in others as fear and ignorance
You had a friend who brought it on
    But if the root is fine it is a friendly grief
Loyalty is a way you have lived for
    Your family is accustomed to honesty
The good of tears as relief is tears
    That patience sends forth in flowing
Where is one who pitied you in war
    When steel was hateful and clashed?
Where is one you left at dawn to
    Meet the Rum as swords split skulls?
The fates allotted two to you openly
    They made your share equal at last
If you measure what they took by
    What they left it frees and consoles
It's certain your happiness is rich
    You are sure your fortune is higher
By my life! you kept fates busy
    With the foe so why do they want?
How many you saved from swords
    As captives, from poverty with gifts
One counts aid against himself
    If attacks are secret wanting revenge
Thoughts deceive you as you labor
    You remain in peace and not tested

وَلَقَدْ رَامَاكَ العُداةُ كَما رَمَ   فَلَمْ يجرَحوا لشَخصِكَ ظِلَّا
وَلَقَدْ رُمْتَ بالسَّعادَةِ بَعْضاً   مِن نُفُوسِ العِدى فأدركتَ كُلَّا
قارَعَتْ رُمْحَكَ الرِّماحُ وَلَكِنْ   تَرَكَ الرَّامِحِينَ رُمْحُكَ عُزْلا
لَوْ يكونُ الذي وَرَدْتَ مِنَ الفَجْـ   ـعَةِ طَعناً أوْرَدْتَهُ الخيلَ قُبْلا
وَلَكَشَّفْتَ ذا الحَنينِ بضَرْبٍ   طالَما كَشَّفَ الكُروبِ وجَلَّى
خِطْبَةٌ للحِمامِ ليسَ لَها رَدٌّ   وَإِنْ كانَتِ المُسَمَّاةَ ثُكْلَا
وَإذا لم تَجِدْ مِنَ النَّاسِ كُفْـ   ـذاتُ خِدرٍ أرادَتِ المَوْتَ بَعْلا
وَلَذيذُ الحَياةِ أنْفَسُ في النَّفْـ   ـسِ وأشهَى مِن أنْ يُمَلَّ وَأحْلَى
وَإذا الشَّيخُ قالَ أُفٍّ فَما مَـ   ـلَّ حَياةً وإنَّما الضَّعفَ مَلَّا
آلَةُ العَيشِ صِحَّةٌ وشَبابٌ   فإذا وَلَّيا عَنِ المَرْءِ وَلَّى
أبَداً تَسْتَرِدُّ ما تَهَبُ الدُّنْـ   ـيا فَيا لَيتَ جُودَها كانَ بُخْلا
فكَفَتْ كَوْنَ فُرْحَةٍ تُورِثُ الغَمَّ   وَحِلٌّ يُغادِرُ الوَجْدَ حِلَّا
وَهيَ مَعشوقَةٌ على الغَدْرِ لا تَحْـ   ـفَظُ عَهْداً وَلا تُتَمِّمُ وَصْلا
كُلُّ دَمْعٍ يَسيلُ مِنها عَلَيها   وَبَفَكِّ اليَدَينِ عَنها تخَلَّى
شِيَمُ الغانِياتِ فيها فَما أدْ   ري لذا أنْتَ اسمَها النَّاسُ أم لا
يا مَليكَ الوَرى المُفَرِّقَ مَحياً   وَمَماتاً فيهِمْ وَعِزّاً وَذُلَّا
قَلَّدَ الله دَوْلَةً سَيْفُها أنْـ   ـتَ حُساماً بالمَكْرُماتِ مُحَلَّى
فَبهِ أغْنَتِ المَوالِيَ بَذْلا   وَبِهِ أفنَتِ الأعادِيَ قَتْلا
وَإذا اهتَزَّ للنَّدى كانَ بَحْراً   وَإذا اهتَزَّ لِلرَّدى كانَ نَصْلا
وَإذا الأرضُ أظلَمَتْ كانَ شَمساً   وَإذا الأرضُ أمحَلَتْ كانَ وَبْلا
وَهوَ الضَّارِبُ الكَتيبَةِ والطَّعْـ   ـنَةُ تَغلو والضَّرْبُ أغلى وَأغلَى
أيَّها الباهِرُ العُقولَ فَما تُدْ   رَكُ وَصْفاً أتعَبْتَ فكري فمَهلا
مَنْ تَعاطَى تَشَبَّها بكَ أعْيَا   هُ وَمَنْ دَلَّ في طَريقِكَ ضَلَّا
وَإذا ما اشتَهى خُلودَكَ داعٍ   قالَ لا زُلتَ أوْ تَرى لكَ مِثْلا

The foe may attack you as desired
    They can't harm your person's shadow
Your were charged with joy of some
    Of the souls of the foe, you gave that
The lances struck your lance when
    Your lance left the spearmen unarmed
If you gave an advantage by surprise
    Jousting, you gave it to men eye to eye
You reveal a show of grief in blows
    As long as it means anguish and glory
Death's wooing leaves her no denial
    Even if she is called the one bereaved
If she did not find men good enough
    A harem daughter chose death as spouse
Life's pleasure is precious to the soul
    More tempting and sweeter than disgust
If an old man says: Alas! it's not life
    Bores him, but rather weakness wearies
Life's instrument is health and youth
    When they turn from a man, he expires
The world is ever taking gifts it gave
    O would that its bounty were more stingy
Pleasure's end that inherits is grief
    And friends that betray a friend's love
This is love of betrayal, not with
    Kept contracts, completed embraces
All tears flow from this and for it
    Opening a pair of hands empty of it
It's feminine nature in her, I know
    Not if a man should name her woman
O king of men who allots life, death
    Among them, and glory and humility
God girds you with rule, its sword
    A blade which is the gem of bounty
Clients grow rich with fine gifts by it
    And the enemy are ruined by its force
When it shakes for bounty it's a sea
    When it shakes for battle it has edges
When the earth is dark it is a sun
    When the earth is barren it is rain
A battalion striker as jousting
    Grows thrusts increase and flash
O you dazzle a mind not attaining
    Description, you tire my ideas, slowly!
He who compares you weakens
    He who travels your road goes astray
If a client wants immortality for you
    He says: Live, or till one sees your like

(٢٣٢)

«من الخفيف»

يمدحه ويذكر نهوضه إلى ثغر الحدث لما بلغه أن
الروم أحاطت به وذلك في جمادى الأولى سنة أربع
وأربعين وثلاث مئة (٩٥٥م):

هَكَذا هكَذا وَإِلّا فَلا لا	ذي المَعالي فَليَعلُوَنَّ مَن تَعالى
ــهِ وَعِزٌّ يُقَلقِلُ الأَجبالا	شَرَفٌ يَنطِحُ النُجومَ بِرَوقَي
دَولَةُ ابنِ السُيوفِ أَعظَمُ حالا	حالُ أَعدائِنا عَظيمٌ وَسَيفُ الــ
أَعجَلَتهُم جِيادُهُ الإِعجالا	كُلَّما أَعجَلوا النَذيرَ مَسيراً
مِلُ إِلّا الحَديدَ وَالأَبطالا	فَأَتَتهُم خَوارِقَ الأَرضِ ما تَحــ
ــعُ عَلَيها بَراقِعاً وَجِلالا	خافِياتِ الأَلوانِ قَد نَسَجَ النَقــ
لَتَخوضَنَّ دونَهُ الأَهوالا	حالَفَتهُ صُدورُها وَالعَوالي
ــح مَداراً وَلا الحِصانُ مَجالا	وَلَتَمضِينَّ حَيثُ لا يَجِدُ الرُمــ
مٌ وَإِنْ كانَ ما تَمَنّى مُحالا	لا أَلومُ ابنَ لاوُنَ مَلِكَ الرو
ــهِ وَبانٍ بَغى السَماءَ فَنالا	أَقلَقَتهُ بَنِيَّةٌ بَينَ أُذنَيـ
ي فَغَطّى جَبينَهُ وَالقَذالا	كُلَّما رامَ حَطَّها اِتَّسَعَ البَنـ
غارَ فيها وَتَجمَعُ الآجالا	يَجمَعُ الرومَ وَالصَقالِبَ وَالبُلـ
ــر كَما وافَتِ العِطاشُ الصِلالا	وَتُوافيهِم بِها في القَنا السُمـ
وَأَتَوْا كَي يُقَصِّروهُ فَطالا	قَصَدوا هَدمَ سورِها فَبَنَوهُ
تَرَكوها لَها عَلَيهِم وَبالا	وَاِستَجَرّوا مَكايِدَ الحَربِ حَتّى
ــالَ فيهِ وَتَحمَدُ الأَفعالا	رُبَّ أَمرٍ أَتاكَ لا تَحمَدُ الفِعــ
في قُلوبِ الرُماةِ عَنكَ النِصالا	وَقِسِيٌّ رُمِيتَ عَنها فَرَدَّت
ــلَ فَكانَ اِنقِطاعُها إِرسالا	أَخَذوا الطُرقَ يَقطَعونَ بِها الرُسـ
أَنَّهُ صارَ عِندَ بَحرِكَ آلا	وَهُمُ البَحرُ ذو الغَوارِبِ إِلّا
ــنَّ القِتالَ الَّذي كَفاكَ القِتالا	ما مَضَوْا لَم يُقاتِلوكَ وَلَكِـ

232
He spoke recalling the approach of Saif al-Daula to the border fort of al Hadath when he learned that the Rum had besieged it in Jumadi in the year 344.
(Nimble la)

This is eminence so let him rise who may
    Thus and so, or otherwise he cannot be so
Nobility strikes stars with its horns
    And strength makes the mountains shake
Our foes' power is tremendous but Saif
    Al-Daula, swords' seed, has greater state
If they hurry with warning on a road
    His hoses are faster than they in haste
They come to them as spoilers of earth
    That bears nothing but steel and heroes
His is their color, for dust weaves
    The veils and saddle cloths upon them
Their breasts and the spears swore
    To plunge into terrors that are before him
To go where lance can find no target
    nd where the stallion can never roam
I don't blame Leon's son, king of Rum
    Even if what he desires is the impossible
Does building between his ears shake
    Him if a builder sought the sky and got it?
If he aimed to ruin her, the huge fort
    Covered his forehead and the back of it
He gathered Rum, Slavs and Bulgars
    Against her and then you gathered death
You met them with the brown lances
    As the thirsty one comes to the pools
They aim to ruin her wall but build
    They come to shorten but make longer
They want to drag war engines till
    They leave them as she attacks them
Many an affair befalls you unpraised
    As action, but one praises the results
Many a bow snapped aimed at you
    Reversing shots with arrows from you
They took roads to stop messengers
    Then their interception was a message
They were a sea possessed of waves
    But it became the mirage as your sea
They ran to shun fighting you but
    The fame that sufficed you was fought

وَالَّذي قَطَّعَ الرَّقابِضَ مِنَ الضَّرْ	بِ بِكَفَّيْكَ قَطَّعَ الآمالا
وَالثَّباتُ الَّذي أَجادوا قَديماً	عَلَّمَ الثّابِتينَ ذا الإِجْفالا
نَزَلوا في مَصارِعٍ عَرَفوها	يَنْدُبونَ الأَعْمامَ وَالأَخْوالا
تَحْمِلُ الرّيحُ بَيْنَهُمْ شَعَرَ الها	مِ وَتَذْري عَلَيْهِمُ الأَوْصالا
تُنْذِرُ الجِسْمَ أَنْ يَقومَ لَدَيْها	فَتُرِيهِ لِكُلِّ عُضْوٍ مِثالا
أَبْصَروا الطَّعْنَ في القُلوبِ دِراكاً	قَبْلَ أَنْ يُبْصِروا الرِّماحَ خَيالا
وَإِذا حاوَلَتْ طِعانَكَ خَيْلٌ	أَبْصَرَتْ أَذْرُعَ القَنا أَمْيالا
بَسَطَ الرُّعْبُ في اليَمينِ يَميناً	فَتَوَلَّوْا وَضَفي الشِّمالِ شِمالا
يَنْفُضُ الرَّوْعُ أَيْدِياً لَيْسَ تَدْري	أَسُيوفاً حَمَلْنَ أَمْ أَغْلالا
وَوُجوهاً أَخافَها مِنْكَ وَجْهٌ	تَرَكَتْ حُسْنَها لَهُ وَالجَمالا
وَالعِيانُ الجَلِيُّ يُحْدِثُ لِلظَّـ	ـنِّ زَوالاً وَلِلْمُرادِ انْتِقالا
وَإِذا ما خَلا الجَبانُ بِأَرْضٍ	طَلَبَ الطَّعْنَ وَحْدَهُ وَالنِّزالا
أَقْسَموا لا رَأَوْكَ إِلّا بِقَلْبٍ	طالَما غَرَّتِ العُيونُ الرِّجالا
أَيُّ عَينٍ تَأَمَّلَتْكَ فَلاقَتْـ	ـكَ وَطَرْفٍ رَنا إِلَيْكَ فَآلا
ما يَشُكُّ اللَّعينُ في أَخْذِكَ الجَيْـ	ـشَ فَهَلْ يَبْعَثُ الجُيوشَ نَوالا
ما لَنْ يَنْصِبُ الخَبائِلَ في الأَرْ	ضِ وَمَرْجَحاهُ أَنْ يَصيدَ الهِلالا
إِنَّ دونَ الَّتي عَلى الدَّرْبِ وَالأَحْـ	ـدَبِ وَالنَّهْرِ مِخْلَطاً مِزْيالا
غَصَبَ الدَّهْرَ وَالمُلوكَ عَلَيْها	فَبَناها في وَجْنَةِ الأَرْضِ خالا
فَهِيَ تَمْشي مَشْيَ العَروسِ اخْتِيالاً	وَتَثَنّى عَلى الزَّمانِ دَلالا
وَحَماها بِكُلِّ مُطَّرِدِ الأَكْـ	ـعُبِ جَوْرَ الزَّمانِ وَالأَوْجالا
وَظُبىً تَعْرِفُ الحَرامَ مِنَ الحِـ	ـلِّ فَقَدْ أَفْنَتِ الدِّماءَ حَلالا
في خَميسٍ مِنَ الأَسودِ بَئيسٍ	يَفْتَرِسْنَ النُّفوسَ وَالأَمْوالا
إِنَّما أَنْفُسُ الأَنيسِ سِباعٌ	يَتَفارَسْنَ جَهْرَةً وَاغْتِيالا
مَنْ أَطاقَ التِماسَ شَيْءٍ غِلاباً	وَاغْتِصاباً لَم يَلْتَمِسْهُ سُؤالا
كُلُّ غادٍ لِحاجَةٍ يَتَمَنّى	أَنْ يَكونَ الغَضَنْفَرَ الرِّئْبالا

That which cut the necks with blows
    By your hand has cut off those hopes
Resolution that was strong of old
    Teaches the resolute in a present fear
They descend to death and know it
    Lamenting maternal and paternal kin
The wind blows among the hair of
    Skulls and scatters the limbs on them
They are warned by bodies not to
    Stay, they see in the bones the lesson
They see the thrusts reaching hearts
    Before they see the lances on horses
When horsemen begin your thrusts
    They see the arms extending spears
Fear spreads from right to right to
    Lengthen from left hand to left hand
Terror shakes the hands so they
    Know not if they hold swords or irons
Faces that your face frightens but
    They leave delicacy and beauty in it
Flashing eyes speak thoughts of
    The end and an intention to retreat
If a coward is left alone in a land
    He seeks jousting and attack alone
They swear not to see you but in
    Fancy only thus eyes deceive men
What eye turns to you and meets?
    Many a glance looks and turns away
Cursed ones don't doubt your luck
    But why do they send armies as gifts?
What ails one who sets a trap in
    Hopes to catch the crescent moon?
Before the pass and Ahdab above
    The river are experienced warriors
He forced destiny and kings for her
    Set her as a beauty spot on time's face
She walked proud steps as a bride
    Was praised as coquette with the times
He defended her by driving lances
    From time's tyranny and from terror
Edges to separate forbid and lawful
    And to destroy the blood on the legal
On battalions of courageous lions
    That devoured the souls and the flocks
Indeed the souls of men are beastly
    They eat each other openly and secretly
He who can seize anything conquest
    And by force does not take it by pleading
Each youth in time of need has an idea
    That he must be the fiercest of the lions

(٢٣٣)

«من الوافر»

فقال أبو الطيب ارتجالاً:

حَديثَهُـمُ المُوَلَّـدَ وَالقَديمَـا	رَأَيْتُـكَ تُوسِـعُ الشُّعَـرَاءَ نَيْـلاً
وَتُعْطِـي مَـن مضَى شرَفـاً عَظيمـا	فَتُعْطِـي مَـنْ بَقَـى مـالاً جَسيمـاً
نَشيـداً مِثْـلَ مُنْشِـدِهِ كَريمَـا	سَمِعْتُـكَ مُنْشِـداً بَيْتَـيْ زيـادٍ
غَبَطْـتُ بِذاكَ أَعْظُمَـهُ الرَّميمَـا	فَمَـا أَنكَـرْتُ مَوْضِعَـهُ وَلَكِـنْ

(٢٣٤)

«من الكامل»

يمدحه ويذكر إيقاعه بعمرو بن حابس وبني ضبة سنة إحدى وعشرين وثلاث مئة (٩٣٣م) و لم ينشده إياه:

جَلَبَـتْ حِمامـي قَبْـلَ وَقْـتِ حِمامـي	ذِكْـرُ الصِّبَـى وَمَراتِـعُ الآرامِ
عَرَصاتِهـا كَتَكاثُـرِ اللُّـوّامِ	دِمَـنٌ تَكاثَـرَتِ الهُمُـومُ عَلَـيَّ في
تَبكِـي بَعَيْنَـيْ عُـرْوَةِ بـنِ حِـزامِ	وَكَـأَنَّ كُـلَّ سَحابَـةٍ وَقَفَـتْ بِهَـا
فيهَـا وَأَفْنَـتْ بِالعِتـابِ كَلامـي	وَلَطَالَمـا أَفنَيـتُ ريـقَ كَعابِهـا
وَتَجُـرُّ ذَيْلَـيْ شِـرَّةٍ وَغُـرامِ	قَـد كُنْـتُ تَهْـزَأُ بِالفِـراقِ مَجانَـةً
هُـنَّ الحَيـاةُ تَرَحَّلَـتْ بِسَـلامِ	لَيـسَ القِبـابُ عَلـى الرِّكـابِ وَإِنَّمـا
لَخِفافِهِـنَّ مَفاصِلـي وَعِظامـي	لَيـتَ الـذي فَلَـقَ النَّـوَى جعَـلَ الحَصـى
حَـذَراً مِـنَ الرُّقَبـاءِ في الأَكْمـامِ	مُتَلاحِظَيـنِ نَسُـحّ مـاءَ شُؤونِنـا
مِـن بَعـدِ مـا قَطَـرَتْ علـى الأَقـدامِ	أَرواحُنـا انهَمَلَـتْ وَعِشْنـا بَعدَهـا
عنـدَ الرَّحيـلِ لَكِـنَّ غَـيـرَ سِجـامِ	لَـوْ كُـنَّ يَـوْمَ جرَيْـنَ كُـنَّ كصَبرِنـا
وَذَميـلَ ذِعْلِبَـةٍ كَفَحْـلِ نَعـامِ	لَـم يَـتْرُكُـوا لـي صاحِبـاً إلّا الأَسَـى
إلّا إلَيْـكَ عَلَـيَّ ظَهْـرُ حَـرامِ	وَتَعَـذُّرُ الأَحـرارِ صَيَّـرَ ظَهْرَهَـا
وُلِـدَتْ مَكارِمُهُـمْ لِغَيـرِ تَمـامِ	أَنـتَ الغَريبَـةُ في زَمـانٍ أَهلُـهُ

233

Saif al-Daula recited a verse of al Nabiga as an example: No fault in them except their swords / Are dull from striking battalions * They did well on Halima's day / And the day when they met the greatest test. And Abu Tayyib spoke in reply,
(Exuberant ma)

I know you honor the poets with gifts
    Both those born lately and those of old
You give those who stay huge riches
    And give those who have gone huge honor
I heard you reciting verses of Ziyad
    With a recitation as noble as his poem
I do not deny his rank but I envy
    For that reason his long dead bones

234

He spoke in the year 321 at Rais al-Ain when Saif al-Daula attacked Amr ibn Habis of Banu Dabba. But he did not recite this to him. When he met him it was placed among his praises of him.
(Perfect mi)

Memories of love and grazing gazelles
    Attract my death before my death's time
Camp traces, longing within me grows
    In this place just as the blame increases
It is as if every cloud that hovers
    Weeps with the eyes of 'Urwa ibn Hizam
Long I sucked drops from its breast
    Here, and it ruined my speech in blame
You laughed at parting shamelessly
    And dragged youth's skirts in ill nature
Those are not howdahs on camels
    They're life itself departing in goodbyes
May he who makes distance put stones
    In their hoofpads, my knuckles and bones
Staring we pour water from our eyes
    Being careful of the guards on the hills
Our souls flow and we live after them
    After they have dripped over these feet
If like our patience the day they went
    They would have been no cloudburst
They left me no master but grief
    Trot of fast camel like a male ostrich
Denial of bounty in her back makes
    It forbid as love object except for you
The rare one in this time, a family
    Whose noble acts are without limits

أَكْـثَـرْتَ مِـنْ بَــذْلِ النَّــوَالِ وَلَمْ تَــزَلْ … عَـلَـمـاً عَلَـى الإفْضـالِ وَالإنْعَــامِ
صَغَـرْتَ كُـلَّ كَبـيـرَةٍ وَكَـبُـرْتَ عَـنْ … لَكَأنَّـهُ وَعَـدَدْتَ سِـنَّ غُــلَامِ
وَرَفَـلْـتَ في حُلَـلِ الثَّنـاءِ وَإنَّـمَـا … عَـدَمُ الثَّنـاءِ نِهـايَــةُ الإعْـدامِ
عَيْـبٌ عَلَيْـكَ تُـرَى بِسَيْفٍ في الوَغَـى … مَـا يَصْنَعُ الصَّمْصَـامُ بالصَّمْصَـامِ
إنْ كَـانَ مِثْلُـكَ كـانَ أوْ هُـوَ كَـائِـنٌ … فَـبَـرِئْتَ حِينَئِـذٍ مِـنَ الإسْـلَامِ
مَلِـكٌ زُهِـيَـتْ بِمَكَـانِـهِ أيَّامُـهُ … حتى افتخـرْنَ بِـهِ على الأيّـامِ
وَتخـالُـهُ سَلَـبَ الـوَرَى مِـنْ حِلْـمِـهِ … أحْلَامَهُـمْ فَهُـمْ بِـلَا أحْـلَامِ
وَإذا امتُحِـنْــتَ تَكَشَّـفَـتْ عَزَمَاتُـهُ … عَـنْ أوْحَـدِيّ النَّقْـضِ وَالإبْـرَامِ
وَإذا سَـألْتَ بَنَانَـهُ عَـنْ نَيْلِـهِ … لَمْ يَـرْضَ بالدّنْـيـا قَضَـاءَ ذِمَـامِ
مَهْـلاً ألَا لله مَـا صَنَعَ القَنَـا … في عَمْـرِو حَـابٍ وَضَبَّـةَ الأغْـتَامِ
لَـمـا تَحَكَّمَـتِ الأسِنَّـةُ فيهِـم … جَارَتْ وَهُـنَّ يَجُـرْنَ في الأحكامِ
تَرَكْتَهُـمْ خِلَـلَ البُيُـوتِ كَأنَّـمَـا … غَضِبَـتْ رُؤوسُهُـمْ على الأجْسَامِ
حِجارُ نَاسٍ فَـوْقَ أرْضٍ مِـنْ دَمٍ … وَنُجُـومُ بَيْـضٍ في سَمَـاءِ قَتَـامِ
وَذِراعُ كُـلّ أبِـي فُلَانٍ كُنْيَـةٌ … حَالَـتْ فَصَاحِبُـهَـا أبُـو الأيْتـامِ
عَهْـدي بَمَعْرَكَـةِ الأميـرِ وَخَيْلُـهُ … في النَّقْـعِ مُحْجَمَـةٌ عَنِ الإحجامِ
صَلَّى الإلَـهُ عَلَيْـكَ غَيْـرَ مُـوَدِّعٍ … وَسَقَى ثَـرَى أبَوَيْـكَ صَوْبَ غَمَـامِ
وَكَسَـاكَ ثَـوْبَ مَهَابَـةٍ مِـنْ عِنْـدِهِ … وَأرَاكَ وَجْـهَ شَقِيقِكَ القَمْقَـامِ
فَلَقَـدْ رَمَـى بَلَـدَ العَـدُوِّ بِنَفْسِـهِ … في رَوْقِ أرْعَـنَ كَـالغِطَمِّ لُهَـامِ
قَـوْمٌ تَفَرَّسَـتِ المَنَايَـا فِيكُـمْ … فَرَأتْ لَكُـمْ في الحـرْبِ صَبْـرَ كِـرَامِ
تَـا لله مَـا عَلِـمَ امرُؤٌ لَـوْ لَا كُـمْ … كيفَ السَّخَـاءُ وَكيفَ ضَـرْبُ الْهَـامِ

You often gave huge gifts and didn't
	Stop excelling with virtues and graces
You belittle great things and enlarge
	With: As if . . . and you are in youth's years
You swagger in garments of praise
	Poverty of praise is an extreme poverty
Bad for you to be seen with sword
	A scimitar does not create by scimitar
If one like you has lived he is dead
	Or divinity and then I am free of islam
A king, his days proud of his rank
	So they boast of him to other days
You think he loots men of minds
	Due to him they are lacking reason
If they test it his will is revealed as
	A unity in the twisting and untwisting
If you ask his fingers about his gifts
	He is displeased at the idea of truth
Slowly, O by God what has lance
	Done to Amr Haba and poor Dabba?
If a spear judged against them it
	Was unjust, they unjust to justice
We left them outside their tents
	Their heads were angry with the bodies
Stony men on a land of blood with
	Helmets as stars in a heaven of dust
Armor of every Abu so-and-so
	ltered and its master was Abu Orphan
I see the Amir's battle, his riders
	In dust pursuers of the pursued
God's blessing without farewell
	May he water your father's land by cloud
Dress you in robes of reverence
	Show you your brother's way as chief
He strikes the enemy's lands himself
	The army's vanguard like a pounding sea
Folk in whom death rides horseback
	See in you the patience of virtue in war
By God! men would not know but for
	You what bounty is or striking off heads

(٢٣٥)

«من الكامل»

يمدحه وأنشده إياها بآمد وكان منصرفاً من بلاد الروم وذلك في شهر صفر سنة خمس وأربعين وثلاث مئة (٩٥٦م):

هُوَ أَوَّلٌ وَهِيَ المَحَلُّ الثَّاني	الرَّأيُ قَبلَ شَجاعَةِ الشُّجعانِ
بَلَغَتْ مِنَ العَلْياءِ كُلَّ مكانِ	فَإِذا هُما اجتَمَعا لِنَفْسٍ حُرَّةٍ
بالرَّأيِ قَبلَ تَطاعُنِ الأَقرانِ	وَرُبَّما طَعَنَ الفَتى أَقرانَهُ
أَدنى إِلى شَرَفٍ مِنَ الإِنسانِ	لَوْ لا العُقولُ لَكانَ أَدنى ضَيغَمٍ
أَيدي الكُماةِ عَوالي المُرَّانِ	وَكَما تَفاضَلَتِ النُّفوسُ وَدَبَّرَتْ
لَما سُلِلْنَ لَكِنَّ كَالأَجفانِ	لَو لا سَمِيُّ سُيوفِهِ وَمَضاؤُهُ
أَمِنِ احتِقارٍ ذاكَ أَمْ نِسيانِ	خاضَ الحِمامَ بِهِنَّ حَتّى ما دُرى
أَهلُ الزَّمانِ وَأَهلُ كُلِّ زَمانِ	وَسَعى فَقَصَّرَ عَن مَداهُ في العُلى
أَنَّ السُّروجَ مَجالِسُ الفِتيانِ	تَخِذوا المَجالِسَ في البُيوتِ وَعِندَهُ
هَيجاءَ غَيرَ الطَّعنِ في المَيدانِ	وَتَوَهَّموا اللَّعبَ الوَغى وَالطَّعنُ في الـ
إِلّا إِلى العاداتِ وَالأَوطانِ	قادَ الجِيادَ إِلى الطِّعانِ وَلَم يَقُدْ
في قَلبِ صاحِبِهِ عَلى الأَحزانِ	كُلُّ ابنِ سابِقَةٍ يُغيرُ بِحُسنِهِ
فَدُعاؤُها يُغني عَنِ الأَرسانِ	إِنْ خُلِّيَتْ رُبِطَتْ بِآدابِ الوَغى
فَكَأَنَّما يُبْصِرْنَ بِالآذانِ	في جَحفَلٍ سَتَرَ العُيونَ غُبارُهُ
كُلُّ البَعيدِ لَهُ قَريبٌ دانِ	يَرمي بِها البَلَدَ البَعيدَ مُظَفَّرٌ
يَطرَحنَ أَيديَها بِحِصنِ الرّانِ	فَكَأَنَّ أَرجُلَها بِتُربَةِ مَنبِجٍ
يَنشُرنَ فيهِ عَمائِمَ الفُرسانِ	حَتّى عَبَرْنَ بِأَرسَناسَ سَوابِحاً
يَذَرُ الفُحولَ وَهُنَّ كَالخِصيانِ	يَقمُصنَ في مِثلِ المُدى مِن بارِدٍ
تَتَفَرَّقانِ بِهِ وَتَلتَقيانِ	وَالماءُ بَينَ عَجاجَتَينِ مُخَلِّصٌ
وَثَنى الأَعِنَّةَ وَهْوَ كَالعِقيانِ	رَكَضَ الأَميرُ وَكَاللُّجَينِ حَبابُهُ
وَبَنى السَّفينَ لَهُ مِنَ الصُّلبانِ	فَتَلَ الحِبالَ مِنَ الغَدائِرِ فَوقَهُ

235
He spoke also praising him at the time of his retreat from the lands of the Rum in the year 345.
(Perfect ni)

Wisdom is before bravery of the brave
    It is first but that has the second place
If they are united in a bitter soul
    They achieve eminence in each condition
Often a man jousts his opponent
    By wit, before foes thrust at each other
But for intellect the meanest lion
    Would be nearer to nobility than man is
Souls would not compete for excellence
    Nor warrior hands manage the hard lance
But for one named for his swords and
    Edges drawn they might be like sheathes
He plunged into death with them
    Unknown if from scorn or forgetfulness
He strove but folk of the time and folk
    Of all times came short of its high goal
They had seats in palaces but he had
    The saddle as the seat for the young man
They fancied battle a game but joust
    In war is other than jousting in a field
He led horses to battle only as if
    He led them by habit to their paddocks
Each winner's foal alters by beauty
    Its master's heart in spite of sorrow
If alone they are bound by habits
    A war cry makes a halter unneeded
In an army whose dust veils eyes
    It seems they look with their ears
A conqueror hits distant lands
    Each remote region is drawn close
As if back legs in Manbij dust
    Drove their front legs at Hisn Ran
Until they cross Arsanas swimming
    Scattering turbans of the horsemen
Galloping against knives of cold
    Shrinking stallions as if castrated
The water between two dust clouds
    Is pure, they parted by it and met in it
The Amir came in silver bubbles
    He turned bridle in their red gold
He twists ropes of women's hair
    Builds boats for them of the crosses

عُقِمَ البُطونُ حَوالَيكَ الأَلوانِ	وَحَشاهُ عادِيَةً بِغَيرِ قَوائِمِ
تَحتَ الحِسانِ مَرابِضُ الغِزلانِ	تَأتي بِما سَبَتِ الخُيولُ كَأَنَّها
مِن دَهرِهِ وَطَوارِقِ الحِدثانِ	بَحرٌ تَعَوَّدَ أَن يُذِمَّ لِأَهلِهِ
رَعَاكَ وَاستَثنى بَني حَمدانِ	فَتَرَكتَهُ وَإِذا أَذَمَّ مِنَ الوَرى
ذِمَمَ الدُروعِ عَلى ذَوي التيجانِ	المُخفِرينَ بِكُلِّ أَبيَضَ صارِمٍ
مُتَواضِعينَ عَلى عَظيمِ الشَأنِ	مُتَصَعلِكينَ عَلى كَثافَةِ مُلكِهِم
أَجَلِ الظَليمِ وَرَبقَةِ السِرحانِ	يَتَقَيَّلونَ ظِلالَ كُلِّ مُطَهَّمٍ
وَأَذَلَّ دينَكَ سائِرَ الأَديانِ	خَضَعَت لِمُنصُلِكَ المَناصِلُ عَنوَةً
وَالسَيرُ مُمتَنِعٌ مِن ضِ الإِمكانِ	وَعَلى الدُروبِ وَفي الرُجوعِ غَضاضَةٌ
وَالكُفرُ مُجتَمِعٌ عَلى الإيمانِ	وَالطُرقُ ضَيِّقَةُ المَسالِكِ بِالقَنا
يَصعَدنَ بَينَ مَناكِبِ العِقبانِ	نَظَروا إِلى زُبَرِ الحَديدِ كَأَنَّما
فَكَأَنَّها لَيسَت مِنَ الحَيَوانِ	وَفَوارِسٍ يُحيي الحِمامُ نُفوسَها
ضَرباً كَأَنَّ السَيفَ فيهِ اِثنانِ	ما زِلتَ تَضرِبُهُم دِراكاً في الذُرى
جاءَت إِلَيكَ جُسومُهُم بِأَمانِ	خَصَّ الجَماجِمَ وَالوُجوهَ كَأَنَّما
يَطَأُونَ كُلَّ حَنِيَّةٍ مِرنانِ	فَرَموا بِما يَرمونَ عَنهُ وَأَدبَروا
بِمُهَنَّدٍ وَمُثَقَّفٍ وَسِنانِ	يَغشاهُم مَطَرُ السَحابِ مُفَصَّلاً
آمالَهُ مَن عادَ بِالحِرمانِ	حُرِموا الَّذي أَمَلوا وَأَدرَكَ مِنهُم
شَغَلَتهُ مُهجَتُهُ عَنِ الإِخوانِ	وَإِذا الرِماحُ شَغَلنَ مُهجَةَ ثائِرٍ
كَثُرَ القيلُ بِها وَقَلَّ العاني	هَيهاتِ عاقَ عَنِ العَوادِ قَواضِبٌ
فَأَطَعنَهُ في طاعَةِ الرَحمَنِ	وَمُهَذَّبٌ أَمَرَ المَنايا فيهِمُ
فَكَأَنَّ فيهِ مُسِفَّةَ الغِربانِ	قَد سَوَّدَت شَجَرَ الجِبالِ شُعورُهُم
فَكَأَنَّهُ النارَنجُ في الأَغصانِ	وَجَرى عَلى الوَرَقِ النَجيعُ القاني
كَقُلوبِهِنَّ إِذا التَقى الجَمعانِ	إِنَّ السُيوفَ مَعَ الَّذينَ قُلوبُهُم
مِثلَ الجَبانِ بِكَفِّ كُلِّ جَبانِ	تَلقى الحُسامَ عَلى جَراءَةِ حَدِّهِ
قِمَمَ المُلوكِ مَواقِدَ النيرانِ	رَفَعَت بِكَ العَرَبُ العِمادَ وَصَيَّرَت
أَنسابُ أَصلِهِمُ إِلى عَدنانِ	أَنسابُ فَخرِهِمُ إِلَيكَ وَإِنَّما

He fills it with runners without legs
    Barren of belly and blacker" in color
They take what riders took captive
    Crouching deer, women underneath
A river used to protect its people
    From its fate, blows and misfortune
You left it when it guarded men
    It feared you, except Banu Hamdan
Destroying by all bright swords
    Armored treaties, crown possessors
Seeming poor spite of realms'
    Wealth, humble spite of high rank
Napping at noon in horse's shade
    Death to ostrich, lasso to the wolf
Swords submit to your sword
    Your religion conquers the others
Shame to retreat on mountain passes
    When progress was forbid as impossible
Roads narrow with passage of lances
    Unbelievers gathered against the faithful
They see steel staves as if they are
    Coming up between shoulders of eagles
At riders whose souls death inspired
    As if they were no more among animals
You cease not to hit them on peaks
    Hard as if swords were double there
Especially skulls and faces as if
    Their bodies came to you in security
They threw away what they shot with
    Turned treading on every twanging bow
Rain from clouds covered in waves
    Straight shafts, Indian steel and points
Forbidden their hope yet attained
    The hope of him who returned denied
If lancers engage revenger's breast
    His heart is busy apart from brothers
Alas the swords hinder return, many
    Are the corpses, few are the captives
An expert commands fate for them
    They submit to him, obey the Merciful
The hair blackened mountain trees
    As if the ravens were sitting on them
Crimson blood on the leaves was
    Like oranges growing on the branches
Swords with those whose hearts are
    Hearts of steeds as they meet a rank
You see a sword for all its daring
    Is fearful in the hands of a coward
The Arabs raised as a pillar for
    Heads of kings a torch to light fires
A boastful genealogy traced to you
    A lineage of ancestors back to

أَصْبَحْتُ مِنْ قَتْلاكَ بِالإِحْسانِ	يا مَنْ يُقَتِّلُ مَنْ أَرادَ بِسَيْفِهِ
وَإِذا مَدَحْتُكَ حارَ فيكَ لِساني	فَإِذا رَأَيْتُكَ حارَ دونَكَ ناظِري

(٢٣٦)

«من البسيط»

قال وقد تُحدث بحضرة سيف الدولة أن البطريق أقسم عند ملكه أنه يعارض سيف الدولة في الدرب وسأله أن ينجده ببطارقته وعدده وعُدده ففعل فخاب ظنه. أنشده إياها سنة خمس وأربعين وثلاث مئة (٩٥٦م) وهي آخر ما أنشده بحلب:

ماذا يَزيدُكَ في إِقدامِكَ القَسَمُ	عُقْبى اليَمينِ عَلى عُقْبى الوَغى نَدَمُ
ما دَلَّ أَنَّكَ في الميعادِ مُتَّهَمُ	وَفي اليَمينِ عَلى ما أَنْتَ واعِدُهُ
فَتًى مِنَ الضَرْبِ تُنْسى عِنْدَهُ الكَلِمُ	آلى الفَتى ابْنُ شُمُشْقيقٍ فَأَحْنَثَهُ
عَلى الفِعالِ حُضورُ الفِعْلِ وَالكَرَمُ	وَفاعِلٌ ما اشْتَهى يُغْنيهِ عَنْ حَلِفٍ
يَمَسَّها غَيْرَ سَيْفِ الدَوْلَةِ السَأَمُ	كُلُّ السُيوفِ إِذا طالَ الضِرابُ بِها
تَحَمَّلَتْهُ إِلى أَعْدائِهِ الهِمَمُ	لَوْ كَلَّتِ الخَيْلُ حَتّى لا تَحَمَّلُهُ
بِفُرْقَةِ المُلْكِ وَالزَعْمُ الَذي زَعَموا	أَيْنَ البَطاريقُ وَالحَلْفُ الَذي حَلَفوا
فَهُنَّ أَلْسِنَةٌ أَفْواهُها القِمَمُ	وَلَّى صَوارِمَهُ إِكْذابَ قَوْلِهِمُ
عَنْهُ بِما جَهِلوا مِنْهُ وَما عَلِموا	نَواطِقٌ مُخْبِراتٌ في جَماجِمِهِمْ
مِنْ كُلِّ مِثْلِ وَبارِ أَهْلِها إِرَمُ	اَلراجِعُ الخَيْلَ مُحْفاةً مُقَوَّدَةً
بِأَنَّ دارَكَ قِنَّسْرينَ وَالأَجَمُ	كَتَلِّ بِطْريقِ المَغْرورِ ساكِنِها
إِذا قَصَدْتَ سِواها عادَها الظُلَمُ	وَظَنَّهُمْ أَنَّكَ المِصْباحُ في حَلَبٍ
وَالمَوْتُ يَدْعُونَ إِلّا أَنَّهُمْ وَهَموا	وَالشَمْسُ يَعْنونَ إِلّا أَنَّهُمْ جَهِلوا
إِلّا وَجَيْشُكَ في جَفْنَيْهِ مُزْدَحِمُ	فَلَمْ تُتِمَّ سُروجٌ فَتْحَ ناظِرِها
وَالشَمْسُ تُسْفِرُ أَحْياناً وَتَلْتَثِمُ	وَالنَقْعُ يَأْخُذُ حَرّاناً وَبُقْعَتَها
وَما بِها البُخْلُ لَوْ لا أَنَّها نِقَمُ	سُحْبٌ تَمُرُّ بِحِصْنِ الرّانِ مُمْسِكَةً

He destroys whom he wishes
  I am one of the corpses due his gift
If I see you my vision is perplexed
  If I praise you my tongue is enchanted

236
He spoke
also praising him
and commemorating
the breaking of the oath
of the Patricius
by the head of the king
that he would confront
Saif al Daula in the pass in the year 345.
(Outspread mu)

End of an oath in battle's end is truth
  Can such a vow increase your courage?
Won't such an oath since you vowed it
  Show you, as to reliability, to be rotten??
Ibn Shumishqiq vowed to one and broke
  With him a handclasp forging his word
A doer is one who avoids an oath to be
  Sufficient in the acting and the dispensing
All swords when striking continues long
  Weaken, except Saif al-Dala the impetuous
If a horse wearies in carrying him
  The spirit will carry him on to his enemy
Where are patricians and vows sworn
  By hair of the king and a lie they lived?
He made lies of the words by swords
  They are tongues, chiefs are the mouths
Being informers to their skulls of him
  What they don't know and what they do
He brings horses shoeless as led
  From places like Wabar and Iram folk
Like Teli Batriq whose folk is tricked
  Because your home is Qinnasrin, Ajam
They think you a torch in Aleppo and
  If you go forth without it darkness comes
They fancy a sun but are ignorant
  They shun death but are imagining
Saruj scarcely stopped waking when
  our army pressed between its eyelid
Dust seized on Harran and its vale
  The sun grew pale and veiled itself
Clouds came to Hisn Ran endless
  They weren't stingy but for revenge

فَالأَرْضُ لا أَمَمٌ وَالجَيْشُ لا أَمَمُ	جَيْشٌ كَأَنَّكَ في أَرْضٍ تُطاوِلُهُ
وَإِنْ مَضى عَلَمٌ مِنْهُ بَدا عَلَمُ	إِذا مَضى عَلَمٌ مِنها بَدا عَلَمُ
وَوَسَّمْتَها عَلى آنافِها الحَكَمُ	وَشُرَّبٌ أَحْمَتِ الشَّعْرى شَكائِمَها
تَنِشُّ بِالماءِ في أَشْداقِها اللُّجُمُ	حَتّى وَرَدْنَ بِسِمْنينِ بُحَيْرَتَها
تَرْعى الظُّبى في خَضيبٍ نَبْتُهُ اللَّمَمُ	وَأَصْبَحَتْ بِقُرى هِنْزيطَ جائِلَةً
تَحْتَ التُّرابِ وَلا بازاً لَهُ قَدَمُ	فَما تَرَكْنَ بِها خُلْداً لَهُ بَصَرٌ
وَلا مَهاةً لَها مِنْ شِبْهِها حَشَمُ	وَلا هِزَبْراً لَهُ مِنْ دِرْعِهِ لِبَدُ
مَكامِنُ الأَرْضِ وَالغيطانُ وَالأَكَمُ	تَرْمي عَلى شَفَراتِ الباتِراتِ بِهِمْ
وَكَيْفَ يَعْصِمُهُمْ ما لَيْسَ يَنْعَصِمُ	وَجاوَزوا أَرْسَناساً مُعْصِمينَ بِهِ
وَما يَرُدُّكَ عَنْ طَوْدٍ لَهُمْ شَمَمُ	وَما يَصُدُّكَ عَنْ بَحْرٍ لَهُمْ سَعَةٌ
قَوْماً إِذا تَلِفوا قُدْماً فَقَدْ سَلِموا	ضَرَبْتَهُ بِصُدورِ الخَيْلِ حامِلَةً
كَما تَجَفَّلُ تَحْتَ الغارَةِ النَّعَمُ	تَجَفَّلُ المَوْجَ عَنْ لَبّاتِ خَيْلِهِمِ
سُكّانُهُ رِمَمٌ مَسْكونُها حُمَمُ	عَبَرْتَ تَقْدُمُهُمْ فيهِ وَفي بَلَدٍ
قَبْلَ المَجوسِ إِلى ذا اليَوْمِ تَضْطَرِمُ	وَفي أَكُفِّهِمُ النّارُ الَّتي عُبِدَتْ
بِحَدِّها أَوْ تُعَظِّمْ مَعْشَراً عَظُموا	هِنْدِيَّةٌ إِنْ تُصَغِّرْ مَعْشَراً صَغُروا
أَبْطالُها وَلَكَ الأَطْفالُ وَالحُرَمُ	قاسَمْتَها تَلَّ بَطْريقٍ فَكانَ لَها
عَلى جَحافِلِها مِنْ نَضْحِهِ رَثَمُ	تَلْقى بِهِمْ زَبَدَ التَّيّارِ مُقْرَبَةً
مَكْدودَةٌ وَيَقومُ لا بِها الأَلَمُ	دُهْمٌ فَوارِسُها رُكّابُ أَبْطُنِها
وَما لَها خِلَقٌ مِنْها وَلا شِيَمُ	مِنَ الجِيادِ الَّتي كِدْتَ العَدُوَّ بِها
كَلَفْظِ حَرْفٍ وَعاهُ سامِعٌ فَهِمُ	نِتاجُ رَأْياكَ في وَقْتٍ عَلى عَجَلٍ
أَنْ يُبْصِروكَ فَلَمّا أَبْصَروكَ عَموا	وَقَدْ تَمَنَّوْا غَداةَ الدَّرْبِ في لَجِبٍ
وَسَمْهَرِيَّتُهُ في وَجْهِهِ غَمَمُ	صَدَمْتَهُمْ بِخَميسٍ أَنْتَ غُرَّتُهُ
يَسْقُطْنَ حَوْلَكَ وَالأَرْواحُ تَنْهَزِمُ	فَكانَ أَثْبَتَ ما فيهِمْ جُسومُهُمُ
وَالمَشْرَفِيَّةُ مِلْءُ اليَوْمِ فَوْقَهُمُ	وَالأَعْوَجِيَّةُ مِلْءُ الطُّرْقِ خَلْفَهُمُ
تَوافَقَتْ قُلَلٌ في الجَوِّ تَصْطَدِمُ	إِذا تَوافَقَتِ الضَّرْباتُ صاعِدَةً
أَلّا انْثَنى فَهْوَ يَنْأى وَهْيَ تَبْتَسِمُ	وَأَسْلَمَ ابْنُ شُمُشْقيقٍ أَلِيَّتَهُ

An army, you in a beaten land
    Earth has no front, nor has the army
Landmarks disappear, flags show
    If banners go the landmarks return
Lean horses, a hot star burns
    Halters and brands the nose bridge
They come to drink Simnin's pool
    Bits in their mouths sizzle in water
They burst on Hinzit town in fury
    Grazing the edges on fertile hair
They leave no sightless mole
    Under dust nor hawk with wings
Nor lion with mane for armor
    No wild cow like to the maidens
Caves of earth, valleys and hills
    Cast them on the scimitar edges
They cross Arsanas once a wall
    How defend those who lack guards?
The stream's current won't bar you
    Nor high peaks turn you back down
You win with horse breasts bearing
    Men, if they meet you they must yield
Waves dash against chests of
    Horses like a herd rushing in fury
You crossed it ahead of them to
    Bones of men, homes in flames
The fires were once adored by
    Magi, kept burning for this battle
Indian steel in a troop small of
    Edge, if you enlarge it is great
You share Tell Bitriq with them
    Its men theirs, yours women and kids
The boats cross foaming waves
    The upper lips slaver from the spray
Black, horsemen riding in bellies
    Toilsome, pain is human not wooden
You trick the foes by horsemen
    Not having their nature or deceits
Product of your thought in haste
    Like a word's letters listeners grasp
They long for morning at Darb to
    See you but when blinded they fail
Your army routs them, you a blaze
    Its spears are the forelocks in front
Firmest thing for them their bodies
    Falling about you, souls fleeing away
Awaji horses fill roads behind
    Mashrafi swords filled day above
When blows agree on forward motion
    Heads will come to clash in the distance
Ibn Shumushqiq broke his promise
    Stayed afar while it was mocked here

فَيَسرِقُ النَّفسَ الأَدنى وَيَغتَنِمُ	لا يَأمُلُ النَّفسَ الأَقصى لِمُهجَتِهِ
صَوبُ الأَسِنَّةِ في أَثنائِها دِيَمُ	تَرُدُّ عَنهُ قَنا الفُرسانِ سابِغَةٌ
كَأَنَّ كُلَّ سِنانٍ فَوقَها قَلَمُ	تَخُطُّ فيها العَوالي لَيسَ تَنفُذُها
لَو زَلَّ عَنهُ لَوارَت شَخصَهُ الرَخَمُ	فَلا سَقى الغَيثُ ما واراهُ مِن شَجَرٍ
شُربُ المُدامَةِ وَالأَوتارِ وَالنَغَمُ	أَلهى المَمالِكَ عَن فَخرٍ قَفَلتَ بِهِ
لا تُستَدامُ بِأَمضى مِنهُما النَعَمُ	مُقَلَّداً فَوقَ شُكرِ اللَهِ ذا شُطُبٍ
فَلَو دَعَوتَ بِلا ضَربٍ أَجابَ دَمُ	أَلقَت إِلَيكَ دِماءُ الرومِ طاعَتَها
فَما يُصيبُهُمُ مَوتٌ وَلا هَرَمُ	يُسابِقُ القَتلُ فيهِم كُلَّ حادِثَةٍ
نَفسٌ يُفَرِّحُ نَفساً غَيرَها الحُلُمُ	نَفَت رُقادَ عَلِيٍّ عَن مَحاجِرِهِ
قِيامَهُ وَهَداهُ العُربُ وَالعَجَمُ	القائِمُ المَلِكُ الهادي الَّذي شَهِدَت
بِسَيفَيهِ وَلَهُ كوفانُ وَالحَرَمُ	اِبنُ المُعَفَّرِ في نَجدٍ فَوارِسُها
إِنَّ الكِرامَ بِأَسخاهُم يَداً خُتِموا	لا تَطلُبَنَّ كَريماً بَعدَ رُؤيَتِهِ
قَد أَفسَدَ القَولَ حَتّى أَحمَدَ الصَمَمُ	وَلا تُبالِ بِشِعرٍ بَعدَ شاعِرِهِ

وقال بمصر وهو يريد سيف الدولة:

قَبلَ الفِراقِ أَذى بَعدَ الفِراقِ يَدُ	فارَقتُكُم فَإِذا ما كانَ عِندَكُم
أَعانَ قَلبي عَلى الشَوقِ الَّذي أَجِدُ	إِذا تَذَكَّرتُ ما بَيني وَبَينَكُمُ

(۲۳۸)

«من البسيط»

توفيت أخت سيف الدولة بميافارقين وورد خبرها إلى الكوفة فقال أبو الطيب يرثيها ويعزيه بها وكتب بها إليه من الكوفة سنة اثنتين وخمسين وثلاث مئة (٩٦٣م):

كِنايَةٌ بِهِما عَن أَشرَفِ النَسَبِ	يا أُختَ خَيرِ أَخٍ يا بِنتَ خَيرِ أَبِ
وَمَن يَصِفكِ فَقَد سَمّاكِ لِلعَرَبِ	أَجِلَّ قَدرَكِ أَن تُسَمَّي مُؤَبَّنَةً
وَدَمعَهُ وَهُما في قَبضَةِ الطَرَبِ	لا يَملِكُ الطَربُ المَحزونُ مَنطِقَهُ
بِمَن أُصِبتَ وَكَم أَسكَتَّ مِن لَجَبِ	غَدَرتَ يا مَوتُ كَم أَفنَيتَ مِن عَدَدٍ
وَكَم سَأَلتَ فَلَم يَبخَل وَلَم تَخِبِ	وَكَم صَحِبتَ أَخاها في مُنازَلَةٍ
فَزَعتُ فيهِ بِآمالي إِلى الكَذِبِ	طَوى الجَزيرَةَ حَتّى جاءَني خَبَرٌ
شَرِقتُ بِالدَمعِ حَتّى كادَ يَشرَقُ بي	حَتّى إِذا لَم يَدَع لي صِدقُهُ أَمَلاً

A distant one had no hope in heart
    The nearby robbed or plundered soul
Long armor repels riders' spears
    Lance rain on the folds is lasting
Spears wrote on it but didn't pierce
    Every point on it was as a scribe's pen
May showers not water trees to hide
    If he slips vultures will veil his shape
He plays with lords without honor
    Wine drinkers, lute players, singers
A sword girded over thanks to God
    No favor exceeds in power these two
Rum blood is on you in submission
    If you call without blows, blood replies
Battle surpasses all evil for them
    Neither death nor old age overwhelms
It banishes Ali's sleep from his eyes
    Soul shows soul in ways not in dreams
Enduring king, guided, Arabs witness
    To his honor and favor as do Persians
Dust cloud's son in Najd for riders
    By his sword Kufa and Makka are his
Seek no bounty after his coming
    A noble deed as gift is a sealed hand
Meddle not with poems after a poet
    Speech is corrupt if the deaf eulogize

237
He spoke also and it is said he referred to him in it. (Outspread du)

I leave you, if there is anything with you
    Of evil before parting, afterwards it is a gift
When I remember what was between me
    And you I comfort my heart for the pain that i had

238
He spoke lamenting the elder sister of Saif al Daula offering condolences for her when she died. (Outspread bi)

Best brother's sister, best father's issue
    Your name in them is of most noble lineage
Your rank too glorious to name in an elegy
    He who describes you names you as Arab maid
Deep griefs cannot hold his tongue nor
    Tears but they are in the grip of feelings
You betray O death as many as you ruin
    In one you hit, as many weepers as you quiet
As many of your brothers you conducted
    In war, how many you asked not stingy or shy!
He crossed Jazira till news came to me
    I was frightened at it hoping it was false

وَالبُرْدُ في الطُّرْقِ وَالأَقْلَامُ في الكُتُبِ	تَعَثَّرَتْ بِهِ في الأَفْواهِ أَلْسُنُها
دِيَارَ بَكْرٍ وَلَم تَخْلَعْ وَلَم تَهَبِ	كَأَنَّ فَعْلَةَ لَم تَمْلَأْ مَواكِبُها
وَلَم تُغِثْ داعِياً بِالوَيْلِ وَالحَرَبِ	وَلَم تَرُدَّ حَياةً بَعْدَ تَوْلِيَةٍ
فَكَيْفَ لَيلَ فَتى الفِتْيانِ في حَلَبِ	أَرى العِراقَ طَويلَ اللَّيْلِ مُذْ نُعِيَتْ
وَأَنَّ دَمْعَ جُفُوني غَيْرُ مُنْسَكِبِ	يَظُنُّ أَنَّ فُؤادي غَيْرُ مُلْتَهِبِ
لِحُرْمَةِ المَجْدِ وَالقُصَّادِ وَالأَدَبِ	بَلى وَحُرْمَةِ مَن كانَتْ مُراعِيَةً
وَإِنْ مَضَتْ يَدُها مَوْرُوثَةَ النَّشَبِ	وَمَن مَضَتْ غَيْرَ مَوْرُوثٍ خِلالِها
وَهَمُّ أَتْرابِها في اللَّهْوِ وَاللَّعِبِ	وَهَمُّها في العُلى وَالمَجْدِ ناشِئَةً
وَلَيْسَ يَعْلَمُ إِلَّا اللَّهُ بِالشَّنَبِ	يَعْلَمْنَ حينَ تُحَيّا حُسْنَ مَبْسِمِها
وَحَسْرَةٌ في قُلُوبِ البِيضِ وَاليَلَبِ	مَسَرَّةٌ في قُلُوبِ الطِّيبِ مَفْرِقُها
رَأى المَقانِعَ أَعْلى مِنهُ في الرُّتَبِ	إِذا رَأى وَرَآها رَأْسَ لابِسِهِ
كَريمَةً غَيرَ أُنْثى العَقْلِ وَالحَسَبِ	وَإِنْ تَكُنْ خُلِقَتْ أُنْثى لَقَدْ خُلِقَتْ
فَإِنَّ في الخَمْرِ مَعنىً لَيسَ في العِنَبِ	وَإِنْ تَكُنْ تَغْلِبُ الغَلْباءُ عُنصُرُها
وَلَيْتَ غائِبَةَ الشَّمْسَيْنِ لَم تَغِبِ	فَلَيْتَ طالِعَةَ الشَّمْسَيْنِ غائِبَةٌ
فِداءُ عَينٍ الَّتي زالَتْ وَلَم تَؤُبِ	وَلَيْتَ عَينَ الَّتي آبَ النَّهارُ بِها
وَلا تَقَلَّدَ بِالهِنْدِيَّةِ القُضُبِ	فَما تَقَلَّدَ بِاليَاقُوتِ مُشْبِهُها
إِلَّا بَكَيْتُ وَلا وُدٌّ بِلا سَبَبِ	وَلا ذَكَرْتُ جَميلاً مِن صَنائِعِها
فَما قَنِعْتِ لَها يا أَرْضُ بِالحُجُبِ	قَدْ كانَ كُلُّ حِجابٍ دُونَ رُؤْيَتِها
فَهَلْ حَسَدْتِ عَلَيها أَعْيُنَ الشُّهُبِ	وَلا رَأَيْتِ عُيُونَ الإِنْسِ تُدْرِكُها
فَقَدْ أَطَلْتُ وَما سَلَّمْتُ مِن كَثَبِ	وَهَلْ سَمِعْتِ سَلاماً لي أَلَمَّ بِها
وَقَدْ يُقَصِّرُ عَن أَحْيائِنا الغِيَبِ	وَكَيفَ يَبْلُغُ مَوْتانا الَّتي دُفِنَتْ
وَقُلْ لِصاحِبِهِ يا أَنْفَعَ السُّحُبِ	يا أَحْسَنَ الصَّبْرِ زُرْ أُولى القُلُوبِ بِها
مِنَ الكِرامِ سِوى آبائِكَ النُّجُبِ	وَأَكْرَمَ النّاسِ لا مُسْتَثْنِياً أَحَداً
وَعاشَ دِرْهَمُها المَفْدِيُّ بِالذَّهَبِ	قَدْ كانَ قاسَمَكَ الشَّخْصَينِ دَهْرُهُما
إِنّا لَنَغْفُلُ وَالأَيّامُ في الطَّلَبِ	وَعادَ في طَلَبِ المَتْرُوكِ تارِكُهُ
كَأَنَّهُ الوَقْتُ بَينَ الوِرْدِ وَالقَرَبِ	ما كانَ أَقْصَرَ وَقْتاً كانَ بَيْنَهُما

Until his trust left me no hope and I
    Choked with tears as he nearly choked me
Their tongue stumbled with it in mouths
    Couriers on the road and pens in a letter
As if Fala's parades had not been full
    At Diyar Bakr no honor given or gifts sent
She gave back no life after transferal
    Nor asked for help with alas! or calamity!
I knew Iraq's long nights since she died
    But how are nights for the hero at Aleppo?
He suspects my heart untouched by heat
    And that tears from my eyes are not flowing
No! by the chastity that was well kept
    By glory's holiness, purpose and culture
She went with none to inherit a nature
    Even if her hand left inheritance of wealth
Her care for eminence, glory in youth
    But others' care was for play and games
They knew her smile's beauty in love
    But for God none knew her teeth's cool
Her hair happiness to grains of musk
    Grief to the souls of the helmet and strap
If one looks beyond at heads with those
    He sees the veil on top of them hung free
If she was made female yet she was
    Noble, not feminine in mind or feeling
If she was Taglib's with many kin
    Yet in wine is truth not found in grapes
Would suns that shine were absent
    And absent sun had not disappeared
Would the eye day brings back with it
    Was ransom for that gone not to return
None who wear ruby collars are as her
    And none who gird on the Indian scimitar
I can't think of beauty in her goodness
    Unweeping, this is no love without cause
Before her face every kind of veil
    You were not content O earth without it
You did not see men's eye reach her
    But did you envy the stare' eyes for her?
Did you hear my greeting made to her?
    I was far and did not salute her nearby
How can news reach the buried one?
    If it fell short of their living absent one
O best courage, visit the best houri
    Say to its owner: O most useful cloud
Most noble of men not second to any
    In generosity except your noble fathers
Their times shared two souls with you
    Their pearls lived, one ransom, one gone
One returned to seek one left behind
    For we forget but days are searching
Only the shortest time was between
    Time between approach and drinking

فحُزْنٌ كلَّ أخي حزنٍ أخو الغضَبِ	جَزَاكَ ربُّكَ بالأحزانِ مَغْفِرَةً
بِمَا يَهَبْنَ ولا يَسْخونَ بالسَّلَبِ	وأنتُمْ نَفَرٌ تَسْخو نُفوسُكُمُ
مَحَلَّ سُمرِ القَنا من سائرِ القَصَبِ	حَلَلْتُمُ من مُلوكِ الأرضِ كلِّهمِ
إذا ضَرَبْنَ كَسَرْنَ النَّبْـعَ بالغَرَبِ	فَلا تَنَلْكَ اللَّيَالـي، إنَّ أَيْدِيَهـا
فإنَّهنَّ يَصِدْنَ الصَّقـرَ بالخَرَبِ	ولا يُعِنّ عَدُوّاً أنـتَ قاهِرُهُ
وقَـد أتَيْنَـكَ في الحالَيـنِ بالعَجَبِ	وإنْ سَرَرْنَ بِمَحْبُوبٍ فجَعْـنَ بِهِ
وفاجَأتْـهُ بـأمرٍ غـيرِ مُحْتَسَبِ	ورُبَّما أحْتَسَبَ الإنسانُ غايَتَها
ولا أنتَهـى أرَبٌ إلاّ إلى أرَبِ	ومـا قَضـى أحَـدٌ منهـا لَبَانَتَـهُ
إلاّ على شَجَبٍ والخُلْفِ في الشَّجَبِ	تخالَفَ النَّاسُ حتـى لا اتّفاقَ لَهُـمْ
وقيـلَ تَشـرَكُ جسْمَ المـرءِ في العَطَبِ	فقيـلَ تَخلُـصُ نَفـسُ المَـرءِ سالمةً
أقامَـهُ الفِكْـرُ بَيـنَ العَجـزِ والتَّعَـبِ	ومَـنْ تَفكَّـرَ في الدُّنْيـا ومُهْجَتَـهِ

(٢٣٩)

«من الخفيف»

أنفذ إليه سيف الدولة ابنه من حلب إلى الكوفة ومعه هدية وكان ذلك بعد خروجه من مصر ومفارقته لكافور، فقال يمدحه وكتب بها إليه من الكوفة سنة اثنتين وخمسين وثلاث مئة (٩٦٣م):

أنا أهـوى وقَلبُـكَ المتبُـولُ	ما لَنا كُلِّنـا جَـوٍ يا رَسُـولُ
غـارَ منّـي وخَـانَ فيمـا يقُـولُ	كلَّمـا عـادَ مَـنْ بَعَثْـتُ إليْهـا
هـا وخَانَـتْ قُلُوبَهُـنَّ العُقُـولُ	أفسَـدَتْ بَيْنَنـا الأمانـاتُ عَيْنـا
قٍ إليها والشَّـوْقُ حيـثُ النُّحُـولُ	تَشْتَكي ما اشْتَكيتُ من ألَمِ الشَّوْ
فَعَلَيْـهِ لكـلِّ عَيـنٍ دَليـلُ	وإذا خامَـرَ الهـوى قلبَ صَبٍّ
مَ فَحُسْـنُ الوُجـوهِ حـالٍ تَحـولُ	زوَّدِينـا من حُسـنِ وجهِكِ ما دا
يـا فإنّ المُقـامَ فيها قَليـلُ	وصِلينـا نَصِلْـكِ في هـذِهِ الدُّنـ

Your lord rewards by pardon for grief
    For sorrow in grief is like anger for all
You are folk whose souls are fine
    In what they give and not as plunder
You settled among mankind's kings
    In brown lance place among the others
May nights not reach you for they if
    They strike break hard wood with soft
May they not aid the foe you conquer
    They hunt the falcon with the buzzard
If they rejoice in love they also plague
    It's wonderful that they bring both states
Often a man thinks he gains by them
    But they surprise with the unexpected
No one obtains from them his needs
    Noris one goal attained without another
Men disagree till no agreement lasts
    Except in ruin and discord lies in ruin
One says man's soul is saved wholly
    One says it shares with man's body loss
If one thinks of the world and its heart
    Memory suspends between sleep and toil

239
He spoke also praising him and he had sent him a present to Iraq and gift after gift in Shawwal of the year 351.
(Nimble lu)

What is wrong O messenger if all are ill
    Am I in love or is your heart apprehensive?
Each time the one I sent to him returns
    He envies me and is false in what he says
Her eyes corrupted the faith between us
    And the minds are betrayed by the hearts
You suffer what I suffer of love's pain
    For her and love shows where emaciation is
If love stirs in the lover's heart
    Then that is the hint to every eye
Our provision is in your face's beauty
    But beauty of face is a changing thing
Embrace us, we embrace you in this world
    For the permanent things in it are the fewest

مَـنْ رَآهَـا بِعَيْنِهَـا شَـاقَهُ القُطّـ	ـانُ فيهَـا كَمَـا تَشُـوقُ الحُمُـولُ
إنْ تَرَيْنِـي أَدِمْـتُ بَعْـدَ بَيَـاضٍ	فَحَمِيـدٌ مِـنَ القَنـاةِ الذُّبُـولُ
صَحِبَتْنـي علـى الفَـلاةِ فَتـاةٌ	عـادةُ اللَّـوْنِ عندهـا التّبديـلُ
سَتَرَتْكَ الحِجَـالُ عَنهَـا ولَكِـنْ	بـكِ مِنهَـا مِـنَ اللَّمَـى تَقبيـلُ
مِثْلُهَـا أَنـتِ لَوَحَتْنِـي وأَسْقَمْـتِ	وَزَادَتْ أَبْهاكُمَـا العُطْبُـولُ
نَحْـنُ أَدْرَى وَقَـدْ سَـأَلْنا بِنَجْـدٍ	أَطَويـلٌ طَريقُنَـا أَمْ يَطُـولُ
وَكَثيـرٌ مِـنَ السُّـؤالِ اشتيـاقٌ	وَكَثيـرٌ مِـنْ رَدِّهِ تَعْليـلُ
لا أَقَمْنـا عَلـى مَكـانٍ وإنْ طَـابَ	ولا يُمْكِـنُ المَكـانَ الرَّحيـلُ
كُلَّمـا رَحَبَـتْ بنـا الرَّوْضُ قُلْنـا	حَلَـبْ قَصْدُنَـا وَأَنْـتِ السَّبيـلُ
فيـكِ مَرْعَـى جيادِنَـا والمَطَايـا	وَإلَيْهَـا وَجِيفُنَـا والذَّميـلُ
والمُسَـمَّوْنَ بالأميـرِ كَثيـرٌ	والأميـرُ الـذي بهـا المَـأْمُولُ
الَّـذي زُلْـتُ عَنْـهُ شَـرْقاً وَغَرْبـاً	وَنَـداهُ مُقـابلي مَـا يَـزُولُ
وَمَعـي أَيْنَمـا سَـلَكْتُ كَـأَنّي	كُـلُّ وَجْـهٍ لَـهُ بِوَجْهـي كَفيـلُ
وَإِذا العَـذْلُ في النَّـدَى زَارَ سَـمْعاً	فَفِـداهُ العَـذُولُ والمَعْـذُولُ
ومَـوالٍ تُحَيِّيهِـمْ مِـنْ يَدَيْـهِ	نِعَـمٌ غَيْرُهُـمْ بهَـا مَقْتُـولُ
فَـرَسٌ سَـابحٌ وَرُمْـحٌ طَويـلٌ	ودِلاصٌ زَغْـفٌ وَسَـيْفٌ صَقيـلُ
كُلَّمـا صَبَّحَـتْ ديـارَ عَـدُوٍّ	قـالَ تِلـكَ الغيـوثُ هـذي السّـيُولُ
دَهِمَتْـهُ تُطـايرُ الـزَّرَدَ المُحْـشَ	كَـمَ عَنْـهُ كَمَـا يَطيـرُ النَّسـيلُ
تَقْنِـصُ الخَيـلَ خَيْلُـهُ قَنـصَ الوَحْـشِ	ويَسْتَأسِـرُ الخَميـسَ الرَّعيـلُ
وإذا الحَـرْبُ أَعرَضَـتْ زَعَـمَ الهَـوْلُ	لِعَيْنَيْـهِ أَنَّـهُ تَهْويـلُ
وَإذا صَـحَّ فَالزَّمـانُ صَحيـحٌ	وَإذا اعْتَـلَّ فَالزَّمـانُ عَليـلُ
وَإذا غَـابَ وَجْهُـهُ عَـنْ مَكَـانٍ	فَبِـهِ مِـنْ ثَنَـاهُ وَجْـهٌ جَميـلُ
لَيْـسَ إلاَّكَ يـا عَلـيُّ هُمَـامٌ	سَـيْفُهُ دونَ عِرْضِـهِ مَسْـلُولُ
كَيْـفَ لا تَأْمَـنُ العِـراقُ وَمِصْـرٌ	وَسَـراياكَ دونَهـا والخُيُـولُ
لَـوْ تَحَرَّفْـتَ عَـنْ طَريـقِ الأَعـادي	رَبَـطَ السِّـدْرَ خَيْلَهُـمْ والنَّخيـلُ
وَدَرَى مَـنْ أَعَـزَّهُ الدفـعُ عَنـهُ	فيهمـا أَنَّـهُ الحَقيـرُ الذَّليـلُ

One knows from looking that dwellers
    Yearn like the loaded camels are longing
If you see me grow dark after white
    It is praise only for the flexible lance
A maid has been with me in the desert
    Change is the custom of colors with her
A bride's tent veils you from her but
    For you the crimson kiss comes from her
Like her you alter my color and find me
    Ill and beauty increases your bright body
We knew yet we asked about Najd
    Is our road long or is it farther away?
Many were the longing questions
    And many were the consoling replies
We did not stay in one place though
    Good, nor was motion possible for it
If a meadow spread wide we said:
    We go to Aleppo, you are the highway
You are pasture for horses, camels
    Toward that is our trotting and gallop
Many there are who are called Amir
    But the Amir who is there is a pledge
He whom I parted from east and west
    Had gifts before men without any end
With me wherever I go it seems
    All of his ways are guarantee for mine
If censure of bounty comes to listen
    Censor and censured are his ransom
Favor gives life to many clients by
    His hand, others struck dead by that
Winning horses and long lances
    Long coats of mail and bright swords
Each time it dawned in a foe's camp
    He said: It's a downpour and a torrent
They take by surprise tearing off
    Chain mail like feathers are plucked
His riders chase them as wild beasts
    The small band takes prisoner an army
And when war appears fear asserts
    By his eyes that he is the terrible one
If he is well the times are healthy
    When he is sick the times are ailing
If his face is absent from a place
    There is in his fame a fine display
None beside you O Ali as a hero
    Whose sword is set before his honor
How could Iraq and Misr not be safe
    If your raids and riders are before them?
If you turn away from the foe's path
    Lote tree and palm ties up their horses
Pride that rejects him knows it well
    The meanness and lowness is in them

فَمَتَى الوَعْدُ أَنْ يكونَ القُفُولُ	أَنْتَ طُولَ الحَيَاةِ للرُّومِ غازِ
فَعَلَى أَيِّ جَانِبَيْكَ تَمِيلُ	وَسِوَى الرُّومِ خَلْفَ ظَهرِكَ رُومٌ
كَالَّذِي عِنْدَهُ تُدارُ الشَّمُولُ	قَعَدَ النَّاسُ كُلُّهُمْ عَنْ مَساعِي
كَالَّذِي عِنْدَهُ تُدارُ الشَّمُولُ	ما الَّذِي عِنْدَهُ تُدارُ المَنَايا
وَزَمَانِي بِأَنْ أَرَاكَ بَخِيلُ	لَسْتُ أَرْضَى بِأَنْ تَكُونَ جَوَاداً
مَرْتَعِي مُخْصِبٌ وَجِسْمِي هَزِيلُ	نَغِصَ البُعْدُ عَنكَ قُرْبَ العَطايا
وَأَتَانِي نَيْلٌ فَأَنْتَ المَنِيلُ	إنْ تَبَوَّأْتُ غَيْرَ دُنيايَ دَاراً
رَوِيَ مِنْ نَداكَ رِيفٌ ونِيلُ	مِنْ عَبِيدِي إنْ عِشْتَ لِي أَلْفُ كافو
مَّنْ دَهَتْهُ حُبُولُها والخُبُولُ	مَا أُبالِي إذا اتَّقَتْكَ اللَّيَالِي

(٢٤٠)

«من المتقارب»

أنفذ إليه سيف الدولة كتاباً بخطه يسأله المسير إليه فأجابه بهذه القصيدة وأنفذها إليه في ميافارقين وكان ذلك في شهر ذي الحجة سنة ثلاث وخمسين وثلاث مئة (٩٦٤م):

فَسَمْعاً لأَمْرِ أَمِيرِ العَرَبْ	فَهِمْتُ الكِتابَ أَبَرَّ الكُتُبْ
وَإِنْ قَصَّرَ الفِعْلُ عَمَّا وَجَبْ	وَطَوْعاً لَهُ وَانْتِهاجاً بِهِ
وَإِنَّ الوِشاياتِ طُرْقُ الكَذِبْ	وَمَا عَاقَنِي غَيرُ خَوْفِ الوُشاةِ
وَتَقْرِيبِهِمْ بَيْنَنا والخَبَبْ	وَتَكْثِيرَ قَوْمٍ وَتَقْلِيلِهِمْ
وَيَنْصُرُنِي قَلْبُهُ والحَسَبْ	وَقَدْ كانَ يَنصُرُهُمْ سَمْعُهُ
وَمَا قُلْتُ لِلشَّمسِ أَنْتَ الذَّهَبْ	وَمَا قُلْتُ لِلبَدْرِ أَنْتَ اللُّجَينْ
وَيَغْضَبُ مِنهُ البَطِيءُ الغَضَبْ	فَيَقْلَقَ مِنهُ البَعِيدُ الأَناةِ
وَلَا اعْتَضْتُ مِنْ رَبِّ نَعْمايَ رَبَّ	وَمَا لاقى بَلَدٌ بَعْدَكُمْ
دٍ أَنْكَرَ أَظْلافَهُ والغَبَبْ	وَمَنْ رَكِبَ الثَّوْرَ بَعْدَ الجَوا

You all your life long battle the Rum
    When is the promise of return fulfilled?
Aside from Rum behind you are Rum
    To which of the two sides do you turn?
All their men sit on your run's sidelines
    The swords and spears stand beside them
None with him pass around death as
    One with him passes round the cool wine
I no longer enjoy your generosity
    My times as I recall you are miserly
Distance from you chokes, bounty is
    Near, the pasture rich, my body emaciate
If I found no house in my world and
    Gifts came to me, you'd be the giver
One of my slaves beside you is many
    Kafurs, your bounty all Iraq and a Nile
If mishap shuns you I do not worry
    About any whom discord and danger doom

240
Saif al-Daula wrote to him inviting him and he replied with this qasida in Shawwal in the year 353.
(Tripping b)

I read the letter, the best of letters
    Obedience is due the Arab Amir's orders
Submissive to him, made happy by him
    Even if the act is short of what is my duty
Nothing hinders me but fear of slander
    For the ways of slanderers are falsehood
Boasting people and their belittling
    And their trotting between us and ambling
Indeed his ears were aiding them
    But his heart and mind were helping me
I did not tell a moon: You are silver
    Nor did I tell the sun: You are fine gold
But a distant friend was shaken by it
    And slowness to anger was enraged by it
No country has held me after you nor
    Substituted a lord for my lord's favors
He who rides the ox after the horse
    Rejects a cloven hoof and a dew lap

وَمـا قِسـتُ كُـلَّ مُلُـوكِ البـلادِ … فَـدَعْ ذِكْـرَ بَعـضِ بَمَـن فـي حلَـبْ
ولَـوْ كُنْـتَ سَـمَّيْتُهُمْ باسْـمِهِ … لَكــانَ الحَديـدَ وكِّـانُوا الخَشَـبْ
أفي الـرَّأي يُشـبِهُـهُ أمْ فـي السَّـخا … ءِ أمْ فـي الشَّـجاعةِ أمْ فـي الأدبْ
مُبَــارَكُ الإسْــمِ أغَــرُّ اللَّقَــبْ … كَريــمُ الجرشَـى شـريفُ النَّسَـبْ
أخـو الحـرْبِ يُخـدِمُ مِّـا سَـبى … قَنـاهُ ويَخلَــعُ مِّــا سَـلَبْ
إذا حــازَ مــالاً فَقَـدْ حــازَهُ … فَتــى لا يُسَــرّ بمَــا لا يَهَــبْ
وإنِّــي لأتْبَــعُ تَذْكــارَهُ … صَـلاةَ الإلَـهِ وسَـقْيَ السُّـحُبْ
وأثْنِــي عَلَيْــهِ بـآلائِــهِ … وأقـرُبُ منْــهُ نَـأى أو قَـرُبْ
وإنْ فــارَقَتْنِـي أمْطــارُهُ … فَـأكثَرُ غُدْرانِهـا مـا نَضَــبْ
أيــا سَـيفَ رَبِّـكَ لا خَلقَــهْ … ويـا ذا المكـارمِ لا ذا الشُّـطَبْ
وأبْعَــدَ ذي هِمَّــةٍ همَّــةً … وأعـرَفَ ذي رُتْبَــةٍ بـالرُّتَبْ
وأطعَـنَ مَــنْ مَــسَّ خَطِّيَّــةً … وأضـرَبَ مَـنْ بحُسَـامٍ ضَـرَبْ
بـذا اللَّفْـظِ نـاداكَ أهْـلُ الثّغُـورِ … فلَبَّيْــتَ والهــامُ تحْــتَ القُضُـبْ
وقَــدْ يَئِسُـوا مِـنْ لَذيـذِ الحَيـاةِ … فَعَيـنٌ تَغُـورُ وقَلـبٌ يَجِـبْ
وغـرَّ الدُّمُسْـتُقَ قَـولُ العُـدَا … ةِ إنَّ عَلِيًّــا ثَقيـلٌ وَصِــبْ
وقَـدْ عَلِمَـتْ خَيلُـهُ أنَّــهُ … إذا هَـمَّ وهْـوَ عَليـلٌ ركِـبْ
أتــاهُم بأوْسَــعِ مِـنْ أرضِهِـمْ … طِـوَالِ السَّـبيبِ قِصَارِ العُسُـبْ
تَغيـبُ الشَّـواهِقُ في جَيشِـهِ … وتَبْـدُو صِغــاراً إذا لَـم تَغِـبْ
ولا تَعْبُــرُ الريـحُ في جَــوِّهِ … إذا لَمْ تَخَــطَّ القَنـا أو تَثِـبْ
فَغـرَّقَ مُدْنَهُــمْ بـالجيُـوشِ … وأخْفَــتَ أصواتَهُــمْ باللَّجَـبْ
فـأخِبْث بـهِ طالِبـاً قَتْلَهُــمْ … وأخِبْــثْ بـهِ تـاركـاً مَـا طَلَـبْ
نـأيْتَ فَقـاتَلْهُمْ باللَّقَــاءِ … وجِئْــتَ فَقـاتَلْهُم بـالـهَرَبْ
وكـانُوا لَـهُ الفخـرَ لَمَّـا أتَـى … وكُنْـتَ لَـهُ العُـذرَ لَمَّـا ذَهَـبْ
سـبَقْتَ إلَيْهِـمْ مَنـايـاهُمْ … ومَنْفَعَــةُ الغَـوْثِ قَبْـلَ العَطَـبْ
فَخَــرّوا لخـالِقِهِمْ سُـجَّداً … ولَـوْ لَـم تُغِـثْ سَـجَدوا للصُّلُبْ

I have matched no kings of the land
    Not to mention some, with one in Aleppo
And if I were to name one by his name
    He would be steel and they would be wood
Is his likeness to mind or character
    Or is it to bravery or is it to his culture?
The name is blessed, surname brilliant
    Generous the soul and noble in ancestry
War's brother, served by ones he takes
    As his slaves, he bestows as he plunders
If he gathers wealth, he gathers it as
    Youth who grieves unless he bestows it
Indeed I follow him with his memories
    blessings of God and showers of clouds
My praises on him for his benefits
    I am near to him whether far or near
If his showers have departed from me
    Yet most of their pools have water yet
O sword of the Lord, not his creatures
    O owner of nobility, not the sword ridge
Most spirited of those having spirit
    Widest of those possessed of rank
Best jouster of those with a Khatti
    Strongest of those who use the sword
By these words I call you O border men
    Be present with skulls under the blades
They despaired of life's pleasures
    Eyes perplexed and fluttering hearts
Enemy words confused Domesticus:
    Truly Ali is seriously sick and ailing
But his horsemen knew that indeed
    If he wishes he will ride even if he is ill
He brings them from land's breadth
    With long manes and short tailbones
All the peaks are hid by his armies
    They appear small if they aren't hid
The wind cannot pass through ranks
    Without being scratched by spear or held
He drowns their cities with his armies
    He makes the voices faint in the uproar
How ugly he is in seeking their death!
    How ugly he is in leaving what he seeks!
You were far, he fought them in battle
    You came, he fought them in their flight
They were his in honor when he came
    You were the excuse for him as he fled
You outdistanced them with death
    The advantage of rescue before ruin
They bowed to their Creator prostrate
    And if not rescued they bowed to a cross
How many you saved from death by death
    And snatched from agony with an agony

وَكَشَفْتَ مِنْ كُرَبٍ بِالكُرَبْ	وَكَمْ ذُدْتَ عَنْهُمْ رَدَّى بِالرَّدَى
يَعُدُّ مَعَهُ المَلِكُ المُعْتَصِبْ	وَقَدْ زَعَمُوا أَنَّهُ إِنْ يَعُدْ
وَعِنْدَهُمَا أَنَّهُ قَدْ صُلِبْ	وَيَسْتَنْصِرانِ الَّذي يَعْبُدانِ
فَيا لِلرِّجالِ لِهَذا العَجَبْ	لِيَدْفَعَ ما نالَهُ عَنْهُمَا
نَ إِمَّا لِعَجْزٍ وَإِمَّا رَهَبْ	أَرَى المُسْلِمينَ مَعَ المُشْرِكي
قَليلُ الرُّقادِ كَثيرُ التَّعَبْ	وَأَنْتَ مَعَ اللهِ في جانِبٍ
وَدانَ البَرِيَّةُ بِابْنٍ وَأَبْ	كَأَنَّكَ وَحْدَكَ وَحَّدْتَهُ
إِذا ما ظَهَرْتَ عَلَيْهِمْ كَئِبْ	فَلَيْتَ سُيوفَكَ في حاسِدٍ
وَلَيْتَكَ تَجْزي بِبُغْضٍ وَحُبْ	وَلَيْتَ شَكاتَكَ في جِسْمِهِ
كَ أَضْعَفَ حَظٍّ بِأَقْوَى سَبَبْ	فَلَوْ كُنْتَ تَجْزي بِهِ نِلْتُ مِنْ

(٢٤١)

«من الطويل»

فارق أبو الطيب سيف الدولة ورحل إلى دمشق وكاتبه الأستاذ كافور بالمسير إليه، فلما ورد مصر أخلى له كافور داراً وخلع عليه وحمل إليه آلافاً من الدراهم فقال يمدحه وأنشده إياها في جمادى الآخرة سنة ست وأربعين وثلاث مئة (٩٥٧م):

وَحَسْبُ المَنايا أَنْ يَكُنَّ أَمانِيا	كَفَى بِكَ داءً أَنْ تَرَى المَوْتَ شافِيا
صَديقاً فَأَعْيا أَوْ عَدُوّاً مُداجِيا	تَمَنَّيْتُها لَمَّا تَمَنَّيْتُ أَنْ تَرَى
فَلا تَسْتَعِدَّنَّ الحُسامَ اليَمانِيا	إِذا كُنْتَ تَرْضَى أَنْ تَعيشَ بِذِلَّةٍ
وَلا تَسْتَجيدَنَّ العِتاقَ المَذاكِيا	وَلا تَسْتَطيلَنَّ الرِّماحَ لِغارَةٍ
وَلا تَتَّقِي حَتَّى تَكونَ ضَوارِيا	فَما يَنْفَعُ الأُسْدَ الحَياءُ مِنَ الطَّوَى
وَقَدْ كانَ غَدَّاراً فَكُنْ أَنْتَ وافِيا	حَبَبْتُكَ قَلْبي قَبْلَ حُبِّكَ مَنْ نَأَى

They thought that if he returned he
    Would bring with him the crowned king
Both asked help of him they served
    According to them he was crucified
They put from themselves what he
    Obtained, O men what a wonder is this!
I see Arabs along with polytheists
    Now in weakness or now terror struck
You with God are on a mountain side
    With little sleep and yet much of labor
You by yourself serve the Unity in him
    And the world submits to father and son
I wish your swords would bring sorrow
    To a jealous one when you appear to him
I wish your pains were on his body
    And what you repaid with hate and love
For if you repay what I got from you
    Weakest joys will be strongest reasons

III: *al-Misriyat*: Egyptian Poems
241
Abu Tayyib spoke praising Kafur the Ikhshid in Jumadi in the year 346.
(Long ye)

Enough ill for you to see death as cure
    And enough deaths that they are desired
You wanted it when you wanted to see
    A friend who failed or an enemy who hid
If you are content live basely
    Then don't get ready the Yamani sword
Don't extend the long lance for war
    And don't make friends with a fine horse
Modesty is no use for hungry lions
    They are not feared except when famished
I knew you, my heart, before your far love
    But he was a betrayer so do you be faithful
I see parting makes you complain of him
    But you are not my heart if I see you fretting

فَلَسْتَ فُؤادي إنْ رَأَيْتُكَ شاكِيا	وَأَعْلَمُ أَنَّ البَيْنَ يُشكيكَ بَعْدَهُ
إذا كُنّ إثْرَ الغادِرينَ جَوارِيا	فإنّ دُموعَ العَيْنِ غُدْرٌ بِرَبِّها
فَلا الحَمْدُ مَكْسوباً وَلا المالُ باقِيا	إذا الجُودُ لَمْ يُرْزَقْ خَلاصاً مِنَ الأذى
أكانَ سَخاءً ما أتى أمْ تَساخِيا	وَلِلنَّفْسِ أخْلاقٌ تَدُلُّ عَلَى الفَتى
رَأَيْتُكَ تُصْفي الوُدَّ مَنْ لَيْسَ صافِيا	أقِلّ اشْتِياقاً أيُّها القَلْبُ رُبَّما
لَفارَقْتُ شَيْبي مُوجَعَ القَلْبِ باكِيا	خُلِقْتُ أَلوفاً لَوْ رَجَعْتُ إلى الصِّبى
حَياتي وَنُصْحي وَالهَوى وَالقَوافِيا	وَلَكِنْ بالفُسْطاطِ بَحْراً أَزَرْتُهُ
فَبِتْنَ خِفافاً يَتْبَعْنَ العَوالِيا	وَجُرْداً مَدَدْنا بَيْنَ آذانِها القَنا
نَقَشْنَ بِهِ صَدْرَ البُزاةِ حَوفِيا	تَماشى بأيْدٍ كُلَّما وَافَتِ الصَّفا
يُرَيْنَ بَعيداتِ الشُّخوصِ كَما هِيا	وَتَنْظُرُ مِنْ سودٍ صَوادِقَ في الدُّجى
يَخَلْنَ مُناجاةَ الضَّميرِ تَنادِيا	وَتَنْصِبُ للجَرْسِ الخَفيّ سَوامِعاً
كَأنَّ عَلى الأَعْناقِ مِنْها أفاعِيا	تُجاذِبُ فُرْسانَ الصَّباحِ أعِنَّةً
بِهِ وَيَسيرُ القَلْبُ في الجِسْمِ ماشِيا	بِعَزْمٍ يَسيرُ الجِسْمُ في السَّرْجِ راكِباً
وَمَنْ قَصَدَ البَحْرَ اسْتَقَلّ السَّواقِيا	قَواصِدَ كافورٍ تَوارَكَ غَيْرِهِ
وَخَلَّتْ بَياضاً خَلْفَها وَمَآقِيا	فَجاءَتْ بِنا إنْسانَ عَيْنِ زَمانِهِ
نَرَى عِنْدَهُمْ إحْسانَهُ وَالأَيادِيا	نَجوزُ عَلَيْها المُحْسِنينَ إلى الَّذي
إلى عَصْرِهِ إلّا نُرَجّي التَّلاقِيا	فَتًى ما سَرَيْنا في ظُهورِ جُدودِنا
فَما يَفْعَلُ الفَعَلاتِ إلّا عَذارِيا	تَرَفَّعَ عَنْ عَوْنِ المَكارِمِ قَدْرُهُ
فإنْ تَبْدُ مِنْهُمْ أبادَ الأَعادِيا	يُبيدُ عَداواتِ البُغاةِ بِلُطْفِهِ
إلَيْهِ وَذا اليَوْمُ الَّذي كُنْتُ راجِيا	أبا المِسْكِ ذا الوَجْهُ الَّذي كُنْتُ تائِقاً
وَجُبْتُ هَجيراً يَتْرُكُ الماءَ صادِيا	لَقيتُ المَروْرى وَالشَّناخيبَ دونَهُ
وَكُلَّ سَحابٍ لا أَخُصّ الغَوادِيا	أبا كُلِّ طيبٍ لا أبا المِسْكِ وَحْدَهُ
وَقَدْ جَمَعَ الرَّحْمَنُ فيكَ المَعانِيا	يَدُلُّ بِمَعْنًى واحِدٍ كُلّ فاخِرٍ
فَإنَّكَ تُعْطي في نَداكَ المَعالِيا	إذا كَسَبَ النّاسُ المَعالِيَ بالنَّدى
فَيَرْجِعُ مَلْكاً لِلعِراقَيْنِ وَالِيا	وَغَيْرُ كَثيرٍ أنْ يَزورَكَ راجِلٌ
لِسائِلِكَ الفَرْدِ جاءَ عافِيا	فَقَدْ تَهَبُ الجَيْشَ الَّذي جاءَ غازِيا

Eye's tears are betrayers to their lord
  If the channels are tracks for deceivers
If bounty makes no provision free of evil
  Praise is not earned nor does wealth stay
Soul has a nature that shows the man
  Was it bounty came or pretended generosity?
Diminish the longing, O heart, for often
  I see you loving one who does not respond
I was created tame, if I return to youth
  I'll leave my gray with hurt heart weeping
But in all Fustat is a sea I will visit
  With my life, my counsel, love and rhymes
Horses between whose ears we set spears
  They spend night easy following lanceheads
Running on feet that as they touch stones
  Will print unshod the falcon's breast marks
They look with dark trusty eyes into
  Gloom seeing distant shapes as they are
The prick up ears to faint whispers
  Thinking of secret words that are spoken
They pull the dawn riders by the reins
  As if on their necks were coils of snakes
Firmly a body in the saddle moves as if
  Riding beside, as heart in body goes apace
Seeking Kafur and leaving all others
  Who seeks a sea thinks little of the creeks
Taking us to a man eye's apple of an age
  Leaving the white behind and the corners
We cross on them as bounty to one whom
  We know from his gifts and favors in them
A man, we came on backs of our past kin
  To his times only in hopes of the meeting
His rank rises above nobility's aid
  So he performs no acts but virgin ones
He erases hate in rivals by his mildness
  If they don't perish by them he kills foes
Father Musk, this is the face I wanted
  This is the moment that I was hoping for
I faced deserts and mountains before
  Passed at noonday leaving water thirsty
Father of all good not only Abu Musk
  And of every cloud not only an early one
Every boaster points to a single idea
  The Merciful gathered in you all meaning
Though a man gain eminence by bounty
  You give high rank with your generosity
It's not much a man visits you on foot
  And returns as viceroy of the two Iraqs
You give an army which comes raiding
  To one of your clients who comes begging

وَتَحتَقِرُ الدُّنيا احتِقارَ مُجَرِّبِ   يَرى كُلَّ ما فيها وَحاشاكَ فانِيا
وَما كُنتَ مِمَّن أَدرَكَ المُلكَ بِالمُنى   وَلَكِن بِأَيّامٍ أَشَبنَ النَواصِيا
عِداكَ تَراها في البِلادِ مَساعِياً   وَأَنتَ تَراها في السَماءِ مَراقِبا
لَستَ لَها كُدرَ العَجاجِ كَأَنَّما   تَرى غَيرَ صافٍ أَن تَرى الجَوَّ صافِيا
وَقُدتَ إِلَيها كُلَّ أَجرَدَ سابِحٍ   يُؤَدّيكَ غَضبانَ وَيَثنيكَ راضِيا
وَمُخَترَطٍ ماضٍ يُطيعُكَ آمِراً   وَيَعصي إِذا استَثنَيتَ أَو صِرتَ ناهِيا
وَأَسمَرَ ذي عِشرينَ تَرضاهُ وارِداً   وَيُرضاكَ في إيرادِهِ الخَيلَ ساقِيا
كَتائِبَ ما انفَكَّت تَجوسُ عَمائِراً   مِنَ الأَرضِ قَد حاسَت إِلَيها فَيافِيا
غَزَوتَ بِها دورَ المُلوكِ فَباشَرَت   سَنابِكُها هاماتِهِم وَالمَغانِيا
وَأَنتَ الَّذي تَغشى الأَسِنَّةَ أَوَّلاً   وَتَأنَفُ أَن تَغشى الأَسِنَّةَ ثانِيا
إِذا الهِندُ سَوَّت بَينَ سَيفَي كَريهَةٍ   فَسَيفُكَ في كَفٍّ تُزيلُ التَساوِيا
وَمِن قَولِ سامٍ لَو رَآكَ لِنَسلِهِ   فِدى اِبنِ أَخي نَسلي وَنَفسي وَمالِيا
مَدى بَلَّغَ الأُستاذَ أَقصاهُ رَبُّهُ   وَنَفسٌ لَهُ لَم تَرضَ إِلّا التَناهِيا
دَعَتهُ فَلَبّاها إِلى المَجدِ وَالعُلى   وَقَد خالَفَ الناسُ النُفوسَ الدَواعِيا
فَأَصبَحَ فَوقَ العالَمينَ يَرَونَهُ   وَإِن كانَ يُدنيهِ التَكَرُّمُ نائِيا

(٢٤٢)

«من الطويل»

يهجو كافوراً وكان قد نظر إلى شقوق في رجليه:

أُريكَ الرِضى لَو أَخفَتِ النَفسُ خافِيا   وَما أَنا عَن نَفسي وَلا عَنكَ راضِيا
أَمينَاً وَإِخلافاً وَغَدراً وَخِسَّةً   وَجُبناً، أَشَخصاً لُحتَ لي أَم مَخازِيا
تَظُنُّ اِبتِساماتي رَجاءً وَغِبطَةً   وَما أَنا إِلّا ضاحِكٌ مِن رَجائِيا
وَتُعجِبُني رِجلاكَ في النَعلِ، إِنَّني   رَأَيتُكَ ذا نَعلٍ إِذا كُنتَ حافِيا
وَإِنَّكَ لا تَدري أَلَونُكَ أَسوَدٌ   مِنَ الجَهلِ أَم قَد صارَ أَبيَضَ صافِيا
وَيُذكِرُني تَخييطُ كَعبِكَ شَقَّهُ   وَمَشيَكَ في ثَوبٍ مِنَ الزَيتِ عارِيا

You scorn a world in learned scorn
    That sees all but yourself as dying in it
You did not reach kingship by wishing
    But rather by days that whitened forelocks
Your foes see them as land's turmoils
    But you see them as stairways to the sky
For them you wore the turbid dust as if
    You saw unclearly to see the clearest air
You led to them all shorthaired swimmers
    Bringing you angry, returning you content
Drawn out, blades submit to you on order
    Transgress if you make exception or oppose
A twenty cubit shaft you favor at water
    Approves your aiming at horsemen it drinks
Detachments cease not to trample tribes
    Hoofs break their skulls and their valleys
Troops ever attack the towns
    Of earth the deserts spied upon
You are one who covers spearpoint first
    And refuses to cover the spearpoint second
If Indians balance a dread pair of swords
    Your sword in hand makes an end of equality
Sam's words to his progeny if he saw you:
    Soul, sons and wealth ransom brother's son
His Lord brought the ustadh to far limits
    His soul not not content except with that goal
One called, he replied, to glory and rank
    While other men rejected the call of spirit
He rose above the world that sees him
    Afar even if nobility makes him come close

242
He came to him after reciting this qasida and the black smiled at him and arose. But he had no shoes on and Abu Tayyib saw the cracks in his feet so he spoke mocking him.
(Long ye)

I'd show you content if soul could hide
    Not being content with myself or with you
Are lying, perjury, betrayal, foulness
    Due? you close to me as person or shame?
You think smiles are hope and emulation
    But I am merely mocking ridiculous wishes
I wonder at your feet in shoes since I
    Saw you in sandals as you went barefoot
You didn't know if your color was black
    Or if it was purest white due to stupidity
Laces on your ankle cracks remind me
    That you walked in oily clothes bare assed

وَلَوْ لا فُضُولُ النّاسِ جِئْتُكَ مادِحاً		بِما كُنتُ في سِرّي بِهِ لَكَ هاجِيا
فَأَصْبَحْتَ مَسْروراً بِما أَنا مُنْشِدٌ		وَإِنْ كانَ بِالإِنْشادِ هَجْوُكَ غالِيا
فَإِنْ كُنتَ لا خَيراً أَفَدْتَ فَإِنّي		أَفَدْتُ بِلَحْظي مِشْفَرَيكَ المَلاهِيا
وَمِثلُكَ يُؤْتى مِنْ بِلادٍ بَعيدَةٍ		لِيُضْحِكَ رَبّاتِ الحِدادِ البَواكِيا

(٢٣٤)

«من الخفيف»

بنى كافور دارا بإزاء الجامع الأعلى على البركة وطالب أبا الطيب بذكرها فعال فعلًا يهنئا بها:

إنَّما التَّهْنِئَاتُ لِلأَكْفَاءِ		وَلِمَنْ يَدَّنى مِنَ البُعَدَاءِ
وَأَنا مِنْكَ لا يُهَنَّىءُ عُضْوٌ		بِالمَسَرّاتِ سَائِرَ الأَعْضَاءِ
مُسْتَقِلٌ لَكَ الدِّيارَ وَلَوْ كَا		نَ نُجوماً آجُرُّ هذا البِناءِ
وَلَوْ أَنَّ الَّذي يَخِرُّ مِنَ الأَمْواهِ		فيها مِنْ فِضَّةٍ بَيْضَاءِ
أَنْتَ أَعْلى مَحَلَّةً أَنْ تُهَنّى		بِمَكانٍ فِي الأَرْضِ أَوْ فِى السَّماءِ
وَلَكَ النّاسُ وَالبِلادُ وَما يَسْرَحُ		بَيْنَ الغَبْرَاءِ وَالخَضْرَاءِ
وَبَساتِينُكَ الجِيادُ وَما تَحْمِلُ		مِنْ سَمْهَرِيَّةٍ سَمْرَاءِ
إنَّما يَفْخَرُ الكَريمُ أَبو المِسْكِ		بِما يَبْتَني مِنَ العَلْيَاءِ
وَبِأَيّامِهِ الَّتي انْسَلَخَتْ عَنْـهُ		وَما دارُهُ سِوى الهَيْجَاءِ
وَبَما أَثَّرَتْ صَوَارِمُهُ البِيـ		ـضُ لَهُ في جَماجِمِ الأَعْدَاءِ
وَمَسْكٌ يُكَنّى بِهِ لَيْسَ بِالمِسْـ		ـكِ وَلَكِنَّهُ أَرِيجُ الثَّنَاءِ
لا بَما يَبْتَني الحَواضِرُ في الرِّيـ		ـفِ وَما يُطَيِّبي قُلوبَ النِّساءِ
نَزَلَتْ إذْ نَزَلْتَها الدّارُ في أَحْـ		ـسَنَ مِنها مِنَ السَّنى وَالسَّناءِ
حَلَّ في مَنْبِتِ الرَّياحينِ مِنها		مَنْبِتُ المَكْرُماتِ وَالآلاءِ
تَفْصَحُ الشَّمْسَ كُلَّما ذَرَّتِ الشَّمْـ		ـسُ بِشَمْسٍ مُنيرَةٍ سَوْدَاءِ
إنَّ في ثَوْبِكَ الَّذي المَجْدُ فيهِ		لَضِياءً يُزْرى بِكُلِّ ضِيَاءِ

But for men's curiosity I'd praise you
  By what I have mocked you with in secret
You would be happy with what I recited
  Even if the recitation was wild burlesque
If you had nothing good for your ransom
  I'd ransom with my view of the flabby lips
Your likes are brought from far lands
  To make women in mourning clothes laugh!

243

Kafur built a palace at the corner of the high mosque on a lake and moved there. Then he asked Abu Tayyib to commemorate it.

(Nimble i)

Congratulations belong to equals
  And to those who approach from afar
I am not a limb to rejoice for you
  With the rejoicing of the other limbs
I think palaces small for you even
  If the bricks of the building were stars
And what murmurs in its pool was
  Made of the brightest silvery waves
You have the highest rank desired
  Whether the place is earth or heaven
Yours are the men and the land and
  What pastures between green and dusty
Your gardens of fine horses and what
  They bear by way of long brown lances
Truly noble Father Musk can boast
  Of what he has built in these heights
Of battles which ended for him
  When he had no palace but the wars
What those bright swords of his
  Imprinted on the skulls of the enemy
He is named for musk and is not
  Musk but rather the perfume of praise
Nor a city built in the country
  Nor what attracts the heart of women
A house is dwelt in if you have it
  By a finer thing, by light and by rank
He gives the flowers their perfume
  The growths of nobility and elegance
He shames a sun when sun appears
  With the sun of his shining blackness
Glory dwells with your clothes
  In a brightness scorning every beam

نَفْسٍ خَيْرٌ مِنِ ابيِضَاضِ القَبَاءِ	إنما الجِلدُ مَلبَسٌ وابيضاضُ الـ
في بَهَاءٍ وقُدرَةٍ في وَفَاءِ	كَرَمِ في شَجَاعَةٍ وذَكَاءِ
نَ بلَوْنِ الأسـتاذِ والسَّحْنَاءِ	مَن لبِيضِ المُلُـوكِ أن تُبـدَلَ اللوْ
ن تَرَاهُ بِهَا غَـداةَ اللِّقَاءِ	فَتَرَاهَا بَنُـو الحُـرُوبِ بِأعْيَـا
لَم يكُنْ غَيـرَ أنْ أراكَ رَجَائي	يا رَجاءَ العُيّـونِ في كـلّ أرضٍ
قَبـلَ أن نَلتَقي وزَادي وَمَـائي	ولقَـدْ أفْنَـتِ المَفَـاوزُ خَيْلـي
أسَدُ القَلْـبِ آدَمـيُّ الـرُّوَاءِ	فَارْمِ في مـا أرَدْتَ مـني فَإني
نَ لِسَـاني يُـرَى مِـنَ الشُّعَـراءِ	وفُـؤادي مِـنَ المُلُـوكِ وإنْ كا

(٢٤٤)

«من البسيط»

يمدحه وأنشده إياها في سلخ شهر رمضان سنة ست وأربعين وثلاث مئة (٩٥٧م):

حُمْـرُ الحُلَى والمَطَايَـا والجَلابيبِ	مَـنِ الجَـآذِرُ في زِيّ الأعـاريبِ
فَمَنْ بَـلاكَ بتَسـهيدٍ وتَعـذيبِ	إنْ كُنـتَ تَسـألُ شَكّـاً في مَعارفِهـا
تَجزي دُموعي مَسكوباً بمَسكُوبِ	لا تَجزِني بِضَنّى بي بَعْدَهَـا بَقَـرٌ
منيعـةً بَيـنَ مَطعُـونٍ ومَضـرُوبِ	سَـوَائرٌ رُبّمَـا سـارَتْ هَوادِجُـهَـا
على نَجِيعٍ مِنَ الفُرسـانِ مَصبُوبِ	ورُبّمـا وَخَـدَتْ أيـدي المَطيّ بهـا
أدهى وقَد رَقَـدوا مِن زَورَةِ الذيبِ	كـم زَورَةٍ لَـكَ في الأعـرابِ خافيَـةٍ
وأنْـتِ وبَيَـاضُ الصبـحِ يُغـري بي	آزورُهُـم وسَـوادُ الليـلِ يَشـفَـعُ لي
وخالَفُوهـا بتَقويـضٍ وتَطنيـبِ	قد وَافقوا الوَحشَ في سُكنى مَراتِعِهـا
وصَحبُهَـا وهُـمْ شَـرُّ الأصَاحـبِ	جيرانُهـا وهُـمْ شَـرُّ الجِـوارِ لهـا
وَمَالُ كُلِّ أخيـذِ المالِ مَحـرُوبِ	فُـؤادُ كُـلِّ مُحِـبٍّ في بُيُوتِهِـم
كَأوْجُـهِ البَدَويّـاتِ الرَّعَـابيبِ	مـا أوْجُـهُ الحَضَـرِ المُستَحسَنَـاتُ بـهِ
وفي البَداوَةِ حُسْـنٌ غيـرُ مَجلُوبِ	حُسْـنُ الحِضَـارَةِ مَجلُـوبٌ بتَطرِيَـةٍ

Only courage wears it and soul fire
    It is better than the glittering garment
You are noble in wisdom and bravery
    Of visage and in power for faithfulness
Who will not change white king's hue
    For the professor's color and his face?
War's sons see them with eyes that
    See him with them on battle morning
O hope of the eyes in all of earth
    No one else that I see can be my hope
The desert wearied my horse before
    We found the food and water set for me
Cast on me what you wish for me
    I am lion hearted with a bloody face
My heart belongs to kings even if
    My tongue seems to be that of the poet

244
He spoke praising Kafur the Ikhshid in Shawwal of the year 346 with this unique pearl of a qasida. It is one of the beauties of his poetry.
(Outspread bi)

Who are the wild heifers in bedouin garb?
    Red the ornaments and camels and clothing
If you ask complaining at their goodness
    Who harms you with wakefulness and worry?
May cows not repay me with grief after
    They repay my tears with flow after flow
Travelers, maybe their howdahs as they go
    Are protected in the jousting and the striking
Perhaps hoofs of camels will tread with
    Them on the blood spilled by their horsemen
Many your sly visits among fearful Arabs
    As they slept through the visit of the wolf
I visited them as black night interceded
    I turned away as the white dawn warned me
Like wild animals grazing in their yards
    They differ in breaking and setting tents
Their neighbors, worst neighbors to them
    And their masters are the worst of masters
Every beloved's heart is in their tents
    The flocks of all the flocks taken as plunder
Faces of town women thought fine are
    Not like the faces of these plump bedouins
A town woman's beauty is won by art
    Among the bedouin beauty is not artificial

وَغَيرَ ناظِرَةٍ في الحُسنِ وَالطيبِ	أينَ المَعيزُ مِنَ الآرامِ ناظِرَةٌ
مَضغَ الكَلامِ وَلا صَبغَ الحَواجيبِ	أفدي ظِباءَ فَلاةٍ ما عَرَفنَ بِها
أوراكُهُنَّ صَقيلاتِ العَراقيبِ	وَلا بَرَزنَ مِنَ الحَمّامِ مائِلَةً
تَرَكتُ لَونَ مَشيي غَيرَ مَخضوبِ	وَمِن هَوى كُلِّ مَن لَيسَت مُمَوَّهَةً
رَغِبتُ عَن شَعَرٍ في الرَأسِ مَكذوبِ	وَمِن هَوى الصِدقِ في قَولي وَعادَتِهِ
مِنّي بِحِلمي الَّذي أعطَت وَتَجريبي	لَيتَ الحَوادِثَ باعَتني الَّذي أخَذَت
قَد يوجَدُ الحِلمُ في الشُبّانِ وَالشيبِ	فَما الحَداثَةُ مِن حِلمٍ بِمانِعَةٍ
قَبلَ اكتِهالٍ أديباً قَبلَ تَأديبِ	تَرَعرَعَ المَلِكُ الأستاذُ مُكتَهِلاً
مُهَذَّباً كَرَماً مِن غَيرِ تَهذيبِ	مُجَرَّباً فَهُما مِن قَبلِ تَجرِبَةٍ
وَهَمُّهُ في ابتِداءاتٍ وَتَشبيبِ	حَتّى أصابَ مِنَ الدُنيا نِهايَتَها
إلى العِراقِ فَأرضِ الرومِ فَالنوبِ	يُدَبِّرُ المُلكَ مِن مِصرٍ إلى عَدَنٍ
فَما تَهُبُّ بِها إلّا بِتَرتيبِ	إذا أتَتها الرِياحُ النَكبُ مِن بَلَدٍ
إلّا وَمِنهُ لَها إذنٌ بِتَغريبِ	وَلا تُجاوِزُها شَمسٌ إذا شَرَقَت
وَلَو تَطَلَّسَ مِنهُ كُلُّ مَكتوبِ	يُصَرِّفُ الأمرَ فيها طينُ خاتَمِهِ
مِن سَرجِ كُلِّ طَويلِ الباعِ يَعبوبِ	يَحُطُّ كُلَّ طَويلِ الرُمحِ حامِلَهُ
قَميصَ يوسُفَ في أجفانِ يَعقوبِ	كَأنَّ كُلَّ سُؤالٍ في مَسامِعِهِ
فَقَد غَزَتهُ بِجَيشٍ غَيرِ مَغلوبِ	إذا غَزَتهُ أعاديهِ بِمَسأَلَةٍ
مِمّا أرادَ وَلا تَنجو بِتَجييبِ	أو حارَبَتهُ فَما تَنجو بِتَقدِمَةٍ
عَلى الحِمامِ فَما مَوتٌ بِمَرهوبِ	أضرَت شَجاعَتُهُ أقصى كَتائِبِهِ
إلى غُيوثِ يَدَيهِ وَالشَآبيبِ	قالوا هَجَرتَ إلَيهِ الغَيثَ قُلتُ لَهُم
وَلا يَمُنَّ عَلى آثارِ مَوهوبِ	إلى الَّذي تَهَبُ الدَولاتِ راحَتُهُ
وَلا يُفَزِّعُ مَوفوراً بِمَنكوبِ	وَلا يَروعُ بِمَغدورٍ بِهِ أحَداً
ذا مِثلِهِ في أحَمّ النَقعِ غِرّيبِ	بَلى يَروعُ ذي جَيشٍ يُجَدِّلُهُ
ما في السَوابِقِ مِن جَريٍ وَتَقريبِ	وَجَدتُ أنفَعَ مالٍ كُنتُ أذخَرُهُ
وَفَينَ لي وَوَفَت صُمُّ الأنابيبِ	لَمّا رَأَينَ صُروفَ الدَهرِ تَغدُرُ بي
ماذا لَقينا مِنَ الجُردِ السَراحيبِ	فُتنَ المَهالِكَ حَتّى قالَ قائِلُها

Where are equals of the goats of Iram?
　　There are no equals for beauty or goodness
I ransom desert deer who do not know
　　How to chew their words or dye their veils
They do not come out of bath strutting
　　Rather their thighs have smoother tendons
Of my loves none try to gild the silver
　　I leave my gray hair's color without a dye
Among loving friends in word and habit
　　I do not like hair on the head that pretends
Would fate would sell me what it took
　　From me by a mind and experience it gave
For youth is not excluded from experience
　　Intelligence is found in the young and old
The royal tutor grew up and was mature
　　Before maturity, cultured before educated
Experienced in wisdom without passion
　　Cultured in nobility before he was taught
Until he attained the world's limit and
　　His desire in the beginning and youth
He ruled Egypt's kingdom up to Aden
　　And to Iraq and the Rum lands and Nubia
If strange winds come from other lands
　　They do not blow here except predictably
The sun does not cross when it rises
　　Except it has permission from him to set
His seal's clay would dispatch business
　　Even if every writing were erased by him
Its bearer brings down all the lances
　　From saddles of all strong fast steeds
As if every request in his eyes were
　　The coat of Joseph to the eyes of Jacob
If his enemies press him with a request
　　They press him with an invincible army
If they make war they do not escape by
　　Advance or by flight from what he intends
His bravery bribes his weakest troops
　　For death, so death is not to be dreaded
They said:You fled to him for aid, I:
　　To showers of his hands and cloudbursts
To one whose fingers give governments
　　Nothing is desired in these gifts' outcome
Nor does he frighten anyone by betrayal
　　Nor does he scare with violent afflictions
No, he frightens any army he strikes
　　It is like him in the thickest black dust
I found most useful wealth I stored
　　Fast horses' winning gaits and gallops
If they see time's changes betraying me
　　They and the spear point are true to me
They pass deserts till their voices say:
　　What sort of huge, lean ones are these?

لِلُبْسِ ثَوْبٍ ومَأكولٍ ومَشرُوبِ	تَهْوِي بمُنْجَرِدٍ لَيْسَتْ مَذاهِبُهُ
كأنَّها سَلَبٌ في عَيْنِ مَسلُوبِ	يَرَى النُّجومَ بعَيْنِي مَنْ يُحاوِلُها
تَلْقَى النُّفُوسَ بفَضْلٍ غَيْرِ مَحجُوبِ	حتَّى وَصَلْتُ إلى نَفْسٍ مُحَجَّبَةٍ
خلائِقُ النَّاسِ إضْحاكَ الأعاجِيبِ	في جِسْمِ أرْوَعَ صافي العَقْلِ تُضْحِكُهُ
وَللقَنا وَلِإدلاجِي وَتأوِيبي	فالحَمْدُ قَبْلُ لَهُ والحَمْدُ بَعْدُ لها
وَقَدْ بَلَغْتُكَ بي يا كُلَّ مَطْلُوبي	وَكَيْفَ أكْفُرُ يا كافُورُ نِعْمَتَها
في الشَّرْقِ والغَرْبِ عَنْ وَصْفٍ وتلقِيبِ	يا أيُّها المَلِكُ الغاني بتَسْمِيَةٍ
مِنْ أنْ أكُونَ مُجِبّاً غَيْرَ مَحْبُوبِ	أنْتَ الحَبِيبُ ولكِنِّي أعُوذُ بِهِ

(٢٤٥)

«من الطويل»

يمدحه في شهر ذي الحجة من هذه السنة:

وأشكُو إلَيْها بَيْنَنا وَهْيَ جُنْدُهُ	أودُّ مِنَ الأيّامِ ما لا تَوَدُّهُ
فكَيْفَ بجُبٍّ يَجْتَمِعْنَ وَصَدُّهُ	يُواعِدْنَ جِبّاً يَجْتَمِعْنَ وَوَصْلُهُ
فَما طَلَبي مِنها حَبِيباً تَرُدُّهُ	أبَى خُلُقُ الدُّنْيا حَبِيباً تُدِيمُهُ
تَكَلَّفُ شَيْءٍ في طِباعِكَ ضِدُّهُ	وأسْرَعُ مَفْعُولٍ فَعَلْتَ تَغَيُّراً
مَهاً كُلُّها يُولى بجَفْنَيْهِ خَدُّهُ	رَعَى اللهُ عِيساً فارَقَتْنا وَفَوْقَها
وَقَدْ رَحَلُوا جِيدٌ تَنَاثَرَ عِقْدُهُ	بِوَادٍ بِهِ ما بالقُلُوبِ كأنَّهُ
تَفاوَحَ مِسْكُ الغانِياتِ وَرَنْدُهُ	إذا سَرَتِ الأحداجُ فَوْقَ نَباتِهِ
ومِنْ دُونِها غُولُ الطَّرِيقِ وَبُعْدُهُ	وَحالَ كإحداهُنَّ رُمْتُ بُلُوغَها
وَقَصَّرَ عَمَّا تَشْتَهي النَّفْسُ جُدُّهُ	وأتْعَبُ خَلْقِ اللهِ مَنْ زادَ هَمُّهُ
فيَنحَلُّ مَجْدٌ كانَ بالمالِ عَقْدُهُ	فَلا يَنحَلِلْ في المَجْدِ مالُكَ كُلُّهُ
إذا حارَبَ الأعْداءَ والمالُ زَنْدُهُ	وَدَبِّرْهُ تَدْبِيرَ الذي المَجْدُ كَفُّهُ
وَلا مالَ في الدُّنْيا لِمَنْ قَلَّ مَجْدُهُ	فَلا مَجْدَ في الدُّنْيا لِمَنْ قَلَّ مالُهُ
ومَرْكُوبُهُ رِجْلاهُ والثَّوْبُ جِلْدُهُ	وفي النَّاسِ مَنْ يَرْضَى بمَيْسُورِ عَيْشِهِ
مَدَىً يَنْتَهي بي في مُرادي أحُدُّهُ	ولكِنَّ قَلْباً بَيْنَ جَنْبَيَّ ما لَهُ

They love active men whose goals are
    Not putting on clothes, or food and drink
He aims at stars with eyes to steal as
    If they were loot to a plunderer's eyes
So I ran to the one who was veiled
    In order to meet souls of virtue unveiled
A strong body and pure laughing mind
    At the nature of men as ridiculous marvel
His praise is first, their praise after his
    And to lances late at night and in the day
How shall I deny O Kafur your favors?
    As recounted by me O all of my goals
O king of wealth by which you're seen
    In the east and west by fame and name
You the darling but yet I take refuge
    Lest! be the lover without the beloved

245
He spoke praising Kafur in Dhu'l Hijja in the year 346.
(Long hu)

I want from the days what they do not
    I weep our parting but they are its army
They split love as they unite but how
    Unite its embracing and its denying love?
The world's nature opposes lasting love
    So how can I ask it to bring back a lover?
The fastest thing you do to bring change
    Is attempt what is contrary to your nature
May God guard camels gone, on them
    Wild cows, as cheeks' eyes feel late rain
At a wadi something in hearts for him
    As if as they go a neck loses its necklace
When howdahs moved over greenery
    The myrtle and musk of beauties mingled
Many a turn like these I tried to master
    Less than them perils of road and distance
Weariest of God's folk as care grows
    Soul's power falls short of what it wants
Spend not all your wealth for glory
    For glory whose knot is wealth is lost
Use it the way the hand of glory does
    As it attacks a foe and wealth is its arm
No worldly fame for one of little wealth
    No worldly wealth for one of small glory
Among men one content with low life
    His vehicle his legs, his coat his skin
A heart is in my breast without a goal
    Whose limits end now in my intentions

فَيَختارُ أَن يُكسى دُروعاً تَهُدُّهُ	يَرى جِسمَهُ يُكسى شُفوفاً تَرُبُّهُ
عَلَيقي مَراعيهِ وَزادي رُبَدُّهُ	يُكَلِّفُني التَهجيرَ في كُلِّ مَهْمَهٍ
رَجاءُ أَبي المِسكِ الكَريمِ وَقَصدُهُ	وَأَمضى سِلاحِ قَلَّدَ المَرءُ نَفسَهُ
وَأَمرَةُ مَن لَم يُكثِرِ النَسلَ جَدُّهُ	هُما ناصِراً مَن خانَهُ كُلُّ ناصِرٍ
لَنا وَالِدٌ مِنهُ يُفَدِّيهِ وُلْدُهُ	أَنا اليَومَ مِن غِلمانِهِ في عَشيرَةٍ
وَمِن مالِهِ دَرُّ الصَغيرِ وَمَهْدُهُ	فَمِن مالِهِ مالُ الكَبيرِ وَنَفسُهُ
وَتَردي بِنا قُبُّ الرِباطِ وَجُرْدُهُ	نَجُرُّ القَنا الخَطِّيَّ حَولَ قِبابِهِ
دَوِيُّ القِسِيِّ الفارِسِيَّةِ رَعدُهُ	وَنَمتَحِنُ النُشّابَ في كُلِّ وابِلٍ
فَإِنَّ الَّذي فيها مِنَ النَاسِ أَسدُهُ	فَإِن لا تَكُن مِصرُ الشَرى أَو عَرينَهُ
بِصُمِّ القَنا لا بِالأَصابِعِ نَقدُهُ	سَبائِكُ كافورٍ وَعِقيانُهُ الَّذي
وَجَرَّبَها هَزلُ الطِرادِ وَجِدُّهُ	بَلاها حَوالَيهِ العَدُوُّ وَغَيرُهُ
وَلَكِنَّهُ يَفنى بِعُذرِكَ حِقدُهُ	أَبو المِسكِ لا يَفنى بِذَنبِكَ عَفوُهُ
وَيا أَيُّها المَنصورُ بِالسَعيِ جَدُّهُ	فَيا أَيُّها المَنصورُ بِالجَدِّ سَعيُهُ
وَما ضَرَّني لَمّا رَأَيتُكَ فَقدُهُ	تَوَلّى الصَبى عَنّي فَأَخلَفتَ طيبَهُ
لَدَيكَ وَشابَت عِندَ غَيرِكَ مُردُهُ	لَقَد شَبَّ في هَذا الزَمانِ كُهولُهُ
فَتَسأَلَهُ وَاللَيلُ يُخبِرُ بَردُهُ	أَلا لَيتَ يَومَ السَيرِ يُخبِرُ حَرُّهُ
فَتَعلَمَ أَنّي مِن حُسامِكَ حَدُّهُ	وَلَيتَكَ تَرعاني وَحَيرانُ مُعرِضٌ
تَدانَت أَقاصيهِ وَهانَ أَشَدُّهُ	وَأَنّي إِذا باشَرتُ أَمراً أَريدُهُ
إِلَيكَ فَلَمّا لُحتَ لي لاحَ فَردُهُ	وَما زالَ أَهلُ الدَهرِ يَشتَبِهونَ لي
أَمامَكَ رَبٌّ رَبُّ ذا الجَيشِ عَبدُهُ	يُقالُ إِذا أَبصَرتَ جَيشاً وَرَبَّهُ
قَريبٌ بِذي الكَفِّ المُفَدّاةِ عَهدُهُ	وَأَلقى الفَمَ الضَحّاكَ أَعلَمُ أَنَّهُ
وَفي النَاسِ إِلّا فيكَ وَحدَكَ زُهدُهُ	فَزارَكَ مِنّي مَن إِلَيكَ اِشتِياقُهُ
وَيَأتي فَيَدري أَنَّ ذَلِكَ جُهدُهُ	يُخَلِّفُ مَن لَم يَأتِ دارَكَ غايَةً
شَرِبتُ بِماءٍ يُعجِزُ الطَيرَ وِردُهُ	فَإِن نِلتُ ما أَمَّلتُ مِنكَ فَرُبَّما
نَظيرٌ فَعالَ الصادِقِ القَولِ وَعدُهُ	وَوَعدُكَ فِعلٌ قَبلَ وَعدٍ لِأَنَّهُ
يَبينُ لَكَ تَقريبُ الجَوادِ وَشَدُّهُ	فَكُن في اِصطِناعي مُحسِناً كَمُجَرِّبٍ

It sees a body dress lightly to please
    But it prefers an armor that is heavier
It loads me with noon trips in desert
    My barley its food, its ostrich my meat
Sharpest weapons a man girds on
    Hope of generous Abu Musk as a goal
They aid him when all aid betrays
    Family for one with kin of few progeny
I am now of his family due to slaves
    We have a father in him and a ransom
In his wealth great good and himself
    From his flocks cradle and milk for two
We hold the Khatti around his tent
    Stallions, lean ones, in squadons trot
We feel the arrows in each downpour
    Thunder echoes the bows of cavalry
If Egypt is not a haunt of lions or their
    Lair yet the men who are there are lions
Kafur's silver and gold are what is
    On his lance points, not cash in hand
The foe and others have tested them
    Sport of the chase and earnest prove it
Abu Musk's pardon isn't erased by sin
    Rather his rage destroyed by the excuse
O conqueror by sincerity in his effort
    O conqueror in his efforts in sincerity
My youth goes but you replace its
    Sweet, its loss no worry when I see you
Adults in these times grow young as
    Youths grow gray with others than you
O would day's heat in a trip was known
    Known night's coldness as you asked it
Would you had seen me at Lake Hairan
    You'd known I have your sword's edges
If I begin a matter I have planned its
    Distance is near and its hardness easy
Folk of the age ever compare me to
    You as you shine by me, unique light
One said when I saw the army's lord
    Before you a king, lord, an army's slave!
I met a smiling mouth, I knew that he
    Was near whose vow was a kindly hand
One who loves you visited on my behalf
    His disdain for men you alone excepted
Left behind one who finds your house
    No end, coming he knows it is his limit
If I get what I hope from you maybe
    I drink water whose sipping tires birds
Your vow is action before promise
    Its promise equals action true to speech
Favor my work as one tests a horse
    His gallop and fast pace will show you

فإمَّا تَنْفيهِ وإمَّا تُعِدَّهْ	إذا كنتَ في شَكٍّ من السَّيفِ فابْلُهْ
إذا لم يُفارقْهُ النِّجادُ وغِمْدُهْ	وَمَا الصَّارمُ الهِنديُّ إلاَّ كغَيرِهِ
ولَوْ لم يَكنْ إلاَّ البَشاشَةَ رِفدُهْ	وإنَّكَ للمَشْكُورِ في كلِّ حالةٍ
فلَحظَةُ طَرْفٍ منكَ عندي نِدَّهْ	فكُلُّ نَوالٍ كانَ أوْ هُوَ كائنٌ
عَطاياكَ أرْجو مَدَّها وهيَ مَدَّهْ	وإنِّي لَفي بَحْرٍ من الخَيرِ أصْلُهُ
ولَكِنَّها في مَفخَرٍ أسْتَجدَّهْ	وَما رَغبَتي في عَسْجَدٍ أستَفيدُهْ
ويَحمَدُهُ مَن يَفضَحُ الحَمدَ حَمدُهْ	يَجودُ بهِ مَن يَفضَحُ الجودَ جودُهْ
وقابَلْتَهُ إلاَّ ووَجْهُكَ سَعْدُهْ	فإنَّكَ ما مرَّ النُّحوسُ بكَوْكَبٍ

(٢٤٦)

«من الوافر»

دسَّ إليه الأسودُ من قال له قد طال قيامك في مجلس كافور يريد أن يعلم ما في نفسه له فقال ارتجالاً:

وَبَذْلُ المُكرَماتِ منَ النَّفوسِ	يَقِلّ لَهُ القِيامُ على الرُّؤوسِ
فكَيفَ تكُونُ في يَوْمٍ عَبُوسِ	إذا خانَتْهُ في يَوْمِ ضَحُوكٍ

(٢٤٧)

«من البسيط»

دخل على الأستاذ كافور بعد انتقاله من دار البركة إلى الدار الثانية فقال وأنشده إياها في شهر محرم سنة سبع وأربعين وثلاث مئة (٩٥٨م):

دارٌ مُبارَكةُ المَلْكِ الذي فيهَا	أحَقُّ دارٍ بأنْ تُدْعَى مُبارَكةً
دارٌ غَدا النَّاسُ يَستَسقُونَ أهليهَا	وأجْدَرُ الدُّورِ أنْ تُسْقَى بسَاكِنِها

If you doubt a sword you must try it
    You either reject it or reckon upon it
For Indian sword is like the others
    If belt and scabbard do not part from it
Truly you are thanked in every way
    Even if support is only your affability
Each gift is or exists in essence
    A glance of your eye equals it for me
I'm in a sea of goodness whose source
    Is your gifts, a tide whose flow
I hope for It's not my desire to profit from gold
    But rather to try something new in honor
He is generous if bounty shames giving
    He praises him whose praise shames favor
And if an unlucky star comes near you
    You approach it: but your face brings luck

246

**The black
sent someone
to Abu Tayyib
secretly who said:
Your attendance at his majlis
has lasted a long time.
He meant that he knew
what was on his mind.
So he said:
(Exuberant si)**

Standing gladly is a small thing to him
    And spending generously of one's thoughts
Since they betrayed you on smiling days
    What should they do now in these dark days?

247

**Fifty slaves of the black
died in the new palace
to which he had moved in happier days
so he took fright
and left it for another palace.
And Abu Tayyib spoke
(Outspread ha)**

The best of houses that claim a blessing
    Is the house that has its king's approbation
Finest house to pour favor on its inmate
    The house where men ask drink of its folk

فَمَنْ يَمُرَّ عَلَى الْأُولَى يُسَلِّيهَا	هَذِهِ مَنَازِلُكَ الْأُخْرَى نُهَنِّهَا
جَعَلْتَ فِيهِ عَلَى مَا قَبْلَهُ تِيهَا	إِذَا حَلَلْتَ مَكَانًا بَعْدَ صَاحِبِهِ
فَإِنَّ رِيحَكَ رُوحٌ فِي مَغَانِيهَا	لَا يُنْكَرُ الْحِسُّ مِنْ دَارٍ تَكُونُ بِهَا
وَلَا اسْتُرَدَّ حَيَاةً مِنْكَ مُعْطِيهَا	أَتَمَّ سَعْدَكَ مَنْ أَعْطَاكَ أَوَّلَهُ

(٢٤٨)

«من الطويل»

وقاد إليه فرساً فقال يمدحه:

وَأُمٌّ وَمَنْ يَمَّمْتُ خَيْرُ مُيَمَّمِ	فِرَاقٌ وَمَنْ فَارَقْتُ غَيْرُ مُذَمَّمِ
إِذَا لَمْ أُبَجَّلْ عِنْدَهُ وَأُكَرَّمِ	وَمَا مَنْزِلُ اللَّذَّاتِ عِنْدِي بِمَنْزِلِ
مِنَ الضَّيْمِ مَرْمِيًّا بِهَا كُلَّ مَخْرَمِ	سَجِيَّةُ نَفْسٍ مَا تَزَالُ مَلِيحَةً
عَلَى وَكَمْ بَاكٍ بِأَجْفَانِ ضَيْغَمِ	رَحَلَتْ فَكَمْ بَاكٍ بِأَجْفَانِ شَادِنٍ
بِأَجْزَعَ مِنْ رَبِّ الْحُسَامِ الْمُصَمَّمِ	وَمَا رَبُّهُ الْقُرْطِ الْمَلِيحِ مَكَانَةً
عَذَرْتُ وَلَكِنْ مِنْ حَبِيبٍ مُعَمَّمِ	فَلَوْ كَانَ مَا بِي مِنْ حَبِيبٍ مُقَنَّعٍ
هَوًى كَاسِرٌ كَفِّي وَقَوْسِي وَأَسْهُمِي	رَمَى وَاتَّقَى رَمْيِي وَمِنْ دُونِ مَا اتَّقَى
وَصَدَّقَ مَا يَعْتَادُهُ مِنْ تَوَهُّمِ	إِذَا سَاءَ فِعْلُ الْمَرْءِ سَاءَتْ ظُنُونُهُ
وَأَصْبَحَ فِي لَيْلٍ مِنَ الشَّكِّ مُظْلِمِ	وَعَادَى مُحِبِّيهِ بِقَوْلِ عُدَاتِهِ
وَأَعْرِفُهَا فِي فِعْلِهِ وَالتَّكَلُّمِ	أُصَادِقُ نَفْسَ الْمَرْءِ مِنْ قَبْلِ جِسْمِهِ
مَتَى أَجْزِهِ حِلْمًا عَلَى الْجَهْلِ يَنْدَمِ	وَأَحْلُمُ عَنْ خِلِّي وَأَعْلَمُ أَنَّهُ
جَزَيْتُ بِجُودِ التَّارِكِ الْمُتَبَسِّمِ	وَإِنْ بَذَلَ الْإِنْسَانُ لِي جُودَ عَابِسٍ
نَجِيبٌ كَصَدْرِ السَّمْهَرِيِّ الْمُقَوَّمِ	وَأَهْوَى مِنَ الْفِتْيَانِ كُلَّ سَمَيْذَعٍ
بِهِ الْخَيْلُ كَبَّاتِ الْخَمِيسِ الْعَرَمْرَمِ	خَطَتْ تَحْتَهُ الْعِيسُ الْفَلَاةَ وَخَالَطَتْ
وَلَكِنَّهَا فِي الْكَفِّ وَالطَّرْفِ وَالْفَمِ	وَلَا عِفَّةٌ فِي سِنِّهِ وَسِنَانِهِ
وَلَا كُلُّ فَعَّالٍ لَهُ بِمُتَمِّمِ	وَمَا كُلُّ هَاوٍ لِلْجَمِيلِ بِفَاعِلٍ
سَوَابِقُ خَيْلٍ يَهْتَدِينَ بِأَدْهَمِ	فِدًى لِأَبِي الْمِسْكِ الْكِرَامُ فَإِنَّهَا
إِلَى خُلُقٍ رَحْبٍ وَخَلْقٍ مُطَهَّمِ	أَغَرَّ بِمَجْدٍ قَدْ شَخَصْنَ وَرَاءَهُ

Your second dwelling we congratulate
  For he who passes the first forgets that
If you settle in a place after its lord
  You do it proud over what it was before
Feeling deserts no house if you stay
  Your perfume is a soul for its quarters
Who gave you the first completed your joy
  And he will not take back the life he gave you

248
He spoke also praising him and he had sent him a black colt in the last of the month of Rabia in the year 347.
(Long mi)

Parting, one I part from is not to blame
  Journey and one I went to was best of goals
But my stay is not happy in an abode if
  I find no respect and no true generosity
It's soul's nature not to cease from fear
  Of evil as all mountain roads are probed
I saddle up, many weepers with fawn eyes
  For me, and many a tear in the lion's eyes
No fine earringed mistress in the place
  Anxious for the master of the sharp swords
If my trouble were due a veiled lover
  I'd excuse it but it's a lover with a turban
He shot wary of my shot and what else
  In love, breaking my hand, bow and arrows
If a man's act is bad, his ideas are bad
  What he is used to true to those fancies
He attacks his love with hostile words
  And in the night the evil doubts will come
I'm friendly to a man's soul before body
  I know it from his actions and his speech
I'm forgiving to my friend and I know
  If I give him clemency he repents unblamed
If a man lavishes bounty on me frowning
  I'll repay him by leaving gifts with a smile
I love a man who is a true, noble chief
  Of the finest, like a straight lance shaft
A white camel crosses deserts, guard
  For him horsemen of a huge raiding army
No continence in his sword or spear
  But it is in his hand, genitals and mouth
Not every lover of beauty attains it
  And not all of his actions are perfection
Generosity ransom for Abu Musk, it is
  The leader of horses guided by the black
Bright in glory they look up behind him
  To the ample nature and perfect visage

فَقِفْ وَقْفَةً قُدّامَهُ تَتَعَلَّمِ	إذا مَنَعَتْ مِنكَ السِّياسَةُ نَفسَها
ضَعيفَ المَساعي أوْ قَليلَ التَكَرُّمِ	يَضيقُ على مَن راءَهُ العُذْرُ أن يُرى
وكانَ قَليلاً مَنْ يقولُ لها اقدِمي	ومَن مثلُ كافورٍ إذا الخَيلُ أحجَمَتْ
إلى لَهَواتِ الفارِسِ المُتَلَثِّمِ	شَديدُ ثَباتِ الطِّرْفِ والنقعُ واصِلٌ
وآمُلُ عِزّاً يَخضِبُ البيضَ بالدّمِ	أبا المسكِ أرجو منكَ نصراً على العِدى
أُقيمُ الشَّقا فيها مَقامَ التَنَعُّمِ	ويَوماً يَغيظُ الحاسِدينَ وحالةً
مَواطِرَ مِن غَيرِ السَّحائِبِ يَظلِمِ	ولم أرْجُ إلاّ أهلَ ذاكَ ومَن يُرِدْ
بقَلبِ المَشوقِ المُستَهامِ المُتَيَّمِ	فَلَوْ لم تكنْ في مصرَ ما سِرتُ نحوَها
كأنَّ بها في اللَيلِ حَمَلاتِ دَيلَمِ	ولا نَبَحَتْ خَيلي كِلابُ قَبائِلٍ
فَلَم تَرَ إلاّ حافِراً فَوقَ مَنسِمِ	ولا اتَّبَعَتْ آثارَنا عَينُ قائِفٍ
من النيلِ واستَذَرَتْ بظلِّ المُقَطَّمِ	وسِمْنا بها البيداءَ حتى تَغَمَّرَتْ
عَصَيْتُ بقَصدَيهِ مُشيري ولَومي	وأبلَجَ يَعصي باختِصاصي مُشيرَهُ
وسُقْتُ إلَيهِ الشُّكرَ غَيرَ مُجَمجَمِ	فَساقَ إليَّ العُرفَ غَيرَ مُكَدَّرِ
حَديثاً وقد حَكَّمتُ رَأيَكَ فاحكُمِ	قدِ اختَرتُكَ الأملاكَ فاختَرْ لهم بنا
وأيمَنُ كَفٍّ فيهمْ كَفُّ مُنعِمِ	فأحسَنَ وَجهٍ في الوَرى وَجهُ مُحسِنٍ
وأكثَرَ إقداماً على كلِّ مُعظَمِ	واشرَفُهُم مَن كان اشرَفَ هِمّةً
سُرورُ مُحِبٍّ أو مَساءَةُ مُجرِمِ	لمَن تَطلُبُ الدنيا إذا لم تُرَدْ بها
من اسمِكَ ما في كلِّ عُنقٍ ومَعصَمِ	وقد وَصَلَ المُهرُ الذي فوقَ فَخذِهِ
وإنْ كانَ بالنيرانِ غَيرَ مُوَسَّمِ	لكَ الحَيوانُ الرّاكِبُ الخَيلَ كلُّهُ
وصَيَّرتُ ثُلثَيها انتِظارَكَ فاعلَمِ	ولَوْ كنتُ أدري كم حَياتي قَسَمتُها
فَجُدْ لي بحَظِّ البادِرِ المُتَغَنِّمِ	ولكن ما يَمضي من الدَهرِ فائِتٌ
وقُدتُ إلَيكَ النَفسَ قَودَ المُسَلَّمِ	رَضيتُ بمَا تَرْضى بهِ لي مَحَبَّةً
فَكَلَّمَهُ عَنّي ولَمْ أتَكَلَّمِ	ومِثلُكَ مَن كانَ الوَسيطَ فُؤادُهُ

If authority defends itself from you
    Stand still in front of it to learn by it
Excuse is hard for one who sees him
    He seems weak in effort, small in giving
Who is like Kafur when riders attack?
    It is easy for one to order them: Advance!
Sturdy the stallions as the dust rises
    Down the throats of riders who have veils
Abu Musk I hope your aid against foes
    I hope for help to dye a sword in blood
To enrage the envious today and soon
    To fix pain upon them in place of favor
I hope only in such as you for whoever
    Wants rains without clouds is benighted
If you were not in Egypt I'd not come
    With heart enslaved by a passion of love
Nor would bedouin dogs bark at me
    As when Dailamis attack in the night
Pursuer's eye could not follow our track
    Seeing only a horse track on a camel trail
We mark desert with them till they wade
    In Nile, or settle Muqattam's dusty shade
Haughty, it defies my talent in a hint
    I exceed my mark or blame by seeking him
He pours perfume untroubled on me
    And I pour thanks on him without mumbling
I chose you from kings, chose for them
    A story, for I judged your mind and judge
Finest face among men a patron's face
    Trustiest hand among them that is gracious
Most noble he who is noble in spirit
    Farthest advanced over all the magnified
Some seek a world they do not want
    Joy of the beloved or evil of a criminal
The foal arrived having on its withers
    Your brand that is on every neck or wrist
Yours the living, riders on horseback
    Even on sun and moon out of known world
If I knew my life's span I'd share it
    I'd have a third wait for you, now you know'
Yet what has passed of life is past
    So endow me with swift joy and plunder
I am happy you want to be my lover
    I lead a soul to you as surrender is led
Such as you are the core of one's heart
    So say it for me and then I need not speak

(٢٤٩)

«من السريع»

وحرج من عبده يوماً فقال:

مَنْ حَكَّمَ الْعَبْدَ عَلَى نَفْسِهِ	أنـوكُ مِنْ عَبْدٍ وَمِنْ عِرْسِهِ
تَحَكَّمَ الْإِفْسَادِ فِي حِسِّهِ	وَإِنَّمَا يُظْهِرُ تَحْكِيمُهُ
كَمَنْ يَرَى أَنَّكَ فِي حَبْسِهِ	مَا مَنْ يَرَى أَنَّكَ فِي وَعْدِهِ
عَنْ فَرْجِهِ الْمُنْتِنِ أَوْ ضِرْسِهِ	أَلْعَبْدُ لَا تَفْضُلُ أَخْلَاقُهُ
وَلَا يَعِي مَا قَالَ فِي أَمْسِهِ	لَا يُنْجِزُ الْمِيعَادَ فِي يَوْمِهِ
كَأَنَّكَ الْمَلَّاحُ فِي قَلْسِهِ	وَإِنَّمَا تَحْتَالُ فِي جَذْبِهِ
مَرَّتْ يَدُ النَّخَّاسِ فِي رَأْسِهِ	فَلَا تَرَجَّ الْخَيْرَ عِنْدَ امْرِيءٍ
بِحَالِهِ فَانْظُرْ إِلَى جِنْسِهِ	وَإِنْ عَرَاكَ الشَّكُّ فِي نَفْسِهِ
إِلَّا الَّذِي يَلْؤُمُ فِي غِرْسِهِ	فَقَلَّمَا يَلْؤُمُ فِي ثَوْبِهِ
لَمْ يَجِدِ الْمَذْهَبَ عَنْ قَنْسِهِ	مَنْ وَجَدَ الْمَذْهَبَ عَنْ قَدْرِهِ

(٢٥٠)

«من الخفيف»

جرت وحشة بين الأستاذ كافور والأمير أبي القاسم مدة ثم اصطلحا فقال:

وَأَذَاعَتْهُ أَلْسُنُ الْحُسَّادِ	حَسَمَ الصُّلْحُ مَا اشْتَهَتْهُ الْأَعَادِي
رَكَ مَا بَيْنَهَا وَبَيْنَ الْمُرَادِ	وَأَرَادَتْهُ أَنْفُسٌ حَالَ تَدْبِي
مِنْ عِتَابٍ زِيَادَةً فِي الْوِدَادِ	صَارَ مَا أَوْضَعَ الْمُخَبِّنُونَ فِيهِ
بَابَ، سُلْطَانَةٌ عَلَى الْأَضْدَادِ	وَكَلَامُ الْوُشَاةِ لَيْسَ عَلَى الْأَحْ
ءِ إِذَا وَافَقَتْ هَوًى فِي الْفُؤَادِ	إِنَّمَا تُنْجِحُ الْمَقَالَةُ فِي الْمَرْ
لَ فَأُلْفِيتَ أَوْثَقَ الْأَطْوَادِ	وَلَعَمْرِي لَقَدْ هُزِزْتَ بِمَا قِي
كُنْتَ أَهْدَى مِنْهَا إِلَى الْإِرْشَادِ	وَأَشَارَتْ بِمَا أَبَيْتَ رِجَالٌ
هَدْ وَيُشْوِي الصَّوَابَ بَعْدَ اجْتِهَادِ	قَدْ يُصِيبُ الْفَتَى الْمُشِيرُ وَلَمْ يَجْ

249
He went from him and mocked him.
(Swift hi)

More fool than slave or than his wife
    He who makes a slave judge over him
He who sees that you hold his pledge
    Is not one who sees you in his prison
However he will show his judgment
    By this corrupt working of his tastes
A slave's nature doesn't go beyond
    His stinking crotch and his grinders
He won't perform a vow on its day
    Nor recall what he said in the evening
He only plays false in his pulling
    As if you were a boatman on his rope
Hope not for success from a fellow
    If slaver's hand passed over his head
And if doubt takes you about him
    And his condition, look at his class
Rarely does one blame his coat
    Without blaming how he was planted
He who finds escape from his power
    Won't find any escape from his roots

250
Some of the military joined with Ibn al Ikhshid the lord of Kafur seeking a rebellion among them. And the rumors were current for several days. Then he brought them back to his side and peace was restored. So Abu Tayyib spoke.
(Nimble di)

Peace was cut off as the enemy wanted
    The tongues of the envious published that
Some wanted your government to change
    From what they had to what they intended
What the betrayers plotted was altered
    From blame to an increase of affection
A slanderer's word had no power
    Over the lover and was to the contrary
Speech only succeeds in a man when
    It concurs with the love firm in his heart
My life, if you shook at the gossip
    You met it more firmly than a mountain
One counseled what you rejected but
    You were more guided than that to truth
A counselor was hit and didn't oppose
    He missed the target after the struggle

نِلْتَ ما لا يُنالُ بالبيضِ والسُّمْرِ   وَصُنْتَ الأرْواحَ في الأجْسادِ
وَقَنا الخَطِّ في مَراكِزِها حَوْلَكَ   والمُرْهَفاتُ في الأغْمادِ
ما دَرَوْا إذ رَأَوْا فُؤادَكَ فيهمْ   ساكِناً أنَّ رَأْيَهُ في الطِّرادِ
فَفَدى رَأْيَكَ الذي لم تُفِدْهُ   كلُّ رَأيٍ مُعَلَّمٍ مُسْتَفادِ
وَإذا الحِلْمُ لم يَكُنْ عن طِباعٍ   لم يَكُنْ عَن تَقادُمِ المِيلادِ
فَبِهَذا وَمِثْلِهِ سُدْتَ يا كافورُ   واقْتَدْتَ كلَّ صَعْبِ القِيادِ
وَأَطَاعَ الذي أطاعَكَ والطَّاعَةُ   لَيْسَتْ خلائِقَ الآسادِ
إنَّما أنْتَ والِدٌ والأبُ القاطِعُ   أحْنى مِنْ واصِلِ الأوْلادِ
لا عَدا الشَّرُّ مَنْ بَغى لكُما الشَّرَّ   وَخُصَّ الفَسادُ أهلَ الفَسادِ
أنْتُما ما اتَّفَقْتُما الجِسْمُ والرُّوحُ   فَلا احْتَجْتُما إلى العُوَّادِ
وَإذا كانَ في الأنابيبِ خُلْفٌ   وَقَعَ الطَّيشُ في صُدورِ الصِّعادِ
أشْمَتَ الخُلْفُ بالشُّراةِ عِداها   وَشَفى رَبِّ فارِسٍ مِن إيادِ
وَتَوَلَّى بَني اليَزيديِّ بالبَصْرَةِ   حتى تَمَزَّقوا في البِلادِ
وَمُلوكاً كأمْسِ في القُرْبِ مِنَّا   وَكَطَسْمٍ وأُخْتِها في البِعادِ
بِكُما بَتَّ عَائِذاً فيكُما مِنْهُ   وَمِنْ كَيدِ كلِّ باغٍ وَعادِ
وَبِلَيْكُمَا الأصيلَيْنِ أنْ تَفْتَرِقَ   صُمُّ الرِّماحِ بَينَ الجِيادِ
أوْ يَكونَ الوَلِيُّ اشْقى عَدُوٍّ   بالذي تَذخَرانِهِ مِنْ عَتادِ
هَلْ يَسُرَّنَّ باقِياً بَعْدَ ماضٍ   ما تَقولُ العُداةُ في كلِّ نادِ
مَنَعَ الوُدَّ والرِّعايَةَ والسُّؤدُدُ   أنْ تَبْلُغَا إلى الأحْقادِ
وَحُقوقٌ تُرَقِّقُ القَلْبَ للقَلْبِ   وَلَوْ ضُمِّنَتْ قُلوبَ الجَمادِ
فَغَدا المُلْكُ باهِراً مَنْ رآهُ   شاكِراً ما أتَيْتُما مِنْ سَدادِ
فيهِ أيْديكُما عَلى الظَّفَرِ الحُلْوِ   وَأيْدي قَوْمٍ عَلى الأكبادِ
هَذِهِ دَوْلَةُ المَكارِمِ والرَّأْفَةِ   وَالمَجْدِ والنَّدى والأيادي
كسَفَتْ ساعَةً كما تكسِفُ الشَّمْسُ   وَعادَتْ ونُورُها في أزْديادِ
يَزْحَمُ الدَّهرَ رَكْبُها عَنْ أذاها   بفَتىً مارِدٍ على المُرادِ
مُتْلِفٍ مُخْلِفٍ وَفِي أبيٍّ   عَالِمٍ حازِمٍ شُجاعٍ جَوادِ

You got what's not in sword or lance
    And you guarded the souls in the bodies
Khatti lances in their ranks about you
    And the polished ones in their scabbards
They knew not when they met cool heart
    That its counsels were in pursuit of them
He ransoms your mind who is not so
    Every opinion taught wants to ransom it
If intelligence is not in a nature
    Growth cannot make it mature after birth
By this and the like of it you ruled
    O Kafur, and you led the intractables
Those who yielded to you submitted
    But submission is not in a lion's nature
You as true parent, a whipping father,
    Longed for reconciliation with his child
May penalty not miss him who plots
    May discord single out discord's folk
You, while you live, are the body
    And soul, may you not need a nurse
If a break shows between the joints
    Lightness falls on the breast of a lance
Broken promises rejoiced Shura foes
    And healed Persia's lord from the Iyad
One ruled over Banu Yazid at Basra
    Till they were torn to bits in the town
Kings like these in our own times
    Like Tasm and its sister in early ages
For you I spent nights seeking aid
    From tricky ambitions and evil people
For your firm wits lest sharp lances
    Among the steeds should make division
Or near ones should split in enmity
    ith what they hoarded up as weapons
Can they be happy after what passed
    What will the foe say in the assemblies?
Love and trust and leadership forbid
    That you should carry out such revenge
This loyalty softens heart to heart
    Even if it were surety for stony hearts
If the king is victorious one sees
    Gratefully what you bring of stability
Thus your gifts are sweet with reward
    The people's hand are on their livers
This a government of noble deeds
    And mercy, glory and bounty and gifts
Absent an hour as the sun is absent
    But they return and their light increases
His forces defend times from evil
    With proud young men against rebels
Violent, solitary, trusted and proud
    Sagacious, strict, brave and generous

أجفلَ النّاسُ عن طريقِ أبي المِسْـ ـكِ وَذَلَّتْ لَهُ رِقابُ العِبادِ
كَيْفَ لا يُتْرَكُ الطّريقُ لِسَيْلٍ ضَيِّقٍ عَنْ أتِيّهِ كُلُّ وادِ

(٢٥١)

«من الطويل»

يمدحه في شوال سبع وأربعين وثلاث مئة (٩٥٨م):

أغالِبُ فيكَ الشَّوْقَ والشَّوْقُ أغْلَبُ وَأعجبُ مِن ذا الهجرِ وَالوَصلُ أعجبُ
أما تَغْلَطُ الأيّامُ فيَّ بأنْ أرى بَغيضاً تَنائي أوْ حَبيباً تُقَرِّبُ
وللّهِ سَيْري ما أقلَّ تَئِيّةً عَشِيَّةَ شَرقيَّ الحِدالى وَغرَّبُ
عَشِيَّةَ أحفى النّاسِ بي مَنْ جَفوْتُهُ وَأهدَى الطّريقَينِ التي أتَجَنَّبُ
وَكَمْ لِظَلامِ اللّيلِ عندكَ مِنْ يَدٍ تُخَبِّرُ أنَّ المانَوِيَّةَ تَكْذِبُ
وَقاكَ رَدى الأعداءِ تَسْري إليْهِمْ وَزارَكَ فيهِ ذو الدَّلالِ المُحَجَّبُ
وَيَوْمٍ كَلَيْلِ العاشِقينَ كَمَنْتُهُ أراقِبُ فيهِ الشَّمسَ أيَّانَ تَغْرُبُ
وَعَيْني إلى أُذْني أغرَّ كأنَّهُ مِنَ اللّيلِ باقٍ بَينَ عَيْنَيهِ كَوْكَبُ
لَهُ فَضْلَةٌ عَنْ جِسْمِهِ في إهابِهِ تَجيءُ عَلى صَدْرٍ رَحيبٍ وَتَذهَبُ
شَقَقْتُ بهِ الظَّلماءَ أدْني عِنانَهُ فَيَطْغى وَأُرخيهِ مِراراً فيَلعَبُ
وَأصرَعُ أيَّ الوَحشِ قَفَّيْتُهُ بهِ وَأنزِلُ عنهُ مِثلَهُ حينَ أركَبُ
وَما الخَيلُ إلّا كالصَّديقِ قَليلَةٌ وَإنْ كَثُرَتْ في عَينِ مَنْ لا يُجَرِّبُ
إذا لم تُشاهِدْ غَيرَ حُسْنِ شِياتِها وَأعضائِها فالحُسْنُ عَنكَ مُغَيَّبُ
لحى اللهُ ذي الدّنيا مُناخاً لراكبٍ فَكُلُّ بَعيدِ الهَمِّ فيها مُعَذَّبُ
ألا لَيتَ شِعري هَلْ أقولُ قَصيدَةً فَلا أشتَكي فيها وَلا أتَعَتَّبُ
وَبي ما يَذودُ الشِّعرَ عَنّي أقلُّهُ وَلَكِنَّ قَلبي يا ابنَةَ القَومِ قُلَّبُ
وَأخلاقُ كافورٍ إذا شِئْتَ مَدْحَهُ وَإنْ لم أشَأْ تُملي عَلَيَّ وأكْتُبُ
إذا تَرَكَ الإنسانُ أهلاً وَراءَهُ وَيَمَّمَ كافوراً فَما يَتَغَرَّبُ
فَتًى يَملأُ الأفعالَ رأياً وَحِكمَةً وَنادِرَةً أحياناً يَرضى وَيَغضَبُ

Men leave the way free to Abu Musk
    The necks of slaves now submit to him
Should not way be left to a torrent
    If each wadi is too narrow for the current?

251
He spoke praising him in Shawwal in the year 347 and he had just sent him 600 dinars.
(Long bu)

I fight longing for you but desire wins
    I wonder at flight but union is stranger
Do the days trick me in that I behold
    The hateful afar or the beloved nearby?
By God! how small delay in my trip
    Evening at Hadali and Gurrab to the east
At eve, one kindest to me was one I hurt
    And the more guided of two ways I avoided
Many a helper hand for you in dark night
    Has proved that the Manichaeans were liars
Saved you from death by foe as you went
    And the one modestly veiled came to visit you
Many a day like lover's night I hid in
    When I watched for the sun to set there
My eye was on elegant ears as if they
    Were a bit of night, between its eyes a star
He has a fine skin over his body which
    Is coming and going upon his broad breast
I cut through dark with him on taut rein
    He rebels so l relax at times and he plays
Many a beast I kill with him as I track
    I dismount him, he's like when I mounted
Horses like friends are only too few
    Though they are manly to an untrained eye
If you only see the beauty of marking
    And of limb, then beauty is hid from you
God damn a world as rest for rider
    For all of high ambition are punished here
O would I knew how to speak a qasida
    Without a complaint in it or reproaching
A thing in me a bit of it repels poetry
    Yet my heart alters O daughter of the camp
Kafur's nature, if I wish to praise it
    Or if I don't, dictates to me and I write
If a man leaves his family behind him
    And journeys to Kafur it is not strange
A man filling deeds with wisdom, wit
    And rarities when pleased or displeased

تَبَيَّنْتَ أَنَّ السَّيفَ بالكَفِّ يَضرِبُ	إذا ضرَبتْ في الحربِ بالسَّيفِ كَفُّـهُ
وَتَلْبَثُ أَمْواهُ السَّحابِ فَتَنضُبُ	تَزيدُ عَطاياهُ على اللَّبثِ كَثرَةً
فإنّي أُغَنّي مُنذُ حِينٍ وَتَشرَبُ	أبا المِسْكِ هل في الكَأسِ فَضلٌ أَنالُهُ
وَنَفسِي على مِقدارِ كَفَّيكَ تَطلُبُ	وَهَبْتَ على مِقدارِ كَفَّي زَمانِنا
فَجودُكَ يَكسُوني وَشُغلُكَ يَسلُبُ	إذا لم تَنُطْ بي ضَيعَةً أَوْ وِلايَةً
حِذائي وَأَبكي مَنْ أُحِبُّ وأَندُبُ	يُضاحِكُ في ذا العِيدِ كُلُّ حَبيبَهُ
وَأَينَ مِنَ المُشتاقِ عَنقاءُ مُغرِبُ	أَحِنُّ إلى أَهلي وَأَهوَي لِقاءَهُمْ
فإنَّكَ أَحلى في فُؤادي وَأَعذَبُ	فإنْ لم يَكُنْ إلّا أبو المِسكِ أوْ هُمُ
وَكلُّ مَكانٍ يُنبِتُ العِزَّ طَيِّبُ	وَكلُّ امرئٍ يُولي الجَميلَ مُحَبَّبُ
وَسُمرُ العَوالي وَالحَديدُ المُذَرَّبُ	يُريدُ بِكَ الحُسّادُ ما الله دافِعٌ
إلى المَوتِ مِنهُ عِشتَ والطِّفلُ أَشيَبُ	وَدُونَ الذي يَبغُونَ ما لَوْ تَخَلَّصُوا
وَإِنْ طَلَبُوا الفَضلَ الذي فيكَ خُيِّبُوا	إذا طَلَبُوا جَدواكَ أَعطوا وَحُكِّمُوا
وَلَكِنْ مِنَ الأَشياءِ ما لَيسَ يُوهَبُ	وَلَوْ جازَ أَن يَحُوزُوا عُلاكَ وَهَبتَها
لِمَنْ باتَ في نَعمائِهِ يَتَقَلَّبُ	وَأَظلَمُ أَهلِ الظُّلمِ مَن باتَ حاسِداً
وَلَيسَ لَهُ أُمٌّ سِواكَ وَلا أَبُ	وَأَنتَ الذي رَبَّيتَ ذا المُلكِ مُرضَعاً
وَما لَكَ إلّا الهِندُوانِيُّ مِخلَبُ	وَكُنتَ لَهُ لَيثَ العَرينِ لِشِبلِهِ
إلى المَوتِ في الهَيجاءِ مِن العارِ تَهرُبُ	لَقيتَ القَنا عَنهُ بِنَفسٍ كَريمَةٍ
وَيَحتَرِمُ النَّفسَ التي تَتَهَيَّبُ	وَقَد يَترُكُ النَّفسَ التي لا تَهابُهُ
وَلَكِنَّ مَنْ لاقَوا أَشَدُّ وأَنجَبُ	وَما عَدِمَ اللّاقوكَ بَأساً وَشِدَّةً
عَلَيهِم وَبَرقُ البِيضِ في البِيضِ خُلَّبُ	ثِناهم وَبَرقُ البِيضِ في البِيضِ صادِقٌ
على كلِّ عُودٍ كَيفَ يَدعُو وَيَخطُبُ	سَلَلْتَ سُيُوفاً عَلِمَتْ كلُّ خاطِبٍ
إلَيكَ تَناهى المَكرُماتُ وَتُنسَبُ	وَيُغنيكَ عَمّا يَنسُبُ النّاسُ أَنَّهُ
مَعَدُّ بنُ عَدنانَ فِداكَ وَيَعرُبُ	وَأَيُّ قَبيلٍ يَستَحِقُّكَ قَدرُهُ
لَقَد كُنتُ أَرجُو أَنْ أَراكَ فأَطرَبُ	وَما طَرَبي لَمّا رَأَيتُكَ بِدْعَةً
كَأنّي بِمَدْحٍ قَبلَ مَدحِكَ مُذنِبُ	وَتَعذُلُني فيكَ القَوافي وَهِمَّتي
أَفَتِّشُ عَن هَذا الكَلامِ وَيُنهَبُ	وَلَكِنَّهُ طالَ الطَّريقُ وَلَم أَزَلْ

If his hand strikes in war with a sword
    It is plain the sword strikes by a hand
His gifts increase in number by delays
    But the waters of clouds dry up with time
Abu Musk is there a bit in the cup for
    Me to take? since I sing while you drink
You gave to the extent of time's hand
    My soul seeks from your hand's grasp
If you dress me not in estate or rule
    Your bounty cloaks, your work plunders
Every man at feast smiles at his love
    But me and I weep for one I love, mourn
I long for family, want to meet them
    Where is a western griffin for the lovers?
If there were only Abu Musk or them
    You'd be sweeter to my heart and tastier
Each man who grants favors is beloved
    Every place that grows glory is sweetest
Envy wants for you what God forbids
    As do brown spears and the keen steel
Before their wish is that, if they shun
    In ruin, you'd thrive on as the kids gray
If they seek your gift they take, aided
    If they seek your virtue they are balked
If it were right to take your rank you'd
    Give it but some things are not bestowed
Most evil of evil ones is he who nightly
    Envies one darkly planning his good acts
You are one who raised a suckling king
    Who had neither mother or father but you
You were a lion of the den to this cub
    You had no other claw but Indian sword
You met lances with kindly soul to him
    Fleeing to death in battle far from shame
It leaves a soul alone that is not base
    While it ruins the soul that is terrified
Your foes lack no bravery or energy
    But one they met is stronger and nobler
You won, sword flash true on helmet
    For them but helmet flash alone useless
You drew swords to teach the preacher
    On all the pulpits how to pray and preach
Useless if men trace your genealogy
    Noble acts aim at and return for you
What tribe has worth to deserve you
    Maadd ibn Adnan ransoms and Yarub
My joy when I saw you wasn't new
    I hoped to see you and was satisfied
My verses, ambition blames me as
    If in praising before your poem I sinned
The road was long and I was ever
    Sought after for poetry as for plunder

(٢٥٢)

«من البسيط»

اتصل بأبي الطيب أن قوما نعوه في مجلس سيف الدولة بحلب فقال و لم ينشدها كافورا:

وَلا نَديمٌ وَلا كَأسٌ وَلا سَكَنُ	بِمَ التَّعَلُّلُ لا أَهلٌ وَلا وَطَنُ
مـا لَيسَ يَبلُغُهُ مِن نَفسِهِ الزَّمَنُ	أُريدُ مِن زَمَنــي ذا أَن يُبَلِّغَني
ما دامَ يَصحَبُ فيهِ روحَكَ البَدَنُ	لا تَلـقَ دَهرَكَ إِلّا غَيـرَ مُكتَـرِثٍ
وَلا يَرُدُّ عَلَيكَ الفائِتَ الحَزَنُ	فَمـا يَديـمُ سُـرورُ مـا سُـرِرتَ بِهِ
هَوّوا وَما عَرَفوا الدُنيا وَما فَطِنوا	مِمّـا أَضَـرَّ بِأَهـلِ العِشـقِ أَنَّهُـمُ
في إِثرِ كُلِّ قَبيـحٍ وَجهُهُ حَسَـنُ	تَفنى عُيونُهُمُ دَمعـاً وَأَنفُسُـهُمُ
فَكُلُّ بَيـنٍ عَلَـيَّ اليَـومَ مُؤتَمَـنُ	تَحَمَّلـوا حَمَلَتكُـمْ كُـلُّ ناجِيَـةٍ
إِن مُـتُّ شَوقـاً وَلا فيها لَها ثَمَنُ	ما في هَوادِجِكُم مِن مُهجَتي عِوَضٌ
كُلٌّ بِمـا زَعَـمَ النـاعونَ مُرتَهَـنُ	يا مَن نُعيتُ عَلى بُعدٍ بِمَجلِسِهِ
ثُمَّ اِنتَفَضتُ فَزالَ القَبرُ وَالكَفَنُ	كَم قَد قُتِلتُ وَكَم قَد مِتُّ عِندَكُمُ
جَماعَـةٌ ثُمَّ ماتـوا قَبلَ مَن دَفَنـوا	قَد كانَ شاهَدَ دَفني قَبلَ قَولِهِمُ
تَجري الرِياحُ بِما لا تَشتَهي السُفُنُ	ما كُلُّ مـا يَتَمَنّـى المَرءُ يُدرِكُـهُ
وَلا يَـدِرُّ عَلـى مَرعاكُـمُ اللَبَـنُ	رَأَيتُكُم لا يَصونُ العِرضَ جارُكُـمُ
وَحَظُّ كُلِّ مُحِبٍّ مِنكُمُ ضَغَـنُ	جَزاءُ كُلِّ قَريـبٍ مِنكُمُ مَلَـلٌ
حَتّى يُعاقِبَـهُ التَنغيـصُ وَالمِنَـنُ	وَتَغضَبونَ عَلى مَن نالَ رِفدَكُـمُ
يَهمـاءَ تَكذِبُ فيها العَينُ وَالأُذُنُ	فَغادَرَ الهَجـرُ ما بَيني وَبَينَكُـمُ
وَتَسـأَلُ الأَرضَ عَن أَخفافِها الثَفِنُ	تَحبو الرَواسِمُ مِن بَعدِ الرَسيـمِ بِها
وَلا أَصاحِبُ حِلمي وَهوَ بي جُبُنُ	إِنّـي أُصاحِبُ حِلمي وَهوَ بي كَرَمٌ
وَلا أَلَـذُّ بِمـا عِرضـي بِـهِ دَرِنُ	وَلا أُقيـمُ عَلى مالٍ أَذِلُّ بِـهِ

وَغَــرَّبَ حَتّى لَيسَ لِلغَـربِ مَغـرِبُ | فَشَـرَّقَ حَتّى لَيسَ لِلشَّـرقِ مَشـرِقٌ
جِـدارٌ مُعَلّـى أَو خِبـاءٌ مُطَنَّـبُ | إِذا قُلتُـهُ لَم يَمتَنِـعْ مِـن وُصولِـهِ

It went east till east was not casts
    And to the west till west was not west
When I spoke it the arrival was not
    Forbid by towered wall or rope held tent

252
Abu Tayyib learned that some folk at the Aleppo majlis of Saif al Daula announced his death so he spoke in 348.
(Outspread nu)

Where is solace without family or land?
    Neither drinking pal nor cup nor a home
I desire my time to achieve for me
    What the time cannot achieve for itself
Meet not your fate unless without grief
    So long as body accompanies your spirit
For happiness you enjoy does not last
    And grief does not return the past to you
What hinders love's people is that they
    Love but know not the world or understand
Their eyes fade with tears and souls
    Track each ugly one whose face is pretty
Load up! let any fast camel carry you
    For every parting for me today is desired
No mate for my heart in your howdahs
    Nor any value in it if I die with my passion
O you for whom I was dead in far court
    Crepe hangers' creams all pledged to be
How often I am killed and dead for you
    Then I give a shake as tomb and coffin go
Crowds saw my burial before they spoke
    Then they died before they dug the grave
Not all man desires can he achieve
    Winds blow where boats don't want to go
I see your neighbor saves not his honor
    Nor does the milk flow over your pastures
Boredom requites all those near you
    Each lover's gift from you is in hatred
Angry at those who receive your favor
    Till bother and blame are the end of it
Separation left what was between us
    A desert in which eye and ear deceived
A fast camel crawls after having raced
    And callouses ask earth about food pads
I accept clemency so long as generous
    But not forbearance when it is cowardly
I do not stay with wealth that demeans
    Nor do I enjoy that which fouls my honor

ثـمَّ اسـتَمَرَّ مريري وَارْعَـوَى الوَسَـنُ	سَهِرْتُ بَعدَ رَحيلي وَحشَـةً لَكُـمُ
فَإِنَّـني بِفِـراقٍ مِثْلِـهِ قَمِـنُ	وَإِنْ بُليتُ بـوُدٍّ مِثـلَ وُدِّكُـمُ
وَبُـدِّلَ العُـذْرُ بِالفُسـطاطِ وَالرَّسَـنُ	أَبْلـى الاجِلَّـةَ مُهْري عِنـدَ غَيرِكُـمُ
في جُـودِهِ مُضَـرُ الحَمـراءِ وَاليَمَـنُ	عِندَ الهُمامِ أَبي المِسكِ الذي غَرِقَتْ
فَمـا تَــأَخَّرَ آمـالي وَلا تَهِـنُ	وَإِنْ تَــأَخَّرَ عَنِّـي بَعـضُ مَوْعِـدِهِ
مَـوَدَّةٌ فَهْـوَ يَبْلوهَـا وَيَمْتَحِـنُ	هُـوَ الوَفِـيُّ وَلَكِنِّـي ذَكَـرْتُ لَـهُ

(٢٥٣)

«من الخفيف»

ومما قال بمصر ولم ينشدها الأسود ولم يذكره فيها:

وَعَنَّاهُـمْ مِـنْ شَـأْنِهِ مَـا عَنَانَـا	صَحِبَ النّـاسُ قَبلَنَـا ذَا الزَّمَانَـا
ـهِ وَإِنْ سَـرَّ بَعْضَهُـمْ أَحْيَانَـا	وَتَوَلَّـوْا بِغُصَّـةٍ كُلُّهُـمْ مِنْـ
ـهِ وَلَكِـنْ تُكَـدِّرُ الإِحْسَـانَا	رُبَّمَـا تُحسِـنُ الصَّنيـعَ لَيالِيـ
دَهْـرٍ حَتَّـى أَعَانَـهُ مَـنْ أَعَانَـا	وَكَأَنَّـا لَم يَـرْضَ فينَـا بِرَيْبِ الـ
رَكَّـبَ المَـرْءُ في القَنـاةِ سِنَانَـا	كُلَّمـا أَنْبَـتَ الزَّمَـانُ قَنَـاةً
تَتَعَـادَى فيـهِ وَأَنْ تَتَفَانَـى	وَمُـرادُ النُّفـوسِ أَصْغَـرُ مِـنْ أَنْ
كَالحَيَـاتِ وَلا يُلاقِـي الهَوَانَـا	غَيْـرَ أَنَّ الفَتَـى يُلاقِـي المَنايَـا
لَعَدَدْنَـا أَضَلَّنَـا الشُّجْعَانَـا	وَلَـوْ أَنَّ الحَيَـاةَ تَبْقَـى لِحَـيٍّ
فَمِـنَ العَجْـزِ أَنْ تَمـوتَ جَبَانَـا	وَإِذا لَم يَكُـنْ مِـنَ المَـوْتِ بُـدٌّ
ـفْسِ سَهْـلٌ فيهـا إذا هُـوَ كَانَـا	كُلُّ ما لَم يكُنْ مِنَ الصَّعبِ في الأَنْـ

I awaken after my journey lonely for you
    Then my rope holds firm, my sleep yields
If I suffered from a love like your love
    I would be ready for a parting like that
I wore out my foal's cloth among others
    Cheekstrap and halter changed at Fustat
With hero Abu Musk in whose bounty
    Mudar the golden and Yaman are drowned
If some of his promises are slow
    My hopes are not, nor are they weak
He's my faithful one, I only remind him
    Of love, but he is testing and proving it

253
Among those which he spoke in Egypt and did not recite to the black and did not mention him in them.
(Nimble na)

Men before us submitted to the times
    Worried about great things as we worry
All of them turned away choking on it
    Even if some of them were happy at times
Often the nights accomplish good deeds
    Then one finds their beauties are turbid
As if one is not content with doubts of
    Destiny, so he attacks one it torments
Each time fate makes the shafts grow
    Men fit the lances with their spearheads
No young man should meet this death
    In a gloomy fashion nor meet it basely
If life were preserved only for living
    We'd count our brave men as most lost
If there were no necessity in death
    It would be only weakness to be coward
All that is difficult before it occurs
    Is easy for the soul whenever it befalls

(٢٥٤)

«من الطويل»

يذكر قيام شبيب العقيلي على الأستاذ كافور وقتله بدمشق سنة ثمان وأربعين وثلاث مئة (٩٥٩م):

وَلَوْ كَانَ مِنْ أعدائِكَ القَمَرانِ	عَدُوُّكَ مَذمومٌ بكُلِّ لِسانِ
كَلامُ العِدَى ضَرْبٌ مِنَ الهَذَيانِ	وللهِ سِرٌّ في عُلاكَ وإنّما
قِيامَ دَليلٍ أو وُضوحَ بَيانِ	أتَلتَمِسُ الأعداءُ بَعدَ الَّذي رَأتْ
بغَدْرِ حَياةٍ أو بغَدْرِ زَمانِ	رَأتْ كلَّ مَنْ يَنوى لكَ الغَدرَ يُبتَلى
وكانا على العِلّاتِ يَصطَحِبانِ	برَغْمِ شَبيبٍ فارقَ السَّيفُ كَفَّهُ
رَفيقُكَ قَيسِيٌّ وأنْتَ يَمانِ	كأنَّ رِقابَ النّاسِ قالَتْ لسَيفِهِ
فإنَّ المَنايا غَايَةَ الحَيَوانِ	فإنْ يَكُ إنساناً مَضَى لسَبيلِهِ
تُثيرُ غُباراً في مكانِ دُخانِ	وَمَا كانَ إلّا النّارَ في كُلِّ مَوْضِعٍ
ومَوْتاً يُشَهّي المَوتَ كلَّ جَبانِ	فَنالَ حَياةً يَشتَهيها عَدُوُّهُ
ولَم يَخشَ وَقعَ النَّجمِ والدَّبَرانِ	نَفَى وَقعَ أطرافِ الرِّماحِ برُمحِهِ
مُعارَ جَناحٍ مُحسِنِ الطَّيَرانِ	ولَم يَدرِ أنَّ المَوتَ فَوقَ شَواتِهِ
بأضْعَفِ قِرْنٍ في أذَلِّ مَكانِ	وقَد قَتَلَ الأقرانَ حتى قَتَلَتْهُ
على كلِّ سَمْعٍ حَوْلَهُ وعِيانِ	أتَتْهُ المَنايا في طَريقٍ خَفِيَّةٍ
بطُولِ يَمينٍ واتِّساعِ جَنانِ	ولَوْ سَلَكَتْ طُرقَ السِّلاحِ لرَدَّها
على ثِقَةٍ مِنْ دَهرِهِ وأمانِ	تَقَصَّدَهُ المِقدارُ بَينَ صِحابِهِ
على غَيرِ مَنصُورٍ وغَيرِ مُعانِ	وهَل يَنفَعُ الجَيشُ الكَثيرُ التِفافُهُ
ولَم يَدِهِ بالجامِلِ العَكَنانِ	ودَى ما جَنى قَبلَ المَبيتِ بنَفسِهِ
وتَمسِكَ في كُفرانِهِ بعِنانِ	أتُمسِكُ ما أوْلَيْتَهُ يَدُ عاقِلٍ
ويَركَبُ للعِصْيانِ ظَهرَ حِصانِ	ويَركَبُ ما أركَبتَهُ مِنْ كَرامَةٍ
وقَد قَبَضَتْ كانَتْ بغَيرِ بَنانِ	تُنى يَدَهُ الإحسانُ حتى كأنَّها
شَبيبٌ وأوْفَى مَنْ تَرى أخوانِ	وعِندَ مَنِ اليَوْمَ الوَفاءُ لصاحِبٍ

254
He spoke recalling the rebellion of Shabib al-Uqaili in the year 348.
(Long nu)

Your enemy is blamed by every tongue
    Even if the sun and moon were your foes
God has the secret of your exaltation
    Words of the enemy are a kind of madness
Do foes seek after what they have seen
    Established proof or clear demonstration?
They saw all aiming to betray you tried
    By betrayal of life or betrayal of the times
Despite Shabib his hand lost its sword
    They were companions in all difficulties
As if necks of men said to his sword:
    Your friend must be Qais, you are Yamani!
So if he was a man he went his way
    For death is the goal of all living things
But he was only a fire in every place
    Stirring up the dust instead of the smoke
He had a life his enemies longed for
    A death to make every coward want it
He blocked spearpoints by his spear
    Feared not the star force of al Debaran
Didn't he see death above his topknot
    Coming on borrowed wing fine in flight;
He killed warriors till you killed him
    With weakest warrior in lowest place
Death came to him by a hidden path
    To every ear and eye roundabout him
Had it trod war's way he'd been safe
    By right arm's length or heart's depth
Fate aimed at him midst his friends
    Confident of destiny and secure in it
What use a huge army gathered
    Without any succor or divine help?
Before night he paid for his crime
    He did not give the herds of camels
Can rational hand take your gifts
    Hold the reins in such ingratitude?
Did he ride respect you gave him
    Ride a stallion's back to rebellion
Benefits double his hand till it seems
    In grabbing to have no more fingers
Where nowadays is loyalty to masters?
    Shabib and trust you see are brothers!

وَلَيسَ بِقاضٍ أَن يُرى لَكَ ثانِ	قَضى اللَهُ يا كافورُ أَنَّكَ أَوَّلٌ
عَنِ السَعدِ يُرمى دونَكَ الثَقَلانِ	فَما لَكَ تَختارُ القِسِيَّ وَإِنَّما
وَجَدُّكَ طَعّانٌ بِغَيرِ سِنانِ	وَما لَكَ تُعنى بِالأَسِنَّةِ وَالقَنا
وَأَنتَ غَنِيٌّ عَنهُ بِالحَدَثانِ	وَلَم تَحمِلِ السَيفَ الطَويلَ نِجادُهُ
فَإِنَّكَ ما أَحبَبتَ في أَتاني	أَرِد لي جَميلاً جُدتَ أَو لَم تَجُد بِهِ
لَعَوَّقَهُ شَيءٌ عَنِ الدَورانِ	لَوِ الفَلَكُ الدَوّارُ أَبغَضتَ سَعيَهُ

(٢٥٥)

«من الوافر»

نالت أبا الطيب بمصر حمى فقال يصفها ويعرض بالرحيل عن مصر وذلك في ذي الحجة سنة ثمان وأربعين وثلاث مئة (٩٥٩م):

وَوَقعُ فَعالِهِ فَوقَ الكَلامِ	مَلومُكُما يَجِلُّ عَنِ المَلامِ
وَوَجهي وَالهَجيرُ بِلا لِثامِ	ذَراني وَالفَلاةُ بِلا دَليلٍ
وَأَتعَبُ بِالإِناخَةِ وَالمُقامِ	فَإِنّي أَستَريحُ بِذي وَهَذا
وَكُلُّ بُغامِ رازِحَةٍ بُغامي	عُيونُ رَواحِلي إِن حِرتُ عَيني
سِوى عَدّي لَها بَرقَ الغَمامِ	فَقَد أَرِدُ المِياهَ بِغَيرِ هادٍ
إِذا احتاجَ الوَحيدُ إِلى الذِمامِ	يُذِمّ لِمُهجَتي رَبّي وَسَيفي
وَلَيسَ قِرى سِوى مُخِّ النَعامِ	وَلا أُمسي لِأَهلِ البُخلِ ضَيفاً
جُزِيتُ عَلى ابتِسامٍ بِابتِسامِ	وَلَمّا صارَ وُدُّ الناسِ خِبّاً
لِعِلمي أَنَّهُ بَعضُ الأَنامِ	وَصِرتُ أَشُكُّ فيمَن أَصطَفيهِ
وَحُبُّ الجاهِلينَ عَلى الوَسامِ	يُحِبُّ العاقِلونَ عَلى التَصافي
إِذا ما لَم أَجِدهُ مِنَ الكِرامِ	وَآنَفُ مِن أَخي لِأَبي وَأُمّي
عَلى الأَولادِ أَخلاقُ اللِئامِ	أَرى الأَجدادَ تَغلِبُها كَثيراً
بِأَن أُعزى إِلى جَدٍّ هُمامِ	وَلَستُ بِقانِعٍ مِن كُلِّ فَضلٍ

God judges, O Kafur, you are prince
    It's not decreed a second to you exists
Why do you choose the bow when one
    Shoots for you, men and, favorably
Why take care of spear and lance if
    Your joy is jousting without the lance?
Why does the belt bear a long sword
    Since you are freed from it by the event?
Wish me well if you give it or not
    Whatever you want for me comes to me
If you hate the turning sky's motion
    Something will hinder it from its rolling

255
He spoke
in Egypt
recalling a fever
that seized him
in Dhu'l Hijja of the year 348.
(Exuberant mi)

The blame of you two exceeds the fault
    The force it has is beyond words for that
Let me alone for desert has no guide
    And my face and the midday have no veil
I wish to find relief in this and that
    I am exhausted by stopping and staying
My mount's eyes are as my eyes in fever
    Every groan of the weary beast is my groan
I can reach water with no other guide
    Than my count of flashes from its cloud
My sword and my Lord protect my heart
    When the single person requires a guard
I say no good eve as guest of misers
    No hospitality but ostrich bone marrow
If men's friendship becomes betrayal
    I repay their smiles with others like them
I have my doubts about one I've chosen
    Due to my knowledge he's one of mankind
Intelligent people love by qualities
    Ignorant love is according to appearance
I reject a brother, my father mother's
    Son, if I find he is not of a noble nature
I see that parents are often overcome
    By the evil nature in their own children
I am not satisfied with any virtues
    That are traced to illustrious ancestors

وَيَنْبُو نَبْوَةَ القَضِمِ الكَهامِ	عَجِبْتُ لِمَنْ لَهُ قَدٌّ وَحَدٌّ
فَلا يَذَرُ المَطِيَّ بِلا سَنامِ	وَمَنْ يَجِدُ الطَّريقَ إلى المَعالي
كَنَقْصِ القادِرينَ عَلى التَّمامِ	وَلم أرَ في عُيوبِ النّاسِ شَيْئاً
تَخُبُّ بِيَ الرِّكابُ وَلا أمامي	أقَمْتُ بِأَرْضِ مِصرَ فَلا وَرائي
يَمَلُّ لِقاءَضِهِ في كُلِّ عامِ	وَمَلَّنِيَ الفِراشُ وَكانَ حِضْني
كَثيرٌ حاسِدي صَعْبٌ مَرامي	قَليلٌ عائِدي سَقِمٌ فُؤادي
شَديدُ السُّكْرِ مِنْ غَيرِ المُدامِ	عَليلُ الجِسْمِ مُمْتَنِعُ القِيامِ
فَلَيسَ تَزورُ إلّا في الظَّلامِ	وَزائِرَتي كَأَنَّ بِها حَياءً
فَعافَتْها وَباتَتْ في عِظامي	بَذَلْتُ لَها المَطارِفَ وَالحَشايا
فَتوسِعُهُ بِأَنواعِ السَّقامِ	يَضيقُ الجِلدُ عَنْ نَفْسي وَعَنها
كَأنّا عاكِفانِ عَلى حَرامِ	إذا ما فارَقَتْني غَسَّلَتْني
مَدامِعُها بِأَرْبَعَةٍ سِجامِ	كَأَنَّ الصُّبحَ يَطْرُدُها فَتَجري
مُراقَبَةَ المَشوقِ المُسْتَهامِ	أَراقِبُ وَقْتَها مِنْ غَيرِ شَوْقٍ
إذا ألْقاكَ في الكُرَبِ العِظامِ	وَيَصْدُقُ وَعْدُها وَالصِّدْقُ شَرٌّ
فَكَيفَ وَصَلْتِ أَنتِ مِنَ الزِّحامِ	أبِنْتَ الدَّهرِ عِندي كُلُّ بِنتٍ
مَكانٌ لِلسُّيوفِ وَلا السِّهامِ	جَرَحْتِ مُجَرَّحاً لم يَبقَ فيهِ
تَصَرَّفَ في عِنانٍ أَو زِمامِ	أَلا يا لَيتَ شِعرَ يَدي أَتُمسي
مُحَلّاةِ المَقاوِدِ بِاللِّغامِ	وَهَلْ أَرْمي هَوايَ بِراقِصاتٍ
بِسَيرٍ أَوْ قَناةٍ أَوْ حُسامِ	فَرُبَّتَما شَفَيْتُ غَليلَ صَدْري
خَلاصِ حَميرٍ مِنْ نَسْجِ الفِدامِ	وَضاقَتْ خُطَّةٌ فَخَلَصْتُ مِنها
وَضَوَّعْتُ البِلادَ بِلا سَلامِ	وَفارَقْتُ الحَبيبَ بِلا وَداعِ
وَدائُكَ في شَرابِكَ وَالطَّعامِ	يَقولُ لِيَ الطَّبيبُ أَكَلتَ شَيْئاً
أَضَرَّ بِجِسمِهِ طولُ الجَمامِ	وَما في طِبِّهِ أَنّي جَوادٌ
وَيَدْخُلُ مِنْ قَتامٍ في قَتامِ	تَعَوَّدَ أَنْ يُغَبِّرَ في السَّرايا
وَلا هُوَ في العَليقِ وَلا اللِّحامِ	فَأَمْسِكَ لا يُطالُ لَهُ فَيَرْعى
وَإنْ أَحُمَّ فَما حُمَّ اعتِزامي	فَإنْ أَمْرَضْ فَما مَرِضَ اصطِباري

I'm surprised at one with power, edge
    Glancing off a blunt, dull sword's blow
One who finds the way to heights but
    Wears down no camel till it has no hump
I saw nothing so blamable among men
    As defection of the able from perfection
I settled in Egypt's land, and back nor
    Forward has the camel moved with me
The bed disgusts me, though my side
    Incline to meet it only once in the year
Few are my visitors, sick is my heart
    Many the jealous and difficult my goal
My body is ailing, rising forbidden
    Violent the giddiness without any wine
She who comes to me seems ashamed
    She does not visit except in the darkness
I lavished on her a gown and a bed
    She declined them and slept in my bones
Skin too tight for my breath and her
    So she stretched it in the way of ills
When she left me she washed me for
    We two were addicted to a sacred ritual
As if dawn drove her off so her tears
    Ran from all the four corners in showers
I waited for her moment without love
    An expectation of a passionate yearning
Her promise true but an evil truth
    When it hits in the agony of the bone
O time's daughter, for me each maid
    How could you alone get past a crowd?
You wounded me with such wounds
    There is no place for swords or arrows
O will my hand ever know the touch
    That manages the reins or the tether?
Shall I attain my object on a trotter
    Whose bridle is silvered with a sweat;
Maybe I'll heal my chest's boiling
    With a journey or a lance or the sword
The way is blocked, I want to be free
    With wine's freedom from sieve's web
If I left this lover without a goodbye
    I'd part from this land without farewell
A doctor says to me: You ate a thing
    Your illness is in eating and drinking
It's not in his skill, I'm thoroughbred
    The long stay in stable injures my body
He's used to getting dirty in a sortie
    Rushing from dust cloud to dust cloud
He's restrained, not loose to graze
    He's not in barley nor is he bridled if
I am sick my courage is not sick
    If I am fevered yet my will is not ill

وَإِنْ أَسْلَمْ فَمَا أَبْقَى وَلَكِنْ … سَلِمْتُ مِنَ الحِمَامِ إِلى الحِمَامِ
تَمَتَّعْ مِنْ سُهَادٍ أَوْ رُقَادٍ … وَلا تَأْمُلْ كَرًى تَحْتَ الرِّجَامِ
فَإِنَّ لِثَالِثِ الحَالَيْنِ مَعْنًى … سِوَى مَعْسَى انْتِبَاهِكَ وَالمَنَامِ

(٢٥٦)

«من الطويل»

يمدحه وأنشده إياها في شوال سنة تسع وأربعين وثلاث مئة (٩٦٠م) وهي آخر ما أنشده و لم يلقه بعدها:

مَنَّى كُنَّ لِي أَنَّ البَيَاضَ خِضَابُ … فَيَخْفَى بِتَبْيِيضِ القُرُونِ شَبَابُ
لَيَالِيَ عِنْدَ البِيضِ فَوْدَايَ فِتْنَةٌ … وَفَخْرٌ وَذَاكَ الفَخْرُ عِنْدِيَ عَابُ
فَكَيْفَ اذُمُّ اليَوْمَ مَا كُنْتُ أَشْتَهِي … وَأَدْعُو بِمَا أَشْكُوهُ حِينَ أَجَابَ
جَلَا اللَّوْنُ عَنْ لَوْنِ هُدًى كُلَّ مَسْلَكٍ … كَمَا انْجَابَ عَنْ ضَوْءِ النَّهَارِ ضَبَابُ
وَفِي الجِسْمِ نَفْسٌ لَا تَشِيبُ بِشَيْبِهِ … وَلَوْ أَنَّ مَا فِي الوَجْهِ مِنْهُ حِرَابُ
لَهَا ظُفُرٌ إِنْ كَلَّ ظُفْرٌ أَعَدَّهُ … وَنَابٌ إِذَا لَمْ يَبْقَ فِي الفَمِ نَابُ
يُغَيِّرُ مِنِّي الدَّهْرُ مَا شَاءَ غَيْرَهَا … وَأَبْلُغُ أَقْصَى العُمْرِ وَهْيَ كَعَابُ
وَإِنِّي لَنَجْمٌ تَهْتَدِي صُحْبَتِي بِهِ … إِذَا حَالَ مِنْ دُونِ النُّجُومِ سَحَابُ
غَنِيٌّ عَنِ الأَوْطَانِ لَا يَسْتَخِفُّنِي … إِلَى بَلَدٍ سَافَرْتُ عَنْهُ إِيَابُ
وَعَنْ ذَمَلَانِ العِيسِ إِنْ سَامَحَتْ بِهِ … وَإِلَّا فَفِي أَكْوَارِهِنَّ عُقَابُ
وَأَصْدَى فَلَا أُبْدِي إِلَى المَاءِ حَاجَةً … وَلِلشَّمْسِ فَوْقَ اليَعْمَلَاتِ لُعَابُ
وَلِلسِّرَّ مِنِّي مَوْضِعٌ لَا يَنَالُهُ … نَدِيمٌ وَلَا يُفْضِي إِلَيْهِ شَرَابُ
وَلِلخَوْدِ مِنِّي سَاعَةٌ ثُمَّ بَيْنَنَا … فَلَاةٌ إِلَى غَيْرِ اللِّقَاءِ تُجَابُ
وَمَا العِشْقُ إِلَّا غِرَّةٌ وَطَمَاعَةٌ … يُعَرِّضُ قَلْبٌ نَفْسَهُ فَيُصَابُ
وَغَيْرُ فُؤَادِي لِلْغَوَانِي رَمِيَّةٌ … وَغَيْرُ بَنَانِي لِلزُّجَاجِ رِكَابُ
تَرَكْنَا لِأَطْرَافِ القَنَا كُلَّ شَهْوَةٍ … فَلَيْسَ لَنَا إِلَّا بِهِنَّ لَعَابُ
نَصَرْفُهُ لِلطَّعْنِ فَوْقَ حَوَادِرٍ … قَدِ انْقَصَفَتْ فِيهِنَّ مِنْهُ كِعَابُ
أَعَزُّ مَكَانٍ فِي الدُّنَى سَرْجُ سَابِحٍ … وَخَيْرُ جَلِيسٍ فِي الزَّمَانِ كِتَابُ

If I surrender I will not stay but
    I am safe from one death in another
Enjoy the waking or the sleeping
    Do not hope for dozing in the tomb
For in the third state the meaning is
    Another meaning than waking or sleep

256
He spoke praising Kafur the Ikhshid and he recited it in Shawwal of the year 347. And he did not see him after that.
(Long bu)

Wishes once were mine that dye was white
    Thus youth was hidden by those gray locks
My nights with beauties, my curls a charm
    And an honor but my boast now is a fault
How can I blame today what I wanted
    Or pray for what I'd deprecate if granted?
One color succeeds another, guided
    Like a mist that rised at the beams of day
In body soul grows not gray by its fading
    Even if what was on its face showed bravely
She has claws if I pull back every claw
    And fangs when no teeth remain in mouth
Destiny changes me as it wants, not he
    As I reach life's goal, but she is a maid
I have a star to guide my companions
    When the clouds shift beneath the stars
Homelands are unneeded, returns to
    Town don't provoke me once I go from it
As fast trotting camels when they go
    And if not, an eagle has their saddles
I'm thirsty but I have no need of water
    While the heat rays weave above a camel
Among my secrets is one a drinking pal
    Will not receive, nor will the wine get it
I had a pretty woman an hour, we parted
    The desert was crossed to another union
Love is nothing but perplexity, lust
    A heart opposed to itself, overwhelmed
My heart is not target for singing girls
    Nor my fingers mounts for wine glasses
We leave each passion for lance heads
    No playing at war for us except with them
We bear them to joust on heavy ones
    And by that their ferrules are split open
Best place in a world is a fast swimmer
    Best of sittings at times is with the book

عَلى كُلِّ بَحرٍ زَهرَةٌ وَعُبابُ	وَبَحرُ أَبي المِسكِ الخِضَمُّ الَّذي لَهُ
بِأَحسَنِ ما يُثنى عَلَيهِ يُعابُ	تَجاوَزَ قَدرَ المَدحِ حَتّى كَأَنَّهُ
كَما غالَبَت بيضُ السُّيوفِ رِقابُ	وَغالَبَهُ الأَعداءُ ثُمَّ عَنَوا لَهُ
إِذا لَم تَصُنَّ إِلّا الحَديدَ ثِيابُ	وَأَكثَرُ ما تَلقى أَبا المِسكِ بِذلَةٍ
رِماءٌ وَطَعنٌ وَالأَمامَ ضِرابُ	وَأَوسَعُ ما تَلقاهُ صَدراً وَخَلفَهُ
قَضاءُ مُلوكِ الأَرضِ مِنهُ غِضابُ	وَأَنفَذُ ما تَلقاهُ حُكماً إِذا قَضى
وَلَو لَم يَقُدها نائِلٌ وَعِقابُ	يَقودُ إِلَيهِ طاعَةَ النّاسِ فَضلُهُ
وَكَم أَسُدٍ أَرواحُهُنَّ كِلابُ	أَيا أَسَداً في جِسمِهِ روحُ ضَيغَمٍ
وَمِثلُكَ يُعطى حَقَّهُ وَيُهابُ	وَيا آخِذاً مِن دَهرِهِ حَقَّ نَفسِهِ
وَقَد قَلَّ إِعتابٌ وَطالَ عِتابُ	لَنا عِندَ هَذا الدَّهرِ حَقٌّ يَلُطُّهُ
وَتَنعَمِرُ الأَوقاتُ وَهِيَ يَبابُ	وَقَد تُحدِثُ الأَيّامُ عِندَكَ شيمَةً
كَأَنَّكَ سَيفٌ فيهِ وَهوَ قِرابُ	وَلا مُلكَ إِلّا أَنتَ وَالمُلكُ فَضلَةٌ
وَإِن كانَ قُرباً بِالبِعادِ يُشابُ	أَرى لي بِقُربي مِنكَ عَيناً قَريرَةً
وَدونَ الَّذي أَمَّلتُ مِنكَ حِجابُ	وَهَل نافِعي أَن تُرفَعَ الحُجبُ بَينَنا
وَأَسكَتُّ كَيما لا يَكونَ جَوابُ	أَقِلُّ سَلامي حُبَّ ما خَفَّ عَنكُمُ
سُكوتي بَيانٌ عِندَها وَخِطابُ	وَفي النَّفسِ حاجاتٌ وَفيكَ فَطانَةٌ
ضَعيفُ هَوىً يُبغى عَلَيهِ ثَوابُ	وَما أَنا بِالباغي عَلى الحُبِّ رِشوَةً
عَلى أَنَّ رَأيي في هَواكَ صَوابُ	وَما شِئتُ إِلّا أَن أَدُلَّ عَواذِلي
وَغَرَّبتُ أَنّي قَد ظَفِرتُ وَخابوا	وَأَعلِمَ قَوماً خالَفوني فَشَرَّقوا
وَأَنَّكَ لَيثٌ وَالمُلوكُ ذِئابُ	جَرى الخُلفُ إِلّا فيكَ أَنَّكَ واحِدٌ
ذِئاباً وَلَم يُخطِىء فَقالَ ذُبابُ	وَأَنَّكَ إِن قَوَّيسَت صَحَّفَ قارِىءٌ
وَمَدحُكَ حَقٌّ لَيسَ فيهِ كِذابُ	وَإِنَّ مَديحَ النّاسِ حَقٌّ وَباطِلٌ
وَكُلُّ الَّذي فَوقَ التُّرابِ تُرابُ	إِذا نِلتُ مِنكَ الوُدَّ فَالمالُ هَيِّنٌ
لَهُ كُلَّ يَومٍ بَلدَةٌ وَصِحابُ	وَما كُنتُ لَو لا أَنتَ إِلّا مُهاجِراً
فَما عَنكَ لي إِلّا إِلَيكَ ذَهابُ	وَلَكِنَّكَ الدُّنيا إِلَيَّ حَبيبَةٌ

A sea full of water is Abu Musk who has
    Above all seas rising tides that overflow
It exceeds the power of praise until
    The best one can honor him with blame
A foe contends with him and submits
    As a neck contends with a sword's sheen
Most don't see Abu Musk in men's dress
    Clothing is no guard unless it be of iron
Broad chest to those who meet him with
    Archers and spearmen, and in front a foe
Keen in judgment on those who face him
    He judges a case as earth's kings enrage
His virtues lead. men submitting to him
    And if not, then his gifts and fines do so
Lion whose body has a fierce soul
    How many lions have the souls of dogs?
He takes from the times his soul's due
    Such as you are given by right and feared
For us it is right he disown this age
    For content is small and blame is long
The days adopted a new habit for you
    Times flourish though they were a waste
No king but you, kingship is external
    You are the sword and that the scabbard
I know I by being near you calm my eye
    Even if nearness mingles with distance
What use a curtain between us is up
    If before what I hoped from you is a veil
My greeting small shows easy love
    I stay silent, there need be no response
In me are wants, in you is sagacity
    My silence is plain and holds a prayer
I want no bribe for love's sake
    It's weak love to want love as reward
I ask nothing but to humble my foes
    So my idea may be true to your kindness
I know people oppose me in the east
    I went west, I conquered and they lost
Discord came except with you alone
    You are the lion, other kings are wolves
If you check meter as reader misreads
    Wolves, he'd not mistake if he said flies
The praise of men is both true and vain
    Your praise is true no falsehood in that
If I have your love wealth is no use
    And all that is above earth is but dust
I 'm nothing but a pilgrim, but for you
    Each day a new land, comrades for him
Through you the world is a beloved
    No parting for me from you but a return

(٢٥٧)

«من البسيط»

يهجوه أيضاً:

أيـنَ المَحاجِمُ بـا كـافورُ والجَلَـمُ	مـن آيَـةِ الطُّـرْقِ يـأتي مثلَـكَ الكَـرَمُ
فعُرِّفـوا بِـكَ أنَّ الكَلْـبَ فوْقَهُـمُ	جـازَ الألى ملَكَـتْ كَفّـاكَ قَدْرَهُـمُ
تَقـودُهُ أمَـةٌ لَيْسَـتْ لَهـا رَحِـمُ	لا شَـيءَ أقْبَـحُ مِـنْ فَحْـلٍ لَـهُ ذَكَـرُ
وسـادةُ المُسلِمـينَ الأعْبُـدُ القُـزُمُ	سـاداتُ كـلِّ أُنـاسٍ مِـنْ نُفوسِـهِمِ
يـا أُمَّـةً ضَحِكَـتْ مِـن جَهلِها الأُمَـمُ	أغايَـةَ الدِّيـنِ أنْ تُحفُـوا شَواربَكُـمْ
كَيمـا تـزولَ شكـوكُ النّـاسِ والتُّهَـمُ	ألا فتًـى يـوردُ الهِنـدِيَّ هامَتَـهُ
مِـنْ دِينِـهِ الدَّهـرِ والتَّعطيـلِ والقِـدَمِ	فإنَّـهُ حُجَّـةٌ يُـؤذي القُلُـوبَ بهـا
ولا يُصَـدِّقَ قَومـاً في الذي زَعَمـوا	مـا أقـدَرَ اللهَ أنْ يُخْـزي خَليقَتَـهُ

(٢٥٨)

«من الوافر»

وقال يهجوه أيضاً:

تَـزولُ بِـهِ عـنِ القلْـبِ الْهُمـومُ	أمَـا في هَـذِهِ الدُّنْيـا كَريـمٌ
يُسَـرَّ بأهلِـهِ الجـارِ المُقيـمُ	أمَـا في هَـذِهِ الدُّنيـا مَكـانٌ
عَلَينـا والمَـوالي والصَّميـمُ	تَشـابَهَتِ البَهائِـمُ والعبِـدَّى
أصـابَ النّـاسَ أمْ داءٌ قديـمُ	ومـا أدري أذا داءٌ حديـثٌ
كأنَّ الحُـرَّ بَينَهُـمُ يَتيـمُ	حَصَلـتُ بأرْضِ مِصـرَ عـلى عَبيـدِ
غُـرابٌ حَولَـهُ رَخَـمٌ وَبُـومُ	كأنَّ الأسـوَدَ اللابـيَّ فيهِـمْ
مَقـالي لِلأُحَيْمِـقِ يـا حَليـمُ	أخِـذْتُ بِمَدْحِـهِ فَرأيْـتُ لَهْـواً
مَقـالي لابـنِ آوى يـا لَئيـمُ	ولَمّـا أنْ هَجَـوْتُ رأيْـتُ عِيّـاً
فَمَدْفـوعٌ إلى السَّقَـمِ السَّقيـمُ	فَهَـلْ مِـنْ عـاذِرٍ في ذا وَفي ذا
ولَـم أُلِـمِ المُسـيءَ فَمَـنْ ألُـومُ	إذا أتَـتِ الإساءَةُ مِـنْ وَضيـعٍ

257
He spoke mocking Kafur.
(Outspread mu)

By what paths could nobility come to you
  Where is the leech cup and knife O Kafur?
Those your hand owns betrayed rank
  As they found in you a dog was above them
None more ugly than stallion with a cock
  Having a slave to lead him without a cunt!
Rulers of people come from themselves
  But the ruler of Muslims is the basest slave
Is religion's aim to shave your mustache
  O you people whose ignorance nations mock?
Will no man wet a blade with his head
  To end complaints and suspicions of folk?
He proves evil in hearts, those whose
  Religion is fate and delay and favoritism
How great is God to shame his creation
  And not to support people who think thus!

258
He spoke also mocking him
(Exuberant mu)

Is there in this world no nobility
  Has compassion ceased from hearts?
Is there in this world no place for
  Settled neighbor to enjoy his family?
Beasts and servants of God are
  To us as freed and those of lineage
I know not if it is a new sickness
  That plagues men or an old disease
I came among slaves in Egypt
  The free among them seem orphans
As if the Black blacks there were
  Crows, around them vultures or owls
I hated to praise him, I saw my words
  Delighted fools O as well as the wise!
When I mocked I saw the weakness
  Of my terms to a jackal, O the vile one!
What excuse for this and for that
  The sick man can't avoid his illness
When the evil comes from vileness
  And I hurt no victim, whom do I blame?

(٢٥٩)

«من السريع»

وقال فيه:

ضَيْفاً لأَوْسَعْناهُ إحْسَانا	لَوْ كانَ ذا الآكِلُ أَزْوادَنا
يُوسِعُنا زُوراً وَبُهْتَانا	لكِنَّنا في العَينِ أضْيافُهُ
أَعَانَهُ اللهُ وَإيّانا	فَلَيْتَهُ خَلَّى لَنا طُرُقَنا

(٢٦٠)

«من الوافر»

استأذنه في الخروج إلى الرمة ليقضي مالاً كتب له به وإنما أراد أن يعرف ما عند الأسود فمنعه وحلف عليه أن لا يخرج وقال: نحن نوجه من يقضيه لك فقال في ذلك:

إلى بَلَدٍ أُحاوِلُ فيهِ مَالا	أتَحْلِفُ لا تُكَلِّفُني مَسِيراً
وَأَبْعَدَ شُقَّةً وَأَشَدَّ حَالا	وَأَنْتَ مُكَلِّفي أنْبَى مَكَاناً
فَلَقَّنيَ الفَوارِسَ وَالرِّجَالا	إذا سِرْنا عَنِ الفُسْطَاطِ يَوْماً
وَأنَّكَ رُمْتَ مِنْ ضَيْمي مُحَالا	لتَعْلَمَ قَدْرَ مَنْ فَارَقْتَ مِنّي

(٢٦١)

«من البسيط»

وقال عند خروجه من مصر:

بِمَا مَضَى أمْ لأمْرٍ فيكَ تَجْديدُ	عيدٌ بأيَّةِ حالٍ عُدتَ يا عيدُ
فَلَيْتَ دونَكَ بيداً دونَها بيدُ	أمَا الأحِبَّةُ فَالبَيْداءُ دونَهُمْ
وَجْنَاءُ حَرْفٌ وَلا جَرْداءُ قَيْدودُ	لوْ لا العُلَى لَمْ تَجُبْ بي ما أجوبُ بها
أشْباهُ رَوْنَقِهِ الغِيدُ الأماليدُ	وَكَانَ أطْيَبَ مِنْ سَيفي مُعَانَقَةً
شَيْئاً تَتَيَّمُهُ عَيْنٌ ولا جيدُ	لمْ يَتْرُكِ الدَّهْرُ مِنْ قلبي ولا كبدي

259
He looked at the black
one day and spoke.
(Swift na)

If this food was our provision for
    The guess we'd take it courteously
But we are his guests and obviously
    He spreads only lies and falsehoods
Would he'd leave our way free
    To us, may God help him and us!

260
Abu Tayyib wrote to him about a trip
to Ramia to take care of some property
of his there, however he knew want
the black would say about a journey.
He replied No by God,
we do not allow the trip
but we will send someone to take of it for you
(Exuberant la)

Have you sworn not to permit me to go
    To the country to take care of my things
You allowed me this unlucky place
    In utmost exile and in worst condition
Someday when we travel from Fustat
    As one pursues me with horses and men
You'll know the value you lost in me
    And that you aimed at my hurt in vain

261
He spoke on the day
of Arafat and departed
from Egypt in the year 350.
(Outspread du)

Feast in what state do you return O feast
    With what past and what new things to come
My dear ones, desert between them and me
    O for desert before you as that before them
But for eminence no strong camel nor
    Lean horse would cross what I have crossed
Sweeter than my sword as bedmate is
    The slender girl like it in her brightness
Time left not for my heart or my liver
    Anything that eye or neck could enslave

أَمْ في كُووسِكُما هَمٌّ وَتَسهيدُ؟	يا سَاقِيَيَّ أَحسِرَّ في كُووسِكُما
هَذِي المُدامُ وَلا هَذي الأَغاريدُ	أَصَخرَةٌ أَناءَ مالي لا تُحَرَّكُني
وَجَدُّتْهَا وَحَبيبُ النَّفسِ مَفقُودُ	إذا أَرَدْتُ كَمَيتَ اللَّونِ صافِيَةً
أَنّي لَما أَنا شاكٍ مِنْهُ مَحْسُودُ	ماذا لَقيتُ مِنَ الدُّنْيا وَأَعْجَبُهُ
أَنا الغَنِيُّ وَأَمْوالي المَواعيدُ	أَمْسَيتُ أَرْوَحَ مُثْرٍ خازنًا وَيَداً
عَنِ القِرَى وَعَنِ التَّرحالِ مَحدُودُ	إِنّي نَزَلْتُ بِكَذّابينَ، ضَيفُهُمْ
مِنَ اللِّسانِ، فَلا كانوا وَلا الجُودُ	جُودُ الرِّجالِ مِنَ الأَيدي وَجُودُهُمْ
إلّا وَفي يَدِهِ مِنْ نَتْنِها عُودُ	ما يَقبِضُ المَوتُ نَفساً مِنْ نفوسِهِم
لا فِي الرِّحالِ وَلا النِّسْوانِ مَعْدُودُ	مِنْ كُلِّ رِخوِ وِكاءِ البَطنِ مُنْفَتِقِ
أَوْ خانَهُ فَلَهُ في مِصرَ تَمْهيدُ	أَكُلَّما اغتالَ عَبدُ السَّوءِ سَيِّدَةً
فالحُرُّ مُسْتَعْبَدٌ والعَبْدُ مَعْبُودُ	صارَ الخَصِيُّ إمامَ الآبِقينَ بِها
فَقَدْ بَشِمْنَ وَما تَفنى العَناقيدُ	نامَتْ نَواطِيرُ مِصرٍ عَنْ ثَعالِبِها
لَوْ أَنَّهُ في ثِيابِ الحُرِّ مَولُودُ	العَبْدُ لَيسَ لِحُرٍّ صالِحٍ بِأَخٍ
إنَّ العَبيدَ لأَنجاسٌ مَناكيدُ	لا تَشتَرِ العَبدَ إلّا والعَصا مَعَهُ
يُسيءُ بي فيهِ عَبْدٌ وَهْوَ مَحْمُودُ	ما كُنْتُ أَحسِبُني أَحيا إلى زَمَنٍ
وَأَنَّ مِثلَ أَبي البَيْضاءِ مَوْجُودُ	وَلا تَوَهَّمتُ أَنَّ النّاسَ قَدْ فُقِدُوا
تُطيعُهُ ذِي العَضاريطُ الرَّعاديدُ	وَأَنَّ ذا الأَسْوَدَ المَثقُوبَ مِشفَرُهُ
لِكَيْ يُقالَ عَظيمُ القَدرِ مَقْصُودُ	جَوْعانُ يَأْكُلُ مِنْ زادي وَيُمسِكُني
لِمُسْتَضامٍ سَخينِ العَينِ مَفْقُودُ	إنَّ أُمراً أَمَةٌ حُبلى تُدَبِّرُهُ
لِمِثْلِها خُلِقَ المَهرِيَّةُ القُودُ	وَيُلْمِهَا خُطَّةً وَيُلِمُّ قابِلُها
إنَّ المَنِيَّةَ عِندَ الذُّلِّ قِنديدُ	وَعِندَها لَذَّ طَعْمَ المَوتِ شارِبُهُ
أَقَومُهُ البيضُ أَمْ آباؤُهُ الصِّيدُ	مَنْ عَلَّمَ الأَسْوَدَ المَخصِيَّ مَكرُمَةً
أَمْ قَدرُهُ وَهْوَ بالفَلسَينِ مَرْدُودُ	أَمْ أُذنُهُ في يَدِ النَّخاسِ دامِيَةً
في كُلِّ لُؤمٍ، وَبَعْضُ العُذْرِ تَفنيدُ	أَوْلى اللِّئامِ كُمَيفيرٌ بِمَعْذِرَةٍ
عَنِ الجَميلِ فَكَيفَ الخِصيَةُ السُّودُ؟	وَذاكَ أَنَّ الفُحُولَ البيضَ عاجِزَةٌ

O my two saqis do your cups have wine
    Or is care and wakefulness in your cups?
Am I rock? what's wrong that the wine
    Does not rouse me nor yet this singing?
When I wanted the pure red wine I
    Found it by my soul's darling was gone
What have I found in the world? I am
    Surprised that what I wept for was envied
I am easy in riches in store and cash
    I am wealthy but my property is promises
I settled with liars as their guest
    Was forbid hospitality and departure
Bounty is men's hands, but the gift
    Tongues, and they and their gift failed
Death takes no single soul of them
    Unless its hand has a stick for the stink
With each fart the belly band breaks
    Not counted among the men or women
Each time a slave murders his lord
    Or betrays his training was in Egypt
A eunuch leader of runaway slaves
    The free man enslaved, slave obeyed
Egypt's overseers sleep while foxes
    Eat too much, still grapes aren't gone
Slave is no brother to the free men
    Even if born in noblemen's clothes
Buy no slave unless with a stick
    For slaves are a filthy rebellious lot
I never thought I'd live to a time
    A dog would do me dirt and praised
Nor think that men would be lost
    Or the likes of Abu Baida be found
Or a pierced black with camel lips
    Have trembling sycophants obey him
Hungry, he eats my food, detains me
    So he be named: Great Power, Sought!
A pregnant slave girl guides him
    Oppressed by bleary eyes, weak heart
Alas her mistake, alas her midwife!
    For her likes Mahari camels were made
For her drinkers enjoy death's taste
    Death for one humiliated is sweetest
Who taught a black eunuch giving
    His white folks or his runaway fathers?
His ears bloody in a slaver's hand
    His value rejected at two farthings?
Little Kafur first in vile excuses
    In every fault excuses are to blame
If the while stallions are feeble
    Effeminate, what about black eunuchs?

(٢٦٢)

«من الطويل»

كتب إلى عبد العزيز بن يوسف الخزاعي في بلبيس يطلب منه دليلا فأنفذه إليه فقال يمدحه:

جَزَى عَرَباً أَمْسَتْ بِبُلْبَيْسَ رَبَّها	بِمَسْعَاتِهَا تَقْرَرُ بِذاكَ عُيُونُها
كَرَاكِرَ مِـنْ قَيْسِ بْنِ عَيْلَانَ ساهِراً	جُفُونُ ظُبَاها لِلْعُلَى وَجُفُونُها
وَخَصَّ بِـهِ عَبْـدَ العَزيزِ بْـنَ يُوسُفٍ	فَمَا هُـوَ إلَّا غَيْثُهَـا وَمَعِينُـها
فَتَى زَانَ في عَيْنَيَّ أقْصَى قَبِيلِـهِ	وَكَـمْ سَيِّدٍ في حِلّـةٍ لا يَزِينُها

(٢٦٣)

«من الوافر»

نزل أبو الطيب في أرض حسمى برجل يقال له وردان ابن ربيعة الطائي فاستغوى وردان عبيد أبي الطيب فجعلوا يسرقون له من أمتعته، فلما شعر أبو الطيب بذاك ضرب أحد عبيده بالسيف فأصاب وجهه وأمر الغلمان فأجهزوا عليه وقال يهجو وردان:

لَئِنْ تَكُ طَيِّءٌ كَانَتْ لِئَامـاً	فَألأمُهَـا رَبيعَـةُ أَوْ بَنُــوهُ
وَإِنْ تَكُ طَيِّءٌ كَانَتْ كِراماً	فَـوَرْدانُ لِغَيْرِهِمْ أَبُــوهُ
مَرَرْنَـا مِنْـهُ في حِسْـمَى بِعَبْـدٍ	يَمُجُّ اللَّـؤمَ مَنْخِـرُهُ وَفُـوهُ
أَشَدَّ بِعُرْسِـهِ عَنِّـي عَبيـدي	فَأتْلَفَهُـمْ وَمَـالي أَتْلَفُـوه
فَإِنْ شَقيتُ بِأيدِيهِمْ جِيَادي	لقَدْ شَقِيَتْ بِمُنصُلِيَ الوُجُـوهُ

262
He spoke in Egypt and wrote to Abd al Aziz ibn Yusuf al-Khuzai.
(Long ye)

May their lord repay Arabs at Balbais
    For their kindness may their eyes be cool
Folk of Qais ibn 'Ailan are alert
    Their eyelids and sword sheaths are lofty
Especially Ibn al-Aziz ibn Yusuf
    For he is their rain shower and stream
A man in my eyes adorns a tribe afar
    As many a chief in the land fails to adorn

263
He spoke mocking Wardan ibn Rabi'a of the Tai with whom he stayed on his way from Egypt
(Exuberant hu)

If you are of Tai they are blameworthy
    And their forebears Rabia and his sons
Or if you are of Tai they were noble
    But Wardan's father is not one of theirs
At Hisma we passed one of his slaves
    He dripped filth from his nose and mouth
He seduced my slaves with his woman
    He destroyed them and they destroyed him
If my horse was unhappy with their hands
    His face must now be unhappy with my sword

(٢٦٤)

لَـهُ كَسْبُ خِنزيرٍ وخُرطُومُ ثَعْلَبِ	لَحَا اللهُ وَرْدانًا وأمَّا أَتَتْ بِهِ
عَلَى أنَّهُ فيهِ مِنَ اللُّؤْمِ وَالْأَبِ	فَمَا كَانَ فيهِ الْغَدْرُ إلّا دَلالَةً
فَيَا لُؤْمَ إنْسَانٍ وَيَا لُؤْمَ مَكْسَبِ	إذا كَسَبَ الإنْسَانُ مِنْ هَنِ عِرْسِهِ
هُمَا الطَّالِبَانِ الرِّزْقَ مِنْ شَرِّ مَطْلَبِ	أَهَذا اللّذَيَّا بِنْتُ وَرْدَانَ بِنْتُهُ
فَلَا تَعْذِلَانِي رُبَّ صِدْقٍ مُكَذَّبِ	لَقَدْ كُنْتُ أَنْفِي الْغَدْرَ عَنْ تُوسِ طَيِّءٍ

(٢٦٥)

«من المنسرح»

وقال في العبد الذي قتله:

أَجْدَعُ مِنْهُمْ بِهِنَّ آنَافَا	أَعْدَدْتُ لِلْغَادِرِينَ أَسْيَافَا
أَطَرْنَ عَنْ هَامِهِنَّ أَقْحَافَا	لا يَرْحَمُ اللهُ أَرْؤُسًا لَهُمْ
وَأنْ تَكُونَ المِئُونَ آلافَا	ما يَنْقِمُ السَّيفُ غَيْرَ قِلَّتِهِمْ
وَزَارَ للخَامِعَاتِ أَجْوَافَا	يا شَرَّ لَحْمٍ فَجَعْتُهُ بِدَمٍ
مَنْ زَجَرَ الطَّيْرَ لِي وَمَنْ عَافَا	قَدْ كُنْتَ أُغْنِيتَ عَنْ سُؤالِكَ بِي
وَخِفْتُ لَمَّا اعْتَرَضْتَ إخْلافَا	وَعُدْتُ ذا النَّصْلَ مَنْ تَعَرَّضَهُ
تَتْبَعُكَ المُقْلَتَانِ تَوْكَافَا	لا يُذْكَرُ الخَيْرُ إنْ ذُكِرْتَ وَلا
أَوْرَدْتُهُ الغَايَةَ الّتي خَافَا	إذا امْرُؤٌ رَاعَنِي بِغَدْرَتِهِ

(٢٦٦)

«من المتقارب»

لما بلغ أبو الطيب إلى بسيطة رأى بعض عبيده نورًا
فقال: هذه منارة الجامع، ورأى آخر نعامة فقال:
وهذه نخلة، فضحك أبو الطيب وقال:

تَرَكْتِ عُيُونَ عَبِيدي حَيَارَى	بُسَيْطَةُ مَهْلاً سُقِيتِ القِطَارَا
وَظَنُّوا الصِّوَارَ عَلَيْكِ المَنَارَا	فَظَنُّوا النَّعَامَ عَلَيْكِ النَّخِيلَ
وَقَدْ قَصَدَ الضَّحْكُ فيهمْ وَحَارَا	فَأَمْسَكَ صَحْبِي بِأَكْوَارِهِمْ

264
He spoke
also mocking him.
(Long bi)

May God curse Wardan and his broad
    His profit of a pig and the snout of a fox
His betrayal was only an indication
    Of what his mother and his father were
If a man profits from his wife's sex
    O he's worst of men O worst of profits!
O tiny pair, lady Wardan and daughter
    Earning their living in the worst of trades
I reject betrayal of the Tai truth
    Don't blame me, many a friend is belied

265
He spoke also
about the slave
who tried to steal
his horse and sword
(Flowing fa)

I count them betrayers of swords
    So I cut off their noses with these
May God not pity heads if they
    Send flying the tops of their skulls
A sword avenges not a few
    Would it were a hundred thousand
O worst flesh whose life I took
    And that went to the hyena's belly
You could have avoided doubts
    Taking omens of bird in auguries
I promised this blade what it met
    I was afraid of mutiny as you came
Goodness knows you not if named
    Nor do two eyes follow you weeping
If a man alarms me with betrayal
    I bring him to a goal that he fears

266
He said also.
(Tripping ra)

Busaita you make the rain fall slow
    You leave my servants' eyes confused
They think an ostrich near you a palm
    They thought the deer near you minarets
My friends hung on to their saddles
    Laughter got to them and was hard on them

(٢٦٧)

«من المتقارب»

قال عند وروده إلى الكوفة يصف منازل طريقه ويهجو كافورا في شهر ربيع الأول سنة إحدى وخمسين وثلاث مئة (٩٦٢م):

فِدَى كُلِّ ماشِيَةِ الْهَيْذَبَى	ألا كُلُّ ماشِيَةِ الْخَيْزَلَى
خَنوفٍ وَمَا بِي حُسْنُ الْمِشَى	وكُلُّ نَجَاةٍ بُجَاوِيَّةٍ
وكَيدُ العُداةِ وَمَيْطُ الأذَى	ولَكِنَّهُنَّ حِبَالُ الحَيَاةِ
رِ إِمَّا لهذا وإمَّا لِذَا	ضَرَبْتُ بهَا التِّيهَ ضَرْبَ القِمَا
وَبِيضُ السُّيوفِ وَسُمْرُ القَنَا	إذا فَزِعَتْ قَدَّمَتْهَا الجِيَا
عَنِ العَالمينَ وَعَنْهُ غِنى	فَمَرَّتْ بِنَخْلٍ وَفِي رَكْبِهَا
بِ وادي المِياهِ وَوَادي القُرَى	وأَمْسَتْ تخَيَّرُنَا بالنَّقَا
فَقَالَتْ ونَحْنُ بتُرْبَانَ هَا	وقُلْنَا لَهَا أَيْنَ أَرْضُ العِرَاقِ
مُسْتَقْبَلاتِ مَهَبَّ الصَّبَا	وهَبَّتْ بِجِسْمي هُبُوبَ الدَّبُو
وَجَارِ البُوَيْرَةِ وَادي الغَضَى	رَوَامِي الكِفَافِ وَكِبْدِ الوِهَادِ
ءِ بَيْنَ النَّعَامِ وَبَيْنَ المَهَا	وَجَابَتْ بُسَيْطَةَ جَوْبَ الرِّدَا
بِمَاءِ الجَرَاوِيِّ بَعْضَ الصَّدَى	إلى عُقْدَةِ الجَوْفِ حتى شَفَتْ
وَلَاحَ الشَّغُورُ لَهَا والضُّحَى	ولاحَ لهَا صَوَّرٌ والصَّبَاحَ،
وَغَادَى الأضارعَ ثُمَّ الدَّنَا	ومَسَّى الجُمَيْعِيَّ دِئْدَاؤُهَا
أَحَمَّ البِلادِ خَفِيَّ الصُّوَى	فَيا لَكَ لَيْلًا على أعْكُشٍ
وَبَاقِيهِ أَكْثَرُ مِمَّا مَضَى	وَرَدْنَا الرُّهَيْمَةَ في جَوْزِهِ
حَ بَيْنَ مَكَارِمِنَا والعُلَى	فَلَمَّا أَنَخْنَا رَكَزْنَا الرِّمَا
ونَمْسَحُهَا مِنْ دِمَاءِ العِدَى	وبِتْنَا نُقَبِّلُ أَسْيافَنَا
ومَنْ بالعَواصِمِ أنَّى الفتَى	لتَعْلَمَ مِصْرُ وَمَنْ بالعِراقِ
وأنِّي عَتَوْتُ على مَنْ عَتَا	وأنِّي وَفَيْتُ وأنِّي أبَيْ
ولا كُلُّ مَنْ سِيمَ خَسْفًا أبَى	وَمَا كُلُّ مَنْ قَالَ قَوْلًا وَفَى

267
He spoke when he entered Kufa describing his journey from Egypt and he mocked Kafur in the first of the month of Rabi a in the year 351.
(Tripping bi)

O all the mincing women's walks are
    Ransom for every fast she-camel's gait
Every Bajawi that can rescue, though
    Clumsy, for a graceful pace is nothing
But they are life lines, deceits
    To the foe and defenses against evil
By her I beat desert in gambler's luck
    That might have been one way or other
When she took fright horsemen were
    Ahead, bright swords and brown lances
She passed Nakhla in her going
    Did without the people and the place
At eve she gave a choice of Nigab
    Of the Water Wadi or the Town Wadi
We said to her: Where's Iraqi soil?
    She said as we were at Turban: There!
In Hisma she went with a west wind
    Motion, facing the force of east winds
Aiming at Kifaf and Kibd al Wihad
    And after that Buwaira and Wadi Gada
She cut through Busaita as a sword
    Among the ostriches and the wild cows
To Uqdat al Jauf until she slaked
    At Jarawi Water some of her thirst
Sawwar and dawn shone on her
    As Shagur appeared in the forenoon
Her gallop took us at eve to Jumai
    nd morning to Adari and then to Dana
O that was a night for you at Akush
    The land all dark and signposts hidden
We came to Ruhaima in the midst of it
    The remainder more than what was past
We made camels kneel to set spears
    Between our generous deeds and rank
We spent night kissing our swords
    Wiping them clean of enemies brood
So Egypt might know and the Iraqs
    And those in Awasim that I'm a man
And I'm true and I rejected for not
    All forced to shame will then reject it
Not everyone speaks a true word
    Nor does everyone deny an eclipse

يَشُقُّ إلى العِزِّ قَلْبَ التَّوَى	وَمَنْ يَكُ قَلْبٌ كَقَلْبِي لَهُ
ورَأيٍ يُصَدِّعُ صُمَّ الصَّفا	ولا بُدَّ لِلقَلْبِ مِنْ آلةٍ
على قَدَرِ الرَّجُلِ فيهِ الخُطى	وكُلُّ طَريقٍ أتاهُ الفَتى
وقَدْ نامَ قَبْلَ عَمّى لا كَرى	ونامَ الخُوَيْدِمُ عَنْ لَيْلِنا
مَهامِهُ مِنْ جَهْلِهِ والعَمى	وكانَ على قُرْبِنا بَيْنَنا
أنَّ الرُّؤوسَ مَقَرُّ النُّهى	لَقَدْ كُنْتُ أحْسِبُ قَبْلَ الخِصِّى
رَأيْتُ النُّهى كُلَّها في الخُصى	فَلَمّا نَظَرْتُ إلى عَقْلِهِ
ولكِنَّهُ ضَحِكٌ كالبُكا	ومَاذَا بِصِرَ مِنَ المُضْحِكاتِ
يُدَرِّسُ أنْسابَ أهلِ الفَلا	بها نَبَطِيٌّ مِنَ اهلِ السَّوادِ
يُقالُ لَهُ أنْتَ بَدْرُ الدُّجى	واسْوَدُّ مِشْفَرُهُ نِصْفُهُ
بَينَ القَريضِ وبَينَ الرُّقى	وشِعْرٌ مَدَحْتُ بهِ الكَرْكَدَنْ
ولكِنَّهُ كانَ هَجْوَ الوَرى	فَما كانَ ذلِكَ مَدْحاً لَهُ
وأمَّا بِزِقِّ رِياحٍ فَلا	وقَدْ ضَلَّ قَوْمٌ بأصْنامِهِمْ
إذا حَرَّكوهُ فَسا أوْ هَذى	وتِلْكَ صُمُوتٌ وذا ناطِقٌ
رَأى غَيْرُهُ مِنْهُ ما لا يَرى	ومِنهُ جَهِلَتْ نَفْسُهُ قَدْرَهُ

(٢٦٨).

«من الطويل»

وقال يهجوه:

نَحيبٌ وأمَّا بَطْنُهُ فَرَحيبُ	وأسْوَدُ أمَّا القَلْبُ مِنهُ فَضَيِّقٌ
كما ماتَ غَيظاً فاتِكٌ وشَبيبُ	يَموتُ بهِ غَيظاً على الدهرِ أهْلُهُ
يُتَبَّعُ مِنّى الشَّمْسَ وهي تَغيبُ	أعَدْتُ على مَخْصاهُ ثُمَّ تَرَكْتُهُ
فَما لِحَياةٍ في جَنابِكَ طِيبُ	إذا ما عدِمتَ الأصلَ والعقلَ والنَّدى

He who has a heart like my heart
    Splits destruction's heart to glory
Some toot is needed for the mind
    And some idea to split the hardest rock
Every path that the youth takes finds
    His step by the measure of his legs
The little slave slept in our night
    Before he slept blindly, no slumber
In spite of closeness, between us
    Deserts of ignorance and blindness
Indeed I thought before the eunuch
    Conscience was placed in the skull
When I observed his wit's scope
    I knew all conscience was in the balls
O the ridiculous in Egypt's land
    It was laughter very close to tears
A Nabataean of the Sawad folk
    Teaching pedigrees of desert people
And the black who was half lip, one
    Must address as: You moon of darkness!
In poetry I praised him as rhinoceros
    At times with verses at times by spells
But this praise was not for him
    Rather it was a satire on mankind
Some people have gone astray by
    heir idols, but with a windbag, O no!
Those were deaf and he talkative
    But farts moved him or those stutters
If one's self is ignorant of worth
    Others see in him what he can't see

268
He spoke
mocking the black.
(. . . bu)

Black but his heart is too narrow
    A toast but the belly is too flabby
His folk die in rage at the time
    As Fatik and Shabib died of hatred
I loved his castration and left
    He followed me like a sun but dark
If you lack roots, reason, bounty
    There's nothing good in life for you

(٢٦٩)

«من البسيط»

قدم أبو شجاع فاتك المعروف بالمجنون من الفيوم إلى مصر فوصل أبا الطيب وحمل إليه هدية قيمتها ألف دينار فقال يمدحه:

لَا خَيْلَ عِنْدَكَ تُهْدِيهَا وَلَا مَالُ	فَلْيَسْعِدِ النُّطْقُ إِنْ لَمْ تُسْعِدِ الحَالُ
واجْزِ الأَمِيرَ الَّذِي نُعْمَاهُ فَاجِئَةٌ	بِغَيْرِ قَوْلٍ وَنُعْمَى النَّاسِ أَقْوَالُ
فَرُبَّمَا جَزَتِ الإِحْسَانَ مُولِيَهُ	خَرِيدَةٌ مِنْ عَذَارَى الحَيِّ مِكْسَالُ
وَإِنْ تَكُنْ مُحْكَمَاتِ الشَّكْلِ تَمْنَعُنِي	ظُهُورَ جَرْيِي فَلِي فِيهِنَّ تَصْهَالُ
وَمَا شَكَرْتُ لِأَنَّ المَالَ فَرَّحَنِي	سِيَّانَ عِنْدِيَ إِكْثَارٌ وَإِقْلَالُ
لَكِنْ رَأَيْتُ قَبِيحًا أَنْ يُجَادَ لَنَا	وَأَنَا بِقَضَاءِ الحَقِّ بُخَّالُ
فَكُنْتَ مَنْبِتَ رَوْضِ الحَزْنِ بَاكِرَةً	غَيْثٌ بِغَيْرِ سِبَاخِ الأَرْضِ هَطَّالُ
غَيْثٌ يُبَيِّنُ لِلنُّظَّارِ مَوْقِعَهُ	أَنَّ الغُيُوثَ بِمَا تَأْتِيهِ جُهَّالُ
لَا يُدْرِكُ المَجْدَ إِلَّا سَيِّدٌ فَطِنٌ	لِمَا يَشُقُّ عَلَى السَّادَاتِ فَعَّالُ
لَا وَارِثٌ جَهِلَتْ يُمْنَاهُ مَا وَهَبَتْ	وَلَا كَسُوبٌ بِغَيْرِ السَّيْفِ سَآّالُ
قَالَ الزَّمَانُ لَهُ قَوْلًا فَأَفْهَمَهُ	إِنَّ الزَّمَانَ عَلَى الأَمْسَاكِ عَذَّالُ
تَدْرِي القَنَاةُ إِذَا اهْتَزَّتْ بِرَاحَتِهِ	أَنَّ الشَّقِيَّ بِهَا خَيْلٌ وَأَبْطَالُ
كَفَاتِكٍ وَدُخُولُ الكَافِ مَنْقَصَةٌ	كَالشَّمْسِ قُلْتُ وَمَا لِلشَّمْسِ أَمْثَالُ
أَلْقَائِدُ الأَسْدَ غَذَّتْهَا بَرَاثِنُهُ	بِمِثْلِهَا مِنْ عِدَاهُ وَهْيَ أَشْبَالُ
القَاتِلِ السَّيْفَ فِي جِسْمِ القَتِيلِ بِهِ	وَلِلسُّيُوفِ كَمَا لِلنَّاسِ آجَالُ
تُغِيرُ عَنْهُ عَلَى الغَارَاتِ هَيْبَتُهُ	وَمَالُهُ بِأَقَاصِي الأَرْضِ أَهْمَالُ

269
He spoke praising Abu Shuja Fatik nicknamed Majnun in the year 348.
(Outspread lu)

No horses as your gift and no flocks so
    Speech brings joy if things do not rejoice
Repay the Amir who is kind unforeseen
    Without plea though men's gifts are begged
Often she repays kindness of one near her
    This lazy pearl among the virgins of the tribe
And if strong hobbles now prevent me
    From running free, yet there is whinnying
I do not give thanks because the wealth
    Lures me, little or much is equal with me
I think it is ugly he is generous with us
    And we by authority's decree are miserly
I was wasteland meadow growth, showers
    Came at dawn, a downpour on no salt earth
A shower with effect clear to onlookers
    But showers know not what they bring here
Only a master of sagacity attains glory
    When any action is difficult for masters
None inherit whose hand ignores a gift
    None acquire without a sword demanding
Time spoke a word to him, he understood
    For time is censorious of the tight fisted one
A lance knows if shaken by his hand
    A horseman and hero are unhappy with it
Like Fatik . . .but comparison is lacking
    Like sun I had said, but sun is no trope
Leader of lions whose claws feed some
    Who are his cubs with the like of his foes
Sword killer the body of one killed
    For there is an end for swords as for men
Fear for him protects him in battle
    His flocks unshepherded for far pasture

عَيْرٌ وهَيْقٌ وخَنْسَاءٌ وذَيَّالُ	لَهُ مِنَ الوَحشِ ما اختارَتْ أسِنَّتُهُ
كَأنَّ أوقاتَها في الطِّيبِ أصالُ	تُمْسِي الضُّيُوفُ مُشَهَّاةً بعَقْوَتِهِ
خَرَادِلٌ مِنهُ في الشِّيزَى وأوْصَالُ	لَوِ اشْتَهَتْ لَحمَ قارِيها لَبَادَرَها
إلّا إذا حَفَزَ الضِّيفانَ تَرْحَالُ	لا يَعرِفُ الرُّزءَ في مالٍ ولا وَلَدٍ
مَحْضُ اللِّقاحِ وَصَافي اللَّوْنِ سَلْسَالُ	يُروي صَدى الأرضِ مِن فَضَلاتِ ما
كَأنَّما السَّاعُ نُزَّالٌ وَقُفَّالُ	تَتَوَلَّى صَوَارِمُهُ السَّاعاتِ عَبطَ دَمٍ
مِنها عُداةٌ وَأغْنامٌ وآبالُ	تَجري النُّفوسُ حَوالَيْهِ مُخَلَّطَةً
وَغَيرُ عاجِزَةٍ عَنْهُ الأَطَيْفَالُ	لا يَحرِمُ البُعْدُ أهلَ البُعْدِ نائلَهُ
والبيضُ هادِيَةٌ وَالسُّمْرُ ضُلَّالُ	أمضَى الفَرِيقَيْنِ في أقرانِهِ ظُبَةً
بَينَ الرِّجالِ وَفيها الماءُ وَالآلُ	يُريكَ مَخبَرُهُ أضعافَ مَنظَرِهِ
إذا اختَلَطْنَ وَبَعضُ العَقلِ عُقَّالُ	يدٌ يُلَقِّبُهُ المَجْنونَ حاسِدُهُ
مِن شَقِّهِ وَلَوْ أنَّ الجَيشَ أجبَالُ	يَرمي بها الجَيشَ لا بُدَّ لَهُ وَلَها
لَم يَجتَمِعْ لَهُمْ حِلمٌ وَرِئْبَالُ	إذا العِدَى نَشِبَتْ فيهِم مَخالِبُهُ
مُجَاهِرٌ وَصُرُوفُ الدَّهرِ تَغتَالُ	يُرَوِّعُهُم مِنهُ دَهرٌ صَرفُهُ أبَداً
فَما الَّذي بِتَوَقّي ما أتى نَالوا	أنالَهُ الشَّرَفَ الأعلى تَقَدُّمُهُ
مُهَنَّدٌ وَأصَمُّ الكَعبِ عَسَّالُ	إذا المُلوكُ تَحَلَّتْ كانَ حِلْيَتَهُ
هَوْلٌ نَمَتْهُ مِنَ الهَيجاءِ أهوالُ	أبُو شُجَاعٍ أبُو الشُّجعانِ قاطِبَةً
في الحَمْدِ حاءٌ وَلا ميمٌ وَلا دَالُ	تَمَلَّكَ الحَمْدَ حتّى ما لِمُفتَخِرٍ
وَقَدْ كَفاهُ مِنَ الماذِيِّ سِرْبَالُ	عَلَيهِ مِنهُ سَرَابِيلٌ مُضَاعَفَةٌ
وَقَدْ غَمَرْتَ نَوالاً أيُّها النَّالُ	وَكَيفَ أستُرُ ما أوْلَيْتَ مِن حَسَنٍ
إنَّ الكَرِيمَ عَلى العَليَاءِ يَختَالُ	لَطَفْتَ رَأيَكَ في بَرّي وَتَكرمَتي
وَلِلكَواكِبِ في كَفَّيكَ آمَالُ	حَتَّى غَدَوْتَ وَللأخبارِ تَجوَالُ
إنَّ الثَّنَاءَ عَلى التَّنَّالِ تِنْبَالُ	وَقَدْ أطَالَ ثَنَائي طُولُ لابِسِهِ
فإنَّ قَدْرَكَ في الأقدارِ يَختَالُ	إنْ كُنتَ تَكبُرُ أنْ تَختَالَ في بَشَرٍ
إلّا وَأنْتَ عَلى المِفضَالِ مِفضَالُ	كأنَّ نَفسَكَ لا تَرضاكَ صاحِبَها
إلّا وَأنْتَ لَها في الرَّوْعِ بَذَّالُ	وَلا تَعُدُّكَ صَوَّاناً لِمُهجَتِها

His whatever wild game his spear sees
    Wild asses, ostrich, boars and wild bulls
Guests at eve fill up his courts
    As if sunset's cool was brought for them
If they want meat their host hurries
    A cut on a platter and even the haunch
He knows no bad luck in wealth or child
    Except as he sends the guests on the way
He waters avid earth with drink's dregs
    Camel's milk cream and pure color wine
His sword is host wet hourly in blood
    As momently guests arrive and return
Life flows around him in mixed ways
    Some of it foes', some sheep and camel
Distance prohibits no gifts to men, no
    Children are kept by weakness from them
Keenest sword in two armies for a foe
    Swords are guided while spears stray
His fame weaker than sight of him
    Among men some are water, some mirage
The jealous call him Majnun the mad one
    As swords clash for sometimes reason clogs
He hits armies with them, no escape then
    In his blow even if armies are as mountains
So when his claws are in the enemy
    Pity and lions cannot be joined for them
Destiny's course in him ever terrible
    Openly but fate's mishaps are unforeseen
His boldness attains nobility's height
    They gain it not who guard against a comer
If kings adorn themselves his gems are
    Indian swords and shaken lance nipples
Abu Shuja father of the bold one, all
    Terror feeds him with the feared conflicts
You take praise, until for boasters
    There is neither hah, nor mim, nor dal
Upon him there is double coat of it
    So that he has no need of a coat of mail
How should I hide gifts you conferred
    You overflowed with riches O bounteous!
You were kind to think of my virtue and
    Honor, the generous are the height of tact
You made it known and the news spread
    And hope in your hands reached the stars
My praise is long as he who wears it
    Is tall, the praise for dwarfs is dwarflike
If you are proud as conceited men
    Your worth by their worth is haughty
As if not content with yourself as
    A friend until you excel in qualities
You didn't see yourself sure of heart
    Until you were spendthrift of fear for it

لَوْ لا المَشَقَّةُ سادَ النّاسُ كُلُّهُمُ	الجُودُ يُفقِرُ والإقْدامُ قَتّالُ
وَإنَّما يَبلُغُ الإنْسانُ طاقَتَهُ	ما كُلّ ماشِيَةٍ بالرَّحلِ شِمْلالُ
إنّا لَفي زَمَنٍ تَركُ القَبيحِ بِهِ	مِن أكثَرِ النّاسِ إحْسانٌ وَإجْمالُ
ذِكرُ الفَتى عُمرُهُ الثّاني وَحاجَتُهُ	ما قاتَهُ وفُضولُ العَيشِ أشغالُ

(٢٧٠)

«من الكامل»

توفي أبو شجاع فاتك بمصر سنة خمسين وثلاث مئة (٩٦١م) فقال يرثيه بعد خروجه منها:

الحُزنُ يُقلِقُ والتَّجَمُّلُ يَردَعُ	والدَّمعُ بَينَهُما عَصِيٌّ طَيِّعُ
يَتَنازَعانِ دُموعَ عَينٍ مُسَهَّدٍ	هذا يَجيءُ بِها وَهذا يَرجِعُ
ألنَّومُ بَعدَ أبي شُجاعٍ نافِرٌ	واللَّيلُ مُعيٍ والكَواكِبُ ظُلَّعُ
إنّي لأحبُنُ عَن فِراقِ أحِبَّتي	وَتُجِسُّ نَفسي بِالحِمامِ فَأشجَعُ
وَيَزيدُني غَضَبُ الأعادي قَسوَةً	وَيَلِمَ بي عَتبُ الصَّديقِ فَأجزَعُ
تَصفُو الحَياةُ لِجاهِلٍ أوْ غافِلٍ	عَمّا مَضى فيها وَما يَتَوَقَّعُ
وَلَمَن يُغالِطُ في الحَقائِقِ نَفسَهُ	وَيَسومُها طَلَبَ المُحالِ فَتَطمَعُ
أينَ الَّذي الهَرَمانِ مِن بُنيانِهِ	ما قَومُهُ، ما يَومُهُ، ما المَصرَعُ؟
تَتَخَلَّفُ الآثارُ عَن أصحابِها	حيناً وَيُدرِكُها الفَناءُ فَتَتبَعُ
لَم يُرضِ قَلبَ أبي شُجاعٍ مَبلَغٌ	قَبلَ المَماتِ وَلَم يَسَعهُ مَوضِعُ
كُنّا نَظُنُّ دِيارَهُ مَملوءَةً	ذَهَباً فَماتَ وَكُلُّ دارٍ بَلقَعُ
وَإذا المَكارِمُ والصَّوارِمُ والقَنا	وَبَناتُ أعوَجَ كُلُّ شَيءٍ يَجمَعُ
المَجدُ أخسَرُ والمَكارِمُ صَفقَةً	مِن أن يَعيشَ لَها الهُمامُ الأروَعُ
والنّاسُ أنزَلُ في زَمانِكَ مَنزِلاً	مِن أن تُعايِشَهُم وَقَدرُكَ أرفَعُ
بَرِّد حَشايَ إن استَطَعتَ بِلَفظَةٍ	فَلَقَد تَضُرُّ إذا تَشاءُ وَتَنفَعُ
ما كانَ مِنكَ إلى خَليلٍ قَبلَها	ما يُستَرابُ بِهِ وَلا ما يوجِعُ

But for hardship all men would rule
>   Generosity be poor and boldness death
Even if each one reaches capacity
>   Not every runner has a fast racing gait
The time left off ugliness in him
>   For most men he is the best and finest
Hero's memory is second life, urgent
>   Needs feed him not nor exuberant life

270
Abu Shuja Fatik died in Egypt on the first day of the last eleven of Shawwal in the year 350. And he spoke lamenting him.
(Perfect u)

Grief disquiets, reflection restrains
>   Tears between these two rebel and submit
These dispute my sleepless Byes' tears
>   One brings them and the other takes them
Sleep after Abu Shuia'a is frightened
>   And the night tired and the stars are lame
I'm a coward at my beloved's departure
>   But as my soul tastes of death I feel brave
My foe's anger increases my harshness
>   Blame of a friend pains me and I'm anxious
Life for a fool or the forgetful is simple
>   Both what is past and what is yet to come
And for him who mistakes his own value
>   Making endless search for the impossible
Where is he who built two pyramids
>   What were his folk, his time, his death?
A trace remained for their friends
>   Then ruin overtook them and they went
Money did not hold Abu Shuja's heart
>   Before his death nor rank he had gained
We thought his house was filled with
>   Gold but he died and the house is empty
Nobility and scimitars and lance and
>   Awaji daughters are all he had gathered
Glory is loss, nobility a hand clasp
>   And nobility's beauty cannot live by them
Men go to too low a level in your time
>   For you to live by them, you rank higher
Cool my heart with a word if you can
>   You could hurt if you wish or be useful
Never before this did you give a friend
>   Anything that made him doubt or suffer

إلّا نَفاها عنـكَ قلبٌ أصمَعُ	ولقَد أراكَ وَما تُلِمَّ مُلِمَّةٌ
فَرضٌ يحِقّ عَلَيـكَ وَهـوَ تبـرّعُ	وَيَدٌ كـأنَّ نَوالَها وَقِشـتالَها
أنّــى رَضيـتَ بخُلّـةٍ لا تُنـزَعُ؟	يـا مَـن يُبَـدّلُ كُـلّ يَـوْمِ حُلّـةً
حتى لَبِسْـتَ اليَـومَ مـا لا تخلعُ	مـا زِلْـتَ تَخْلَعُهـا عَلـى مَـن شـاءَها
حتى أتى الأمـرُ الـذي لا يُدفَـعُ	مـا زَلْـتَ تدفـعُ كُـلّ أمْـرٍ فـادِحٍ
فيمـا عَــرَاكَ وَلا سُيـوفُكَ قُطَّـعُ	فظَلِلْـتَ تنظُـرُ لا رِماحُـكَ شُـرَّعٌ
يكـي وَمَنْ شَرّ السّلاحِ الأدْمَـعُ	بـأبي الوَحيـدُ وَجَيشُـهُ مُتكـاثِرٌ
فحَشاكَ رُعْـتَ بـهِ وخَـدَّكَ تقـرَعُ	وَإذا حصَلـتَ مِن السّـلاحِ على البُكـا
بـازي الأشَيْـهَبُ وَالغُـرابُ الأبْقَـعُ	وَصَلـتْ إليـكَ يَـدٌ سَـواءٌ عِنْدَهـا الـ
فَقَــدَتْ بفَقْـدِكَ نَيّـراً لا يَطْلُـعُ	مَـن للمَحـافِلِ وَالجَحـافِلِ وَالسُّـرَى
ضـاعُوا وَمِثلُـكَ لا يكـادُ يُضَيَّـعُ	وَمَـن اتّخذَتْ على الضّيـوفِ خَليفَـةً
وَجهـاً لَـهُ مِـن كُـلّ قُبْـحٍ بُرْقُـعُ	قُبْحـاً لِوَجهـكَ يـا زَمـانُ فإنّـهُ
وَيَعيشَ حاسِـدُه الخصيُّ الأوكَـعُ	أيَمـوتُ مِثـلُ أبـي شُجـاعٍ فـاتِكٍ
وَقفـاً يَصيـحُ بهـا: ألا مَـن يَصفَـعُ	أيـدٍ مُقَطَّـعَةٌ حَوَالَــيْ رَأسِــهِ
وَأخذتَ أصْـدَقَ من يقـولَ وَيسمَـعُ	أبْقَيْـتَ أكْـذَبَ كـاذِبٍ أبْقَيْـتَـهُ
وَسَلَبْـتَ أطيَـب ريحَـةٍ تَتَضَـوّعُ	وَتَركْـتَ أنتَـنَ ريحَـةٍ مَذمُومَـةٍ
دَمــهُ وَكـانَ كأنّـهُ يَتَطَلَّــعُ	فاليَوْمَ قَـرّ لكُـلّ وَحْـشٍ نـافِرٍ
وَأوَتْ إلَيها سُـــوقُها وَالأذرُعُ	وَتَصَالحَتْ ثَمَـرُ السّياطِ وَخَيْلُـهُ
فَـوْقَ القَنـاةِ وَلا حُسـامٌ يَلمَـعُ	وَعَفا الطّـرَادُ فَـلا سِنانٌ راعِـفٌ
بَعْـدَ اللّـزُومِ مُشَيِّـعٍ وَمُـوَدِّعُ	وَلّـى وَكُـلّ مُحـالِمٍ وَمُنـادِمٍ
وَلسَـيفِهِ في كـلّ قَـومٍ مَرْتَـعُ	مَــنْ كـانَ فيـهِ لكُـلّ قَـومٍ مَلجـأً
كسرى تـذلّ لـهُ الرّقـابُ وَتخضَـعُ	إنْ حَـلّ في فُـرسٍ فَفيها ربُّهـا
أو حَـلّ في عَـرَبٍ فَفيها تُبَّـعُ	أو حَـلّ في رومٍ فَفيهـا قَيصَـرٌ
فَرَسـاً وَلَكِـنّ المنِيَّـةَ أسْـرَعُ	قـد كـانَ أسْـرَعَ فارِسٍ في طَعْنةٍ
رُمحـاً وَلا حمَلَـتْ جَـوَاداً أربَـعُ	لا قَلَبَـتْ أيـدي الفَـوارِسِ بَعْـدَهُ

I saw you, no trouble came near you
    But what a wise heart drove off from you
Or hand making its battles and gifts
    Duties and you undertook voluntarily
O you changed your garments daily
    Now content with a garment not taken
You ever robed those who wanted
    Until one day you took one unhonored
You always repelled the hard thing
    Until a burden, unavoidable, was given
You stayed to see your lance not ready
    For what attacked nor would the sword cut
By my father alone! a numerous army
    Wept, but tears are the worst of weapons
When you were left with weeping arms
    You feared in your heart, your cheeks wet
A hand came to you finding equal value
    In the gray falcon and the speckled crow
Who now for assembly, army or raid?
    Lost in your loss, a star rising no more
Who takes you as deputy for guests
    Who lose heir way while you remain?
Ugly be your face O time, for it is
    A face that is veiled with all disgust!
Must such as Shuja Fatik die, he
    Who envied him, stub-toed eunuch, live?
Chopped off hands lie near his head
    A neck cries to them: Will no one hit him?
You let stay the worst liar you had
    But took the best who spoke and heard
Left the most stinking damned weed
    Stole sweetest perfume that ever spread
Today blood of all frightened animals
    Is calm and it is as if he loomed far off
Knots of whips and his horses calm
    Back legs and forelegs are together
Sortie canceled, no spearpoint drips
    Blood above a shaft, no sword glitters
He turns, each friend, drinking pal
    After privacy takes a walk for goodbye
He who was refuge for every people
    Found food for his sword in each nation
If he was among Persians he was lord
    Kisra, necks bowed to him and stopped
If he came among Rum he was Caesar
    Or stayed with Arabs then he was Tubba
He was fastest rider in the jousting
    On horseback, but yet death was quicker
May hand of rider not grip the lance
    After him, nor four feet carry the steed

(٢٧١)

«من المتقارب»

دخل عليه صديق له بالكوفة وبين يديه تفاحة من الند مكتوب عليها إسم فاتك وكان قد أهداها إليه فاستحسنها الرجل فقال أبو الطيب:

وَشَيْءٌ مِنَ النَّدِّ فيهِ اسمُهُ	يُذَكِّرُني فاتِكاً حِلْمُهُ
يُجَدِّدُ لي ريحَهُ شَمُّهُ	وَلَسْتُ بِناسٍ وَلَكِنَّني
نْ لم تَدْرِ ما وَلَدَتْ أُمُّهُ	وَأَيُّ فَتًى سَلَبَتْني المَنو
وَلَوْ عَلِمَتْ هالَها ضَمُّهُ	وَلا ما تَضُمُّ إلى صَدْرِها
وَلَكِنَّهُمْ ما لَهُمْ هَمُّهُ	بِمِصْرَ مُلُوكٌ لَهُمْ مالُهُ
وَأحمَدُ مِنْ حَمدِهِمْ ذَمُّهُ	فَأجوَدُ مِنْ جودِهِمْ بُخْلُهُ
وَأنفَعُ مِنْ وَجدِهِمْ عُدْمُهُ	وَأشرَفُ مِنْ عَيشِهِمْ مَوْتُهُ
لَكالخَمرِ سُقْيَةُ كَرْمُهُ	وَإنَّ مَنيَّتَهُ عِنْدَهُ
وَذاكَ الَّذي ذاقَهُ طَعْمُهُ	فَذاكَ الَّذي عَبَّهُ ماؤُهُ
حَرًى أن يَضيقَ بِها جِسمُهُ	وَمَن ضاقَتِ الأرضُ عَنْ نَفسِهِ

(٢٧٢)

«من البسيط»

قال بالكوفة يرثيه ويذكر مسيره من مصر:

وَما سُراهُ على خُفٍّ وَلا قَدَمِ	حَتّامَ نَحنُ نُساري النَّجمَ في الظُّلَمِ
فَقدَ الرُّقادَ غَريبٌ باتَ لم يَنَمِ	وَلا يُحِسُّ بِأَجفانٍ يُحِسُّ بِها
وَلا تُسَوِّدُ بيضَ العُذرِ وَاللِّمَمِ	تُسَوِّدُ الشَّمسُ مِنّا بيضَ أوجُهِنا
لَو احتَكَمْنا مِنَ الدُّنيا إلى حَكَمِ	وَكانَ حالُهُما في الحُكمِ واحِدَةً
ما سارَ في الغَيمِ مِنهُ سارَ في الأَدَمِ	وَنَترُكُ الماءَ لا يَنفَكُّ مِن سَفَرٍ
قَلبي مِنَ الحُزنِ أو جِسمي مِنَ السَّقَمِ	لا أَبغَضُ العيسَ لَكِنّي وَقَيتُ بِها
حَتّى مَرَقْنَ بِها مِن جَوْشَ وَالعَلَمِ	طَرَدتُ مِن مِصرَ أيديَها بِأَرْجُلِها

271
He spoke to a friend from Kufa: (Tripping hu)

Its mildness reminded me of Fatik
    Something of spice is in his name
I am not forgetful, but still
    Its smell renews for me his perfume
What a youth death plundered! not
    Even his mother knew what she bore
Nor what she took to her breast
    If she knew his embrace had scared her
The kings in Egypt had its wealth
    But they, not they, have not his spirit
Larger than their bounty his economy
    Better than their eulogy was his blame
Nobler than their lives is his death
    More use than their riches his poverty
In truth his death in his house
    Was like a wine that nobility pours
For it is water which one drinks
    And it is his taste which one savors
Earth was too narrow for his spirit
    It is nature his body was cramped by her

272
Abu Tayyib spoke after leaving Madina recalling his journey from Egypt and Fatik. (Outspread mi)

How long do we follow stars in darkness
    If their journey is not with hoof or on foot?
Not feeling in eyelids what a traveler
    Feels from lost sleep as he wakes at night
Sun blackened our white faces but
    Blackened not our white locks or braids
Their state will be under one judgment
    If we judge by the judgment of the world
We let no water cease from traveling
    Going from clouds through the water bag
I chide no camel, for by her I protect
    My heart from grief, my body from illness
With back legs I drove her front legs
    From Egypt till we passed Jawsh and Islam
Desert ostriches raced the saddled ones
    Matching camels' soft tethers with bridles
With boys who risk their souls and joy
    In what comes, content with arrow's luck
They display as they toss off turbans
    Their turbans created black without veil
Pale checked, jousting horsemen they
    Pursue them as they drive off the camels
They take by spear what's beyond force
    But achieve not the limit of their desires
It is Jahiliya time except that they
    In their good nature are in truce month
Casting spears that cannot talk yet
    Are taught birds' screams for the brave

تَجري لَهُنَّ نَعامَ الدَوِّ مُسرَجَةً تُعارِضُ الجُدَّلَ المُرخاةَ بِاللُجُمِ
في غِلمَةٍ أَخطَرُوا أَرواحَهُم وَرَضوا لَمّا لَقينَ رِضى الأَيسارِ بِالزَلَمِ
تَبدو لَنا كُلَّما أَلقَوا عَمائِمَهُم عَمائِمٌ خُلِقَت سوداً بِلا لُثُمِ
بيضُ العَوارِضِ طَعّانونَ مَن لَحِقوا مِنَ الفَوارِسِ شَلّالونَ لِلنَعَمِ
قَد بَلَغوا بِقَناهُم فَوقَ طاقَتِهِ وَلَيسَ يَبلُغُ ما فيهِم مِنَ الهِمَمِ
في الجاهِلِيَّةِ إِلّا أَنَّ أَنفُسَهُم مِن طيبِهِنَّ بِهِ في الأَشهُرِ الحُرُمِ
ناشُوا الرِماحَ وَكانَت غَيرَ ناطِقَةٍ فَعَلَّموها صِياحَ الطَيرِ في البُهَمِ
تَخدي الرِكابُ بِنا بيضاً مَشافِرُها خُضراً فَرائِسُها في الرُغلِ وَاليَنَمِ
مَكعومَةً بِسِياطِ القَومِ نَضرِبُها عَن مَنبِتِ العُشبِ نَبغي مَنبِتَ الكَرَمِ
وَأَينَ مَنبِتُهُ مِن بُعدِ مَنبِتِهِ أَبي شُجاعٍ قَريعِ العُربِ وَالعَجَمِ
لا فاتِكٌ آخَرٌ في مِصرَ نَقصِدُهُ وَلا لَهُ خَلَفٌ في النّاسِ كُلِّهِمِ
مَن لا تُشابِهُهُ الأَحياءُ في شِيَمٍ أَمسى تُشابِهُهُ الأَمواتُ في الرِمَمِ
عَدِمتُهُ وَكَأَنّي سِرتُ أَطلُبُهُ فَما تَزيدُني الدُنيا عَلى العَدَمِ
ما زِلتُ أُضحِكُ إِبلي كُلَّما نَظَرَت إِلى مَنِ اِختَضَبَت أَخفافُها بِدَمِ
أَسيرُها بَينَ أَصنامٍ أُشاهِدُها وَلا أُشاهِدُ فيها عِفَّةَ الصَنَمِ
حَتّى رَجَعتُ وَأَقلامي قَوائِلُ لي المَجدُ لِلسَيفِ لَيسَ المَجدُ لِلقَلَمِ
أُكتُب بِنا أَبَداً بَعدَ الكِتابِ بِهِ فَإِن غَفَلتُ فَدائي قِلَّةُ الفَهَمِ
أَسمَعتِني وَدَوائي ما أَشَرتِ بِهِ فَإِن غَفَلتُ فَدائي قِلَّةُ الفَهَمِ
مَنِ اِقتَضى بِسِوى الهِندِيِّ حاجَتَهُ أَجابَ كُلَّ سُؤالٍ عَن هَلَ بِلَمِ
تَوَهَّمَ القَومُ أَنَّ العَجزَ قَرَّبَنا وَفي التَقَرُّبِ ما يَدعو إِلى التُهَمِ
وَلَم تَزَل قِلَّةُ الإِنصافِ قاطِعَةً بَينَ الرِجالِ وَلَو كانوا ذَوي رَحِمِ
فَلا زِيارَةَ إِلّا أَن تَزورَهُمُ أَيدٍ نَشَأنَ مَعَ المَصقولَةِ الخُذُمِ
مِن كُلِّ قاضِيَةٍ بِالمَوتِ شَفرَتُهُ ما بَينَ مُنتَقِمٍ مِنهُ وَمُنتَقِمِ
صُنّا قَوائِمَها عَنهُم فَما وَقَعَت مَواقِعَ اللَومِ في الأَيدي وَلا الكَزَمِ
هَوِّن عَلى بَصَرٍ ما شَقَّ مَنظَرُهُ فَإِنَّما يَقَظاتُ العَينِ كَالحُلُمِ
وَلا تَشَكَّ إِلى خَلقٍ فَتُشمِتَهُ شَكوى الجَريحِ إِلى الغِربانِ وَالرَخَمِ

The camels speed with frothy lips
    Their hoofs green with grass and brush
We beat with drivers' whips kept from
    The bushy growth, we want glory's growth
Where is its growth after his growth?
    Abu Shuja chosen of Arabs and non-Arabs
No other Fatik in Egypt that we went to
    Nor a successor to him among all mankind
Those unlike him in nature when alive
    Are as him when dead amid rotting bones
I have lost him, I go to seek him
    The world will not repay me for the loss
I can't stop smiling at my camel as she
    Looks at what colors her hoofs with blood
I led her among idols to show them
    But I found among them no idols' chastity
So I returned as my pen spoke to me:
    Glory is a sword, glory is not in the pen
Write ever with us after writing with it
    For indeed we are servants to the swords
It made he hear, my cure was its advice
    If I slip my ransom is that I have little wit
He who fulfills not his need by sword
    Answers each question of How with a
No! People imagine it's weakness brings us
    To them and the approach raises suspicion
A failure of justice won't stop a rift
    Among men, even if they are of one womb
No visits unless you visit them with
    Hands prepared for the polished scimitar
In each case its edges decide for death
    In what is between avenger and avenged
Keep its hilt clean for them and what
    Befalls of blame and stinginess to my hand
What's hard to see is scorned by vision
    For a waking eyes like the dreaming one
Do not distrust people and gloat in
    Complaints of wounds for crow or vulture
Be on your guard with men but hide it
    And let not a smiling mouth confuse you
Faith is rare, you don't often meet it
    Trust scarce, either in word or promise
Praise to my soul's Creator, her joy is
    What other souls sees as a peak of pain
Fate wonders at my bearing calamity
    At my body's patience in crushing events
Time seduces, would the time of life
    Were among other folk of bygone nations
When sons came in time's growth and
    Made them happy, but we come in old age

(٢٧٣)

مَـا أَنْصَـفَ الْقَـوْمُ ضَبَّـهْ	وَأُمُّــهُ الطُّرْطُبَّــهْ
رَمَـوْا بِـرَأْسِ أَبْشِـيْهِ	وَبَــاكَوا أَلَامَّ غُلْبَّــهْ
فَــلَا بِمَــنْ مَــاتَ فَخْــرٌ	وَلَا بِمَـنْ نِيـكَ رَغْبَـهْ
وَإِنَّمَـا قُلْـتُ مَـا قُلْـ	ـتُ رَحْمَـةً لَا مَحَبَّـهْ
وَحِيلَــةً لَــكَ حَتَّــى	عُـذِرْتَ لَـوْ كُنْـتَ تِيبَـهْ
وَمَـا عَلَيْـكَ مِـنَ الْقَتْـ	ـلِ إِنَّمَـا هِـيَ ضَرْبَـهْ
وَمَـا عَلَيْـكَ مِـنَ الْغَـدْ	رِ إِنَّمَـا هُـوَ سُبَّـهْ
وَمَـا عَلَيْـكَ مِـنَ الْعَـا	رِ إِنَّ أُمَّـكَ قَحْبَـهْ
وَمَـا يَشُـقُّ عَلَـى الْكَلْـ	ـبِ أَنْ يَكـونَ ابْـنَ كَلْبَـهْ
مَـا ضَرَّهَـا مَـنْ أَتَاهَـا	وَإِنَّمَـا ضَـرَّ صُلْبَـهْ
وَلَــمْ يَنِكْهَــا وَلَكِــنْ	عِجَانُهَــا نَــاكَ زُبَّــهْ
يَلُــومُ ضَبَّــةَ قَــوْمٌ	وَلَا يَلُومُــونَ قَلْبَــهْ
وَقَلْبُــهُ يَتَشَــهَّى	وَيُــلْزِمُ الْجِسْـمَ ذَنْبَـهْ
لَــوْ أَبْصَــرَ الْجِذْعَ شَـيْئاً	أَحَـبَّ فِي الْجِـذْعِ صُلْبَـهْ
يَـا أَطْيَـبَ النَّـاسِ نَفْسـاً	وَأَلْيَـنَ النَّـاسِ رُكْبَـهْ
وَأَخْبَـثَ النَّـاسِ أَصْـلاً	فِي أَخْبَـثِ الأرْضِ تُرْبَـهْ
وَأَرْخَــصَ النَّــاسِ أُمًّـا	تَبِيـعُ الْفَــاَ بِحَبَّــهْ
كُــلُّ الْفُعُــول سِــهَامٌ	لِمَرْيَــمٍ وَهْــيَ جَعْبَـهْ

273
He spoke mocking Dabba ibn Yazid al Ainy and scorned him in his qasida. al-Mutanabbi disliked it. (Amputated h)

How unjust folk are to Dabba
    And to his long breasted mamma
They hit his dad on the head
    And fucked the overcome mother
No honor for one who is dead
    Nor love for those fucked with
I have said what I have said
    Out of pity and not from passion
It is hidden from you for
    You'd be excused if repentant
It's not your fault that he
    Was killed, for it was a fight
You were not betrayed
    For she was only an asshole
It's not your fault that
    Your mamma was a dirty whore
It's no hardship to the dog
    That he is the son of a bitch
No matter to her who got her
    And it did not bother her thighs
He did not fuck her, yet
    Her ass bothered his cock
Some folk blame Dabba
    They do not blame his heart
It was not his heart lusted
    Forced the body with his tail
If he sees a thing's stalk
    He loves the stump's hardon
O best of men in himself
    Softest of men for a rimming
O trickiest of men in root
    In the smelliest dusty grave
Cheapest of men to his ma
    She sells to a thousand guys
All on the make are arrows
    For Miriam and she the quiver

وَمَا عَلَى مضن بِهِ الدَّاءُ	مِنْ لِقَاءِ الأَطِبَّهْ
وَلَيْسَ بَيْنَ هَلُوكٍ	وَحُرَّةٍ غَيْرَ خِطْبَهْ
يَا قَاتِلاً كُلَّ ضَيْفٍ	غَنَّاهُ ضَيْحٌ وَعُلْبَهْ
وَخَوْفُ كُلِّ رَفِيقٍ	أَبَاتَكَ اللَّيْلُ جَنْبَهْ
كَذَا خُلِقْتَ وَمَنْ ذَا الَّــ	ــذِي يُغَالِبُ رَبَّهْ
وَمَنْ يُيَالِي بِذَمٍّ	إذا تَعَوَّدَ كَسْبَهْ
أَمَا تَرَى الْخَيْلَ فِي النَّخْـ	ـلِ سُرْبَةً بَعْدَ سُرْبَةْ
عَلَى نِسَائِكَ تَجْلُــوا	فَعُولَهَا مُنْذُ سَنْبَهْ
وَهُنَّ حَوْلَكَ يَنْظُــرْ	نَ والأَحْيَرَاحُ رَطْبَهْ
وَكُلُّ غُرْمُــول بَغْــلٍ	يَرَيْـــنَ يَحْسَدْنَ قُنْبَهْ
فَسَــلْ فُؤَادَكَ يَا ضَبْــــبُّ أَيْــنَ خَلَّــفَ عُجْبَهْ
وَإِنْ يَخُنْــكَ لَعَمْــري	لَطَالَمَــا خَــانَ صَحْبَهْ
وَكَيْــفَ تَرْغضبُ فِيهِ	وَقَــدْ تَبَيَّنْــتَ رُعْبَهْ
مَــا كُنْــتَ إِلاَّ ذُبَابــاً	نَفَتْــكَ عَنَّــا مِذَبَّهْ
وَكُنْــتَ تَفْخَــرُ تِيهــاً	فَصِــرْتَ تَضْــرِطُ رَهْبَهْ
وَإِنْ بَعُدْنَــا قَلِيــلاً	حَمَلْــتَ رُمْحــاً وَحَرْبَهْ
وَقُلْــتَ لَيْــتَ بِكَفِّــي	عِنَـــانَ جَــرْدَاءَ شَطْبَهْ
إِنْ أَوْحَشَــتْكَ الْمَعَــالِي	فَإِنَّهَـــا دَارُ غُرْبَهْ
أَوْ آنَسَــتْكَ الْمَخَــازِي	فَإِنَّهَـــا لَــكَ نِسْبَهْ
وَإِنْ عَرَفْــتَ مُــرَادِي	تَكَشَّـــفَتْ عَنْــكَ كُرْبَهْ
وَإِنْ جَهِلْــتَ مُــرَادِي	فَإِنَّـــهُ بِــكَ أَشْبَهْ

It's nothing for one with clap
    To have a meeting with doctors
No difference between a drab
    And proper girl but go between
O you murder a guest for
    Profit in water milk and bags
For fear of every comrade
    You stay the night beside him
Thus you were created
    And who can overcome his Lord?
Who cares about the blame
    If he is accustomed to a profit?
Don't you see stallions in
    The palms, in herd after herd?
They show among your hens
    Their cocks for the longest time
Roundabout you they watch
    And their big cunts are juicy
All the inflamed mules
    Show that they envy that herd
Solace your heart O Dabba
    Where can one leave conceit?
If one betrays you, my life
    He long betrayed his companion
Why ever do you want it?
    For you already display fear
You are only a flea that
    Ruins you as a woman's guard
When you snored proudly
    You were farting out of terror
If you went off a little
    You seized the spear or sword
You said: Would I had in
    Hand short hair horse's reins
If heights abandoned you
    The house was still an exile's
Or shame was friendly to you
    And yet this was in your lineage
If you know my meaning
    You'll discover your affliction
If you're ignorant of my idea
    Then it is similar to yourself

(٢٧٤)

«من الطويل»

يمدح أبا الفوارس وليّ بن لشكروز وكان قد أتى الكوفة لقتال الخارجي الذي نجم بها من بني كلاب وانصرف الخارجي قبل وصول دلير إليها:

وَمَنْ ذا الَّذي يَدري بِما فيهِ مِنْ جَهْلِ	كَدَعْواكَ كُلٌّ يَدَّعي صِحَّةَ العَقْلِ
وَأحْوَجُ مِمَّنْ تَعذِلينَ إلى العَذْلِ	لَهَنَّكِ أَوْلَى لائِمٍ بِمَلامَةٍ
جِدي مِثْلَ مَنْ أحْبَبْتُهُ تَجِدي مِثْلي	تَقولينَ ما في النّاسِ مِثْلَكَ عاشِقٌ
وَبِالحُسْنِ في أجْسامِهِنَّ عَنِ الصَّقْلِ	مُجِبٌّ كَنى بِالبيضِ عَنْ مُرْهَفاتِهِ
جَناها أحِبّائي وَأطْرُفُها رُسْلي	وَبِالسُّمْرِ عَنْ سُمْرِ القَنا غَيرَ أَنَّني
لِغَيرِ الثَّنايا الغُرِّ وَالحَدَقِ النُّجْلِ	عَدِمْتُ فُؤاداً لَمْ تَبِتْ فيهِ فَضْلَةٌ
وَلا بَلَّغَتْها مَنْ شَكا الهَجْرَ بِالوَصْلِ	فَما حَرَمَتْ حَسْناءُ بِالهَجْرِ غِبْطَةً
فَصَعْبُ العُلى في الصَّعْبِ وَالسَّهلُ في السَّهْلِ	ذَريني أنَلْ ما لا يُنالُ مِنَ العُلى
وَلِلمَجْدِ دونَ الشَّهدِ مِنْ إبَرِ النَّحْلِ	تُريدينَ لُقيانَ المَعالي رَخيصَةً
وَلَمْ تَعلَمي عَنْ أيِّ عاقِبَةٍ تَجْلي	حَذِرْتُ عَلَينا المَوْتَ وَالخَيلُ تَدَّعي
بِإكْرامِ دِلَّيرِ بنِ لَشْكَرَوزَ لي	وَلَسْتُ غَبيناً لَوْ شَرِبْتُ مَنِيَّتي
وَنَذْكُرُ إقْبالَ الأميرِ فَتَحْلَوْلي	تَمُرُّ الأنابيبُ الخَواطِرُ بَيْنَنا
لَزادَ سُروري بِالزِّيادَةِ في القَتْلِ	وَلَوْ كُنْتُ أدْري أنَّها سَبَبٌ لَهُ
دَعَتْكَ إلَيها كاشِفَ البَأْسِ وَالمَحْلِ	فَلا عَدِمَتْ أرْضُ العِراقَينِ فِتْنَةً
بِجَرْدٍ ذَكَرْنا مِنْكَ أمْضى مِنَ النَّصْلِ	ظَلِلْنا إذا أنْبى الحَديدُ نِصالَنا
بِأنْفَذَ مِنْ نُشّابِنا وَمِنَ النَّبْلِ	وَنَرْمي نَواصيها مِنَ اسمِكَ في الوَغى
فَقَدْ هَزَمَ الأعْداءَ ذِكْرُكَ مِنْ قَبْلِ	فَإنْ تَكُ مِنْ بَعدِ القِتالِ أتَيْتَنا
عَلى حاجَةٍ بَينَ السَّنابِكِ وَالسُّبْلِ	وَما زِلْتُ أطْوي القَلْبَ قَبلَ اجْتِماعِنا
غَرائِبَ يُؤْثِرْنَ الجِيادَ عَلى الأهْلِ	وَلَوْ لَمْ تَسِرْ سِرْنا إلَيكَ بِأنْفُسٍ
أَبَتْ رَعْيَها إلّا وَمِرْجَلُنا يَغْلي	وَخَيلٍ إذا مَرَّتْ بِوَحْشٍ وَرَوْضَةٍ
فَكانَ لَكَ الفَضْلانِ بِالقَصْدِ وَالفَضْلِ	وَلَكِنْ رَأيْتَ القَصْدَ في الفَضْلِ شِرْكَةً

274

He spoke praising Dallar ibn Kashkarawuzz who had come to Kufa to fight the Kharajites who had gathered there from the Banu Kilab But the Kharajites were dispersed before Dallar arrived at Kufa. (Long li)

As you claim each claims his logic good
    Who knows the ignorance that is in a self?
You are the first to blame by reproof
    More in need of guilt than ones you blame
You said: No lover like you among men
    Find one like I love and you find my equal
A lover compares women to a thin sword
    And fineness in their bodies to the polish
Brunettes to buff lances except for me
    Their prey is my love, spears my messages
I lost a heart when virtue departed
    A night but as bright teeth and dark eyes
Beauty denies no ambition in her parting
    No one who weeps loss wins her by union
Let me take rank no one yet has taken
    Difficult heights are hard, the easy gentle
You like one to get to the top cheaply
    But before honey no way but a bee's sting
You warned me of death in ricers' crash
    You did not know the goals they rushed to
I am no fool if I drink of my death
    With favors of Dallar Kashkarawuzz
Dangerous lances are biker between us
    So we recall the Amir's great successes
If I knew these things as cause of his
    Coming, my joy would grow as battles do
The two Iraqs would lack no discord
    To call you to expose fear and sterility
If our blades' steel was dull we rose
    To draw your memory sharper than edge
We hurl forelocks with your name in war
    More piercing than our darts and arrows
If it was after a battle you came to us
    Your fame put a foe to flight beforehand
I ceased not to travel before we met
    With desire of horse's hoof for the road
If you came not to us we'd come to you
    For exiles choose a horse over their folk
Many a fine one passes desert or field
    Denying the fodder till our pot is boiled
You see the favor of a visit is shared
    Yours double favor in intent and action

كَمَنْ جاءَهُ في دارِهِ رائِدُ الوَبْلِ	وَلَيْسَ الذي يَتَّبِعُ الوَبْلَ رائِداً
وَيَحْتَجُّ في تَرْكِ الزِّيارَةِ بالشُّغْلِ	وَما أَنا مِمَّنْ يَدَّعي الشَّوقَ قَلْبُهُ
لِمَنْ تَرَكَتْ رَعْيَ الشُّوَيْهاتِ والإِبْلِ	أَرادَتْ كِلابٌ أَنْ تَفوزَ بِدَوْلَةٍ
وَإِنْ يُؤمِنِ الضَّبُّ الخَبيثُ مِنَ الأَكْلِ	أَبى رَبُّها أَنْ يَتْرُكَ الوَحْشَ وَحْدَها
تَنيفُ بِخَدَّيها سِحوقٌ مِنَ النَّخْلِ	وَقادَ لَها دَلّيرُ كُلَّ طِمِرَّةٍ
بِأَغْنى عَنِ النَّعْلِ الحَديدِ مِنَ النَّعْلِ	وكُلَّ جَوادٍ تَلْطِمُ الأَرْضَ كَفُّهُ
وَتَطْلُبُ ما قَدْ كانَ في اليَدِ بالرِّجْلِ	فَوَلَّتْ تُريغُ الغَيْثَ والغَيْثُ خَلَّفَتْ
وَأَشْهَدُ أَنَّ الذُّلَّ شَرٌّ مِنَ الهُزْلِ	تُحاذِرُ هُزْلَ المالِ وَهيَ ذَليلَةٌ
كَريمُ السَّجايا يَسْبِقُ القَوْلَ بالفِعْلِ	وَأَهْدَتْ إِلَيْنا غَيْرَ قاصِدَةٍ بِهِ
نَتَّبِعُ آثارَ الأَسِنَّةِ بالفَتْلِ	تَتَبَّعَ آثارَ الرَّزايا بِجودِهِ
مِنَ الدّاءِ حَتّى الشّاكِلاتِ مِنَ الثُّكْلِ	شَفى كُلَّ شاكٍ سَيْفُهُ وَنَوالُهُ
فَلَوْ نَزَلَتْ شَوْقاً لَحادَ إِلى الظِّلِّ	عَفيفٌ تَروقُ الشَّمْسَ صورَةُ وَجْهِهِ
إِذا زارَها فَدَّتْهُ بِالخَيْلِ وَالرَّجْلِ	شُجاعٌ كَأَنَّ الحَرْبَ عاشِقَةٌ لَهُ
وَصَدْيانُ لا تَرْوى يَداهُ مِنَ البَذْلِ	وَرَيّانُ لا تَصْدى إِلى الخَمْرِ نَفْسُهُ
شَهيدٌ بِوَحْدانِيَّةِ اللَّهِ وَالعَدْلِ	فَتَمْليكُ دَلّيرٍ وَتَعْظيمُ قَدْرِهِ
فَلا نابَ في الدُّنْيا لِلَيْثٍ وَلا شِبْلِ	وَما دامَ دَلّيرٌ يَهُزُّ حُسامَةً
فَلا خُلِقَ مِنْ دَعْوى المَكارِمِ في حِلِّ	وَما دامَ دَلّيرٌ يُقَلِّبُ كَفَّهُ
لِمَنْ لَمْ يُطَهِّرْ راحَتَيْهِ مِنَ البُخْلِ	فَتىً لا يُرَجّى أَنْ تَتِمَّ طَهارَةٌ
فَإِنّي رَأَيْتُ الطَّيِّبَ الطَّيِّبَ الأَصْلِ	فَلا قَطَعَ الرَّحْمَنُ أَصْلاً أَتى بِهِ

(٢٧٥)

«من الكامل»

خرج أبو الطيب من الكوفة إلى العراق فراسله ابن العميد أبو الفضل محمد بن الحسين وزير ركن الدولة من أرجان فسار إليه وقال يمدحه:

وَبُكاكَ إِنْ لَمْ يَجْرِ دَمْعُكَ أَوْ جَرى	بادٍ هَواكَ صَبَرْتَ أَمْ لَمْ تَصْبِرا

He who follows a shower seeking grass
    Is not one to whose camp showers come
I'm one whose heart pretends love
    But is busy with affairs to shun a visit
Kilab intended to seize a government
    To whom did they leave lambs and colts?
Their Lord left beasts in their wilds
    To make safe the filthy lizards they eat
Dallar led to them all the war horses
    Palm fronds were topped by the prancing
His hand pounded earth with horses
    Whose hooves were without iron shoes
They turned, wanting aid they left it
    They sought what was in hands and feet
They feared lost flocks, that is shame
    They found out defeat is worse than loss
They guided to us without intending
    A generous nature who wins words by acts
He follows the track of war with bounty
    As spear wounds are tended by a doctor
His sword and gifts heal each complaint
    Of the sick, even bereavement in a mother
Modest, his face's beauty melts a sun
    If they came in love he'd turn to a shade
He is brave, war seems his lover, he
    Visits, she pays with horses and men
Watered, his s, isn't thirsty for wine
    Thirsty, his hand is not slaked by gifts
Dallar's authority and his great rank
    Are witness to God's unity and justice
While Dallar exists he shakes a sword
    No lion or cubs show teeth in the world
While Dallar lives his hand will open
    No creature pretends to lawful giving
A man, let not purity hope to be perfect
    In those whose hands are not free of greed
May Mercy not cut the root of him
    For I see goodness comes of a good root

IV: *al-Amidiyat*: Poems for Ibn Amid
275
He spoke praising Abu Fadl Muhammad ibn al-Husayn al Amid and came to him in Arajan, Arajan.
(Perfect ra)
Your love is known if you hide it or not
    As your weeping, if your tears flow or not

كَمْ غَرَّ صَبْرُكَ وابْتِسامُكَ صاحِباً   لَمّا رَآهُ وَفي الحَشا ما لا يُرى
أمَرَ الفُؤادُ لِسانَهُ وجُفونَهُ   فَكَتَمْنَهُ وكَفى بجِسمِكَ مُخبِرا
تَعِسَ المَهاري غَيرَ مَهريَّ غَدا   مُصَوَّرٌ لَبِسَ الحَريرَ مُصَوَّرا
نافَسْتُ فيهِ صُورَةً في سِتْرِهِ   لَو كُنتُهُ لَخَفيتُ حتّى يَظهَرا
لا تَتْرُبُ الأَيْدي المُقيمَةُ فَوقَهُ   كِسرى مَقامَ الحاجِبَينِ وقَيصَرا
يَقِيانِ في أَحَدِ الهَوادِجِ مُقلَةً   رَحَلَتْ وكانَ لَها فُؤادي مَحجِرا
قَد كُنتُ أَحْذَرُ بَينَهُم مِن قَبْلِهِ   لَو كانَ يَنفَعُ حائِناً أن يَحذَرا
ولَو اسْتَطَعْتُ إذِ اغْتَدَتْ رُوّادُهُم   لَمَنَعْتُ كُلَّ سَحابَةٍ أَن تَقطُرا
فَإذا السَّحابُ أَخو غُرابِ فِراقِهِم   جَعَلَ الصِّياحَ بَينَهُم أن يَمطُرا
وَإذا الحَمائِلُ ما يَخِدْنَ بِنَفْنَفٍ   إلّا شَقَقْنَ عَلَيهِ ثَوباً أَخْضَرا
يَحمِلنَ مِثلَ الرَّوضِ إلّا أَنَّها   أَسْبى مَهاةً للقُلوبِ وجُؤذُرا
فَبِلَحْظِها نَكِرَتْ قَناتي راحَتي   ضُعْفاً وأَنكَرَ خاتِمايَ الخِنصِرا
أَعطى الزَّمانُ فَما قَبِلْتُ عَطاءَهُ   وأَرادَ لي فَارَدْتُ أن أَتَخَيَّرا
أَرَحانَ أَيَّتُها الجِيادُ فَإنَّهُ   عَزْمي الَّذي يَذَرُ الوَشيجَ مُكَسَّرا
لَو كُنتُ أَفعَلُ ما اشْتَهَيْتُ فَعالَهُ   ما شَقَّ كَوكَبُكِ العَجاجَ الأَكدَرا
أُمّي أَبا الفَضلِ المُبِرَّ الَّتي   لَأُيَمِّمَنَّ أَجَلَّ بَحرٍ جَوْهَرا
أَفْتى بِرُؤيَتِهِ الأَنامُ وحاشَ لي   مِن أَن أَكونَ مُقَصِّراً أَو مُقْصِرا
صُغْتُ السِّوارَ لِأَيِّ كَفٍّ بَشَّرَتْ   بابنِ العَميدِ وأَيِّ عَبدٍ كَبَّرا
إنْ لَمْ تُغِثْني خَيلُهُ وسِلاحُهُ   فَمَتى أَقودُ إلى الأَعادي عَسكَرا
بِأبي وأُمّي ناطِقٌ في لَفظِهِ   ثَمَنٌ تُباعُ بِهِ القُلوبُ وتُشْتَرى
مَن لا تُريهِ الحَربُ خَلقاً مُقبِلاً   فيها ولا خَلْقٌ يَراهُ مُدَبِّرا
خَشّى الفُحولَ مِن الكُماةِ بِصَبغِهِ   ما يَلْبَسونَ مِنَ الحَديدِ مُعَصفَرا
يَتَكَسَّبُ القَصَبُ الضَّعيفُ بِكَفِّهِ   شَرَفاً على صُمِّ الرِّماحِ ومَفخَرا
ويَبينُ فيما مَسَّ مِنهُ بَنانُهُ   تيهُ المُدِلِّ فَلَو مَشى لَتَبَخْتَرا
يا مَن إذا وَرَدَ البِلادَ كِتابُهُ   قَبلَ الجُيوشِ ثَنى الجُيوشَ تَحَيُّرا
أَنتَ الوَحيدُ إذا رَكِبتَ طَريقَةً   وَمَنِ الرَّديفُ وقَد رَكِبتَ غَضَنفَرا

Many a friend your patient smiles cheat
    If they see you but within is what is unseen
The heart orders the tongue and eyelids
    To hide it but your body is enough to tell
Mahri camels stumble at dawn but for one
    Like a picture, wearing those painted silks
I envy it the paintings on its curtains
    If I were them I'd hide till one appeared
May hands not be poor who wove them
    Kisra is standing guard and a Caesar too
Both guard eyes in one of the howdahs
    That go and my heart makes the eye hollow
I was warned of their departure before
    If it were useful for a fear to be cautious
If able when their scouts left camp
    I'd have forbidden every cloud's dripping
A cloud is brother to parting's raven
    Whose cry at their leaving produces rain
The camels cannot plod through valleys
    Without splitting the green garment on it
They seem to bear gardens except they
    Seize hearts as wild cows and their young
By glances they deny my week hand its
    Spear and my finger disowns my two rings
Time gave me what I accept as no gift
    It planned for me but I wanted it better
To Arajan O horse, for this is my
    Will that shatters spears to splinters
If I were to do what you want done
    our stars wouldn't split the turbid dust
Take me to Abu Fadl who fulfills my vow
    To come to the sea most filled with gems
Men judge for his face and may I avoid
    Unable to fulfill or falling short of that?
I made a bracelet for a hand greeting
    Ibn Amid as in a slave's: God is great!
If his horses and weapons do not deny
    When shall I lead an army against a foe?
My father and mother, an orator! his word
    The price that buys hearts and sells them
One whom war shows none advancing
    Nor yet does anyone see his retreating
Gelded stallion warriors have his
    Saffron dye whatever they wear as armor
A feeble reed in his hand earns honor
    . And eminence over the stone deaf spear
His fingers if they touch it give it
    A coquette's pride, if it walks it swaggers
O you who when his letters reach a land
    Before armies, armies turn into disorder
You are alone when you ride on a way
    And who goes behind if you ride a lion?

وَقَطَفْتَ أنْتَ القَوْلَ لَمّا نَوَّرا	قَطَفَ الرّجالُ القَوْلَ وَقتَ نَباتِهِ
وهوَ المُضاعَفُ حُسنُهُ إنْ كُرِّرا	فهوَ المُشَيَّعُ بالمَسامِعِ إنْ مَضَى
قَلَمٌ لكَ اتّخَذَ الأنامِلَ مِنْبَرا	وَإذا سَكَتَّ فإنّ أبْلَغَ خاطِبٍ
فَرَأوْا قَناً وَأسِنّةً وَسَنَوَّرا	وَرَسائِلٍ قَطَعَ العُداةَ سِحاها
وَدَعاكَ خالِقُكَ الرّئيسَ الأكْبَرا	فدَعاكَ حُسّدُكَ الرّئيسَ وَأمْسَكوا
كاخَطّ يَمْلأُ مِسمَعَيْ مَن أبصَرا	خَلّفتَ صِفاتِكَ في العُيونِ كَلامَهُ
نَقَلَتْ يَداً سُرحاً وَخفّاً مُجمَرا	أرَأيتَ هِمّةَ ناقَتي في ناقَةٍ
طَلَباً لَقَومٍ يوقِدونَ العَنْبَرا	تَرَكّتْ دُخانَ الرّمْثِ في أوْطانِهَا
تَقَعانِ فيهِ وَلَيسَ مِسكاً أذفَرا	وَتَكرّمَتْ رُكَباتُها عن مَبرَكٍ
حُذِيَتْ قَوائِمُها العَقيقَ الأحْمَرا	فأتّكَ دامِيَةَ الأظَلّ كَأنّما
وَجَدَّتْهُ مَشغولَ اليَدَينِ مُفكّرا	بَدَرَتْ إلَيكَ يَدُ الزّمانِ كَأنّها
جالَستْ رَسطاليسَ والإسكَندَرا	مَن مُبلِغُ الأعرابِ أنّي بَعْدَها
مَنْ يَنحَرُ البَدرَ النُضارَ لِمَن قَرَى	وَمَلِلْتُ نَحرَ عِشارِها فأضافَني
مُتَمَلّكاً مُتَبَدّياً مُتَحَضِّرا	وَسَمِعْتُ بَطليموسَ دارسَ كُتبِهِ
رَدّ الإلَهُ نُفوسَهُمْ والأعْصُرَا	وَلَقِيتُ كُلّ الفاضِلينَ كَأنّما
وَأتَى فذلِكَ إذ أتَيتَ مُؤخَّرا	نُسِقوا لَنا نَسَقَ الحِسابِ مُقَدَّما
نَظَرَتْ إلَيكَ كَما نَظَرْتَ فتَعذَّرا	يا لَيتَ باكِيَةً شَجاني دَمْعُها
الشّمسُ تُشرِقُ والسّحابُ كَنَهوَرا	وَتَرى الفَضيلَةَ لا تَرُدُّ فَضيلَةً
وَأسَرُّ راحِلَةً وَأربَحُ مُتَّجَرا	أنا مِن جَميعِ النّاسِ أطيَبُ مَنزِلاً
لَوْ كانَ مِنكَ لكانَ أكرَمَ مَعْشَرا	زُحَلٌ على أنّ الكَواكِبَ قَومُهُ

(٢٧٦)

«من المتقارب»

أحضرت بجمرة قد حشيت بالنرجس والآس حتى خفيت نارها فكان الدخان يخرج من خلالها فقال:

وَأطْيَبُ ما شَمَّهُ مَعْطِسُ	أحَبُّ امرِئٍ حَبَّتِ الأنْفُسُ

Men pluck the word as it grows at times
    But you take the word whenever it blooms
It is escorted by listeners as it goes
    And its beauty doubles if it is repeated
If you are quiet the best speaker is
    The pen that takes your fingers as pulpit
Letters of which the foe cuts envelopes
    To read spearshafts, points, chain mail
Those who envy, call you lord now
    But your Creator calls you great chief
Your traits restore to eyes His words
    Like writing fills the ears of the readers
Do you see my camel's spirit in a gait
    That moves her leg and hard hoof easy?
She left tamarisk smoke in her land
    Seeking people who burn the ambergris
Her knees show bounty by not kneeling
    Lest she fall where no fragrant musk lies
She came to you with bleeding pads
    Her feet seem shod with red carnelians
She hurried to you before time's hand
    She found it busy as both hands thought
Who will inform Arabs that I after them
    Witnessed both Aristotle and Alexander?
I tired of camel killing so I am a guest
    Of one killing gold purses for his friend
I heard Ptolemy explain his books as
    A ruler, a bedouin and a city dweller
I met all men of learning as if
    God brought back their souls and times
Set out for us in order from the start
    Then came summation as you came at last
O would the weeper whose tears grieve
    Looked at you, as I looked, for my pardon
She'd see virtue not repelled by virtue
    The east sun rising and clouds as rivers
I of all men have the best of places
    Happiest in my camel, profiting in trade
Zuhal, though stars are his folk, if he
    Were with you, would be in nobler company

276
A censer hid the coals of its smoke coming from the incense.
So Abu Tayyib spoke. (Tripping su)

Loveliest of things soul can love
    And sweetest that the nose can smell

496 Diwan al-Mutanabbi

مَجامِرُهُ الآسُ والنَّرْجِسُ	وَنَشْرٌ مِنَ النَّدِّ لكِنَّما
فهَلْ هاجَهُ عِزُّكَ الأقْعَسُ	وَلَسْنا نَرى لَهَبًا هاجَهُ
لَتَحْشُدُ أرْجُلَها الأرْؤُسُ	فإنَّ القِيامَ التي حَوْلَهُ

(٢٧٧)

«من الخفيف»

يمدحه ويهنئه بالنيروز ويصف سيفا قلده إياه
وفرسا حمله عليه وجائزة وصله بها وكان
قد عاب القصيدة الرائية عليه:

وَوَرَتْ بالذي أرادَ زِنادُهْ	جاءَ نَيْروزُنا وأنْتَ مُرادُهْ
ــكَ إلى مِثْلِها مِنَ الحَوْلِ زادُهْ	هذِهِ النَّظْرَةُ التي نالَها مِنْــ
ناظِرٌ أنْتَ طَرْفُهُ ورُقادُهْ	يَنْثَني عَنكَ آخِرَ اليَوْمِ مِنْهُ
ذا الصَّباحُ الذي نَرى ميلادُهْ	نَحْنُ في أرضِ فارسٍ في سُرورٍ
كُلُّ أيّامِ عامِهِ حُسّادُهْ	عَظَمْتْهُ مَمالِكُ الفُرْسِ حتى
لَبِسَتْها تِلاعُهُ ووِهادُهْ	ما لَبِسْنا فيهِ الأكاليلَ حتى
سانَ مُلكاً بهِ ولا أوْلادُهْ	عندَ مَنْ لا يُقاسُ كسرى أبو سا
رَأيُهُ فارِسِيَّةٌ أعْيادُهْ	عَرَبيٌّ لِسانُهُ فَلْسَفيٌّ
سَرَفٌ قالَ آخِرٌ ذا اقْتِصادُهْ	كُلَّما قالَ نائِلٌ أنا منهُ
والنِّجادُ الذي عَلَيهِ نِجادُهْ	كَيْفَ يَرْتَدُّ مَنكِبي عن سَماءٍ
أعقَبَتْ منهُ واحِداً أجْدادُهْ	قَلَّدَتْني يَمينَهُ بحُسامٍ
تَزعُمُ الشَّمسُ أنَّها أرآدُهْ	كُلَّما اسْتُلَّ ضاحَكَتْهُ إياةٌ
دِ فَفي مِثْلِ أثَرِهِ إغْمادُهْ	مَثْلُوهُ في جَفْنِهِ خيفَةَ الفَقْــ
مِثلُ بَحْرٍ فِرِنْدُهُ إزْبادُهْ	مُنْعَلٌ لا مِنَ الحَفا ذَهَباً يَحْــ

The spreading incense is as if
    Its coals were myrtle and narcissus
We do not see the flame to stir it
    Does your continuous glory feed it?
For those who stand round about it
    Have heads which are envious of feet

277
He spoke praising and congratulating him on the New Year
(Nimble h)

Our Nairuz comes and you its purpose
    These firesticks kindling the fire it desires
This glance which it receives from you
    Feeds it until its likeness in another year
It swerves with you till its last day
    You are its overseer, its eye and sleep
We in the Persian land have the joy
    This dawn which we see is its birthday
The Persian kings magnified it ill
    All the days of the year envied this
We do not put on crowns for it until
    The hills and valleys send them out
Among them no comparison of Kisra
    Abu Sasan, or his children with his rule
Arabic his language, philosophic
    His thought, Persian are his festivals
Each time a gift says: I am his bounty
    A second says: This is his economy gift
How should my shoulder not touch sky
    When the sword belt on it is his belt?
His right hand girded me with a sword
    His ancestors produced only one of them
Each time it unsheathes, lights beam
    As if the sun thinks she is shining on it
They paint it on the sheath in fear of
    Loss, the effect of its image is a guard
It is not barefoot, but shod with gold
    It bears a sea whose crazing is the foam

لَـمْ مِـنْ شَـفْرَتَيْهِ إِلاّ بَدَادُهْ	يَقْسِمُ الفَارِسَ المُدَجَّجَ لا يَسْـ
وَتُضِنِّـائي فاسْـتَجْمَعَـتْ آحـادُهْ	جَمَـعَ الدَّهْـرُ حَـدَّهُ وَيَدَيْـهِ
جِلْدُهـا مُنْفِسـاتُهُ وَعَتـادُهْ	وَتَقَلَّـدْتُ شامَةً في نَـداهُ
فـارَقَتْ لِبْـدَهُ وفيهـا طِـرادُهْ	فَرَّسَتْنـا سَـوابِقٌ كُـنَّ فيـهِ
وَبِـلادٌ تَسِـيرُ فيهـا بِلادُهْ	وَرَحَـتْ راحَـةً بنـا لا تَراهَـا
ـلِ قَبُـولُ سَـوادُ عَينـي مِدادُهْ	هل لعُذْري عند الْهُمامِ أبي الفضْـ
مَكْرُمـاتُ الْمُعلَّـهِ عُـوّادُهْ	أنـا مِـنْ شِـدّةِ الحَيـاءِ عَليلٌ
عَنْ عُـلاهُ حتى تَنـاهُ انتِقادُهْ	ما كَفاني تَقصيـرُ ما قلتُ فيـهِ
أَجَـلَّ النّجُـومِ لا أَصْطـادُهْ	إنّـي أَصيـدُ البُـزاةِ وَلكِـنَّ
والـذي يُضمِـرُ الفُـؤادُ اعتِقـادُهْ	رُبَّ ما لا يُعَبِّـرُ اللَّفْـظُ عَنْـهُ
ـلِ وَهَذا الـذي أَتـاهُ اعتِيـادُهْ	ما تَعَـوَّدْتُ أن أرى كأبي الفضْـ
واضِحـاً أَنْ يَفُوتَـهُ تَعْـدادُهْ	إنّ في المَوْجِ للغَريـقِ لعُـذْراً
ـرُ عِمـادي وَابْنُ العميـدِ عِمـادُهْ	للنَّـدَى الغَلَـبُ إنَّـهُ فـاضَ والشِّعْـ
لَيْـسَ لي نُطْقُـهُ وَلا في آدُهْ	نـالَ طِبّـي الأُمُـورَ إلاّ كَريمـاً
سِـيمَ أَنْ تَحمِـلَ البِحـارَ مَـزادُهْ	ظالِـمُ الجُـودِ كُلَّمـا حَـلَّ رَكْبٌ
أَنْ يَكـونَ الكَـلامُ مِمّـا أَفـادُهْ	غَمَرَتْنـي فَوائِـدٌ شـاءَ فيهـا
فاشْـتَهَى أنْ يَكـونَ فيهـا فُـؤادُهْ	مـا سَـمِعْنا بِمَنْ أَحَـبَّ العَطَايـا
في مَكـانٍ أَعْرابُـهُ أَكْـرادُهْ	خَلَـقَ اللهُ أَفْصَـحَ النّـاسِ طُـرّاً
في زَمـانٍ كُـلُّ النّفُـوسِ جَـرادُهْ	وَأَحَـقَّ الغُيُـوثِ نَفْسـاً بِحَمْـدٍ
لم والبَعْـثُ حِيـنَ شـاعَ فَسـادُهْ	مِثْلَمـا أَحْدَثَـتْ النُّبُـوّةَ في العـا
ـعَ فيـهِ وَلم يَشِـنْها سَـوادُهْ	زانَـتِ اللَّيْـلَ غُـرّةُ القَمَـرِ الطّا
ـسَـدَتْ إلى رَبِّها الرَّئيسِ عِبـادُهْ	كَثُـرَ الفِكْـرُ كيفَ نُهْدي كما أَهْـ
ـلِ فَمِنْـهُ هِباتُـهُ وَقيـادُهْ	والـذي عنـدَنـا مِـنَ المَـالِ والخَيْـ
كُـلُّ مُهْـرٍ مَيدانُـهُ إنْشـادُهْ	فَبَعَثْنـا بِـأَرْبَعيـنَ مِهـاراً
أَرَبـاً لا يَـراهُ فيمَـا يُـزادُهْ	عَـدَدَ عِشْـتَهُ يَـرَى الجِسْـمُ فيـهِ
مَرْبِـطٌ تَسْـبِقُ الجِيـادَ جِيـادُهْ	فَارْتَبِطْهـا فَـإِنّ قَلْبـاً نَمَاهَـا

It splits the armored warrior, not
    Yielding its edges until his saddle top
Destiny joined its edges, his hand and
    My praise so its unique things are joined
A beauty spot in his bounty, a necklace
    Its skin is precious with their pock marks
Fast horses, his gift, taught us riding
    They left his saddle pad and his pursuits
They hope for rest with us but see it not
    The lands they traveled in were his lands
Shall my excuse to gallant Abu Fadl be
    The offer of my eye's black as his own ink'
I am sick with an intensity of shame
    The gifts of one who caused it tended it
A fault did not hinder what I said of his
    Rank until he praised it by the criticism
I was a hunter of the falcon's mistress
    But the highest stars I could never reach
Often what words can't express about him
    Is what a heart conceals as its conviction
I am not used to see Abu Fadl's like
    This that I bring him is the usual to him
An excuse for one drowning in waves!
    Plainly he should not try to count them
Victory is the bounty he spreads, poetry
    Is my support and Ibn Amid supports that
My ideas had experience but not nobility
    I had not his eloquence or strength in me
He wrongs bounty if riders stop with him
    He arranges that providers bring out a sea
They overwhelm me, a heart wishes now
    That words were among things he ransoms
We never heard of anyone who gave gifts
    And wished that among them was his heart
God created him most eloquent of men
    Though native Kurd he made himself Arab
Most worthy praise showers for himself
    In times when all men are his grasshoppers
As when prophets appear in the world
    A mission occurs while corruption spreads
The brightness of a rising moon adorns
    The night, and darkness does not harm it
Thoughts are many how we are guided
    As his slaves are guided to their country
For what we have of flocks and horses
    Are his as are his gifts and guidance
We are sending forty of the Mahri kind
    Each Mahri recited in its parade ground
A number, may you live it, body sees as
    Goal but sees not how it is to be doubled
Station them for a heart trained them
    As station to excel that of finest horses

(٢٧٨)

«من المتقارب»

قال عند قراءة كتاب ورد عليه من أبي الفتح ابن العميد:

بِكُتْبِ الأَنامِ كِتابٌ وَرَدْ	فَـدَتْ يَـدَ كاتِبِـهِ كُـلُّ يَـدْ
يُعَبِّرُ عَمَّا لَـهُ عِنْدَنـا	وَيَذْكُـرُ مِن شَـوْقِهِ مـا نَجِدْ
فَأَخْرَقَ رائِيَـهُ ما رَأَى،	وَأَبْـرَقَ نـاقِدَهُ ما انْتَقَـدْ
إذا سَـمِعَ النّاسُ أَلْفاظَـهُ	خَلَقْـنَ لَـهُ في القُلوبِ الحَسَـدْ
فَقُلْـتُ وَقـدْ فَـرَسَ النّاطِقينَ	كَـذا يَفْعَـلُ الأَسَـدُ ابنُ الأَسَـدْ

(٢٧٩)

«من الطويل»

ورد عليه كتاب عضد الدولة يستزيره فقال عند مسيره مودعا ابن العميد سنة أربع وخمسين وثلاث مئة (٩٦٥م):

نَسيتُ وَما أَنسى عِتاباً على الصَّدِّ	وَلا خَفَراً زادَتْ بِهِ حُمْرَةُ الخَدِّ
وَلا لَيْلَـةً قَصَّرْتُهـا بِقَصيـرَةٍ	أَطالَتْ يَدي في جيدِها صُحْبَةَ العِقْدِ
وَمَـنْ لي بِيَـوْمٍ مِثـلِ يَـوْمٍ كَرِهْتُـهُ	قَرُبْتُ بِـهِ عِنـدَ الـوَداعِ مِن البُعْـدِ
وَأَلّا يُخِـصَّ الفَقْـدُ شَـيْئاً لِأَنَّـني	فَقَدْتُ فَلَم أَفْقِـدْ دُموعي وَلا وَجْدي
تَمَنّىٰ يَلَـذَّ المُسْـتَهامُ بِذِكْـرِهِ	وَإِنْ كـانَ لا يُغْـني فَتيـلاً وَلا يُجْدي

278
A letter
from Abu Fath ibn al-Amid
came to
Abu Tayyib recalling
his joy and love
so he spoke impromptu.
(Tripping d-)

In the writing of men a letter came
    Every hand ransoms the writer's hand
It tells his reltionship to us
    And recalls what we found in his love
It rends the reader by what he sees
    Flashes of lightning at faults he find
When mankind hears its words
    They become jealous in their hearts
I spoke, it devoured the speeches
    Like the lion who is son of the lion

279
He spoke also
bidding farewell
to Ibn Amid
on his journey
to the land of Fars in the year 354.
(long di)

I forgot but forget not refusal's blame
    Nor shame increasing the cheeks' blushing
Nor a night I found short within a tent
    And my hand long on her neck and necklace
Who aids me on a day like one I hate
    At farewell when I am close to one afar?
Though loss is not a particular thing
    I lose but not my tears and my passions
This is desire, lust enjoys its memory
    Even if it hasn't a farthing nor begs it

وَلَكِنَّـهُ غَيـظُ الأَسيـرِ عَلـى القِـدِّ	وَغَيـظٌ عَلى الأَيّـامِ كالنّـارِ في الحَشَـا
فآفَـةُ غِمـدي في دُلوقـي وَفي حَـدّي	فَإِمّـا تَرَيْنـي لا أُقيـمُ بِبَلْـدَةٍ
فَأحرِمُـهُ عِرْضـي وَأَطْعِمُـهُ جِلدي	يُحِـلُّ القَنـا يَـوْمَ الطِّعـانِ بِعَقْوَتـي
بَحائِـبُ لا يُفَكِّـرْنَ فـي النحـسِ وَالسَّعـدِ	تُبَـدِّلُ أَيّامـي وَعَيْشـي وَمَنـزِلـي
عَلَيْهِـنَّ لا خَـوْفٌ مِـنَ الحَـرِّ والبَـرْدِ	وَأَوْجُـهُ فِتيـانٍ حَيـاءً تَلَثَّمـوا
وَلَكِنَّـهُ مِـنْ شيمَـةِ الأَسَـدِ الـوَرْدِ	وَلَيـسَ حَيـاءُ الوَجْـهِ في الذِّئـبِ شيمَـةً
أَجـازَ القَنـا وَالخَـوْفُ خَيـرٌ مِـنَ الـوُدّ	إِذا لَـمْ تُجِـزْهُـمْ دارَ قَـوْمٍ مَـوَدَّةٌ
تَوَفَّـرَ مِـن بَيـنِ المُلُـوكِ عَلـى الجَـدّ	يَحيـدونَ عَـن هَـزْلِ المُلوكِ إلى الّـذي
يَسيـرُ بَيـنَ أَنيـابِ الأَسـاوِدِ وَالأَسْـدِ	وَمَـنْ يَصْحَـبِ اسمَ ابـنِ العَميـدِ مُحَمَّـدٍ
وَيَعْبُـرُ مِـنْ أَفواهِهِـنَّ عَلـى دُرْدِ	يَمُـرُّ مِـنَ السَّـمِّ الوَحِـيِّ بِعاجِـزٍ
فَجاءَتْـهُ لَم تَسمَـعْ حُـداءً سِـوى الرَّعـدِ	كَفانـا الرَّبيـعُ العيـسَ مِـن بَرَكاتِـهِ
كَرَعْـنَ بِسِبْـتٍ في إِنـاءٍ مِـنَ الـوَرْدِ	إِذا مـا استَجَنَّ المـاءَ يَعـرِضُ نَفسَـهُ
فَلَـمْ يُخِلْنـا جَـوٌّ هَبَطناهُ مِـن رِفدِ	كَأَنّـا أَرادَت شُكرَنـا الأَرضُ عِندَهُ
وَإِتيانِـهِ نَبْغـي الرَّغائِـبَ بِالزُّهْـدِ	لَنـا مَذْهَـبُ العُبّـادِ فـي تَـرْكِ غَيـرِهِ
بِأَرجانَ حَتّـى ما يَئِسنـا مِـنَ الخُلْـدِ	رَجَوْنـا الّـذي يَرْجـونَ في كُـلِّ جَنَّـةٍ
تَعَـرُّضَ وَحـشٍ خائِفـاتٍ مِـنَ الطَّـرْدِ	تَعَـرُّضُ لِلـزُّوّارِ أَعنـاقُ خَيْلِـهِ
وَرُودَ قَطـاً صُـمٍّ تَشـايَحنَ في وِرْدِ	وَتَلقَـى نَواصيَهـا المَنايـا مُشيـحَـةً
إِلَيْـهِ وَيَنْسُبْـنَ السُّيـوفَ إلى الهِنـدِ	وَتَنسُـبُ أَفعـالَ السّيـوفِ نُفوسَهـا
أَتـى نَسَـبٌ أَعْلـى مِـنَ الأَبِ وَالجَـدّ	إِذا الشُّرَفـاءُ البيـضُ مَتّـوا بِقَتـوِهِ
فَمـا أَرمَـدَتْ أَجفانَـهُ كَثـرَةُ الرُّمْـدِ	فَتـىً فاتَـتِ العَـدْوى مِـنَ النّـاسِ عَينَـهُ
فَقَد جَـلَّ أَنْ يُعـدي بِشَـيْءٍ وَأَنْ يُعـدي	وَخالَفَهُـمْ خَلْقـاً وَخُلْقـاً وَمَوْضِعـاً
بِمَنشـورَةِ الرّايـاتِ مَنصـورَةِ الجُنـدِ	يُغَيِّـرُ أَلـوانَ اللَّيالـي عَلـى العِـدى
كَتائِـبَ لا يَرْدي الصَّبـاحُ كَمـا تَـرْدي	إِذا ارتَقَبُـوا صُبحـاً رَأَوْا قَبـلَ ضَوْئِـهِ
وَلا يَحتَمـى مِنهـا بِغَـورٍ وَلا نَجْـدِ	وَمَبثـوثَـةً لا تَتَّقـى بِطَليعَـةٍ
مِـنَ الكُثْـرِ غـانٍ بِالعَبيـدِ عَـنِ الحَشْـدِ	يَغِضْـنَ إِذا مـا عُـدْنَ فـي مُتَفـاقِـدٍ
فَهُـنَّ عَلَيْـهِ كَالطَّرائِـقِ فـي البُـرْدِ	حَثَّـتْ كُـلُّ أَرضٍ تَرْبَـةً في غُبـارِهِ

Anger at destiny is as fire in vitals
    But it is rage of a prisoner at his bonds
If you see I don't stay long in a land
    The ruin of my sheath is unsheathed edge
On jousting day the lances fall near me
    I defend my honor and my courage enjoys it
My days change as my life and dwelling
    Camels think not about bad or good times
Young men's faces are veiled modestly
    They have no fear of the heat or the cold
A modest face is not the wolf's nature
    Rather it is the nature of the red lions
If love doesn't pay them in a folk camp
    A spear is reward fear better than love
They love the weakness of kings for
    What abounds among the kings of bounty
A user of Muhammad ibn Amid's name
    Can travel amid fangs of snakes and lions
He changes swift poison to weakness
    And recalls what we found in his love
By his favor meadows suffice for camels
    Flashes of lightning at faults he finds
They come to water presenting itself
    Sip with lips at pools rimmed by roses
Earth wants our thanks to be given
    Plains won't let us descend due to gifts
Our view ascetic in leaving all others
    In coming to him we seek content in rule
What they hope we hope in all gardens
    Of Arajan so we despair not of paradise
Horses' necks turn from his guests
    With beasts' turning fearful of the hunt
They toss the forelocks fast at death
    As deaf watering grouse flying to a drink
Actions of swords trace themselves
    To him thoughswords are traced to India
When fine noble men come to service
    The lineage is higher than father or kin
A hero whose eyes destroy men's rage
    Much sickness cannot make sick his eyes
His nature, class, rank is not theirs
    He is too great to hate but he may do so
He changes nights' colors for the foe
    By flutter of flags for soldiers' victory
If they watch dawn they see before light
    Cavalry plunging on as dawn cannot burst
Scattered they guard against no attack
    Nor look for that in hollows or on heights
Loaded when they turn from the melee
    With much booty for slaves apart from men
Each land stirs dust for his clouds
    They are like the stripes on the burda

فَهَـذا وَإِلّا فَـالهُدى ذا فَمـا المَهـدي	فَإِنْ يَكُـنِ المَهدِيُّ مَـنْ بـانَ هَدْيُـهُ
وَيَخْـدَعُ عَمّـا في يَدَيْـهِ مِـنَ النَقْـدِ	يُعَلِّلُنـا هَـذا الزَّمـانُ بِـذا الوَعْـدِ
أَمِ الرَّشْدُ شَيءٌ غـائِبٌ لَيسَ بِالرَّشْدِ	هَلِ الخَيْرُ شَيءٌ لَيسَ بِالخَيْـرِ غـائِبٌ
وَأَسْجَعَ ذي قَلْبٍ وَأَرحَمَ ذي كَبِـدِ	أَأَحْزَمَ ذي لُـبٍّ وَأَكْـرَمَ ذي يَـدٍ
عَلى المِنبَرِ العيلي أَوِ الفَرَسِ النَّهْدِ	وَأَحْسَـنَ مُعْتَـمٍّ جُلوسـاً وَرَكبَـةً
فَلَمّـا حَمِدْنـا لَـم تَـدِمْنـا عَلى الحَمدِ	تَفَضَّلَـتِ الأَيّـامُ بِالجَمْـعِ بَيْنَنـا
جَمـالِكَ وَالعِلْـمُ المُبَـرِّحُ وَالمَجْـدِ	جَعَلْـنَ وَداعـى وَاحِـداً لِثَلاثَـةٍ
يُعَيِّرُني أَهْلي بِإِدراكِهـا وَحْـدي	وَقَد كُنتُ أَدْرَكْتُ المُنى غَيْرَ أَنَّـني
أَرى بَعدَهُ مَـنْ لا يَرى مِثْلَـهُ بَعدي	وَكُـلُّ شَريـكٍ في السُرورِ مُصَبِّحي
مُخَـلَّفُ قَلبي عِنـدَ مَـن فَضلُهُ عِنـدي	فَجُـدْ لي بِقَلْـبٍ إِنْ رَحِمْـتَ فَـإِنَّني
لَقُلْـتُ أَصـابَتْ غَيـرَ مَذمومَـةِ العَهْدِ	وَلَـوْ فـارَقَتْ نَفْسـي إِلَيكَ حَياتَـها

(٢٨٠)

«من المنسرح»

يمدح عضد الدولة عند قدومه عليه بشيراز:

لِمَـنْ نَـأَتْ وَالبَديـلُ ذِكْراهـا	أَوّهْ بَديـلٌ مِـنْ قَوْلَتـي واهـا
وَأَصْـلُ واهـاً وَأَوّهْ مَرآهـا	أَوّهْ لِمَـنْ لا أَرى مَحاسِنَهـا
تُبصِـرُ في نـاظِري مُحَيّاهـا	شـامِيَّةٌ طالَمـا خَلَـوْتُ بِهـا
وَإِنَّمـا قَبَّلَـتْ بِـهِ فاهـا	فَقَبَّلَـتْ نـاظِري تُغالِطُنـي
وَلَيْتَـهُ لا يَـزالُ مَأْواهـا	فَلَيْتَهـا لا تَـزالُ آوِيَـةً
إِلّا فُـؤاداً رَمَتْـهُ عَيناهـا	كُـلُّ جَريـحٍ تُرْجـى سَلامَتُـهُ
مِـنْ مَطَـرٍ بَرقُـهُ ثَناياهـا	تَبُـلُّ خَدَّيَّ كُلَّمـا اِبْتَسَمَـتْ
جَعَلْتُـهُ في المُـدامِ أَفواهـا	مـا نَفَضَـتْ في يَدي غَدائِرُهـا
عَلى حِسـانٍ وَلَسْـنَ أَشْباهـا	في بَلَـدٍ تُضـرَبُ الحِجالُ بِـهِ
وَهُـنَّ دُرٌّ فَذِبْـنَ أَمْواهـا	لَقيـنَنـا وَالحُمـولُ سـائِرَةٌ
تَقـولُ إِيّـاكُـمْ وَإِيّاهـا	كُـلُّ مَهـاةٍ كَأَنَّ مُقْلَتَهـا

If a Mahdi is guided as foretold, he
  Is it, if not, he is guided and no Mahdi
These times make us sick with hopes
  And deceive one in whose hand is cash
Is not the best thing a good not hid
  Or if guidance is hid isn't it unguided?
O keener wit, most generous in gifts
  Braver in heart, most merciful in bowels
And finest turban or seated or riding
  Whether on a great horse or high pulpit
Days were gracious in bringing us near
  We praised and they stayed not for praise
They made a single farewell in triple form
  Your beauty, known wisdom and your glory
I attain a reward except that I am
  Ashamed for my people I alone attain it
Everyone who shares in my joy's morn
  Knows one will not see its like once more
Be generous at heart as I go, for
  I leave my heart to one who is my virtue
If my body leaves its life with you
  I say it happened without blame to a bond

V. *al-Adudiyat*: Poems for Adud al-Daula
280
He spoke praising Abu Shuja Adud al-Daula Fannakhusra.
(Flowing ha)

O pain! and the word means, O wonder!
  And her memory's idea for one who goes
Alas for one whose beauties I saw not
  Wonder's root and pain's in her sight
A Syrian who as long as I was alone
  With her showed her visage in my vision
She kissed my eyes as she cheated me
  For so she kissed her own mouth in them
Would she'd continue to give me refuge
  And may he continue to give me shelter
All the wounded whose peace was hope
  She struck with her eyes but for a heart
When she smiled my cheeks grew wet
  With rain whose lightning was her teeth
She was one to shake her braids into
  My hand as I put spice into this wine
In a land where the veil is required
  For beauties who are not compared to her
They met us and camels were on the move
  And they were pearls whose water dripped
It was as if all the wild cows' eyes said
  You should beware, and they should too!

إِذا لِسانُ المُحِبِّ سَمّاها	فيهِنَّ مَن تَقطُرُ السُيوفُ دَماً
وَكُلُّ نَفسٍ تُحِبُّ مَحياها	أَحِبُّ حِمصاً إِلى خُناصِرَةٍ
نَّانِ وَنَغري عَلى حُمَيّاها	حَيثُ التُقى خَدُّها وَتُفّاحُ لُبْـ
شَتَوْتُ بِالصَحصَحانِ مَشتاها	وَصِفتُ فيها مَصيفَ بادِيَةٍ
أَوْ ذُكِرَتْ حِلّةٌ غَزَوْناها	إِنْ أَعشَبَتْ رَوضَةٌ رَعَيْناها
صِدْنا بِأُخرى الجِيادِ أُولاها	أَوْ عَرَضَتْ عانَةٌ مُقَزَّعَةٌ
تَكوسُ بَينَ الشُروبِ عَقراها	أَوْ عَبَرَتْ هَجمَةٌ بِنا تَرَكَتْ
تَجُرُّ طولى القَنا وَقُصراها	وَالخَيلُ مَطرودَةٌ وَطارِدَةٌ
يُنَظِّرُها الدَهرُ بَعدَ قَتلاها	يُعجِبُها قَتلُها الكُماةَ وَلا
وَسِرْتُ حَتّى رَأَيْتُ مَوْلاها	وَقَدْ رَأَيْتُ المُلوكَ قاطِبَةً
يَأمُرُها فيهِمْ وَيَنْهاها	وَمَنْ مَناياهُمْ بِراحَتِهِ
لَـةِ فَناخُسْرُوا شَهَنْشاها	أَبا شُجاعٍ بِفارِسَ عَضُدَ الدَوْ
وَإِنَّما لَذَّةٌ ذَكَرْناها	أَسامِياً لَمْ تَزِدْهُ مَعرِفَةً
كَما تَقودُ السَحابَ عُظماها	تَقودُ مُستَحسَنَ الكَلامِ لَنا
أَنفَسُ أَموالِهِ وَأَسْناها	هُوَ النَفيسُ الَذي مَواهِبُهُ
لَمْ يُرضِها أَنْ تَراهُ يَرْضاها	لَوْ فَطِنَتْ خَيْلُهُ لِنائِلِهِ
إِذا انتَشى خَلَّةً تَلافاها	لا تَجِدُ الخَمرَ في مَكارِمِهِ
فَتَسقُطُ الراحُ دونَ أُذْناها	تُصاحِبُ الراحُ أَريحِيَّةً
ثُمَّ تُزيلُ السُرورَ عُقْباها	تَسُرُّ طَرَباتُهُ كَرائِنَهُ
قاطِعَةٍ زيرَها وَمَثناها	بِكُلِّ مَوهوبَةٍ مُوَلوَلَةٍ
مِنْ جودٍ كَفِّ الأَميرِ يَغشاها	تَعومُ عَوْمَ القَذاةِ في زَبَدٍ
إِشراقَ أَلفاظِهِ بِمَعناها	تُشرِقُ تيجانُهُ بِغُرَّتِهِ
وَنَفسُهُ تَستَقِلُّ دُنياها	دانَ لَهُ شَرقُها وَمَغرِبُها
مِلْءُ فُؤادِ الزَمانِ إِحداها	تَجَمَّعَتْ في فُؤادِهِ هِمَمٌ
أَوسَعَ مِنْ ذا الزَمانِ أَبْداها	فَإِنْ أَتى حَظُّها بِأَزمِنَةٍ
تَعثُرُ أَحياؤُها بِمَوْتاها	وَصارَتِ الفَيلَقانُ واحِدَةً
تَسجُدُ أَقمارُها لِأَبْهاها	وَدارَتِ النَيِّراتُ في فَلَكٍ

For them the swords dripped blood
    When the tongue of a lover named her
I love the land of Hims to Khunasri
    As everyone loves those that live there
Where her cheeks and Lubnan apples
    And my teeth met over the Humai wine
I spent summers in the desert heat
    I spent winters on those cold plains
If meadows had shrubs we grazed them
    If a settlement was seen we raided that
Or if wild asses came scudding up1
    We chased their first with last horses
Or a camel herd passed we left them
    To wander hamstrung among drinkers
And horsemen pursued and were now
    Running with long lances and with short
The killing surprised mailed warriors
    They never looked at killing after that
And I observed kings by the dozens
    And traveled until I saw their master
Those whose fates were in his hands
    To command themselves or to forbid
Abu Shuja of Persia, Adud al-Daula
    Called the Fannakhusra, Shahanshah
Names that do not increase his fame
    But rather pleasure as we recall them
You bring the benefit of words to us
    As those clouds bring their greatness
He is most glorious whose gifts come
    Most dear in his wealth and their fire
If his horses knew of his gifts he'd
    Not like them to see his content in them
Wine has no part in his generosity
    So if he feels dizzy it remedies
Wine accompanies his liberal moods
    But it falls short of the lowest of them
His pleasure rejoices singing girls
    But then he brings their joy to its end
Each girl makes lament when given
    Breaking the strings and the lute itself
They float like motes in the foam of
    Bounty of the Amir's overflowing hand
Their east and west submit to him
    He himself thinks little of their world
His crown shines on his forehead
    His words make a dawn of meaning
Desires gather in his heart, one of
    Them would fill the heart of the time
If its joy would come in ages more
    Spacious than these it would be eternal
Opposed armies would become one
    The living would stumble over the dead
Two linked fires would turn in heaven
    Its moons prostrate before the splendor

مُثْنِي عَلَيْهِ الوَغَى وَخَيْلاهَا	ألفَارِسُ المُتَّقَى السِّلاحُ بهِ الـ
في الحَرْبِ آثارَهَا عَرَفْناهَا	لَوْ أَنْكَرَتْ مِنْ حَيائِهَا يَدُهُ
وَناقِعُ المَوْتِ بَعْضُ سِيماهَا	وَكَيْفَ تَخْفَى الَّتِي زِيادَتُهَا
دُنْيا وَأَبْنائِهَا وَمَا تاهَا	الوَاسِعُ العُذْرِ أَنْ يَتِيةَ على الـ
لَمَّا عَدَتْ نَفْسُهُ سَجَايَاهَا	لَوْ كَفَرَ العالَمُونَ نِعْمَتَـهُ
مَعْرِفَةً عِنْدَهُمْ وَلا جَاهَا	كالشَّمسِ لا تَبْتَغِي بِمَا صَنَعَتْ
والجاءَ إِلَيْهِ تَكُنْ حُدَيَّاهَا	وَلِّ السَّلاطِينَ مَنْ تَوَلَّاهَا
غَيرَ أَمِيرٍ وَإِنْ بهَا باهَى	وَلا تَغُرَّنَّكَ الإِمَارَةُ في
قَدْ أَفْعَمَ الخافِقَيْنِ رَيَّاهَا	فَإِنَّما المَلْكُ رَبُّ مَمْلَكَةٍ
سِلْمُ العِدَى عِنْدَهُ كَهَيْجَاهَا	مُبْتَسِمٌ وَالوُجُوهُ عَابِسَةٌ
وَعَبْدُهُ كَالمُوَحِّدِ اللَّهَا	النَّاسُ كالعَابِدِينَ آلِهَةً

(٢٨١)

«من الوافر»

يمدح عضد الدولة ويذكر في طريقه إليه شِعب بوان:

بِمَنْزِلَةِ الرَّبِيعِ مِنَ الزَّمانِ	مَغَانِي الشِّعْبِ طِيباً في المَغَانِي
غَرِيبُ الوَجْهِ وَاليَدِ وَاللِّسَانِ	وَلَكِنَّ الفَتَى العَرَبِيَّ فيها
سُلَيْمانٌ لَسارَ بِتَرْجُمَانِ	مَلاعِبُ جِنَّةٍ لَوْ سَارَ فيها
خَشِيتُ وَإِنْ كَرُمْنَ مِنَ الحِرانِ	طَبَتْ فُرْسانُنا وَالخَيْلَ حَتَّى
على أَعْرافِها مِثْلَ الجُمَانِ	غَدَوْنَا تَنْفُضَ الأَغْصَانُ فيها
وَجُئْنَ مِنَ الضِّياءِ بِمَا كَفَانِي	فَسِرْتُ وَقَدْ حَجَبْنَ الحَرَّ عَنِّي
دَنانِيراً تَفِرُّ مِنَ البَنَانِ	وَأَلْقَى الشَّرْقُ مِنْهَا في ثِيَابِي
بِأَشْرِبَةٍ وَقَفْنَ بِلا أَوَانِ	لَها ثَمَرٌ تُشِيرُ إِلَيْكَ مِنْهُ
صَلِيلَ الحَلْيِ في أَيْدِي الغَوَانِي	وَأَمْواهٌ تَصِلُّ بهَا حَصَاهَا

Rider who guards himself as armor
    Battles praise him as do their horsemen
If his hand disowned itself modestly
    In war, we would know it by its tracks
How should what is its scourge be hid
    The sting of death or some of its marks?
Reason for his excuse if he is proud
    Of a world and its sons and kills them
If the universe denied his favors
    His soul would not oppose her nature
Like sun they ask not of their acts
    Any profit for themselves or reward
Let sultans rule what you give them
    Take refuge with him who is their foe
Do not deceive yourself that command
    Is another Amir's even if he boasts of it
Truly kingship is lord of the kingdom
    Whose perfume clings from east to west
Smiling though the face be darkened
    Enemy's peace for it like their battles
Men are as servants of heathen gods
    His servants like those unified by God

281
He spoke praising him and recalling his journey to him in the Shi'b Bawwan (Exuberant ni)

Abodes of Shib, sweetest among abodes
    As this time of spring among these seasons
Even though an Arab youth is here
    A stranger in face and hand and tongue
Playground of jinn, if Solomon were
    To travel here he'd need an interpreter
It is good to our horsemen and our horses
    Yet I fear though thoroughbred they'll balk
We go at dawn with branches dripping
    The like of seed pearls on their manes
I travel on as they veil sun from me
    Bringing me enough of the rays of light
The east threw some of it on my shirt
    Like dinars that fled from these fingers
They had fruits that were offered
    By way of drink ready without the cups
Waters rustling there over pebbles
    Purling bracelets on a singer's hands

لَبيقُ التَّرَدُّدِ صِيِّيُ الجَفانِ	وَلَوْ كانَتْ دِمَشْقَ ثَنى عِناني
بِهِ النّيرانُ نَدِّيُ الدَّخانِ	يَلَنْجوجي ما رُفِعَتْ لِضَيفٍ
وَتَرْحَلُ مِنهُ عَن قَلْبٍ جَبانِ	تَحِلَّ بِهِ عَلى قَلْبِ شُجاعٍ
يُشَيِّعُني إلى النُّوَبَنْذَجانِ	مَنازِلُ لَمْ يَزَلْ مِنها خَيالٌ
أَجابَتْهُ أَغاني القَيْنانِ	إذا غَنَّى الحَمامُ الوُرْقُ فيها
إذا غَنّى وَناحَ إلى البَيانِ	وَمَنْ بِالشِّعْبِ أَحْوَجُ مِنْ حَمامٍ
وَمَوْصوفاهُما مُتَباعِدانِ	وَقَدْ يَتَقارَبُ الوَصْفانِ جِدّاً
أَعَنْ هَذا يُسارُ إلى الطِّعانِ	يَقولُ بِشِعْبِ بَوّانَ حِصاني:
وَعَلَّمَكُمْ مُفارَقَةَ الجِنانِ	أَبوكُمْ آدَمٌ سَنَّ المَعاصي
سَلَوْتُ عَنِ العِبادِ وَذا المَكانِ	فَقُلتُ: إذا رَأَيْتُ أَبا شُجاعٍ
إلى مَنْ ما لَهُ في النّاسِ ثانِ	فَإِنَّ النّاسَ وَالدُّنْيا طَريقٌ
كَتَعْليمِ الطِّرادِ بِلا سِنانِ	لَقَدْ عَلَّمْتُ نَفْسي القَوْلَ فيهِمْ
وَلَيْسَ لِغَيرِ ذي عَضُدٍ يَدانِ	بِعَضْدِ الدَّوْلَةِ امْتَنَعَتْ وَعَزَّتْ
وَلا حَطٌّ مِنَ السُّمْرِ اللَّدانِ	وَلا قَبْضٌ عَلى البيضِ المَواضي
لِيَوْمِ الحَرْبِ بِكْرٍ أَوْ عَوانِ	دَعَتْهُ بِمَفزَعِ الأَعْضاءِ مِنها
وَلا يَكْني كَفَنّا خُسْرَ كانِ	فَما يُسْمي كَفَنّا خُسْرَ مُسْمٍ
وَلا الإخْبارُ عَنْهُ وَلا العِيانِ	وَلا تُحْصى فَضائِلُهُ بِظَنٍّ
وَأَرْضُ أَبي شُجاعٍ مِنْ أَمانِ	أَروضُ النّاسِ مِنْ تُرْبٍ وَخَوْفٍ
وَيَضْمَنُ لِلصَّوازِمِ كُلَّ جانِ	يُزِمُّ عَلى اللُّصوصِ لِكُلِّ تَجْرٍ
دُفِعْنَ إلى المَحاني وَالرِّعانِ	إذا طَلَبَتْ وَدائِعُهُمْ ثِقاتٍ
تَصيحُ بِمَنْ يَمُرُّ: أَلا تَراني	فَباتَتْ فَوْقَهُنَّ بِلا صِحابٍ
لِكُلِّ أَصَمَّ صِلٍّ أَفْعَوانِ	رُقاهُ كُلَّ أَبْيَضَ مَشْرَفِيٍّ
وَلا المالُ الكَريمُ مِنَ الهَوانِ	وَما تُرْقى لُهاهُ مِنْ نَداهُ
يَحُضُّ عَلى التَّباقي بِالتَّفاني	حَمى أَطْرافَ فارِسَ شَمَّرِيٌّ
سِوى ضَرْبِ المَثالِثِ وَالمَثاني	بِضَرْبٍ هاجَ أَطْرابَ المَنايا
كَسا البُلْدانَ ريشَ الحَيْقُطانِ	كَأَنَّ دَمَ الجَماجِمِ في العَناصي

If at Dimashq my reins were taken
    By one good at shard in Chinese bowls
Aloes wood piled up for the guests
    With fires that are spicy as they smoke
One stops with the heart of a hero
    And leaves there with a coward's heart
A home from which ghosts did not go
    As those that follow me to Naubandijan
And when the gray doves sing here
    The songs of singing girls respond
Those in the Shib, more than doves
    Need clarity as they sing and lament
The two songs approach each other
    But two descriptions are very far apart
In the Shib Bawwan my horse said:
    We have to leave here for a jousting?
Your father Adam used disobedience
    And taught you how to go from gardens
And I said: When I saw Abu Shuja
    I was consoled for worlds and this place
For men and the world are a highway
    To one who has no second in creation
I taught myself to speak about them
    Like learning jousting without a spear
By Adud al Daula defended honor
    Two hands belong to no other forearm
Nor any grip on the cutting sword
    Nor joy in the brown flexible lance
They name him refuge of their men
    On a day of virgin war or an old one
No one is named as Fannakhusra
    Nor called by Fannakbusra's surname
His virtues not understood by thought
    Nor by tales about him or by eyewitness
The lands of men are dust and fear
    But the land of Abu Shuja is security
He guards each merchant from thieves
    Guarantees the sword to every criminal
If their cargoes require a safeguard
    They are defended on plain or mountain
They spend night without a guard here
    Saying to passersby: Why don't you see?
His magic is in every Mashrafi sword
    Against every deaf basilisk among snakes
His wealth not charmed against bounty
    Nor his generous flocks against contempt
A hero defends Persian borders swiftly
    Urging survival with destruction's help
With a blow to stir fate's feelings
    Not on second and third lute strings
As if skulls' blood on scattered hair
    Dressed the land with feathers of grouse

لَمَّا خافَتْ مِنَ الحَدَقِ الحِسانِ	فَلَوْ طُرِحَتْ قُلوبُ العِشْقِ فيها
كَشِبْلَيْهِ ولا مُهْرَيْ رِهانِ	وَلَم أرَ قَبْلَهُ شِبْلَيْ هِزَبْرٍ
وأشْبَهَ مَنْظَراً بأبٍ هِجانِ	أشَدَّ تَنازُعاً لكَريمِ أصْلٍ
فُلانٌ دَقَّ رُمْحاً في فُلانِ	وأكْثَرَ في مَجالِسِهِ اسْتِماعاً
فَقَدْ عَلِقا بها قَبْلَ الأوانِ	وأوَّلُ رَأيَةٍ رَأيَ المَعالي
أغاثَةُ صارِخٍ أوْ فَكَّ عانِ	وأوَّلُ لَفْظَةٍ فَهْماً وَقالا:
فكيفَ وقَد بَدَتْ مَعَها اثْنَتانِ	وَكُنْتَ الشَّمْسَ تَبْهَرُ كلَّ عَينٍ
بضَوْئِهِما ولا يَتَحاسَدانِ	فَعاشا عيشةَ القَمَرَينِ يُحْيِيا
ولا وَرِثا سِوَى مَنْ يَقْتُلانِ	ولا مَلِكاً سِوَى مُلْكِ الأَعادي
لَهُ ياءَيْ حُروفٍ أنيسيانِ	وكانَ ابْناً عَدُوٌّ كاثَراهُ
يُؤدِّيهِ الجَنانُ إلى الجِنانِ	دُعاءٌ كالثَّناءِ بِلا رِئاءِ
وأصْبَحَ منكَ في عَضْبٍ يَمانٍ	فَقَدْ أصْبَحْتَ مِنهُ في فِرِنْدٍ
هُراءً كالكَلامِ بِلا مَعانِ	وَلَوْ لا كَوْنُكُمْ في النَّاسِ كانوا

(٢٨٢)

«من المنسرح»

قال في يوم الجلسان وقد نثر عليهم الورد وهم قيام بين يديه حتى غرقوا فيه:

أنَّكَ صَيَّرْتَ نَثْرَهُ دِيَمَا	قَدْ صَدَقَ الوَرْدُ في الذي زَعَمَا
بَحْرٌ حَوَى مِثْلَ مائِهِ عَنَمَا	كأَنَّما مائِجُ الهَواءِ بِهِ
وكُلَّ قَوْلٍ يَقولُهُ حِكَمَا	ناثِرُهُ النَّاثِرُ السُّيوفَ دَماً
والنِّعَمَ السَّابِغاتِ والنِّقَمَا	والخَيْلُ قَدْ فَصَّلَ الضِّياعَ بها
أحْسَنَ مِنهُ مِنْ جودِها سَلِمَا	فَلْيُرِنا الوَرْدُ إنْ شَكا يَدَهُ
وإنَّما عَوَّذَتْ بكَ الكَرَمَا	فَقُلْ لَهُ لَسْتَ خَيْرَ ما نَثَرَتْ
أصابَ عَيْناً بها يُصابُ عَمَى	خَوْفاً مِنَ العَينِ أنْ يُصابَ بها

If lovers' hearts were driven there
    They'd not fear glances of lovely women
I had not seen before him two lion cubs
    Like to his cubs nor yet two Mahri racers
Stronger in fighting for a noble stock
    More like in form to pure blooded father
More often in assembly listening to:
    Such a one broke a spear on such a one
The first vision they saw was heights
    Were attached to them before their time
First words understood or spoken were:
    Rescue suppliants! Freedom to captives
You were the sun dazzling every eye
    How now since two others have risen
They live sun and moon lives reviving
    Each other by their light and not envy
May they rule only enemy kingdoms
    And inherit only what they battle for
May the foe's two sons increase for
    Him with the two ya letters diminutive
A prayer like praise without hypocrisy
    When the heart brings it to one's heart
I appear in it like the temper of
    Yamani sword which it becomes in you
Be nonsense like words without meaning

282
He spoke praising him and recalling the roses.
(Flowing ma)

The rose is true to what it asserts
    That you make its continued scattering
As if a sea stirred by the wind
    Held in its water the red anam fruit
His strewing is swords' bloody scatter
    Every word that he speaks is intelligent
Horses, with estates interspersed
    And the perfect flocks and vengeance
The rose shows us in blaming his hand
    Those finer things in its bounty's peace
Tell it: You're not the best it gives
    It shelters generosity with you indeed
For fear of an eye overcome let
    Blindness hit an eye with what it wants

«من الكامل الأحذّ»

بمدحه ويذكر وقعة كانت مع دهشوذان ابن محمد الكردي بالطرم:

نَبْكــي وتُـرزم تَحْتَنــا الإبــلُ	إثلـتْ! فإنّــا أيّهــا الطَلَـلُ
إنّ الطُّلــولَ لمثلِهــا فُعُـلُ	أوْ لا فَـلا عَتْـبٌ عَلـى طَلَـلْ
بي غَيـرُ مـا بـاكَ أيّهـا الرّجُـلُ	لَـوْ كُنْـتَ تَنْطِـقُ قلتَ مُعتَـذِراً
لم أبـكِ أنّـي بعـضَ مَـن قَتَلـوا	أبكـاكَ أنّـكَ بعـضُ مَـن شَـغَفوا
أيّامُـهُـمْ لديـارهِـمْ دُوَلُ	إنّ الذيـنَ أقَمْـتَ وارْتَحَلُـوا
مَعَـهُـم ويَنْـزِلُ حيثُمـا نَزَلُـوا	الحُسْـنُ يَرْحَـلُ كُلّمـا رَحلُـوا
بَدَويّــةٌ فُتِنْـتُ بِهــا الحِلَـلُ	في مُقْلَتَــيْ رَشــا تُديرُهُـمـا
وصُدودَهـا ومَـن الـذي تَصِـلُ	تَشكُو المَطاعِـمَ طـولَ هِجرَتِهـا
تَرَكتــهُ وهـوَ المِسْــكُ والعَسَـلُ	ما أسـأرَتْ فـي القَعْبِ مـن لَبَـنِ
أعْلَمْتِنـي أنّ الهَـوَى ثَمَـلُ	قالـتْ ألا تَصحُـو فقلـتُ لَهَـا
وبَـرَزْتِ وحْـدَكِ عاقَـهُ الغَـزَلُ	لَـوْ أنّ فَناخُسْـرَ صبّحَكُــمْ
إنّ المِـلاحَ خَــوادِعٌ قُتُـلُ	وتَفَرَّقَـتْ عنكُــمْ كَتائبُـهُ
مَلِـكُ المُلـوكِ وشـأنُكِ البَخَـلُ	مـا كُنْـتِ فاعِلــةً وضَيْفُكُــمْ
أمْ تَبْذِلِيـنَ لَـهُ الـذي يَسَـلُ	أتَمَنّعِـيـنَ قِـرَى فتَفتَضِحـي
بُخْـلٌ ولا خَـوَرٌ ولا وَجَـلُ	بَـلْ لا يَحِـلّ بَحَيْـثُ حَـلّ بـهِ
طَنِـبٌ ذَكَرْنـاهُ فَيَعْتَـدِلُ	مَلِـكٌ إذا مَـا الرُّمْـحُ أدرَكَـهُ
عَمّـا يَسُـوسُ بـهِ فقـد غَفَلُـوا	إنْ لم يَكُـنْ مَـن قَبلَـهُ عَجَـزُوا
فشكَا إليْـهِ السّـهلُ والجَبَـلُ	حتّى أتَـى الدّنيــا ابـنُ بَجدَتِهـا
أنْ لا تَمُـرّ بجِسْـمِهِ العِلَـلُ	شَكوَى العَليـلِ إلى الكفيـلِ لَـهُ
أقْـدِمْ فنفسُـكَ مَـا لَهـا أجَـلُ	قالَـتْ فَـلا كَذَبَـتْ شَجاعَتُـهُ
أوْ قيـلَ يــومَ وغًـى مِـن البَطَـلْ	فَهـوَ النّهايَـةُ إنْ جَـرَى مَثَـلٌ
دونَ السِّــلاحِ الشَّــكْلُ والعَقْـلُ	عُـدَدُ الوُفُـودِ العَامِدينَ لَـهُ

283
He spoke praising him and the news had come of the defeat of Wahsudnan the Kurd.
(Perfect u)

Be a third with us, O tell, for we
    Weep and the camel graons beneath
Or do not, it is no blame for a tell
    Tells have their own kind of activity
If you spoke you'd say in excuse:
    My trouble is other than yours O man
I'd weep for you as one who suffers
    But I weep not for I am one they kill
They saddle up wile I stay here
    The days of their camp have seasons
Beauty travels every time they go
    And settles with them where they do
A gazelle in my eyes governs them
    A bedouin, the folk are charmed by her
Food complains of her long asence
    Her aloofness, but who can hold her?
What she leaves in the milk cup's
    Bottom, she leaves as musk or honey
She said: Are you not well? I said:
    You've taught me love is drunkenness
If Fannakhusra overtook you at dawn
    As you came alone, wooing were heard
His riders would stand off from you
    Because beauty is clever at a killing
You are doing nothing, your guest
    Is a king of kings and you are stingy
Do you refuse hospitality and insult
    Or do you favor him in what he asks?
No, not right as to what is proper
    The stinginess, the bad temper or fear
He's a king who if lance reaches him
    It bends, we think of him, and it's firm
If those before him were not weak in
    Their rule they were lax in comparison
One who has wisdom came to a world
    As plain and mountina came with pleas
Sick man's lament to one who is his
    Help, if illness may pass from his body
They say: Let bravery not trick you
    Go on, for your soul has no limit on it
He's the idea if a proverb is current
    Or if asked on battle day: Who's a hero?
Numerous client troops come to him
    Without any gear but hobbles and clogs
Hobbles used for the horses and
    Clogs are fixed on the Bactrian camels

وَلِعُقْلِهِـــمْ فِي بُخْتِـــهِ شُـــغُلُ	فَلِشُكْلِهِمْ فِي خَيْلِـــهِ عَمَـــلُ
هِــيَ أَوْ بَقِيَّتُهَـــا أَوِ البَــدَلُ	تُمْسِــي عَلَــى أَيْــدِي مَوَاهِبِــهِ
شَرْقـاً إِلَيْــهِ يَنْبُــتُ الْأَسَــلُ	يَشْتَاقُ مِــنْ يَــدِهِ إِلَى سَبَلٍ
وَالمَجْـــدُ لَا الحَـــوْذَانُ النَّفَـــلُ	سَبَـلٌ تَطُـولُ المَكْرُمَـاتُ بِـهِ
بِالنَّــاسِ مِــنْ تَقْبِيلِــهِ يَلَــلُ	وَإِلَى حَصَــى أَرْضٍ أَقَــامَ بِهَــا
فَلِمَــنْ تُصَــانُ وَتُدَّخَــرُ الفُبَــلُ	إِنْ لَمْ تُخَالِــطْ ضَوَاحِكَهُـــمْ
غُرَرٌ هِــيَ الآيَــاتُ وَالرُّسُـــلُ	فِي وَجْهِهِ مِـــنْ نُــورِ خَالِقِــهِ
سَجَدَتْ لَــهُ فِيهِ القَنَـــا الذُّبُـــلُ	فَإِذَا الخَمِيسُ أَبَى السُّجُـــودَ لَـــهُ
رَضِيَــتْ بِحُكْـــمِ سُيُوفِهِ القَلَلُ	وَإِذَا القُلُــوبُ أَبَــتْ حُكُومَتَـــهُ
أَمْ تَسْــتَزِيدُ لَأَمَـــاكَ الْهَبَـــلُ	أَرْضِيــتَ وَهِشُّـــوذَانُ مَـــا حَكَمَـــتْ
وَكَأَنَّهَـــا بَــيْنَ القَنَــا شُعَـــلُ	وَرَدَتْ بِـــلَادَكَ غَيْــرَ مُغْمَــدَةٍ
وَالخَيْـــلُ فِي أَعيَانِهَــا قَبَــلُ	وَالقَــوْمُ فِي أَعيَانِهِمْ حَــزَرٌ
بِهِمْ وَلَيْــسَ بِمَنْ نَــأَوْا خَلَــلُ	فَأَتَوْكَ لَيْسَ بِمَــنْ أَتَـوْا قِبَــلُ
فَصَلُّــوا وَلَا يَــدْرِي إِذَا قَفَلُــوا	لَمْ يَــدْرِ مَـــنْ بِالرَّيِّ أَنَّهُــمْ
وَمَضَيْــتَ مُنْهَزِمَــاً وَلَا وَعِــلُ	وَأَتَيْــتَ مُعْتَزِمَــاً وَلَا أَسَــدٌ
مَــا لَمْ تَكُــنْ لَتَنَالَــهُ المُقَــلُ	تُعْطِــي سِلَاحَهُــمْ وَرَاحَهُــمْ
مَــنْ كَــادَ عَنْــهُ الــرَّأْسُ يَنْتَقِــلُ	أَسْخَى المُلُوكِ بِنَقْــلِ مَمْلَكَــةٍ
قَــوْمٌ غَرِقْــتَ وَإِنَّمَــا ثَقَلُــوا	لَــوْلَا الجَهَالَــةُ مَـــا دَلَفْــتَ إِلَى
غَــدْرَاً وَلَا نَصَرْتْهُـــمُ الغِيَــلُ	لَا أَقْبَلُــوا سِــرَّاً وَلَا ظَفِــرُوا
إِلَّا إِذَا مَـــا ضَاقَــتِ الحِيَــلُ	لَا تَلْــقَ أَفْرَسَ مِنْكَ تَعْرِفُــهُ
نَضْلُــوكَ آلَ بُوَيْــهِ أَوْ فَضَلُــوا	لَا يَسْتَــحِي أَحَــدٌ يُقَــالُ لَــهُ
أَغْنَــوْا عَلَــوْا أَعْلَــوْا وَلُــوا عَدَلُــوا	قَــدَرُوا عَفَــوْا وَعَــدَوا وَفَــوْا سُــئِلُوا
فَإِذَا أَرَادُوا غَايَـــةً نَزَلُــوا	فَــوْقَ السَّمَـــاءِ وَفَــوْقَ مَـــا طَلَبُــوا
فَإِذَا تَعَـــذَّرَ كَــاذِبٌ قَبِلُــوا	قَطَعَــتْ مَكَارِمُهُمْ صَوَارِمَهُــمْ
سَيْفَــاً يَقُــومُ مَقَامَــهُ العَــذَلُ	لَا يَشْهَـــرُونَ عَلَـــى مُخَالِفِهِمْ
وَأَبُــو شُجَاعٍ مَــنْ بِــهِ كَمَلُــوا	فَأَبُو عَلِيٍّ مَـــنْ بِــهِ قَهَــرُوا
فِي المَهْــدِ أَنْ لَا فَاتَــهُ أَمَــلُ	حَلَفَــتْ لِــذَا بَرَكَــاتُ غُــرَّةِ ذَا

They come with hands full of gifts
    As those, or what is left, or the cash
Men desire a shower from his hand
    Spear shafts grow by yearning for him
A shower generosity lengthens for him
    And glory not mere trefoil and waterlily
It flows to earth's rocks and stays
    To shorten men's teeth with lapping it
If the front teeth were not worn down
    For whom would kisses be saved, held?
In his face from the Creator's light
    A sign kept for miracles and prophets
When baKalions refuse to submit
    They bend to him with pliant lances
When hearts reject his judgments
    Heads must enjoy his sword's decrees
Wahsudhan do you accept judgment
    Want to increase your mother's sorrow?
They come to your land, unsheathed
    It was as if flames were on their lances
The men narrowed the eyes to slits
    And horses looked wild with crosseyes
They came to you and had no front
    No break between them and one afar
Those at Rayy knew not whether
    They decamped or returned to camp
You came with conceit not as a lion
    You left in flight not as the hill goat
You gave them weapons and hands
    And something that no eye could take
Most generous king at yielding rule
    Who almost handed over his head
But for ignorance you'd not gone
    To folk who can drown you by spit
They come not secretly nor conquer
    By deceit, nor are aided by treachery
You thought you'd meet none beKer
    Except when cunning was put to test
No one need feel shame if it's said:
    The Buwaid house fought you or won
They rule, bear, vow, give, are sought
    Enrich, rise, elevate, entrust, are just
Above the heavens and what they see
    When they aim at a goal they stoop to it
Their noble acts cut as their swords
    If traitors make excuse they accept it
They make no show to their opponents
    With swords if reproof can take its place
For Abu Ali is one who has victories
    And Abu Shuja one who has perfection
One's best blessing was sworn to other
    In the cradle: May hope never leave them

(٢٨٤)

«من السريع»

توفيت عمة عضد الدولة ببغداد فقال يرثيها ويعزّ به بها:

هـذا الــذي أثّــر في قَلْبِـهِ	آخِـرُ مَــا المَلْــكُ مُعَــزًّى بــهِ
أنْ يَقْــدِرَ الدّهْــرُ علـى غَصْبِـهِ	لا جَزَعــاً بَــلْ أنَفــاً شــابَهُ
لا ســتَحْيَتِ الأيّـامُ مِــن عَتَبِــهِ	لَــوْ دَرَتِ الدّنْيــا بمَــا عِنــدَهُ
لَيْــسَ لَدَيْــهِ لَيْــسَ مِــن جِزْبِـهِ	لَعَلّهَــا تَحْسَــبُ أنّ الــذي
لَيْسَ مُقيمـاً في ذَرا عَضْبِـهِ	وَأنّ مَــنْ بَغْدادَ دارٌ لَــهُ
مَـن ليسَ منهـا ليسَ مـن صُلْبِـهِ	وَأنّ جَــدّ المَــرْءِ أوْطانُــهُ
فَيُجْفِلُـوا خَوْفـاً إلـى قُرْبِـهِ	أخَافُ أنْ تَفْطَــنَ أعْداؤهُ
لا تَقْلِـبُ المُضْجَـعَ عـن جَنبِـهِ	لا بُــدّ للإنْســان مــن ضَجعَـةٍ
وَمَـا أذاقَ المَــوْتَ مِـن كَرْبِـهِ	يَنسـى بهـا مـا كـانَ مِـن عُجْبِـهِ
نَعَافُ مَـا لا بُــدّ مِـن شُـرْبِهِ	نحــنُ بنُــو المَوْتــى فَمَـا بالُنَـا
على زَمَــانٍ هِــيَ مِــن كَسْبِــهِ	تَبْخَــلُ أيْدينَــا بِأرْواحِنَـا
وَهَــذِهِ الأجْسَــامُ مِـنْ تُرْبِــهِ	فَهَــذِهِ الأرْواحُ مِــنْ جَــوّهِ
حُسْـنُ الـذي يَسْبِيهِ لم يَسْبِـهِ	لَـوْ فكّــرَ العاشِــقُ في مُنتَهــى
فَشَكّـتِ الأنْفُـسُ في غَرْبِـهِ	لم يُــرَ قَــرْنُ الشّمس في شَرْقِـهِ
ميتـــةَ جَــالينُوسَ في طِبِّـهِ	يَمُــوتُ راعــي الضّـأن في جَهْلِـهِ
وَزادَ في الأمْـن علـى سِـرْبِهِ	وَرُبَّمَــا زادَ علــى عُمْــرِهِ
كَغَايَــةِ المُفْــرِطِ في حَرْبِــهِ	وَغَايَــةُ المُفْــرِطِ في سِلْمِـهِ
فُــؤادُهُ يَخفِــقُ مِــنْ رُعْبِــهِ	فَـلا قَضَى حاجَتَــهُ طالِــبٌ
كــانَ نَــداهُ مُنتَهَــى ذَنْبِـهِ	أسْتَغْفِرُ اللهَ لشَخْـصٍ مَضَى
كأنّمَــا أفْــرَطَ في سَــبِّهِ	وَكــانَ مَــنْ عَــدّدَ إحْسَــانَهُ
ولا يُريــدُ العَيْــشَ مِــن حُبِّـهِ	يُريـدُ مِـنْ حُبّ العُلـى عَيْشَـةً
وَمَجـدُهُ في القبـرِ مِــن صَحْبِـهِ	يَحْسَـبُهُ دافِنُــهُ وَحْــدَهُ

284
He spoke consoling Abu Shuja
Adud al-Daula for his paternal aunt. (Nimble ha)

The last that a king is consoled for
    This which was imprinted on his heart
Not with fear but shame gripping him
    When fate got power over him violently
If the world knew what grief he had
    Days would be ashamed of their censure
Maybe they think that one who is not
    At home with him is not of his family
That one who has a house in Bagdad
    Is not within the scope of his weapons
That a man's ancestors are his land
    One who is not in it is not of his loins
I fear his foes will start thinking
    And so hurry out of terror to his side
No escape from that couch
    No turning one's side from that bed
One forgets what his pleasure was
    And death has no taste of its agony
Death's sons, why should it bother us?
    We hate what we cannot escape drinking
Our hands greedy for our souls as
    Rivals to time but they're his realty
For these souls belong to its air
    And these bodies belong to its dust
If a lover thought of beauty's end
    Enslaving him, he'd not be enslaved
A sun's horn is not seen in the east
    But souls will complain of its setting
A sheep's keeper dies in ignorance
    A death of Galen with his medicine
And often he outlives him
    And is more secure in his journey
The end of one who excels in peace
    Is as the end of who excels in wartime
May the seeker not attain his end
    Whose heart is flattered by his fears
I ask God's pardon for a soul gone
    Its bounty was the far limit of its sin
Telling over the good deeds made
    The lavish gifts as a curse upon it
It wanted its life for the high love
    But wanted no life for love of itself
The gravedigger thought it was alone
    But its glory was its companion below

وَيُسْتَرُ التَّأْنِيثُ في حُجْبِهِ	وَيُظْهِرُ التَّذْكِيرُ في ذِكْرِهِ
فَقَالَ جَيْشٌ للقَنَا: لَبَّهِ	أُخْتُ أَبِي خَيْرِ أَمِيرٍ دَعَا
أَبُوهُ وَالقَلْبُ أَبُو لُبِّهِ	يَا عَضُدَ الدَّوْلَةِ مَنْ رُكْنُهَا
كَأَنَّهَا النَّوْرُ عَلَى قُضْبِهِ	وَمَنْ بُنُوَّةٍ زَيَّنَ آبَاءِهِ
وَمُنْجِبٌ أَصْبَحْتَ مِنْ عَقْبِهِ	فَخْراً لِلدَّهْرِ أَنْتَ مِنْ أَهْلِهِ
وَسَيْفُكَ الصَّبْرُ فَلَا تُنْبِهِ	إنَّ الأَسَى القِرْنُ فَلَا تُحْيِهِ
يُوحِشُهُ المَفْقُودُ مِنْ شُهْبِهِ	مَا كَانَ عِنْدِي أَنَّ بَدْرَ الدُّجَى
تَحَمَّلَ السَّائِرُ فِي كُتْبِهِ	حَاشَاكَ أَنْ تَضْعُفَ عَنْ حَمْلِ مَا
فَأَغْنَتِ الشِّدَّةُ عَنْ سَحْبِهِ	وَقَدْ حَمَلْتَ الثِّقْلَ مِنْ قَبْلِهِ
وَيَدْخُلُ الإِشْفَاقُ فِي ثَلْبِهِ	يَدْخُلُ صَبْرُ المَرْءِ فِي مَدْحِهِ
وَيَسْتَرِدُّ الدَّمْعَ عَنْ غَرْبِهِ	مِثْلُكَ يَثْنِي الحُزْنَ عَنْ صَوْبِهِ
إيمَا لتَسْلِيمٍ إلى رَبِّهِ	إيمَا لإِبْقَاءٍ عَلَى فَضْلِهِ
سِوَاكَ يَا فَرْداً بِلَا مُشْبِهِ	وَلَمْ أَقُلْ مِثْلَكَ أَعْنِي بِهِ

(٢٨٥)

«من المنسرح»

يمدحه ويذكر هزيمة وهشوذان:

أَمْ عِنْدَ مَوْلَاكَ أَنَّنِي رَاقِدْ	أَزَائِرٌ يَا خَيَالُ أَمْ عَائِدْ
فَجِئْتَنِي فِي خِلَالِهَا قَاصِدْ	لَيْسَ كَمَا ظَنَّ، غَشْيَةٌ عَرَضَتْ
أَلْصَقَ ثَدْيَيْ بِثَدْيَكَ النَّاهِدْ	عُدْ وَأَعِدْهَا فَحَبَّذَا تَلَفٌ
مِنَ الشَّتِيتِ المُؤَشَّرِ البَارِدْ	وَجُدْتَ فِيهِ بِمَا يَشِحُّ بِهِ
أَضْحَكَهُ أَنَّنِي لَهَا حَامِدْ	إذا خَيَالَاتُهُ أَطَفْنَ بِنَا
مِنَّا فَمَا بَالُ شَوْقِهِ زَائِدْ	وَقَالَ إِنْ كَانَ قَدْ قَضَى أَرَباً
مَا لَمْ يَكُنْ فَاعِلاً وَلَا وَاعِدْ	لَا أَجْحَدُ الفَضْلَ رُبَّمَا فَعَلَتْ
كُلُّ خَيَالٍ وِصَالُهُ نَافِدْ	مَا تَعْرِفُ العَيْنُ فَرْقَ بَيْنَهُمَا
عَلَى البَعِيرِ المُقَلَّدِ الوَاخِدْ	يَا طَفْلَةَ الكَفِّ عَبْلَةَ السَّاعِدْ

Manliness was manifest in its memory
    The femininity was hid beneath the veil
Father's sister of best Amir to call
    Thus: Warriors to arms! and they reply
Adud al-Daula whose support O his
    Father, the heart is the mind's father
His sons are his father's ornaments
    As if they were flowers on his stalk
Honor to an age of whose folk you are
    In nobility you show as one of its sons
Grief a beaten foe, may it not revive
    Your sword courageous, may it not dull
It seems to me the moon in a dark sky
    Won't let a lost star make him desperate
Beware of weakening under a burden
    Of what another brings you in his letters
You have borne a heavy load before
    Strength relieves you from dragging it
The courage of a man leads him to
    Praise, as fear leads only to calamity
Such as you turn back grief's attack
    And drive back the tears in their fall
Truly permanence depends on virtue
    And truly submission is to one's Lord
I should not say such as you but say:
    But for you, O unique without compare

285
He spoke also praising him
and commemorating the rout of Wahsudhan.
(Flowing d)

Are you a visitor, O dream, or a nurse
    Or does your friend think I am sleeping?
It's not as he thinks, a faint came on
    And you came seeking me in the interval
Come back, restore her, wonderful dying!
    My breast pressed to her swelling breast
You're generous just as he was stingy
    With widespaced handsome, cool teeth
When his fancies circle about us
    I laugh at him since I praised her
He said: If he fulfilled his need with
    Us he'd not bother to increase his love
I deny no favor they perhaps have done
    Something accomplished or yet promised
Eye cannot tell of parting between two
    The union in dreams is only exhaustion
O soft hand filled with happiness
    On the swift camel with the necklace

زيدي أذى مُهجَتي أزدكِ هَوى	فأجْهَلُ النّاسِ عاشِقٌ حاقِدِ
حَكَيْتَ يا لَيْلُ فَرْعَها الوارِدُ	فاحكِ نَواها لجَفني السّاهِدِ
طالَ بكُائي على تَذَكّرها	وَطُلْتَ حتى كِلاكُما واحِدِ
ما بالُ هَذي النّجُومِ حائِرةً	كأنّها العُمْيُ ما لَها قائِدِ
أوْ عُصبَةٌ مِنْ مُلُوكِ ناجِيَةٍ	أبُو شُجاعٍ عَلَيْهِم واحِدِ
إنْ هَرَبوا أدرَكوا وَإنْ وَقَفوا	خَشُوا ذَهابَ الطّريفِ والتّالِدِ
فهُمْ يُرَجّونَ عَفْوَ مُقْتَدِرِ	مُبارَكِ الوَجْهِ جائِدٍ ماجِدِ
أبْلَجَ لَوْ عاذَتِ الحَمامُ بِهِ	ما خَشِيَتْ رامِياً وَلا صائِدِ
أوْ رَعَتِ الوُحْشُ وَهْيَ تَذكرُهُ	ما رَاعَها حابِلٌ وَلا طارِدِ
تُهدي لَهُ كُلَّ ساعَةٍ خَبَراً	عَن جَحفَلٍ تَحتَ سَيفِهِ بائِدِ
وَمُوضِعاً في فِتانِ ناجِيَةٍ	يَحمِلُ في التّاجِ هامَةَ العاقِدِ
يا عَضُداً رَبّهُ بهِ العاضِدُ	وَسارِياً يَبعَثُ القَطا الهاجِدِ
وَمُمطِرَ المَوتِ والحَياةِ مَعاً	وَأنتَ لا بارقٌ وَلا راعِدِ
نِلتَ وَما نِلتَ مِن مَضَرَّةٍ وَهْـ	شوذانَ ما نالَ رَأيُهُ الفاسِدُ
ـيَيبدَأُ مِنْ كَيدِهِ بِغَايَتِـهِ	وَإنّما الحَرْبُ غايَةُ الكائِدِ
ماذا على مَن أتى يُحارِبُكُم	فَذَمّ ما اختارَ لَوْ أتى وافِدِ
بِلا سِلاحٍ سِوى رَحائِبِكُم	فَفازَ بالنّصرِ وانثَنى راشِدِ
يُقارِعُ الدّهرُ مَن يُقارِعُكُم	على مَكانِ المَسُودِ والسّائِدِ
وَلَيتَ يَومي فَناءَ عَسْكَرِهِ	وَلَمْ تَكُنْ دانِياً وَلا شاهِدِ
وَلَمْ يَغِبْ غائِبٌ خَليفَتُـهُ	جَيشُ أبيهِ وَجَدُّهُ الصّاعِدِ
وَكُلُّ خَطّيّةٍ مُثَقَّفَـةٍ	يَهُزّها مارِدٌ على مارِدِ
سَوَافِكٌ ما يَدَعْـنَ فاصِلَـةً	بَينَ طَريءِ الدّماءِ والجاسِدِ
إذا المَنايا بَدَتْ فَدَعَوْتَها	أُبدِلَ نُوناً بدالِهِ الحائِدِ
إذا دَرى الحِصْنُ مَن رَماهُ بِها	خَرَّ لَها في أساسِهِ ساجِدِ
ما كانَتِ الطِّرمُ في عَجاجَتِها	إلا بَعِيراً أضَلَّـهُ ناشِدِ
تَسأَلُ أهلَ القِلاعِ عَنْ مَلِكٍ	قَدْ مَسَختْهُ نَعامَةً شارِدِ

If you hurt my heart I'll return love
    The most ignorant man is an angry lover
You told O night of her long hair
    Tell of her absence to my wakeful eye
My weeping was long in memory of her
    You too are long till both of you embrace
What's wrong with meandering stars
    As if they were blind and had no leader
Or like the mob of kings on one side
    Abu Shuja alone is over against them
If they flee he takes them, if they stay
    They fear loss of their gains and legacy
They hope for firm forgiveness of one
    Whose face is blessed by generous glory
Serene, if dove has shelter with him
    She does not fear the archer or trapper
If wild beasts graze they think of
    Him so no hunter or fowler scares them
Every hour news is brought to him
    Of the armies destroyed by his swords
Covered with blood the camels swiftly
    Bring him heads with crowns attached
O forearm whose Lord is the Forearm
    Traveling by night you wake red grouse
Rain cloud of death and life at once
    But you are not lightning or thunder
You gave but took not from Wahsudhan
    Injuries that his corrupt mind would take
He began with his tricks as a goal
    But war is the goal of the trickster
What's due one who wars on you?
    He blames that even if troops come
Without weapons except your hope
    He wins by aid, flees with guidance
Fate strikes one who hits at you
    Whether he is the ruler or the ruled
You gave two days to his army's ruin
    You were neither victor not a witness
Absent he did not hide, his vicars
    His father's army, eminent ancestors
All the Khatti straight ones too
    Giants shook them on huge beasts
Blood shedders ask for no marks
    Between fresh blood or deadly stink
If death appears then I call to it:
    Change *dal* to *nun* in *had*: Death!
If a horse knows who attacks, he
    Falls down prostrate to his authority
Tarm was so enveloped in the dust
    That camels seeking it had to be lost
One asks the fort folk about the king
    He had changed to a running ostrich

تَسْتَوْحِشُ الأرضُ أَنْ تُقِرَّ بِهِ   فكُلُّها مُنْكِرٌ لَهُ جَاحِدْ
فَلا مُشادٌ وَلا مُشيدٌ حَمَى   وَلا مَشيدٌ أغنى وَلا شائِدْ
فاغْتَظْ بقَوْمٍ وَهشودٍ ما خلقوا   إلّا لغَيظِ العَدوِّ والحاسِدْ
رَأوْكَ لَمّا بَلَوْكَ نابتَةً   يأكُلُها قَبْلَ أَهْلِهِ الرّائِدْ
وَحَلَّ زَيّاً لِمَنْ يُحَقِّقُهُ   ما كُلُّ دامٍ جَبينُهُ عابِدْ
إنْ كانَ لَمْ يَعْمِدِ الأميرُ لِما   لَقيتَ مِنْهُ فَيُمْنُهُ عامِدْ
يُقْلِقُهُ الصّبحُ لا يَرى مَعَهُ   بُشرى بفَتْحٍ كأنَّهُ فاقِدْ
والأمرُ للهِ، ربَّ مُجْتَهدٍ   ما خابَ إلّا لأنَّهُ جاهِدْ
ومُنْفِقٍ والسِّهامُ مُرْسَلَةٌ   يَحيدُ عَنْ حابضٍ إلى صارِدْ
فَلا يَزَلْ قاتِلٌ أعاديَهُ   أقائماً نالَ ذاكَ أمْ قاعِدْ
لَيتَ ثَنائي الذي أصُوغُ فِدى   مَنْ صِيغَ فيهِ فإنَّهُ خالِدْ
لَوَيْتُهُ دُمْلُجاً عَلى عَضُدٍ   لِدَوْلَةٍ رُكْنُها لَهُ وَالِدْ

(٢٨٦)

«من الرجز»

يمدحه ويذكر خروجه للصيد بموضع
يعرف ببدشت الارزن:

ما أجْدَرَ الأيّامَ واللّيالي   بأنْ تَقولَ ما لَهُ وَما لي
لا أنْ يكونَ هكذا مَقالي   فتًى بنيرانِ الحُروبِ صالِ
مِنْها شَرابي وَبها اغْتِسالي   لا تَخطُرُ الفَحْشاءُ لي بَبالِ
لَوْ جَذَبَ الزَّرّادُ مِنْ أذْيالي   مُخَيِّراً لي صَنْعَتَيْ سِرْبالِ
ما سُمْتُهُ زَرَدَ سِوى سِرْوالِ   وَكيفَ لا وَإنَّما إدْلالي
بفارسِ المَحْروحِ والشَّمالِ   أبي شُجاعٍ قاتِلِ الأبطالِ
ساقي كُؤوسِ المَوْتِ والجِريالِ   لَمّا أصارَ القُفْصَ أمْسِ الخالي
وَقَتَلَ الكُرْدَ عَنِ القِتالِ   حتى اتَّقَتْ بالفَرِّ والإجْفالِ
فَهالِكٌ وَطائِعٌ وَحالِ   وَاقْتَنَصَ الفُرْسانَ بالعَوالي

The land is waste lest he rest in it
    ll of it groans ungratefully at him
No fort or house for protection
    No building can enrich or builder
So rage at these folk O Wahsudhan
    Not made except for foe's hate or envy
They look at you to test you in a bite
    Before his people return with provision
Abandon the robe to a worthy one
    Not everyone prays as forehead bleeds
If the Amir had not commanded as you
    Met him he'd given success to the deputy
Dawn shook him for he did not see
    The victory messenger in his mourning
The event is God's, many a striver
    would not lose except as he struggles
Many a cautious one when arrows fly
    Flees a weak arrow to one that strikes
The killer cares not if the enemy
    Who receives it is standing or sitting
May the praise I fashion be ransom
    To a man described and be immortal
I twisted a bracelet for the arm
    Of a state whose support is a father

286
He spoke praising Adud al-Daula and recalling his hunt at a place named Dasht Arzan.
(Nimble li)

How natural for the days and the nights
    To say: What's wrong with him or with me?
It is not my way of talking, a youth
    Who has burned in the double fires of war?
Drinking from them, bathing in them
    Nor did whoring touch me in my heart
If an armorer were to tug my skirts
    Offering one of two kinds of garments
I'd not name mail coats but pants
    And why not since there is my guide
The rider of Majruh and Shamal
    Abu Shuja the conqueror of warriors
Winebearer of death's cup and blood
    As he routed the Qufs in former times
He beat down Kurds in war till they
    Took shelter in a flight and retreat
Destroyer bringing defeat and exile
    Hunting down horsemen with lances

سَارَ لِصَيدِ الوَحشِ في الجِبَالِ	وَالعُتُقِ المُحْدَثَةِ الصِّقَالِ
عَلى دِمَاءِ الإنْسِ وَالأوْصَالِ	وَفي رِقَاقِ الأرْضِ وَالرِّمَالِ
مِنْ عِظَمِ الهِمَّةِ لا المَلَالِ	مُنْفَرِدُ المُهْرِ عَنِ الرِّعَالِ
مَا يَتَحَرَّكْنَ سِوَى انْسِلَالِ	وَشِدَّةِ الضِّنِّ لا الاسْتِبْدَالِ
كُلُّ عَلَيهِ فَوقَهَا مُخْتَالِ	فَهُنَّ يُضرَبْنَ عَلى التَّصْهَالِ
مِن مَطْلَعِ الشَّمسِ إلى الزَّوَالِ	يُمْسِكُ فَاهُ خَشْيَةَ السُّعَالِ
وَمَا عَدَا فَانْغَلَّ في الأدْغَالِ	فَلَمْ يَنِلْ مَا طَارَ غَيرَ آلِ
مِنَ الحَرَامِ اللَّحْمِ وَالحَلَالِ	وَمَا احْتَمَى بِالمَاءِ وَالدِّحَالِ
سَقْياً لِدَشْتِ الأرْزَنِ الطُّوَالِ	إنَّ النُّفُوسَ عَدَدُ الآجَالِ
مُجَاوِرِ الخِنْزِيرِ لِلرِّئْبَالِ	بَينَ المُرُوجِ الفِيحِ وَالأغْيَالِ
مُشتَرِفِ الدُّبِّ عَلَى الغَزَالِ	دَانِي الخَنَانِيصِ مِنَ الأشْبَالِ
كَأنَّ فَنَاخُسْرَ ذَا الإفْضَالِ	مُجْتَمِعِ الأضْدَادِ وَالأشكَالِ
فَجَاءَهَا بِالفِيلِ وَالفَيَّالِ	خَافَ عَلَيهَا عَوَزَ الكَمَالِ
طَوْعَ وُهُوقِ الخَيلِ وَالرِّجَالِ	فَقيَّدَتِ الأيَّلَ في الجِبَالِ
مُعْتَمَّةً بِبَيسِ الأجْدَالِ	تَسِيرُ سَيرَ النَّعَمِ الأرْسَالِ
قَدْ مَنَعَتْهُنَّ مِنَ التَّفَالِي	وُلِدْنَ تَحتَ أثْقَلِ الأحْمَالِ
إذَا تَلَفَّتْنَ إلى الأظْلَالِ	لا تَشْرَكُ الأجْسَامَ في الهُزَالِ
كَأنَّمَا خُلِقْنَ لِلإذْلَالِ	أرَيْنَهُنَّ أشْنَعَ الأمْثَالِ
وَالعُضْوُ لَيسَ نَافِعاً في حَالِ	زِيَادَةً في سُبَّةِ الجُهَّالِ
وَأوْفَتِ الفُدْرُ مِنَ الأوْعَالِ	لِسَائِرِ الجِسْمِ مِنَ الخَبَالِ
نَوَاجِسَ الأطْرَافِ لِلأكْفَالِ	مُرْتَدِيَاتٍ بِقِسِيِّ الضَّالِ
لَها لِحًى سُودٌ بِلا سِبَالِ	يَكَدْنَ يَنْفُذْنَ مِنَ الآطَالِ
كُلُّ أثِيثٍ نَبْتُهَا مِتْفَالِ	يَصْلُحْنَ لِلإضْحَاكِ لا الإجْلَالِ
تَرْضَى مِنَ الأدْهَانِ بِالأبْوَالِ	لَمْ تُغْذَ بِالمِسْكِ وَلَا الغَوَالِي
لَو سُرِّحَتْ في عَارِضَي مُحْتَالِ	وَمِنْ ذَكِيِّ الطِّيبِ بِالدَّمَالِ
بَينَ قَضَاةِ السَّوْءِ وَالأطْفَالِ	لَعَدَّهَا مِنْ شَبَكَاتِ المَالِ

With newly polished heirlooms he
    Goes chasing beats in the mountains
In soft places of meadow and sand
    Over the blood of men and their limbs
Apart from the troop on a young horse
    Out of greatness of spirit not weariness
Restrained, not desiring substitutes
    They make no commotion except to move
They have been beaten for neighing
    Everyone on them is sick with awe of him
Their mouths held in fear for a cough
    From the sun's rising now to its setting
Whatever flies far cannot escape
    Nor whatever runs into thickets to hid
No protection in waters or lakes
    For fles either forbidden or permitted
Truly souls are prepared for death
    Poured down the length of Dasht Arzan
Between wide praries and woods
    In the pathways of the boards and lions
The piglets are close to the cubs
    And bear towers over the gazelles
Uniting the opposites and the shapes
    In Fannakhusra most perfect in virtues
Fearing they'd lack completeness
    He brings elephants and their riders
Mountain goats hobbled with rope
    Submissive to lassoes of men and horses
Walking a gait of sheep and camels
    Turbaned with those dried-out roots
Born beneath the heaviest of burdens
    As it keeps them from being deloused
They share not in bodies' leanness
    When they turn to look at the shadows
They show them the ugliest shapes
    As if they were created for baseness
Increasing the shame of ignorance
    With members not useful in any case
To the rest of the body a defect
    The buck of the antelope lives higher
Horns bent back like a boew of yew
    With the point of the tip on the flank
They almost pierce the haunces
    With a black beard without a mustache
Good for a laugh but not for fear
    It grows all thickened with spittle
Not anointed with musk or unguent
    It is content with oil and with urine
And with piercing spice and manure
    If fixed to the cheeks of the deceiver

لا تُؤْثِرُ الوَحْشَةَ على القَذَالِ	شَبيهَةَ الإدْبارِ بالإقْبالِ
مِنْ أسْفَلِ الطَّوْدِ ومَنْ مُعَالِ	فاخْتَلَفَتْ في وابِلَيْ نِبَالِ
في كلِّ كِبْدٍ كَبِدَيْ نِصَالِ	قَدْ أوْدَعَتْها عَتَلُ الرِّحالِ
مَقْلُوبَةُ الأظْلافِ والأرْقالِ	فَهُنَّ يَهْوِينَ مِنَ القِلالِ
في طُرُقٍ سَريعَةِ الإيصالِ	يُرْقِلْنَ في الجَوِّ على المَحالِ
على القُفِّيِّ أعْجَلَ العِجالِ	يَنمْنَ فيها نِيمَةَ المِكسالِ
ولا يُحاذِرْنَ مِنَ الضَّلالِ	لا يَتَشَكَّيْنَ مِنَ الكَلالِ
تَشْويقُ إكْثارٍ إلى إقْلالِ	فكانَ عَنْها سَبَبَ التَّرْحالِ
يَخَفْنَ في سَلْمَى وفي قَيالِ	فَوَحْشُ نَجْدٍ مِنْهُ في بَلْبالِ
والخاضِبَاتِ الرُّبْدِ والرِّئالِ	نَوافِرَ الضِّبابِ والأوْرالِ،
يَسْمَعْنَ مِنْ أخْبارِه الأزْوالِ	والظَّبي والخَنْساءِ والذَّيَّالِ
فُحُولَها والعُوذَ والمَتالي	ما يَبْعَثُ الخُرْسَ على السُّؤالِ
يَرْكَبُها بالخَطْمِ والرِّحالِ	تَوَدُّ لَوْ يُتْحِفُها بوالِ
ويَخْمُسُ العُشْبَ ولا تُبالي	يُؤْمِنُها مِنْ هَذِهِ الأهْوالِ
يا أقْدَرَ السُّفارِ والقُفَّالِ	ومَاءَ كُلِّ مُسْبِلٍ هَطَّالِ
أوْ شِئْتَ عرَّقتَ العِدَى بالآلِ	لَوْ شِئْتَ صِدْتَ الأسْدَ بالثَّعالي
لآئِماً قَتَلْتَ باللآلي	ولَوْ جَعَلْتَ مَوْضِعَ الألالِ
في الظُّلَمِ الغائِبَةِ الهِلالِ	لم يَبْقَ إلّا طَرَدُ السَّعَالي
فَقَدْ بَلَغْتَ غايَةَ الآمالِ	على ظُهُورِ الإبِلِ الأبّالِ
في لا مَكانٍ عِنْدَ لا مَنَالِ	فَلَمْ تَدَعْ منها سِوَى المُحالِ
النَّسَبُ الحَلْيُ وأنتَ الحالي	يا عَضُدَ الدَّوْلَةِ والمَعَالي
حَلْياً تَحَلَّى مِنْكَ بالجَمالِ	بالأبِ لا بالشَّنْفِ والخَلْخالِ
أحسَنُ منها الحُسْنُ في المِعطالِ	ورُبَّ قُبْحٍ وحِلًى ثِقَالِ
مِنْ قَبْلِهِ بالعَمِّ والأخْوالِ	فخرُ الفتَى بالنَّفْسِ والأفْعالِ

He has it serve as a net for riches
    Between evil judgments and children
With pretense that back is front
    It does not show a face from the rear
They are left to arrow's downpour
    From the mountain slopes and heights
The men's bows bid them farewell
    In every liver two arrowheads' weight
So they plummet away from peaks
    Upside down the hoofs and bounding
Leaping through air on their backs
    On the fastest way down to the depths
They sleep the sleep of the lazy
    On their necks they hurry the fastest
They don't complain of weariness
    Nor do they take care about straying
One has a reason to go from them
    The desire of the much for the little
Upland beasts grieve due to that
    They were frightened in Salma and Qiyal
With the fear of lizards and iguanas
    Dust colored ostriches and the chicks
Fawns and wild cows and buffalo
    They listened for his stunning news
They sent to no dumb beasts to ask
    Their barren, foals, and young camels
Wishing he'd send them a governor
    To rule them with bridle and saddle
To make them safe from these fears
    And shade, a pasturage and not anxiety
And water of every flowing shower
    O power of those who travel and turn
If you wish you hunt lions with foxes
    And drown the foe with desert mirages
Or put in place weapons of war
    Pearls so you can kill them with joy
Nothing remains but to pursue
    Goblins in the dark of an absent moon
On backs of camels not needing water
    You could reach the top of your hopes
You leave nothing but the impossible
    That exists nowhere and is unobtainable
O Forearm of State and of heights
    The lineage is gems and your are owner
Of a father not of earring or bracelet
    A gem from yourself to adorn by beauty
Many an ugly one is heavily bejeweled
    Finer than her is the unadorned beauty
A man's honor is in himself and acts
    Of mother and father's kin before him

(٢٨٧)

«من الوافر»

قال عند وداعه لعضد الدولة في أول شعبان سنة أربع وخمسين وثلاث مئة (٩٦٤م) وهي آخر شعر قاله:

فَلا مَلِكٌ إِذَنْ إِلّا فَداكا	فِدًى لَكَ مَنْ يُقَصِّرُ عَنْ مَداكا
دَعَوْنا بِالبَقاءِ لِمَنْ قَلاكا	وَلَوْ قُلْنا فِدًى لَكَ مَنْ يُساوي
وَلَوْ كانَتْ لِمَمْلَكَةٍ مَلاكا	وَآمَنّا فِداءَكَ كُلَّ نَفْسٍ
وَيَنصَبُّ تَحتَ ما نَثَرَ الشِّباكا	وَمَنْ يَظُنُّ نَثْرَ الحَبِّ جوداً
وَإِنْ بَلَغَتْ بِهِ الحالُ السُّكاكا	وَمَنْ بَلَغَ الحَضيضَ بِهِ كَراهُ
لَقَدْ كانَتْ خَلائِقُهُمْ عِداكا	فَلَوْ كانَتْ قُلوبُهُمْ صَديقاً
إِذا أَبصَرْتَ دُنياهُ ضَناكا	لِأَنَّكَ مُبغِضٌ حَسَباً نَجيفاً
بِحُبِّكَ أَنْ يَحِلَّ بِهِ سِواكا	أَروحُ وَقَدْ خَتَمتَ عَلى فُؤادي
ثَقيلاً لا أُطيقُ بِهِ حَراكا	وَقَدْ حَمَّلتَني شُكراً طَويلاً
فَلا تَمشي بِنا إِلّا سِواكا	أُحاذِرُ أَنْ يَشُقَّ عَلى المَطايا
يُعينُ عَلى الإِقامَةِ في ذَراكا	لَعَلَّ اللهَ يَجعَلُهُ رَحيلاً
فَلَمْ أُبصِرْ بِهِ حَتّى أَراكا	فَلَوْ أَنّي اِستَطَعتُ خَفَضتُ طَرْفي
نَداكَ المُستَفيضُ وَما كَفاكا	وَكَيفَ الصَبرُ عَنكَ وَقَدْ كَفاني
فَتَقطَعَ مَشيَتي فيها الشِّراكا	أَتَترُكُني وَعَينُ الشَمسِ نَعلي
فَكَيفَ إِذا غَدا السَّيرُ اِبتِراكا	أَرى أَسَفي وَما سِرْنا شَديداً
وَها أَنا ما ضُرِبتُ وَقَدْ أَحاكا	وَهَذا الشَوقُ قَبلَ البَينِ سَيفٌ
عَلَيكَ الصَّمتَ لا صاحَبتَ فاكا	إِذا التَوديعُ أَعرَضَ قالَ قَلْبي
مُعاوَدَةٌ لَقُلْتُ: وَلا مُناكا	وَلَوْ لا أَنَّ أَكثَرَ ما تَمَنّى
فَأَقتَلُ ما أَعَلَّكَ ما شَفاكا	إِذا اِستَشْفَيتَ مِنْ داءٍ بِداءٍ

287
**He spoke bidding farewell
to Adud al-Daula
and this is the last he spoke.
It was a bad omen
for his soul in its subject.
(Exuberant ka)**

Your ransom is one short of your limit
    No kings exist but those who ransom you
If we say: Your ransom is equal to you
    We'd ask life for those who dislike you
We'd grant as your ransom every soul
    Even if the chief support of the kingdom
Or he who thinks strewing corn bounty
    But sets up traps under what he scatters
Or he who grovels in dirt and sleeps
    Though rank he attained touched the sky
Even if their hearts were faithful
    Yet their characters would be your foes
Since you hate a worldly thin esteem
    When you see that its property is fatness
I go and you have sealed my heart
    With your love lest other than you come
And you loaded me with large thanks
    And heavy so I can scarcely move with it
I am afraid it will be hard on camels
    They cannot go with us without wavering
Perhaps God sets this departure so
    It helps us remain under your protection
If I were able I would lower my eyes
    And not look anywhere until I see you
Can I be patient far from you if your
    Bounty contents me but contents not you?
You leave me with my shoe in sun's eye
    So my walking with it cuts the shoelace
I see I weep and we not yet far gone
    How can the journey be if it increases?
Passion before departure is a sword
    Here am I not yet hit, but I am marked
As farewell came to us my heart said:
    Keep quiet, don't let your mouth run on
If it weren't that the most you desire
    Was return, I'd say: Don't have your way
You healed from illness with ills
    The most deadly sickness is what heals

هُمُومـاً قَدْ أَطَلْتُ لَهَا العِرَاكَـا	فَأَسْتُرُ مِنــكَ نَجْوَانَـا وأُخْفِـي
وَإِنْ طاوَعْتُها كانَتْ رِكَاكَــا	إِذَا عَاصَيْتُهَـا كانَـتْ شِـدَاداً
يَقُـولُ لَـهُ قُدُومِـي ذَا بذاكَــا	وَكَـمْ دُونَ الثَّوِيّـةِ مِـنْ حَزِيـنٍ
يُقَبِّـلُ رَحْـلَ تُـرْوكَ والوَرَاكَـا	وَمِـنْ عَـذْبِ الرُّضَـابِ إذَا أَنَخْنَـا
وَقَـدْ عَبِـقَ العَبِيـرُ بِـهِ وَصَاكَـا	يُحَـرِّمُ أَنْ يَمَـسَّ الطّيـبَ بَعْـدِي
وَيَمْنَحُـهُ البَشَامَـةَ والأَرَاكَـا	وَيَمْنَـعُ ثَغْـرَهُ مِـنْ كُـلِّ صَـبٍّ
فَلَيْتَ النَّـوْمَ حَـدَّثَ عَنْ نَدَاكَـا	يُحَـدِّثُ مُقْلَتَيْـهِ النَّـوْمُ عَنِّـي
وَقَدْ أَنْضَى العُذَافِـرَةَ اللِّكَاكَـا	وَأَنَّ البُخْـتَ لا يُعْرَقْـنَ إلاَّ
إذَا انْتَبَهَـتْ تَوَهَّمَـهُ ابْتِشَـاكَـا	وَمَـا أَرْضَى لِمُقْلَتِـهِ بِحُلْـمٍ
فَلَيْتَـكَ لا يُتَيِّمُـهُ هَوَاكَــا	وَلا إلاّ بـأَنْ يُصْغِـي وأَحْكِـي
أَيَعْجَـبُ مِـنْ ثَنَائِـي أَمْ عُلاكَـا	وَكَمْ طَرِبِ المَسَامِعِ لَيْسَ يَـدْرِي
وَهَـذَا الشِّعْـرُ فِهْرِي والمَدَاكَـا	وَذَاكَ النَّشْـرُ عِرْضُـكَ كانَ مِسْكاً
إذَا لَمْ يُسْـمِ حَامِـدُهُ عَنَاكَــا	فَـلا تَحْمَدْهُمَـا وَاحْمَـدْ هُمَامـاً
غَـداً يَلْقَـى بَنُـوكَ بِهَـا أَبَاكَـا	أَغَـرَّ لَـهُ شَمَائِـلُ مِـنْ أَبِيـهِ
وَآخَـرُ يَدَّعِـي مَعَـهُ اشْتِرَاكَـا	وَفِي الأَحْبَابِ مُخْتَـصٌّ بِوَجْـدٍ
تَبَيَّـنَ مَـنْ بَكَـى مِمَّـنْ تَبَاكَـى	إذَا اشْتَبَهَـتْ دُمُـوعٌ فِي خُـدُودٍ
لِعَيْنِـي مِنْ نَـوَايَ عَلَى أُلاكَـا	أَذَمَّـتْ مَكْرُمَـاتُ أَبِـي شُجَـاعٍ
لَهَـا وَقْـعُ الأَسِنَّـةِ فِي حَشَاكَـا	فَزُلْ يَـا بُعْـدُ عَـنْ أَيْـدِي رِكَابٍ
أَذَاةً أَوْ نَجَـاةً أَوْ هَلاكَــا	وأَنَّـى شِئْـتِ يَا طُرُقِـي فَكُونِـي
رَأَوْنِـي قَبْـلَ أَنْ يَـرَوْا السِّمَاكَـا	فَلَـوْ سِرْنَـا وَفِي تِشْرِيـنَ خَمْـسٌ
قَنَـا الأَعْـدَاءِ والطَّعْـنَ الدِّرَاكَـا	يُشَـرِّدُ يُمْـنٌ فَنَاحُِسُـرَ عَنِّـي
سِلاحـاً يَذْعَـرُ الأَعْـدَاءَ شَاكَـا	وَأَلْبَـسُ مِـنْ رِضَـاهُ فِي طَرِيقِـي
وَكُلُّ النَّاسِ زُورٌ مـا خَلاكَــا	وَمَـنْ أَعْتَـاضُ مِنْـكَ إذَا افْتَرَقْنَـا
يَعُـودُ وَلَمْ يَجِـدْ فِيـهِ امْتِسَاكَـا	وَمَـا أَنَـا غَيْـرُ سَهْـمٍ فِي هَـوَاءٍ
وَقَـدْ فَارَقْـتُ دَارَكَ وَاصْطِفَاكَـا	حَيِـيٍّ مِـنْ إلهِـي أَنْ يَرَانِـي

I veiled from you our whispers, I hid
    Desires which I have long been fighting
If I opposed them they were strong
    If I submitted to them they were weak
To many a one this side of Thawiya
    My approach says in grief: This for that!
Many with sweet saliva as camels kneel
    Will kiss Turwak's saddle and saddle rug
He is forbidden to touch perfume after
    I am gone for scent clings and lingers
He refuses his lips to every lover
    But gives them to the toothpick wood
Sleep whispered to his eyes about me
    Would that sleep told about your bounty
Of camels not reaching Iraq except
    They grew thin, once strong, and fleshy
I do not want his eyes to dream
    And when he awakes he thinks it a lie
Nor yet that he listen and I tell so
    He may not be enslaved by love for you
How much joy for listener who ignores
    If he marvels at my words or at your rank
That perfume, your honor, is musk
    This poetry is my pestle and mortar
Praise them not but praise a hero
    Who if his praise won't name him is you
Noblest, his qualities from his father
    Soon your sons meet your father there
Among friends is one marked with
    Love others claim to share with him
When tears on cheeks are compared
    It is clear who weeps and who pretends
The virtues of Abu Shuja condemn
    The laker, for my eyes which are far
Distance, move from a camel's feet
    They are spearpoint blows in your side
Whatever you wish my way let it be
    Suffering or escape or my destruction
If we go and Tishrin has five days
    They see me before they see the Simak
Fannakhusra's favor drives from me
    Enemy spears and thrusts that are cast
I wear by his good pleasure on my way
    Bristling armor that frightens the heroes
Who substitutes for you when we part
    When all men are false except you alone?
I am nothing but an arrow in the air
    Returning if it finds nothing to hold it
Ashamed that my God can see me when
    I left your house and he has chosen you

References
This list shows selections which I have made for my Arab Translations Series ATS,to illustrate poets which Mutanabbi may have used as models for his own poetry or poets who used the poems Of Mutanabbi as models in their pins.

Abu 'Ala al Ma'ari, ATS 2, 39
Abu 'Atahiya, ATS 59
Abu Husaina, ATS 125
Abu Hayyan, ATS 120
Abu Nuwas, ATS 8, 50
Abu Tammam, ATS 11. 14
'Ajjaj, ATS 67
Akhtal, ATS 6
'Alqama, ATS 45
'Amid), ATS 12
'Antara, ATS 10
Bashshar ibn Burd, ATS 21
Buhturi, ATS 16
Dhu'l Rumma, ATS 62
Hassan ibn Numair, ATS 123
Hassan ibn Thabit, ATS 69
Hatim al Tai, ATS 77
Hutaia, ATS 46
Ibn Dahhan, ATS 126

314
Ibn Duraid, ATS 58
Ibn Hamdis, ATS 116
Ibn Hani al Andalusi, ATS 79
Ibn al Mu'tazz, ATS 38, 44
Ibn Qutaiba, ATS 4
Ibn al Rumi, ATS 26
Ibn Slna al Maliki, ATS 121
    Ibrahim ibn Sahl, ATS 57
    'Imr al Qais, ATS 15
    Ibn 'Unain, ATS 97
    Ibn Zaidun, ATS 3
    Jamil Buthaina, ATS 64
    Jarir wa Farazdaq, ATS 7
    Khansa, ATS 5
    Ka'b ibn Zuhair, ATS 18
    Labid, ATS 25
    Maimun al 'Asha, ATS 72
    Murtadi, ATS 102
    Muslim al Walid, ATS 54
    Mutanabbi, ATS I, 31
37, 52
    Nabiga, ATS 30
    Nusaib, ATS 42
Qadi al Fadl, 113
Qais al Ruqayya, ATS 43
Sahib, ATS 9
Sanaubari, ATS 23

Sharaf al Din al Ansari, ATS 118
Shushtari, ATS 128
Sultan al Khattab, ATS 130
Tarafa, ATS 41
Tha'alibi, ATS 17, 18, 20, 22, passim
'Umar ibn Abu Rabi'a, ATS Z8
'Urwa ibn al Ward, ATS 40
Walid ibn Yazid, ATS 74
Zuhair ibn Abu Sulma, ATS 20